San Francisco

timeout.com/sanfrancisco

D0951109

Published by Time Out Guides Ltd, a wholly owned subsidiary of Time Out Group Ltd.
Time Out and the Time Out logo are trademarks of Time Out Group Ltd.

© **Time Out Group Ltd 2006**
Previous editions 1996, 1998, 2000, 2002, 2004.

10 9 8 7 6 5 4 3 2 1

This edition first published in Great Britain in 2006 by Ebury Publishing
Ebury Publishing is a division of The Random House Group Ltd,
20 Vauxhall Bridge Road, London SW1V 2SA

Random House Australia Pty Limited 20 Alfred Street, Milsons Point, Sydney, New South Wales 2061, Australia
Random House New Zealand Limited 18 Poland Road, Glenfield, Auckland 10, New Zealand
Random House South Africa (Pty) Limited Isle of Houghton, Corner Boundary
Road & Carse O'Gowrie, Houghton 2198, South Africa

Random House UK Limited Reg. No. 954009

Distributed in USA by Publishers Group West
1700 Fourth Street, Berkeley, California 94710

Distributed in Canada by Penguin Canada Ltd
10 Alcorn Avenue, Toronto, Ontario, Canada M4V 3B2

For further distribution details, see www.timeout.com

ISBN
To 31 December 2006: 1-904978-11-8
From 1 January 2007: 9781904978114

A CIP catalogue record for this book is available from the British Library

Colour reprographics by Icon, Crowne House, 56-58 Southwark Street, London SE1 1UN

Printed and bound in Germany by Appl

Papers used by Ebury Publishing are natural, recyclable products made from wood grown in sustainable forests

All rights reserved. No part of this publication may be reproduced, stored in a retrieval system, or transmitted in any
form or by any means, electronic, mechanical, photocopying, recording or otherwise, without prior permission from the
copyright owners.

Time Out Guides Limited
Universal House
251 Tottenham Court Road
London W1T 7AB
Tel + 44 (0)20 7813 3000
Fax + 44 (0)20 7813 6001
Email guides@timeout.com
www.timeout.com

Editorial

Editor Will Fulford-Jones
Consultant Editor Bonnie Wach
Sub Editors Simon Coppock, Sally Davies, Robert Dimery, Janice Fuscoe
Researchers Tony Hayes, Patrick Welch
Proofreader Sylvia Tombesi-Walton
Indexer Sam Le Quesne

Editorial/Managing Director Peter Fiennes
Series Editor Ruth Jarvis
Deputy Series Editor Lesley McCave
Business Manager Gareth Garner
Guides Co-ordinator Holly Pick
Accountant Kemi Olufuwa

Design

Art Director Scott Moore
Art Editor Tracey Ridgewell
Senior Designer Josephine Spencer
Graphic Designer Henry Elphick
Digital Imaging Dan Conway
Ad Make-up Jenny Prichard

Picture Desk

Picture Editor Jael Marschner
Deputy Picture Editor Tracey Kerrigan
Picture Researcher Helen McFarland

Advertising

Sales Director Mark Phillips
International Sales Manager Ross Canadé
International Sales Executive Simon Davies
Advertising Assistant Kate Staddon

Marketing

Marketing Director Mandy Martinez
Marketing & Publicity Manager, US Rosella Albanese

Production

Production Director Mark Lamond
Production Controller Marie Howell

Time Out Group

Chairman Tony Elliott
Managing Director Mike Hardwick
Group Financial Director Richard Waterlow
Group Commercial Director Lesley Gill
Group General Manager Nichola Coulthard
Group Circulation Director Jim Heinemann
Group Art Director John Oakey
Online Managing Director David Pepper
Group Production Director Steve Proctor
Group IT Director Simon Chappell

Contributors

Introduction Will Fulford-Jones. **History** Michael Ansaldo (*Tales of the city: Emperor Norton* Simon Littlefield). **San Francisco Today** Bonnie Wach. **Architecture** Erin Cullerton (*Five to avoid* Elise Proulx). **Literary San Francisco** Heidi Kriz (*Write to perform* Kimberly Chun). **The Politics of Progress** Matt Markovich. **Where to Stay** Robert Farmer; *additional reviews* Will Fulford-Jones, Bonnie Wach (*Tales of the city: Palace Hotel* Matt Markovich). **Sightseeing: Introduction** Will Fulford-Jones. **Downtown** Matt Markovich (*The cable guys* Will Fulford-Jones; *Bridge of sighs* Bonnie Wach; *Tales of the city: O'Farrell Theatre* Dayvid Figler). **SoMa & South Beach** Matt Markovich (*Statues: Willie McCovey* Will Fulford-Jones). **Nob Hill & Chinatown** Michael Ansaldo (*Statues: Goddess of Democracy* Will Fulford-Jones). **North Beach to Fisherman's Wharf** Michael Ansaldo (*Walk: The North Beach beat* Jake Bumgardner; *Statues: Fire Department, What the flock?* Matt Markovich; *Barbary Lane* Simon Coppock). **The Mission & the Castro** Ken Taylor (*Statues: Fr Junípero Serra* Jonathan Cox, Will Fulford-Jones). **The Haight & Around** Matt Markovich (*Tales of the city: Mary Pleasant* Kimberly Chun). **Sunset, Golden Gate Park & Richmond** Matt Markovich (*Statues: John McLaren* Bonnie Wach). **Pacific Heights to the Golden Gate Bridge** Matt Markovich. **The East Bay** Elise Proulx. **Restaurants & Cafés** Robert Farmer; *additional reviews* Will Fulford-Jones (*After a fashion* Robert Farmer; *Get connected* Will Fulford-Jones; *Crack one open, The Latin quarter, Out of this world* Matt Markovich). **Bars** Matt Markovich (*Walk: Crawling the Tenderloin, Smoke 'em if you got 'em* Will Fulford-Jones). **Shops & Services** Heather Bradley (*Corporate punishment* Bonnie Wach). **Festivals & Events** Tony Hayes (*Only in San Francisco...* Michael Ansaldo). **Children** Laura Moorhead. **Film** Michael Ansaldo (*Faster than a speeding Bullitt* Tony Hayes). **Galleries** Jackie Bennion (*Opening source* Kimberly Chun). **Gay & Lesbian** Robin S Dornan. **Music** Kimberly Chun (*Tales of the city: The Fillmore* Matt Markovich). **Nightclubs** Ken Taylor. **Sports & Fitness** Tony Hayes (*Walking back to happiness* Dan Epstein; *Shark attack!* Lena Katz). **Theatre & Dance** Robert Avila (*Pyromania* Matt Markovich). **Trips Out of Town: Getting Started** Will Fulford-Jones. **Heading North** Elise Proulx. **Wine Country** Will Fulford-Jones, Doreen Schmid. **Heading East** Ann Marie Brown, Ruth Jarvis. **Heading South** Will Fulford-Jones, Grace Krilanovich. **Directory** Will Fulford-Jones.

Maps JS Graphics (john@jsgraphics.co.uk), except: page 320, used by kind permission of Reineck & Reineck.

Photography by Elan Fleisher, except: page 10 Janine Wiedel; page 12 North Wind Picture Archives; page 13 Mary Evans Picture Library; page 14 Corbis; pages 15, 23, 245 Getty Images; page 16 Time Life Pictures/Getty Images; page 38 Associated Press; page 98 © 2001 by Jamie Morgan; page 211 Warner Bros/The Kobal Collection; page 221 Jane Philomen-Cleland, courtesy of the San Francisco Lesbian/Gay Freedom Band; pages 258, 265, 266, 267, 268, 271, 273, 275, 276, 279 Héloise Bergman. The following images were provided by the featured establishments/artists: pages 125, 198, 201, 229, 252.

The Editor would like to thank Laurie Armstrong at the SFCVB, Nyx Bradley, and all contributors to previous editions of *Time Out San Francisco* and *Time Out California*, whose work forms the basis for parts of this book.

© Copyright Time Out Group Ltd
All rights reserved

Contents

Introduction

Run through a checklist of ideals for city living, and you'll get nothing but superlatives from San Francisco. The climate is comfortable and the public transportation decent; the shopping is terrific and the restaurants outstanding; the politicians are tolerant and the people accepting; the culture is adventurous and thrilling, the nightlife sharp and vibrant; the parks are inviting and the surrounding landscape spectacular. And yet for all that, San Francisco is something other than the sum of its parts, something altogether richer, stranger and more characterful. It was ever thus; rarely is a city's past more revealing of its present and future than here.

San Francisco grew dramatically in the late 1840s and early 1850s, its population expanding forty-fold in a single year after newspaper proprietor Sam Brannan stood in Portsmouth Square, waved a vial of precious metals at the gathering crowds and started the Gold Rush. The Cantonese followed in its wake, establishing America's first Chinatown. In the 1950s, Jack Kerouac, Allen Ginsberg and other writers of the so-called Beat Generation school issued their visions of a whole new American dream from the city; the late 1960s drew thousands to the drug-inflected, generation-changing Summer of Love; the 1970s saw the gay rights movement grow in a way rivalled only in New York City. And then there was the spectacular dot-com boom and bust of the 1990s: nothing less than a second Gold Rush, the mother lode not nuggets but chips.

The adventurous, trailblazing spirit that defines all these key events in the city's history, and more besides, remains very much in evidence today. For at its heart, San Francisco still feels like a pioneer town: occasionally opportunist, sure, and a little ragged around the edges, but always looking for the way forward while never taking its eye off what got it there. Few cities balance history and modernity with such élan.

The locals don't have it all their own way: San Francisco is a famously, fearsomely expensive place in which both to buy property and park a car. But for visitors, who can take advantage of numerous good-value hotel rooms and get around using buses, trains, bicycles and even feet, these problems are incidental. Just as crucially, San Francisco is that rare and joyous place: a town in which tourists and the famously laid-back, anything-goes locals co-exist in harmony. Have a wonderful time.

ABOUT TIME OUT CITY GUIDES

The sixth edition of *Time Out San Francisco* is one of an expanding series of around 50 Time Out guides produced by the people behind the successful listings magazines in London, New York, Chicago and other cities around the globe. Our guides are all written by resident experts who have striven to provide you with all the most up-to-date information you'll need to explore the city or read up on its background, whether you're a local or a first-time visitor.

THE LOWDOWN ON THE LISTINGS

Above all, we've tried to make this book as useful as possible. Telephone numbers, websites, transport information, opening times, admission prices and credit card details are included in our listings. And we've given details on facilities, services and events, all checked and correct at press time. However, owners and managers can change their policies with little notice. Before you go out of your way, we strongly advise you to call and check opening times, dates of exhibitions and other particulars. While every effort has been made to ensure the accuracy of the information in this guide, the publishers cannot accept responsibility for any errors it may contain.

PRICES AND PAYMENT

Our listings detail the major credit cards – American Express (AmEx), Diners Club (DC), Discover (Disc), MasterCard (MC) and Visa (V) – taken by each venue. Many will also accept travellers' cheques issued by a major financial institution, such as American Express.

The prices we've supplied should be treated as guidelines, not gospel. Fluctuating exchange rates and inflation can cause prices to change rapidly, especially in shops and restaurants. If costs vary wildly from those we've quoted, then ask whether there's a good reason – and please email us to let us know. We aim to give the best and most up-to-date advice, so we always want to know if you've been badly treated or overcharged.

THE LIE OF THE LAND

San Francisco's various neighbourhoods have very distinct characters, but the boundaries that separate them are occasionally fuzzy. We have used the most commonly accepted demarcations; see page 308 for a map that defines these areas.

In addition to this overview map, the back of this book also includes street maps of much of San Francisco, along with a comprehensive street index. The street maps start on page 312, and now pinpoint specific locations of hotels (**❶**), restaurants and cafés (**❶**), and bars (**❶**). For all addresses throughout the book, we've given both a cross-street and a map reference, so finding your way around should be simple.

TELEPHONE NUMBERS

There are various telephone area codes that serve the Bay Area: 415 for San Francisco and Marin County, 510 for Berkeley and Oakland, 650 for the peninsula cities and 707 for Napa and Sonoma Counties. Phone numbers throughout the guide are listed as if you're dialling from within San Francisco. If you're dialling from outside your area code, you'll have to add an initial 1 (1-415, 1-510 and so on). Numbers beginning 1-800, 1-866, 1-877 and 1-888 can be dialled free of charge within the US. For more on telephones and codes, *see p292.*

ESSENTIAL INFORMATION

For any practical information you might need for visiting the city, including visa, customs and immigration information, disabled access, emergency telephone numbers, a list of useful websites and the ins and outs of the local transport network, see the Directory (*pp282-296*) at the back of this guide.

LET US KNOW WHAT YOU THINK

We hope you enjoy *Time Out San Francisco*, and we'd like to know what you think of it. We welcome tips for places that you believe we should include in future editions and appreciate your feedback on our choices. Please e-mail us at guides@timeout.com.

Advertisers

We would like to stress that no establishment has been included in this guide because it has advertised in any of our publications and no payment of any kind has influenced any review. The opinions given in this book are those of Time Out writers and entirely independent.

There is an online version of this book, along with guides to over 100 other international cities, at **www.timeout.com**.

Boston

HAVE US.
WILL
TRAVEL.

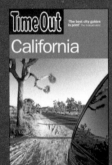

California

Chicago

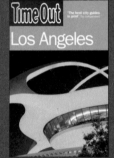

Los Angeles

Miami
& the Florida Keys

San Francisco

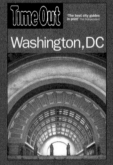

Washington, DC

In Context

Mission Dolores. *See p11*.

Black Panthers in Oakland. *See p18.*

History

Boomtown, earthquake zone, hotbed of counterculture, gay village *in excelsis* – welcome to San Francisco.

When excavation began in 1969 for BART's Civic Center station, workers uncovered the body of a young woman. Experts dated the remains to approximately 2,950 BC, the city's earliest known burial. It was a glimpse into the rich indigenous culture of the Bay Area.

During the last Ice Age, 15,000 years ago, nomadic tribes migrated across the Bering Strait from Asia and eventually settled along the shores of the Bay. Ringed by reeds and hills covered with pastures, the Bay Area sustained more than 10,000 Northern Californian natives of different tribes, later collectively dubbed Costanoans ('coast dwellers') by the Spanish.

Despite its current name, the San Francisco Bay is an estuary, mixing the cold Pacific Ocean with the San Joaquin and Sacramento rivers, which originate from the fresh snowmelt of the Sierra Nevada. The Bay reached its present size about 100,000 years ago, when melting glaciers flooded the world's oceans. Rising sea water flowed inland through the Golden Gate, the point where prominent coastal hills jostling around two peninsulas almost meet. This estuary protects three natural islands, Alcatraz, Angel and Yerba Buena, and the artificial Treasure Island.

At first, the Ohlone people lived here in harmony both with their Miwok neighbours and the land, which provided them with rich pickings of game, fish, shellfish, fruit and nuts (it was, in the words of a later French explorer, a land of 'inexpressible fertility'). They lived a successful hunter-gatherer existence until the arrival of Spanish missionaries. Their previous contacts with Europeans had been friendly, but the Spanish brought with them the dubious gifts of Christianity, hard labour and diseases such as smallpox, which eventually annihilated half the native population of California in 75 years.

THEY CAME, THEY SAW

Looking at the Golden Gate today, it's not hard to imagine how early navigators missed the mile-wide opening. The Bay and its native peoples were hidden by 'stynkinge fogges' (as Francis Drake later complained), which prevented numerous explorers over a period of 200 years from discovering the harbour entrance.

An early series of Spanish missions sent up the coast by Hernán Cortés, notorious conqueror of Mexico and the Aztecs, never got as far as Upper California. In 1542, under the flag of Cortés's successor, Antonio de Mendoza, Portuguese explorer Juan Rodríguez Cabrillo became the first European to visit the area. Inspired by a popular 16th-century novel, the Spanish named their new-found land California. Cabrillo passed the Bay's entrance on his way north and on his way back again, but failed to discover its large natural harbour.

An Englishman got even closer, yet still managed to miss it. In 1579, during a foraging and spoiling mission in the name of the Virgin Queen, Elizabeth I, the then-unknighted Francis Drake landed in Miwok Indian territory just north of the Bay. With one ship, the *Golden Hind*, and a crew in dire need of rest and recreation, he put in for a six-week berth on the Marin coastline, probably near Point Reyes. Long before the Pilgrims landed at Plymouth Rock or the English settled Cupid's Cove at Newfoundland, Drake claimed California for Elizabeth I as 'Nova Albion' or 'New Britain'.

It would be 190 years before another white man set eyes on the Bay. Spurred on by the pressure of British colonial ambitions in America, the Spanish sent northbound missions to stake out their own territories, intent on converting the *bestias* and claiming land for the Spanish crown. Sailing under the Spanish flag in 1595, Portuguese explorer Sebastian Rodríguez Cermeno was shipwrecked just north of the Golden Gate at what is now known as Drake's Bay. Before he made his way back to Mexico in a small boat saved from the ship, he named the protected cove Bahia de San Francisco.

In 1769 came the 'sacred expedition' of Gaspar de Pórtola, a Spanish aristocrat who would later become the first governor of California, and the Franciscan priest Junípero Serra (*see p100* **Statues**), who set off with 60 men on a gruelling march across the Mexican desert with the aim to establish a mission at San Diego. Once they'd done so, the party worked its way north to Monterey, building missions and baptising Indians as they went. During the expedition, an advance party discovered an unexpectedly long bay 100 miles further up the coast. They mistook it for Cermeno's Bahia de San Francisco and, since the expedition's brief was only to claim Monterey, returned to San Diego.

It was not until August 1775 that the *San Carlos*, a Spanish supply vessel, became the first ship to sail into the Bay. Meanwhile, a mission set off to establish a safer land route to what would eventually become San Francisco. Roughly concurrent with the signing of the American Declaration of Independence, Captain Juan Bautista de Anza led an advance party to the southern point of the Golden Gate, which he declared a perfect location for a Spanish military garrison, or *presidio*. Three miles inland to the south-east, a suitable site was found for a mission. Before the year was out, the *presidio* was erected, and the mission – named Misión San Francisco de Asís after the holy order operating in Upper California, but popularly known as Mission Dolores – was established by the indefatigable Serra.

FOLLOW THE BEAR

A mix of favouritism, authoritarianism and religious fervour eventually helped sow the seeds of resentment and resistance in territories colonised by Spain. The country's hold on its American empires first began to crumble in Mexico, which declared itself a republic in 1821. The Mexican annexation of California in the same year opened up the area to foreign settlers; among them were American pioneers such as fur trapper Jedediah Smith, who in 1828 became the first white American to reach California over the Sierra Nevada mountain range. His feat was impressive, but the more sedate arrival by whaler ship of an Englishman had more lasting impact. Captain William Richardson, who in 1835 built the first dwelling on the site of the future San Francisco, is credited with giving the city its first name: Yerba Buena, named after the sweet mint (literally 'good herb') the Spanish used for tea.

That same year, the US tried unsuccessfully to buy the whole of the Bay Area from the Mexicans. In the long run, however, they got California for free: the declaration of independence of the territory of Texas, and its subsequent annexation by the US, triggered the Mexican-American war in June 1846. The resulting Guadalupe-Hidalgo Treaty of 1848 officially granted the Union all the land from Texas to California and from the Rio Grande to Oregon. But before the treaty could be nailed down, a few hotheads decided to 'liberate' the territory from Mexico themselves.

The short-lived Mexican rule of California coincided with the era of idealistic frontiersmen such as Kit Carson and Captain John Fremont, who, in June 1846, convinced a motley crew to take over the abandoned *presidio* to the north of Yerba Buena in Sonoma. Fremont proclaimed his new state the 'Bear Flag Republic', after the ragged banner he raised over Sonoma's square (the design was eventually adopted as the state flag), and he named the mouth of San Francisco

There's gold in them there hills! **Prospectors** arrive in 1849.

Bay the 'Golden Gate' after Istanbul's Golden Horn. A few weeks after the Bear Flaggers annexed Sonoma, the US Navy captured Yerba Buena without a struggle and the whole of California became US territory.

The infant Yerba Buena was a sleepy trading post of 500 people. The newly appointed mayor, Lieutenant Washington A Bartlett, officially renamed it San Francisco on 30 January 1847. But unknown to its residents, the tiny settlement was about to change dramatically.

ALL THAT GLITTERS

Californians have the eagle eye of one James Marshall to thank for their current prosperity. Marshall it was who, while building a mill on the American River near Sacramento in January 1848, spotted what he thought was gold in a sawmill ditch. Along with John Sutter, the Swiss-born rancher who was Marshall's landlord, he attempted to keep his findings secret, but when newspaper publisher Sam Brannan dramatically waved a bottle of gold dust in San Francisco's town square, gold fever went global. The Gold Rush was on.

The news brought droves of drifters and fortune-seekers to the Bay Area, their fever fanned by people like Brannan, whose *California Star* newspaper told of men digging up a fortune in an hour. (Brannan eventually became California's first millionaire by selling goods to prospectors. Pure coincidence.) Many never made it: by land, the journey meant months of

exposure to blizzards, mountains, deserts and hostile tribes; by sea, they faced disease, starvation or brutal weather. Still, more than 90,000 prospectors appeared in California in the first two years after gold was discovered, and 300,000 had arrived in the state by 1854, one out of every 90 people then living in the US. Though they called themselves the Argonauts, after the mythical sailors who accompanied Jason in search of the Golden Fleece, locals named them after the year the Rush began: the Forty-Niners.

The port town in which they arrived was one without structure, government or even a name (to many, it was still Yerba Buena). They found more hardship than gold: on their way to the mines, predatory merchants fleeced them; when they returned, broke, they were left to grub mean existences from the city streets, seeking refuge in brothels, gambling dens and bars. Within two years of Marshall's discovery, nearly 100,000 men had passed through the city; the population grew from 600 in 1848 to 25,000 in 1849, swelling the tiny community into a giant, muddy campsite. Despite a fire that levelled the settlement on Christmas Eve 1849, a new town rose up to take its place and the population exploded. Still, this brave new boomtown was not a place for the faint-hearted. Lawlessness and arson ruled; frontier justice was common.

The opening of a post office marked the city's first optimistic stab at improving links with the rest of the continent. John White Geary, appointed postmaster by President James Knox

Tales of the city Emperor Norton

Like so many thousands from around the globe, Joshua A Norton – born in England, raised in South Africa – arrived in San Francisco in 1849 with high hopes of making his fortune from the Gold Rush. While those around him discovered untold riches to the east of San Francisco, before losing them in the fleshpots of the newly emerging city, Norton steadily increased his capital, dealing in real estate and speculating on the markets. Within a few years, he had become one of the wealthiest and most powerful figures in San Francisco.

Disaster struck Norton in 1858, when he lost all his money investing in rice, an important foodstuff in San Francisco. Declared bankrupt, he disappeared from the city, tail between his legs. A year later, though, he returned, and in some style. In letters he wrote to several San Francisco newspapers, he proclaimed himself to be 'Emperor Norton of These United States and Protector of Mexico', immediately declaring the dissolution of the US Government and Constitution in his favour.

While few bowed down to his reign, Norton quickly became a local celebrity. He spent his days wandering the streets of the city with his two dogs, Bummer and Lazarus, who were also the focus of much gossip. (When Bummer died, Mark Twain wrote his obituary.) Although he would return every night to the squalor of a rented room at 624 Commercial Street, Norton ate for free at the finest restaurants in San Francisco and always had a box at local theatres; indeed, it's reputed

that he conducted a passionate affair with a leading actress of the day. Some considered him mad, and many others saw him as at least eccentric, but he was much loved by the citizens of San Francisco, and was saluted by every city policeman as he strolled around town. The census taker even listed his occupation as 'emperor'.

As Emperor of the United States, Norton corresponded with European royalty, including Queen Victoria. He also issued regular proclamations that quickly passed into legend through newspapers: attempting to dissolve Congress, demanding free rooms from the Grand Hotel. So famous was Norton, in fact, that the local newspapers frequently fabricated his proclamations to boost sales; one Norton diktat, the origins of which remain open for debate, had the emperor levying a $25 fine on anyone who referred to San Francisco as 'Frisco'.

However, it wasn't all fun and games. Norton was concerned with the political issues of the day, such as slavery, the Civil War and the general evils of 19th-century society. He implored his 'subjects' to strive for a more equitable society and, in 1872, urged the city to erect a bridge across the Golden Gate.

Upon Norton's sudden death in 1880, 30,000 people lined the streets of San Francisco to pay their respects. He was buried with full honours, at the city's expense, in the Masonic Cemetery, though his body was later moved to Woodlawn Cemetery in Colma.

Polk, rented a room at the corner of Montgomery and Washington Streets, where he marked out a series of squares for each letter of the alphabet and began filing letters. This crude set-up was San Francisco's first postal system. In April 1850, the year California became the Union's 31st state, San Francisco's city charter was approved; the city elected Geary its first mayor.

Geary's council later bought the ship *Euphemia* to serve as San Francisco's first jail. It proved a sound investment. Gangs of

hoodlums controlled certain districts: the Ducks, led by Australian convicts, lived at a spot known as Sydney Town and, together with New York toughs the Hounds, roamed Telegraph Hill, raping and pillaging the orderly community of Chilean merchants who occupied Little Chile. Eventually, right-minded citizens decided to take the law into their own hands. Whipped into a fury by rabble-rouser Brannan, vigilantes lynched their first victim, John Jenkins, at Portsmouth Square in June 1851.

They strung up three more thieves during the following weeks; the other Ducks and Hounds wisely cut out for the Sierras.

Though their frontier justice temporarily curbed the area's excesses, the vigilantes were viewed by Mayor Geary as part of the problem, not the solution. But his crusade was hardly helped when the riverbed gold started running dry. Boom had turned to bust by 1853, and the resulting depression set a cyclical pattern oft-repeated through the city's history.

And sure enough, a second boom arrived. Henry Comstock's 1859 discovery of a rich blue vein of silver (the 'Comstock Lode') in western Nevada triggered a second invasion by fortune-seekers, nicknamed the Silver Rush. This time, though, the ore's nature demanded more elaborate methods of extraction, with high yields going to a small number of companies and tycoons rather than individual prospectors. Before the supply had been exhausted, silver barons had made enough money to transform San Francisco, establishing a neighbourhood of nouveaux riches atop Nob Hill (the name was adapted from the word 'nabob').

If the nabobs took the geographical and moral high ground, those on the waterfront were busy legitimising their reputation as occupants of the 'Barbary Coast'. Naive newcomers and drunken sailors were seen as fair game by gamblers and hoods waiting to 'shanghai' them (shanghai, like 'hoodlum', is a San Francisco expression), as were the immigrant women who found themselves trapped into lives of prostitution or slavery. At one low point, the female population numbered just 22; many a madam made fortune enough to buy her way on to Nob Hill.

COME ONE, COME ALL

The seeds of San Francisco's present-day multiculturalism were sown during this period, when a deluge of immigrants poured in from all over the world. French immigrants vying with Italians to make the best bread started baking sourdough in North Beach. A young German garment-maker named Levi Strauss started using rivets to strengthen the jeans he made for miners. In Chinatown, *tongs* (Mafia-like gangs)

1869. **May 10th.** 1869.
GREAT EVENT
Rail Road from the Atlantic to the Pacific
GRAND OPENING
— OF THE —
Union Pacific
RAIL ROAD
PLATTE VALLEY ROUTE.
PASSENGER TRAINS LEAVE
OMAHA
ON THE ARRIVAL OF TRAINS FROM THE EAST
THROUGH TO SAN FRANCISCO
In less than Four Days, avoiding the Dangers of the Sea!
Travelers for Pleasure, Health or Business
LUXURIOUS CARS & EATING HOUSES
ON THE UNION PACIFIC RAIL ROAD
PULLMAN'S PALACE SLEEPING CARS
RUN WITH ALL THROUGH PASSENGER TRAINS
GOLD, SILVER AND OTHER MINERS!
CHEYENNE for DENVER, CENTRAL CITY & SANTA FE
Be Sure they Read via Platte Valley or Omaha

controlled the opium dens and other rackets; a Chinese immigrant, Wah Lee, opened the city's first laundry. The building in the 1860s of the transcontinental railroad, which employed thousands of Chinese labourers at low pay rates, led to further expansion of Chinatown. Still, despite their usefulness as cheap labour, the Chinese became the targets of racist anti-immigrant activity; indeed, proscriptive anti-Chinese legislation persisted until 1938.

Even in those days, entertainment was high on the agenda for San Franciscans. By 1853, the city boasted five theatres and some 600 saloons and taverns serving 42,000 customers. Locals downed seven bottles of champagne for every bottle swallowed in Boston (San Francisco still leads the US in alcohol consumption per capita). Lola Montez, entertainer to European monarchs and thieves, arrived on a paddle-steamer from Panama in 1853; her 'spider dance' became an instant hit at the American Theater.

San Francisco's relative isolation from the rest of the continent meant the city was hardly affected by the Civil War that devastated the American South in the early 1860s. The rest of the country seemed remote; mail sometimes took six months to arrive. However, communications were slowly improving. Telegraph wires were being strung across the continent; where telegraph poles ran out, the Pony Express picked up messages, relaying up to 75 riders across the West to the Pacific coast. Even so, when the telegraph pole had all but rendered the Pony Express obsolete, the transcontinental railroad was its coup de grâce.

The completion of the Central Pacific Railroad in 1869 was the signal for runaway consumption in the city. The biggest spenders were the 'Big Four', Charles Crocker, Collis P Huntington, Mark Hopkins and Leland Stanford, brutally competitive millionaires who were the powerful and influential principal investors behind the Central Pacific. Their eagerness to impress the West with their flamboyantly successful business practices manifested itself in the mansions they built on Nob Hill. By 1871, 121 businessmen controlled $146 million, according to one newspaper – but others got in on the act. In particular, four Irishmen – the 'Bonanza Kings': James Flood, William O'Brien, James Fair and John Mackay – made the ascent to Nob Hill, having started out as rough-hewn miners and bartenders chipping out their fortunes from the Comstock Lode.

A Scottish-Irish banker, William Ralston, opened the Bank of California on Sansome Street in 1864. Partnered by Prussian engineer Adolph Sutro, later famous for building the first Cliff House and the Sutro Baths, Ralston was determined to extract every last ounce of silver from the Comstock's Sun Mountain. Unfortunately, he did so too quickly: the ore ran out before he could recoup his investment, and his bank collapsed. Ralston drowned himself, leaving behind the luxurious Palace Hotel and a lasting contribution towards San Francisco's new civic pride: Golden Gate Park. Ralston's company provided the water for William Hammond Hall's audacious project, which transformed a barren area of sand dunes into a magnificent expanse of trees, flowers and lakes.

THE BIG ONE

The city continued to grow, and by 1900 its population had reached more than a third of a million, making it the ninth-largest city in the Union. But shortly after 5am on 18 April 1906, dogs began howling and horses whinnying –

noises that, along with glasses tinkling and windows rattling, marked the unnerving moments before an earthquake.

When the quake hit – a rending in the tectonic plates 25 miles beneath the ocean bed that triggered the shifting of billions of tons of rock – it generated more energy than all the explosives used in World War II. The rip snaked inland, tearing a gash now known as the San Andreas Fault down the coastline. Cliffs appeared from nowhere, cracks yawned, ancient redwoods toppled and part of the newly built City Hall tumbled down. A second tremor struck, ripping the walls out of buildings, destroying the city alarms and disrupting the water pipes that fed the fire hydrants, leaving the city's firefighters helpless. The blaze that followed compounded the damage; it only ceased when, in desperation, Mayor Eugene Schmitz and General Frederick Funston blew up the mansions along Van Ness Avenue, creating a firebreak.

The earthquake and three-day inferno were initially thought to have killed around 700, but military records now reveal that the figure probably ran to several thousand. Around 250,000 people were left homeless and thousands of acres of buildings were destroyed; on Schmitz's orders, anyone suspected of looting in the ensuing chaos was shot dead.

If the **1906 earthquake** didn't affect the locals, the fire that followed did.

Tales of the city Robert Stroud

A military jail from the 1870s onwards and a federal prison from 1934 to 1963, Alcatraz hosted many of America's most incorrigible criminals, among them Al Capone, George 'Machine Gun' Kelly and Alvin 'Creepy' Karpis. Still, no previous inmate has inspired quite so much interest as Robert Stroud, aka the Bird Man of Alcatraz.

The public image of Stroud is built around Burt Lancaster's sympathetic turn as Stroud in the 1962 film *Birdman of Alcatraz*, which portrays him as a brilliant but troubled man, a benevolent bird lover and a righteous foe of the inhuman prison regime. He was certainly a man of uncommon intellect, but the rest? Pure Hollywood.

In the Alaskan town of Juneau in 1909, the 18-year-old Stroud shot and killed a bartender who had allegedly refused to pay Stroud's prostitute girlfriend for services rendered. As he left the scene, he coolly stole the $10 fee from the dead man's wallet. A 12-year sentence for manslaughter didn't mellow him: while inside, he stabbed a hospital orderly, and generally gained a reputation as a difficult and dangerous individual. In 1916, after learning that his brother had tried to visit

on a non-designated day and been turned away, he murdered a prison guard in front of 1,100 inmates in the prison mess hall. Originally sentenced to death for the killing, Stroud eventually had his term commuted to life without parole, albeit in solitary confinement.

While incarcerated at Leavenworth in Kansas, Stroud discovered an injured sparrow in the recreation yard, and soon grew interested in birds. The administration encouraged his sudden interest in ornithology, allowing him to breed some 300 canaries in his cell. The concession proved problematic, though. After performing autopsies on birds as part of his research (he even wrote two books on canaries, and developed medicines for their various ailments), Stroud left their carcasses in the cell, and laboured in his informal lab covered in bird excrement. He received so many letters that it was impossible to screen his mail; the stacks of bird cages made searching his cell impossible. Guards eventually discovered that the ever-resourceful Stroud had built an alcohol still out of some of his lab equipment.

In 1942 Stroud was transferred to Alcatraz, where he was to spend 17 years of his life in 'deep lockdown'. However, the privileges he enjoyed at Leavenworth were not extended to him on the island. In other words, the Birdman of Alcatraz never kept birds on Alcatraz. He was transferred to the Medical Center for Federal Prisoners in Missouri, where he died in 1963. *Birdman of Alcatraz* was on general release, but Stroud was never allowed to see it. Still, it hardly matters: a vicious, dislikeable man prone to violent outbursts who may also have been a stool pigeon and a predatory homosexual, he probably wouldn't have recognised himself.

On the third day of the catastrophe, the wind changed direction, bringing rain. By 21 April the fire was out.

ONWARDS AND UPWARDS

Before the ashes cooled, citizens set about rebuilding; within ten years, San Francisco had risen from the ruins. Some claimed that in the rush to rebuild, planners passed up the chance to replace the city's grid street system with a more sensible one that followed the area's

natural contours. But there's no doubt San Francisco was reborn as a cleaner, more attractive city – within three years of the fire, it could boast half of the nation's concrete and steel buildings. Such statistical pride was not out of keeping with the boosterism that accelerated San Francisco's post-Gold Rush growth into a large, modern city. The most potent symbol of restored civic pride was the new City Hall, the construction of which was secured by an $8-million city bond.

Completed in 1915, it rose some 16 feet higher than its model, the Capitol building in Washington, DC.

In the years following the catastrophe, two waterways opened that would prove critical to California's economic vitality. The Los Angeles aqueduct was completed in 1913, beginning the transformation of a sleepy Southern California cowtown into the urban sprawl of modern LA. Then, in 1915, the opening of the Panama Canal considerably shortened shipping times between the Atlantic and Pacific coasts, an achievement celebrated in San Francisco by the Panama-Pacific Exposition. Not even the outbreak of World War I in Europe could dampen the city's high spirits. Its optimism was well founded: the war provided a boost to California's mining and manufacturing industries. But, as elsewhere in America, the good times were quickly swallowed up in the world depression signalled by the Wall Street Crash of 1929.

The crisis hit the port of San Francisco especially badly; half the workforce was laid off. On 9 May 1934, under the leadership of Harry Bridges, the International Longshoremen's Association declared a coast-wide strike. Other unions, including the powerful Teamsters, came out in sympathy, shutting down West Coast ports for three months. Blackleg workers managed to break through the picket on 5 July – Bloody Thursday – but with disastrous results. As violence escalated, police opened fire, killing two strikers and wounding 30. A general strike was called for 14 July, when 150,000 people stopped work and brought San Francisco to a standstill for three days. The strike fizzled out when its leaders couldn't agree on how to end the stalemate, but the action wasn't completely futile: the longshoremen won a wage increase and control of the hiring halls.

At the same time, San Francisco managed an amazing amount of construction. The Opera House was completed in 1932; the following year, the island of Alcatraz was transferred from the army to the Federal Bureau of Prisons, which set about building a high-security lock-up. The San Francisco Museum of Modern Art, the first West Coast museum to feature exclusively 20th-century works, opened in 1935. The same decade saw the completion of the San Francisco–Oakland Bay Bridge – six months before work started on the Golden Gate Bridge's revolutionary design. In 1939, on man-made Treasure Island, the city hosted another fair: the Golden Gate International Exposition, described as a 'pageant of the Pacific'. Those who attended were dubbed 'the Thirty-Niners' by local wits. It was to be San Francisco's last big celebration for a while: in 1941 the Japanese attacked Pearl Harbor, and America entered World War II.

The war changed the city almost as much as the Gold Rush or the Great Quake. More than 1.5 million men and thousands of tons of material were shipped to the Pacific from the Presidio, Travis Air Force Base and Treasure Island. Between 1941 and 1945, almost the entire Pacific war effort passed under the Golden Gate. The massed ranks of troops, not to mention some half a million civilian workers who flooded into San Francisco, turned the city into a milling party town hell-bent on sending its boys into battle with smiles on their faces.

Towards the end of the war in Europe, in April 1945, representatives of 50 nations met at the San Francisco Opera House to draft the United Nations Charter. It was signed on 26 June 1945 and formally ratified in October at the General Organisation of the United Nations in London. Many people felt that San Francisco would be the ideal location for the UN's headquarters, but the British and French thought it too far to travel. To the city's great disappointment, the UN moved to New York.

BEATNIK BLUES AND HIPPIE HIGHS

The immediate post-war period was coloured by the return of the demobilised GIs, among them Lawrence Ferlinghetti. While studying at the Sorbonne in the early 1950s, the poet had discovered Penguin paperbacks, which inspired him to open his tiny, wedge-shaped bookshop at 261 Columbus Avenue. Called City Lights, the shop became a mecca for the bohemians later dubbed the Beat Generation by Jack Kerouac.

The Beats reflected the angst and ambition of a post-war generation attempting to escape both the shadow of the Bomb and the rampant consumerism of ultra-conformist 1950s America. In Kerouac's definition, Beat could stand for either beatific or beat – exhausted. The condition is best explained in his novel *On the Road*, which charts the coast-to-coast odysseys of San Francisco-based Beat saint Neal Cassady (thinly disguised as Dean Moriarty), poet Allen Ginsberg and Kerouac himself (named Sal Paradise).

'The emergence of the Beat Generation made North Beach the literary centre of San Francisco and nurtured a new vision that would spread far beyond its bounds,' reflected Ferlinghetti 40 years on. 'The Beats prefigured the New Left evolution and the impulse for change that swept eastward from San Francisco.' The attention of the world might have been on the beret-clad artists and poets populating North Beach cafés, but an event in Anaheim, 500 miles to the south, was more reflective of mainstream America. In 1955, Disneyland opened its gates.

Despite the imaginary perfect world portrayed by Disney, the media exposure received by Kerouac and Ginsberg established the Bay Area as a centre for the burgeoning counterculture, generating mainstream America's suspicions that San Francisco was the fruit-and-nut capital of the US. Its fears were about to be confirmed by the hippie explosion of the 1960s. The Beats and hippies might have shared a love of marijuana and a common distaste for 'the system', but Kerouac – now an embittered alcoholic – abhorred what he saw as the hippies' anti-Americanism. (It was, in fact, the Beats who coined the term 'hippie' to refer to those they saw as second-rate, lightweight hipsters.) Kerouac's distaste for these new bohemians was shared by John Steinbeck, who shied away from the recognition he received in the streets.

The original Beats had no interest in political action, but the newer generation embraced it. A sit-in protest against a closed session of the House of Representatives Un-American Activities Committee (HUAC) at the City Hall in 1961 drew protesters from San Francisco State University and the University of California's Berkeley campus. It quickly degenerated into a riot, establishing the pattern for later protests and police responses. In 1964 Berkeley students, returning from a summer of civil rights protests in the South, butted heads with university officials over the right to use campus facilities for their campaigns. The conflict signalled the beginning of the 'free speech movement', led by student activist Mario Savio; it marked the split between the politically conscious and those who chose to opt out of the system altogether. America's escalating involvement in the Vietnam War added urgency to the voices of dissent; Berkeley students remained at the forefront of protests on campuses around the country.

The availability of LSD, its popularity boosted in San Francisco by such events as the Human Be-In and the Acid Tests overseen by Owsley Stanley and the Grateful Dead, drew an estimated 8,000 hippies from across America. Over half stayed, occupying the cheap Victorian houses around the Haight-Ashbury district (dubbed 'the Hashbury'). Combined with the sun, drugs and acid-induced psychedelic music explosion, the local laissez-faire attitude gave rise to the famous Summer of Love. By 1968, however, the spread of hard drugs, notably heroin, had taken the shine off the hippie movement; the fatal stabbing by Hell's Angels of a Rolling Stones fan at the Altamont Speedway during the band's 1969 concert there seemed to confirm darker times ahead.

Like its drugs, the city's politics were getting harder. Members of the Black Panther movement, a radical black organisation founded across the Bay in Oakland by Huey Newton and Bobby Seale, asked themselves why they should ship out to shoot the Vietnamese when the real enemy was at home. Around Oakland, the Panthers took to exercising the American right to bear arms. Gunfights inevitably followed: Panther leader Eldridge Cleaver was wounded and 17-year-old Bobby Hutton killed in a shoot-out with Oakland police in April 1968. The Black Panther movement had petered out by the early 1970s, its leaders either dead, imprisoned or, like Cleaver, on the run. The kidnapping in 1974 of Patty Hearst, heir to the Hearst newspaper fortune, was the point at which the 1960s revolution turned into deadly farce. When she was captured, along with the other members of the tiny Symbionese Liberation Army, Hearst seemed to have been brainwashed into joining the cause.

Despite the violence that characterised the student and anti-war protests, however, the enduring memory of 1960s San Francisco is as the host city to the Summer of Love. The psychedelic blasts of the Grateful Dead, Janis Joplin, Country Joe and the Fish and Jefferson Airplane defined both the San Francisco sound and its countercultural attitude. Berkeley student Jann Wenner founded *Rolling Stone* magazine in 1967 to explain and advance the cause, helping to invent New Journalism in the process.

THE RAINBOW REVOLUTION

San Francisco's radical baton was taken up in the 1970s by the gay liberation movement. Local activists insisted that gay traditions had always existed in the city, first among the Ohlone and later during the 1849 Gold Rush, when women in the West were more scarce than gold. Early groups such as the Daughters of Bilitis, the Mattachine Society and the Society for Individual Rights (SIR) paved the way for more radical new political movements. Gay activists made successful forays into mainstream politics in 1977: SIR's Jim Foster became the first openly gay delegate at a Democratic Convention, and Harvey Milk was elected to the city's Board of Supervisors.

Then Dan White changed everything. A former policeman from a working-class background, White had run for supervisor as an angry, young, blue-collar populist – and won. He suffered poor mental health and had to resign under the strain of office, but quickly changed his mind and asked Mayor Moscone to reinstate him. Milk, who held the deciding vote, persuaded the mayor not to let the unstable

White back in, with catastrophic consequences: on 28 November 1978 White entered City Hall and shot Milk and Moscone. He turned himself in after the deed; in the poorly prosecuted court case, the jury returned two verdicts of voluntary manslaughter, and White was sentenced to seven years. His 'Twinkie Defense' was notorious: his attorney argued that White's lousy diet, especially the eponymous foodstuff, had led to diminished mental capacity.

The killings stunned San Francisco, and the verdict outraged the populace. White's sentence prompted one journalist to wonder why the jury had not posthumously convicted Milk of 'unlawful interference with a bullet fired from the gun of a former police officer'. Gay men and women responded by storming City Hall and hurling rocks through the windows. The disturbance escalated into a full-blown battle, known as the White Night Riot. White committed suicide not long after his release.

Gay life and politics changed radically and irrevocably with the onset of the HIV virus, which tore the gay community apart and caused controversy when the city's bathhouses, a symbol of gay liberation and promiscuity, were closed in panic over the spread of the disease. Gay radicals branded *Chronicle* writer Randy Shilts a 'fascist Nazi, traitor and homophobe' when he criticised bathhouse owners who refused to post safe-sex warnings, but his book *And the Band Played On* is still the definitive account of the period.

Since its identification, AIDS has claimed the lives of some 18,000 San Franciscans. The levelling-out of numbers of new cases and the dangerous misperception that the epidemic is ebbing have endangered fundraising efforts, but the city remains home to the most efficient volunteers in the country. Preventionists continue to make inroads into all sexually active communities; caretakers have taken charge of housing, food and legal problems for the roughly two per cent of the city who have been diagnosed as HIV-positive. As sufferers live longer thanks to new drugs, the city continues to need more resources to assist them.

COLLAPSE AND RECOVERY
Because of its location on the San Andreas Fault, San Francisco has always lived in anticipation of a major earthquake to rival the 1906 disaster. It came in October 1989: the Loma Prieta quake, named after the ridge of mountains at its epicentre, registered 7.1 on the Richter scale (the 1906 quake was an estimated 7.8). Part of the West Oakland Freeway collapsed, crushing drivers; the Marina district was devastated by fires; and 50 feet (15 metres) of the Bay Bridge's upper deck

collapsed. In just 15 seconds, more than 19,000 homes were damaged or destroyed; 62 people were killed and 12,000 were displaced.

As the 1990s progressed, changes in the city reflected those in the world beyond. The end of the Cold War meant cuts in military spending, and the Presidio – which operated as a US military base for almost 150 years – was closed in 1994. As part of the Base Closure and Realignment Act, the land was transferred to the the National Park Service. The collapse of the Soviet Union also brought in a wave of Russian immigrants, many of them settling in the already ethnically diverse Richmond District.

San Francisco also experienced a remarkable renaissance. Its proximity to Silicon Valley's economic boom rejuvenated the city's business structure and reshaped the skyline. In the wake of the Loma Prieta earthquake, the Embarcadero Freeway was torn down and the city's historic bayside boulevard turned into a palm-tree-lined haven for walkers, joggers, in-line skaters and cyclists. Numerous major projects were brought to completion and others begun: in 1995, the San Francisco Museum of Modern Art moved into a new building in burgeoning SoMa, and voters passed a bond allowing for the restoration of City Hall. Five years later, Pac Bell Park (now SBC Park), the first privately funded Major League Baseball park in nearly 40 years, opened its gates. The Yerba Buena Center and Zeum children's museum also opened their doors during this time.

As the 20th century rolled into the 21st, San Francisco suffered from many of the same social problems that plagued other major US cities. Homelessness was particularly severe, with up to 14,000 destitute men and women sleeping without nightly shelter. The problem was compounded by the late '90s internet boom, which brought workers from around the world into an increasingly tight housing market and gentrified working-class neighbourhoods.

But by the end of the decade, fortunes had turned, rents had started to drop and the city had begun to reinvent itself yet again. San Francisco maintains its best-of-the-West-Coast reputation for magnificent food, stylish design, charming architecture and a multicultural, ideas-driven population. In 1889, Rudyard Kipling described San Francisco as a 'mad city inhabited for the most part by perfectly insane people'. His conclusion is one shared by many residents even today: ''Tis hard to leave.'

▶ For more on **City Hall**, *see p78*.
▶ For more on **the Beats**, *see p33*.
▶ For more on **Harvey Milk**, *see p40*.

Key events

c10,000 BC The Ohlone and Miwok Indians begin to settle the Bay Area.
1542 Juan Cabrillo sails up the California coastline.
1579 Francis Drake lands north of the San Francisco Bay, claiming the land for Elizabeth I and calling it 'Nova Albion'.
1769 Gaspar de Pórtola and Father Junípero Serra lead an overland expedition to establish a mission at San Diego. An advance party is sent to scout the coast; they become the first white men to see the San Francisco Bay.
1775 The *San Carlos* is the first ship to sail into the bay.
1776 On 4 July, 13 American colonies declare their independence from Great Britain. In the autumn, a Spanish military fort is founded by Fort Point; Serra establishes Mission Dolores.
1821 Mexico declares its independence from Spain and annexes California.
1828 Fur trapper Jebediah Smith becomes the first white man to reach California across the Sierra Nevada mountain range.
1835 English-born sailor William Richardson sets up a trading post he calls 'Yerba Buena'.
1846 The Bear Flag Revolt takes place against Mexican rule in California. Captain John B Montgomery takes possession of Yerba Buena and claims it for the US.
1847 Yerba Buena is renamed San Francisco.
1848 A US–Mexican treaty confirms American dominion over California. James Marshall finds gold in the low Sierras near Sacramento.
1849 The Gold Rush swells the city's population from 800 to 25,000 in less than a year. A fire levels the city on Christmas Eve.
1850 California becomes the 31st state of the Union.
1859 The Comstock Lode is discovered in western Nevada, triggering the Silver Rush.
1861 The Civil War breaks out between the Union and the Confederacy. California remains largely untouched by hostilities.
1868 The University of California is established at Berkeley.
1869 The transcontinental railroad connects San Francisco with the rest of the US.
1873 Andrew Hallidie builds the first cable car.
1906 A massive earthquake hits the city; a fire follows. Thousands die, and 28,000 buildings are destroyed.
1915 San Francisco celebrates the opening of the Panama Canal with the Panama-Pacific Exposition.

1932 San Francisco Opera House opens.
1934 On 5 July (Bloody Thursday), police open fire on striking longshoremen, leaving two dead and prompting a three-day general strike that brings the Bay Area to a standstill. Also this year, Alcatraz opens as a federal prison.
1936 The Bay Bridge is completed.
1937 The Golden Gate Bridge is completed.
1941 The Japanese attack Pearl Harbor, and the US enters World War II.
1945 Fifty nations meet at the San Francisco Opera House to sign the UN Charter.
1955 Allen Ginsberg reads 'Howl' at the Six Gallery.
1961 UC Berkeley students stage a sit-in protest against a closed session of the House of Representatives Un-American Activities Committee at City Hall.
1964 Student sit-ins and mass arrests grow as the civil rights, free-speech and anti-Vietnam War movements gain momentum.
1967 The Human Be-In pre-empts the Summer of Love.
1968 Teenager Bobby Hutton is killed in a Black Panther shoot-out with Oakland police.
1972 The Bay Area Rapid Transit system (BART) opens.
1978 Mayor George Moscone and Harvey Milk, a gay member of the Board of Supervisors, are shot and killed by former official Dan White.
1981 The city's first known cases of AIDS.
1989 Another major earthquake hits the city.
1992 Fire sweeps through the Oakland hills, killing dozens and destroying 3,000 homes.
1994 After 220 years with the military, the Presidio transfers to the National Park Service.
1995 The San Francisco 49ers win the Super Bowl for the fifth time. Willie Brown Jr becomes the city's first African-American mayor.
1997 Damaged in the 1989 quake, the San Francisco Opera House finally reopens.
2000 Pacific Bell Park (now SBC Park), the new home of the San Francisco Giants baseball team, opens to great acclaim.
2003 Establishment Democrat Gavin Newsom pips progressive Green Party member Matt Gonzalez in the city's mayoral elections.
2004 Newsom grants the first same-sex marriage licenses in the US, setting off a storm of controversy. Barry Bonds hits his 661st home run, moving past godfather and fellow Giants icon Willie Mays on the all-time list.
2005 The de Young Museum reopens in a dramatic building in Golden Gate Park.

San Francisco Today

The dot-com bubble may have burst, but the City by the Bay is back on the rise again.

Some people have said that the '90s in San Francisco were just the '60s upside down (and with more cash). If that's the case, then the '00s are looking like the '70s sideways: sky-rocketing real estate and petrol prices, along with a shift from a heady, adrenaline-pumped, go-get-'em approach to a increasingly mellow outlook, and an apparent return to the introversion of the 'Me Generation'.

This current self-absorption is surely due, at least in part, to the 2004 presidential election, and to the unprecedented recall election that put muscle-bound Republican actor Arnold Schwarzenegger in power as the governor of California. Both events hit this famously liberal stronghold right in the solar-panelled plexus; anti-war protesters, Bush bashers, and political and environmental activists of every stripe were devastated. For a time, they retreated to

lick their collective wounds, but the familiar rumble of defiance and dissent didn't take too long to rear its head once more.

In 2004, the newly crowned boy-mayor Gavin Newsom rocketed into the national spotlight by granting marriage licences to gay couples. Thousands of same-sex pairs flocked to City Hall to exchange their vows, before the Feds stepped in and blocked the whole permit process. The battle rages on, however, with other states joining the fray on both sides. A big showdown in the Supreme Court and the corridors of Congress is looming on the horizon.

Whatever the outcome, Bonnie Prince Newsom, whose hands-on style and Kennedy-esque good looks recall a bygone era of Democratic idealism, has scored points with both the city's old-school liberals and the young anti-establishment activists; more so with the

Roads to ruin

Getting around San Francisco efficiently has always been something of a challenge: all those steep hills and giant bodies of water, not to mention the recurring bouts with earthquakes that inconveniently upend major transportation arteries, and the waves of population explosions that made already-crowded commuter routes nearly impassable. Yet the city planners, in their rush to find immediate solutions, have frequently ended up cutting down the trees only to turn around and complain about the lack of forest.

In the early 1970s, after smoothing over the last bit of asphalt following a decade of construction on the BART system, the city proceeded to tear up Market Street all over again to build the underground Muni Metro streetcar network. South of Market, the streetcar service that ran up and down 3rd Street in the early 20th century was deemed inefficient (read: unprofitable) just before World War II, and dismantled. A half-century later, they thought better of it, and Muni is nearing completion on a 3rd Street light-rail line that will cover much of the same territory.

No doubt the biggest transportation quagmire, however, is the convoluted saga of the elevated Central Freeway. It was long considered a blot on the urban landscape, and most San Franciscans were pleased to see the bulk of it razed in 1992 after the

1989 Loma Prieta earthquake rendered the freeway unsafe. The same year, the Board of Supervisors voted to ban new ramps north of Market Street, but the California Department of Transportation (aka Caltrans) intervened, insisting that a single deck was necessary to streamline traffic to the west end of the city.

What followed was a game of political badminton, with battling grassroots groups succeeding in first halting and then restarting the freeway project several times over. In 1997, voters narrowly passed a bill to rebuild the Fell Street off-ramp. The following year, opponents passed another initiative to stop construction. Finally, in 1999, a third vote put the freeway revolt to rest with the approval of a pedestrian-friendly boulevard at Octavia Street that would accommodate transportation requirements without having to put up another double-decker eyesore.

But the tale doesn't quite end there. After tearing down the last pylon of the old Central in 2002, construction crews reappeared and began erecting giant concrete supports in practically the same place as before. The resulting egress and boulevard, while an aesthetic improvement for Hayes Valley, again casts the businesses along Duboce and Mission streets into sub-freeway hell. Unfortunately, this time, barring another big quake, the purgatory looks to be permanent.

latter, now that he's single again. His latest bid – a call for city-wide free wireless internet access and more widespread healthcare – should keep him on the front pages well into the next election cycle.

This fresh infusion of purpose seems to have shaken the locals out of their post-election stupor. Emboldened by Bush's falling approval ratings and a tide of sentiment that seemed to be turning against his White House, San Franciscans led California in defeating all of Governor Schwarzenegger's proposed state initiatives in a controversial and extremely costly special election in November 2005. A humbled Schwarzenegger is now in for an uphill battle as he fights for re-election in 2006.

As vitriolic as they were about the substance of the special election, San Franciscans were apoplectic about how much it all cost: upwards of $50 million was spent simply on holding it. Their rage appears justified. While employment has been improving incrementally since the dot-bomb era, the Bay Area's economy still lags

behind the rest of the country, particularly in terms of available white-collar jobs. Meanwhile, interest rates keep on rising, and the cost of living continues to break all records. A tiny two-bedroom house in the city goes easily for a million bucks these days, and gas has topped $3 a gallon. Even a day at the revolving-name ballpark (originally Pacific Bell Park, then SBC Park, and, with SBC now using AT&T's name, doubtless something different in 2006) can put the average San Francisco Giants baseball fan out of pocket by a three-figure sum.

The same young wuppies – white urban professionals – who sailed into the city on a wave of internet stock options with a what's-in-it-for-me attitude tacked to the foremast are now discovering the harsh realities of feeding, clothing, housing and schooling their brood in a place that's consistently rated second only to Manhattan as the priciest urban centre in the US. While not as dramatic as the exodus after the bust, the resulting white flight has had a deep impact on the city's infrastructure and its reputation as an adults-only playground. A *New York Times* survey recently reported that San Francisco has fewer children per capita than any other city its size in the USA.

'Projects fuelled by the 1990s internet gold rush are slowly coming to fruition.'

TECHNOPOLIS
Still, economic hope springs eternal for a city that always manages to be in the vanguard of technological discovery. In 2005, it beat half a dozen competitors for the rights to play home to a new $3-billion stem-cell research centre, which will be built in SoMa over the next few years. Now Mayor Newsom and the city's business leaders are banking on the centre to spark a bio-tech boom across San Francisco.

On the other side of town, *Star Wars* mogul George Lucas has opened his state-of-the-art Digital Arts Center on the grounds of the Presidio, an old army base that's now a national park. The complex, comprising 24 acres of office and studio space, positions San Francisco at the hub of the digital film and

video-game revolution; among other innovations, each desktop in the four buildings is wired with fibre-optic cables that enable workers to share digital files instantly.

Down in Silicon Valley, venture capitalism also appears to be climbing out of the doldrums, spurred on by companies such as Google; its 2004 IPO set Wall Street aflame and immediately made its owners into billionaires. This internet search engine, now so ingrained in everyday life as to have become a verb, proceeded to defy doomsday forecasters who predicted its $100 stock value would plummet. As of late 2005, its price was creeping up to nearly $400 a share.

Elsewhere, projects fuelled by the 1990s internet gold rush are slowly coming to fruition. The first phase of construction has been completed on Mission Bay, more than 13 million square feet of research, retail, office, residential and recreation development in China Basin, next to the baseball stadium. A previously lifeless area of industrial warehouses has been transformed into a neighbourhood for the 21st century. The high-rise condominiums, upscale grocers, trendy restaurants, warehouse-size bookstore and an impressive new campus for the University of California are just a few of

Mayor Gavin Newsom (left) still has yet to solve the city's homeless problem.

the components already in place, with more to follow. Indeed, the city's south waterfront is in the process of being entirely, dramatically reshaped. In this very small city, where space is invariably at a premium and where almost everything new is reconstituted from something old, the fresh face of China Basin is something of a revelation. It's not really surprising that everything takes forever to get done here, especially new buildings; approval processes and beauty contests take time. What's really surprising is that it's still possible to invent a brand new neighbourhood from the ground up.

'For the hungry culturati, the de Young is but the first boulder in an avalanche of new arts institutions.'

FEED YOUR HEAD
With tech money starting to flow back into town, and free-spending tourists returning in higher numbers (more than 15 million came in 2004), San Franciscans can finally get back to the things that really matter: what's the next hot food trend, and how do you wangle a reservation at the current 'it' spot? The city's ever-vigilant foodies seem to be growing bored with the craze of the last few years – tapas-style small plates – and are already rooting around for a new taste sensation. Early bets are on Asian comfort food, as exemplified by such popular dishes as Coca-Cola-braised short ribs and congee (a kind of Chinese porridge). Raw fish – in the forms of crudo, tartare and sushi – is also on the rise, wriggling its way into the positions formerly occupied by French bistro fare and *nueva cocina latina*. In general, the cyclical restaurant scene, usually a reliable bellwether for the local economy, is feeling pretty confident these days, with dozens of high-end places opening to packed crowds who hardly hesitate before throwing $40 at a choice piece of organic, grass-fed Niman Ranch beef.

Renewed optimism has also taken hold in the arts; most spectacularly in autumn 2005, when the long-awaited de Young Museum finally opened in Golden Gate Park. The controversial copper-mesh-clad building with its crow's-nest tower, designed by the renowned Swiss team of Herzog and de Meuron, teetered at the sharp edge of critics' tongues for about ten minutes before they swallowed it, art, line and sinker.

It's but the first boulder in an avalanche of new arts institutions scheduled to open in San Francisco over the next few years. Across from the de Young, the California Academy of Sciences, home to the Steinhart Aquarium

and Morrison Planetarium, is in the process of building a groundbreaking new facility that will include a 'living' green roof; it's scheduled for completion in 2008. And over on the other side of town, the Yerba Buena district is a hive of construction activity. The Museum of the African Diaspora opened in the huge St Regis hotel tower in December 2005; come 2008, the Mexican Museum, designed by noted Mexican architect Ricardo Legorreta, and the Contemporary Jewish Museum, due to be housed in an historic Willis Polk power substation made over by famed New York architect Daniel Libeskind, will also have welcomed their first visitors.

Even on issues as seemingly intractable as traffic congestion and the city's chronic indigent problem, there appears to be forward momentum. Following a tumultuous debate over mayor Newsom's 'care not cash' initiative, which provides the homeless with housing and services rather than simple cash handouts, agencies are reporting that the number of homeless on the rolls has dropped dramatically; critics counter that they've simply relocated to friendlier climes. And after a 12-year stalemate, civic leaders finally agreed to start construction on a new eastern span for the Bay Bridge (*see p73* **Bridge of sighs**). Cranes toil away day and night to finish the project – which is already billions over budget and hopelessly behind schedule – in the hope that it might finally be completed some time in 2012.

Meanwhile, an overhaul of the bridge approaches and on-ramps has created nearly round-the-clock gridlock for commuters, who continue to seek creative ways to avoid spending their lives sitting bumper to bumper and paying enormous parking fees and tolls. Hundreds of office workers have taken to casual carpooling, a practice that involves suburban residents standing on street corners and hitching rides into town, enabling the vehicle's driver to take advantage of free carpool lanes.

Those without their own set of wheels have found alternatives such as the City Carshare, a programme that lets members borrow a car at an hourly rate, minus gas charges and parking hassles (subscribers get their own parking spots). Others have opted to retrofit their old Mercedes to run on 'biodiesel' (used cooking oil), which they collect from the backsides of the city's gourmet kitchens, leaving the fumes of French fries trailing in their wake. Whether founded in stubbornness, a propensity for bucking convention or an abiding sense of self-reliance, it's this spirit of inventiveness that long ago earned San Francisco the moniker 'the City that Knows How', and which seems likely to continue driving the town.

Ferry Building. *See p29.*

Architecture

World-class architectural aspirations abound
for the City by the Bay.

Walking through this tiny metropolis in
recent years, you could almost feel the
ground underfoot rumbling with construction
work. Well known for its architectural
conservatism, San Francisco is finally starting
to turn over a new leaf when it comes to
building. By 2008, the city will have seen
the construction of four new major museums,
one sizeable federal building complex and
several new centres for architecture and urban
design. But the old favourites still stand…

FRAGILE FOUNDATIONS
The oldest building in the city is **Mission
Dolores** (*see p100*), where the thick adobe
walls and painted hammer beams represent
the early European settlement of Yerba Buena.
Founded in 1776 and completed 15 years later,
the simple chapel sits north of a cemetery
where Native Americans, outlaws and the
city's first Irish and Hispanic mayors are
buried. The mission was one of 21 built in
California by the Spanish; only two others,
at Carmel and Monterey, rival it for authentic
atmosphere. Along with a portion of the original
walls of the Officers' Club in the Presidio,

it's the sole piece of colonial architecture
to have outlived the city's steep progress
from hamlet to metropolis.

The town inhabited by the Forty-Niners –
or 'Argonauts', as the Gold Rush immigrants
dubbed themselves – suffered a series of fires.
Portsmouth Square in today's Chinatown
(*see p87*), the heart of the early outpost,
was levelled by two blazes; the surrounding
streets perished in the fire following the 1906
earthquake. The most impressive buildings
from the Gold Rush era are in the **Jackson
Square Historical District** (best viewed
on Jackson between Montgomery and Sansome
Streets; *see p71*).

WEST COAST VICTORIANA
A burst of 19th-century prosperity quickly
filled San Francisco's once-empty sloping
streets with what have become its signature
Victorian terraced houses. Built by middle-
class tradesmen in the Mission and Lower
Haight districts, and by rich merchants in
Presidio Heights and around **Alamo Square**
(*see p106*), these famous '**Painted Ladies**'
provide San Francisco's most characteristic

architectural face. One of the most popular views of the city is framed by a row of six painted Victorians along Steiner Street between Hayes and Grove Streets ('**Postcard Row**'), but there are more than 14,000 examples of this eye-catching architectural vernacular, some even more fanciful.

'This most curious of cities boasts many curiosities.'

Built of wooden frames and decorated with mass-produced ornamentation, San Francisco's Victorians come in four distinct styles: Gothic Revival, Italianate, Stick-Eastlake and Queen Anne. The earliest Gothic Revival houses have pointed arches over their windows and were often painted white, rather than in the bright colours of the later styles. The Italianate style, with tall cornices, neo-classical elements and add-on porches, are best exemplified in the Lower Haight, notably

on Grove Street near Webster Street, but there are other examples at **1900 Sacramento Street** (near Lafayette Park) and at 1818 California Street in the shape of the **Lilienthal-Pratt House**, built in 1876.

The Italianate was succeeded by the Stick-Eastlake style, named after furniture designer Charles Eastlake and characterised by square bay windows framed with angular, carved ornamentation. The 'Sticks' are the most common of the Victorian houses left in the city; a shining example is the over-the-top extravaganza at **1057 Steiner Street**, on the corner of Golden Gate Avenue.

With its turrets, towers and curvaceous corner bay windows, the so-called Queen Anne style is amply demonstrated by the **Wormser-Coleman House** in Pacific Heights (1834 California Street, at Franklin Street). The most extravagant example is the **Haas-Lilienthal House**; it was built in 1886 by Bavarian grocer William Haas, who treated himself to a home

Five to avoid

The Golden Gate Bridge, the Transamerica Pyramid, the Painted Ladies... San Francisco has architectural charm aplenty. But it's also home to a handful of engineering losers, from the merely misguided to the truly hideous. These are the five ugliest; readers should note that the **de Young Museum** – a dazzling piece of 21st-century design, or an ungainly copper-mesh-covered Yucatan pyramid sitting atop an aircraft carrier? – only missed the cut after a heated editorial debate...

CHINATOWN HILTON
Just across the street from Portsmouth Square sits this monstrous cement phallus (750 Kearny Street), surging into the sky in thoroughly intrusive fashion. Formerly a Holiday Inn building, it was undergoing a renovation in 2005, but only a miracle can really save it. Or a wrecking ball.

SAN FRANCISCO MARRIOTT
Known by residents as 'the jukebox', the late-'80s Marriott (55 4th Street, between Market & Mission Streets) is an example of architectural whimsy gone awry. *Way* awry. With its rounded, mirrored façade, punctuated by cheap-looking peach-coloured concrete, this behemoth is held by some to be the pinnacle of tackiness. Worse still, it's the most prominent thing in the city's skyline from the southern perspective.

SAN FRANCISCO MUSEUM OF MODERN ART
While the grey-and-white-striped SFMOMA (151 3rd Street, at Mission & Howard Streets; *see p81*), which opened to much fanfare in 1995, may be architecturally significant, its concrete block does nothing to warm up the SoMa locale where it squats. The tubular motif on its façade has been compared to a lamprey, a type of eel with a jawless sucking mouth and rasping teeth.

SUTRO TOWER
Dubbed 'one of the worst structures, visually, I have an opportunity to view' by California lawmaker Dianne Feinstein, this spindly red-and-white-striped antenna even dwarfs even the largest hills of Twin Peaks below it. The only charm of the 977-foot (297-metre) tower stems from the fact that the city's fog bank tends to peter out at the bottom of its three-antennaed apex, which then takes on the character of a three-masted ghost galleon hovering over the Barbary Coast.

WURSTER HALL
This ghastly, neo-brutalist carbuncle, devoid of any charm whatsoever, is the undisputed lowlight of the UC Berkeley campus. Perhaps inevitably, then, it's home to the university's Architecture Department.

SF's **'Painted Ladies'**. *See p25*.

with 28 rooms and six bathrooms. Now a museum, the house is one of the few Victorians open to the public (*see p117*).

OPULENCE AND INTRIGUE

Another example of the ostentation that accompanied San Francisco's booming late 19th-century lifestyle can be seen at the **Palace Hotel** (*see p47* **Tales of the city**), where guests have included everyone from Rudyard Kipling to European royalty. Opened in 1875, it epitomised local entrepreneur Billy Ralston's dreams and his inability to resist Italian marble and solid-gold dinner services, still on display in the lobby. Locals mourned the original building after it burned down in the 1906 fire, but the city rebuilt it, glassing in the atrium for elegant dining and adding fashionable art deco murals in the bar. It is still wonderful, combining echoes of Old Vienna and a Prohibition-era speakeasy.

Engineer Adolph Sutro was Ralston's friend and his equal in ambition. He eventually came to own most of the western side of the city, including the sandy wasteland on its westerly edge, which he bought in 1881 for his **Sutro Baths**. Annexed by the new Golden Gate Park, the therapeutic baths were the most elaborate in the western world. Much in need of repair by the 1960s, and badly burned in a fire, they were sold to developers for high-rise apartments

that remained unbuilt, and are now unofficially the city's favourite ruins. The adjoining **Cliff House** hotel (*see p115*) burned twice: the rebuilt eight-storey 'castle' was destroyed again in 1907, then went through further incarnations before reopening in 2004 as a bar and restaurant.

Closer to downtown, San Francisco's 'Big Four' businessmen – Mark Hopkins, Leland Stanford, Collis P Huntington and Charles Crocker – made their architectural mark in the late 19th century by building grand edifices. Their mining investments funded railroads and public transport, banks and businesses, but also paid for some baronial mansions on Nob Hill. Many were destroyed in the 1906 fire; their sites have since been filled in suitably grand fashion. Two old mansions have been replaced by hotels: the **Stouffer Renaissance Court** (905 California Street, at Powell Street) and the **Mark Hopkins Inter-Continental** (1 Nob Hill, at California & Mason Streets), while the site that once held the **Crocker Mansion**, a Queen Anne manor built in 1888, is now occupied by **Grace Cathedral** (*see p84*).

However, the nearby **Flood Mansion** (1000 California Street, at Mason Street), survived the blaze and remains a brilliant example of the grandeur of the homes that once perched on Nob Hill. The 42-room sandstone marvel was built in 1886 by silver baron James C Flood and now houses a private club. Another grand old survivor, albeit one that post-dates the quake, is the **Spreckels Mansion**, an impressive Beaux Arts building in Pacific Heights (2080 Washington Street, at Octavia Street). Built in 1912 for sugar baron Adolph Spreckels, it's now owned by mega-selling novelist Danielle Steel.

Unsurprisingly, this most curious of cities boasts many architectural curiosities. Perhaps chief among them is the **Octagon House** (*see p117*). Built in 1861 during a city-wide craze for eight-sided buildings (they were considered healthier because they let in more light), it's one of just two octagonal buildings left in the city. Furnished in early colonial style, the upper floors have now been fully restored, with a central staircase leading to a domed skylight.

Another oddity is the **Columbarium** (*see p115*), a neo-classical temple built in 1898 that now holds the ashes of thousands of San Franciscans. Its interior is decorated with mosaic tiling and elaborate urns in imaginatively bedecked niches. Oriental promise meets occidental vulgarity at the **Vedanta Temple** (*see p117*), an eccentricity built in 1905 for the Hindu Vedanta Society. Its bizarre mix of styles includes a Russian Orthodox onion-shaped dome, a Hindu cupola, castle-like crenellations and Moorish arches. The building is open to the public for Friday night services.

Guides

**To advertise
in the next edition of
Time Out San Francisco**

Please contact us on:
020 7813 6020
or email
guidesadvertising@timeout.com

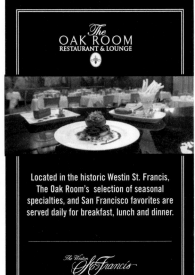

OAK ROOM
RESTAURANT & LOUNGE

Located in the historic Westin St. Francis,
The Oak Room's selection of seasonal
specialties, and San Francisco favorites are
served daily for breakfast, lunch and dinner.

335 Powell Street, San Francisco
Located on Union Square • 415.774.0495

CAMPTON PLACE
SAN FRANCISCO

THE GILT EDGE OF UNION SQUARE

340 STOCKTON STREET SAN FRANCISCO CA 94108 T 415 781 5555 RESERVATIONS 866 332 1669
KORHOTELGROUP.COM I ANGUILLA BEVERLY HILLS LOS ANGELES MIAMI PALM SPRINGS RIVIERA MAYA
SAN FRANCISCO SANTA MONICA SOUTH BEACH WASHINGTON DC WEST HOLLYWOOD

CIVIC ART

When the growing city began to burst at its peninsula seams, a ferry network evolved to carry passengers to and from the Bay Area cities. Intended as a symbol of civic pride for the young city, with a clock tower inspired by the Moorish campanile of Seville Cathedral, the **Ferry Building** was built on the Embarcadero in 1896. It's been renovated in recent years; the impeccably restored Great Nave, a 660-foot-long (200-metre) steel-framed, two-storey interior now houses everything from office space to a hugely popular farmers' market.

After the 1906 earthquake, a passion for engineering spurred an interest in Chicago architect Daniel Burnham's 'City Beautiful' project. Arising from it was a proposal for an heroic new Civic Center planted below a terraced Telegraph Hill, laced with tree-lined boulevards that would trace the city's contours. The plan was the result of Burnham's two-year consultations with leading city architects Bernard Maybeck and Willis Polk (the latter the designer of the wonderful **Hobart Building** at Market & Montgomery Streets), and countered the city's impractical grid street pattern. However, it never came to fruition.

Under Mayor 'Sunny Jim' Rolph, the thrust of the 1915 Civic Center complex eventually came from public contests; many were won by Arthur Brown, architect of the mighty domed **City Hall** (*see p78*). Several other Civic Center buildings date back to this era, among them Brown's **War Memorial Opera House** (*see p227*), completed in 1932, and the **Bill Graham Civic Auditorium** (*see p232*). All reflect the Imperial, Parisian Beaux Arts style, sometimes described as French Renaissance or classical baroque, boasting grandiose proportions and ornamentation, as well as theatrical halls and stairways. The former main library, built by George Kelham in 1915, was recently redesigned by Italian architect Gae Aulenti, best known for her transformation of Paris's Musée d'Orsay; it now offers a spectacularly modern experience as the **Asian Art Museum** (*see p78*).

It was largely Rolph's idea to host the huge Panama-Pacific Exposition in 1915, for which he commissioned Bernard Maybeck to build the **Palace of Fine Arts** and its myriad pavilions. Originally made of wood and plaster (but rebuilt using reinforced concrete in the 1960s), it's the only building left from the Exposition. Around this time, Julia Morgan, another Arts and Crafts architect, was designing buildings around the East Bay, at least when she wasn't working for San Francisco newspaper magnate William Randolph Hearst on the extravagant Hearst Castle. In San Francisco, she designed the old

Willis Polk's 1914 **Hobart Building**.

Chinese YMCA building, now home to the **Chinese American National Museum & Learning Center** (*see p86*).

Passionate rebuilding continued during the Depression, with two staggering landmarks leading the way. The **Golden Gate Bridge** (*see p122*) opened to traffic in 1937, one year after the completion of the **San Francisco–Oakland Bay Bridge** (*see p73* **Bridge of sighs**); the latter is undergoing renovations to protect it from future earthquakes, work that's scheduled to be completed in 2012. The Works Progress Administration (WPA), part of President Roosevelt's post-Depression New Deal job-creation scheme, was responsible for many structures, such as the **Coit Tower**, designed by Arthur Brown in 1932 (*see p91*), and the prison buildings on **Alcatraz** island (*see p93*). Other examples from this period include the 1932 **Herbst Theatre** (with murals by Frank Brangwyn; *see p253*), the 1930 **Pacific Coast Stock Exchange** (complete with mural by Diego Rivera; *see p71*) and the Rincon Annex Post Office Building, built in 1940 to include Anton Refregier's murals and now part of the **Rincon Center** (*see p74*).

While Frank Lloyd Wright's **Marin Civic Center**, completed after his death in 1972 and located further north in San Rafael, is his most stunning civic work, there is one other Lloyd

In Context

Building the future

As San Francisco takes to modern architecture as never before, so its residents develop a greater interest in it. With more architects and designers per capita than anywhere else in the US, the city has become a virtual breeding ground for all things design-related. Following suit, a centre devoted to the region's design arts has sprung to life.

Founded by the local chapter of the American Institute of Architects (www.aiasf. org), the **Center for Architecture & Design** (130 Sutter Street, 362 7397, www.cadsf. org) will be the first AIA enterprise of its kind on the West Coast when it opens in June 2006. Designed by local architect Fred Quezada and located in the historic Hallidie Building, a 1917 Willis Polk creation that features one of the world's first glass curtains, the centre will feature sustainable principles in its 5,000-square-foot space, notably a radiant heating and cooling system.

The centre will offer a year-round programme of lectures, tours, exhibitions and other events on the work of local architects and designers; past AIA exhibitions have focused on alternative practice, architectural photography, furniture design and issues relevant to housing and building in San Francisco. Every September, the AIA stages the Architecture and the City festival, a month-long event that celebrates local construction with tours, film screenings, talks and exhibitions. The Home Tours Weekend, which showcases a wide variety of residential projects in the city, takes place on the third weekend of the month.

Wright building in the city, at 140 Maiden Lane. Wright designed the edifice in 1948, originally a gift store, as a prototype Guggenheim (notice the winding, circular stair). It now houses a tribal- and folk-art gallery, and is open to the public as **Folk Art International** (*see p69*)

ROLLING OUT THE NEW

After a quiet spell, the 1970s saw a small wave of construction that had a big impact on the city's image. Pietro Belluschi and Pier Luigi Nervi completed the **Cathedral if St Mary of the Assumption** (*see p108*) in 1972; a 255-foot (78-metre) concrete structure supporting a cross-shaped, stained-glass ceiling, it's a 1970s symbol of anti-quake defiance, nicknamed St Maytag because it resembles a giant washing-machine agitator. The same year saw the completion of the 853-foot (260-metre) **Transamerica Pyramid**, one of San Francisco's most iconic buildings. The $34-million, seismic-proofed structure boasts an internal suspension system, which served to protect its 48 storeys and 212-foot (65-metre) spire in the 1989 quake. At first unpopular, the pyramid now has few detractors, instead becoming to many a symbol for the city itself. It's even featured in the *Beach Blanket Babylon* revue, a sure sign of civic affection.

Following another relatively restrained period, the last decade has seen a flurry of construction in the city. Unlike LA, which has the space, money and creative chutzpah to build lavishly, grandly and boldly, San Francisco has always taken a quiet approach to construction, zealously protecting its past and only begrudgingly embracing its future. But of late, San Francisco has begun to introduce bold new works into the cityscape. Credit some smart decision-making for the change: by city planners, sure, but also by museum trustees. Increasingly, world-renowned architects are being selected for some of the city's defining projects.

Designed by architects James Ingo Freed of Pei Cobb Freed and Cathy Simon of Simon Martin-Vegue Winkelstein Moris, the **San Francisco Main Library** (1996; *see p78*) is a marriage of Beaux Arts and more recent styles. One side links the building to the more contemporary Marshall Plaza; the other echoes the old library to the north, with grandiose, neo-classical columns. The dramatic interior centres around a five-storey atrium below a domed skylight designed to let natural light filter throughout the building.

However, it's SoMa that's really been transformed. Most dramatic, at least for now, is the **San Francisco Museum of Modern Art** (*see p81*): designed by Mario Botta and opened in 1995, it features a series of stepped boxes and a signature squared circle facing west. Just west of SFMOMA is a great triumph of recent urban planning: Yerba Buena's **Esplanade Gardens** (*see p79*) is a beautiful urban park, framed by museums, theatres and shops and replete with lush greenery, fountains, sculptures, cafés and the **Metreon** (*see p176*), a hyper-modern urban mall. Directly opposite is Moscone West, the latest addition to the **Moscone Convention Centre** (*see p285*). The stunning glass structure incorporates a graphic display screen designed by New York artists/architects Elizabeth Diller and Ricardo Scofidio.

Perhaps the most dramatic of the new SoMa projects is the **San Francisco Federal Building** at 7th and Mission Streets. Designed by Thom Mayne, the architect of LA's new Caltrans District 7 Headquarters Building, the structure will rise a full 18 storeys; its innovative, energy-efficient sunscreen façade promises to reduce overall energy use. Nearby are two more museums, both due to open in 2008. The most eagerly anticipated, in part because it's been delayed for eons, is architect Daniel Libeskind's strikingly modern update of a 1907 Willis Polk substation, which will house the **Contemporary Jewish Museum** (*see p74*). Inside, the quixotic design calls for gold-toned extensions clad in stainless steel that will jut out of the original power station. On the same block will sit Ricardo Legorreta's **Mexican Museum** (*see p118*), a sophisticated, layered box made of red stone. Legorreta also recently completed the **UCSF Community Center** at the UC San Francisco campus, not far from here in Mission Bay, a building that echoes the architect's Mexican roots with its brilliant-red clay and fuchsia-toned palette.

Across town in Golden Gate Park, there's been plenty of activity. The **de Young Museum** (*see p111*) opened its doors in October 2005, after structural damage suffered during the Loma Prieta earthquake rendered it unsound. The ultra-modern design by Swiss architects Herzog & de Meuron, responsible for London's Tate Modern, caused huge controversy when it was first unveiled. Angular in shape, the museum's helix-like viewing tower rises high above the park; the dabbled, copper façade,

which will develop a patina over time, offers a burst of colour in the otherwise mild-mannered park setting.

Just nearby, the **California Academy of Sciences** is currently receiving a facelift from world-renowned architect Renzo Piano, which will turn the 152-year-old institution into a top-class planetarium, aquarium and rainforest with a 'living' roof that will undulate according to the building's shape. The park's oldest building, the whimsical **San Francisco Conservatory of Flowers**, just received a full-scale seismic upgrade. Even the iconic Cliff House has a new, state-of-the-art, contemporary face.

The Presidio has also seen plenty of action over the last few years, as work continues on converting and upgrading the old army properties on the site for public habitation. However, the decision to allow filmmaker George Lucas to build the $350-million **Letterman Digital Arts Center** on a 24-acre plot at the eastern edge of the park has not been without its controversy, however sympathetic the buildings might be to their surroundings.

Finally, there's the 2005 opening of the **St Regis Hotel** (*see p52*). The city's first new luxury hotel in four years has been designed by Skidmore, Owings & Merrill architect Craig Hartman, who lent his touch to the sparkling International Terminal at **San Francisco International Airport** (*see p282*). As well as housing one of the city's most luxurious hotels, the building will shelter the three-storey, non-profit **Museum of the African Diaspora** (*see p81*). Very San Francisco: even the newest buildings have a touch of the old about them.

The **de Young Museum**.

City Lights. *See p33.*

Literary San Francisco

Read all about it.

A wealth of characters, soothing Left Coast liberalism, atmospheric foghorns and alleys and views… It's little wonder San Francisco has long been a mecca for writers, from Mark Twain reporting on the quest for gold to Tom Wolfe writing about a very different kind of rush. From Dashiell Hammett and Jack London to Gertrude Stein and Danielle Steel, some of the country's best-known writers have called the city home. And what's more, the supply of new novelists and poets shows no sign of drying up.

ARRIVALS AND DEPARTURES

A little less than two decades after the city of Yerba Buena was renamed San Francisco by the Americans, journalist and budding fiction writer **Mark Twain** arrived in town. Like many of the writers based here in the city's early years, Twain came to create himself and his persona, only heading for the brighter literary lights of New York once *The Celebrated Jumping Frog of Calaveras County* had hit the

big time in 1867. Along with contemporaries **Bret Harte** and **Ambrose Bierce**, both of whom also worked in newspapers, Twain built on a foundation of journalistic irony and muckraking that gave the West a piercingly independent literary culture in the 1860s and 1870s. Nowhere was that spirit more evident than at the Bohemian Club, an outgrowth of raucous newsman breakfasts hosted by *San Francisco Chronicle* writer **James Bowan**.

In 1879, long after Twain had left the city, **Robert Louis Stevenson** arrived here in pursuit of his darling Fanny Osbourne. He lived at 868 Bush Street while Osbourne waited for a divorce in Oakland; the two married the next year. Stevenson left San Francisco for Hawaii and Samoa, but he wrote about the city in *The Wrecker* (1892) and about his Napa Valley honeymoon in *The Silverado Squatters* (1883). His former house is in St Helena in Napa Valley; Robert Louis Stevenson State Park is nearby.

As an adolescent in his native Oakland, **Jack London** spent time doing numerous menial seafaring jobs. He didn't start writing until he was in his twenties, but found success first with short stories and then with novels such as *The Call of the Wild* (1903). London spent his latter years in the part of the northern Sonoma Valley known as the Valley of the Moon; he's buried in what is now Jack London State Historic Park in Glen Ellen. Oakland's Jack London Square bears little resemblance to the waterfront of the author's youth, but the cabin he occupied in the Yukon was moved here in 1970.

Like London, **Gertrude Stein** was raised in Oakland; unlike him, Stein made her name not on the West Coast but among the expat modernists and artistic avant-garde of early 20th-century Paris, hosting a salon with San Francisco-born secretary and partner **Alice B Toklas**. A return to Oakland spawned one of Stein's famously gnomic utterances: 'There is no there there,' she said of the town.

Born two decades after Stein, **Dashiell Hammett** came to the city as a 27-year-old in 1921. He had spent time as a detective in Baltimore, and it was this work that informed his writing. Starting in 1923, Hammett published his 'Continental Op' stories in *Black Mask*, 'tec tales set in the city and written while the tubercular writer was living at 620 Eddy Street. Later, at 891 Post Street, he wrote the novels – *Red Harvest*, *The Dain Curse* (both 1929), *The Maltese Falcon* (1930) and *The Glass Key* (1931) – that established the hard-boiled 'tec novel as *the* American genre. However, by 1934, Hammett had virtually stopped writing; by the time he was jailed after refusing to testify during the 1951 McCarthy trials, he had vanished from public life. The plaque on Burritt Street (off Bush Street) acknowledges *The Maltese Falcon* and its protagonist Sam Spade, but not their creator.

BEAT DOWN TO YOUR SOUL

Popular imagination has it that the Beat Generation was founded in San Francisco. In truth, the scene's leading writers – **Jack Kerouac**, **Allen Ginsberg** and **William Burroughs** – cut their literary teeth on the East Coast, meeting in New York City during the 1940s. However, San Francisco provided a sympathetic environment for them and their contemporaries, fostering a literary scene – centred on North Beach bars such as **Gino & Carlo's** (548 Green Street) and **Vesuvio** (255 Columbus Avenue), both still there – that's since assumed legendary status.

Kerouac arrived in the city in 1949 with charismatic companion (and occasional writer) **Neal Cassady**, at the end of a trip he later wrote up – on a single continuous scroll of paper, sold to a collector in 2001 for a record-breaking $2.4 million – as *On the Road* (written 1950, published 1957). His time in the city was productive. The poem 'San Francisco Blues' was written in the Cameo Hotel, since bulldozed to make way for the Moscone Center, but *The Subterraneans* (written 1953, published 1958), while set in North Beach, is actually a New York story transposed to protect the characters.

Kerouac did write often about San Francisco itself, most notably in *The Dharma Bums* (1958). Among the highlights of the novel is a report of the epochal Six Gallery reading on 7 October 1955, at which the then-unknown Ginsberg read the first part of his eventually notorious poem 'Howl'. The central image of the work is the Moloch-face of the Drake Hotel on Powell Street, as observed by Ginsberg while high on peyote. Also on the bill at the Six Gallery that night were surrealist poet and SF native **Philip Lamantia**, Buddhist writers **Gary Snyder** and **Philip Whalen**, and **Michael McClure**. The latter trio were raised in the Pacific Northwest but soon moved to San Francisco; Snyder is now a professor of English at UC Davis. The introductions were delivered by literary guru **Kenneth Rexroth**, an irascible pacifist who had worked tirelessly to keep Japanese Californians out of internment camps during World War II. Rexroth's salon at 250 Scott Street was the centre of what was later called the San Francisco Poetry Renaissance.

Lawrence Ferlinghetti, former poet laureate of the city and long-time owner of City Lights bookshop, published the now-legendary pocket-sized edition of *Howl and Other Poems* in 1956. An obscenity trial targeting Ferlinghetti and the book catapulted the Beats to fame and began the collapse of the American obscenity laws in the 1960s. Neither Ginsberg nor Ferlinghetti have yet had streets named in their honour, but one of their compadres has: just by City Lights store stands Jack Kerouac Alley.

FURTHER TALES OF THE CITY

The Haight-Ashbury scene of the 1960s doesn't have much of a literary monument – perhaps because, in the words of Tom Wolfe, if you can remember it, you weren't really there. Still, it didn't go totally undocumented. **Ken Kesey** and the reborn Cassady hosted the psychedelic Trips Festival at the Longshoreman's Hall on Fisherman's Wharf in 1966, before the scene moved to the Avalon Ballroom on Polk Street, the Fillmore Auditorium on Geary Boulevard, and eventually to the Haight. *The Electric Kool-Aid Acid Test* by Tom Wolfe (1968) is the best account of the times, though *Ringolevio* (1972), Diggers founder **Emmet Grogan**'s memoir, is also worth a read. Kesey and **Robert Stone**, who wrote about the era's psychic fallout in *Dog Soldiers* (1974), were both products of Pulitzer Prize-winning novelist **Wallace Stegner**'s writing programme at Stanford University.

The Castro hasn't produced its literary testament yet. Before his death, **Randy Shilts** wrote an account of the coming of AIDS in *And the Band Played On* (1987), as well as a biography of Harvey Milk (1982). However, **Armistead Maupin**, the most flamboyant SF author to embrace queer themes, sets his *Tales of the City* series outside the Castro: on Macondray Lane on Russian Hill.

BRING ME YOUR HUDDLED MASSES

Though they haven't always been welcome here, immigrant cultures are now very much a part of San Francisco. The development of the city was made possible by the railroad system, the construction of which relied heavily on Chinese immigrant slave workers; the community that arose has grown into one of the most vibrant deposits of this ethnic group in the world, and has produced some of the country's leading Chinese-American authors.

Maxine Hong Kingston, a current resident of the Bay Area, was the first of six children born to a gambling-house owner in Stockton,

California. Her work, best epitomised by *The Fifth Book of Peace* (2003), is a mirror of her cultural heritage, its postmodernist arch defined by its effective blend of non-fiction and fiction. A committed activist, she was arrested in Washington, DC, in 2003, for crossing a police line during a protest against the war in Iraq.

Born in 1952, **Amy Tan** is another product of blended culture. Mixing American cool with Chinese contemplativeness, Tan started writing only at the age of 33, but found worldwide fame four years later with *The Joy Luck Club* (1989), the story of which demonstrates a kind of crash convergence between those two worlds. Ineluctably cool herself, Tan is also one of the Rock Bottom Remainders, a covers band that also counts Stephen King and Dave Barry among its members.

THE NEW, NEW THING

Out of punk rock came a kind of literary voice. Intent on shattering the classical mould of literature, a new school was born in the mid to late 1980s, known as the New Narrative. The writers often wore many hats, starting out as performance artists and/or musicians, and evolving into an off-key collective described by one critic as purveyors of 'victim art'.

Write to perform

San Francisco is a mite pricier than it was back when Mark Twain roamed its fog-cloaked side streets. However, despite the invasion of the techies, the city is as hospitable towards young writers as ever. The progressive political climate and innumerable coffeehouses constitute something of a support system for local scribes, so much so that living here as a writer feels less a solitary pursuit than an invitation into an exclusive but sizeable gang.

The impression is reinforced by the enviable literary performance scene. The **Poetry Center** at San Francisco State University (1600 Holloway Avenue, 338 2227, www.sfsu.edu/~poetry) stages regular readings, while the programme run by **Small Press Traffic** at the California College of the Arts (1111 8th Street, 551 9278, www.sptraffic.org) takes in everything from discussion groups to read-throughs of new plays. Both **826 Valencia** (*see p35*) and the **San Francisco Public Library** (*see p78*) offers author readings and other literary events.

An outgrowth of the Beat 'happenings' of the 1950s, the city's slam and spoken-word scene remains vital. An extension

to the circuit is Beth Lisick's enjoyable **Porchlight** series (monthly at Café du Nord, www.porchlightsf.com; *see p234*), at which local scribes extemporise ten-minute tales on a given theme. Poetry and performance also cross over at events run by the **Kearny Street Workshop** (www.kearnystreet.org), a vibrant home for Asian-American writers, and **YouthSpeaks** (www.youthspeaks.org), a spoken-word workshop for younger scribblers.

Alongside authors of national renown, local writers get a platform at October's ten-day, citywide **Litquake** (www.litquake.org) and July's day-long **Books By the Bay** (www.books bythebay.com) at Yerba Buena Gardens. Even outside these events, San Francisco is a popular stop on the touring circuit: as well as being great places to track down works by local pen men and women, bookstores such as **A Clean Well-Lighted Place for Books**, **City Lights** and **Cody's** (for all, *see pp178-180*) regularly host promotional events with both big-name and no-name authors. Those in the former category also discuss their lives and work as part of the excellent **City Arts & Lectures** series (www.cityarts.net).

A plaque marks a key murder in **Dashiell Hammett**'s *The Maltese Falcon. See p33.*

Autobiographical and semi-autobiographical novels poured out of the group. Perhaps its most famous figure was **Kathy Acker**, a controversial performance artist famous for once sticking a can of yams into her vagina on stage. The bare-all, tell-all books of fellow Bay Area writer **Dodie Bellamy**, which take in such subjects as feminism and queer sex, are no less controversial but more highly regarded by critics; *Cunt-Ups*, a feminist revision of William Burroughs' pioneering cut-up techniques, won the Firecracker Alternative Book Award for Poetry in 2002. However, San Franciscan writer **Dennis Cooper** might be the king of the scene. His books teem with sexually driven fantasies of fucking and murdering troubled boys; indeed, his depictions even led to one group of satirists sending him a mock death threat – 'Dennis Cooper Must Die! Must Die! Must Die!' for killing young boys – when Cooper gave a reading from his book *Frisk* here in 1991.

Of course, the world of literary endeavours is not limited to the standard forms of fiction and non-fiction. In the views of many critics, comic books are just as valid as art and literature. One exponent of the genre is the precocious **Adrian Tomine**, first published at 16 and now a regular in the *New Yorker*. Tomine's naturalistically drawn art and storytelling manner captivate his Gen-X fans, most notably in the comic book series *Optic Nerve*.

At the opposite end of the literary spectrum from Tomine is **Starhawk** (aka Miriam Samos), a local writer, activist, teacher of paganism and practising witch. The author of numerous non-fiction bestsellers, among them *Dreaming the Dark* (1982) and *The Earth Path* (2004), Starhawk works with the Reclaiming tradition of witchcraft she helped found, through classes, workshops, camps and public rituals.

WORD UP

Dave Eggers moved to the Bay Area in his early twenties, after the death of his parents, to raise his young brother. His experiences form the basis of *A Heartbreaking Work of Staggering Genius* (2000), his dazzling first book. Two years later, rather than simply sit on his hands after its success, Eggers used a good chunk of the change he earned from it to set up **826 Valencia**, a non-profit youth literacy centre. The same Mission building is also home to Eggers' *McSweeney's* literary journal and publishing house, and a pompous, self-regarding and generally excellent periodical called *The Believer*.

Eggers, though, is merely one of hundreds of young writers, based in the city but making waves beyond it, whose writing draws heavily on personal experience. **Po Bronson**'s non-fiction has found both critical acclaim and commercial success, while **Caroline Paul**'s 1998 memoir *Fighting Fire* drew great reviews; both are members of local writing collective the Grotto (www.sfgrotto.org). Notable writers whose work straddles the boundaries between fiction and autobiography include **Sean Wilsey**, **Michelle Tea** and **Beth Lisick**, who crept on to the bestseller lists with her 2005 novel *Everybody into the Pool*. Both Tea and Lisick are also performance poets; others worth seeing include **Bucky Sinister**, **Justin Chin** and **Daphne Gottlieb**. To track down books by these authors and others, try City Lights or A Clean Well-Lighted Place for Books; *SF Weekly* and the *San Francisco Bay Guardian* carry listings for literary events.

▶ For **bookshops**, *see pp178-180.*
▶ For **books about the city**, *see p295.*
▶ For **literary tours**, *see p65.*

the *heart* **of the city**

City Parks Foundation
people + parks

Central Park
SummerStage

free!

music

dance

film

word

in
Central Park!

New Yorks's premiere **free** performing arts festival

www.SummerStage.org

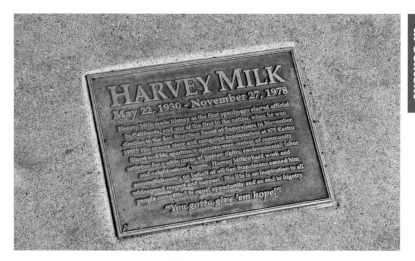

The Politics of Progress

How San Francisco became the nonconformist jewel of the Left Coast.

In some regards, San Francisco has always been a liberal city. Witness, for example, how its early inhabitants were largely left to go about their boozing, gambling and whoring by the city's authorities during the Gold Rush. However, the city's current status as an oasis of liberal political values has been only recently acquired. The powerhouse of military-industrial expansionism and the home to media outlets that served as a bullhorn of imperial avarice in the early 19th century is today the epicentre of an American counterculture that stands in direct and vociferous opposition to US foreign policy and corporate dominance.

San Francisco, once the western beachhead of the growing American empire, quickly came to symbolise what became known as 'Manifest Destiny', the belief that America deserved – nay, had an obligation and a quasi-divine right – to conquer the North American continent. And beyond that conquest, San

Francisco was pinned as a gateway to an all-encompassing imperial vision that, to some, stretched west to the Philippines, Japan and, ultimately, China.

During the 19th century, liberal writers such as Mark Twain openly opposed this drive for conquest. In the same era, John Muir established the modern environmental movement, challenging the city's massive mining and water interests. However, these liberal voices came up against stiff opposition from the city's power base, which colluded with the press to get its message across. Early 20th-century media baron William Randolph Hearst (thought to be the inspiration for *Citizen Kane*), whose family fortune came from mining, used his newspapers as pro-war propaganda tools and awarded such men as Nazi general Hermann Goering a syndicated column in his papers; as Dr Gray Brechin wrote in *Imperial San Francisco: Urban Power, Earthly Ruin*, his

Tales of the city Rev Cecil Williams

As a youngster in the South, Cecil Williams experienced what he has described as a 'nervous breakdown'. Though he despaired for weeks, the young African-American boy eventually came to see the breakdown as a kind of existential crisis precipitated by the injustice of the segregation through which he was forced to live. However, the experience also inspired in him a vision of standing in front of a congregation of all colours, ages and nations. Without that vision, religious life in San Francisco would be very different today.

After attending college and then seminary, the young minister joined the conservative Glide Memorial United Methodist Church (*see p75*) in 1963. Founded in 1929, the same year Williams was born, and located in the raggedy Tenderloin district, Glide was a conservative church, but wouldn't remain so for very long. Arriving at his post, Williams saw the effects of police harassment on gays and the homeless first hand. He was determined to fight back with the power of the pulpit, a decision that was to lead to the creation of the largest non-profit community-service organisation in the city.

Revolution came apace. In 1964 Williams helped to create the Council on Religion and Homosexuality (CRH), promoting dialogue, tolerance and understanding between gays and the religious communities. Three years later, he removed the crucifix from the sanctuary: his church, he decided, would henceforth celebrate life, not death. Under the stewardship of Williams and his wife, activist and writer Janice Mirikitani, Glide attracted a supremely inclusive congregation, its members welcome regardless of race, nationality, sexual orientation, socio-economic status or even religious belief. Williams's fiery preaching, jazz-charged Sunday celebrations and progressive political views made him a controversial figure to conservatives.

Today, Glide claims a congregation of around 10,000, employs over 170 people, and offers more than 80 different services to the community. Free meals are served every day, totalling around one million each year. AIDS testing and prevention programmes are run from the church, as are medical and case management services for the homeless, a licensed child-care facility, academic tutoring and vocational training, counselling, shelters for battered women and children, and even housing for 140 people.

Now well into his 70s, Williams is still fully committed to his ideals, proudly acting as Grand Marshal of San Francisco's Gay Pride Parade in 2003. To those who regularly attend his celebrations, or who simply peek in to get a taste of a truly 'only in San Francisco' experience, it's pretty plain to see that Rev Cecil Williams's childhood vision has been fully realised.

scathing exposé of the city's rise to prominence, Hearst gave '30 million Americans the Nazi point of view without space for rebuttal'.

Indeed, the years around the war saw the city allow some of the most egregious examples of racism, human abuse and environmental debasement in the history of the US. During World War II, Japanese-American citizens were dragged from their homes and sent to internment camps. During the same period, the natural riches of northern California and Nevada were wrecked by environmentally catastrophic deforestation, mining and damming operations from which they're still recovering.

THE WAVE OF CHANGE

San Francisco's political shift began in earnest in the late 1950s and early 1960s. Ethnically diverse populations in urban areas began to gain political strength after 'white flight' sent more affluent families to the suburbs just as many gays and lesbians left the armed forces and settled here. These developments, along with the city's hedonistic reputation, began to draw a bohemian element that flowered with the ascendancy of the Beats.

The early 1960s ushered in more widespread political awareness. The bohemian subculture of San Francisco began to gain strength and voice in literature, art and music. After John F Kennedy was assassinated in 1963, the growth of the civil-rights movement and the start of the Vietnam War in 1965 caused more turbulence. A considerable number of baby boomers came to question the wisdom of the country's political and social leadership, and many embraced full-bore rebellion.

Well before 1967's Summer of Love, the Haight-Ashbury neighbourhood was home to politically conscious cultural ensembles, among them the Diggers. Evolving out of the San Francisco Mime Troupe, a guerrilla theatre group known for its biting social satire, the Diggers took their political ideals off the stage and into the streets, experimenting with communal living, 'free' stores that used a barter system and other non-traditional forms of social cooperation. At the same time, the national civil-rights movement was coming to a head; with the notable exceptions of Malcolm X and the later Black Power movement, Gandhian principles of non-violent protest became the organising principle of virtually all social movements.

Marijuana had been a staple among the artistic community for some time, since the days of the city's early opium dens. But it was the consciousness-altering properties of new and powerful psychedelic compounds such as LSD that led many to question traditional western mores, religions and political theories. The culture of experimentation not only made its way into the work of the area's artists, writers and musicians, but also into the pursuits of academics, technologists, physicians and citizens of the Bay Area in general. The free and easy atmosphere enabled social, personal and sexual experiences without traditional boundaries, contributing to the lore of the 1960s and, in turn, coming to inform the politics of modern-day San Francisco.

To many in modern America, the rise of the hippie culture marked the beginning of the decay of so-called 'American values'. This more conservative strain of political and social thinking is based on a sense of nostalgia for a largely revisionist interpretation of American history. It holds that American political systems were founded on the tenets of Judeo-Christian and Puritan belief systems rather than the truly radical, intellectual roots of the Founding Fathers, whom many dissenters and activists in the '60s felt were their spiritual

kinsmen. Indeed, many hippies considered it their patriotic duty to oppose events they held to be grossly un-American. They railed against racial and gender segregation and inequality, illegal wars resulting in mass killing, and the abridgement of the very rights the traditional political establishment cynically claimed to protect even as they covertly infiltrated and sabotaged student and political groups.

GEEKS ON ACID

As the 1960s came to a close, a group of researchers funded by the US military were labouring at Stanford University, just south of San Francisco, to make computing more powerful. But in nearby Los Altos, pioneering LSD guru and psychologist Dr Timothy Leary and author Ken Kesey were spreading a gospel of psychedelics through the intellectual and research community surrounding the college. A number of technology researchers, influenced by the political movements surging through the Bay Area, began to conceive alternative uses for the military and business computers they were designing.

'Global information-sharing is now the stuff of daily life, thanks to Bay Area hippies.'

John Markoff's *What the Dormouse Said: How the '60s Counterculture Shaped the Personal Computer* (the title refers to the acid-rock lyric of Jefferson Airplane's 'White Rabbit') relates how the development of home computers and the internet is directly attributable to the desire of those Bay Area designers to help people communicate and organise more effectively, both politically and socially. It was an unrivalled power-to-the-people coup that fundamentally reconfigured the daily lives of millions worldwide and resulted in what one Silicon Valley venture capitalist called 'the largest legal accumulation of wealth in the history of the world'. Counterculture researchers and electronics-club geeks took the cream of the US Defense Department's Advanced Research Projects Agency's top-secret work and put it in homes, schools, libraries and businesses around the world. Global communications, collaboration and information-sharing inconceivable just five to ten years ago are now the stuff of daily life, thanks to the efforts of those Bay Area hippies.

Many jumped on the internet bandwagon. As with the Gold Rush and the 1960s, the dot-com boom of 25 years later made San Francisco the centre of a cultural and technological revolution. But before long, the excesses of the late 1990s

In Context

and the dawn of the 21st century washed over the city. The bubble burst and San Francisco was again left to sort through the remains of an era that swept away many of the wealth-seekers, but that left rich soil for those willing to do the hard work of realising its potential.

THE MILK-MAN COMETH

Like the researchers behind the PC, San Francisco's gay community arose from the Bay Area's military past to become a thriving subculture by the early 1970s, and eventually grew into something far greater. According to a 2001 article in *American Demographics* magazine, the 94114 zip code – San Francisco's Castro neighbourhood – has more gay residents than any other in the country. The 2000 census determined that the city holds six of the top ten densest concentrations of self-identified same-sex couples; in four of those six areas, same-sex couples represent over 40 per cent of the total population. With numbers like these, it's difficult to overstate the impact that San Francisco's gay and lesbian population has had on the culture – and politics – of the city.

San Francisco has virtually always had some sort of queer scene; there were well-known drag bars here in the 1920s and '30s. But it was during the 1950s and '60s, when gay and lesbian servicemen and -women returned to live in the city, that San Francisco became known as a haven in an otherwise intolerant country. When the social movements of the 1960s geared up, so did gay pride. The queer population began to organise, realising that the surest way to gain power was at the ballot box.

Success came in 1977, when Harvey Milk, a beloved figure and businessman in the Castro, was elected to the city's Board of Supervisors, becoming the nation's first openly gay elected official. The triumph was short-lived, however: along with Mayor George Moscone, Milk was assassinated in City Hall by Dan White, a former city supervisor, the following year. When White received only a light sentence, the city's gay and lesbian community exploded in grief and anger, prompting the White Night Riot of 21 May 1979: police cars were torched and City Hall was ransacked.

Perhaps ironically, the tragedy galvanised the community into becoming a formidable political force. Through the establishment of many queer political organisations, voter registration and education campaigns, San Francisco's gay voters have undoubtedly become among some of the most mobilised and educated in the world. Although deeply scarred by the AIDS crisis of the 1980s and 1990s, the community has grown stronger. Today, it wields substantial political clout across the Bay Area.

GOING DUTCH

San Francisco is something of a Californian Amsterdam, its liberal political and social views coupled with a fierce resistance to change. The city's footprint may be small, but the impact of San Franciscan politics and innovation is undisputedly global.

Since the 1960s, both the city of San Francisco and the state of California have been at the forefront of progressive politics locally, nationally and internationally. The Bay Area has played a major role in advancing worker protection, the minimum-wage, environmental regulation, workplace safety and curbing emissions, not to mention issues concerning civil rights, the GLBT communities, women, undocumented workers and illegal aliens. The northern California chapter of the American Civil Liberties Union is the nation's largest.

The city has also been in the vanguard of the move to legalise same-sex marriage and medicinal marijuana, and advance stem-cell research; it's also become a stronghold of the anti-war and slow-growth property-development movements. Congressional leaders from the Bay Area are among the most outspoken liberal voices in US government. California was, in fact, the first state to be simultaneously represented by two women in the US Senate: Barbara Boxer and Dianne Feinstein, the latter a former mayor of San Francisco, are both residents of the Bay Area.

The 2003 mayoral election provided the most accurate indicator of the city's current political climate. The event became a down-to-the-wire contest between Democratic candidate Gavin Newsom, a young, wealthy business owner with establishment ties (and, it should be added, politically liberal leanings), and Green Party representative Matt Gonzalez, an über-liberal lawyer and president of San Francisco's Board of Supervisors known for wearing combat boots with his business suit.

In any other city in the US, the Greens wouldn't have got a look-in. But though Newsom spent ten times more than Gonzalez on his campaign, in the process enlisting the help of the national Democratic Party (former president Bill Clinton even came out on the stump), the contest was tight. Newsom edged it, but only by 53 per cent of the vote against 47 per cent for Gonzalez. A big Green spanner had been thrown into the Democratic machine.

Newsom emerged humbled by San Francisco's outpouring of support for his grass-roots rival. Had Gonzalez won the office, he would have been the first Green mayor of a major city in the US. Newsom publicly conceded that he had got the message loud and clear: in all senses of the word, San Francisco is a liberal town.

Where to Stay

W Hotel. *See p52.*

Where to Stay

Hot properties.

Whether impossibly posh or fun and funky, San Francisco's hotels have your tastes covered. The biggest problem is deciding which option to take, something that itself depends a good deal on where you want to stay. Do you want to shop? See the sights? Explore the town? Simply relax? Whatever your intention, there's a good hotel nearby. Once you've figured your budget, all you've got to work out is whether you'd rather stay somewhere plush or minimalist, modern or historic, large or small, with its own bar or its own spa…

The **Union Square** area is home to most of the city's large hotels, many run by major-name companies (the likes of Marriott and Hyatt; for details, *see p61* **The chain gang**). In addition to the monolithic, impersonal hotels on or near the square, there are a number of smaller, more charming properties run by 'boutique' operators who don't forsake comfort or style in the name of economy; many are in the **Tenderloin** and **Nob Hill**. Indeed, the city is home to two chains, each of which has expanding empires of chic hotels in the city. Both **Joie de Vivre** (www.jdvhospitality.com), which has an astonishing 18 properties in the city, **Kimpton** (www.kimptonhotels.com), which operates ten hotels here, have created something of an industry for attention to customer care and unexpected luxury at reasonable prices.

San Francisco's hotels continue to suffer below-optimum occupancy rates, which ebbed a couple years ago in the aftermath of 9/11. While occupancy continued to climb in 2005, it's still a way off the record numbers enjoyed in the late 1990s. Nonetheless, optimism in the city's travel and tourism markets is riding high. The industry is still basking in the glow of its newest gem, Joie de Vivre's **Hotel Vitale** (*see p48*); directly on its heels followed the eagerly awaited **St Regis Hotel** (*see p52*).

INFORMATION & PRICES

Accommodation prices vary wildly here. From hotel to hotel, sure, but also for the same room within a single property, which might double in price from a dreary midwinter Tuesday to

> ▶ ❶ Green numbers given in this chapter correspond to the location of each hotel on the street maps. *See pp312-319.*

The best Hotels

For the lap of luxury
Four Seasons (*see p43*); **Mandarin Oriental** (*see p46*); **St Regis Hotel** (*see p52*); **Huntington Hotel** (*see p53*).

For animal lovers
Campton Place Hotel (*see p43*); **Golden Gate Hotel** (*see p55*).

For tech-heads
Hotel Diva (*see p45*); **Hotel Vitale** (*see p48*); **St Regis Hotel** (*see p52*); **W Hotel** (*see p52*).

For Dead-heads
Hotel Triton (*see p45*); **Red Victorian** (*see p59*).

a July weekend or even during a big convention. The rates we've quoted here, obtained from the hotels, reflect this disparity: always shop around. Bear in mind, too, that quoted rates exclude a gasp-inducing 14 per cent room tax.

Always call the hotel directly when making reservations. Or, better still, book online on the hotel's website: many hotels offer internet-only specials that can shave as much as $50 from the room rates. Higher availability means that savvy travellers can typically find bargain prices even for peak travel times and dates: if the rates quoted on individual hotel websites aren't low enough, check reservation systems such as **hotels.com** and **priceline.com**, which may have better deals. Always ask about cancellation policies when booking, so you don't get stuck paying for a room you can't use. Most hotels require notice of cancellations at least 24 hours in advance; however, this may not be the case if you booked via an outside website, or with a service such as **San Francisco Reservations** (1-800 677 1570, 1-510 628 4440, www.hotelres.com).

We've listed a selection of services for each hotel at the bottom of each review, everything from the in-room entertainment options (all hotel rooms have TVs unless stated, but others feature CD and/or DVD players) to the often

Hotel Nikko. *See p45.*

prohibitive cost of parking. Regarding the internet, the vast majority of hotels feature dataports for dial-up users; however, many hotels also offer high-speed options. 'Wireless' denotes a hotel that has a wireless connection throughout; 'DSL' is used for hotels where a high-speed connection is available only via a cable; and 'shared terminal' refers to a computer in the hotel's lobby or business centre that offers high-speed net access. All hotels are required by law to provide accommodation for disabled visitors and, thanks to California's strict anti-smoking policies, all hotels have no-smoking rooms. Indeed, many hotels are now completely non-smoking, so we've made special note of hotels that still offer rooms for smokers.

Downtown

Union Square & around

Expensive

Campton Place Hotel

340 Stockton Street, between Post & Sutter Streets, CA 94108 (1-800 235 4300/781 5555/fax 955 5536/www.camptonplace.com). BART & Metro to Montgomery/bus 2, 3, 4, 15, 30, 38, 45, 76 & Market Street routes/cable car Powell-Hyde or Powell-Mason. **Rates** $360-$450 double; $575-$2,050 suite. **Credit** AmEx, DC, Disc, MC, V. **Map** p315 M5 ❶

Though it sits just a half-block from Union Square, this sleek, refined hotel has attracted a very discreet, and wealthy, following. Neatly packing 110 rooms into a small space on Stockton Street, it offers exceptional service, including valet-assisted packing and unpacking. Small dogs are allowed to stay with their owners; staff will even walk them. Room amenities are excellent; there's an elegant restaurant downstairs, plus a handsome and popular cocktail lounge. *Bar. Concierge. CD. DVD. Gym. Internet (DSL, shared terminal). Parking ($38). Restaurant. Room service. Smoking rooms.*

Four Seasons

757 Market Street, between 3rd & 4th Streets, CA 94103 (1-800 819 5053/633 3000/fax 633 3001/www.fourseasons.com). BART & Metro to Powell/bus 27, 30, 45 & Market Street routes/cable car Powell-Hyde or Powell-Mason. **Rates** $405-$500 double; $760 suite. **Credit** AmEx, DC, Disc, MC, V. **Map** p315 M6 ❷

The sleek, 36-storey Four Seasons is situated nicely on the south side of Market Street, convenient for both Union Square and SoMa. Its 277 rooms and suites, 142 residential condos, high-end shops and upscale restaurant create the feeling of a city unto

San Francisco's Most Unique Collection of Boutique Hotels

Receive Our Exclusive "Time Out" City Guide Discount

Use promo code "TIMEOUT" at
www.jdvhospitality.com

Scott Brooks

Archbishops Mansion
Hotel Adagio
Hotel Bijou
Hotel Carlton
Commodore Hotel
Hotel Del Sol
Hotel Drisco
Galleria Park Hotel
Laurel Inn
Maxwell Hotel
Nob Hill Lambourne
Hotel Rex
Petite Auberge
Phoenix Hotel
White Swan Inn

Joie de Vivre
HOSPITALITY

www.jdvhospitality.com

itself. The general design and ambience are pretty similar to other Four Seasons around the world: as you might expect, the rooms are sumptuously appointed, with no corner-cutting. The list of on-site amenities is lengthy and all-encompassing; perhaps the jewel is the two-storey health club, which includes an indoor pool and a jacuzzi.

Bar. Business centre. CD. Concierge. Gym. Internet (DSL, shared terminal). Parking ($44). Pool. Restaurant. Room service. Smoking rooms. Spa.

Hotel Nikko
222 Mason Street, between Ellis & O'Farrell Streets, CA 94102 (1-800 645 5687/394 1111/fax 394 1106/www.hotelnikkosf.com). BART & Metro to Powell/bus 2, 3, 4, 15, 30, 38, 45, 76 & Market Street routes/cable car Powell-Hyde or Powell-Mason. **Rates** $159-$365 double; $399-$2,000 suite. **Credit** AmEx, DC, MC, V. **Map** p315 M6 ③

Part of the Japan Airlines hotel chain, the 25-storey Nikko is incredibly popular with Japanese visitors. The 510 rooms and 22 suites are large, bright and reasonably handsome, furnished with luxurious fabrics, lightwood furniture and lush green plants. Elsewhere, the design is clean with Asian touches throughout; some subtle, some plain as daylight. There's an indoor pool that lets in light through a glass ceiling, a gym and a sauna (or, to be precise, a *kamaburo*, the Japanese equivalent), and the Anzu sushi bar and steak house isn't a bad place to eat. **Photo** *p43*.

Bar. Business centre. CD. Concierge. Gym. Internet (DSL). Parking ($39). Pool. Restaurant. Room service. Smoking rooms. Spa.

Pan Pacific
500 Post Street, at Mason Street, CA 94102 (1-800 533 6465/771 8600/fax 398 0267/ http://sanfrancisco.panpacific.com). Bus 2, 3, 4, 27, 38, 76/cable car Powell-Hyde or Powell-Mason. **Rates** $149-$429 double; $479-$2,200 suite. **Credit** AmEx, DC, Disc, MC, V. **Map** p314 L5 ④

This sleek-looking hotel is far enough from Union Square that guests can avoid the crush, but close enough that the shops are mere steps away. The dazzling lobby, with its soaring 18-storey ceiling, is the focal point of the design. The brass-railed hallways circle the atrium and lead to 329 rooms, which are now comfortable and well appointed: a recent refurbishment added such amenities as flat-screen TVs and upscale bath accessories. The third-floor restaurant is a serene place to start or end your day.

Bar. Business centre. CD. Concierge. DVD. Gym. Internet (wireless (lobby areas only), DSL). Parking ($48). Restaurant. Room service. Smoking rooms.

Moderate

Hotel Diva
440 Geary Street, between Mason & Taylor Streets, CA 94102 (1-800 553 1900/885 0200/fax 346 6613/www.hoteldiva.com). Bus 2, 3, 4, 27, 38, 76/cable car Powell-Hyde or Powell-Mason. **Rates** $99-$169 double; $250-$450 suite. **Credit** AmEx, DC, Disc, MC, V. **Map** p314 L5 ⑤

Located in the heart of the city's Theatre District, just a block from Union Square, the Diva is, it hopes, on the up: already stylish, the hotel is promising to unveil a new look in 2006, which will run to new deluxe bedding, artwork and lighting throughout the property. A few quirky touches add character: there are CD players in the rooms, and the front desk offers iPod rentals if the SF streets don't make for a pleasing soundtrack. Its owners also look after the Metropolis (*see p51*) and Hotel Union Square (*see p45*), designed and run along similar lines.

Business centre. CD. Concierge. Gym. Internet (wireless, DSL, shared terminal). Parking ($30-$35). Smoking rooms.

Hotel Milano
55 5th Street, at Market Street, CA 94103 (543 8555/fax 543 5885/www.hotelmilanosf.com). BART & Metro to Powell/bus 27, 30, 45 & Market Street routes. **Rates** $99-$199 double. **Credit** AmEx, DC, Disc, MC, V. **Map** p315 M6 ⑥

The often-overlooked Milano boasts some of the best-value rooms in Downtown, and one of the best locations: right next door to the San Francisco Shopping Centre, a block from Yerba Buena and five minutes' walk from Union Square. The 1913 neo-classical façade gives way to modern Italian decor that's homey, if a bit nondescript. A two-storey fitness center with a steam room, a sauna and a jacuzzi, plus a well-priced Thai restaurant, put this a cut above the average business hotel.

Gym. Internet (wireless). Parking ($30). Restaurant. Smoking rooms.

Hotel Rex
562 Sutter Street, between Powell & Mason Streets, CA 94102 (1-800 433 4434/433 4434/fax 433 3695/www.thehotelrex.com). Bus 2, 3, 4, 27, 38, 76/cable car Powell-Hyde or Powell-Mason. **Rates** $129-$279 double; $269-$379 suite. **Credit** AmEx, DC, Disc, MC, V. **Map** p315 M5 ⑦

Named after Kenneth Rexroth, MC for the fabled Six Gallery reading that provided a launchpad for the Beat Generation, the recently renovated Rex is one of the city's most appealing small hotels, aiming to come off like a 20th-century salon and almost succeeding. There are books scattered throughout the place, and the walls are adorned with caricatures of writers with local ties (Allen Ginsberg, Dashiell Hammett, Gertrude Stein). Literary events are often held in the back salon, and the business centre even has antique typewriters alongside the modern amenities. The matchbox-sized bistro Café Andrée is named after Rexroth's wife.

Bar. Business centre. CD. Concierge. Internet (wireless, DSL). Parking ($34). Restaurant. Room service.

Hotel Triton
342 Grant Avenue, between Bush & Sutter Streets, CA 94108 (1-800 800 1299/394 0500/fax 394 0555/www.hoteltriton.com). Bus 2, 3, 4, 15, 30, 38, 45, 76. **Rates** $159-$239 double; $249-$329 suite. **Credit** AmEx, DC, Disc, MC, V. **Map** p315 M5 ⑧

The right-on **Triton**. *See p45.*

This hotel, across from the ornate Chinatown gate, succeeds in being both fun and funky. Especially opular with celebrities and musicians, the Triton is a leader in 'green hotel' practices, with environmentally friendly rooms and amenities. The 140 rooms offer organic cotton bedlinen and 'Earthly Beds' made entirely of recycled materials. Also on the hotel's eclectic menu are on-site yoga classes, nightly tarot readings, and free wine and beer in the lobby. Much of the joy, though, is in the design quirks: the small 'Zen Dens' have incense, books and Buddhism and daybeds, and there are suites designed by Jerry Garcia, the Red Hot Chili Peppers and even Woody Harrelson.
Business centre. CD. Concierge. Gym. Internet (wireless). Parking ($37). Restaurant. Room service.

Orchard Hotel

665 Bush Street, between Stockton & Powell Streets, CA 94108 (1-888 717 2881/362 8878/fax 362 8088/www.theorchardhotel.com). Bus 30, 45/cable car Powell-Hyde or Powell-Mason. **Rates** $139-$299 double; $239-$499 suite. **Credit** AmEx, DC, Disc, MC, V. **Map** p315 M5 **9**

The Orchard is one of only a handful of recently opened San Francisco boutique hotels to be housed in a new building rather than an old conversion. The main advantage to this is that the rooms – 105 of them, spread over ten stories, including nine suites – are all a decent size, something that can't be said about some of its neighbours. The styling throughout is gentle and never overwhelming, and the rooms themselves are nicely appointed and extremely comfortable. All in all, a very pleasant place to spend a few days. The Orchard Garden, a sister operation built to full LEED Project 'green' specifications, is scheduled to open two blocks away in June 2006 (466 Bush Street, at Grant Street).
Bar. Business centre. CD. Concierge. DVD. Gym. Internet (wireless, DSL, shared terminal). Parking ($34). Restaurant. Room service.

Also recommended

The stylish **Hotel Union Square** (114 Powell Street, CA 94102, 1-800 553 1900, 397 3000, www.hotelunionsquare.com, $99-$199 double).

The Financial District

Expensive

Mandarin Oriental

222 Sansome Street, between Pine & California Streets, CA 94104 (1-800 622 0404/276 9888/fax 433 0289/www.mandarinoriental.com). Bus 1, 10, 12, 15, 41/cable car California. **Rates** $415-$735 double; $1,400-$3,000 suite. **Credit** AmEx, DC, Disc, MC, V. **Map** p315 N4 **10**

Few hotels in the world can boast such extraordinary views, or such decadent means of enjoying them, as the Mandarin Oriental. Its lobby is on the ground floor of the city's third-tallest edifice, the 48-storey First Interstate Building, but all of its 158 rooms, including four suites, are on the top 11 floors, affording breathtaking vistas of the city and the Bay. The rooms contain blond wood furnishings and Asian artwork, and are decked out in sumptuous fabrics. All of them have binoculars and some, more importantly, have glass-walled bathtubs beside the windows. Service is predictably exemplary: the moneyed guests wouldn't have it any other way.
Bar. Business centre. CD. Concierge. Gym. Internet (DSL, shared terminal). Parking ($40). Restaurant. Room service. Smoking rooms.

Omni San Francisco

500 California Street, at Montgomery Street, CA 94104 (1-888 444 6664/677 9494/fax 273 3038/ www.omnihotels.com). Bus 1, 10, 12, 15, 41/cable car California. **Rates** $209-$519 double; $599-$799 suite. **Credit** AmEx, DC, Disc, MC, V. **Map** p315 N4 **11**

With a great central location right on the cable car line, this business-friendly hotel is relatively new, but feels as though it's been part of the landscape for years. That's partly because it's been built into a historic structure, but it's also due to the exceptional service. The 362 rooms are larger than you might expect and appointed with comfortable amenities, including upscale bath accessories and plush robes. Features include large work desks and three two-line telephones in each room. The lobby-level restaurant, Bob's Steaks & Chops, is one of the better steakhouses in town.
Bar. Business centre. CD. Concierge. DVD. Gym. Internet (wireless, DSL, shared terminal). Parking ($45). Restaurant. Room service. Smoking rooms.

Palace Hotel

2 New Montgomery Street, at Market Street, CA 94105 (1-800 325 3589/512 1111/fax 243 8062/www.sfpalace.com). BART & Metro to Montgomery/bus 2, 3, 4, 31 & Market Street routes. **Rates** $199-$449 double; $775-$4,00 suite. **Credit** AmEx, DC, Disc, MC, V. **Map** p315 N5 **12**

See p47 **Tales of the city.**

Tales of the city Palace Hotel

In 1873, financier William Ralston began to build the **Palace Hotel** (*see p46*), the crowning vision of his plan to make San Francisco a world-class metropolis. Two years later, days before his dream was to become reality, Ralston was dead. William Sharon, one of his partners, had created a run on the Bank of California, which Ralston had co-founded in 1864, by selling massive portions of his holdings. As depositors panicked and attempted to withdraw their money, it was found that Ralston had been using the bank's capital to fund his private investments. Early on the morning of 27 August 1875, Ralston resigned and went to take his daily swim off North Beach; his body was recovered later that day. The cause of death was ruled to be a stroke so that Ralston's widow could collect an insurance settlement, but it was clear to all that the banker had committed suicide.

Barely five weeks later, on 2 October 1875, the Bank of California reopened its doors. The same day, on schedule despite his death, Ralston's Palace Hotel also welcomed the first members of the public. At the time, it was the largest and most lavish hotel on earth, with modern innovations that included electric call buttons in each room, plumbing and private toilets, and hydraulic elevators.

The hotel survived the 1906 earthquake, but not the ensuing fire. The blaze threatened to destroy Market Street, and firemen tapped the Palace's massive reservoir system in an attempt to fight the flames. But after several hundred thousand gallons of water in the hotel's emergency tanks were exhausted,

the 'Grande Dame of the West' was left defenceless. The building was demolished, a Herculean task taking 18 months and generating some 15,000 cartloads of debris.

A very different Palace soon rose in its place. American illustrator Maxfield Parrish was commissioned to paint a mural for the hotel's 1909 opening; the result was the seven-foot by 16-foot *Pied Piper of Hamelin* which still hangs behind the bar in Maxfield's, the hotel's watering hole. On the opposite wall are photos of the hotel's many famous guests, who have included Thomas Edison, Winston Churchill, Charlie Chaplin, Oscar Wilde and US president Ulysses S Grant. Warren G Harding passed away in the hotel's Presidential Suite in August 1923, though no one has been able to say for sure whether he died of a heart attack, a stroke, a cerebral haemorrhage, food poisoning or even suicide.

The hotel suffered the effects of another earthquake in 1989, when the Loma Prieta tremor shook the Bay Area. The damage wasn't extensive, but the hotel's owners took the opportunity to close it for restoration. Following a $150-million renovation, it opened again in 1991. The new Palace dining rooms and public spaces are simply breathtaking, with a spectacular 80,000 panes of stained glass in the Garden Court's ceiling dome and a covered swimming pool that is by far the finest in the city. No matter that the 553 rooms seem rather modest nowadays: the Palace stands as a testament to a Californian golden age. If you aren't staying, do make a point of visiting for afternoon tea.

Bar. Business centre. Concierge. Gym. Internet
(wireless (lobby areas only), DSL, shared terminal).
Parking ($40). Pool. Restaurants (3). Room service.
Smoking rooms. Spa.

Also recommended

A pair of businessfolks' favourites: the **Hyatt
Regency** (5 Embarcadero Center, CA 94111,
1-888 591 1234, 788 1234, http://sanfranciscoregency.
hyatt.com, $149-$349 double) and the **Park
Hyatt** (333 Battery Street, CA 94111, 1-888 591
1234, 392 1234, http://parksanfrancisco.hyatt.com,
$179-$499 double).

The Embarcadero

Expensive

Hotel Vitale

*8 Mission Street, at Embarcadero, CA 94105
(1-888 890 8688/278 3700/fax 278 3750/www.
hotelvitale.com). BART & Metro to Montgomery/
bus 2, 3, 4, 31 & Market Street routes.* **Rates** $269-
$399 double; $699-$1,200 suite. **Credit** AmEx, DC,
Disc, MC, V. **Map** p315 O4 ⑬
For our money, this is the most impressive hotel
opening in San Francisco over the last few years.
Blessed with a truly dramatic location on the
Embarcadero (many rooms have great views of the
Bay Bridge, and the spa is atop a penthouse suite),
the Vitale is otherwise discreet in its stylishness: the
capacious rooms are done out in light colours, all the
better to reflect the light, with wildly comfortable
beds and excellent amenities (including, in the
suites, a Bose SoundDock for travellers with iPods).

Downstairs is a bar and restaurant (Americano; *see
p134*) that conforms immaculately to the comfortably chic ambience. Highly recommended.
*Bar. Business centre. CD. Concierge. Gym. Internet
(wireless, DSL, shared terminal). Parking ($42).
Restaurant. Room service. Spa.*

Moderate

Harbor Court Hotel

*165 Steuart Street, between Mission & Howard
Streets, CA 94105 (1-866 792 6283/882 1300/fax
882 1313/www.harborcourthotel.com). BART &
Metro to Embarcadero/bus 1, 12, 41 & Market
Street routes.* **Rates** $159-$309 double. **Credit**
AmEx, DC, Disc, MC, V. **Map** p315 O5 ⑭
On the Embarcadero waterfront, the Harbor Court
is something of an underdiscovered treat. The 131
stylishly cosy rooms look out to San Francisco Bay
and the bridge; in addition to niceties such as
bathrobes and a top-notch Japanese restaurant and
sake bar, guests get free use of the adjacent YMCA,
a chi-chi facility with swimming pool, sauna and
steam room.
*Business centre. Concierge. Gym. Internet (wireless).
Parking ($35). Pool. Room service. Smoking rooms.*

The Tenderloin

Expensive

Clift Hotel

*495 Geary Street, at Taylor Street, CA 94102
(1-800 697 1791/775 4700/fax 441 4621/www.
clifthotel.com). Bus 2, 3, 4, 27, 38, 76/cable car*

Hotel Vitale.

Powell-Hyde or Powell-Mason. **Rates** $255-$395 double; $355-$1,200 suite. **Credit** AmEx, DC, Disc, MC, V. **Map** p314 L6 ⓕ
Built into the fabric of a historic hotel, this deeply chic property is the creation of impresario Ian Schrager and designer Philippe Starck. In comparison to some of the duo's other, somewhat overdesigned properties, it's a surprisingly comfortable place. The 373 rooms and suites contain relatively peaceful colour schemes, comfortable beds and elegant fittings, plus a top-drawer range of amenities. Downstairs, it's a little more over the top, both in the Redwood Room bar (*see p161*) and the immensely fashionable Asia de Cuba restaurant (*see p136*). At night, the hotel draws many of SF's more beautiful people, who have attitudes to match. Bring a torch to help you navigate the deliberately dark hallways.
Bar. Business centre. CD. Concierge. DVD. Gym. Internet (wireless (lobby areas only), DSL, shared terminal). Parking ($45). Restaurant. Room service. Smoking rooms. Spa.

Hotel Monaco

501 Geary Street, at Taylor Street, CA 94102 (1-866 622 5284/292 0100/fax 292 0111/www.monaco-sf. com). Bus 2, 3, 4, 27, 38, 76/cable car Powell-Hyde or Powell-Mason. **Rates** $219-$349 double; $289-$559 suite. **Credit** AmEx, DC, Disc, MC, V. **Map** p314 L6 ⓖ
Perhaps the signature Kimpton Group property in San Francisco, this Beaux Arts wonder has been converted in eye-catching, indulgent fashion. The common areas are done out with hand-painted ceiling domes and grandiose art nouveau murals, but, if anything, the rooms are even more extravagant: check the canopy-draped beds and the outlandish striping. Be sure to get a pet goldfish (maintenance

free) in your room for the duration of your stay. The sumptuous Grand Café in the lobby has the feel of a Parisian train station in the 1920s, and offers a first-rate menu. Rates include wine and cheese receptions, neck massages and tarot readings.
Bar. Business centre. CD. Concierge. DVD. Gym. Internet (wireless, DSL). Parking ($39). Restaurants (2). Room service. Smoking rooms. Spa.

Moderate

Hotel Adagio

550 Geary Street, between Taylor & Jones Streets, CA 94102 (1-800 228 8830/775 5000/fax 775 9388/www.thehoteladagio.com). Bus 2, 3, 4, 27, 38, 76. **Rates** $139-$289 double; $169-$895 suite. **Credit** AmEx, DC, Disc, MC, V. **Map** p314 L6 ⓗ
Now owned by Joie de Vivre Hospitality, the Adagio has been in town in one incarnation or another since 1929. Its current version is the best yet: the casual, mellow decor combines muted colours and arty photos, making the hotel feel comfortable as well as chic and smart without ever being too business-like. Aveda bathroom products, hi-definition TVs and on-the-spot room service help guests feel pampered. Having Pascal Rigo's Cortez (*see p137*) as the bar/restaurant and breakfast room is another major boon.
Bar. Business centre. CD. Concierge. Gym. Internet (wireless (lobby only), DSL, shared terminal). Parking ($33). Restaurant. Room service. Smoking rooms.

Hotel Bijou

111 Mason Street, at Eddy Street, CA 94102 (1-800 771 1022/771 1200/fax 346 3196/www. hotelbijou.com). BART & Metro to Powell/bus 27,

Hotel Monaco.

1050 Van Ness Avenue
San Francisco • CA 94109
Tel: 415-673-6400
Fax: 415-673-9362
www.laquintasf.com

The La Quinta Inn and Suites- San Francisco is conveniently located at Van Ness Avenue and Geary Street in the Civic Center-Cathedral Hill neighborhood of downtown San Francisco. The hotel offers daily complimentary expanded continental breakfast and complimentary Wireless, and in room DSL.

The California Street Cable Car just steps from the hotel, allows easy access to Union Square, the Nordstrom Shopping Centre, Fisherman's Wharf, San Francisco's Chinatown, Pier 39, the Embarcadero, Financial District, and all of the other sites that San Francisco is famous for.

Clear your mind. Rest your soul.

415.394.1111 · 1.800. IKKO.US
222 MASON STREET
SAN FRANCISCO, CA 94102
AAA FOUR DIAMOND AWARD
WWW.HOTELNIKKOSF.COM

hotel nikko san francisco
travel to a different place

30, 45 & Market Street routes/cable car Powell-Hyde or Powell-Mason. **Rates** $89-$159 double. **Credit** AmEx, DC, MC, V. **Map** p315 M6 ⑱
If you're happy in this slightly edgy pocket of the Tenderloin, you'll appreciate the Bijou's proximity to Market Street. Cinephiles with a sense of humour will love the cleverly executed (albeit occasionally over-cutesy) homage to 1930s movie houses: walls are covered in black-and-white images of cinema marquees and local film schedules are posted on a board. Best of all, there's a mini-theatre, with real vintage cinema seating, in which guests can enjoy nightly viewings (on a television, though, not a big screen). All 65 of the comfortably stylish rooms are named after a movie shot in the city, but there's nothing to distinguish *Vertigo* from *Mrs Doubtfire* besides a film still on the wall.
Concierge. Internet (wireless, DSL, shared terminal). Parking ($25).

Hotel Metropolis

25 Mason Street, at Turk Street, CA 94102 (1-800 553 1900/775 4600/fax 775 4606/www.hotel metropolis.com). BART & Metro to Powell/bus 27, 30, 45 & Market Street routes/cable car Powell-Hyde. **Rates** $99-$189 double; $195-$350 suite. **Credit** AmEx, DC, Disc, MC, V. **Map** p315 M6 ⑲
The Metropolis is eco-friendly yin meets mid-priced yang, with each floor colour-coded in shades of olive green (earth), taupe (wind), yellow (fire) and aquamarine (water). The 105 rooms and five suites have nicely understated furnishings: one of the suites, specially designed for kids, has bunk beds, a blackboard and toys, including a Nintendo. There's a small library and a lovely painted ceiling in the lobby. Cable TV and better-than-average toiletries complete the comforts. From the tenth floor, where some rooms have balconies, there are splendid views over Potrero Hill to the Oakland hills beyond.
Business centre. CD. Concierge. Gym. Internet (wireless, DSL (some rooms), shared terminal). Parking ($29). Smoking rooms.

Hotel Serrano

405 Taylor Street, at O'Farrell Street, CA 94102 (1-866 289 6561/885 2500/fax 474 4879/www. serranohotel.com). Bus 2, 3, 4, 27, 38, 76/cable car Powell-Hyde. **Rates** $159-$259 double; $229-$329 suite. **Credit** AmEx, DC, MC, V. **Map** p314 L6 ⑳
Right next door to the more lavish and expensive Monaco (*see p49*), this 17-storey Spanish Revival building is no less decoratively daring. The lobby is in a Moorish style – jewel-tones, rich dark woods and high, elaborately painted ceilings – but the rooms are cosier, with buttery yellow damask walls, cherrywood furniture and warm red striped curtains. The upper floors have good city views. Pet-friendly and kid-friendly, the Serrano has a games library; guests are invited, at check-in, to play a round of blackjack for prizes. Ponzu, the hotel's hip Asian-fusion restaurant, is a great place for dinner.
Bar. Business centre. Concierge. Gym. Internet (wireless, DSL). Parking ($39). Restaurant. Room service. Smoking rooms.

Monticello Inn

127 Ellis Street, at Powell Street, CA 94102 (1-866 778 6169/392 8800/fax 398 2650/www.monticello inn.com). BART & Metro to Powell/bus 27, 30, 45 & Market Street routes/cable car Powell-Hyde or Powell-Mason. **Rates** $139-$229 double. **Credit** AmEx, DC, Disc, MC, V. **Map** p315 M6 ㉑
This charming, pet-friendly hotel, tucked away near Union Square and the Theatre District, is meant to recall the gracious Colonial-era Virginia home of Thomas Jefferson. As odd as this may sound, it's actually quite snug. Each of the 91 rooms and 20 two-room suites is small, but they're also tidy and comfortably appointed. The hotel offers room service from Puccini & Pinetti, the excellent Italian restaurant downstairs. Order a book from the Borders nearby, and it'll be delivered within an hour.
Bar. Concierge. Internet (wireless). Parking ($30). Restaurant. Room service. Smoking rooms.

Phoenix Hotel

601 Eddy Street, at Larkin Street, CA 94109 (1-800 248 9466/776 1380/fax 885 3109/www. thephoenixhotel.com). Bus 19, 31. **Rates** $99-$219 double; $229-$279 suite. **Credit** AmEx, DC, Disc, MC, V. **Map** p314 K6 ㉒
Add funky styling to affordable rates and an edgy neighbourhood, then sit back and watch the hipsters come in their droves. That's certainly the way things have worked at the Phoenix, which has housed a who's who of upcoming musical talent on their way through town – everyone from Red Hot Chili Peppers to British Sea Power. The rooms, somewhat surprisingly, aren't anything special, but the adjoining Bambuddha restaurant and cocktail lounge (*see p239*), which serves exotic Asian-themed cocktails and Asian tapas, and its heated pool are both popular places to lounge.
Bar. Internet (wireless). Parking (free). Pool. Restaurant.

Also recommended

The old-fashioned, good-value **Savoy Hotel** (580 Geary Street, CA 94102, 1-800 227 4223, 441 2700, www.thesavoyhotel.com, $129-$189 double).

Budget

The **Adelaide Hostel** (*see p62*) also has private rooms, six of them en suite.

Touchstone Hotel

480 Geary Street, between Mason & Taylor Streets, CA 94109 (1-800 620 5889/771 1600/fax 931 5442/www.thetouchstone.com). Bus 2, 3, 4, 27, 38, 76/cable car Powell-Hyde or Powell-Mason. **Rates** $79-$129 double. **Credit** AmEx, DC, Disc, MC, V. **Map** p314 L5 ㉓
Formerly the Hotel David, this recently spruced-up family-run hotel offers comfortable rooms and good value in an excellent location (it's two blocks from Union Square and virtually next door to the more expensive Clift). The 42 nicely appointed rooms have few frills, but are all clean and nicely appointed. The

W Hotel: the lore of the letter. *See p53.*

Jewish delicatessen downstairs is a local institution, popular with theatregoers for the pastrami on rye, and with guests for the made-to-order breakfasts. *Concierge. Internet (wireless, shared terminal). Parking ($26). Restaurant. Smoking rooms.*

Civic Center

Moderate

Inn at the Opera
333 Fulton Street, between Gough & Franklin Streets, CA 94102 (1-800 590 0157/863 8400/fax 861 0821/www.innattheopera.com). BART & Metro to Civic Center/bus 21, 47, 49 & Market Street routes. **Rates** $139-$159 double; $159-$259 suite. **Credit** AmEx, DC, Disc, MC, V. **Map** p318 J7 ❷
Tagged by crooner Tony Bennett as the 'best romantic hotel I know', this charmer is popular with a culturally motivated older crowd, thanks to its handy location near the Opera House, the Davies Symphony Hall and the shops of Hayes Valley. Framed portraits of composers hang on the walls, sheet music lines some bureau drawers, and the sound systems in every room are tuned to classical stations. The 30 rooms and 18 suites are mainly handsome and fairly spacious, and most have kitchenettes. The restaurant, Ovation, is popular for pre- and post-performance dinners. *Bar. CD. Concierge. Internet (wireless, shared terminal). Parking ($25). Restaurant. Room service.*

Budget

Edwardian Inn
1668 Market Street, between Rose & Haight Streets, CA 94102 (1-888 864 8070/864 1271/ fax 861 8116/www.edwardiansfhotel.com). Metro to Van Ness/bus 6, 7, 66, 71. **Rates** $89-$169 double; $189-$249 suite. **Credit** AmEx, DC, Disc, MC, V. **Map** p318 K8 ❷
This European-style hotel is one of the best bargains in the area, offering charm and tidiness for a relative song. Close to various performing-arts venues and with easy access to Market Street transportation, each of the 40 rooms has been recently renovated; most of them offer private bathrooms, some have jetted tubs, and all are warmly appointed with good-quality bedlinens and nice touches such as freshly cut flowers. The only drag is that some of the rooms are on the small side. *Bar. Concierge. Internet (wireless). Parking ($16).*

SoMa & South Beach

SoMa

Expensive

St Regis Hotel
125 3rd Street, at Mission Street, CA 94103 (1-877 787 3447/284 4000/fax 284 4030/www. stregis.com). BART & Metro to Montgomery/bus 9, 12, 15, 30, 45, 76. **Rates** $279-$699 double; $749-$2,500 suite. **Credit** AmEx, DC, Disc, MC, V. **Map** p315 N6 ❷
The latest addition to San Francisco's growing collection of luxury hotels, this high-rise property opened in November 2005, next to SFMOMA and central to the entire burgeoning SoMa arts scene. The 260 guestrooms are spacious and sleek, appointed with the very top line of indulgences, including 42-inch plasma-screened televisions, deep-soak bathtubs and fingertip electronic controls to adjust everything from lighting and window coverings to the do-not-disturb sign on the door. The new building, which also includes private residences, a top-rated spa and an excellent restaurant, is state of the art in every respect. *Bar. Business centre. CD. Concierge. DVD. Gym. Internet (wireless, DSL, shared terminal). Parking ($40). Restaurant. Room service. Smoking rooms. Spa.*

W Hotel
181 3rd Street, at Howard Street, CA 94103 (1-888 625 5144/777 5300/fax 817 7823/www.whotels.com). BART & Metro to Montgomery/bus 12, 15, 30, 45, 76. **Rates** $189-$429 double; $1,000-$1,800 suite. **Credit** AmEx, DC, Disc, MC, V. **Map** p315 N6 ❷

This trailblazing, chic and ever so slightly snooty urban hotel chain continues to expand around the country, but it hasn't yet reached the point at which hip and fashionable turns to yesterday's thing. For that, full credit goes to the design, which eschews grand flourishes in favour of a simple and unobtrusive stylishness in both the rooms and the public spaces. Immediately on entering the hotel, you'll find yourself in a buzzing lobby bar, crowded with visitors and after-work locals making the scene. The 423 rooms are as modern as the lobby and loaded up with all the latest gadgets: CD players, 27-inch TV screens, wireless keyboards, high-speed internet access and goose-down duvets. Service is swift and professional. **Photo** *p52*.
Bar. Business centre. CD. Concierge. DVD. Gym. Internet (wireless (lobby areas only), DSL, shared terminal). Parking ($45). Pool. Restaurant. Room service. Smoking rooms. Spa.

Moderate

Courtyard San Francisco Downtown

229 2nd Street, between Howard & Folsom Streets, CA 94105 (1-800 321 2211/947 0700/fax 947 0800/www.marriott.com/courtyard). BART & Metro to Montgomery/bus 9, 12, 15, 30, 45, 76. **Rates** $129-$269 double; $269-$429 suite. **Credit** AmEx, DC, Disc, MC, V. **Map** p315 N6 ㉓
Although it's run by a large chain, this comfortable, modern hotel feels like a one-off property. The service is friendly and professional, and amenities are far nicer than those provided by most hotels of this calibre. The 405 rooms and 31 suites are appointed with modern fittings and plenty of accessories designed to cater to the needs of the business traveller. The location, close to the ballpark and within walking distance from the Financial District, is also a selling point. Coffee addicts will appreciate the on-site branch of Starbucks.
Bar. Business centre. Concierge. Gym. Internet (wireless (lobby areas only), DSL, shared terminal). Parking ($35). Pool. Restaurant. Room service. Smoking rooms.

Nob Hill & Chinatown

Expensive

Huntington Hotel

1075 California Street, at Taylor Street, CA 94108 (1-800 227 4683/474 5400/fax 474 6227/www.huntingtonhotel.com). Bus 1/cable car California, Powell-Hyde or Powell-Mason. **Rates** $339-$399 double; $490-$1,199 suite. **Credit** AmEx, DC, Disc, MC, V. **Map** p314 L5 ㉙

Making an entrance: the **Ritz-Carlton**.

One of the truly iconic San Francisco hotels, this old-world, family-owned and -operated property exemplifies understated luxury. The hotel is perched high on Nob Hill, near to Grace Cathedral, and has 137 lovely, well-appointed rooms and 32 suites, offering eye-popping views of the city. What could be better than a swimming pool overlooking Union Square or indulgent treatments at the lush Nob Hill Spa (345 2888)? Of course, you'll pay for the privilege: if you have to check the room rates before booking, you're probably in the wrong place. The California cable car line rambles past the front door.
Bar. Business centre. CD. Concierge. DVD. Gym. Internet (wireless). Parking ($29). Pool. Restaurant. Room service. Spa.

Ritz-Carlton

600 Stockton Street, at California Street, CA 94108 (1-800 241 3333/296 7465/fax 291 0288/www.ritzcarlton.com). Bus 1, 15, 30, 45/cable car California. **Rates** $279-$595 double; $525-$2,000 suite. **Credit** AmEx, DC, Disc, MC, V. **Map** p315 M4 ㉚
The Ritz-Carlton has been the de facto choice for dignitaries and heads of state for years. As you might expect, then, the rooms are sumptuously appointed, immaculately clean, stocked with luxurious treats and rather on the staid side. Amenities include an indoor spa with gym, swimming pool, whirlpool and sauna; the Dining Room (*see p142*), a top-class French restaurant; daily piano performances in the Lobby Lounge; and an armada of valets to meet your

Fairmont Hotel & Tower.

every need. Mere mortals can pop in for the Sunday Jazz Brunch, held on a sunken roof terrace and surrounded by roses and bougainvillea.

Bars (2). Business centre. Concierge. DVD. Gym. Internet (wireless, DSL, shared terminal). Parking ($55). Pool. Restaurants (2). Room service. Smoking rooms. Spa.

Also recommended

The impossibly swanky **Fairmont Hotel & Tower** (950 Mason Street, CA 94108, 1-800 527 4727, 772 5000, www.fairmont.com, $199-$469 double); the similarly moneyed **Mark Hopkins Inter-Continental** (1 Nob Hill, CA 94108, 1-800 662 4455, 392 3434, http://sanfrancisco.intercontinental. com, $199-$379 double); the **Renaissance Stanford Court Hotel** (905 California Street, CA 94108, 1-800 227 4736, 989 3500, www. marriott.com, $195-$299 double).

Moderate

Executive Hotel Vintage Court

650 Bush Street, at Powell Street, CA 94108 (1-800 654 1100/392 4666/fax 433 4065/www. vintagecourt.com). Bus 2, 3, 4, 27, 38, 76/cable car Powell-Hyde or Powell-Mason. **Rates** $109-$189 double; $225-$349 suite. **Credit** AmEx, DC, Disc, MC, V. **Map** p315 M5 ③①

Despite the deeply uninspiring name, this elegant, relaxed hotel gives guests a taste of Wine Country within a stroll of both Union Square and Chinatown. Each of its 107 rooms is named after a Californian winery, and there are daily tastings (sometimes hosted by a local winemaker) beside the grand marble fireplace in the lobby. Rooms have bay windows with venetian blinds, handsome writing desks and green-striped, padded headboards. The penthouse Niebaum-Coppola Suite boasts views of the bay, a jacuzzi, a wood-burning fireplace and a stained-glass window that dates back to 1912. But the very best reason to bunk here is that guests get jumped up the waiting list for reservations at Masa's (*see p132*), the hotel's deservedly well-regarded and notoriously hard-to-access French restaurant.

Bar. Concierge. DVD. Internet (wireless, DSL, shared terminal). Parking ($24-$32). Restaurant.

White Swan Inn

845 Bush Street, between Taylor & Mason Streets, CA 94108 (1-800 999 9570/775 1755/fax 775 5717/www.whiteswaninnsf.com). Bus 2, 3, 4, 27, 38, 76/cable car Powell-Hyde or Powell-Mason. **Rates** $139-$259 double; $229-$309 suite. **Credit** AmEx, DC, Disc, MC, V. **Map** p314 L5 ③②

Essentially, California's version of an English B&B, and how you just reacted to that sentence will be pretty much how you react to the hotel itself. It's

almost the definition of the old 'different strokes for different folks' gambit: some will find its lodgings quaint and delightful, while others will take one look, throw both hands in the air, holler 'Chintz!' and run screaming from the premises. Either way, the early-evening wine receptions are a nice touch, and the staff are charmers. Next door, sister property the Petite Auberge is a cheaper, country-French version of the Swan, with many of the same amenities, that feels cosier and more romantic.
Business centre. CD. Concierge. DVD. Gym. Internet (wireless, DSL, shared terminal). Parking ($30).

Also recommended
The century-old **Nob Hill Inn** (1000 Pine Street, CA 94102, 1-888 982 2632, 673 6080, www.nobhill inn.com, $125-$165 double).

Budget

Andrews Hotel
624 Post Street, between Jones & Taylor Streets, CA 94109 (1-800 926 3739/563 6877/fax 928 6919/www.andrewshotel.com). Bus 2, 3, 4, 27, 38, 76. **Rates** $99-$169 double; $139-$189 suite. **Credit** AmEx, MC, V. **Map** p314 L5 ㉝
It's something of a mystery why American hotels continue to describe themselves as 'European-style'; seasoned travellers are aware that, in Europe itself, that often means creaky bedsprings, rude staff and a toilet several miles down the corridor. Still, this handsome old Queen Anne structure, formerly the opulent Sultan Turkish Baths, isn't on that particular radar. The rooms are well kept, if hardly stylish; the public spaces are considerably more charming, and Fino, the hotel's restaurant, is a decent spot. The main drawback: walls are on the thin side.
Bar. CD. Concierge. Internet (DSL). Parking ($25). Restaurant. Room service.

Ansonia Abby Hotel
711 Post Street, between Leavenworth & Jones Streets, CA 94109 (1-800 221 6470/673 2670/fax 673 9217/www.ansoniahotel.com). Bus 2, 3, 4, 27, 38, 76. **Rates** $56-$79 double; $105 suite. **Credit** AmEx, MC, V. **Map** p314 L5 ㉞
Staying at this heartwarming bed and breakfast is a bit like kipping over at grandma's, albeit a little more expensive. It's a deceptively large place, with halls that feel like an Old West hotel, a lobby like the sitting room of a railroad tycoon and rooms in which your great-aunt would be totally at home. With own-cooked breakfast and dinner included, you can't beat the prices, and it's only five minutes from Union Square and Market Street. There's also an entrance around the block at 630 Geary.
Internet (shared terminal). Parking ($18). Restaurant.

Commodore Hotel
825 Sutter Street, between Jones & Leavenworth Streets, CA 94109 (1-800 338 6848/923 6800/fax 923 6804/www.thecommodorehotel.com). Bus 2, 3, 4, 27, 38, 76. **Rates** $79-$169 double. **Credit** AmEx, DC, Disc, MC, V. **Map** p314 L5 ㉟

Designed to a 1920s ocean liner (no, really, stick with this), this colourful hotel offers style and attitude at decidedly keen prices. The colourful lobby is a Lido Deck, complete with chaises longues, while the tiny Canteen restaurant holds some of the hottest stools in town, thanks to rising star chef Dennis Leary. Each of the 110 spacious rooms has large bathtubs and big closets; you can also request one of the post-modern deco rooms with custom furnishings by local artists. It's also a fashionable spot: the Red Room bar (*see p164*) is as popular as the hotel.
Bar. Business centre. Concierge. Internet (wireless, DSL, shared terminal). Parking ($21-$36). Restaurant.

Cornell Hotel de France
715 Bush Street, between Powell & Mason Streets, CA 94108 (1-800 232 9698/421 3154/fax 399 1442/ www.cornellhotel.com). Bus 30, 45/cable car Powell-Hyde or Powell-Mason. **Rates** $80-$170 double. **Credit** AmEx, DC, Disc, MC, V. **Map** p315 M5 ㊱
One of a number of small hotels and B&Bs up along Bush Street, the Cornell makes no secret of its origins: the Lamberts, who've run the Cornell for decades, are French imports. Downstairs is a restaurant, Jeanne d'Arc, serving complimentary breakfast and non-complimentary dinners; the place is a blast on Bastille Day. The lack of air-conditioning means that when it's warm outside, it can get pretty warm inside.
Internet (shared terminal). Parking ($17). Restaurant.

Dakota Hotel
606 Post Street, at Taylor Street, CA 94109 (931 7475/fax 931 7486/www.hotelsanfrancisco.com). Bus 2, 3, 4, 27, 38, 76/cable car Powell-Hyde or Powell-Mason. **Rates** $55-$89 double. **Credit** MC, V. **Map** p314 L5 ㊲
The sign says 'Kick off your boots and stay awhile'. Once past the typical lobby and fin-de-siècle elevator, pink walls tease you all the way into the rooms, brightly lit by the sunlight coming through bay windows. The rooms aren't anything special design-wise, to put it mildly, but they're in decent nick and you can't argue with the prices.
Parking ($20).

Golden Gate Hotel
775 Bush Street, between Powell & Mason Streets, CA 94108 (1-800 835 1118/392 3702/fax 392 6202/www.goldengatehotel.com). Bus 30, 45/cable car Powell-Hyde or Powell-Mason. **Rates** $85-$130 double. **Credit** AmEx, DC, Disc, MC, V. **Map** p315 M5 ㊳
This 1913 Edwardian hotel is a real charmer; a little creaky in places, certainly, but generally delightful nonetheless. The rooms vary in style a fair bit, thanks to the presence throughout of one-of-a-kind antiques, but the majority are cosy and easy on the eye. The welcome from owners John and Renate, not to mention the hotel dog and cat, couldn't be warmer. The traffic noise from busy Bush Street isn't as bad as you might expect, but light sleepers may do well to take a room at the back of the building. There's no a/c, and rooms can get warm during summer.
Internet (wireless, shared terminal). Parking ($16).

 **San Francisco Airport South**

Great for Late Night Arrivals or Early Morning Departures

- 1 mile from San Francisco Airport (SFO)
- Only airport hotel next to BART (Rapid Transit) & CalTrain; for quick trips to/from San Francisco
- Plush pillow-top beds for a sound sleep

- Free 24-hour airport shuttle, expanded continental breakfast, wireless internet and overnight parking.
- Quiet, safe suburban location with 15 restaurants and other services within 3 blocks

For Reservations:

info@travelodgesfairport.com
001.650.697.7373
Mention Time Out for Special Savings

110 S. El Camino - Millbrae - California - 1.800.697.7370 (US) - www.travelodgesfairport.com

CUDDLE UP!

HAVE SOMEONE SPECIAL IN YOUR LIFE?

ROMANCE ABOUNDS IN SAN FRANCISCO!

OUR UPSCALE BOUTIQUE OF EUROPEAN STYLING
IS ON THE WATERFRONT. CONTINENTAL BREAKFAST INCLUDED.

155 STEUART STREET
HOTEL RESERVATIONS (800) 321-2201

WWW.HOTELGRIFFON.COM

VOTED "BEST BOUTIQUE HOTEL, BEST OF THE BAY AREA 2004"
SAN FRANCISCO MAGAZINE

York Hotel

940 Sutter Street, between Leavenworth & Hyde Streets, CA 94109 (1-800 808 9675/885 6800/fax 885 2115/www.yorkhotel.com). Bus 2, 3, 4, 27, 38, 76. **Rates** *$89-$189 double.* **Credit** *AmEx, Disc, MC, V.* **Map** *p314 K5* ⓭

The York Hotel is a delightful throwback to the speakeasy era when gents and dames would knock on a door across the street and were then escorted via an underground tunnel to the Empire Plush Room, where they could drink bootleg booze. While you enter through the front door these days, the cabaret venue still feels somewhat clandestine. The hotel itself has original 1920s pillars and a marble lobby floor, and the rooms, though fairly perfunctory, are more spacious than many. The adjacent Empire Bar is a local favorite nightspot. This was the hotel where Alfred Hitchcock filmed *Vertigo*; Kim Novak's character lived in room 501.
Bar. Concierge. Gym. Internet (wireless). Parking ($25). Room service. Smoking rooms.

Also recommended

The affordable **Grant Hotel** (753 Bush Street, CA 94108, 1-800 522 0979, 421 7540, www.granthotel.net, $55-$100 double); the cheap but nicely located **Hotel Astoria** (510 Bush Street, CA 94108, 1-800 666 6696, 545 8889, www.hotelastoria-sf.com, $40-$80 double).

Chinatown

Budget

Grant Plaza Hotel

465 Grant Avenue, at Pine Street, CA 94108 (1-800 472 6899/434 3883/fax 434 3886/www.grantplaza. com). Bus 2, 3, 4, 15, 30, 38, 45, 76/cable car California. **Rates** *$59-$89 double; $109-$129 suite.* **Credit** *AmEx, DC, Disc, MC, V.* **Map** *p315 M5* ⓰

As long as you don't need to find somewhere to park, the Grant Plaza Hotel, located right in the middle of busy Chinatown, is an excellent deal. The 72 immaculately clean (if rather on the small side) rooms are hardly stacked with amenities (basically a bath, a TV and a phone), but it's all about the location, location, location for most people who choose to stay here, and not without good reason.
Internet (shared terminal).

North Beach to Fisherman's Wharf

North Beach

Moderate

Hotel Bohème

444 Columbus Avenue, between Vallejo & Green Streets, CA 94133 (433 9111/fax 362 6292/
www.hotelboheme.com). Bus 12, 15, 30, 39, 41, 45. **Rates** *$149-$169 double.* **Credit** *AmEx, DC, Disc, MC, V.* **Map** *p315 M3* ⓿

First set up after the 1906 earthquake by an Italian immigrant family and reopened as the Hotel Bohème in 1995, this hotel positively brims with North Beach Beat-era history. The walls are lined with smoky black and white photos of 1950s jazz luminaries, fragments of poetry turn up everywhere and, if you're very lucky, you can even sleep in Allen Ginsberg's room (No.204): in his last years he was often to be seen here, looking out over Columbus Avenue from the bay window, tapping away on his laptop. The 16 rooms are fairly tiny, on the whole, but at least you're surrounded by cafés and restaurants, with City Lights (*see p179*) just across the street. For quieter nights, request a room not facing bustling Columbus Avenue.
Concierge. Internet (wireless).

Washington Square Inn

1660 Stockton Street, between Union & Filbert Streets, CA 94133 (1-800 388 0220/981 4220/ fax 397 7242/www.wsisf.com). Bus 12, 15, 30, 39, 41, 45. **Rates** *$145-$235 double; $265 suite.* **Credit** *AmEx, Disc, MC, V.* **Map** *p315 M3* ⓯

Close to one of San Francisco's prettiest urban parks, in one of the quieter parts of North Beach, this is a convivial little inn, beautifully decorated with large gilt mirrors, pots of exotic orchids and lots of character. Each of the 15 rooms is furnished with antiques and luxurious fabrics, and the service is excellent: the guests are provided with tea, wine and hors d'oeuvres every afternoon. The rates also include continental breakfast, though it's a foolish soul who chooses to eat it here instead of stepping across the square for the outstanding breakfasts served at Mama's (*see p144*).
Concierge. Internet (wireless, DSL, shared terminal). Parking ($16).

Budget

San Remo Hotel

2337 Mason Street, at Bay Street, CA 94133 (1-800 352 7366/776 8688/fax 776 2811/ www.sanremohotel.com). Bus 10, 15, 30, 39, 47/ cable car Powell-Mason. **Rates** *$55-$75 double; $155 suite.* **Credit** *AmEx, DC, MC, V.* **Map** *p314 L2* ⓭

It's difficult to imagine this meticulously restored Italianate Edwardian serving time as a boarding house for dockworkers displaced by the Great Fire. Though the rooms are on the small side and the spotless shower rooms are shared (there's also one bath), you would be hard-pressed to find finer hotel in San Francisco at this price. The 63 rooms have either brass or cast-iron beds, wicker furniture and antique armoires, but otherwise are fairly basic, with no phones or TVs. Ask for a room on the upper floor facing Mason Street or, if the penthouse is free, book it: you'll never want to leave. **Photo** *p58.*
Bar. Concierge. Parking ($12.50-$14). Restaurant. Smoking rooms.

The penthouse is sweet at the **San Remo**. *See p57.*

Fisherman's Wharf

Moderate

Argonaut Hotel

495 Jefferson Street, at Hyde Street, CA 94109 (1-866 415 0704/563 0800/fax 563 2800/ www.argonauthotel.com). Metro F to Fisherman's Wharf/bus 10, 19, 30, 47/cable car Powell-Hyde. **Rates** $139-$379 double. **Credit** AmEx, DC, Disc, MC, V. **Map** p314 K2 **44**

Built into an historic fruit-packing warehouse, this beautiful luxury hotel is the best in the area by far. Located directly opposite Hyde Street Pier, the property celebrates the city's seafaring past, evidenced in the blue-and-yellow maritime decor and the abundant nautical props. The 252 carefully furnished rooms have all the mod cons you might need, but it's in the suites that the hotel excels itself: hot tub with a sea view, tripod telescope in the lounge by the dining table. Staff are helpful and friendly. Breakfast is served in the Blue Mermaid (*see p147*) on the ground floor. If you want a sea view, ask for a north-facing room on the third floor or above. There's a small nautical museum off the lobby.

Bar. Business centre. CD. Concierge. DVD. Gym. Internet (wireless (lobby areas only), DSL). Parking ($36). Restaurant. Room service. Smoking rooms.

Hyatt Fisherman's Wharf

555 North Point Street, between Jones & Taylor Streets, CA 94133 (1-888 591 1234/563 1234/fax 486 4444/http://fishermanswharf.hyatt.com). Metro F to Fisherman's Wharf/bus 10, 15, 30, 39, 47/ cable car Powell-Mason. **Rates** $129-$299 double. **Credit** AmEx, DC, Disc, MC, V. **Map** p314 K2 **45**

A good choice if you want to be near Pier 39 and the Wharf but aren't interested in much adventure when it comes to where you stay. The 313 rooms at this well-run property are fairly standard, but they do offer home comforts, including nice bedding and – by no means a given in adult-oriented San Francisco – family-friendly service. The rooms on the top floor have good views. Another perk: if you time your visit right, the online rates can be very cheap.

Bar. Business centre. Concierge. Gym. Internet (wireless, shared terminal). Parking ($36). Room service. Smoking rooms.

Wharf Inn
2601 Mason Street, at Beach Street, CA 94133 (1-877 786 4721/673 7411/fax 776 2181/ www.wharfinn.com). Metro F to Pier 39/bus 10, 15, 30, 39, 47/cable car Powell-Mason. **Rates** $99-$199 double. **Credit** AmEx, DC, Disc, MC, V. **Map** p314 L2 ⁴⁶

This little hotel doesn't look like much from the outside. And, if we're being totally honest, it doesn't look like much from the inside, either. However, the location is perfect for those travelling with children, the rates are decent (the free parking is a real bonus), the service is friendly and personal, and most of the 51 rooms and three suites have balconies, some of which overlook Pier 39. Rooms have been done out with a playful retro beach-motel theme. There's fresh coffee available in the lobby.
Internet (wireless). Parking (free). Smoking rooms.

The Haight & Around

Haight-Ashbury

Moderate

Stanyan Park Hotel
750 Stanyan Street, at Waller Street, CA 94117 (751 1000/fax 668 5454/www.stanyanpark.com). Metro N to Cole & Carl/bus 7, 33, 66, 71. **Rates** $130-$185 double; $265-$315 suite. **Credit** AmEx, Disc, MC, V. **Map** p317 E9 ⁴⁷

This beautifully maintained, three-storey Victorian building on the edge of Golden Gate Park has been accommodating travellers in fine style since 1904; it's even listed on the National Register of Historic Places. The 30 handsome rooms, of varying sizes, are filled with authentic Victorian antiques, right down to the drapes and quilts. Large groups may be attracted to the six big suites with full kitchens, dining rooms and living spaces. Rates include breakfast and even – hurrah! – afternoon tea.
Concierge. Internet (wireless). Parking ($12).

Budget

Red Victorian
1665 Haight Street, between Belvedere & Cole Streets, CA 94117 (864 1978/fax 863 3293/ www.redvic.com). Bus 6, 7, 33, 43, 66, 71. **Rates** $86-$126 double; $200 suite. **Credit** AmEx, Disc, MC, V. **Map** p317 E9 ⁴⁸

While the Stanyan Park Hotel offers a glimpse of the Haight as it was a century or so ago, the history on display at the Red Vic is a little more recent: about 40 years old, to be precise. The hotel – a red Victorian, funnily enough – wears its hippie heart on its sleeve: wildly colourful rooms revel in names

Red Victorian, beloved by homey hippies.

such as Flower Child and Summer of Love, there's a Peace Café downstairs, and the delightful artist-owner even rejoices in the name Sami Sunchild. Six rooms have private baths, the rest share; a continental breakfast is included in the price. Rooms don't have TVs, and the hotel is no-smoking – that's tobacco *and* grass, folks – throughout.
Internet (shared terminal). Parking ($12). Restaurant.

Lower Haight

Budget

Metro Hotel
319 Divisadero Street, between Oak & Page Streets, CA 94117 (861 5364/fax 863 1970/www.metrohotel sf.com). Bus 6, 7, 22, 24, 66, 71. **Rates** $66-$120 double. **Credit** AmEx, Disc, MC, V. **Map** p317 G8 ⁴⁹

The 22-room Metro is cheap, convenient and a good base for exploring neighbourhoods somewhat off the tourist track. The decor is bare-bones, the walls are a little thin, and the street-side rooms are noisy at night; all rooms have shower stalls only. Still, at these prices, complaining seems a little churlish. Request a room overlooking the back garden, which the hotel shares with an excellent French bistro. Around the corner, and belonging to the same people, is a plain two-room studio apartment with kitchenette, available for around $100 a night. *Restaurant. Smoking rooms.*

The Western Addition

Moderate

Archbishop's Mansion
1000 Fulton Street, at Steiner Street, CA 94117 (1-800 543 5820/563 7872/fax 885 3193/ www.thearchbishopsmansion.com). Bus 5, 21, 22. **Rates** $129-$269 double; $219-$599 suite. **Credit** AmEx, DC, Disc, MC, V. **Map** p317 H7 ⑤⓪
Judging by this opulent French-style chateau, being archbishop of San Francisco wasn't a bad gig in 1904. Right on Alamo Square Park and facing the famous Painted Ladies (*see p106*), the hotel is certainly more magisterial than cosy, but friendly service makes the heavy atmosphere manageable. Decked out with belle époque fittings (chandeliers, heavy antiques and canopy beds), the ten rooms and five suites are named after operas: the Don Giovanni suite has a hand-carved four-poster bed, two fireplaces and a seven-headed shower (one to wash away each of the seven deadly sins – honestly). Breakfast and afternoon wine and cheese are included.
Business centre. Concierge. DVD. Internet (wireless, shared terminal). Parking (free). Room service.

Hotel Majestic
1500 Sutter Street, at Gough Street, CA 94109 (1-800 869 8966/441 1100/fax 673 7331/www. thehotelmajestic.com). Bus 2, 3, 4, 38. **Rates** $115-$135 double; $175-$250 suite. **Credit** AmEx, DC, Disc, MC, V. **Map** p310 F4 ⑤①
The Majestic is the oldest hotel in the city to have remained in continuous operation: it welcomed its first guests in 1904, only two years after it was completed as a railroad magnate's private residence. Living up to the hotel's name, each of the 58 rooms and nine suites in this white five-storey Edwardian has canopied four-poster beds with quilts, a host of French Imperial and English antiques, and tons of Crabtree & Evelyn goodies. Free hors d'oeuvres and wine are served in the evening.
Bar. CD. Concierge. Internet (wireless, DSL). Parking ($20). Restaurant. Room service.

Queen Anne
1590 Sutter Street, at Octavia Street, CA 94109 (1-800 227 3970/441 2828/fax 775 5212/www. queenanne.com). Bus 2, 3, 4, 38. **Rates** $99-$205 double; $179-$350 suite. **Credit** AmEx, Disc, MC, V. **Map** p314 J6 ⑤②
One of the more successful olde-worlde hotel operations in San Francisco, the Queen Anne is, as its name suggests, housed in an extremely handsome old Victorian property. Having begun life as a finishing school for the city's posh young debs (the headmistress, one Mary Lake, is rumoured to haunt her former office, now Room 410), it was converted into a hotel only 25 or so years ago. However, it wears its history on its sleeve: every room contains Victorian antiques, and the lobby area is a splendid space. The amenities are in keeping with the era, but it's all perfectly charming.
Concierge. Parking ($15).

Radisson Miyako Hotel
1625 Post Street, at Laguna Street, CA 94115 (1-800 333 3333/922 3200/fax 921 0417/ www.miyakohotel.com). Bus 2, 3, 4, 22, 38. **Rates** $99-$199 double; $199-$299 suite. **Credit** AmEx, DC, Disc, MC, V. **Map** p314 J6 ⑤③
With its fountains and Zen gardens, this efficient hotel is a favourite of Japanese business travellers. Most of the 211 rooms and 17 suites are standard-issue western style, enlivened with Asian touches such as Japanese bathing stools and tubs a foot deeper than the usual, but visitors who want to experience a serene traditional Japanese *tatami* suite can avail themselves of two here, each with futons, sliding *shoji* screens and deep soaking tubs. Overlooking the Peace Pagoda, the Miyako is just steps from dozens of sushi restaurants, shops and a Japanese bathhouse.
Bar. Business centre. Gym. Internet (wireless, shared terminal). Parking ($22). Restaurant. Smoking rooms.

Sunset, Golden Gate Park & Richmond

Richmond

Budget

Seal Rock Inn
545 Point Lobos Avenue, at 48th Avenue, CA 94121 (1-888 732 5762/752 8000/fax 752 6034/www.seal rockinn.com). Bus 18, 38. **Rates** $85-$134 double; $97-$158 suite. **Credit** AmEx, DC, MC, V.
San Francisco doesn't really do beach motels, but this 1960s motorcourt lodge comes close: most of the 27 large and spotless rooms have at least partial ocean views and, when things quieten down at night, you can fall asleep to the sound of distant foghorns. Furnishings won't win any interior-design awards, but most third-floor rooms have wood-burning fireplaces: these book up early, so grab one if you can. Seal Rock is next to Sutro Heights Park and has free covered parking, a patio and, for the thick of skin, a heated outdoor pool.
Internet (DSL). Parking (free). Pool. Restaurant.

Where to Stay

Pacific Heights to the Golden Gate Bridge

Pacific Heights

Moderate

Hotel Drisco
2901 Pacific Avenue, at Broderick Street, CA 94115 (1-800 634 7277/346 2880/fax 567 5537/www.hotel drisco.com). Bus 3, 24, 43. **Rates** $150-$245 double; $315-$405 suite. **Credit** AmEx, DC, Disc, MC, V. **Map** p313 F5 ⑤④

It might be yet another in the seemingly endless list of Joie de Vivre properties around town, but this hotel has actually been in business for over a century. These days, the 24 rooms and 19 suites pay a kind of gentle homage to the hotel's history: the decor is a crisp, modern update of past trends and fashions, the various fittings as handsome and refined as the neighbourhood in which the hotel sits. Business travellers will be grateful for the morning towncar service to the Financial District (weekdays only); only teetotallers will fail to appreciate the free wine served each evening.

Business centre. CD. Concierge. DVD. Gym. Internet (DSL). Room service.

Jackson Court
2198 Jackson Street, at Buchanan Street, CA 94115 (1-800 738 7477/929 7670/fax 929 1405/www.jacksoncourt.com). Bus 3, 12, 24. **Rates** $145-$235 double. **Credit** AmEx, MC, V. **Map** p314 H4 ⑤⑤

This fantastic neighbourhood B&B is still, happily, flying under most visitors' radar. Located on a calm residential stretch of Pacific Heights, Jackson Court is built into a beautiful 19th-century brownstone mansion and is as quiet as a church. Each of the ten rooms is furnished with a soothing combination of antiques and tasteful contemporary pieces, and has a private bath. Request the Library Room, with its brass bed and working fireplace. Rates include continental breakfast and afternoon tea.

Concierge. Internet (shared terminal). Parking (free).

Laurel Inn
444 Presidio Avenue, between California & Sacramento Streets, CA 94115 (1-800 552 8735/567 8467/fax 928 1866/www.thelaurelinn.com). Bus 1, 3, 4, 43. **Rates** $125-$190 double. **Credit** AmEx, DC, Disc, MC, V. **Map** p313 F5 ⑤⑥

A motor inn renovated in mid-century modern style a few years ago, this neighbourhood gem packs plenty of hip into a modest shell. The 49 rooms are chicly appointed, including great bathroom amenities and modern accessories; some have kitchenettes and city views. Located well off the downtown path, the Laurel nonetheless has easy transport options

The chain gang
The following hotel chains have branches in or on the outskirts of San Francisco.

Moderate
Hilton 1-800 445 8667/www.hilton.com.
Hyatt 1-888 591 1234/www.hyatt.com.
Marriott 1-888 236 2427/www.marriott.com.
Radisson 1-800 333 3333/www.radisson.com.
Sheraton 1-888 625 5144/www.starwoodhotels.com.

Budget
Best Western 1-800 780 7234/www.bestwestern.com.
Comfort Inn 1-877 424 6423/www.comfortinn.com.
Holiday Inn 1-800 465 4329/www.holiday-inn.com.
Motel 6 1-800 466 8356/www.motel6.com.
Travelodge 1-800 578 7878/www.travelodge.com.

just out front. The lobby level is home to the popular G Bar (*see p170*), which brings in the scenesters on weekend nights. Service tends to be exceptional, and there are great restaurants close at hand.

Bar. CD. Concierge. Internet (wireless, DSL, shared terminal). Parking (free). Smoking rooms.

Cow Hollow

Moderate

Hotel Del Sol
3100 Webster Street, at Greenwich Street, CA 94123 (1-877 433 5765/921 5520/fax 931 4137/www.thehoteldelsol.com). Bus 28, 30, 43, 76. **Rates** $109-$199 double; $149-$269 suite. **Credit** AmEx, DC, Disc, MC, V. **Map** p313 H3 ⑤⑦

Those ubiquitous Joie de Vivre folks (*see p42*) have dusted a bit of funky West Coast magic over this 1950s motel. Each of the 47 rooms and 11 suites is decorated with bright and splashy tropical colours; cool details include clock radios that wake guests to the sound of rain or waves. The family suite has bunk beds, toys, books and games, and guests can go to the quirky Pillow Library to choose their own luxury headrests. Complimentary coffee, tea and muffins are served by the outdoor pool each morning, and the free parking is a valuable commodity in this crowded neighbourhood.

CD. DVD. Internet (wireless, DSL). Parking (free). Pool.

Union Street Inn

2229 Union Street, between Fillmore & Steiner Streets, CA 94123 (346 0424/fax 922 8046/ www.unionstreetinn.com). Bus 22, 41, 45. **Rates** $179-$289 double. **Credit** AmEx, MC, V. **Map** p313 G4 ⑱

A haven on bustling Union Street, the six rooms at this B&B are furnished in traditional style, with canopied or brass beds, feather duvets and fresh flowers. All have private bathrooms, some of them with jacuzzi tubs. Alternatively, you could opt for the private Carriage House behind the Inn, which has its own garden. An extended continental breakfast can be taken in the parlour, in your room or on a terrace overlooking the hotel garden. Evening pampering is available in the form of hors d'oeuvres and cocktails, included in the room price.
Concierge. DVD. Internet (wireless, DSL). Parking ($15).

Budget

Edward II Inn & Pub

3155 Scott Street, between Greenwich & Lombard Streets, CA 94123 (922 3000/fax 931 5784/ www.edwardii.com). Bus 28, 30, 43, 76. **Rates** $69-$149 double; $169-$249 suite. **Credit** AmEx, MC, V. **Map** p313 G3 ⑲

There's a wide array of room styles at the Edward II, catering to almost every whim and budget and, in the main, really quite pleasant with it. You can choose from 25 rooms – some with shared baths – or seven suites and cottages, with kitchens, living rooms and whirlpool baths. All the rooms contain antique furnishings and fresh flowers, and complimentary breakfast and evening drinks are served in the adjoining pub. The inn's location is a little traffic-heavy, but it's near the shops and restaurants of Chestnut and Union Streets.
Bar. Internet (wireless, DSL). Parking ($12).

Also recommended

The basic but affordable **Cow Hollow Motor Inn** (2190 Lombard Street, CA 94123, 921 5800, www.cowhollowmotorinn.com, $86-$135 double) is also a decent option..

The Marina & the waterfront

Budget

The **HI–Fisherman's Wharf** hostel (*see below*) has some private rooms.

Marina Inn

3110 Octavia Street, at Lombard Street, CA 94123 (1-800 274 1420/928 1000/fax 928 5909/www.marinainn.com). Bus 28, 30, 76. **Rates** $75-$125 double. **Credit** AmEx, DC, MC, V. **Map** p314 H3 ⑳

It might be located on one of the city's busiest streets, but the Marina Inn has surprisingly quiet rooms. Spread over the four storeys of this Victorian-style inn (it actually dates to 1924), all 40 rooms are also stylishly furnished with pine fittings and four-poster beds. A continental breakfast is included in the price, as is – in a nicely civilised touch – afternoon sherry, on request.

Also recommended

Basic, affordable rooms at the **Marina Motel** (2576 Lombard Street, CA 94123, 1-800 346 6118, 921 9406, www.marinamotel.com, $89-$129 double).

Hostels

Budget-conscious travellers have almost 20 hostels to choose from in San Francisco; what's more, most of them are in good locations. Go to **www.hostels.com/us.ca.sf.html** for a full listing of such establishments.

Adelaide Hostel

5 Isadora Duncan Lane, off Taylor Street, between Post & Geary Streets, Tenderloin, CA 94102 (1-877 359 1915/359 1915/fax 276 2366/www.adelaidehostel.com). Bus 2, 3, 4, 27, 38, 76/cable car Powell-Hyde or Powell-Mason. **Rates** $20 dorm bed; $55-$80 private room. **Credit** AmEx, MC, V. **Map** p314 L5 ㉑

Until 2003, the Adelaide was a friendly, old-fashioned pension, but in early 2004 the owners expanded the 18 rooms to add six en suites and two 12-bed dormitories. The rooms have TVs but no phones (there is a hotel payphone), while breakfast and internet use are free to guests. The hostel itself is tucked into a quiet alley.

HI–Downtown

312 Mason Street, at O'Farrell Street, Union Square & Around, CA 94102 (1-888 464 4872/ 788 5604/fax 788 3023/www.sfhostels.com). BART & Metro to Powell/bus 2, 3, 4, 15, 30, 38, 45, 76 & Market Street routes/cable car Powell-Hyde or Powell-Mason. **Rates** $20-$25 dorm bed; $60-$67 private room. **Credit** MC, V. **Map** p315 M6 ㉒

Make your reservation at least five weeks in advance during the high season to stay at this extremely popular 260-bed hostel. It prides itself on its privacy and security, with guests accommodated in small single-sex rooms; some larger rooms also have their own bathroom. Beds for walk-ins are available on a first-come, first-served basis: bring ID or you'll be turned away.

Hostelling International also run two other hostels in San Francisco. The 75-room **HI–City Centre** (685 Ellis Street, between Larkin & Hyde Streets, Tenderloin, 474 5721) was refurbished to a decent standard in 2005, and is worth a try, while **HI–Fisherman's Wharf** (Building 240, Fort Mason, at Bay & Franklin Streets, Marina, 771 7277) offers a wide variety of rooms, free breakfast and some quite astonishing views of the bay. As with HI–Downtown, both are accessible via 1-888 464 4872 or www.sfhostels.com.

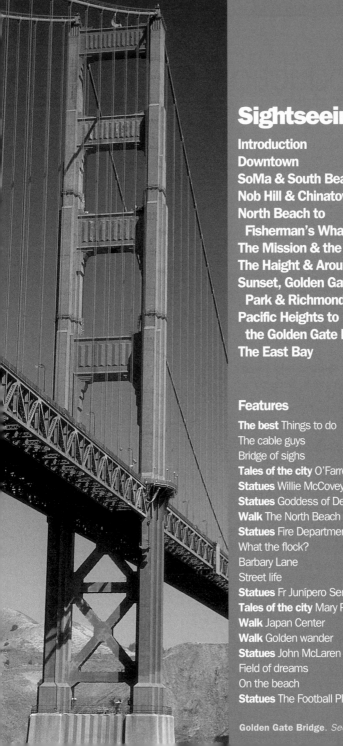

Sightseeing

Features

Golden Gate Bridge. *See p120.*

Introduction

Your two-page primer to seeing the sights.

Every city worth its salt can be said to offer something for everyone. The astonishing thing about San Francisco is that it does so within such a small area, just seven miles long by seven miles wide. The city feels squeezed together at times, as well it might: the streets around Union Square are packed with both buildings and people, the latter a mix of workaday commuters and curious tourists. But you don't have to travel far from the centre to encounter a variety of different worlds: buzzing ethnic 'hoods, chi-chi shopping corridors, eye-catching new buildings, expansive old parks… The variety here is virtually endless.

Getting around San Francisco is relatively simple. As befits a city its size, it's pedestrian-friendly; indeed, the best way to see the place is on foot. If the hills get a little too much, worry not: there's an excellent public transportation network in place, a mix of buses, streetcars, trains and the world-famous cable cars. For more on getting around town, *see pp282-285.*

THE NEIGHBOURHOODS

Arranged by area, our sightseeing chapters start at **Union Square**, where visitors are most likely to have procured a hotel or emerged from public transport. From here, we explore the rest of Downtown north of Market Street: the high-rise **Financial District**, the lovely **Embarcadero**, the run-down **Tenderloin** and the grand **Civic Center**. Then we go south of Market into **SoMa**: centre of the dot-com boom and bust, but now up and coming again. From Downtown, we move north towards the water, through posh **Nob Hill**, vibrant **Chinatown**, espresso-scented **North Beach** and on to the tourist heaven of **Fisherman's Wharf**.

We then go south to the Latino-meets-hipster **Mission**, its neighbour **Potrero Hill**, the city's gay heartland in the **Castro** and pretty **Noe Valley**. From here, it's to the still-lively **Haight**, the sprawling **Western Addition** (including **Japantown**) and smart **Hayes Valley**. West of here are the largely residential areas of the **Richmond** and the **Sunset**, with **Golden Gate Park** in between. North from the Western Addition, meanwhile, lie the upmarket trio of **Pacific Heights**, **Cow Hollow** and the **Marina**, the former military base of the **Presidio** and the **Golden Gate Bridge**. Finally, we cross the Bay Bridge to the **East Bay**, to ethnically diverse **Oakland** and the People's Republic of **Berkeley**.

A few things about the city never change: its relative safety (*see p291*) and its topography. Lace up your boots, and remember: for every uphill climb, there's a downslope to follow.

BASIC NAVIGATION

As a rule of thumb, blocks in San Francisco work in units of 100 heading north or south away from **Market Street**, west from the **Embarcadero** or (for the numbered avenues)

Top ten — Things to do

Catch a ballgame
… In America's most handsome major-league stadium. *See p244.*

Cross the Golden Gate Bridge
Ditch the car and go by bike or on foot: it's far more dramatic. *See p120.*

Get lost in the Presidio
Formerly an army base, now a sizeable national park. *See p119.*

Go back to school
Take the BART across the Bay to collegiate Berkeley. *See p125.*

Head out on a tour of Alcatraz
The city's best attraction is a mile and a half from its edge. *See p93.*

Hit the beach
Sunny SoCal it ain't, but dramatic it certainly is. *See p122.*

Read all about it
San Francisco and Berkeley are both full of stupendous bookstores. *See p178.*

Ride a cable car
Ding ding! Hold on tight… *See p68.*

Scoff a Mission burrito
And skip lunch first if you want to finish it. *See p150.*

Take a stroll in the park
Golden Gate Park, to be precise. *See p109.*

south from the **Presidio**. Thus 250 24th Avenue is the third block south of the Presidio; 375 Mason on the fourth block north of Market. Most street signs indicate whether you're heading towards larger or smaller numbers.

Tours

Vehicle tours

Fire Engine Tours & Adventures

333 7077/www.fireenginetours.com. **Tours** 1pm Mon, Wed-Sun; call for details of additional tours. **Cost** $35; $30 13-17s; $25 under-13s. **Credit** MC, V.
A shiny red 1955 Mack fire engine whisks you from Beach Street, behind the Cannery, through the Presidio across the Golden Gate Bridge and back in 75 minutes. Wearing a fireman's coat. Well, why ever not? Book ahead.

San Francisco Helicopter Tours

1-800 400 2404/1-650 635 4500/www.sfhelicopter tours.com. **Tours** 10am, 12.30pm, 3pm, 5.30pm daily. **Cost** $130-$275. **Credit** AmEx, MC, V.
See San Francisco from the skies. The Vista ($130, $95 children; 15-20mins) and Vista Grande ($170, $120 children; 25-30mins) tours soar up from SFO over San Francisco; the latter also takes in the Marin Headlands and Sausalito. The views, predictably, are truly stunning, especially when the fog holds off. Other options include a helicopter ride followed by dinner on a yacht ($265). Booking is essential for all tours; ground transportation to and from your hotel is included.

San Francisco Seaplane Tours

332 4843/732 7526/www.seaplane.com. **Tours** 10.30am, 12pm, 1.30pm, 12.30pm, 3pm, 4.30pm daily. 9am-5pm daily. **Cost** $129; $99 2-12s; $169 sunset Champagne tour. **Credit** MC, V.
Starting from Pier 39, this de Havilland Beaver zooms round the Bay for half an hour.

Rendezvous Charters

543 7333/www.rendezvouscharters.com. **Tours** *Sunset* from 2hrs before sunset Wed, Fri, Sat. *Brunch* 11am-2pm Sun. *Afternoon* 3-5pm Sun. **Cost** *Sunset, Afternoon* $25; $20 discounts. *Brunch* $40; $35 discounts. **Credit** AmEx, MC, V.
A variety of boat trips, leaving from Pier 40 in South Beach Harbor. Book well in advance.

Walking tours

All About Chinatown

982 8839/www.allaboutchinatown.com. **Tours** 10am daily. **Cost** $25; $10-$15 discounts; free under-6s. *With lunch* add $15. **No credit cards.**
Everything you need to know about perhaps the city's most fascinating neighbourhood, told from a genuine insider's perspective: chief guide Linda Lee was raised here. Tours last two hours, or three if you stay for a dim sum lunch. Reservations are essential; when you've booked, you'll be told the meeting point.

Cruisin' the Castro

255 1821/www.webcastro.com/castrotour. **Tours** 10am Tue-Sat. **Cost** $45 with lunch. **No credit cards.**
Founded by recently-retired Trevor Hailey, the Castro's most entertaining tour points out historic queer landmarks and traces the origins of the gay community. The tour lasts four hours and starts at the corner of Castro and Market Street above Castro Metro station. Reservations are required.

Dashiell Hammett Walking Tour

www.donherron.com. **Tours** *May, Sept* noon Sun; check website for others. **Cost** $10. **No credit cards.**
For four hours, you can walk in the footsteps of the city's most famous thriller writer and see the places about which he wrote in his novels. Meet by the Main Library, at Fulton and Larkin Streets; reservations aren't necessary.

Flower Power Walking Tour

863 1621. **Tours** 9.30am Tue, Sat. **Cost** $15. **No credit cards.**
A 2.5-hour walk that relives 1967's Summer of Love, exploring and celebrating the Haight's brief moment at the forefront of global youth culture. Meet at the corner of Stanyan and Waller Streets. Tours for groups of four or more can be arranged at other times; booking ahead is necessary for all tours.

San Francisco Architectural Heritage Tours

441 3000/www.sfheritage.org. **Tours** 1.30pm Sat; 12.30pm Sun. **Cost** $8; $5 discounts. **No credit cards.**
SF Architectural Heritage runs a number of different tours: Civic Center architecture (1st Sat of mth); Broadway (2nd Sat); Cow Hollow (3rd Sat); Van Ness Avenue (4th Sat); and the mansions, Victorian homes and classic row houses of Pacific Heights (every Sun). Most walks meet at the Haas-Lilienthal House (*see p117*) and last a couple of hours; reservations aren't necessary. The exception is the Civic Center tour, for which reservations are required; when you book, you'll be told the meeting point.

San Francisco Literary Tours

441 0140/www.sfliterarytours.com. **Tours** noon Sat. **Cost** $25. **No credit cards.**
A two-hour jaunt around North Beach and Chinatown in the company of local writer Jake Montana. Keeping in the Beat spirit, the admission price includes a free drink. The tour meets in front of the City Lights bookstore (*see p178*) at noon every Saturday, though other tour times can be arranged.

Victorian Home Walk

252 9485/www.victorianwalk.com. **Tours** 11am daily. **Cost** $20 **No credit cards.**
Irrepressible enthusiast Jay Gifford leads these terrific tours of some of the city's loveliest Victorian houses. Meet in the lobby of the Westin St Francis on Union Square, and bring a camera. Transport from the Westin to the Victorians is included in the tour price. Reservations aren't necessary.

6 MAJOR ATTRACTIONS
ONE LOW PRICE
UNLIMITED CABLE CAR RIDES

VALID 9 DAYS

Only **$49.00**
A $104.50 Value!
(Youth 5-17 $39.00)

CityPass is on sale at all of the above attractions.
Ask for it at the first one you visit! For more information
visit **www.citypass.com** or call **(707) 256-0490**.
Prices change 4/1/07

CityPass includes
admission to:

**7-Day Unlimited Use
Cable Car & MUNI
Transportation Pass**

Plus admission to:
**Blue & Gold Fleet
Bay Cruise**

Exploratorium

Museum of Modern Art

**de Young Museum /
Legion of Honor**

Aquarium of the Bay

And your choice of:
Asian Art Museum or
**Academy of Sciences &
Steinhart Aquarium**

Boston · Chicago · Philadelphia · New York City · Seattle · So. California · Toronto · Hollywood

ORCHARD HOTEL
665 Bush Street
San Francisco
California 94108
+1-888-717-2881
www.theorchardhotel.com

Intimate and elegant, the Orchard
Hotel near Union Square on Nob Hill
is a premier boutique hotel, catering
to both business and pleasure travelers.

Just 105 guest rooms including nine
suites, with service that entices the
discriminating traveler looking for the
finest in San Francisco luxury hotels.
Tantalizing cuisine awaits in Vignette
Restaurant where wining and dining
pleases the finest palates.

Downtown

Retail heaven, terrific museums… and those picturesque cable cars.

San Francisco's Downtown is perhaps the only thing that saves the city from being seen simply as a series of villages linked by a common name. The city isn't even close to being one of the ten largest in the country: by population, Phoenix, Arizona, is twice its size. However, the top-class museums and terrific shopping Downtown have helped it maintain a reputation for cosmopolitanism while other, less culturally impressive cities have expanded around it. Just as crucially, at least for the tourist industry, the tightly packed streets, daunting hills and clattering cable cars continue to lend it an appealing old-world character.

The epicentre of the action is **Union Square** (*see below*), a handsome space ringed with shops and hotels. East of here sits the **Financial District** (*see p70*), one of the few places where one can see northern Californians in business attire; beyond it is the elegant **Embarcadero** (*see p72*), which meanders towards the Pacific Coast. To the west of Union Square, it's all very different: after the **Tenderloin** (*see p75*), a gritty area defined by dive bars and panhandlers, comes the **Civic Center**, the city's grand seat of government (*see p77*).

Union Square & around

In 1997, a competition was launched to create a 'new Union Square' to replace the 1941 design by Timothy Pflueger (the Bay Area architect famous for his cinemas, especially the glorious Castro Theatre; *see p209*). April Phillips and Michael Fotheringham's winning design was eventually unveiled in July 2002; at a stroke, the entire flavour of the area changed.

San Francisco's homeless population once hung out here. These days, though, **Union Square** is a mecca only for tourists and shoppers. With little greenery and few benches, the $25-million renovation seems, on the surface, reluctant to welcome visitors. However, initial expectations have been confounded by the square's popularity. Both tourists and locals sprawl on the strips of lawn along the southern edge of the square (designed for, but thankfully never used by, street performers), taking a break from the shops, connecting to the square's free Wi-Fi network on their laptops, or simply enjoying a bit of sun before heading back to the daily grind at the shops and offices nearby.

Not everything was made over. The square, which takes its name from the pro-Union rallies held here on the eve of the Civil War, is still anchored by a 97-foot (30-metre) Corinthian column that soars upwards from its middle. The column, designed by Robert Aitken and dedicated by President Theodore Roosevelt in 1903, commemorates Admiral Dewey's 1898 victory at Manila during the Spanish-American War, a monument to imperialism that might irk the locals if they actually knew what it stsood for. At the corner of Post and Stockton Streets, the names of the city's mayors are etched into the granite.

The square contains a kiosk that holds the San Francisco's Parks Store and TIX Bay Area (*see p252*), plus the Emporio Rulli café, which offers sandwiches, strong espressos and frosty-mugged beers. However, the real commerce is around the outside: the square is ringed by upscale stores and hotels. At No.335, right on the square, the once-glamorous **Westin St Francis Hotel** is where silent-era film star Fatty Arbuckle's lethal libido ignited Hollywood's first sex scandal in 1921.

Once you've maxed out the credit cards, head to the **Rotunda** restaurant at Neiman Marcus (150 Stockton Street, between Geary & O'Farrell Streets, 362 4777, www.neimanmarcus.com) for a lobster club sandwich and a glass of wine beneath the breathtaking stained-glass dome. Built in 1909 for the City of Paris department store that first occupied this site, the dome was shipped across the country for repair when Neiman Marcus took over the building; each of its 26,000 pieces was individually cleaned

The cable guys

Installed in 1873 by wily Scotsman Andrew Hallidie, cable cars were an ingenious solution to San Francisco's eternal problem: how to get up the damn hills. Nob Hill and Russian Hill in particular were tempting morsels of real estate, yet remained mostly undeveloped. Horse-drawn carriages could barely make the climb, and Victorian gentlefolk were unwilling to exhaust themselves by slogging up and down on foot. Enter Hallidie and his idea of introducing cable-drawn transport to the city streets, a method he had first used hauling ore carts in California's gold mines. When, to everyone's amazement, his first cars worked flawlessly, imitators sprang up overnight. Soon, more than 100 miles of tracks criss-crossed the city, operated by seven cable-car companies.

It didn't last. Earthquakes, fires and the advent of automobiles and electric trolleys spelled doom for most of the cable-car lines; by 1947, the city had proposed tearing up the last lines and replacing them with diesel buses. Happily, the outraged citizenry stopped the plan going ahead. Since then, the government has declared the system a National Historic Landmark, which means the beloved cars are here to stay. Three lines survive, covering a total of eight miles: the Powell-Mason and Powell-Hyde lines, both of which depart from the Powell Street turnaround (where Powell meets Market Street) and run to, respectively, North Beach and Fisherman's Wharf; and the California line, which runs straight along California Street between Market Street and Van Ness Avenue.

If you're expecting to see a network of cable cars dangling in the air above the city, think again. San Francisco cable cars remain firmly grounded. Visitors are often surprised to learn that cable cars have no engine or other means of propulsion. All they need is a 'grip', a steel clamp that grabs on to a subterranean cable, running under the streets at a constant 9.5mph. The cables never stop moving: you can hear them humming even when there are no cable cars in sight. Every car has two operators: a gripman, who works the cranks and levers that grab on to and release the underground cable; and a conductor, who takes fares and somehow manages to cram 90-plus passengers, many of them hanging off the running boards, on to a single vehicle.

Visit the **Cable Car Museum** (*see p84*) to inspect the system's inner workings: as well as Hallidie's original 1873 car, you'll get to see the immense winding turbines that power the cables. From the balcony you can watch the ten-foot wheels spinning, as gears and pulleys whir.

While the cable cars are a legendary part of San Francisco history, so is the hassle of waiting for one at the Powell Street turnaround. So don't. Instead, walk up Powell a few blocks and board the car at O'Farrell or Union Square. Or, if you aren't going anywhere in particular, take the rarely crowded California line. The views aren't as good as on the Powell lines, but it's still a cable car. If you're tired of forking over the $5 fare, cable-car rides are included in the price of various travel passes. Cars run every 12-15 minutes from 6.30am to midnight; the Powell Street ticket booth is open from 8.30am until 8pm. For more on the cable cars, *see p283*.

Sightseeing

and restored. There's more history at nearby jeweller **Shreve & Co** (200 Post Street, at Grant Avenue, 421 2600, www.shreve.com): founded in 1852, it's the city's oldest retail store.

The stretch of **Powell Street** that links Union Square to Market Street is among the city's busiest thoroughfares. However, watching the cable cars clatter past, only to realise that the cables are still humming under your feet, is a quintessential San Francisco experience. At the foot of Powell, where it joins Market Street, huge queues of tourists hang around and wait to catch a cable car. (If you want to cut the time, we've a spot of advice; *see p68* **The cable guys.**)

Market Street itself is a fairly unbecoming thoroughfare, dominated at its Powell Street junction by the **San Francisco Centre** mall (*see p177*). The crowds are here for the big chain stores: a huge branch of clothing retailer **Old Navy** looms large on the south side, with a capacious **Virgin Megastore** also doing swift business. The most handsome building in the area is arguably the triangular **Phelan Building**, on the north side of Market Street, between Stockton and O'Farrell Streets. Built in 1908 as part of Mayor James Phelan's post-quake reconstruction programme, it's the largest of San Francisco's 'flat-iron' structures. How Phelan would have felt about the giant **CompUSA** store on the bottom floor is not a matter of public record. Levity is provided across the street at the historic **Mechanics' Institute** (*see p285*), home to the nation's oldest chess club and a 150-year-old library that contains more than 160,000 books on every subject under the sun. Free tours are offered every Wednesday at noon.

The streets north of Market Street and east of Union Square are home to several handsome little alleyways, missed by most tourists but treasured by locals for the relative peace and quiet they afford. **Maiden Lane**, mere steps away, was once one of the city's most notorious thoroughfares, where randy townsfolk headed to pick up the town's cheapest prostitutes. Now gated by day to keep out cars, it's considerably more handsome, awash with chic boutiques and one-off stores such as **Folk Art International** (No.140, 392 9999). The swooping circular interior of the building, which was designed in 1948 by Frank Lloyd Wright, is filled with wonderful and exotic merchandise, everything from coffee-table books on South Seas art to nandi masks from 17th-century India.

Further north sit two more notable alleys. **Belden Place**, a small street between Kearny and Montgomery Streets, is the main artery of Downtown's emerging French Quarter, offering dining both fine and casual plus

Union Square. *See p67.*

the most enthusiastic Bastille Day (14 July) celebrations in the city. Nearby **Mark Lane**, another tiny road just off Bush Street, forgoes the red, blue and white in favour of green: it's home to the Irish Bank, an old-school Irish pub. Post-work revellers spill out into the alley clutching pints of the dark stuff; the annual St Patrick's Day celebrations (17 March) are the stuff of legend.

The other streets surrounding Union Square are dominated by shops and hotels, although there are a handful of landmarks that may please literary buffs. Head two blocks north of Union Square up Stockton Street and take a left down Bush Street, and you'll come to **Burritt Street**; it is in this alley that the byzantine plot of Dashiell Hammett's *The Maltese Falcon* begins, with a murder. The street opposite is even named after the author, who, like fictional alter ego Sam Spade, used to visit regularly the century-old **John's Grill** (63 Ellis Street, between Market and Powell Streets, 986 0069).

San Francisco Museum of Craft & Design

550 Sutter Street, between Powell & Mason Streets (396 2619/www.wellsfargohistory.com). Bus 1, 10, 12, 15, 41/cable car California. **Open** 10am-5pm Tue, Wed, Fri, Sat; 10am-7pm Thur; noon-5pm Sun. **Admission** *Suggested donation* $3; $2 discounts. **Map** p315 M5.

This modest, three-room museum, which celebrated its first anniversary in 2005, highlights how contemporary craft and design enrich everyday life. Exhibitions have included comparing and contrasting contemporary studio furniture from Tanzania and the United States, and the confluence of art and wine label design.

The Financial District

Bounded by Market, Kearny and Jackson Streets, plus the Embarcadero to the east, the Financial District has been the business and banking hub of San Francisco since the Gold Rush of the mid 19th century. It's a curious place, at least architecturally. While walking through it, you're constantly aware that you're surrounded by skyscrapers. However, the layout of the streets still allows those trapped in its canyons to admire one of San Francisco's finest features: vast expanses of sky.

The Financial District's northern edge is overlooked by the **Transamerica Pyramid** (600 Montgomery Street, between Washington & Clay Streets). Built on the site of the Montgomery Block, a four-storey office building that formerly housed writers, artists and radicals such as Rudyard Kipling and Mark Twain, the structure provoked public outrage when William Pereira's designs for it were unveiled, and public reaction to its completion in 1972 was mixed. However, the 853-foot (260-metre) building has long since become an iconic spike on the city's skyline. The pyramid sits on giant rollers that allow it to rock safely in the event of an earthquake. It sounds a little wacky, but it must work: the building wasn't damaged by the 1989 Loma Prieta tremor. Sadly, the only people who get access to the observation deck are those who work in the building.

On the pyramid's east side, tiny **Redwood Park** is a cool refuge that lunching workers share with sculptures of bronze frogs frozen mid-leap in the pond. Across from the Transamerica, in front of the **California Pacific Bank**, a plaque marks another classic piece of vanished Americana: the Western Headquarters of Russell, Majors & Waddell, founders and operators of the Pony Express (1860-1). Further south, on nearby Commercial Street, in the city's former mint, the modest **Pacific Heritage Museum** (*see p71*) holds an art collection that's small but worth a peek.

Continuing south from the Transamerica, the area's thrall to finance remains to the fore. The **Omni** hotel (500 California Street, at Montgomery Street; *see p46*) was built in 1926 as a bank and wears its origins proudly; just up the road is the small but nonetheless enjoyable **Wells Fargo History Museum** (*see p71*).

However, both are dwarfed by the nearby **Bank of America Center** (555 California Street, at Kearny Street), which towers over the Financial District. The skyscraper is 75 feet (23 metres) shorter than the Transamerica, but it's much more *massive*, its carnelian granite zigzag frame often disappearing into the clouds. On the 52nd floor sits the **Carnelian Room** (433 7500, www.carnelianroom.com), a cocktail lounge, upscale restaurant and favourite dating spot among locals, not all of whom remember its role in the 1974 disaster epic *The Towering Inferno*.

A block east of the Bank of America Center sits the **Merchant's Exchange** (465 California Street, between Sansome & Montgomery Streets, 421 7730). The building is no longer used by share traders, but its historic spaces illustrate the important role it once played in the financial life of the city. The lavish trading hall, designed by Julia Morgan, is now the lobby of the California Bank & Trust offices and home to an impressive collection of William Coulter seascapes.

There's further financial heritage close by, at the Union Bank of California's **Museum of the Money of the American West** (400 California Street, at Sansome Street, no phone). The bank's doors and imposing columns may seem disproportionately massive next to the museum's small Wild West collection, but the rare gold coins, three-dollar bills, nuggets and even pistols (used in a fateful 1859 duel between two politicians) make it worth a peek.

The museum also reveals a little about William Chapman Ralston, the bank's founder, a major figure in the development of the city and the man responsible for the lavish **Palace Hotel** (2 New Montgomery Street, at Market Street; *see p49* **Tales of the city**). To learn more about these posh lodgings, take one of the thrice-weekly tours of the hotel run by San Francisco City Guides (10am Tue & Sat, 2pm Thur). However, if you've not got time, a visit to the hotel's Pied Piper Bar is a must, both to wet one's whistle with a fine cocktail and to see the huge Maxfield Parrish painting of the Pied Piper behind the bar. Just across from here – and, strictly speaking, in SoMa – stands the venerable **House of Shields** (39 New Montgomery Street, at Jessie Street, 495 5436), the mahogany bar of which was originally meant for the Pied Piper. However, a careless cabinet-maker made it to such dimensions that the room couldn't hold both the bar and the Parrish painting, and so the bar had to go.

A block east, at the intersection of Market, Kearny and Geary Streets, a uniquely San Franciscan ritual is played out every year. At 5.13am on 18 April, the last survivors of the 1906 earthquake gather around the ornate,

Skyscrapers dominate Downtown, none more than the **Transamerica Pyramid** (*right*). *See p70.*

lion-headed **Lotta's Fountain** (named after the popular vaudevillian Lotta Crabtree, who donated it to the city), just as they did a century ago when families separated by the huge quake used the fountain as a meeting point. Few survivors remain these days, but the meetings continue.

Pacific Coast Stock Exchange

301 Pine Street, at Sansome Street (tours 202 9700 ext 721/www.mexicanmuseum.org). Bus 1, 10, 12, 15, 41/cable car California. **Open** *Tours 3pm 1st Wed of mth.* **Admission** $5 donation. **Map** p315 N5.

The Exchange was modernised in 1928 by architect Timothy Pflueger, who believed art should be an integral part of architecture. He commissioned sculptor Ralph Stackpole to create the two granite statues outside, which represent Agriculture and Industry (the twin sources of wealth), while above the entrance is a figure called *Progress of Man*, with arms outstretched.

The building's main attraction is on the tenth floor: Diego Rivera's 1930 mural *Allegory of California*. It's richly ironic that Rivera, a committed communist, should have been allowed to create such a magnificent work within the heart of capitalism; Stackpole, an old friend of Rivera, had recommended him for the job. The mural shows Bay Area industries, including aviation and oil, with Mother Earth in the centre and the emphasis firmly on workers rather than bosses, highlighting Rivera's socialist penchant for stickin' it to the authorities. For the monthly tours to the mural (*see above*), meet in the lobby of the City Club of San Francisco (155 Sansome Street).

Pacific Heritage Museum

608 Commercial Street, at Montgomery Street (399 1124/www.ibankunited.com/phm). Bus 1, 10, 12, 15, 41/cable car California. **Open** *10am-4pm Tue-Sat.* **Admission** free. **Map** p315 N4.

Once the city's mint, this structure is now a Bank of Canton, and also a museum. Emphasising the city's connections with the Pacific Rim, the museum features changing exhibits of contemporary artists from countries such as China, Taiwan, Japan and Thailand. Much of what is displayed here is on loan from private collections rarely seen elsewhere.

Wells Fargo History Museum

420 Montgomery Street, between California & Sacramento Streets (396 2619/www.wellsfargo history.com). Bus 1, 10, 12, 15, 41/cable car California. **Open** *9am-5pm Mon-Fri.* **Admission** free. **Map** p315 N4.

If you're in the area during business hours, pop into the headquarters of Wells Fargo, California's oldest bank. This collection of Gold Rush memorabilia also gives a history of banking in California. You'll find gold nuggets, an old telegraph machine and a Concord stagecoach, built in 1867, plus some interesting historical photos. It's certainly worthy of at least a quick stop.

Jackson Square

The northern edge of the Financial District is marked by the **Jackson Square Historical District** (bounded by Washington, Kearny and Sansome Streets and Pacific Avenue).

It's the last vestige of San Francisco's Barbary Coast, once a seething mass of low-life bars and 19th-century sex clubs the floor shows of which made modern-day Tijuana seem like an ice-cream social. Today, the few blocks of 1850s-era brick buildings – housing upmarket antiques shops and lovingly restored offices – stand far from the waterfront, though they once stood on the shoreline itself. Indeed, their foundations are made from the hulls of ships abandoned by eager gold-seekers.

Stroll along **Jackson Street** (between Sansome and Montgomery Streets) and **Hotaling Street** to see what is the only neighbourhood left in San Francisco that pre-dates the ubiquitous Victorian style. It was spared during the 1906 quake and subsequent fire, not least because several of the buildings were liquor warehouses that had been built of stone to protect the precious booze. By the 1930s, Jackson Square was popular with a number of bohemian artists and writers; John Steinbeck and William Saroyan, among others, used to drink at the now long-vanished Black Cat Café (710 Montgomery Street). Local establishments popular with after-work drinkers today include **Bix** (*see p160*), where bartenders pour top-shelf Martinis surrounded by authentic 1930s decor.

The Embarcadero

For decades, San Franciscans old enough to recall the majesty of the original Embarcadero became misty-eyed for the old days when it was a palm-lined thoroughfare as opposed to a double-decker freeway with all the charm of Chicago's Lower Wacker Drive. Then came the devastating 1989 Loma Prieta earthquake. Although the quake wreaked havoc throughout the region, it also felled the Embarcadero's ill-considered upper deck, returning it to its former glory. Today, refurbished antique streetcars from all over the world – Milan, Moscow, Oporto, Japan, even a popular roofless number from the English resort town of Blackpool – provide tourists with a little hint as to how the area might once have looked.

At the foot of Market Street stands the centrepiece of the Embarcadero: the beautifully restored **Ferry Building**, which divides even-numbered piers (to the south) from odd (to the north). Major renovations to this California landmark, originally completed in 1898, were unveiled in 2003; the building now bustles every weekend with the unmatched **Ferry Plaza Farmers' Market** (*see p189*), at which stallholders sell organic produce, artisanal bread, cheeses and other gourmet delicacies.

Boats come and boats go, but at the **Ferry Building**, the attraction is really the food.

Bridge of sighs

Built in 1936, the **San Francisco–Oakland Bay Bridge** has always been considered the ugly stepsister to the Golden Gate Bridge's Cinderella: grey and clunky, short on charm, and always trying to cram more cars on to its steel-toed decks than it has room to hold. Still, for locals, it's the more important of the two bridges, carrying more than twice the traffic load of its showy sibling (some 270,000 cars a day) over an 8.4-mile stretch. Divided into two by Yerba Buena Island, it's actually three separate bridges linked together: two suspension spans placed end to end on the west side of Yerba Buena, and a cantilever span on the east side. Combined, they make one of the world's longest bridges.

Completed a year before the Golden Gate Bridge, the Bay Bridge was even more of an engineering challenge because of the greater distances. The engineers' solution to the sheer scale was to build a concrete pylon of massive proportions in the middle of the bay, as an anchor point for two different suspension spans. Because much of it is underwater, this central pylon draws little notice from the thousands who cross it each day, even though it remains one of the largest structures ever built in California, a solid concrete tower nearly as tall as the Transamerica Pyramid.

Designed by Charles H Purcell, the bridge has two levels, each with five lanes of traffic that cruise straight through Yerba Buena Island inside the largest vehicular tunnel on earth. Impressed? You will be when you emerge on the top deck heading west. It's a breathtaking way to enter the city, well worth the $3 toll that's levied each time you cross it from west to east (there's no charge in the other direction).

The bridge came under serious threat in 1989, when the 7.1 Loma Prieta earthquake shook a chunk of the eastern span loose and dropped it on to the lower deck. Aside from the obvious safety implications, the Oakland half of the Bay Bridge was suddenly poised for an extreme makeover, as engineers warned that 'the Big One', the quake Californians have been expecting since Loma Prieta, could take out the bridge's entire eastern half. Civic planners and designers, who had long seen it as a utilitarian eyesore, were positively giddy over the prospects; a movement even started to name the new span after Emperor Norton (*see p13* **Tales of the city**). Politicians and bean counters were less enthused, pushing for a swift and cheap retrofit rather than a complete overhaul. Between bureaucratic bickering, budgetary overruns, design debates and a nasty squabble involving ex-mayor Willie Brown, CalTrans and the Navy over how the new span would affect development on Yerba Buena and Treasure Islands, it took a decade for the city to agree to move forward on a new wing for the bridge.

And then, just when it seemed like things were finally going to get under way, in stepped Arnold Schwarzenegger. In 2004, citing the high cost of the chosen design – a graceful single-span self-anchored suspension bridge by TY Lin International – the Governator proposed to scuttle already-approved plans in favour of a generic causeway. Some 18 months and billions of tax dollars later, a compromise was finally reached in the legislature that gave the green light to the bridge. Meanwhile, the dollar signs have rolled over and over like a runaway slot machine, from an initial cost estimate of $1.3 billion to – at last count – $6.3 billion. The completion date, originally slotted for 2005, has now been pushed back to around 2012. A series of vast cranes are in periodic operation along the northern side, while the constant roadworks cause truly maddening traffic delays.

The 660-foot (200-metre) Grand Nave gets packed with foodies, as daytrippers pile out of the back to hop on ferries to Marin or the East Bay. But even during the week, the building isn't without its culinary attractions, among them a branch of venerable burger business **Taylor's Refresher** (see p135).

Opposite the Ferry Building is **Justin Herman Plaza**, where you'll be confronted by Benecia-born artist Robert Arneson's bronze sculpture *Yin and Yang*. Looming behind it is a mysteriously dry series of square pipes that together make up a fountain by French-Canadian artist Armand Vaillancourt; at the foot of the **Hyatt Regency** hotel (see p48) is Jean Dubuffet's *La Chiffonière*, a stainless-steel sculpture of a larger-than-life figure. The phalanx of wafer-thin towers behind the plaza, at the foot of Sacramento Street, comprises the **Embarcadero Center** (see p175), a maze-like shopping/dining/theatre complex. The **Embarcadero Cinema** (see p209) screens artsy movies.

Walk south from the Ferry Building along the Embarcadero to Howard Street, and you'll see low cement walls where bronze starfish, turtles and octopi have 'washed up' on the shore. Nearby, and easy to miss, is the small sign that marks **Herb Caen Way**, named after the late and ever-popular *Chronicle* columnist. Lovers who come down this way may feel they've walked into their destiny when they spy an immense Cupid's bow in gold, complete with a silver and red arrow. This is Claes Oldenburg and Coosje van Bruggen's *Cupid's Span*, installed in 2002 in a field of native grass.

After taking in the wonderful views of the **Bay Bridge** (see p73 **Bridge of sighs**), perhaps also stopping in for a spot of lunch at the Hotel Vitale's **Americano** restaurant (8 Mission Street, at Embarcadero; see p48 and p135), continue south to **Red's Java House** (Pier 30, 777 5626), a small and quirky snack shack that's been a favourite for coffee and burgers since the 1920s. Between Brannan and Townsend Streets, you'll see a cement marker reading 'Great Seawall'. This is exactly what the Embarcadero was built to be. Work on the seawall started in 1878 and continued for nearly five decades.

Once you've had your fill of waterside views, head inland to the **Rincon Center**, at the intersection of Mission and Spear Streets. This former main post office, containing a number of impressive art pieces and historic murals, is clear of San Franciscans on the weekends except for the dim-sum crowd at **Yank Sing** (49 Stevenson Street, between 1st & 2nd Streets; see p136). Also nearby is the **Contemporary Jewish Museum** (see below).

Alternatively, head north. From the Ferry Building, the Embarcadero grows into a long, gently curving promenade along the waterfront, extending all the way to the confounding tourist magnet of Fisherman's Wharf. Skaters meet at 9pm each Friday for the **Midnight Rollers**, a 12-mile skate through the city (www.cora.org). Pier 7, a wide-open public pier jutting out into the Bay, offers lovely views of **Treasure Island** (see p74). North and a little inland, where Green and Sansome Streets meet, you'll find the offices of Philo TV, which occupy the former laboratory of boy-genius Philo T Farnsworth. Here, in 1927, Farnsworth invented the current system of TV transmission; a small plaque marks the achievement.

Contemporary Jewish Museum

121 Steuart Street, between Mission & Howard Streets (344 8800/www.jmsf.org). BART & Metro to Embarcadero/bus 1, 12, 41 & Market Street routes. **Open** noon-6pm Mon-Thur, Sun. **Admission** $5; $4 discounts; free under-12s. **Credit** MC, V. **Map** p315 O4.
Devoted to linking the art of the Jewish community with the community at large, the Jewish Museum runs educational programmes and shows works by students and established artists, many of them political or controversial in nature. The museum has had a new home planned for the better part of a decade, next to Yerba Buena Gardens, in a Willis Polk power substation that dates to 1907. However, designed by superstar architect Daniel Libeskind (who started work on the project in 1998), the new premises look likely to open in the relatively near future. The museum doesn't expect to be leaving Steuart Street until late 2007, but it has already joined collections with Berkeley's Judah L Magnes Museum.

Rincon Center

101 Spear Street, at Mission Street (243 0473). BART & Metro to Embarcadero/bus 1, 12, 41 & Market Street routes. **Open** 24hrs daily.
Admission free. **Map** p315 O4.
The lobby (facing Mission Street) of this art deco post office and residential/office tower has intriguing WPA-style murals. Painted in 1941 by the Russian Social Realist painter Anton Refregier, this luscious historical panorama was hugely controversial at the time of its unveiling; not only because it was the most expensive of the WPA mural projects, but also because it includes many dark moments from California's past. The central atrium has a unique all-water sculpture dubbed *Rain Column*. Designed by Doug Hollis, the sculpture's 50 gallons-plus (190l) of recycled water fall 85ft (26m) into a central pool every minute.

Treasure Island

Bus 108.
Flat-as-a-griddle Treasure Island, built on the shoals of neighbouring Yerba Buena Island, is entirely man-made from boulders and sand. Originally constructed as a site for 1939's Golden Gate

Sightseeing

Starfish on the
Embarcadero. *See p74.*

Sightseeing

International Exposition, the island was seized by
the US Navy in 1942 near the outbreak of World War
II, provoking ire and alarm. No matter: it served as
a troop deployment staging area for many years,
until it was returned to the city in 1997. At around
this time it was determined that the entire island
sinks a bit deeper into the Bay each year. Despite
this, the island is now a sort of mid-bay suburb, with
some lucky San Franciscans moving into the former
military housing. Why lucky? The views are spectacular, as many Hollywood location scouts have
realised: parts of *The Caine Mutiny* and two of the
Indiana Jones movies were filmed here.

Adjoining Yerba Buena Island – literally, 'Good
Herb Island', though the Yerba Buena referred to
is actually an aromatic perennial herb from the
mint family used in medicinal tea by Native
Americans – is an important Coast Guard station.
It's mostly closed to tourism: you can drive on the
island's one road, but there's nowhere to stop.

The Tenderloin

There are two competing stories as to how
the Tenderloin got its name. The first is that
police who worked the beat here in the 19th
century were paid extra for taking on such
a tough neighbourhood, and could therefore
afford to buy better cuts of meat. The second
is similar, but with one key change: the cops
got their extra cash not from police chiefs
in the form of wages, but from local hoods
in the form of bribes. No one is sure which tale
is correct, but neither reflects especially well
on an area that's always lived on the wild side.

The Tenderloin is a far cry from the retail
mecca of Union Square a few blocks to the east.
The area is home to a spirited and close-knit
community, and its reputation shouldn't put
people off visiting the local theatres, staying
in one of its stylish hotels or checking out
its myriad terrific bars. That said, there's not
much reason to visit the area during the day,
when the only streetlife comes courtesy of the
panhandlers and drug addicts who cluster on
corners. Depending on where you're planning to
walk (Geary Street and points north are usually
safe, streets south of it can get a bit sketchy),
it may also be best to hail a cab at night.

While the city struggles with the question of
how best to care for the Tenderloin's dissolute
souls (it's been a key issue in every mayoral
contest for at least two decades), soup kitchens
provide a partial solution. In particular, one pair
of churches share a long and compassionate
history. **St Boniface Catholic Church** (*see
p77*) hosts dozens of benefit programmes and
has a dining room that serves food to the needy,
while the Free Meals programme at **Glide
Memorial Church** (330 Ellis Street, at Taylor
Street; *see p38* **Tales of the city**), started
back in 1969, offers similar sustenance. Both,
of course, also cater to the religious: St Boniface
offers Mass in English, Spanish, Tagalog and
Vietnamese, while at Glide on Sundays, ecstatic
gospel singing drags a mixed congregation to
its feet. Glide runs services at 9am and 11am;
get there early, as the place is usually packed.

Outside of Sundays, the main attractions here
are nocturnal. Dinner (and lunch) is served by
aspiring chefs at the **California Culinary
Academy** (625 Polk Street, at Turk Street, 292
8229), and at a surprisingly decent range of
Indian restaurants on or near O'Farrell Street:
try **Shalimar** (532 Jones Street, at O'Farrell
Street; *see p138*), which serves inexpensive
Pakistani and Indian food or **Naan 'n' Curry**
(478 O'Farrell Street, at Leavenworth Street,
775 1349). Wherever you eat, wash your
dinner down with a beer or a cocktail at one
of countless bars in the locale, which range
from spit 'n' sawdust dives to wannabe-swank
lounges (*see p162* **Walk**). However, the joint
most characteristic of the area's reputation is
the **Mitchell Brothers O'Farrell Theatre**,
a huge porn theatre with a somewhat colourful
history (*see p76* **Tales of the city**). Just down
the street is the **Great American Music
Hall**, said to be the oldest nightclub in San
Francisco and now a beautiful music venue
(859 O'Farrell Street, between Polk & Larkin
Streets; *see p232*). However, even this grand
space isn't as virtuous as it looks: although
it's now unimpeachably respectable, it spent
a number of its best years as a bordello.

Tales of the city O'Farrell Theatre

Sightseeing

A parlour built on prurient rebellion, the **O'Farrell Theatre** is both a far cry from and the inevitable result of its humble beginnings as a constant prick to the tush of moralist crusaders. As youngsters, brothers Artie and Jim Mitchell made a few bucks selling photos to adult theatres of Bay Area hippie gals all too willing to take off their shirts for a five-buck bill. As is commonly known, topless photography is a gateway drug to short-film loops, which in turn invariably lead to full-length porn features, which slide straight into live sex acts on stage… but that's getting a bit ahead.

As twentysomethings, the entrepreneurial Mitchell boys parlayed a little foxy and a lot of moxie into a porn empire. Opening the O'Farrell Theatre in 1969, the brothers soon made both a reputation and a pile of money from the sex films they showed there, then invested $60,000 of it in the production of their own full-length movie. When it opened, *Behind the Green Door* was a sensation, making Marilyn Chambers a global star and the Mitchells a reputed $25 million.

Fuelled by an itch for pushing the latex to its extremes, and emboldened by their love of money, sex, drugs and stickin' it to The Man, the duo were hardly shy about their success (they even took *Behind the Green Door* to the Cannes Film Festival). In the process, they made a number of powerful enemies – Dianne Feinstein chief among them. Feinstein became the city's mayor in 1978 and now represents California in the US Senate, but she made her name as a member of the city's Board of Supervisors, with her relentless attempts to quash into oblivion the Mitchell brothers and all their declarations of First Amendment protection. However, each new bust by the cops brought a fresh trial, more headlines and even greater business to the little sex shop that could.

As the brothers' reputation grew, so did that of the theatre. Soon, the movies were supplemented with live 'dancers', who behaved in increasingly outrageous ways. By the late 1980s, it was not uncommon to pay the cover charge and enter a full-blown bacchanalia, complete with audience participation. Even maverick writer Hunter S Thompson got into the act by masquerading as the night manager for a few months under the pretext of 'research'; he later referred to the O'Farrell as the 'Carnegie Hall of public sex'.

Eventually, though, too much became Too Much. The litigation never ceased, and Artie apparently developed something of a drug problem. In February 1991 Jim went to his brother's house and, in mysterious circumstances, shot and killed Artie in what the defence later called 'an intervention gone wrong'. The story later became fodder for a tepid Movie of the Week starring Emilio Estevez and half-brother Charlie Sheen, with the screen idols donning bald-head wigs (or were they?) and prancing about in what amounted to a third-rate *Boogie Nights*.

After serving three years of a six-year sentence for voluntary manslaughter, Jim is now out of custody and reputedly still overseeing the show at the O'Farrell, but without the brazen peacockery of old. Out of sight, the O'Farrell is hopefully not out of the public mind. The theatre stands as a testament to human sexuality and emotion in an era where moral lines are drawn in thick marker pen, despite the fact that the lines are really as quivering and permeable as the human body itself.

The **Asian Art Museum**: the contents are just as impressive as the exterior. *See p78.*

St Boniface Catholic Church

*133 Golden Gate Avenue, at Leavenworth Street
(863 7515). BART & Metro to Civic Center/bus 19,
31 & Market Street routes.* **Open** *hours vary.*
Map p318 L7.
St Boniface's Romanesque interior, restored in the
1980s, includes some impeccable stencilling and
a beautifully gilded apse topped by a four-storey
cupola. You'll find the church is gated, so ring the
buzzer to get in. Be sure to get there before 1.30pm
during the week, when the church closes for clean-
ing until the next morning.

Civic Center

South-west of the Tenderloin and north of
Market Street, San Francisco's Civic Center
is a complex of imposing government buildings
and immense performance halls centred on
the **Civic Center Plaza**, an expansive and
well-tended lawn. By day, it's populated by
an extreme spread of locals: on the one hand are
the smartly turned-out officials and dignitaries
who work within the buildings; on the other are
the homeless folk who hang around outside
them. At night, the worker bees are replaced
by culture vultures, here to take in a concert
at one of the several music venues.

Facing the plaza, and dominating the area, is
the stunning Beaux Arts **City Hall** (*see p78*), a
glory both inside and out. Across the four lanes
of traffic on Van Ness Avenue is a trio of grand
edifices. The multistorey, curved-glass façade
of the **Louise M Davies Symphony Hall**
(201 Van Ness Avenue, at Hayes Street; *see
p228*) would be unforgettable even without
the reclining Henry Moore bronzes in front,
while just north of Grove Street sits the **War
Memorial Opera House** (301 Van Ness
Avenue, at Grove Street; *see p227*). Directly

behind City Hall, it's in many ways the
building's companion piece, designed by the
same architect (Arthur Brown) in the same
style. This is where the UN Charter was signed
by 51 nations in June 1945 (*see p17*).

The last of the triumvirate of buildings
is the **Veterans' Memorial Building** (Van
Ness Avenue, at McAllister Street), a venerable
workhorse the various spaces of which hold
offices, performance theatres and even galleries.
On its main floor sits the diminutive **San
Francisco Art Commission Gallery**
(*see p213*), which specialises in politically or
sociologically driven art. Take the lift to the
fourth floor, and you'll find the **San Francisco
Performing Arts Library and Museum**
(*see p78*); also here is the beautiful **Herbst
Theatre** (*see p253*).

In the south-east corner of Civic Center Plaza
are two further landmark buildings. Named
after the promoter who almost single-handedly
created the musical juggernaut that was San
Francisco in the 1960s, the 7,000-capacity **Bill
Graham Civic Auditorium** (99 Grove Street,
at Polk Street; *see p232*) now stages gigs by big
names. The nearby **Main Library** (*see p78*) is a
six-storey building mixing Beaux Arts elements
with modernism; the old library is now home to
the world-class collections of art and antiquities
at the **Asian Art Museum** (*see p78*).

On the edge of the Civic Center is **United
Nations Plaza**. A modest farmers' market
operates here on Wednesday and Sunday
mornings, with arts and crafts stalls moving
in on Mondays, Thursdays and Fridays. The
action takes place under the approving gaze
of a mounted statue of Simón Bolívar, the great
liberator of Central America. The plaza, created
to honour San Francisco's role as host of the

signing of the original UN Charter on 26 June 1945, has in recent years become a veritable campground for the city's disenfranchised.

There's little in the way of eating, drinking or shopping options in this particular corner of the city. However, if you can successfully negotiate the legions of homeless, head across Market Street to **Tulan** (8 6th Street, at Market Street; *see p138*). While this hole-in-the-wall diner may look like nothing, it's widely considered to serve the best Vietnamese cuisine in the city. And just up Larkin from the Asian Art Museum are a number of great bare-bones Vietnamese joints.

Asian Art Museum

200 Larkin Street, at Fulton Street (581 3500/www. asianart.org). BART & Metro to Civic Center/bus 21, 47, 49 & Market Street routes. **Open** 10am-5pm Tue, Wed, Fri-Sun; 10am-9pm Thur. **Admission** $10; $6-$7 concessions. **Credit** MC, V. **Map** p318 K7.
This highly popular museum has one of the world's most comprehensive collections of Asian art, spanning 6,000 years of Asian history with over 15,000 displayed objects. Artefacts range from Japanese buddhas to sacred texts to items from the Ming dynasty. The outdoor café, open only to visitors, is a great place to enjoy American- and Asian-inspired dishes on sunny days, and the gift shop is well stocked with high-quality stationery, decorative items and a good selection of coffee-table books.

The museum once resided in Golden Gate Park, but in 2003 it reopened in this building, the former home of San Francisco Public Library. Extensively and beautifully redesigned by Gae Aulenti, the architect responsible for the heralded Musée d'Orsay conversion in Paris, the museum retains remnants of its previous role, including bookish quotes etched into the fabric of the building. **Photo** *p77*.

City Hall

1 Dr Carlton B Goodlett Place (Polk Street), between McAllister & Grove Streets (554 4000/tours 554 6023). BART & Metro to Civic Center/bus 21, 47, 49 & Market Street routes. **Open** 8am-8pm daily. *Tours* 10am, noon, 2pm Mon-Fri. **Admission** free. **Map** p318 K7.
Built in 1915 to designs by Arthur Brown and John Bakewell, City Hall is the epitome of the Beaux Arts style visible across the whole Civic Center. The building has lots of ornamental ironwork, elaborate plasterwork and a dome – modelled on the one at St Peter's in Rome – that is, in fact, 16ft (5m) higher than the one on the nation's Capitol. The central rotunda is a magnificent space and the dome overlooks a five-storey colonnade, limestone and granite masonry, regal lighting and majestic marble floors. Dubbed 'the most significant interior space in the United States' by a New York architectural critic, City Hall inspires a marked feeling of municipal awe. The city capitalises on this by renting it out for private functions. The site fee alone begins at around $12,000.

Beneath its neo-classical exterior, the building hums with modern technology. After it was damaged in the 1989 earthquake, city planners spent $300 million protecting it against future shocks (a system of rubber-and-steel 'base isolators' allows the structure to move a metre in any direction), but also restoring the building to its original grandeur. Its 600 rooms have seen plenty of history. Joe DiMaggio got hitched to Marilyn Monroe on the third floor in 1954, although nobody knows in which office; on a more sombre note, it was here that Dan White assassinated Mayor George Moscone and city supervisor Harvey Milk in 1978 (*see pp18-19*). Today, the building houses the legislative and executive branches of both city and county government, but free tours offering behind-the-scenes views of the Board of Supervisors' chambers (panelled in hand-carved Manchurian oak) are available.

With the exception of some impossibly intricate handmade wooden models of San Francisco landmarks, among them a cross-section of the building's dome, the Museum of the City of San Francisco in South Light Court isn't that impressive. Still, souvenir-hunters will find the City Store, on the main floor in North Light Court, a thrill: SFPD mugs, bricks from Lombard Street, old street signs and city sweatshirts. There's a small café for the weary of feet, and the basement contains art sponsored by the San Francisco Arts Commission.

San Francisco Main Library

100 Larkin Street, between Grove & Fulton Streets (library 557 4400/history room 557 4567/www.sfpl. org). BART & Metro to Civic Center/bus 21, 47, 49 & Market Street routes. **Open** *Library* 10am-6pm Mon, Sat; 9am-8pm Tue-Thur; noon-6pm Fri; noon-5pm Sun. *History room* 10am-6pm Tue-Thur, Sat; noon-6pm Fri; noon-5pm Sun. *Tours* 2.30pm Wed, Fri. **Admission** free; 3mth visitor's card $10. **Map** p318 L7.
Built in 1996 by the architectural firm Pei Cobb Freed, San Francisco's public library is beautifully designed, although locals still complain about the institution's abundance of missing and lost books. On the top floor, the San Francisco History Room hosts changing exhibitions, a large photo archive and knowledgeable, friendly staff. The basement café is mediocre, but the small kiosk on the main floor has good bargains on local titles. Readings by big-name and up-and-coming authors are held here on a regular basis.

San Francisco Performing Arts Library & Museum

4th floor, Veterans' Memorial Building, 401 Van Ness Avenue, at McAllister Street (255 4800/www. sfpalm.org). BART & Metro to Civic Center/bus 21, 47, 49 & Market Street routes. **Open** *Museum* 11am-5pm Tue-Fri; 1-5pm Sat. *Library* 11am-5pm Wed-Fri; 1-5pm Sat. **Admission** free. **Map** p318 K7.
Exhibitions at this enjoyable museum relate to every one of the performing arts, from puppet shows to operas, but the principal attraction for scholars is the prodigious amount of resource material: thousands of books on design, fashion, music, theatre, opera and other art forms. PALM recently added the Costume Image Research Collection, which explores the history of eastern and western dress.

SoMa & South Beach

Major changes are afoot south of Downtown.

For much of the 20th century, the streets south of Market Street and east of 10th Street were an industrial wasteland, filled with warehouses and sweatshops. When the internet boomed, the area regenerated rapidly: the warehouses were converted into high-end loft apartments, bars opened to serve the new locals, and **SoMa** ('South of Market', a nod to SoHo in New York City) took off.

The internet boom bust in a hurry, but SoMa has carried on without it: the San Francisco Giants baseball team draws huge crowds for its 81 home games each summer, while new shops and assorted bars and clubs also do brisk business. Smart eateries are crowding out greasy spoons, and pre-game and post-work cocktailing are taking the place of the grizzled men who once sat in doorways passing bottles shrouded in paper bags.

People live here too. The rental market may be soft, but the market for buyers continues to break records. In this seismically challenged region, building upwards is costly, but there's also limited space to build outwards. As a result, all available space is being snapped up by developers looking for some of the last real estate open for development within the official city borders. **Mission Bay**, an immense mixed-use project that's already redeveloped a swathe of the old Santa Fe railyard with apartments, eateries, shops, a university campus and a biotech research centre, is expected to double in size by 2020. Planned additions including a new streetcar line and subway link, 48 acres of parks, an elementary school and a hotel, all of which ought to transform this former badlands into a bona fide neighbourhood.

Yerba Buena Gardens & around

Bounded by Mission, 3rd, Folsom and 4th Streets, the **Yerba Buena Gardens** complex was renovated as part of a city-funded project in the 1980s and '90s. It's a maze of attractions, gardens and businesses in a purpose-built series of structures that's half above ground and half below it. **Esplanade Gardens** is an urban park with sculpture walks, shady trees and the *Revelations* waterfall, constructed in 1993 in memory of Martin Luther King Jr. A selection of Dr King's quotes is inscribed beneath the waterfall in various languages.

On one side of the block sits the **Yerba Buena Center for the Arts** (*see p82*), an architectural beauty in itself. Filling the other half of the block (4th Street, from Howard to Mission Streets) is the **Metreon** centre (*see p176*), a four-storey futuristic mall where 16 theatres (including a giant-screen IMAX) are backed up by high-tech shops, restaurants, video-game rooms and the country's only official Sony PlayStation store. The 270-foot (86-metre) lobby, which exits out into the Esplanade Gardens, contains amenities such as ATM machines and public restrooms.

Across 3rd Street from Yerba Buena Gardens sits the **San Francisco Museum of Modern Art** (*see p81*), where the permanent collection and temporary exhibits are supplemented by

Esplanade Gardens.

Sightseeing
with an edge

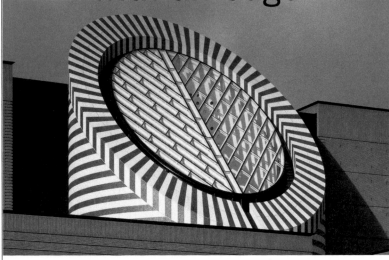

SFMOMA presents an outstanding collection of modern and contemporary art. View painting, sculpture, photography, architecture, design, and media arts—in a landmark building.

- Open daily (except Wednesday) 11 a.m. to 6 p.m.
- Open late Thursday 11 a.m. to 9 p.m.
- Don't miss the award-winning MuseumStore and Caffè Museo

SAN FRANCISCO MUSEUM OF MODERN ART
151 Third Street (between Mission and Howard streets)
415.357.4000 www.sfmoma.org

a top-quality shop and a somewhat pricey café. Next door is the staggering St Regis Museum Tower, where the chief attraction is the **Museum of the African Diaspora** (*see below*). The **Moscone Convention Center** (747 Howard Street, between 3rd & 4th Streets; *see p286*), named after assassinated mayor George Moscone, is a similarly daunting building. Most of it is of little interest to casual visitors, but the Rooftop at Yerba Buena Gardens, ingeniously covering the top of the Moscone Center on the south side of Howard Street, offers the child-friendly attractions of **Zeum** (221 4th Street, at Howard Street; *see p204*). Also here are a delightful carousel, hand-carved by Charles Looff in 1906 (a $2 ticket is good for two rides), an ice rink, a bowling alley and an ultra-cool interactive sculpture by Chico Macmurtrie: sit on the middle pink bench and your weight moves the metal figure up and down on top of its globe. Attempt this only before lunch.

Contrasting with all this modernity is the high-ceilinged **St Patrick's Church** (756 Mission Street, between 3rd & 4th Streets, 777 3211). Built in 1851, the church ministered to the growing Irish population brought to the city by the Gold Rush. It was destroyed by the 1872 earthquake but subsequently restored to its original state; it now hosts both services and concerts (*see p228*). Nearby is a trio of other museums: the **Cartoon Art Museum** (*see below*), the free **California Historical Society** (*see below*) and the **Society of California Pioneers** (*see p82*), as well as the new sites of the **Contemporary Jewish Museum** (*see p74*) and the **Mexican Museum** (*see p118*).

Several blocks south-west of Yerba Buena, **Folsom Street** savours its kinky reputation each autumn during the annual **Folsom Street Fair** (*see p200*), but the **Cake Gallery** (290 9th Street, at Folsom Street, 861 2253) is a year-round thrill: with a nod to the legendary Magnolia Thunderpussy (*see p104*), it's the only bakery in SF that sells pornographic-style cakes. Nearby is the **BrainWash Café** (1122 Folsom Street, between 7th & 8th Streets; *see p140*), a spot about which weary travellers have fantasised for generations: a combo bar/music venue/restaurant/laundromat, where you can sup on suds while your duds get suds of their own.

California Historical Society

678 Mission Street, between 3rd & New Montgomery Streets (357 1848/www.calhist.org). BART & Metro to Montgomery/bus 9, 12, 15, 30, 45, 76. **Open** noon-4.30pm Wed-Sat. **Admission** $3; $1 discounts. **No credit cards**. **Map** p315 N6.

The state's official historical group has focused its efforts on assembling this impressive collection of Californiana. The vaults hold half a million photographs and thousands of books, magazines and paintings, as well as an extensive Gold Rush collection; selections are presented as changing displays on the state's history. The gift shop has an excellent little bookshop and a selection of souvenirs, including California Republic T-shirts.

Cartoon Art Museum

655 Mission Street, between 3rd & New Montgomery Streets (227 8666/www.cartoonart.org). BART & Metro to Montgomery/bus 9, 12, 15, 30, 45, 76. **Open** 11am-5pm Tue-Sun. **Admission** $6; $4 discounts; $2 6-12s. **Map** p315 N6.

The camera that was used to create the first animation for television (it was called *Crusader Rabbit* and produced in 1949-51) graces the lobby of this museum. Boasting over 5,000 pieces of cartoon and animation art, as well as a research library, this is the only museum in the western US dedicated to the form. The bookstore contains a large and eclectic selection of books, 'zines, periodicals and coffee-table tomes covering everything from erotic photography to *Asterix* books. The first Tuesday of each month is 'Pay What You Wish Day'.

Museum of the African Diaspora

90 New Montgomery Street, at Mission Street (358 7200/www.moadsf.org). BART & Metro to Montgomery/bus 9, 12, 15, 30, 45, 76. **Open** 10am-6pm Mon, Wed, Fri, Sat; 10am-9pm Thur; noon-5pm Sun. **Admission** 10am-6pm Mon, Tue, Thur-Sat; 10am-9pm Wed; noon-5pm Sun. **No credit cards**. **Map** p315 N5.

Newly opened in November 2005, in an $11-million, 20,000sq ft centre on the first three floors of the St Regis Museum Tower, the Museum of the African Diaspora (MoAD) is the world's first museum dedicated to exploring the international impact of the spread of African peoples across the globe. Rotating exhibitions highlight the art and culture of the continent, with state-of-the-art multimedia exhibits and first-person accounts underscoring things.

San Francisco Museum of Modern Art (SFMOMA)

151 3rd Street, between Mission & Howard Streets (357 4000/www.sfmoma.org). BART & Metro to Montgomery/bus 9, 12, 15, 30, 45, 76. **Open** *Memorial Day-Labor Day* 10am-5.45pm Mon, Tue, Fri-Sun; 10am-8.45pm Thur. *Labor Day-Memorial Day* 11am-5.45pm Mon, Tue, Fri-Sun; 11am-8.45pm Thur. **Admission** $12.50; $7-$8 concessions; free under-12s. Half price 6-8.45pm Thur; free 1st Tue of mth. **Credit** *Café & shop only* AmEx, MC, V. **Map** p315 N6.

The second-largest US museum devoted to modern art, SFMOMA opened in 1995, reaping enthusiastic approval as much for its $60 million design as for any improvement to the collections. Swiss architect Mario Botta's red-brick building, with its huge, circular skylight, is as dramatic from the outside as within, and still feels brand new. Don't miss the spectacular catwalk just beneath the skylight, accessible from the top-floor galleries: though not recommended for those who suffer from vertigo, it offers a stunning view of the striped marble below.

The four floors of galleries that rise above the stark and stunning black-marble reception area house a solid permanent collection, with some 15,000 paintings, sculptures and works on paper, as well as thousands of photographs and a growing range of works related to the media arts. The collection includes works by artists as varied as Jeff Koons, René Magritte, Piet Mondrian (characteristically geometric) and Marcel Duchamp (a urinal). However, it's the special exhibits that are the real draw. With an evident fondness for electronic and digital works, gallery director David Ross has made efforts to include Bay Area artists in most group shows.

Society of California Pioneers Seymour Pioneer Museum

300 4th Street, at Folsom Street (957 1849/ www.californiapioneers.org). BART & Metro to Montgomery/bus 9, 12, 15, 30, 45. **Open** 10am-4pm Wed-Fri, 1st Sat of mth. *Library* by appt. **Admission** $3; $1 discounts. **Credit** MC, V. **Map** p319 N7.
Operated by descendants of the state's first settlers, this small museum, a treasure trove for the historically inclined, has occasional intriguing displays on California's past, alongside 10,000 books, 50,000 prints and all kinds of other ephemera, such as 19th-century paintings, sculpture and furniture.

Yerba Buena Center for the Arts

701 Mission Street, at 3rd Street (978 2787/www. ybca.org). BART & Metro to Montgomery/bus 9, 12, 15, 30, 45, 76. **Open** noon-5pm Tue, Wed, Fri-Sun; noon-8pm Thur. **Admission** $6; $3 discounts. Free 1st Tue of mth. **Credit** AmEx, MC, V. **Map** p315 N6.
Yerba Buena Center stands opposite SFMOMA and is somewhat in its shadow, yet it seems unintimidated, tugging at the modern art scene's shirt-tails with a scrappy itinerary and great attitude. Housed in Fumihiko Maki's futuristic-looking building, it contains four changing galleries and a 96-seat theatre. The focus is on the new and the challenging (installation and video art, outsider art); shows have included works by such diverse names as Henry Darger, Fred Thomaselli and Kumi Yamashita.

SFMOMA. *See p81.*

South Park & South Beach

If any area in San Francisco embodies the dot-com bust, it's this one. A few years ago, finding a clear space in the green oval of South Park took more time and moxie than snagging one of the coveted parking spaces. Techies would duck out to grab a burrito and end up never returning to the office: they'd been poached by a rival offering an extra 20k a year. Today, though, the 20-year-old studs have had their Beemers repossessed, and the rest of us can now take a picnic and spread out our blankets without stepping on anyone's toes.

South Park was San Francisco's first gated community, until it suffered a string of misfortunes. Getting burned to the ground

early in the 20th century may have been careless, but it was pure bad luck that the invention of the cable car led the local millionaires to abscond to Nob Hill. The area then became an African-American enclave after World War II, but was otherwise neglected until a tornado of young men both fuelled by and fluent in Java arrived in the 1990s.

The madness of Multimedia Gulch has pretty much mellowed, but some remnants of the revival remain in business. Bargain-hunting fashionistas will want to check out **Jeremy's** (2 South Park, off 2nd Street; *see p182*), where women's trousers are sold in sizes 0 to 2; alternatively, try to catch one of the sample sales at the **Isda & Co** outlet (29 South Park, 512 1610). But no single establishment is as representative of new South Park as **Tres Agaves Mexican Kitchen & Tequila Lounge** (130 Townsend Street, between 2nd & 3rd Streets; *see p142*), which features upscale cuisine, premium cocktails made with fresh fruit and a staggering selection of tequilas.

Two further spots merit mention. South-east of South Park at 5th and Bryant Streets, just south of the I-80, you'll find one of the city's oldest murals: John Wehrle's dreamy 1984 seascape *Reflections*, faded but still affecting. A few blocks south, **SBC Park** (24 Willie Mays Plaza, at 3rd & King Streets; *see p243*) is home to the San Francisco Giants baseball team.

Instantly hailed as a classic when it opened in 2000, the bayside ballpark is a wonderful place to catch a game: characterful, handsome and beautifully maintained. It's a shame the same can't be said about the team that plays there. After SBC bought AT&T in 2005, it looked likely that the ballpark would change its name to something AT&T-related in 2006.

Close by stands an intriguing architectural gem: the **Francis 'Lefty' O'Doul Bridge** (3rd Street, near Berry Street), the only working drawbridge in the city. A charming antique, it was designed by JB Strauss, better known for designing the Golden Gate Bridge (*see p120*). Born in San Francisco, 'Lefty' started out as a pitcher but made his name as a hitter in New York and Philadelphia, before eventually returning home to manage the minor league San Francisco Seals. The eponymous bar he opened in 1958 (333 Geary Street, at Powell Street, 982 8900, www.leftyodouls.biz) remains in business to this day.

Statues Willie McCovey

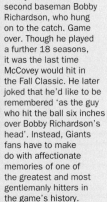

Willie McCovey's start in the major leagues couldn't have been faster. Making his debut for the San Francisco Giants in July 1959, the 21-year-old first baseman had four hits, including two triples, off future Hall of Fame pitcher Robin Roberts. Several months later, he was the baseball writers' pick as the National League Rookie of the Year.

Unlikely as it sounds, McCovey was often booed by Giants fans during his early years. It took a few seasons for his hitting to reach the potential he'd shown in his debut year, but it was his graceless performances in left field that really drew the fans' ire. However, he made some new fans by leading the league in home runs in 1963; and when Orlando Cepeda fell injured in 1965, McCovey was mercifully returned by management to first base.

The move coincided with the most dominating stretch of his career. Matching a good eye with devastating left-handed power, the quietly spoken, likeable McCovey soon came to be regarded by opposing managers as the most feared hitter in the game (only Barry Bonds and Hank Aaron have been intentionally walked more than McCovey). His best year was in 1969, when he won the league's Most Valuable Player award after hitting .320 and leading the league in home runs, RBIs, on-base average and slugging average. However, he couldn't lift the Giants above second place.

Indeed, the one thing missing from his resumé is a World Series ring, though he couldn't have come much closer to winning one. Down 1-0 with just one out left in the deciding game of the 1962 series against the New York Yankees, McCovey stepped to the plate with the potential tying run at third base and the potential winning run at second. McCovey absolutely drilled a Ralph Terry fastball, but it flew directly at Yankee second baseman Bobby Richardson, who hung on to the catch. Game over. Though he played a further 18 seasons, it was the last time McCovey would hit in the Fall Classic. He later joked that he'd like to be remembered 'as the guy who hit the ball six inches over Bobby Richardson's head'. Instead, Giants fans have to make do with affectionate memories of one of the greatest and most gentlemanly hitters in the game's history.

And remember him they do. A dead-pull hitter, McCovey hit the majority of his 521 homers over the right-field fences.

In recognition of his trademark long balls, the team has named the small span of water just beyond SBC Park's right-field wall McCovey Cove in his honour. Just on the other side of it stands this statue, one of three tributes to Giants greats around the ballpark. The others are in honour of two contemporaries of McCovey: outfielder Willie Mays and pitcher Juan Marichal.

Nob Hill & Chinatown

Old-time elegance, splendid churches and a rich helping of Chinese culture.

Nob Hill & Polk Gulch

Overlooking the Tenderloin and Union Square, the **Nob Hill** neighbourhood was named after the wealthy nabobs who built their mansions in the area; Robert Louis Stevenson, who lived briefly on its lower flank, described it as 'the hill of palaces'. A short but incredibly steep walk up from Union Square, the summit stands 338 feet (103 metres) above the Bay. Both the houses and their residents retain an appropriately haughty grandeur.

After a cable car started running up the hill in the 1870s, the once-barren area began to attract wealthy folk, among them the 'Big Four' of the boom-era railroad tycoons: Charles Crocker, Leland Stanford, Mark Hopkins and Collis P Huntington. Their grand mansions were to perish in the fire that followed the 1906 earthquake; and only the 1886 mansion belonging to millionaire silver baron James C Flood survived. Later remodelled by Willis Polk, the brownstone is now the site of the private **Pacific-Union Club** (1000 California Street, at Mason Street). Next to it, at the corner of California and Taylor Streets, is the public but prissy **Huntington Park**, with its fountain modelled on Rome's Fontana delle Tartarughe. Across the park, **Grace Cathedral** (*see below*) is another lovely landmark. Midnight Mass here, sung by the celebrated boys' choir, is a marvellous Christmas tradition.

The park and the club are surrounded by elegant hotels. The **Fairmont Hotel** (950 Mason Street, at California Street; *see p54*) has a plush marble lobby and the fabulous **Tonga Room** (*see p164*). The quieter **Huntington**

Hotel (1075 California Street, at Taylor Street; *see p53*) is known as a royals' hideaway, but you don't have to stay there to use its luxurious **Nob Hill Spa** (345 2888). Nearby, the **Top of the Mark** bar (*see p164*), on the 19th floor of the **Mark Hopkins Inter-Continental Hotel**, offers fabulous views of the city. Moving down from the peak of the hill, the free **Cable Car Museum** (*see below*) displays antique cable cars and the mighty turbines that power the cables beneath the city's streets.

At the base of Nob Hill's western slopes, the stretch of Polk Street between Geary and Washington Streets comprises a small, block-wide neighbourhood known as **Polk Gulch**. Before the middle-class Castro came into its own, this was the city's gay mecca, host to bold bars, adult bookshops and street-corner encounters. The area fell on hard times in the 1970s, and developed an unsavoury reputation as the last resort for runaway teenage boys selling sexual favours. The ambience has mellowed, with shops and restaurants crowding every block. But the teenage boys have grown up into sad-eyed transvestites, and the area still seems to be searching for a new identity.

Cable Car Museum

1201 Mason Street, at Washington Street (474 1887/www.cablecarmuseum.org). Bus 12, 30, 45/ cable car Powell-Hyde or Powell-Mason. **Open** *Jan-Mar, Oct-Dec* 10am-5pm daily. *Apr-Sept* 10am-6pm daily. **Admission** free. **Map** p314 L4.
The sound most often associated with San Francisco is the clanging bell of the cable cars. The best way to study them is to ride one (*see p68* **The cable guys**), but at this entertaining museum you can find out how the cars work, as well as view the cable-winding machinery that actually powers them. You'll also learn about emergency procedures, bell-ringing competitions and the workmanship that goes into each car. Vintage cable cars, associated artefacts and dozens of old photos complete matters.

Grace Cathedral

1100 California Street, at Taylor Street (749 6300/www.gracecathedral.org). Bus 1, 27/cable car California. **Open** *Cathedral* 7.30am-6pm Mon-Fri, Sun; 8am-6pm Sat. *Tours* 1-3pm Mon-Fri; 11.30am-1.30pm Sat; 12.30-2pm Sun. **Admission** donations requested. **Map** p314 L5.
Begun in 1928, this Episcopalian house of worship was once a private mansion. It was later taken over by the Church and is, by the standards of most

The bright lights and busy gift shops of **Grant Avenue** in Chinatown. *See p86.*

cathedrals in the United States, an architectural extravaganza, with a façade modelled on Paris's Notre Dame. Its other features include a fine rose window, a magnificent organ and gilded bronze portals made from casts of the Doors of Paradise in Florence's Baptistery. Murals depict the founding of the United Nations and the burning of Grace's predecessor; the AIDS Interfaith Chapel has an altarpiece by Keith Haring.

Chinatown

The 1849 Gold Rush and its promise of untold prosperity drew shiploads of Cantonese to California. The excitement didn't last, but many immigrants decided to stay, finding work on the transcontinental railroads or the farms of the San Joaquin Valley. Californians both feared and loathed the Chinese, and were enthusiastic about the Chinese Exclusion Act of 1882 (which put a stop to immigration), subjecting those Chinese already here to appalling racism. However, famine and unrest across China gave the immigrants little incentive to return home, and their understandable need for a strong community led to a 20-block area of central San Francisco becoming a focal point for Chinese immigrants of every stripe.

The **Chinatown** that arose in San Francisco soon developed a reputation for its vice; curious Caucasians were lured here round the clock by its cheap whores, opium dens and all-hours gambling. After the 1906 earthquake and fire, which devastated the district, the city fathers tried to clean up the neighbourhood and, crucially, appropriate what had become prime real estate. However, not only did the illicit activity continue, but the Chinese held fast and rebuilt their community.

The crowded streets and dark alleys of Chinatown – bordered today by Bush Street to the south, Broadway to the north, and Powell and Kearny Streets from west to east – evoke an earlier era. Life carries on as it has for more than a century: nearly 100 restaurants serve exotic specialities (taro-root dumplings, duck's feet); herbalists prepare natural remedies; laundry flutters from windows above the streets. Many wealthier Chinese immigrants have moved out to Richmond, Sunset and even other Bay Area towns, but some 10,000 Chinese still live in Chinatown, lending it one of the largest Asian populations outside Asia itself.

Today, Chinatown also feels like two distinct neighbourhoods. Along **Grant Avenue**, one of the two main north–south drags, store owners target tourists with plastic Buddhas and spangly fabrics; conversely, little English is spoken at the ornate temples and food stalls on and near **Stockton Street**. In fact, this contradiction is nothing new. Chinatown has been a thriving, tightly knit community for 150 years, but, since the 1920s, it's also been one of the most visited attractions on the West Coast.

Stockton Street & around

You'll see very few tourists among the throngs of customers that pack the grocery stores of **Stockton Street**. It's easy to understand why. The shops on adjacent Grant Avenue (*see p86*) offer an anaesthetised version of Chinese culture, and fill daily with gift-hunting visitors. However, whether selling medicines or turtles (many of the markets here are 'live', with fish and animals on display in tanks and cages), the enterprises on Stockton cater only to locals, who

Vegetarian options are also available...

conduct their business in a range of dialects. In much the same way, the restaurants on Stockton have a more authentic feel than those on Grant; indeed, for many, Stockton Street constitutes the 'real' Chinatown.

One of the oldest religious structures in San Francisco, the **Kong Chow Temple**, stands on the street (No.855, between Sacramento and Clay Streets). Established in 1857, it was moved to its present home on the fourth floor of the Chinatown Post Office in 1977. Divination sticks, red satin banners and flowers flank a fabulous altar from which a statue of the god Kuan Ti has a keen view of the Bay. Nearby, the façade of the photogenic **Chinese Six Companies Building** (No.843) sports stone lions, ceramic carp and coloured tiles.

Perhaps the truest taste of Chinatown can be found in the alleys a half-block east of Stockton Street, sprouting off Jackson and Washington Streets. In cosy **Ross Alley**, you can watch cookies being made by hand at the **Golden Gate Fortune Cookie Factory** (56 Ross Alley, 781 3956), and even buy some to take home. Sweet **Waverly Place**, just to the south, was the scene of a famous 1879 battle between two *tongs* (mutual-protection societies whose Mafia-style dealings sparked bitter, bloody battles over gambling and prostitution rackets) over the ownership of a prostitute; these days, it's best visited for the historic **Tien Hau Temple** (No.125). Another kind of history was made in adjacent **Spofford Street**, where between 1904 and 1910 Sun Yat-sen launched a revolution against the Manchu dynasty from the **Ghee Kung Tong Building** (No.36).

An intriguing landmark stands just south of here, at 920 Sacramento Street. Named after Donaldina Cameron, the New Zealand crusader who devoted her life to saving San Francisco's Chinese girls from prostitution and slavery, **Cameron House** today provides help to low-income Asian immigrants and residents. However, it's also just about the only place in the city where you can still see traces of the great 1906 fire: misshapen 'clinker' bricks, melted by the heat, protrude from the walls.

Chinese American National Museum & Learning Center

965 Clay Street, between Stockton & Powell Streets (391 1188/www.chsa.org). Bus 1, 12, 15, 30, 45/ cable car Powell-Hyde or Powell-Mason. **Open** noon-5pm Tue-Fri; noon-4pm Sat, Sun. **Admission** $3; $1 discounts; free 1st Thur of mth. **Credit** MC, V. **Map** p315 M4.

Formerly the Chinese Historical Society Museum, this facility opened in November 2001 in improved digs at the historic Chinese YWCA building, designed by renowned local architect Julia Morgan and completed in 1932. The move enabled the museum to continue and expand its mission of promoting the understanding of Chinese history. Displays in English and Chinese follow California's Chinese population from the frontier years to the Gold Rush, through the building of the railroads and the Barbary Coast opium dens. The expanded centre also serves as a useful learning resource for students, with books, videos and CD-Roms.

Grant Avenue & around

A few blocks from Union Square, at Grant Avenue and Bush Street, the dragon-topped **Chinatown Gate** marks Chinatown's southern entrance. A gift from Taiwan in 1970, the green-tiled portal is made to a traditional design, complete with a quotation from Confucius that urges passers-by to work for the common good.

Grant Avenue itself is Chinatown's main thoroughfare and arguably the oldest street in the city. In the 1870s and '80s, when it was called Dupont Street (it was later renamed in honour of President Ulysses Grant after the 1906 earthquake), it was controlled by *tongs*. These days, however, the cash-grabbing is rather more above board; almost as far as the eye can see, souvenir shops sell T-shirts, toys, ceramics, souvenirs and jewellery, the genuine mixed with the junk.

Although most buildings on Grant have been built in undistinguished American styles, a few structures carry a genuine exoticism. The **Ying On Labor Association** building (Nos.745-747) is a gaudy study in chinoiserie; across the street, the **Sai Gai Yat Bo Company** building (No.736) features antiquated ornate balconies and a pagoda-style roof. Slightly more kitsch – check the circular gold entrance – is the **Li**

Po dive bar (No.916, 982 0072), named after the great drunken poet of the T'ang dynasty. Along both sides of the street are streetlamps sculpted in the likeness of golden dragons, created during the tourist boom of the 1920s at the behest of the Chinese Chamber of Commerce.

The shops are a mixed bunch, but one popular stop is the **Ten Ren Tea Company** (No.949, 362 0656, www.tenren.com), which offers free samples to help patrons choose. On the corner of Grant and California Streets, meanwhile, is the Roman Catholic **Old St Mary's Cathedral** (*see below*), a sturdy 1854 edifice made of granite imported from China.

Old St Mary's Cathedral

660 California Street, at Grant Avenue (288 3800/ www.oldsaintmarys.org). Bus 1, 15, 30, 45/cable car California. **Open** 7am-4.30pm Mon-Fri; 11am-6pm Sat; 8am-2.30pm Sun. **Admission** free. **Map** p315 M5. Much early missionary work, and the city's first English lessons for Chinese immigrants, took place under this 19th-century building's foreboding clock tower: 'Son, observe the time and fly from evil', it warns. Observe your time at lunchtime concerts staged in the cathedral's daintily glorious interior.

Portsmouth Square

Many people consider **Portsmouth Square**, which sits on the corner of Clay and Kearny Streets a half-block east of Grant Avenue, as the true birthplace of the city. It was here that Captain John B Montgomery first hoisted the US flag, having captured the city – then known

as Yerba Buena – from the Mexicans on 9 July 1846; the plaza is now named after his ship, the USS *Portsmouth*. Two years later, newspaper boss Sam Brannan stood here and announced to the public that gold had been discovered at Sutter's Mill, sparking the Gold Rush.

Within a few years of Brannan's declaration, Chinese immigrants settled in the area for good. Today, the elderly congregate to practise t'ai chi, argue politics and kibbitz over Chinese chess. Among the monuments is one shaped like the galleon *Hispaniola* and dedicated to Robert Louis Stevenson, who used to sit here during his time in town during 1879. The buildings here, meanwhile, include the **Bank of Canton** (743 Washington Street), one of the most photographed structures in Chinatown. The pagoda-like structure was built back in 1909 for the Chinese American Telephone Exchange; for four decades, multilingual phone operators routed calls throughout Chinatown by memory alone, since there was no area phone directory.

Chinese Culture Center

3rd floor, Hilton Hotel, 750 Kearny Street, at Washington Street (986 1822/www.c-c-c.org). Bus 1, 9, 15/cable car California. **Open** 10am-4pm Tue-Sat. **Admission** free. **Map** p315 M4. Linked to Portsmouth Square by a footbridge and located on the third floor of a Hilton hotel, the Center hosts a variety of events, including Asian-themed art exhibitions and performances, as well as workshops and walking tours. There's also an annual festival to celebrate Chinese New Year.

Sightseeing

Statues Goddess of Democracy

At first glance, the ten-foot bronze statue looking down over one corner of Portsmouth Square appears to be not much more than a curious and not altogether accurate replica of the Statue of Liberty. However, add a little context, and the figure quickly grows into something far more dramatic.

The Goddess of Democracy – some call her the Goddess of Liberty – is a bronze replica of a gigantic papier-mâché-and-styrofoam statue modelled after the Statue of Liberty and created in four days by Beijing art students during the Tiananmen Square protests of 1989. The statue was placed opposite a huge picture of Mao Tse-Tung on the Tiananmen Gate during the uprising, and quickly became a symbol of the students' anti-communist defiance. When the government decided to put an end to the troubles on 4 June 1989, killing hundreds of protestors in the process,

the statue was wrecked by the army. However, by way of tribute, northern Californian sculptor Thomas Marsh constructed this bronze replica of the statue, which was unveiled in Portsmouth Square five years to the day after the original was destroyed.

London's weekly listings bible

OUT EVERY TUESDAY

North Beach to Fisherman's Wharf

The erstwhile home of the Beat Generation continues to interest.

Sightseeing

North Beach is unique among San Francisco neighbourhoods: it's a popular pilgrimage for tourists but also a community beloved by locals. Part of the old Barbary Coast, the area retains ties to the past. Grant Avenue, which runs through the area, is the city's oldest street; along with the North Point docks, the century-old ethnic neighbourhoods of Chinatown (just south of North Beach; see pp85-87) and Little Italy are reminders that San Francisco once served as the gateway to the west. With City Lights and a variety of cafés, the area is also bound to the Beat movement of the 1950s.

Above North Beach is an area that's treasured by tourists but looked upon by locals with something approaching despair, even pity. Once a genuine fishing port, **Fisherman's Wharf** has since been made over into a dreary tourist trap, soaked with T-shirt stalls, tacky museums and overpriced restaurants. It could be anywhere in America; it's just a pity that it has to be here. Looking down on all this tomfoolery are the residents of **Russian Hill**, one of the city's richest neighbourhoods and also, it stands to reason, among its nicest.

North Beach

Situated north and east of Columbus Avenue, North Beach turned San Francisco into the counterculture capital of the US. Originally it was home to the city's Italian community, who rebuilt it after the 1906 earthquake and liked it so much they stayed, but it eventually came to attract leagues of writers and artistic types, drawn not only by the European aura but also by the low rents.

Even after the Beat Generation had come and gone (see p90 **Walk**), the area maintained its reputation for individualism and artistic endeavour. In the early '60s, nightclubs such as the Purple Onion and the Hungry i showcased an array of boundary-pushing comedians such as Woody Allen and Lenny Bruce; later, punk venues solidified the indelible stamp of hipness.

Even today, North Beach has avoided falling victim to homogeny. The mellow streets, with their famously lambent light on sunny days, are still home to elderly Italians playing *bocce*, reading Neapolitan newspapers and nibbling *cannoli*. The brash strip joints along Broadway are another tourist draw, whether locals like it or not; indeed, North Beach has long been as famous for its sex shows as for its literary heritage and its lasagne. But time hasn't stood still here. Amid the long-standing strip joints, the vintage cafés, the cultured dive bars and the Old-World delicatessens sit shops offering handmade and imported goods, restaurants serving all manner of classic, contemporary and international cuisine, and a slew of lively – or, if you prefer, noisy – bars and nightclubs. North Beach's secret, it seems, is that it's figured out that with a little effort, it is possible to be all things to all people.

City Lights & around

Much of North Beach's history and many of its treasures lie along **Columbus Avenue**, and especially close to the three-way junction of Columbus, Broadway and Grant Avenue that represents North Beach's beating heart. At the centre is **City Lights** bookstore (261 Columbus Avenue, at Broadway; see p179): formerly the focal point for the Beat movement, it's still owned by poet Lawrence Ferlinghetti. Next door, **Vesuvio** (255 Columbus Avenue, at Broadway; see p166) welcomes bums, poets and tourists in equal measure, much as it did when Kerouac drank here in the 1950s.

Walk The North Beach beat

After North Beach was destroyed in the 1906 earthquake and fire, it was repopulated with immigrant labourers. Many of them were Italians, who stayed in the neighbourhood once they'd finished rebuilding it. Fantastic *ristoranti* and coffee shops sprang up all over the place, and in time, the cheap *pensioni* began to attract those most notorious of voluntary indigents: writers and musos.

Our walk starts on **Columbus Avenue** and Broadway, where the literary spirits are packed so tightly you practically have to step into the road to avoid them. First, have a peek into **Vesuvio** (No.255; *see p166*); the surprisingly jaunty multicoloured sign has welcomed poets and artists since it opened in 1948. Neither Dylan Thomas or Jack Kerouac could resist when they were in town, nor can the dipsomaniacal poets and poetical dipsomaniacs of today. To the right of Vesuvio is **Jack Kerouac Alley**, renamed by the city in 1988, and the world-famous **City Lights** bookstore (No.261; *see p179*).

Cross Columbus heading east along Broadway. **Tosca** (No.242; *see p166*) can lay proud claim to having ejected Bob Dylan one boisterous evening, and it was at **Spec's** (12 William Saroyan Place; *see p165*) that famed *Chronicle* columnist Herb Caen coined the derogatory term 'Beatnik' to describe the increasingly large numbers of youths heading to North Beach in search of jazz, sex and poetry. They found the former, at least, just away from City Lights along the right-hand side of Broadway: at Nos.471-3, the **Jazz Workshop** once hosted the likes of Miles Davis, Cannonball Adderley, John Coltrane, Sonny Rollins and Ornette Coleman; it was also here that Lenny Bruce was first arrested for obscenity in 1961.

Head up to Montgomery Street for a great view of the Bay Bridge, then cross over Broadway. Allen Ginsberg lived at **1010 Montgomery** with Peter Orlovsky, and probably conceived his epochal poem *Howl* here. The site is now, prosaically, an old folks' home.

There are smarter eating and drinking options hereabouts, however. These days Francis Ford Coppola works from an office in **Columbus Tower**, the turreted green building on the corner of Columbus and Kearny, but long before he set up shop here, the structure was known as the Sentinel Building and was home to **Caesar's**, the restaurant that was credited with popularising the salad of the same name. On its ground floor is elegant **Café Niebaum-Coppola** (291 1700), which sells its own brand of pasta alongside wines from the director's own Napa Valley vineyard.

East of here is **Broadway**, which, between Columbus Avenue and Montgomery Street, is lined with nightclubs offering strippers and sexy floorshows. History was made at the **Condor Club** (300 Columbus Avenue, at Broadway, 781 8222) in 1964 when a buxom waitress named Carol Doda went topless for the first time; more than four decades later,

the Condor is now a sports bar, but the **Hungry i** just down the street (546 Broadway, at Columbus Avenue, 362 7763) keeps the titty-bar flame burning. A new culture of a slightly different stripe was forged in the **Mabuhay Gardens** at 443 Broadway (now the Velvet Lounge restaurant/nightclub), a punk mecca in which both the Dead Kennedys and the Avengers got their starts.

Just down on Kearny Street are two newer adult hangouts, which together represent a pair of contradictory extremes. **Larry Flynt's Hustler Club** (No.1031, 434 1308) is as about crude and modern as they come, every bit the reflection of its famous owner's crass image. Next door sits the **Lusty Lady** (No.1033, 391 3126), a pretty scruffy-looking peep show notable initially for being the first unionised strip joint in the US, and, since 2003, for being the only enterprise of its type to be owned and operated by the girls who work in it.

Sightseeing

Heading back along Broadway you'll pass the Green Tortoise Hostel at No.494. It may not look like much now, but this was once the chic **El Matador**, where Frank Sinatra and Duke Ellington would perform for Marlon Brando's Hollywood set.

Turn right onto Kearny and you're facing more than 100 pretty steps. Locals call them the Kearny Steps, but the official title is the Macchiarini Steps; it's named for a local family who still make jewellery in the area. From the top, it's downhill again (you'll be pleased to hear) for a break at **Caffe Trieste** (No.601; *see p144*). If it is Saturday you'll be treated to some opera, but any day of the week it's worth dropping in for an espresso and some bohemians. Coppola is alleged to have worked on *The Godfather* here, so don't be rude to anybody with a violin case. Drink up, and head back to Columbus.

Turn right down Green Street, skipping the inevitable queue at Club Fugazi for **Beach Blanket Babylon** (*see p253*). If it's a sunny daytime, turn left and head up to **Washington Square** for a glorious mix of tatty old bohemians, wannabe alternative types and discreet Chinese ladies doing t'ai chi. Otherwise, zigzag across the intersection between Green, Columbus and Stockton. Stick on Green Street, passing Caffè Sport at No.574. When this was the **Cellar**, Kenneth Rexroth and Ruth Weiss read to improvised

accompaniment here, a first foray into jazz poetry. Stop when you reach **Gino & Carlo's** (No.548, 421 0896), easily recognisable by the puff of smokers out front and the four-deep mob surrounding the bar inside.

Turn right onto Grant Avenue and head past the Grant & Green Saloon (No.1371) and the Lost & Found Saloon (No.1361), until you reach the plain old **Saloon** (No.1232; *see p231*). This is San Francisco's oldest bar, getting folks drunk since 1861. There's no smoky jazz, but there is live blues. If you still fancy a Martini by the time you stumble out, it's way past time to hail that taxi home.

Washington Square & around

The **Molinari Delicatessen** (373 Columbus Avenue, at Vallejo Street; *see p189*), which boasts a cameo role in *Babycakes*, one of Armistead Maupin's *Tales of the City* series, sells olives, cheeses, salads, a selection of cold cuts and own-made tortellini. Pick up a picnic and take it just up the road to Washington Square, a lovely patch of greenery that really comes into its own at the height of summer. The grassy rectangle is overlooked by the white stucco Romanesque **Church of St Peter and St Paul**, where Marilyn Monroe and local hero Joe DiMaggio had their wedding photos taken. (Since both were divorced and Joe was a Catholic, they actually got married in a civil ceremony at City Hall.) An 1879 statue of Benjamin Franklin stands in the park on a granite-encased time capsule – it's scheduled for to be reopened in 2079.

At **Caffe Roma** (526 Columbus Avenue, at Green Street, 296 7942), coffee comes freshly roasted on the premises, while at **Liguria** (1700 Stockton Street, 421 3786), the locals stand in line for foccacia made in-house, tied up with string, and baked by members of the same family since 1911.

Telegraph Hill, bordered by Grant Avenue and Green, Bay and Sansome Streets, was so named as the site of the West Coast's first telegraph. The landmark **Coit Tower** (*see p92*) sits on top. Two nearby hotels neatly sum up the area. The **Hotel Bohème** (444 Columbus Avenue, between Vallejo & Green Streets; *see p57*) celebrates Beat heritage with framed snapshots of life in bohemian North Beach in the 1950s and '60s, while the *pensione*-like **San Remo Hotel** (2337 Mason Street, at Chestnut Street; *see p57*), a pretty Italianate Victorian, is an ideal base for soaking up the area's Italian ambience.

Statues Fire Department

When unveiled in 1933, the Washington Square statue depicting three of the city's courageous volunteer firemen generated an unexpected reaction: peals of laughter. Someone had apparently placed a bottle of whisky into one the moustachioed figure's outstretched hand. But such a gesture would surely have been appreciated by Lillie Hitchcock Coit, the statue's benefactress.

Coit was raised near the Knickerbocker #5 Volunteer Fire Company. Legend holds that, as a schoolgirl, she happened upon the firemen attempting to haul their engine up steep Telegraph Hill. As their energy flagged, the young Lillie cast down her schoolbooks, grabbed the rope and exhorted the men to pull on. From that day forth, she became the mascot of the #5s; she would embroider their number onto her clothes throughout her life.

The hoydenish Coit grew up to become a global traveller with a talent for cards and a penchant for whisky. However, she never forgot her childhood; when she died in 1929 at the age of 86, Coit bequeathed a massive sum to the city. Part of it went towards the statue; the rest went on the erection of Coit Tower (see p92) atop Telegraph Hill, where Coit first made the firemen's acquaintance.

Coit Tower

Peak of Telegraph Hill, at the end of Telegraph Hill Boulevard (362 0808/www.coittower.org). Bus 39. **Open** 10am-5pm daily. **Admission** *Elevator* $3. **Map** p315 M3.

This 210ft (64m) concrete turret, built by City Hall architect Arthur Brown in 1933, was a gift to the city from the eccentric Lillie Hitchcock Coit. Lillie was a lifelong fan of firemen, but while most assume that the tower represents the nozzle of a fire hose by way of tribute, architects Arthur Brown and Henry Howard always denied it. (Indeed, it's said Coit herself actually hated towers.)

The spectacular views from the top aren't the tower's only attraction. Under the supervision of Diego Rivera, some wonderful murals were created here, a series of socialist-realist images so subversive that, when they were completed in 1934, the opening was delayed in order that an errant hammer and sickle could be erased. **Photo** *p94.*

Fisherman's Wharf

Fisherman's Wharf dates back to the Gold Rush, when Italian and Chinese immigrants plied the Bay for crab and other seafood and sold it right off their boats. There's little evidence of that historic past today: the wharf, roughly bounded by Jefferson, North Point and Kearny Streets and Fort Mason, is little more than a conglomeration of novelty attractions, tacky shops and heavy pedestrian traffic. In surveys, Fisherman's Wharf routinely ranks as the No.1 destination for visitors, despite the fact that its main attractions were built in the late '60s and '70s. Its only real value these days is as a departure point for ferry trips to **Alcatraz** (*see p93*) and **Angel Island** (*see p94*). Still, those with a few hours to kill can find some inexpensive entertainment here, along with unrivalled views of the Bay.

Jefferson Street, the wharf's main drag, is a fairly undignified spectacle. The **Wax Museum** (145 Jefferson Street, between Mason and Taylor Streets, 1-800 439 4305, www.wax museum.com) and **Ripley's Believe It Or Not! Museum** (175 Jefferson Street, at Taylor Street, 771 6188, www.ripleys.com) are clichéd seafront diversions; elsewhere, sidewalk crab stalls and seafood restaurants thrive. For the only remaining glimpse of Fisherman's Wharf as it once was, turn towards the water off Jefferson and on to Leavenworth Street, then

Sightseeing

slip into **Fish Alley**. There, you'll find real fishing boats and real fishermen. Although it's within shouting distance of Jefferson, it feels like miles away.

At the eastern end, **Pier 39** is a sprawling prefab array of seafront shops, attractions and arcade games patently designed to separate you from your money. Luckily, crowds of sea lions barking and belching on nearby pontoons provide a natural respite (their population varies with the seasons). Offshore from H Dock on Pier 39, **Forbes Island** (951 4900) is 700 tons (711,200 kilos) of man-made, engine-propelled, floating lighthouse and restaurant. Further west, at Pier 45, a World War II submarine, the **USS Pampanito** (*see p95*), has ended its ship-sinking days and opened its hull to the public.

A reminder of the area's former industrial life is the **Cannery** (2801 Leavenworth Street, enter on Jefferson or Beach Streets, 771 3112, www.delmontesquare.com). Built in 1907 as a fruit-canning factory, it's now another twee mall modelled on London's Covent Garden Piazza, complete with street performers. The red-brick **Ghirardelli Square** (at North Point and Larkin Streets; *see p175*) dates to the 19th century and housed a famous chocolate factory until the 1960s; the namesake chocolate is still sold, but the building is now a complex of shops and restaurants. You can sort through any tourist monstrosities you've acquired in the central plaza, alongside the lovely *Mermaid Fountain* by local artist Ruth Asawa.

There's more to enjoy a little further west. The shores of **Aquatic Park** (between Hyde Street and Van Ness Avenue) offer one of the best strolls in the city, with a panorama of the Golden Gate Bridge, Alcatraz, windsurfers, sailing boats, wildly coloured kites and dogs catching frisbees. Along the **Municipal Pier** (accessible from the northern end of Van Ness), fishermen try their luck; at the **Hyde Street Pier** (*see p94*), a fleet of carefully restored historic ships is docked permanently and open to the public. The pier is under the same administration as the **San Francisco Maritime Museum** (*see p95*), opposite Ghirardelli Square. A white art deco building that looks like an ocean liner, it recaptures West Coast whaling, steamboating and perilous journeys 'around the Horn'.

The **Golden Gate Promenade** begins here, continuing for three miles along the shoreline to **Fort Point** (*see p102*). The entire waterfront from Aquatic Park to Ocean Beach was incorporated into the Golden Gate National Recreation Area in 1972, with the authorities thankfully stopping Fisherman's Wharf-style tourist kitsch spreading any further.

Alcatraz

www.nps.gov/alcatraz. Blue & Gold ferry from Pier 41, Embarcadero (information 773 1188/tickets 705 5555/www.blueandgoldfleet.com). Metro F to Pier 41/bus 10, 15, 39, 47. **Tickets** *Day tour with audio guide* $16; $10.75-$14.25 discounts. *Day tour without audio guide* $11.50; $8.25-$9.75 discounts. *Evening tours* $23.50; $14.25-$20.75 discounts. **Credit** AmEx, Disc, MC, V. **Map** p314 L1.

'Alcatraz' is Spanish for pelican, but to its inmates it was simply known as 'the Rock'. The West Coast's first lighthouse was built here in 1854, but it was soon decided that the island's isolated setting made it perfect for a prison. It became a military jail in the 1870s, but it wasn't until it was converted into a high-security federal penitentiary in 1934 that the name Alcatraz became an international symbol of punishment. Despite being in operation for less than 30 years, Alcatraz remains fixed in the popular imagination as the ultimate penal colony. (As do some of its inmates; *see p16* **Tales of the city**.) Today, its ominous prison buildings are no longer used (its last inmates left in 1963), but the craggy outcrop, now a National Park, lures well over a million visitors each year.

Despite what you might expect, Alcatraz is far from being a tourist trap. The audio tour of the facility, which features insights from a variety of former prisoners and guards, is wonderfully effective, and the buildings retain an eerie and fascinating appeal. Departure times for both the day

Hard cell: **Alcatraz**.

Sightseeing

tours and the far less frequent (and wildly over-subscribed) evening jaunts vary by season: check the website for details. One word of warning: capacity on the tours is limited, and those who don't book ahead of time may find the only views they get of the island are from the shore.

Angel Island

897 0715/www.angelisland.org. Blue & Gold ferry from Pier 41, Embarcadero (recorded information 773 1188/tickets 705 5555/www.blueandgold fleet.com). Metro F to Pier 41/bus 10, 15, 39, 47. **Tickets** $13.50; $8 discounts. **Credit** AmEx, Disc, MC, V. **Map** p314 L1.

Blue & Gold runs a ferry service to Angel Island; times vary with the season, so check online or call ahead before setting out. Boats arrive at the Ayala Cove visitors' centre, where there are maps, bikes to rent and all-important picnic tables. For more about Angel Island itself, *see pxxx*.

Hyde Street Pier

At the foot of Hyde Street (561 7100/www.maritime. org). Metro F to Fisherman's Wharf/bus 10, 19, 30, 47/cable car Powell-Hyde. **Open** 10am-5pm daily. **Admission** free ($5 for vessels). **No credit cards.** **Map** p314 K1.

Maritime fans, students of history and children will love the historic vessels permanently docked here. Typical of the ships that would have been common here in the 19th and early 20th centuries, they include the 1886 full-rigged *Balclutha*, built to carry grain from California to Europe; the *CA Thayer*, an 1895 sailing ship that carried timber along the West Coast;

the *Alma*, an 1891 scow schooner that hauled cargo throughout the Bay Area; *Hercules*, a 1907 ocean tugboat; and the 1890 commuter ferry *Eureka*.

Along with the new San Francisco Maritime Museum (*see p95*), the set-up is the highlight of what's officially known as the **San Francisco Maritime National Historic Park**. The park's lovely new visitors' centre, at the corner of Jefferson and Hyde Streets (9.30am-7pm daily June-mid October; 9.30am-5pm daily mid October-May; $5), contains a fascinating series of displays on the area's seafaring history, which makes for a welcome contrast with the variety of miserable tourist traps just a few blocks down the street. For more on the park and its various services and attractions, call 447 5000 or visit www.nps.gov/safr.

Musée Mécanique

Pier 45, at the end of Taylor Street (346 2000/ www.museemecanique.org). Metro F to Fisherman's Wharf/bus 10, 19, 30, 47/cable car Powell-Hyde. **Open** 11am-7pm Mon-Fri; 10am-8pm Sat, Sun. **Admission** free. **Map** p314 K1.

Pack a pocketful of quarters before you visit this wonderful museum, actually an arcade housing over 170 old-fashioned coin-operated gizmos that date as far back as the 1880s, ranging from fortune-telling machines to player pianos. Best of all is Laughing Sal, a somewhat scary relic from Whitney's Playland at the Beach, San Francisco's long-defunct coastside amusement park. She's an enormous mechanical figure with a crazy laugh that sends little kids running for their parents.

Coit Tower, up on Telegraph Hill. *See p92.*

What the flock?

When some visitors to San Francisco hear a deafening chorus of squawking accompanied by the sound of hundreds of wings beating overhead, they flee in terror. These are almost certainly the same visitors who recall that parts of Hitchcock's *The Birds* were filmed in the city. However, if you can resist the urge to run, flailing your hands above your head Tippi Hedren-style as you dash for the nearest shelter, crane your neck skyward to get a glimpse of one of San Francisco's wild wonders: its feral parrot population.

Officially classified as *Aratinga erythrogenys* and known variously as the cherry-headed conure, the red-masked parakeet, the red-headed conure and the red-masked conure, the birds that together make up the city's largest flock originally hail from Ecuador and Peru. First spotted here in the early 1970s, parrots were widely sold prior to a ban on the importation of wild-caught birds in 1993. However, the parrots made poor pets: not only do they despise captivity, but they're incredibly noisy and have a tendency to bite. Many were released, while others escaped.

Thanks to their hearty constitution, the cherry-headed conures not only survived but thrived in the city. While their territory ranges all over town from the Presidio to the Sunset, down Dolores Street and all the way out in Noe Valley, they can be seen most often in the Telegraph Hill region; they currently roost in the trees around Ferry Park at Washington and Drumm Streets.

The populations of both cherry-headed conures and canary-winged parakeets (*Brotogeris versicolorus*), the city's other main flock, have grown steadily over the years: there are now 160 of the former and around 40 of the latter, which tend to congregate in the northern parts of the city. Their growth has caused concern for native bird populations, though the parrots normally keep to themselves without disturbing native habitats; non-native parrots tend to roost in non-native trees, such as the eucalyptus and Canary Island date palms scattered through the city. In addition, the flock is culled by the city's imposing raptor population, hawks and peregrine falcons. San Francisco's parrots have always been local celebrities, but their fame is spreading. A recent documentary, *The Wild Parrots of Telegraph Hill*, focused on Mark Bittner, a once destitute caretaker who has looked after the birds for a decade; Bittner has even written a book about his experiences, which crept briefly on to the *New York Times* bestseller list. 'You see them,' he told the *San Francisco Chronicle*, 'and you have to love them.'

San Francisco Maritime Museum

Beach Street, at Polk Street (561 6662/www. maritime.org). Metro F to Fisherman's Wharf/ bus 10, 19, 30, 47/cable car Powell-Hyde. **Open** 10am-5pm daily. **Admission** free. **Map** p314 J2.
This unassuming museum documents US maritime history with the aid of a mixture of photographs and ship models, including miniatures of passenger liners and US Navy ships. Its presentation is a little dated and unlikely to thrill adults who don't already have an interest in the subject, but the interactive exhibits upstairs might distract the children for a half-hour or so, and there's plenty of sea lore to learn if you're prepared to give it your attention.

USS Pampanito

Pier 45 (775 1943/www.maritime.org). Metro F to Fisherman's Wharf/bus 10, 19, 30, 47/cable car Powell-Hyde. **Open** 9am-6pm Mon-Thur, Sun; 9am-8pm Fri, Sat. **Admission** $9; $3-$5 discounts; $20 family. **Credit** AmEx, MC, V. **Map** p314 K1.
The *Pampanito* is a World War II, Balao-class Fleet submarine with an impressive record: it made six patrols in the Pacific at the height of the war, sinking six Japanese ships and damaging four others.

The vessel was recently restored to look much as it would have in its prime in 1945. The sub is still seaworthy: in 1995 it sailed under the Golden Gate Bridge for the first time in 50 years.

Russian Hill

Russian Hill got its name when several Cyrillic-inscribed gravestones were discovered here during the Gold Rush. Local lore has it that a Russian warship put into the harbour of San Francisco in the early 1840s, and a number of the disease-stricken crew died while ashore. As they belonged to the Greek Church, they couldn't be buried in any of the existing Protestant or Catholic cemeteries, so one was created for them in this area. By the late 1800s, the gravestones had disappeared; along with them went any trace of Russian influence.

Today, Russian Hill is a quiet, residential and very pricey neighbourhood roughly bordered by Larkin and North Point Streets, Columbus Avenue, Powell Street and Pacific Avenue. Its most notorious landmark is the

Sightseeing

Barbary Lane

Armistead Maupin's *Tales of the City* column appeared in the *Chronicle* from 1976 but became internationally popular as novels in the '80s. The books offer a convincing snapshot of queer and straight life in San Francisco, but the house at their centre – Anna Madrigal's abode at 28 Barbary Lane – is a chimera. The 'narrow, wooded walkway' is supposed to be found off Leavenworth, between Union and Filbert, but the inquisitive find only the gardens of Havens Street there.

Maupin has claimed the real inspiration behind Barbary Lane was in fact a block away: the miraculously secluded **Macondray Lane**. One of San Francisco's 400 unmarked and overgrown public stairways, it has rickety old wooden stairs and gives, through the idiosyncratic houses that line one side, tantalising views of the Bay. Its signpost is hard to spot (look for the name imprinted in the kerb), but you'll find it just north of Green Street, between Taylor and Jones. To explore more stairways (Adah Bakalinsky's *Stairway Walks in San Francisco* is invaluable for this),

other Russian Hill favourites are Vallejo Street (between Jones and Mason Streets) and Culebra Terrace (Chestnut Street, between Larkin and Polk Streets).

quaint stairs and alleyways: if you don't mind the ups and downs, it can be fun to prowl the neighbourhood for secret passages.

Landmark addresses in the district include **29 Russell Street**, off Hyde Street, where Jack Kerouac lived with Neal and Carolyn Cassady during his most creative period in the 1950s; and the **Feusier Octagon House**, one of the city's oldest dwellings, which is at 1067 Green Street, near Leavenworth. Best viewed from across the street to appreciate its odd shape, the pastel structure is one of only two survivors of the 19th-century octagonal-house craze (the other is in Pacific Heights; *see p117*).

world's 'crookedest' (and no doubt most photographed) thoroughfare: **Lombard Street**, which snakes steeply down from Hyde Street to Leavenworth, packing nine hairpin bends into one brick-paved and over-landscaped block. In summer, tourists queue for the thrill of driving down its hazardous 27 per cent gradient at 5mph, much to the annoyance of local residents. Arrive early or late to avoid the throng. For further thrills, test your skills behind the wheel on the steepest street in the city: Filbert Street between Hyde and Leavenworth descends at a whopping 31.5 per cent gradient. Also up on Russian Hill is the **San Francisco Art Institute** (*see below*), housed in an attractive 1920s Spanish Revival building on Chestnut Street and containing a wonderful Diego Rivera mural.

Struggle up Vallejo Street to take in the views from **Ina Coolbrith Park** at Taylor Street. In truth, it's less a park than a narrow ledge with benches; arrive early in the morning, and you'll catch elderly Chinese practising t'ai chi. Up from the park, the top of the **Vallejo Street Stairway**, designed by Willis Polk and surrounded on each side by landscaped gardens, is the apex of the neighbourhood. Laura Ingalls Wilder, the author of *Little House on the Prairie*, used to live here (at 1019 Vallejo). Indeed, Russian Hill is riven with

San Francisco Art Institute

800 Chestnut Street, between Leavenworth & Jones Streets (771 7020/www.sanfranciscoart.edu). Bus 10, 30, 47/cable car Powell-Hyde or Powell-Mason. **Open** *Diego Rivera Gallery 10am-6pm Tue-Sat.* **Admission** *$6.* **No credit cards. Map** p314 K2.

This hip and prestigious art school offers the full spectrum of fine arts, including painting, film, photography, sculpture and new media. Its student shows are legendary. Most people visit to see Diego Rivera's mural *The Making of a Fresco*, one of various works he completed in San Francisco in the 1930s. If you're worn out from climbing all those hills, have a rest in the pretty open-air courtyard, where plants and benches surround a fountain, or grab a cheap snack in the cafeteria.

The Mission & the Castro

Vibrant culture, amazing food and a world-famous gay mecca.

San Francisco's geographic centre, where the **Mission**, the **Castro** and **Noe Valley** converge, serves up a unique jumble of neighbourhood life. Whether you're looking for rainbow-swathed boutiques, unusual sights and sounds, the oldest building in town or a burrito the size of your baby's arm, these enclaves of queer, yuppie, hip and Latino living are largely responsible for the city's remarkably diverse charm.

The Mission

First settled by the Spanish in the 1770s and later home to Irish, German, Italian and Asian immigrants, the Mission today is the centre of Latino culture in the city. A steady influx of families and workers from Mexico and Central America lends the neighbourhood its distinctive character, especially on **Mission Street** between 14th and Cesar Chavez Streets, the area's main drag. Along here, the scents and sights are plentiful; the mix of sidewalk sausage stands, bootleg-DVD vendors, dollar stores and taquerias colourfully paints the strip of one of the city's tightest ethnic communities.

However, walk two blocks west to **Valencia Street** and you'll see evidence of the area's other main occupants: San Francisco's creative classes. Although the invasion of *nouveaux riches* techies during the dotcom boom drove some rents sky-high, sending some locals on

a scramble to find cheaper quarters, many of the musicians and artists who colonised the area in the 1990s remain in situ. The invasion of the internet millionaires certainly changed the face of the neighbourhood. However, despite fears that the area would gentrify beyond recognition, it seems to have regained its equilibrium: upscale Valencia Street hasn't yet overwhelmed the throbbing pulse of blue-collar Mission Street, and the two coexist in relative harmony.

A quick practical note: unlike Downtown and SoMa, the street numbering along Mission and Valencia Streets doesn't correspond to the numbered streets that cross them. For example, 2000 Mission Street is at the junction not of 20th Street, as you might expect, but of 16th Street; similarly, 2800 Mission is

Down on **Mission Street**.

Street life

The Mission is famous as burrito central. However, the neighbourhood is also home to the most dazzling array of political and spiritual street art in the country. There are more than 200 murals in this single district, many influenced by the craft of noted Mexican muralists Diego Rivera, José Clemente Orozco and David Alfaro Siquieros, and many of them celebrating the struggles and achievements of the area's Hispanic residents. **Precita Eyes** (*see p99*) has been crucial in both the creation and preservation of many of San Francisco's 700-plus murals, encouraging artists and organising tours of their works.

The Mission's murals are in a perpetual state of flux; new works pop up every few months or so. However, some works have lasted decades: take Harrison Street to Precita Avenue and you'll find one of *Family Life and Spirit of Mankind*, painted by Precita Eyes founder Susan Cervantes in 1977 on the side of Leonard R Flynn Elementary School. There are many murals on or near 24th Street between Mission Street and Potrero Avenue, often on the sides of grocery shops and in parks. The area's most decorated street is Balmy Alley, which runs between 24th and 25th Streets east of Harrison Street. During the annual **Día de los Muertos** celebrations (*see p202*), a procession crowds the alley in chaotic fashion.

On the west side of Mission Street, murals are just as plentiful. The Clarion Alley Mural Project (between 17th and 18th Streets and Mission and Valencia Streets) features works with anti-war messages that are conveyed using bold images, such as Uncle Sam spitting bombs. Down nearby Sycamore Alley, you'll find the work of even more urban-art guerillas, with a tad of inventive graffiti mixed in for good measure. And up on 18th Street, the side of the Women's Building (*see p100*) is decorated with a larger-than-life mural entitled *Maestrapeace*, an epic retelling of the history of women in the New World and one of the city's grandest representations of the Central American art tradition.

Tribute to Archbishop Oscar Romero, by Jamie Morgan.

actually at 24th Street. It's a similar story two blocks away: 500 Valencia Street sits at the junction with 16th Street, while 1300 Valencia is at 24th Street. Still, while the numbering doesn't match the streets, it does at least increase at the standard rate of 100 per block, which makes it easy to figure out how far you have to walk.

Mission Street & east

Mission Street is by far the more vibrant of the two main stretches. Cheque-cashing operations, bargain shops, taco stands and grocery stores (selling such exotica as sugar cane and prickly pears) conduct brisk business, while Mexican pop music drifts out of open doors and windows. In a few places, the narrow, crowded pavements are a scene straight out of Guadalajara; it's especially eye-catching in autumn, when Mexican-run shops and art galleries fill with traditional ghoulish items in advance of the **Día de los Muertos** in November (*see p98*).

The neighbourhood can feel a little shady east of Mission Street itself in the inner Mission, particularly north of 19th Street and its environs. The *barrio* has its share of prostitutes, drug addicts and gangs, and doorway drug-deals around the scruffy junction of 16th and Mission Streets are usually enough to scare off the timid. However, it's safer than it once was, and further south, closer to 24th Street, the area seems less urban and more urbane.

Tourist buses tend to limit their explorations to the admittedly fascinating **Mission Dolores** (*see p100*), but there are other worthwhile stops. On Mission Street, the **Mission Cultural Center** (No.2868, at 25th Street, 821 1155, www. missionculturalcenter.org) hosts a theatre and a gallery displaying works by under-the-radar artists. It's also a terrific resource for the area's wealth of public art, as is the **Precita Eyes Mural Arts & Visitor Center** (*see below*) on 24th Street. Also in this area is the **Galeria de la Raza** (*see p212*).

However, the main attraction for most visitors to the Mission in general, and Mission Street in particular, remains the food (*see p150* **The Latin quarter**). The burritos here verge on the legendary, and competition is fierce. Mission Street boasts *mucho* taquerias, but locals swear by **La Taqueria** (No.2889, at 25th Street) and **Taqueria Cancun** (No.2288). At **Pancho Villa** (3071 16th Street, at Valencia Street), Beck has been known to sit in for the roving Mariachi bands when he's in town. Keep in mind that the portions are ungodly and may be more suited to dinner than as a tide-over snack for the fearless foot soldier.

Further south, 24th Street offers numerous culinary temptations, and plenty of Latino *sabor*. **El Nuevo Frutilandia** (No.3077, at Treat Avenue; *see p151*) serves Puerto Rican and Cuban delicacies, but, again, the Mexican food draws the hordes. A half-block west of Mission Street, **Papalote** (No.3409, at Valencia Street) serves delectably fresh fare; if you just want a snack, the intersection of 24th and Alabama Streets is a hub of *típico* Mexican bakeries and quick-bite grills. However, if you're after more American fare, head three blocks east to the delightful **St Francis Fountain & Candy Store** (No.2801, at York Street; *see p149*), a century-old soda fountain that's reputedly the birthplace of the San Francisco 49ers football

team. Once you've eaten, join the hipsters supping suds at one of the area's divey watering holes (*see pp166-167*).

Precita Eyes Mural Arts & Visitors Center

2981 24th Street, at Harrison Street (285 2287/ www.precitaeyes.org). BART 24th Street/bus 12, 48, 67. **Open** 10am-5pm Mon-Fri; 10am-4pm Sat, Sun. **Credit** MC, V. **Map** p318 L12.

Established by Susan Cervantes in 1977, Precita Eyes is dedicated to preserving and promoting the Mission District's 200-plus murals, which it does through this neat visitors' centre and a variety of guided tours. The Mission Trail Mural Walk runs every Saturday and Sunday at 1.30pm ($12); other, slightly shorter walks are also held at 11am on weekends, and private tours are available by appointment. Considering that many of the district's murals were painted by Cervantes and her friends, you can trust that Precita Eyes' docents know the turf inside and out.

Valencia Street & west

While Mission Street retains a headily Latino feel, Valencia Street, parallel to Mission and just two blocks west, is an altogether different kettle of fish. The occasional Mexican business remains, but many of the storefronts have been taken over by boho types, who occupy bar stools and fill seats at the neighbourhood movie house. Vestiges of the dotcom era, such as comparatively upscale restaurant **Luna Park** (694 Valencia Street, at 18th Street; *see p148*), abound in the locale, but gone are the days of whatsitcalled.com, drunk on its fleeting cyberwealth, passing free drinks on to the sidewalk of the **Latin American Club** (3286 22nd Street, at Valencia Street, 647 2732).

The area rewards the happy wanderer. Valencia Street, especially, is a shopaholics' paradise, crammed with independent stores and boutiques. Within a four-block stretch, book lovers get to sift through the shelves of **Dog-Eared Books**, **Modern Times**, **Valencia Street Books** and **Abandoned Planet** (for all, *see pp178-179*), a trove of new and second-hand literary treasures that comes in handy for students of über-liberal New College of California, just blocks away, and the City College of San Francisco. **Aquarius Records** (No.1055, between 21st & 22nd Streets; *see p194*) satisfies the area's hipster contingent.

Local designers also have a presence here, at shops such as **House of Hengst** (No.924, at 20th Street, 642 0841) and **Dema** (No.1038, at 21st Street; *see p180*). At **Paxton Gate** (No.824, between 19th & 20th Streets; *see p190*), a cadre of creative landscapers and taxidermists sells gardening equipment and stuffed vampire mice. However, the most notable commercial landmark

Sightseeing

is the pirate supply store at **826 Valencia** (642 5905). It's said that Dave Eggers, who runs it, opened the shop to meet a commercial-storefront zoning code: its main purpose is as a support centre for young writers.

The Mission's artsy colonies have also opened numerous galleries and performance stages in the area, the majority either on Valencia Street or just off it. The **Women's Building** (3543 18th Street, at Lapidge Street, 431 1180, www.womensbuilding.org) is home to a dozen feminist non-profit groups. Meanwhile, three groups on Valencia Street – **Artists' Television Access** (No.992, 824 3890), the **Marsh** (No.1062, 826 5750) and **Intersection for the Arts** (No.446, 626 2787) – offer a forum for genre-smashing filmmakers, actors, playwrights, artists and musicians.

The best cuppa joe in the area is at **Ritual Coffee Roasters** (1026 Valencia Street, at 21st Street; *see p149*); don't leave without trying the espresso. However, the three-block stretch of 16th Street between Mission and Dolores Streets, is packed full of colourful hangouts, although most are a bit heavier on bohemian atmosphere than they are on taste. Still, a walk along 16th will lead you to the building that gave the city its name: the 225-year-old Misión San Francisco de Asis, better known as **Mission Dolores** (*see below*).

Just south of here, bordered by Dolores, Church, 18th and 20th Streets, is **Mission Dolores Park**. There's great people- and dog-watching during the day; when it's warm,

sunbathers line the park's upper end, earning it the nickname Dolores Beach. Summer evenings offer free film screenings (www.sfneighborhood theater.org), often of classic, SF-centric flicks, but bring a sensible coat and blanket: contrary to Eric Burdon's experience, there's no such thing as 'a warm San Franciscan night'.

Mission Dolores

3321 16th Street, at Dolores Street (621 8203/www. missiondolores.org). BART 16th Street/Metro J to Church/bus 22. **Open** 9am-5pm daily. **Admission** $3-$5. **Credit** (groups only) AmEx, MC, V. **Map** p318 J10.

Founded by a tiny band of Spanish missionaries and soldiers in 1776, and completed 15 years later, historic Mission Dolores is the oldest structure in the city, and San Francisco's Registered Landmark No.1. The building was originally called the Misión San Francisco de Asis (after Saint Francis of Assisi), and provided the town with its name. However, it takes its common name from Laguna de los Dolores, the swampy lagoon on the shores of which it was built.

Although the original mission became an expansive outpost, housing over 4,000 monks and converts, today only the tiny old church remains. The thick-walled adobe structure survived the 1906 earthquake unscathed, while the new church next door crumbled. Small wonder that the cool, dim interior looks and feels authentic: almost everything about it is unreconstructed and original, from the redwood logs holding up the roof to the ornate altars brought from Mexico centuries ago. (The modern-day church next door is a 20th-century basilica with no real architectural significance; it does, however, handle all the mission's religious services.)

Statues Fr Junípero Serra

Born in the Mallorcan village of Petra in 1713, Miguel José Serra travelled to Palma at the age of just 15 and enrolled in a Franciscan school. Within a couple of years, he had been ordained as a priest (and changed his name to Junípero in honour of fellow Franciscan St Juniper).

Serra travelled to Mexico in 1749, and spent the next 18 years engaged in missionary work. However, King Carlos III expelled the Jesuits from Spain's colonies in 1767, and Serra was asked to take over the missions in Baja California. Carlos claimed the west coast of America for Spain the following year; accompanied by a small group of soldiers and priests, Serra trudged north to convert the locals.

Serra and his cohorts spent the following decades travelling the Californian coast on a road they named El Camino Real (the King's Highway) in honour of Carlos III. Beginning with Mission San Diego de Alcalá in 1769, Serra set about establishing missions along this stretch, attempting to convert the natives to Catholicism while simultaneously lending a Spanish presence to the area. Built in 1776, Misión San Francisco de Asís (aka Mission Dolores) was the sixth mission he founded; he set up three others before dying, aged 71, at the Mission of San Carlos Borromeo in Carmel.

This rather contemplative statue, located in the gardens of Mission Dolores, is one of several in California that commemorates Serra's life and work. He was beatified in 1988, since when many in the church have pushed for him to be elevated to sainthood. Native Americans, whom Serra essentially colonised, have been understandably vocal in their opposition.

Mission Dolores. *See p100.*

A small museum on the premises offers volunteer-led tours and access to a picturesque, flower-filled cemetery containing the remains of California's first governor and the city's first mayor, as well as assorted Spanish settlers and the mass grave of 5,000 Costanoan Indians who died in their service. Film buffs may recall that in *Vertigo,* an entranced Kim Novak led Jimmy Stewart to the gravestone of the mysterious Carlotta Valdes in this very cemetery. However, you won't find Carlotta's stone: it was merely a prop and was removed after filming.

Potrero Hill & Bernal Heights

Found on the outskirts of the Mission, the quiet neighbourhoods of **Potrero Hill** (loosely bordered by 16th Street, I-280, Cesar Chavez Avenue and Potrero Avenue) and **Bernal Heights** (south of the Mission) are often sunny, even when the rest of the city is shrouded in fog. Home to a mix of young families, dog-walking lesbians and hipsters who've fled the Mission, both areas are a little off the beaten track, but boast compact, lively commercial districts.

In Potrero Hill, fuel up at **Goat Hill Pizza** (300 Connecticut Street, at 18th Street, 641 1440) before heading to the **Bottom of the Hill** (1233 17th Street, at Missouri Street; *see p234*) for bands and/or a seat on the patio. Bernal Heights, meanwhile, boasts an eclectic mix of hangouts, restaurants and shops on and around Cortland Avenue, including attitude-free lesbian bar **Wild Side West** (No.424, at Bennington Street, 647 3099), which welcomes patrons of all genders and proclivities. Hike up the hill to the car-free stretch that affords spectacular 360° views of the city and bay.

The Castro

Bordered by Market, Church, 20th and Diamond Streets, the Castro is an international gay mecca, one of the few places in the world where being gay is the norm. Straights are welcome, of course, but, for once, they're in the minority. Along this rainbow-flag-festooned stretch of trendy shops and see-and-be-seen cafés and bars, most of them gay-owned, a predominantly male populace enjoys a hard-won social and political influence.

A steadfastly working-class Irish-Catholic stronghold for nearly a century, the Castro changed rapidly in the 1970s, when gay residents began buying businesses and battered Victorian and Edwardian properties at rock-bottom prices, renovating them into what's now some of the city's prettiest and priciest real estate. There's no greater example of the change than the landmark **Twin Peaks Bar** (401 Castro Street, at 17th Street): its 1973 metamorphosis from a traditional pub to a gathering place for a mostly male and conspicuously gay clientele began just as the Castro was, so to speak, coming out. The bar's location on what was fast becoming the gayest corner of the gayest street in the country drew an ever-increasing crowd, who chatted and

Say 'Che...'

socialised unashamedly in its daring, pavement-fronting windows. Frequenting the bar was more than just a good time: it was a political act.

A decade or more later, the AIDS crisis of the 1980s and early 1990s proved socially galvanising. Many feared that the Castro, and perhaps the city itself, would change drastically. However, helped by the increased availability of drugs that can make HIV a manageable condition, and with political clout that has put several mayors and numerous city supervisors into office, Castroites today seem more interested in shopping than storming City Hall.

During the week, the Castro is a relatively quiet, cheerful neighbourhood. However, on the weekends (and, of course, during Pride), the area around Castro and 18th Streets is overrun with visitors and locals who come for the exuberantly queer party atmosphere. Available parking is a rare thing around the densely packed club lane, where visitors and locals mix it up at **Harvey's** (500 Castro Street, 431 4278), **Moby Dick's** (4049 18th Street, 861 1199) and the **Bar on Castro** (456 Castro Street, 626 7220).

Whatever the day, leather chaps and buffed biceps, long blond hair and divine drag are as comfortably at home here as Armani suits. A huge rainbow flag flies over Harvey Milk Plaza (the Muni stop at the corner of Market and Castro Streets), named after the camera-shop owner and activist who, in 1977, became San Francisco's city supervisor and the first openly gay elected official in the US, but was assassinated the following year. Milk's former shop and campaign headquarters, considered as significant in the history of gay politics as New York's Stonewall bar, are now occupied by skincare store **Skin Zone** (575 Castro Street, at 19th Street, 626 7933). Milk is commemorated by a small plaque in the pavement and a modest mural, and elsewhere in the area in the names of a school, a library and a community centre.

The other must-see area landmark is the dazzling art deco **Castro Theatre** (*see p208*). Constructed in 1922, it was the first building designed by noted Bay Area architect Timothy L Pflueger; 55 years after its completion, it became the 100th structure to be designated a US National Historic Landmark. The theatre has retained its original vibe, with a musician banging out showtunes on the original pipe organ before each night's films.

For a great view of the Castro from above, get lunch to go and wander up to **Corona Heights** – walk all the way up 16th Street to Flint Street, then take a right; the bare red rock of Corona will loom overhead. Along with beautiful vistas, you'll see plenty of Castro pooches and their human pets. If you've got tinies in tow, you can also check out the petting zoo at the **Randall Museum** (199 Museum Way, 554 9600, www.randallmuseum.org).

Noe Valley

Quaint Noe Valley, roughly bordered by 20th, Dolores, 30th and Douglass Streets, is a self-contained village cut off from the rest of the city by steep hills on every side. In the 1970s, it housed a fairly bohemian mix of straight, gay, working-class and white-collar residents, before growing more family-oriented in the 1980s and '90s, a place to which well-paid young couples could retreat to raise a family away from the chaos of the rest of the city. **Twin Peaks** overlooks the area from the west and its flanks offer attractive views of the East Bay.

The neighbourhood's main shopping strip, 24th Street, is outfitted with all the amenities you might expect: gourmet grocery stores, romantic restaurants and boutiques where owners and regulars are on first-name terms. When hunger strikes, there's a brunch at **Miss Millie's** (4123 24th Street, at Castro Street, 285 5598) or **Herb's Fine Food** (3991 24th Street, at Noe Street, 826 8937) with your name on it; a few blocks off the main drag, **Lovejoy's Antiques & Tea Room** (*see p152*) seems to think it's in the Lake District, complete with Victorian high teas. If you've got a bit of time, shoot a few blocks south of 24th Street down Church Street and then back up Castro Street for more gourmet and gifty delights. In the mood for something cool? It's a little bit out of the way, but **Mitchell's Ice Cream** (688 San José Street, at 29th Street, 648 2300) is arguably the city's best.

The Haight & Around

Top shopping, a countercultural legacy and some of the city's best views.

Mention the words 'Haight-Ashbury', or even just 'the **Haight**', and members of a certain generation will either sigh with a nostalgic longing or groan in exasperation, depending on their political persuasion and/or their psychological or physical proximity to 1967's legendary Summer of Love. However, once the crowds had tuned out, turned off and dropped back in again, the neighbourhood once again resumed duty as one of the most liveable and vibrant areas of San Francisco. Bordering the Haight, the **Western Addition** has alternately been the heart of the West Coast jazz scene and the centre of its considerable Japanese community, while **Hayes Valley** has emerged as an enclave of considerable hipness.

The Haight

The Haight's history is written in its Victorian buildings, many of them painstakingly restored and elaborately painted. The neighbourhood was considered to be a beach town in the mid 19th century, and many wealthy families from Nob Hill kept vacation homes in the area. However, with the development of Golden Gate Park in 1870, the Haight began to expand, and financially it was to thrive still further in the years following the 1906 earthquake, from which it emerged relatively unscathed.

As the 1950s phenomenon of 'white flight' swept through American urban areas, families left for the suburbs, and the Victorians of the Haight were increasingly left both vacant and affordable. Inevitably, the city's students and burgeoning post-war bohemian culture moved in. Closely allied with the North Beach Beat

scene of the late 1950s, the Haight became the epicentre of hippie culture, the most famous youth movement in history.

In Berkeley and Oakland, the free-speech and black-power movements were already bringing a new political consciousness to the Bay Area. Duly inspired, the hippies were the driving force behind the anti-Vietnam War protests in San Francisco in the 1960s, and a new counterculture emerged. In January 1967, 25,000 gathered for the Human Be-In, a proto-hippie get-together that was the precursor to the Summer of Love. Musicians and artists thronged the area: the Grateful Dead lived at 710 Ashbury Street, and Jefferson Airplane at 2400 Fulton Street; Janis Joplin camped out at 124 Lyon Street, with Robert Crumb down the street at No.301. Yet after speed and heroin replaced marijuana and LSD as the drugs of choice, and free love turned into grim disaffection, unsavoury sorts such as Charles Manson (who lived at 636 Cole Street) emerged as gurus to the impressionable youth, counteracting the work of idealistic political groups such as the Diggers and guerrilla theatre pioneers the San Francisco Mime Troupe.

Just as the bold and the beautiful still flock to Hollywood from all over the world hoping to be 'discovered', so teenage runaways still gravitate to **Haight Street** looking for peace, love and understanding. It's still here, though it takes a keen eye to find it. Traces of the radical past linger at anarchist-run bookshop **Bound Together** (1369 Haight Street, at Masonic Avenue, 431 8355), and the **Haight-Ashbury**

Who needs the modern world?

Strolling on **Haight Street**.

at the height of the hippie era, local bands that went on to fill stadiums (the Grateful Dead, Janis Joplin et al) played free shows here.

More evidence of the neighbourhood's past can be found at the charming **Red Victorian** B&B (1665 Haight Street, between Clayton & Cole Streets; *see p59*), the all-independent **Red Vic** cinema (1727 Haight Street, at Cole Street; *see p209*) and the **Magnolia** brewpub (1398 Haight Street, at Masonic Avenue; *see p168*). This former pharmacy served as a hippie haven called the Drugstore Café back in the 1960s, before becoming the base for Magnolia Thunderpussy and her erotically themed desserts. The new owners have named their brewpub in her honour and covered the walls in psychedelic 1960s murals.

At the corner of Haight Street and Central Avenue is the aptly named, beautifully wooded **Buena Vista Park**, the oldest official park in the city and the unofficial eastern terminus of Upper Haight. In 1867, when the land was still known as Hill Park, the city paid squatters $88,250 (which is equivalent to around $1.1 million today) to gain the rights to the park. It was a wise investment, not only for the city, but in terms of the example it set for the zealous culture of land preservation that still flourishes today across northern California. The paths on the west side of the park are lined with marble gutters and a retaining wall built by WPA workers using Victorian headstones, some laid face up with their inscriptions visible. The walk to the park's 589-foot (180-metre) peak is worth the effort: the views over the city and, on nice days, out to the Golden Gate Bridge and the Marin Headlands, are commanding.

Free Clinic (558 Clayton Street, at Haight Street; *see p288*), while the mellow coffeehouses hark back decades. However, the corner of Haight and Ashbury Streets is now home to a branch of the Gap, the windows of which are usually either spraypainted with graffiti or smashed by the large population of anti-corporate types that tend to haunt an area otherwise consisting almost completely of independently owned businesses.

Haight-Ashbury

The stretch of **Haight Street** that sits between Masonic and Stanyan Streets, known both as **Haight-Ashbury** and **Upper Haight**, makes for a lively scene on weekends and on warm-weather days. Stores hawk new age and eastern esoterica, elaborate hand-blown glass smoking paraphernalia, edgy clothing, high-fashion shoes and mountains of records and CDs, not least at the vast **Amoeba Music** (1855 Haight Street, between Shrader & Stanyan Streets; *see p193*). Shoppers also have to duck the buskers and bums, who add more local flavour than some tourists were expecting. Just west of Amoeba, across Stanyan Street, is **Golden Gate Park** (*see p109*). A couple of blocks north is the **Panhandle**, the park's grand entrance;

Cole Valley

It's only a few blocks from the bustle of Haight-Ashbury, but the cosy enclave of **Cole Valley** is a different world: low-key, smart and upscale. The businesses here are all clustered around a two-block area centred around Cole and Carl Streets. **Zazie** (941 Cole Street, at Carl Street; *see p152*) is a great spot for brunch or lunch; **Le Boulange de Cole** (1000 Cole Street, at Parnassus Street, 242 2442) serves pastries and small baguette sandwiches.

Alternatively, you can pick up supplies from **Say Cheese** (856 Cole Street, between Cole & Frederick Streets, 665 5020), which offers vast selections of gourmet cheeses, meats and wines, and enjoy a picnic on **Tank Hill**. Head one block west from Cole Street to Shrader Street and continue south up the hill until you reach Belgrave Street; turn left (east) on to Belgrave and take the rustic stairway at the end of the street to the top of the hill. It's a bit of a slog,

Sightseeing

but worth the effort. Once home to a water tank (hence the name), the 650-foot (200-metre) peak offers some of the city's best views, yet remains relatively unknown, it's literally overshadowed by nearby **Twin Peaks**.

Lower Haight

While Upper Haight still clings dreamily to its political past, the young, the disenchanted and the progressive have migrated down the hill to **Lower Haight**, on and around Haight Street between Divisadero and Octavia Streets. Hipper and harsher than its neighbour, the area – and specifically, the **Horseshoe** coffeehouse (566 Haight Street, between Fillmore & Steiner Streets, 626 8852) – was headquarters to Green Party candidate Matt Gonzalez, who gave current mayor Gavin Newsom a serious run for his money in the 2003 election.

The area's main intersection is at Haight and Fillmore Streets, from which cool street fashion shops, tattoo parlours, funky bars, ethnic eateries and pile-on-the-pancakes cafés radiate in all directions. Beer lovers would do well to try **Toronado** (547 Haight Street, between Fillmore & Steiner Streets; *see p169*).

The Western Addition

The Western Addition was not only the city's first suburb, but also its first multicultural neighbourhood. Mapped out in the 1860s to accommodate the post-Gold Rush population boom, the area was home to a thriving Jewish community from the 1890s. After the 1906 earthquake, the **Fillmore District**, the area's heart, sprang to life as displaced residents, many Japanese, began arriving.

After the Japanese had been removed to internment camps following Pearl Harbor, thousands of black Southerners, who had come west for work, moved into their houses. Because the area didn't observe the racial covenant laws that prevented African-Americans from owning land elsewhere in the city, the Western Addition soon developed into what became known as the 'Harlem of the West'.

Today it still has a very distinct character, with a mix of African-Americans, Russian seniors, immigrants from other countries and UCSF students who live in everything from amazing Victorians, some of the oldest in the city, to bland high-rises. Gentrification is creeping in, but slowly, and the area remains

Tales of the city Mary Pleasant

San Francisco's most engaging ghost story is set in a house that no longer exists. The south-west corner of Bush and Octavia Streets is now home to a clutch of eucalyptus trees. However, a century or more ago, it was the haunt of one **Mary Ellen 'Mammy' Pleasant**.

Born in Georgia as a slave, the striking, formidable Pleasant came to San Francisco in 1854 at the age of 40, and proceeded to live an extraordinary double life. On the one hand, she worked as a white businesswoman (she had very light skin), and used her business nous to accumulate sizeable piles of money through managing boarding houses, operating brothels and even arranging marriages. With money comes influence, and Pleasant is said to have wielded financial and political power at a pivotal, colourful time in the city's history. She devoted considerable time, money and attention to civil rights campaigning, using her earnings to fund abolitionist causes and becoming a driving force in the campaign to integrate the streetcar network.

However, there may have been a darker side to Pleasant. While she doubtless made some of her money in legitimate fashion, she is also alleged to have resorted to blackmail

in a bid to accrue yet more influence and wealth. Some people claimed she was a nefarious voodoo priestess who used magic rituals to curse and/or unnerve rivals at the upper echelons of society.

Among her closest confidantes was Thomas Bell, the founder of the first Bank of California. No one has ever been able to ascertain exactly what kind of relationship the two enjoyed, however. Bell was married to a younger woman, but Pleasant lived with them in their mansion at Bush and Octavia, and appears to have acted as some sort of mediator when the two grew apart.

In 1892, Bell toppled over the banisters in his mansion and died. A judge ruled that that the death was accidental, but that didn't stop Bell's wife making it plain to society that she thought Pleasant was responsible. Bell's wife inherited her husband's fortune, leaving Pleasant penniless. She's said to have spent her last few years lurking in the fragrant, peeling trees outside her onetime 'House of Mystery' vowing to return to power. After her death in 1904, residents reported seeing a spectre in her image, one that continues to haunt the street even today.

Walk Japan Center

Beginning at the corner of Fillmore and Post Streets, the three-block **Japan Center** mall is home to shops and restaurants that have brought contemporary and traditional Japanese culture and commodities to San Francisco since 1968. At its western end is the **AMC Kabuki 8**, a generic cinema that, in a bid to integrate with the locale, hosts screenings as part of the SF International Film Festival and the SF Asian International Film Festival (for both, see p208 **Festivals**).

Head east on Post Street past the theatre and look for the sign for the Fuku Sushi restaurant; just under it, on your right, are the doors to the **Kinokuniya Building**, named for the famed Japanese bookstore on the second floor. Just inside the entrance is the **Katsura Garden** store. Although it takes its name from the world's first 'stroll-garden', created in 17th-century Japan by Prince Toshihito, the diminutive shop doesn't allow for much strolling. Still, like its selection of bonsai, it's all the more enchanting for its scale.

Diagonally across the hall is **Juban**, one of the city's best *yakiniku* ('grilled meat') houses. Outside, a staircase leads up to the second floor and the aforementioned Kinokuniya Bookstore and **Ma-Shi-Ko Folkcraft**, whose speciality is stoneware. After you've had a look and are ready to leave the store, walk straight ahead into the hallway opposite; it's actually a footbridge over Webster Street to the next building in the complex. On your right are **Asakichi Iron & Bronze**, the perfect place to pick up a traditional Japanese teapot, and its tiny offshoot **Asakichi Incense**.

Emerging from the Webster Street Bridge, you're now in the **Kinetsu Mall**, just across from the doors of the **Ikenobo Ikebana Society of America**. Founded in July 1970 by Sen'ei Ikenobo, it's dedicated to an elaborate, centuries-old style of flower arranging, and offers information, classes, materials and supplies. By way of contrast, head across the hall to the **Mikado Kid Corner** and pick up some *Hello Kitty* hypermerchandising, before heading east around the corner to ceramics and housewares store **Daikoku by Shiki**.

Turning left out of Daikoku by Shiki, go through the doors into **Japantown Peace Plaza**. The heart of Japantown, it's home to the **Cherry Blossom Festival** (see p199) and site of the towering **Peace Pagoda**, the defining symbol of the modern neighbourhood. Across Post Street on Buchanan Street is the pedestrian-only **Buchanan Mall**, where you'll find Japanese stores such as **Soko Hardware** (standard hardware tools plus traditional Japanese implements), **Paper Tree** (origami supplies) and, er, **Aloha Warehouse**, where you can pick up Hawaiian gifts, foodstuffs and CDs and even get a traditional Polynesian tattoo). In the middle of the block is a fountain created in 1976 by sculptor Rai Y Oakmoto, designed to conjure the 'Japanese landscape flowing along a stream'.

Heading back across Post Street and Peace Plaza, turn left into the **Miyako Mall** for some more exotic concerns. The cavernous **Genji Antiques** contains perhaps the highest quality merchandise in the whole complex, from elaborate Shinto shrines to contemporary furniture. Wandering further into the small mall, turn right and continue to the end of the hall to find the **Exhibition of Rare and Exotic Natural Stones**, a showcase (part-museum, part-store) of amazing natural stone formations and stones sculpted and polished to highlight their natural features. Worked up a hunger yet? Climb the ornate staircase to the second floor for two good sushi restaurants, the polar opposite of each other. **Umeko**'s all-you-can eat sushi buffet is perfect for those who want to load up, while **Ino Sushi** offers a more refined and traditional experience. If you end up getting a bit crazy with the saké, stumble down the hallway to the **Radisson Miyako Hotel**, get a room for the night and submerge yourself in one of the in-room Japanese-style soaking tubs.

mostly chain-free. The stretch of **Divisadero Street** between Page and Fulton Streets holds a number of novelty stores, the **Independent** (No.628, at Hayes Street; see p232) and the bar/restaurant **Club Waziema** (No.543, at Fell Street, 346 6641), which offers honey wine, Harar beer and Ethiopian food. At the corner of Divisadero and Fulton, past the incense emporiums and African-American barbershops, sits another couple of notable businesses: **Café Abir** (beers and magazines) and **Tsunami** (sushi and sake).

Alamo Square

San Francisco is crammed full of handsome Victorian houses (commonly known simply as 'Victorians'). However, most tourists choose not

The delightful Victorians of **Alamo Square**.

to roam the city and discover them at random. Instead, they head to the 'Postcard Row' of tidy pastel Victorian houses on the east side of **Alamo Square**, which juxtapose wonderfully with the sweeping view of Downtown behind them. Many visitors are so taken with the homes that they wish they could stay in one; the **Alamo Square Inn** offers just such an opportunity. Still, there are many fine Victorians nearby just to visit; chiefly, perhaps, the ornate Italianate **Westerfield House**, located at the corner of Fulton and Scott Streets, which dates back to 1882.

The Fillmore District

The Fillmore neighbourhood was a mecca for jazz and blues musicians in the 1940s and '50s. Several albums, among them Miles Davis's 1961 *In Person* recordings at the Blackhawk club, are testament to its pedigree. However, the locale was declared a slum by the San Francisco Redevelopment Agency in the 1960s and torn apart in the guise of urban renewal.

The windy intersection of Fillmore and Eddy Streets is a legacy of the city's ill-conceived plan for cultural regeneration, no part of which has yet come to fruition on what remains an empty lot. There is some hope on the horizon, though: **Powell's Place** (1521 Eddy Street, at Fillmore Street, 863 1404), the long-serving Hayes Valley soul-food café, has recently moved here, while renowned Oakland jazz club **Yoshi's at Jack London Square** (*see p234*) is slated to open a branch in 2007. But as of 2006, the musical landmarks here are rock-oriented: the still-extant **Fillmore Auditorium** (*see p232 and p233* **Tales of the city**) and the now-defunct Winterland (formerly at the north-west corner of Post and Steiner Streets), where the Band filmed

The Last Waltz and Johnny Rotten asked the audience 'Ever get the feeling you've been cheated?' at the final Sex Pistols show in 1978.

Yards away, on the wall of the **Hamilton Recreation Center** at the corner of Post and Steiner, is a huge musical mural, created by local musician and painter Santie Huckaby over a two-year span. The mural features dozens of musicians with an SF connection: some lived here, some simply played here, and one, John Lee Hooker, even opened his own club. Hooker died in 2001, but the **Boom Boom Room** (1601 Fillmore Street, at Geary Boulevard; *see p230*), the club in question, is still open for business.

Next to the Fillmore Auditorium, at **1849 Geary Boulevard**, is an eerier landmark. A post office has stood here in recent years, but from 1971 to 1977, this site was the home of the notorious Jim Jones and his People's Temple. Despite running his own legendarily cultish church, Jones was a respectable citizen. However, when reports emerged of physical and sexual abuse within the church, he moved it from here to a Guyanese settlement he named Jonestown. The following year, Jones and almost 1,000 disciples, the majority former Fillmorites, committed mass suicide or were murdered in the now-infamous Jonestown Massacre.

Japantown

Three commercial blocks and a compound-like shopping mall are all that remains of what once may have been the US's largest Japantown. Devastated by the forced relocation of Japanese-Americans during World War II, sent by the government to internment camps after the attack on Pearl Harbor, the community is now home to only a tiny percentage of the city's 12,000 Japanese-Americans. Still, the locale provides support for the elderly, history lessons for the young and a banquet of aesthetic and pop-cultural delights for anyone interested.

At the heart of Japantown is the **Japan Center**, a mostly underground maze of shops, restaurants and other businesses (*see p106* **Walk**). To gain a bit of cultural context on the area, visit the **National Japanese American Historical Society** (684 Post Street, between Buchanan and Laguna Streets, 921 5007, www.nikkeiheritage.org) and/or the nearby **Japanese American Community Center** (1840 Sutter Street, at Webster Street, 567 5505, www.jcccnc.org), which hosts exhibitions on the Japanese-American way of life. To the east of the Japan Center, meanwhile, is the impressively modern **Cathedral of St Mary of the Assumption**.

Cathedral of St Mary of the Assumption

1111 Gough Street, at Geary Boulevard (567 2020/www.stmarycathedralsf.org). Bus 2, 3, 4, 38. **Open** 6.45am-4pm Mon-Fri, Sun; 6.45am-5.30pm Sat. **Admission** free. **Map** p314 J6.

Dominating the skyline, the exterior of this 1970 cathedral is stark, a flowing, sculptural structure (some say it resembles the blades of a washing machine) reaching 198ft (60m) into the sky. The four corner pylons were designed to support over 10 million lbs of pressure and are set 90ft (27m) into the

The new **Hayes Green** (Octavia Boulevard) will host temporary sculptures, such as this 2005 work by David Best.

bedrock beneath the church. Inside, the structure of the cupola is revealed in 1,500 visible coffers, in over 128 sizes, meant to distribute the weight of the roof. The massive organ, on a raised pedestal that floats above the congregation, elevates the cathedral to *Phantom of the Opera* proportions. Large corner windows allow views of the city.

Hayes Valley

Typical San Francisco. Take an urban-planning nightmare – say, a massive road that rips apart a community – and then simply reverse it. Hayes Valley, just west of the Civic Center, was literally overshadowed by the Central Freeway for years. However, when the 1989 earthquake all but destroyed the roadway, it also hurried the transformation of the area from drug- and prostitution-riddled slum to perhaps the hippest urban shopping area in town. Streets that once sat under a tangle of concrete overpasses now have sidewalk cafés, boutiques, galleries and even **True Sake** (560 Hayes Street, at Laguna Street; *see p189*), a specialist sake shop.

The locals know how good they've got it. The community association is active here, and gets results: they've fought to keep out the chains (current score: Hayes Valley 1, Starbucks 0), won the battle to close the major Fell Street highway off-ramp, and established a little tree-lined boulevard along **Octavia Street**, home to great soul-food eaterie **J's Pots of Soul** (No.203, at Page Street; *see p154*). Nearby sits **Dudley Perkins Co** (66 Page Street, at Gough Street, 703 9494, www.dpchd.com): in business since 1914, the city's oldest Harley-Davidson dealership is a veritable museum of gleaming hogs and vintage artefacts. During the day, **Hayes Street** gets busy with well-dressed couples shopping for modernist furniture and brunching on champagne and oysters at **Absinthe** (No.388, at Gough Street; *see p154*), a belle époque French restaurant with tables spilling on to the pavement. Don't miss the stretch of **Market Street** between Gough Street and Van Ness Avenue, a shopping hub for deco antiques and upmarket accessories. But be wary of walking west of Laguna Street at night: the area changes abruptly and can occasionally feel a bit dicey.

The neighbourhood's greatest curiosity is a recent arrival. Based in the city for three decades, the **African Orthodox Church of St John Coltrane** was evicted from its Western Addition premises in 2000. However, it's since found a new home at 930 Gough Street (at Turk Street, 673 3572, www.saintjohn coltrane.com), where it continues to hold jazz-driven services – Coltrane's *A Love Supreme* is their key work – every Sunday at noon.

Sunset, Golden Gate Park & Richmond

Low on crowds, high on charm, and home to one of the world's greatest parks.

To many visitors, and some San Franciscans, the **Richmond** and **Sunset** districts are largely unexplored area that sandwich the verdant expanse of **Golden Gate Park**, one of San Francisco's greatest attractions. And that's fine with the locals, who tend to be a bit more unassuming, a bit less concerned with appearances and a bit more welcoming than those in other neighbourhoods. If Fisherman's Wharf and the Marina represent larger-than-life opera sets, residents of the Richmond and Sunset are the masters of that stagecraft. This happy mélange of active immigrant communities, students, families, working-class folk and, by the ocean, surfers, also enjoys the city's very best coastal trails. Less crowded, less touristy, less flashy and more foggy: for some, this is the real San Francisco.

Sunset & further south

This large southern neighbourhood, west of the Haight and south of Golden Gate Park, usually belies its own name. The sunsets in the Sunset are habitually swathed in fog from June to September, and often in other months. But if you do catch a fair day, they can be spectacular.

The stretch of **Irving Street** between 5th and 10th Avenues, in an area informally known as the Inner Sunset, is the area's shopping corridor. Just off Irving on 9th Avenue sit two fine eateries: sushi stop **Ebisu** (No.1283; *see p155*), and **Park Chow** (No.1240; *see p155*).

However, the Sunset's main attractions are way west, out where the land meets the water. Perhaps chief among them is thin, sandy **Ocean Beach** (*see p122* **On the beach**), which runs for roughly three and a half miles south from the **Cliff House** (*see p115*). It's a good spot for a contemplative wander, a time spent watching the surfers (who sometimes count Sunset homeowner and rocker Chris Isaak among their numbers) battling strong rip tides and chilly water. Take a warming break either over coffee at the **Java Beach Café** (*see p156*) or with a garlic whole-roasted crab at Vietnamese restaurant **Thanh Long** (4101 Judah Street, at 46th Avenue, 665 1146).

Ocean Beach's southernmost point is marked by the **Fort Funston Reservation**, a large natural area in the far south-west of the city. The reservation is criss-crossed with hiking trails, dramatic promontories and jagged beaches, and is both a favourite place for local dog-walkers and a point from which hang-gliders can launch themselves above the waves.

Just over a mile north of Fort Funston is **San Francisco Zoo** (*see p205*), one of the few zoos to house koalas. (Two of them were bear-napped a few years back by some teenage boys who wanted to give them as gifts to their girlfriends; they were safely returned). Beyond the zoo is the **Harding Municipal Park & Golf Course** (*see p248*), cradled by the picturesque Lake Merced and encircled by lovely biking and jogging trails. North of the lake is Stern Grove, just over 60 acres of eucalyptus and redwood that hosts the annual **Stern Grove Festival** (*see p232* **Festivals**). And slightly further inland is **Mount Davidson**, which, at 927 feet (283 metres) in height, is the highest point in San Francisco. If you can ignore the enormous cross that sits at its apex, the views are terrific.

Golden Gate Park

Roughly three miles in length and half a mile wide, **Golden Gate Park** is one of the largest man-made parks in the world and a testament to human dominion over nature. The ambitious

Ocean Beach. *See p109.*

task of creating this pastoral loveliness – 1,000 acres of landscaped gardens, forests, and meadows – from barren sand dunes began in 1870 in an attempt to solidify San Francisco's position as a modern urban centre, to meet the growing public demand for a city park, and, on the part of the wealthy landowners in the area, to stimulate property prices.

William Ralston, founder of the Bank of California and builder of the Palace Hotel, first approached Frederick Law Olmsted, the visionary behind Manhattan's Central Park, to design the project. Believing that the arid landscape of the Outside Lands, as the virtually uninhabited area was then known, could not support such a project, Olmsted's original design proposed a greenbelt that would take advantage of the large natural valley that ran through the city. However, once Olmsted left town, his plan was shelved; the valley he planned to utilise is now Van Ness Avenue.

The project was next awarded to a young civil engineer named William Hammond Hall. The park's wealthy patrons, whose motives were more fiscal- than civic-minded, saw Hall as a like-minded individual who would accede to their plans for the land development, and they were right. Hall's family was hooked into every level of government and industry, and many felt he had been handed an impossible task. Olmsted even wrote to Hall, telling him he 'did not believe it practicable to meet the natural but senseless demand of unreflecting people bred in the Atlantic states and the North of Europe for what is technically termed a park under the climatic conditions of San Francisco'.

Work continued, however, and while it cost the surrounding environment dearly, the result was clearly a marvel. But it wasn't until eccentric Scottish-born John McLaren took over stewardship in 1890 that the park finally came together (*see p112* **Walk**). McLaren spent more than 50 years as park superintendent, expanding on Hall's innovations and planting

by stages, to allow what are now the lakes, meadows and forests of the park to evolve as the substrate could sustain them. In the process, he planted more than a million trees.

The park's public debut came in 1894, when more than 1.3 million people visited for the Midwinter International Exposition. Covering around 200 acres, the six-month fair filled more than 100 temporary buildings. Two still remain: the **Japanese Tea Garden** and the **Music Concourse**. As the park's fame spread in the wake of the exposition, horticulturalists from all over the world sent in seeds and cuttings. Today, a rose garden, a Shakespeare garden, a rhododendron dell and a tulip garden are among hundreds of living delights; the colours dazzle on a sunny day and console on a foggy one. Among all the soaring eucalyptus and pine trees, the city is so rarely in view that it is easily forgotten.

Sampling all the park's attractions, from the assorted natural attractions to the violently modern new **de Young Museum** (*see p111*), would take days. It'll get even more time-consuming in 2008, when the **California Academy of Sciences**, a natural history museum currently based in SoMa (*see p204*), opens in a new and very modern building. The museum will include an aquarium and a planetarium, and will hopefully be a model for 'green' building projects around the country.

However, one great way to see it over the course of a single afternoon is to stroll all the way from the entrance of the park along the pedestrian footpaths beside John F Kennedy Drive, the park's main east–west artery, to the ocean. It takes a few hours if you stop along the way, but your reward will be the crashing waves of the Pacific. If you prefer to travel on wheels, bikes and in-line skates can be rented from various locations (*see p247*). Indeed, if you join the throngs of locals biking, walking, jogging and in-line skating along JFK Drive on a Sunday afternoon, when the road is closed to traffic, you'll soon understand why the park is known as San Francisco's collective backyard.

If you're planning on entering Golden Gate Park from Haight-Ashbury, you can do so at the west end of Haight Street by crossing Stanyan Street. Otherwise, come in via the Panhandle, a couple of blocks north. This was once the grand entrance to the park, designed with paths wide enough to accommodate carriages. It brings you out next to the park headquarters in McLaren Lodge, where you can pick up information. For a self-guided tour of the park, *see p112* **Walk**.

Beach Chalet & Park Chalet

1000 Great Highway (visitor centre 751 2766/ restaurant 386 8439/www.beachchalet.com). Bus 18. **Open** *Visitor centre* 9am-6pm daily. *Beach Chalet* 9am-10pm Mon-Thur, Sun; 9am-11pm Fri, Sat. *Park Chalet* 11am-10pm Mon-Thur, Sun; 11am-11pm Fri, Sat. **Credit** AmEx, MC, V.

A perfect spot for sunset cocktails, this historic Willis Polk-designed building on the coast is home to a fine restaurant and brewpub. The ground-floor walls are awash in WPA frescoes by Lucien Labaudt depicting notable San Franciscans, among them sculptor Benny Bufano and John McLaren. The views of the ocean from upstairs are stupendous.

The newly constructed Park Chalet, which faces Golden Gate Park, doesn't have the views of the Beach Chalet. However, the more mellow atmosphere makes it ideal for whiling away a sunny afternoon in one of the Adirondack chairs arrayed around the beautifully landscaped lawns, or cooling off with a beer after a walk along Ocean Beach.

de Young Museum

50 Hagiwara Tea Garden Drive (863 3330/www.de youngmuseum.org). Bus 5, 44. **Open** 9.30am-5pm Tue-Thur, Sat, Sun; 9.30am-8.45pm Fri. **Admission** $10; $6-$7 discounts; free under-12s. **Credit** AmEx, MC, V. **Map** p316 B9.

The most prominent feature of this controversial new future-primitive building, designed by Herzog & de Meuron, is the massive tower that emerges from the surrounding canopy of trees, making all those who approach from the 10th Avenue entrance to Golden Gate Park feel like the vanguard of an expedition that's just stumbled across an ancient lost city – or an abandoned mothership. Most would agree that the design – seemingly a combination of extraterrestrial metals wedded to sharp angles and organic forms found in ancient structures (like a surreal interpretation of the temples of Machu Picchu) – is at once overwhelming and electrifying. The exterior walls are all made from patterned copper designed to take on the colour of the surrounding greenery as they oxidise over time.

While the jury is still out about the building's exterior, the quality of its contents is not in doubt. Along with its vast collections of American art from the 17th to 20th centuries, the museum showcases an extensive collection from New Guinea and the Oceanias, as well as contemporary craft and textiles. There's also an excellent store and café with large, outdoor seating areas. However, with commanding views over the park, the soaring observation tower is worth the trip alone. The courtyard, café, store, sculpture garden and tower can be entered without paying the admission fee.

Sightseeing

Conservatory of Flowers. See p112.

Walk Golden wander

Sightseeing

Start your tour of Golden Gate Park at the **McLaren Lodge** (John F Kennedy Drive, 831 2700). Once the residence of John McLaren, the lodge is now the site of the park offices and visitors' centre (open 8am-5pm Mon-Fri). Strike out south from the lodge down the tree-lined path running parallel to Stanyan Street, bearing right until you come to **Alvord Lake**. Keep right by the lake and pass under Alvord Lake Bridge, which dates to 1889. It was the first reinforced concrete bridge built in the US and one of few bridges to survive the 1906 earthquake, vindicating its builder's then-controversial faith in concrete construction.

Head through to Mothers' Meadow until you reach a fork. The left branch brings you to the **Children's Playground**, the oldest municipal playground in the nation and home to the 62 hand-painted animals of the wonderful 1912 Herschel-Spillman Carousel. North, past the Sharon Art Building is Sharon Meadow. You'll hear **Hippie Hill**, in the middle of the meadow, before you see it. The hill became the heart of the Summer of Love; the never-ending pick-up drum jams on the hill are still going strong.

Follow the path north to the tennis courts and continue round their right-hand side. Cross John F Kennedy Drive after you emerge from the trees to take in the gleaming, white-domed **Conservatory of Flowers** up to your left. Badly damaged by a storm in 1995, it reopened to considerable excitement in 2003 after an eight-year, $25-million restoration. It's the oldest glass-and-wood Victorian

greenhouse in the western hemisphere, and is home to more than 10,000 plants.

Take the stairs up to JFK Drive and head along Middle East Drive. On your left is the 7.5-acre **National AIDS Memorial Grove**. Inaugurated in 1991, it has the names of some of the city's nearly 20,000 dead engraved in stone amid redwoods, oaks and maples. (For a guided tour, call 750 8340.) Opposite, a path leads north to the beautiful **Lily Pond**. Follow it round the west side to the crossroads. On the right is a grove of ferns that dates to 1898. Head straight on, taking the footpath to your left that parallels JFK Drive, to another botanical delight: the **John McLaren Rhododendron Dell**. Lovingly restored following the same storm that damaged the Conservatory of Flowers, it holds a life-sized statue of McLaren himself (see p114 **Statues**). Further on stands a memorial to another Scotsman, Robert Burns.

Here you have a choice: carry on west towards the newly reopened **de Young Museum** (see p111) before heading south, or amble south along the leafy walkways to the **California Academy of Sciences** complex (closed until 2008). From either venue, press on across the Music Concourse through the arch in the Temple of Music to find yourself at the **Japanese Tea Garden** (752 1171, $3.50). Built in 1893 for the Exposition, the landmark garden – ironically, the spot where the Chinese fortune cookie is said to have been invented – still delights

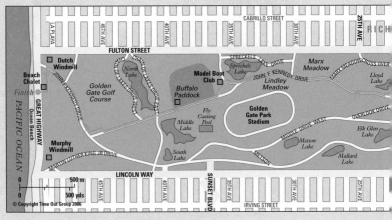

visitors with its steep bridges, bonsai trees, huge bronze Buddha and outdoor tearoom with kimono-clad servers. Another nice stopping-off point are the **Strybing Arboretum & Botanical Gardens** (661 1316), which house some 7,000 species from diverse climates. There's a fragrant garden designed for the visually impaired and a particularly appealing moon-viewing garden. The John Muir Nature Trail focuses on local flora.

Return to MLK Drive, then head west up the hill and take the concrete stairs to Stow Lake. Wandering along the broad path on the south side of the lake, you'll come to the **Rustic Bridge**: cross here to explore Strawberry Hill island and its Chinese pavilion. A gift from the people of Taipei, the pavilion was shipped in 6,000 pieces and reassembled here in 1981. Head round the lake to the **Boathouse**, where paddle boats and canoes are available for rent.

From the Boathouse walk north. Pick up the path to the left of the restrooms across the parking lot, and you'll come out opposite **Rainbow Falls** and the **Prayer Book Cross**, which commemorates Sir Francis Drake's chaplain offering up prayers during their brief holiday in the Bay Area in 1579. Follow the little waterway west under Cross Over Drive Bridge and across Transverse Drive to Lloyd Lake and the **Portals of the Past**, the only memorial in the city devoted to the 1906 earthquake and fire. The ornate marble archway that now stands here was once the front entrance to the Towne Mansion at

1101 California Street, home of Alban Towne; it was the last structure left standing atop Nob Hill following the fire. From there JFK Drive takes you through meadows offering plenty of picnicking opportunities. After about half a mile, you'll come to **Spreckels Lake**, with its ducks and model sailing boats.

When you're ready, get back on to JFK (passing the San Francisco Model Yacht Club on your right) and press ever west. Almost immediately, on your right, you'll pass the large **Buffalo Paddock**, where a small herd of bison roams on a 'prairie'. Pass Chain of Lakes Drive West on your right and keep going for about five minutes. Just past the golf course (watch for stray balls), you'll find a pleasant tree-lined pedestrian path that will take you round to the north, and soon to **Queen Wilhelmina's Tulip Gardens**. A gift from the eponymous Dutch monarch in 1902, the garden is shaded by the commanding **Dutch Windmill**, aka the North Windmill, which boasts the world's largest windmill wings. The windmill functioned as a huge pump, feeding water to the verdant urban wonderland that is now Golden Gate Park but which was once only sand dunes. It's now undergoing a $6.4-million restoration, slated to be complete by spring 2006.

Head south on another wooded path rather than getting on to the Great Highway. You'll soon be at journey's end: the 80-year-old **Beach Chalet** and the new **Park Chalet**. Bus 5 will take you back to civilisation.

Sightseeing

Statues John McLaren

It's no small irony that of the dozens of monuments sprinkled around Golden Gate Park, **John McLaren**'s should be one of the most prominent. The Scottish horticulturalist and spiritual father of Golden Gate Park was a despiser of all things statuary, believing that they detracted from the pastoral nature of a park. During his 53-year reign as park gardener and superintendent (which only ended when he died in 1943 at the age of 96), 'Uncle John' managed to dispose of dozens of 'stookies', as he called them: stowing them away in wooded glens, stashing them behind buildings and shrubbery, and surrounding them with dense plantings chosen for their rapid growth and ability to thrive in the city's cool, damp climate.

One can only imagine how McLaren must have cringed at the life-size statue of himself, a looming contemplative figure in bronze crafted in 1911 by sculptor and park commissioner M Earl Cumming that today crowns the rhododendron dell bearing his name. The legend goes that McLaren hid the monument under an old mattress in the horse stables for years; it was not until after his death in 1943 that park workers discovered it and eventually resurrected it for public display.

Richmond

Bordering the northern edge of Golden Gate Park, from beyond Arguello Boulevard to the ocean and from Fulton to California Streets, the largely residential Richmond is a highly flavoured cultural mix, predominantly but not exclusively made up of Russian, Chinese and Irish immigrants. Once a sandy waterfront wasteland, the region was developed after the construction of the Geary Boulevard tramway in 1906. Eastern European Jews formed a strong community after World War I, and many of their synagogues and delicatessens still thrive.

The **University of San Francisco** and the peculiar **Columbarium** (*see p115*) hover at the easterly edge of the area, but **Clement Street** is the district's primary commercial centre. Stretching from 2nd Avenue all the way to 34th Avenue, the stretch of Clement Street between Arguello and Park Presidio Boulevards arguably offers a more authentic Chinatown than the more famous one in the centre of the city. It's also more pleasant: the wider streets and lack of tourists make browsing the stores for Asian groceries and kitchenware a pleasure.

Literary types have long been enamoured of **Green Apple Books** (506 Clement Street, at 6th Avenue; *see p179*). Just a block north is **Antique Traders** (4300 California Street, at 5th Avenue, 668 4444), whose breathtaking collection of stained-glass windows, salvaged from the city's many Victorians, has many out-of-town shoppers calculating shipping costs. Tucked away behind the misleadingly tiny shopfront, **6th Ave Flowers & Aquarium** (425 Clement Street, between 5th & 6th Avenues, 668 7190, www.6thaveaquarium.com) is a store that rivals many municipal aquariums in its selection of sea creatures, among them dwarf jellyfish and bioluminescent shrimp.

Speaking of shrimp, the takeout dumplings from **Good Luck Dim Sum** (No.736, at 8th Avenue, 386 3388) are authentic and cheap (you can get stuffed for under $5). Super-funky **Q Restaurant** (No.225, at 3rd Avenue; *see p155*) serves up American comfort food in a surreal setting; the Burmese specialties at **Burma Superstar** (No.309, at 4th Avenue, 387 2147) are inspired; and **Chapeau!** (No.1408, at 15th Avenue; *see p155*) offers more upscale ambience, highlighting Provençal cuisine.

One block south of Clement is **Geary Boulevard**, the Richmond's main artery. Fine ice-cream can be found at **Joe's** (No.5351, between 17th and 18th Avenues, 751 1950). Deeper into the avenues is **Tommy's Mexican Restaurant** (No.5929, at 23rd Avenue; *see p170*), with 250 pure agave tequilas. The 'free wine while you wait' is an added bonus at **Pacific Café** (No.7000, at 34th Avenue, 387 7091), with its superfresh seafood.

Now you're at 34th Avenue, turn north back over Clement into Lincoln Park to find the **California Palace of the Legion of Honor** (*see below*), built by George Applegarth to pay homage to the Palais de la Legion d'Honneur in Paris. Just north of the car park is the haunting **Jewish Holocaust Memorial**, created by George Segal. The surrounding wooded and hilly park contains the 18-hole **Lincoln Park Golf Course** (*see p248*), and a number of well-maintained hiking trails, shaded by twisted cypress, which meander along the spectacular cliffs of Land's End.

At the westerly end of the Richmond, **Sutro Heights Park** is a tiny idyll, virtually empty except for a few Russians walking their dogs or playing chess. A statue of the goddess Diana is often decorated with flowers by local pagans. In the nearby garden, enjoy a secluded picnic and marvel at the spectacular panoramic view of the Pacific. If the weather's not good enough, head across the street below Sutro Heights Park to **Louis' Restaurant** (902 Point Lobos Avenue, 387 6330), a 70-year-old classic 'greasy spoon' that serves milkshakes and ham steaks at Formica counters. The views of the ocean rival those from the somewhat touristy and pricey **Cliff House** (*see below*) down the road; both perch on the very edge of the city.

The Cliff House was the brainchild of silver baron and former mayor Adolph Sutro, who owned most of the land on the western side of the city. The remains of Sutro's own mansion are at the western edge of Sutro Heights Park; below the Cliff House to the north are the ruins of Sutro Baths, built by the man himself in 1896 and once the world's biggest swimming baths. Fed by the Pacific, seven pools holding more than six million litres of water could be filled by the tides in one hour. The baths were destroyed by fire in 1966, but the ruins are strangely photogenic. A windswept three-mile coastal path winds north to the Golden Gate Bridge.

California Palace of the Legion of Honor

Lincoln Park, at 34th Avenue & Clement Street (863 3330/www.thinker.org). Bus 1, 2, 18, 38. **Open** 9.30am-5pm Tue-Sun. **Admission** $10; $6-$7 discounts; free under-12s. Free to all Tue. **Credit** AmEx, MC, V.

Built as a memorial to the Californians who died in World War I, and set in a wooded spot overlooking the Pacific Ocean, the Palace of the Legion of Honor is San Francisco's most beautiful museum, its neo-classical façade and Beaux Arts interior virtually unchanged since it was completed in 1924. A cast of *Le Penseur* (aka *The Thinker*) by Rodin dominates the entrance; the French sculptor was the personal passion of Alma Spreckels, the museum's founder, and the collection of his work here is second only to that of the Musée Rodin in Paris. A glass pyramid acts as a skylight for galleries containing more than 87,000 works of art, spanning 4,000 years but with the emphasis on European painting and decorative art (El Greco, Rembrandt, Monet). An expanded garden level houses temporary exhibitions, the Achenbach Foundation for Graphic Arts and the Bowles Collection of porcelain.

Cliff House

1090 Point Lobos Avenue, at the Great Highway (386 3330/www.cliffhouse.com). Bus 18, 38. **Open** *Bar/restaurant* 11.30am-3.30pm, 5-9pm daily. *Bistro* 9am-9.30pm Mon-Sat; 8.30am-9.30pm Sun. *Walkways* 24hrs daily. **Credit** AmEx, MC, V.

After a fire in 1894, a magnificent, eight-storey Victorian turreted palace replaced the original 1860s house on this site. However, only a year after surviving the 1906 earthquake, it also burned. Its 'restoration' appears to have been more demolition and rebuilding; the resulting contemporary structure, completed in 2004, includes an upscale restaurant and bar with floor-to-ceiling glass walls that make the most of its breathtaking Pacific views.

Public walkways allow the less well-heeled to amble around the structure. The whimsical camera obscura, a 19th-century optical marvel, was saved after a public outcry halted its demolition and is still accessible on the walkway; it projects an image of the outside world, including a large stretch of Ocean Beach, on to a giant parabolic screen using mirrors and lenses. The National Park Service maintains a visitor centre (556 8642) on the premises for the Golden Gate National Recreation Area.

Columbarium

1 Loraine Court, off Anza Street (752 7891). Bus 31, 33, 38. **Open** 8am-5pm Mon-Fri; 9.30am-3pm Sat, Sun. **Admission** free. **Map** p316 D7.

This round, domed neo-classical rotunda is honey-combed with hundreds of niches, all filled with lav-ishly and individualistically decorated cremation urns. Among them are the remains of many of the city's first families, such as the Folgers (of coffee fame), the Magnins and the Kaisers. With the exception of the Presidio's military cemetery, it's the only active funereal resting place in the city: a 1901 law made burial illegal within San Francisco, and all graves were moved south to the town of Colma. Indeed, most residents are unaware that their homes were built on a massive 167-acre cemetery now known as the Richmond district, which centred around the Columbarium.

Pacific Heights to the Golden Gate Bridge

Choice architecture, dramatic land restoration… and a genuinely legendary piece of engineering.

Sightseeing

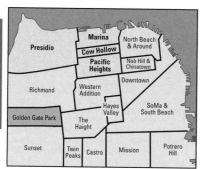

Pacific Heights and San Francisco's northern waterfront command some of the best views the city has to offer, but most people visit for one sight alone: the Golden Gate Bridge. A shame, given that this area, which stretches from Bush Street to the Bay and from Van Ness Avenue to the Presidio, has much more to offer than that single engineering marvel. The Pacific Heights mansions overlook some of the most revered coastline in the United States, while the vast expanses of wooded trails and cliffs throughout the former military base of the Presidio run up against the well-scrubbed opulence of the Marina.

Pacific Heights

True to its name twice over, **Pacific Heights** is perched high over the water, its mansions home to the cream of San Francisco's high society. Billionaire socialites Gordon and Ann Getty have a house here, as do many of the famous 'old' families of San Francisco (the Floods, the Bechtels and others). Thousands of lesser-known millionaires pass unnoticed, shopping for milk and caviar in the corner marts. It's easy to see how the area has picked up the nickname 'Specific Whites' down the years. Visitors head here to try and make rich friends or, if that fails, simply to marvel at the sumptuous real estate. The average price of a home here is in the region of $2.5 million;

in 2005, a one-bedroom condominium appeared on the market priced at $729,000.

The eastern edge of the neighbourhood contains some beautiful Victorian houses. The blue-and-white **Octagon House** (*see p117*) is perhaps the most famous, but there are also rich pickings to the south: the **Haas-Lilienthal House** (*see p117*), for example, which offers visitors a rare chance to see inside a grand old Queen Anne. Nearby is the ornate **Spreckels Mansion**, which spans the entire block between Jackson, Gough, Washington and Octavia Streets. Built by sugar heir Adolph Spreckels for his young wife Alma (the model for the statue that adorns the top of the Dewey Monument in Union Square), the 'Parthenon of the West' has been used as a location in several films. It's now home to novelist Danielle Steel.

Wander west from here, perhaps stopping in **Lafayette Park** (Washington and Gough Streets) to watch pedigreed dogs walking pedigreed owners, to the stretch of **Fillmore Street** between Bush and Jackson Streets. This is the main shopping hub of the area, lined with smart shops and restaurants. A few blocks west, elegant antiques shops, ateliers and boutiques sit on **Sacramento Street** between Presidio Avenue and Spruce Street; **George** (2411 California Street, at Fillmore Street; *see p195*) sells gourmet confections and couture canine sweaters to what must be the most spoiled dogs on the West Coast; and nearby charity shops stock the cast-offs of the rich and famous.

Given the area's current ambience, it comes as some surprise to learn that it was from this now-highfalutin neighbourhood that poet Allen Ginsberg launched a cultural renaissance in 1955, when he gave the first public reading of *Howl* at the long-vanished Six Gallery, the site of which is now home to a furniture store (**Liv**, 3117 Fillmore Street, at Filbert Street). North-west of here, past **Alta Plaza Park** (at Jackson and Steiner Streets), things grow even more handsome. Indeed, the stretch of **Broadway** between Divisadero Street and the Presidio holds some of the best architecture in the city.

Haas-Lilienthal House

2007 Franklin Street, between Washington &
Jackson Streets (441 3000/www.sfheritage.org/
house.html). Bus 1, 12, 27, 47, 49, 76. **Open** noon-
3pm Wed, Sat; 11am-4pm Sun. **Admission** $8; $5
discounts. **Credit** AmEx, MC, V. **Map** p314 J4.
Built in 1886 by Bavarian William Haas, this
28-room house has elaborate wooden gables and a
circular tower, clearly marking it as being in the
Queen Anne style. Fully restored and filled with
period furniture, it also has photos documenting its
history and that of the family that lived in it until
1972. It's maintained by San Francisco Architectural
Heritage, which also organises walking tours.

Octagon House

2645 Gough Street, at Union Street (441 7512). Bus
41, 45. **Open** noon-3pm 2nd & 4th Thur, 2nd Sun of
mth. **Admission** free. **Map** p314 J4 .
The 1861 Octagon House is home to the small
Museum of Colonial and Federal Decorative Arts, but
is most notable as one of two surviving examples of
eight-sided homes in the city. Across the nation, 700
such houses were built, in the belief that they
improved their occupants' health by letting in more
natural light. Once owned by wealthy dairyman
Charles Gough (back when nearby Cow Hollow still
contained cows), the Octagon House stands on the
street to which he magnanimously gave his name
while on the city's naming commission; he also named
an adjacent street 'Octavia' in honour of his sister.

Pretty **Pacific Heights**. *See p116.*

Cow Hollow

From Pacific Heights, it's only a few blocks
downhill towards the Bay to Cow Hollow. Once
a dairy pasture, the area is still serene, but its
grazers are now of the well-heeled, two-legged
kind. The activity is centred on **Union Street**
between Broderick and Buchanan Streets, a chic
and bijou stretch of bars, restaurants (among
them **Betelnut** at No.2030, for which *see p157*)
and boutiques (including wonderful antiques
store **Past Perfect** at No.2224; *see p178*).
Hiding in an alleyway is **Carol Doda's
Champagne & Lace Lingerie Boutique**
(1850 Union Street, between Octavia and
Laguna Streets, 776 6900); Doda, who owns the
store, found fame in the mid 1960s when, while
as a waitress at the Condor Club in North Beach,
she became the city's first-ever topless dancer.

Perhaps even more impressive than Carol's
fabled domes are those atop the nearby
Vedanta Temple (2963 Webster Street, at
Filbert Street). Dating back to 1905, the temple
is dedicated to an ancient strain of Hinduism
that holds all religions to be viable paths to
spiritual awareness. Accordingly, its six domes
each represent a different architectural style,
with elaborate Moorish arches, a Saracenic
crescent, a Russian onion-style dome and
a Victorian gingerbread trim.

The Marina & the waterfront

Built on soft rubble from the 1906 earthquake,
the Marina, between Fort Mason and the
Presidio, shook harder than any other part
of San Francisco in 1989's Loma Prieta quake.
Buildings collapsed hither and thither, but the
only reminders of the damage are the renovated
pavements and suspiciously new structures
among the otherwise-staid townhouses.

In a city justifiably famous for its gay scene,
the pastel-painted Marina is conspicuously
straight. It's also one big pick-up joint. By
night, its bars fill with twentysomethings
sipping cocktails and making eye contact; for
decades, even the local **Safeway** (15 Marina
Boulevard, at Laguna Street) was a pulling
spot, and featured in Armistead Maupin's
Tales of the City. The main commercial drag
is **Chestnut Street**. The stretch between
Fillmore and Divisadero Streets is a shrine
to self-indulgence, with clothing boutiques
and beauty salons seeming to occupy half the
shopfronts. The **House of Magic** (No.2025,
at Fillmore Street, 346 2218) lowers the tone
with fright wigs and fake dog-doo, meanwhile,
and the recently renovated **Presidio Cinema**
(No.2340, at Scott Street, 776 2388) lends the
place a little culture. The **Grove** (No.2250,

Sightseeing

at Avila Street; *see p158*), is a woodsy café, and a good stopping point to watch the preened denizens of the area 'fabu-lapping'.

A little more levity is provided at the eastern edge of the Marina waterfront. **Fort Mason** (*see below*) started out as a US Army command post in the 1850s, and its reconditioned military buildings retain a forbidding mien, but these days they house some fine little museums and exhibitions. For the 1915 Panama-Pacific Exposition, a mile-long swath of temporary structures was erected all the way from here to **Fort Point** (*see p120*). This fantastical city-within-a-city was torn down to make way for the houses we see today, but a small part of the fantasy-scape survived in the shape of the **Palace of Fine Arts** (*see p119*). The original plaster edifice, set in a little park at the western edge of the Marina, was expensively converted to concrete just in time for the opening of the adjacent **Exploratorium** (*see p204*) in 1969. It was one of the world's first hands-on science museums, and is still deservedly popular with children.

The vast, sloping lawns of the **Marina Green** (Marina Boulevard, between Scott and Webster Streets) are the locals' favourite place to fly kites, jog or picnic, offering dizzying views of the Golden Gate Bridge and the Bay.

At the far west side of the green, a path leads past the **Cavern on the Green**, a small stone snack hut perched above a large pool just past the boat marina but before Crissy Field. Stop in for an It's It (a Bay Area-made ice-cream treat) on a warm afternoon.

From here, head west along the edge of Marina Boulevard, around the harbour. Either continue west to the fascinating **Crissy Field** (*see p121* **Field of Dreams**), or follow the signs to the **Golden Gate Yacht Club**, along a kind of expansive promontory. Keep going, past the boats and the boaters and, when you can go no further, you'll get to Peter Richards's amazing **Wave Organ**. Part artwork, part musical instrument, the mostly underwater structure is made up of pipes and benches built from San Francisco's dismantled cemeteries; the tubes make eerie music with the ebb and flow of the Bay. From here the views of the Golden Gate Bridge, the city skyline and Alcatraz are excellent and unobstructed.

Fort Mason

Marina Boulevard, at Buchanan Street (441 3400/ www.fortmason.org). Bus 10, 22, 28, 30, 47, 49. **Map** p314 H2.

This collection of ex-military buildings features various cultural institutions. The Museo ItaloAmericano (Building C, 673 2200, www.museoitaloamericano. org) and the Mexican Museum (Building D, 202 9700, www.mexicanmuseum.org; due to relocate to SoMa in 2008) offer changing exhibitions along ethnic themes. Meanwhile, shows at the Museum of Craft & Folk Art (775 0991, www.mocfa.org) in Building A range from bookbinding to handmade furniture. All the museums are closed on Mondays, and only MoCFA is open on Tuesday; however, all offer free admission on the first Wednesday of the month.

Other enterprises here include the airy SFMOMA Artists' Gallery (Building A, 441 4777, www.sfmoma. org), which sells and rents out contemporary works by northern Californians, and the Book Bay Bookstore (Building C, 771 1076), which sells rejected stock from the public library, as well as LPs and art. Over in Building D is the Magic Theatre (441 8822, www.magictheatre.org), which stages works by a mix of emerging and established playwrights in its two performance spaces; before the performance, have dinner at Greens (Building A, 771 6222, www.greensrestaurant.com): one of the city's favourite vegetarian eateries, it boasts high ceilings that frame a wide view of the Marina and the Bay. A constant array of changing displays is on view at two waterside pavilions (actually reconstituted shipbuilding bays); concerts, gardening competitions and even the local pagan community's major Halloween fête are held here. Also based on site are the administrative offices for the Golden Gate National Recreation Area (GGNRA), responsible for the 75,398 acres that make up one of the largest urban park areas in the world.

Marina: the simplest parking in town.

As good as new? The recently renovated 85-year-old houses of **Pilot's Row**. *See p120.*

Palace of Fine Arts

Lyon Street, at Bay Street (563 6504/www.palaceof finearts.org). Bus 28, 30, 76. **Map** p313 E2.
Local architect Bernard Maybeck's pièce de résistance, the Palace is a neo-classical domed rotunda supported by a curved colonnade topped with friezes and statues of weeping women, and flanked by a pond alive with ducks, swans and lily pads. Initially designed only as a temporary structure, it's been repeatedly saved by generations of San Franciscans, and has served as everything from lighted tennis courts to a motor pool for dignitaries assisting in the creation of the United Nations after World War II. As it fell into neglect and disrepair, it even served as a telephone-book distribution centre and Fire Department headquarters.

The original building was demolished in 1964 – only the shell of the rotunda remained – but it was reconstructed at ten times the original cost. The lagoon and grounds are undergoing a $21-million renovation to retrofit the structure, create an aeration system for the lagoon and restore the landscape; the work is due to be completed in 2007.

The Presidio

The Presidio is sometimes called 'the prettiest piece of real estate in America'; it's certainly among the most valuable. At the northern tip of the city, overlooking the Bay, the Pacific and the Golden Gate Bridge, its location could hardly be more stunning, but for centuries, it endured a workaday existence as a military base, closed to the public. Now completely demilitarised, it has become a national park, complete with 11 miles of hiking trails, 14 miles of bicycle routes and three miles of beaches.

The tip of the San Francisco Peninsula was first established as a military outpost in 1776, when a group led by Captain Juan Bautista de Anza planted the Spanish flag here to protect the newly discovered San Francisco Bay. The site was claimed as a garrison first for Spain (*presidio* means fortress in Spanish) and then for Mexico, but the US took it over, along with the rest of California, in 1848. The US military embarked on a huge landscaping project that converted hundreds of acres of windswept, sandy moors into a tree-lined garden. However, by 1994 they'd had enough. After 220 years, the US Army handed the Presidio over to the Park Service, claiming it could no longer afford the upkeep. The dramatic changeover, from army base to national park, followed soon after.

So far, so good, but the switch hasn't been without its controversies. Among the handful of organisations charged with looking after the immense site is the Presidio Trust; it has also been charged with the unenviable task of making the Presidio self-sustaining by 2013, which it aims to accomplish by renting some buildings as private residences, renting others to businesses, and even allowing some new construction. A plot near the Lombard Gate, formerly home to the Letterman Hospital, has been given over to George Lucas's Industrial Light and Magic film company, which spent $350 million developing the 24-acre plot into the **Letterman Digital Arts Center**, a state-of-the-art complex of offices and studios that opened in 2005. The $5.6 million annual rent that Lucas will pay to the Presidio Trust constitutes around one-sixth of the trust's budget. Conservationists have cried foul, but development looks set to continue. However, it hasn't happened quite yet, and much of the Presidio remains in a state of arrested decay, forlorn and picturesque.

The sheer size of the park, not to mention its inevitably hilly nature, makes exploring it purely on foot something of an adventure. It's definitely worth considering hiring a bike from one of the rental firms at Fisherman's Wharf: the Presidio is arguably best explored by bike. While getting lost in this curious environment is something of a pleasure, maps are available at several information points: the **Crissy Field Center** on Mason Boulevard (enter the Presidio at Marina Boulevard, in its north-east corner, and carry on down the road for around half a mile); the **Visitor Center** in the old Officers' Club at the Main Post, close to the centre of the park (easily accessible from any entrance, but coming in via the Presidio Boulevard Gate at Presidio and Pacific Avenues will take you through fairytale woods, often shrouded in mist); and at the **Battery East Overlook** close to the Golden Gate Bridge.

The centre of the Presidio is the **Main Post**, a complex of old buildings arrayed along parallel streets on the site of the original Spanish fort. Aside from the main visitor centre (561 4323), which contains a few displays on the history of the park and a well-stocked shop selling maps, books and gifts, you'll also find two 17th-century Spanish cannons on Pershing Square, and rows of Victorian-era military homes along Funston Avenue.

Follow Sheridan Avenue west from the Main Post, and you'll soon arrive at the moving **San Francisco National Cemetery**. Among the army officers (and their family members) laid here in hauntingly straightforward fashion are more than 450 'Buffalo Soldiers'. African-American servicemen known to many simply as the subject of the eponymous Bob Marley song, they served not only alongside future president Theodore Roosevelt at the Battle of San Juan Hill (the battle namechecked by Marley), but also throughout the Civil War, the Indian Wars, the Spanish-American War and virtually every conflict up to the Korean War, after which the US armed services were officially integrated.

Continuing along Lincoln and taking the first right (McDowell Avenue), you'll soon stumble upon the **Pet Cemetery**. While its human counterpart sits high on a hill, its gravestones gleaming and its grass immaculately tidy, the pet cemetery, in which servicemen buried their beloved animals, sits directly under the Route 101 overpass, its markers made by hand and its grass unkempt. Still, there's something touching about these crumbling memorials, some of which – complete with poems and drawings – almost constitute folk art.

Much of the rest of the Presidio is a jumble of former servicemen's quarters, now converted into private homes. Around 500 structures from the former military base remain, ranging from Civil War mansions to simple barracks. Some are utilitarian, but others, such as **Pilot's Row** on Lincoln Boulevard near the Golden Gate Bridge toll plaza, are truly delightful. In between these sometimes melancholic clusters run numerous hiking and cycling paths, all marked on the maps available from the visitors' centres. Taking one – or more – is the best way to really get a feel for the Presidio. The easiest is the flat, paved Golden Gate Promenade,

which follows the shoreline up to the foot of the Golden Gate Bridge. However, the rewards are greater with more effort. The hilly, unpaved Coastal Trail runs out past the Golden Gate Bridge to the beginning of the Pacific, with spectacular views of the Marin Headlands. And the Ecology Trail begins directly behind the Officers' Club and follows a pastoral path on to Inspiration Point, which affords terrific views, and picturesque El Polin Spring.

That said, there are other landmarks. A number of haunting old coastal batteries sit along the western edge of the park; **Batteries Godfrey** and **Crosby** are both easily accessible on foot. Below them is **Baker Beach**, a favourite getaway among locals (*see p122* **On the beach**). To the south of the Presidio sits the relaxing idyll of **Mountain Lake Park** (access at Lake Street and Funston Avenue). Just next to it is the public **Presidio Golf Course**, formerly a private club favoured by presidents and generals.

Fort Point

Marine Drive, beneath Golden Gate Bridge (556 1693/www.nps.gov/fopo). Bus 28, 29. **Open** 10am-5pm Fri-Sun. **Admission** free. **Map** p312 A1.
The spectacular brick-built Fort Point was built between 1853 and 1861 to protect the city from a sea attack. The assault never came; the 126 cannons remained idle, and the fort was closed in 1900. Today the four-storey, open-roofed building houses various military exhibitions; children love to scamper among the battlements and passageways. Climb on to the roof for a fabulous view of the underbelly of the Golden Gate Bridge, which was built more than seven decades after the fort was completed.

The fort's pier is famous as the spot where Kim Novak's character 'attempts' suicide in Hitchcock's *Vertigo*. While Novak was only pretending, onlookers often think the surfers plying the point break as it wraps around the fort are legitimately suicidal. They're certainly crazy, but they're not dumb: many wear helmets to guards against the hazards of a wipeout on the jagged, rocky shoreline.

The Golden Gate Bridge

Few cities need bridges like this one. Without the **Golden Gate Bridge** connecting it to the northern half of the state and the **Bay Bridge** (*see p73* **Bridge of sighs**) linking it to the rest of the country, the city would be isolated at the tip of a mountainous peninsula. Sure, it thrived that way for almost a century, but the rise of the automobile meant that ferries and ocean liners were no longer sufficient. Bridges were built, and within a few years they had become the most famous in the US. Now, for $5 (charged only on southbound journeys), motorists can cross one of the greatest bridges in the world.

Field of dreams

Crissy Field, the large expanse of lawn and bucolic wetlands on the northern Presidio shoreline, initially appears to be a supremely bucolic spot. However, the keen eye may spot hints of a militaristic past. The periphery of the field is ringed by ageing hangars and Spanish Mission-style buildings guarded by antique cannons, while the curve of the road has more in common with an oval racetrack than a meandering coastal trail. So what gives?

Originally 130 acres of marshland bounded by coastal dunes, this area was first inhabited by the Ohlone band of Native Americans. From the 1770s, when it was first settled by non-native peoples, it fell successively under the control of the Spanish, Mexican and American militaries – it was the key point for defence of the San Francisco Bay, the most strategically and commercially significant point on the water. Despite its importance, though, it remained as marshland until, in the late 1800s, the US Army paved it for use as drill and parade grounds.

The 1915 Panama-Pacific International Exposition occasioned a building boom all over the city. The Presidio hosted a Grand Prix for the event, competitors circling a 3.84-mile track (the winner clocked a top speed of 56mph). Soon after the expo, it was decided that the expanse would become a full-time army airfield to complement the coastal artillery placements that already ringed the Bay. It was from here in 1919 that Major Dana Crissy set off on a 24-hour transcontinental test flight, but died while attempting to make an emergency landing in Utah. Two years later, the airfield was named in his honour.

Owing to advances in ship-borne artillery (which left the airfield vulnerable to sea attack), the obstruction of the Golden Gate Bridge and the coast's unpredictable weather, Crissy Field was shuttered as a first-line airfield in 1936. The air-mail hangar served as barracks and classrooms for the army's top-secret Military Intelligence Service Language School during World War II, where second-generation Japanese-Americans were trained as battlefield interpreters even as their families were being forcibly interned by the US government. Following the war, the airfield gradually fell into disuse until it was formally closed to air traffic in 1974.

Two decades later, when the land was given back to the city, workers and volunteers began returning Crissy Field to its original state: a pristine marshland home for hundreds of migrating bird species. The regeneration was funded largely by private donors, with over 90 per cent of the $32 million project costs coming from individuals giving $100 or less.

Its success is stunning. The 1.3-mile promenade along the shoreline lures walkers, joggers and spectators admiring daredevil kiteboarders and windsurfers who challenge the notorious waters. Volunteers have planted over 100,000 native plants from the park's nursery; and what was once a landing strip for 'warbird' planes is now a natural shelter for more than 120 species of birds, drawn by the field's 20-acre tidal marsh. Bay shrimp and Dungeness crab have also returned, a source of optimism for those labouring to restore the rich ecosystem of the region. From native lands to storied military airfield to a dramatically reinvigorated ecosystem, Crissy Field reflects the city's history as one of the primary military, industrial and commercial centres of the nation, but also its current role as the champion of environmental restoration, conservation and stewardship.

On the beach

Unlike in Southern California, the majority of beaches in and around San Francisco aren't great for swimming. As if the locals care: between the cavorting families, the picnicking couples, the idle promenaders and, on a couple of beaches, clothes-free pick-up artists, visitors to beaches in San Francisco aren't short of activities.

Most visitors start with the **East Beach**, up close to the Marina in the Presidio. During the week, it can be very pleasant, with dog-walking women, jogging men and cyclists of both sexes (including many tourists bound for the Golden Gate Bridge; *see p120*) passing the time of day along the edge. However, on weekends, it gets a little busier, and space is at a premium.

Running for almost a mile along the craggy western Presidio shoreline, **Baker Beach** is a better bet. It's accessible, for one thing, and offers both great views and easy access to the city's most popular nude beach, the north end of the same stretch. In 1905 the US Army decided to use Baker as the hiding place for a huge 95,000-pound (43,000-kilogramme) cannon. The naval invasion it was built to repel never came, but a replica of the original has been installed for the curious.

Hidden between Baker Beach and Lincoln Park, in the exclusive Seacliff neighbourhood, you'll find the exquisitely sheltered James D Phelan Beach. Better known as **China Beach** (Seacliff Avenue, off 26th Avenue), it takes its nickname from the settlement of Chinese fishermen who camped here in the 19th century. There's plenty of parking and a pleasant hike down to the sand, then a free sundeck, showers and changing rooms once you get there. It's the favourite beach of many locals; should you be around at sunset, with Marin Headlands opposite, the Golden Gate Bridge to your right and sea lions in the ocean ahead of you, it will be your favourite too.

Extending from Cliff House (*see p115*) south towards the city limits, **Ocean Beach** (Great Highway, between Balboa Street and Sloat Boulevard) is by far San Francisco's biggest beach: a three-mile sandy strip along the Pacific. Widening into dunes and plateaus at the end of the fog-bound Sunset District, it's a fine place for strolling, dog-walking and the odd illicit midnight ritual and bonfire. But look, don't taste: tremendous waves come thundering ashore when the weather's up, and even on seemingly calm days the tides and currents can be lethal.

Luminous symbol of San Francisco and of California itself, the **Golden Gate Bridge** (linking the Presidio to Marin County, 921 5858, www.goldengatebridge.org) may not be the longest bridge in the world, but it's among the most beautiful and may well be the most famous. Completed in 1937, it's truly immense: the towers are 746 feet (227 metres) high, the roadway runs for 1.75 miles, and enough cable was used in its construction to encircle the globe three times. However, raw statistics can't convey the sense of awe the bridge inspires, and no trip to the city is complete without walking across it. Drive, walk, ride a bike or take a bus to the toll plaza, and head out on foot along the walkway. Once you feel it thrumming beneath your feet, you'll understand even more why people feel such a strong connection to the span.

The person mainly responsible for making the bridge a reality was one Joseph Strauss, a pugnacious Chicagoan engineer. Strauss spent over a decade lobbying to build a bridge, circumventing innumerable financial and legal hurdles in the process. But it was a little-known freelance architect named Irwin F Morrow who eventually designed it, his brilliantly simple pitch selected in preference to Strauss's hideous and complicated cantilever plans.

The bridge's name has nothing to do with its colour, and everything to do with the name of the narrow strait it spans. The Golden Gate strait was named by Captain John Fremont – not after the Gold Rush (Fremont christened the strait in 1846, more than two years before gold was discovered in the California foothills), as many believe, but after the Golden Horn, the geologically similar channel that links the Black Sea to the Mediterranean. The bridge's stroke-of-genius orange colour was also an accident of fate: San Franciscans were so delighted by the reddish tint of the bridge's primer paint that the builders decided to stick with it, rather than paint the whole bridge in the traditional grey or silver. The bridge has been totally repainted only once, a project completed in 1995 using 2,206 gallons (8,350 litres) of primer and topcoat designed to withstand the corrosive salt and fog that continually bathe it, though it's constantly being repaired and touched up by a 55-strong team of ironworkers and painters.

Reputedly five times stronger than it needs to be, the bridge has survived hurricane-force winds, earthquakes and over 65 years of abuse without the slightest sign of damage. Built to flex under pressure, it can sway 21 feet and sag ten feet while withstanding 100mph winds, and can support the weight of bumper-to-bumper traffic across all six lanes at the same time as shoulder-to-shoulder pedestrians covering the walkways. Although large portions of the

The **Golden Gate Bridge**. *See p119.*

Marina were totally devastated by the 1989 earthquake, the bridge survived unscathed. But the virtual certainty of another earthquake of a similar (if not greater) magnitude prompted officials to undertake a seismic retrofitting project. Vehicle tolls were hiked from $3 to $5 to help pay for the reinforcements, which will require around 22.3 million pounds (10.1 million kilogrammes) of structural steel and 24,000 cubic yards (680 cubic metres) of concrete.

While it is a symbol of strength and triumph, the bridge is also a site of tragedy. A 2005 study in the *San Francisco Chronicle* suggested that more than 1,200 people have been seen jumping off the bridge towards the water some 250 feet (75 metres) below them. However, the actual number of Golden Gate suicides is almost certainly a lot higher, as the bodies are swept out to sea by the Gate's intense currents. This grim subject was recently brought back into the spotlight when it was revealed that after having applied for (and received) permission to film the bridge for a movie about its landmark status, documentary filmmaker Eric Steel wound up filming 19 suicides in the process. For years now debate has raged about whether the city should erect a suicide barrier under the bridge, but opponents of the idea fear any such addition would ruin its aesthetic appeal.

The East Bay

Join the students, foodies and football fans just over the bridge.

San Francisco's attractions are so numerous and well known that many visitors miss the opportunities just a half-hour away by either BART or car. They're making a mistake. **Oakland** and **Berkeley**, the best-known East Bay cities, are between them home to fine museums, a world-renowned university, miles of parkland, numerous great restaurants, some decent nightlife, tons of shops and even two pro sports teams. Need another reason to visit? The temperatures in East Bay run an average 10°F higher than at the Golden Gate.

Oakland

Named after its now-vanished oak forests, San Francisco's stepsister was once the western terminus of the 3,000-mile transcontinental railway. The slow bells of passing freight trains are still strangely evocative of the city's working heritage. However, Oakland faded in the bright light of San Francisco's fame and was soon seen as merely the working-class city across the Bay. Going back there to her childhood home only to discover it existed no longer, modernist author Gertrude Stein wrote: 'What was the use of my having come from Oakland… there is no there there.'

Few would concur these days. Oakland is now on the rise, with luxurious hillside mansions and hip shopping districts. It hasn't entirely turned its back on a more rough-and-tumble past; the once-notorious Black Panthers, who made headlines in the 1960s (along with mob-handed, crystal-meth-snorting Hell's Angels), are now the subject of the two-and-a-half-hour **Black Panther Legacy Tour** (1-510 986 0660, www.blackpanthertours. com). If revolutionary isn't your style, the city offers eight **walking tours** on tamer topics (1-510 238 3234, www.oaklandnet.com), covering everything from churches to the spiffed-up 1930s shopping district or Chinatown.

Oakland is easily accessible from San Francisco. It's a short drive over the Bay Bridge (*see p73*), or take BART to City Center/12th Street or 19th Street, both handy for central Oakland. There's also a regular ferry service from the Ferry Building (*see p72*) and Pier 41 in San Francisco to Oakland's Clay Street Ferry Terminal, near Jack London Square (1-510 522 3300, 1-510 749 5972, www.eastbayferry.com).

On the waterfront lies Oakland's main tourist hive: **Jack London Square** (at Broadway and Embarcadero), named after the noted local author who used to carouse at **Heinold's First & Last Chance** (Jack London Square, at Webster Street; *see p171* **Tales of the city**). Head here for the lovely farmers' market, held from 10am to 2pm on Wednesdays (May-Sept only) and Sundays (year-round). Franklin Delano Roosevelt's 'floating White House', the **USS *Potomac***, is docked to the west; its visitors' centre (540 Water Street, 1-510 627 1215, www.uss potomac.org) arranges tours and bay cruises.

Having undergone huge redevelopment, downtown Oakland is now much more inviting than in years gone by. **Chinatown**, which covers the few blocks south of Broadway around 7th, 8th and 9th Streets, is less tourist-focused than its San Francisco counterpart, but still packed with places to eat and shop. Grab a Vietnamese sandwich, dim sum or Thai barbecue while you're there: all found within steps of the corner of 9th and Franklin. Across Broadway, check out **Swan's Marketplace** (907 Washington Street, at 9th Street, 1-510 444 1935), a renovated 1917 brick building filled with food and wine vendors, and the adjoining **Oakland Museum of Children's Art** (538 9th Street, at Washington Street, 1-510 465 8770, www.mocha.org, closed Mon), which has a wealth of hands-on activities for kids.

Your next stop should be **Oakland Museum of California** (*see p125*), a great place to learn about the state; it's also well worth negotiating the rather unpleasant road that separates it from **Lake Merritt**, which used to boast real gondola rides until the concession owner moved away to the canals of Florida. The lakeside **Children's Fairyland** (699 Bellevue Avenue, at Grand Avenue, 1-510 452 2259, www.fairyland.org) is full of scenarios based on classic nursery rhymes, which tots can access with a 'magic key'. Other notable attractions are a short ride away in East Oakland: the **Chabot Space & Science Center** (*see p125*), **Oakland Zoo** (*see p125*) and **Redwood Regional Park** (7867 Redwood Road, 1-510 562 7275, www.ebparks.org), almost three square miles of sprawling, partially wild park, with horseback riding, 150-foot redwoods and hiking trails.

Just as the dot-com boom priced musicians and artists out of San Francisco, Oakland developed strong theatre, dance, ballet and classical-music scenes, and it now boasts one of the West Coast's best jazz venues: **Yoshi's at Jack London Square** (510 Embarcadero West, at Jack London Square; *see p231*). West of Lake Merritt is the **Paramount Theatre** (2025 Broadway, between 20th & 21st Streets; *see p210*), a fabulous art deco movie house built by renowned Bay Area architect Timothy L Pflueger in 1931. Complete with a Mighty Wurlitzer organ and full bar in the lobby, the cinema screens classic movies and is home to the **Oakland East Bay Symphony** (1-510 444 0801, www.oebs.org) and the **Oakland Ballet** (1-510 286 8914, www.oaklandballet.org).

The best corner for shoppers is the stretch of College Avenue in the ritzy Rockridge district to the north (served by its own BART station). As well as high-end home accessories, pricey children's boutiques and French bistros, you'll find the **Market Hall** (5665 College Avenue, 1-510 652 4680, www.rockridgemarkethall.com), which caters to local yuppies with a butcher, wine shop, bakery, cheese shop, florist and café.

Oakland is also home to two professional sports teams, which boast noticeably rowdier fans than those of neighbouring teams across the bay (and, it should be added, better players). During summer, the **Oakland A's** baseball team gets the attention; in autumn and winter, the **Oakland Raiders** football team dominates sports talk in the city (for both, *see pp243-244*). The team's fans – aka 'Raider Nation' – can be identified by their black-and-silver pirate gear and by the pendants that fly from their pickups. There's many an opportunity for local women to become skimpy-pirate-outfit-wearing 'Raiderettes': huge billboards are regularly posted around town advertising upcoming cheerleading tryouts. Both teams play at the rather bleak McAfee Coliseum, which has its own BART station.

Chabot Space & Science Center

10000 Skyline Boulevard (1-510 336 7300/www. chabotspace.org). **Open** 10am-5pm Tue-Thur; 10am-10pm Fri, Sat; 11am-5pm Sun. **Admission** (inc Planetarium) $13; $9 4-12s, seniors. *MegaDome Theater* $8; $7 4-12s, seniors. **Credit** MC, V.
High in the Oakland Hills, the Chabot combines a superbly equipped, state-of-the-art planetarium with an observatory and film theatre; the latter runs 70mm projections of the internal workings of the human body or the cosmos, seen at both the largest scale and the submolecular level. The three telescopes here include a 36in reflector telescope that is housed in the rotating roof observatory; you can look through all three most Fridays and Saturdays, depending on the weather conditions.

Oakland Museum of California

1000 Oak Street, at 10th Street (1-510 238 2200 www.museumca.org). **Open** noon-5pm Wed-Sat; noon-5pm Sun. **Admission** $8; $5 discounts; free under-5s. Free 2nd Sun of mth. **Credit** AmEx, MC, V.
The art collection includes sketches by early explorers and genre pictures from the Gold Rush, along with sculpture, landscapes and Bay Area figurative, pop and funk works. The Hall of California Ecology uses stuffed mammals, reptiles and birds to show the local range of habitats, while the Cowell Hall of California History houses curiosities going back to the Spanish incursion. The collection of priceless Chinese artefacts also includes some stunning pieces. In March, the museum hosts a huge White Elephant Sale, renowned for unbelievable bargains, in a 96,000sq ft warehouse near the Oakland estuary.

Oakland Zoo

9777 Golf Links Road, off I-580 (1-510 632 9525/ www.oaklandzoo.org). **Open** 10am-4pm daily. **Admission** $9; $5.50 2-14s, discounts; free under-2s. **Credit** MC, V.
Situated in Knowland Park, over the last few years the formerly cramped Oakland Zoo has put effort into creating decent-sized naturalistic habitats for its 400-plus species, including lions and tigers, chimps, elephants, tarantulas and snakes, ibis and toucans. There are also the CP Huntington miniature train, a carousel and the Sky Ride, a children's petting zoo and a chair lift that takes you over the bison and elk on the 'North American Range'.

Berkeley

Berkeley worked hard to earn reputations for its avant-garde arts, leftist politics and marvellous food. Over the decades, it's shown proper

Oakland Zoo. Bless.

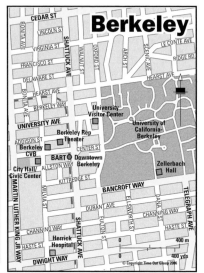

Berkeley

with details of ongoing temporary exhibits, online at www.berkeley.edu/libraries/. However, at the head of the pack are the **Berkeley Art Museum** (*see p128*) and, across the street, the **Pacific Film Archive** (2575 Bancroft Way, between Telegraph Avenue & Bowditch Street; *see p210*). On the peak above the campus, but still run by the university, is the **Lawrence Hall of Science** (*see p128*), a fascinating science museum aimed at children, with the additional attraction of commanding views over the entire Bay Area.

For more information on Cal, drop in on the campus **Visitors' Center** (University Hall, 2200 University Avenue, at Oxford Street, 1-510 642 5215, www.berkeley.edu/visitors) for maps and information. If you've got time, take one of the free 90-minute campus tours, which leave from the Visitors' Center at 10am from Monday to Saturday and at 1pm on Sunday. Bookings are only required for groups of ten or more.

Beyond the college

Even outside the campus, a liberal collegiate vibe dominates Berkeley. Spiking southwards from the university, **Telegraph Avenue** provides a home for street-vendor jewellery, crafts stands, clothes shops and brilliant bookstores. In the latter category, the two essential stops are **Moe's** (No.2476, between Dwight Way & Haste Street; *see p179*) and **Cody's Books** (No.2454, at Haste Street; *see p179*), for a half-century one of the most staunchly independent bookstores in the US and now one of the more successful. Further south are two huge record stores: **Rasputin** (No.2401, at Channing Way; *see p194*) and the superior **Amoeba Records** (No.2455, at Haste Street; *see p193*). Cafés line the university's southern limit, among them **Café Strada** (2300 College Avenue, at Bancroft Way, 1-510 843 5282) and **Café Milano** (2522 Bancroft

dedication to maintaining all three. It remains a fascinating and wonderfully contradictory place, where gourmet eating is accepted as a form of radical liberalism and Noam Chomsky always attracts standing-room-only crowds. Relying on public transport? Downtown Berkeley BART station is convenient for all attractions.

University of California

To suggest that Berkeley is slightly in thrall to its university is to hint that San Francisco gets a little foggy from time to time – the **University of California** campus here, known locally just as 'Cal', is the straw that stirs the Berkeley drink, and it has lent the place a countrywide reputation for its erudite, progressive liberalism. The university was the birthplace of America's youth revolution 30 years ago, with student protests against campus rules and the Vietnam War inspiring a nation of youthful rebels. For more on those heady days, check out Mark Kitchell's documentary *Berkeley in the '60s*.

It's very easy to idle away a few hours just wandering the campus. However, it's worth heading first to the **Sather Tower**: for great views of the campus and the surrounding area, take the lift to the top (open 10am-4pm Mon-Fri). Elsewhere on the campus sit museums dedicated to art, anthropology, palaeontology and plenty of other disciplines. Some operate set hours, while others are open by appointment only; there's a list of all the collections, along

Collegiate life dominates **Berkeley**.

Way, at Telegraph Avenue, 1-510 644 3100). At weekends, students and others loiter around on the corner of Ashby Avenue and Martin Luther King Jr Way for the **Berkeley Flea Market**.

North-west of campus sits the culinary hot zone known as the **Gourmet Ghetto**, which runs along Shattuck Avenue between Delaware and Rose Streets. It's more popular with professors and tutors than with their students, on the whole, but the restaurants are still very egalitarian. The star of the show is undeniably **Chez Panisse** (No.1517, between Cedar & Vine Streets; *see p159*), set up back in the 1970s by Alice Waters, the elfin leader of the revolution in Californian cuisine. It's hardly the only option, though. Next door is **César** (No.1515; *see p159*), which serves an enticing array of cultured tapas; more or less opposite is **Cheese Board Pizza** (No.1512, 1-510 549 3055, http://cheeseboardcollective.coop), an employee-owned collective that offers a single type of vegetarian pizza to crowds that

inevitably begin to form before opening time each evening. Two doors down, the original **Cheese Board** (No.1504, 1-510 549 3183) sells a plethora of cheese. For coffee, try the original **Peet's** (2124 Vine Street, at Walnut Street, 1-510 841 0564, www.peets.com). Opened in 1966, this branch was where the founder of Starbucks got his training. Now you know who to blame.

Other areas of Berkeley hold different fascinations. Trendy **4th Street**, between Hearst Avenue and Virginia Street, near the waterfront, is home to numerous exclusive and stylish shops. Traditionalists can sample the great fish at century-old **Spenger's** (1919 4th Street, at University Avenue, 1-510 845 7771) and **Brennan's** (4th Street & University Avenue, 1-510 841 0960), a cavernous, old-fashioned Irish pub and cafeteria.

Residential South Berkeley, meanwhile, has many California Craftsman-style homes, plus the **Judah L Magnes Museum** (2911 Russell Street, between Claremont & College

Sightseeing

Statues The Football Players

Tucked into a small wooded dale behind one of the Life Sciences Buildings on the UC Berkeley campus sits *The Football Players*, a statue by deaf 19th-century sculptor Douglas Tilden. When it was erected over a century ago, the sculpture simply commemorated Cal's triumph over cross-Bay sporting rival Stanford. However, as gay men and lesbians on campus gained a stronger voice in the 1970s, the sculpture's blatant homoerotic overtones led it to become known by many simply as the 'gay statue'.

Created while Tilden, who was American, was studying art in Paris, the statue depicts two muscular yet sensitive-looking, tousled-haired French models, immortalised in bronze. One of the sportsmen, decked out in what looks more like an extremely skimpy version of British rugby gear than a gridiron uniform, tenderly kneels to bandage the leg of his partner; the injured man elegantly leans on his teammate for support, while delicately lifting his knee over the man's shoulder.

It seems Tilden, though he was married to a woman, had a thing for sculpting almost-nude young men. For another example, check out *The Mechanics Monument* on Market Street back in San Francisco. The statue portrays a trio of impressively muscled young men, each of them barely clad in a loincloth, clambering over a giant printing press.

Avenues, 1-510 549 6950, www.magnes.org),
a large mansion that bursts at the seams
with Jewish history and culture.

Many people visit the area just for its hills.
The lovely and magnificently wild **Tilden
Regional Park** (1-510 562 7275) offers hiking,
nature trails and pony rides, a farm and a
steam train. Those who manage the trek up
to **Inspiration Point** or **Wildcat Peak** are
rewarded with 180° views. For a more leisurely
take on nature, the **UC Berkeley Botanical
Garden** (200 Centennial Drive, 1-510 643 2755,
http://botanicalgarden.berkeley.edu), below
Tilden Park, has cacti, orchids and an
abundance of native California flora.

Berkeley Art Museum

*2626 Bancroft Way, at Telegraph Avenue (1-510
642 0808/www.bampfa.berkeley.edu).* **Open** 11am-
5pm Wed, Fri-Sun; 11am-7pm Thur. **Admission**
$10; $5 discounts; free under-12s. Free 1st Thur of
mth. **Credit** AmEx, DC, MC, V.
Opened in 1970, this dramatic exhibition space is
arranged in terraces so visitors can see the works
from various vantage points. The collection's
strength is 20th-century art, be it sculpture, painting, photography or conceptual work, and there's
also a good collection of Asian pieces. Ten galleries
and a bookstore occupy the upper level, while a
sculpture garden and café share the lower floor.

Lawrence Hall of Science

*Centennial Drive, nr Grizzly Peak Boulevard (1-510
642 5132/www.lhs.berkeley.edu).* **Open** 10am-5pm
daily. **Admission** $9.50; $5.50-$7.50 discounts; free
under-3s. **Credit** Disc, MC, V.
Perched on the hills facing the Bay, this kids' science
museum has computers to explore the inside of your
brain, a Young Explorers Area and a huge DNA
model to scramble over. Fascinating temporary
exhibits – robotic dinosaurs to kapla blocks – appeal
to all ages. It's also a great spot for daytime views
and evening stargazing. Don't miss the telescope
and wind-driven organ pipes at the back.

North of Berkeley

Nestled into Berkeley's north side, the tiny city
of **Albany** may now be famous for excellent
schools and a tidy Downtown, but it was once
renowned for seedy strip joints along San Pablo
Avenue. The clubs have vanished, but the street
retains some kick-ass watering holes – check
out the **Hotsy Totsy** (No.601, at Garfield
Avenue, 1-510 524 1661), **Club Mallard**
(No.752, between Portland & Washington
Avenues; *see p172*) or the **Ivy Room** (No.858,
at Solano Avenue, 1-510 524 9299), the latter
home to a redoubtable roots jukebox.

Albany Mudflats, between the bay shore
and Buchanan Street, is a paradise for wading
birds. Further north, however, you enter an

Telegraph Avenue in Berkeley.

industrial zone. **Richmond**'s shipbuilding
industry is long gone, and the town is now
sustained by an oil refinery: the route into
Marin County via the Richmond–San Rafael
Bridge passes through it. To the north-east
are the Carquinez Straits and **Rodeo**, a tiny
town dwarfed by the neighbouring oil refinery.

The former C&H Sugar company town
Crockett has kept firm hold of the charms
of small-town life – its population hovers
at about 3,000 people – despite being only
a 15-minute drive north of Berkeley. The town
nestles in the hillside over the recently built
Alfred Zampa Memorial Bridge, the first
large suspension bridge built in the US since
1964. It's the gateway to Wine Country (*see
pp264-270*), and is also the first major bridge
to have been named after a blue-collar worker.
Al Zampa worked on all the major Bay bridges,
including the one which stood on this site,
before his namesake bridge.

From here, signs mark a meandering road
east to tiny **Port Costa**, once thriving as a
gateway town for the Sacramento River delta.
There's little to see other than passing boats,
the Warehouse Café and gallery-cum-shop
Theatre of Dreams (11 Canyon Lake Drive,
1-510 787 2164), where Wendy Addison
concocts modern-day Victoriana from old paper
dolls, sheet music, bird's nests and glitter.

Eat, Drink, Shop

Miss Millie's. *See p152.*

YOU KNOW WHO YOU ARE.

Hard Rock CAFE

SAN FRANCISCO • PIER 39 - BLDG. Q-1
BEACH STREET & THE EMBARCADERO
PHONE: 415-956-2013 • HARDROCK.COM

©2005 Hard Rock Cafe International, Inc. All rights reserved.

Restaurants & Cafés

Eat the globe without leaving the city.

San Francisco's reputation for food is now well established, but also well earned. The local culinary landscape is so various and intriguing that even casual endeavours, such as seeking out the perfect bowl of udon noodles, can fast become a life's mission. Conversations that begin as idle discussions about where to find the best Mexican food in town soon escalate towards fisticuffs, and that's before you've even started mulling over the most perfect pad Thai, the finest fries or the choicest crab cakes.

For all the talk of young chefs and pioneering dishes, San Francisco is old-fashioned at heart. The restaurants that continue to thrive in the face of a fickle and spoilt-for-choice public are those serving reliable no-nonsense food with straight-ahead preparations. That's not to deny trails worth trekking are blazed; they are. Still, the days of 'inventing' new ways of eating may be gone. That food pilgrims still make their way to **Chez Panisse** (*see p159*), where Alice Waters established California cuisine, suggests such seismic shifts occur only rarely.

The feeling persists that chefs who make it here can make it anywhere. Many have done so, with major cities throughout the US – notably Las Vegas – boasting of cooks who earned their stripes in San Francisco kitchens. Yet big names such as Nancy Oakes (**Boulevard**; *see p135*) and Gary Danko (**Gary Danko**; *see p146*) prefer to fashion their world-class recipes by staying close to the region's ingredients. The mild weather and rich soil of the Bay Area create great growing conditions for foods of all kinds, and bring excellent fish and meat into easy reach. Lucky chefs, sure, but the dining public are the really fortunate ones. The rich panoply of the world's cuisine is here for them to sample; the intrepid diner can try fare from all points round the globe.

The weekend brings the other essential aspect of SF eating into its own. Few cities in the world are as serious about café culture as this one. As in Paris or Prague, the café here is akin to a church, visited religiously and advocated with a rigour usually saved for theological controversy. In truth, locals show little regard for the day of

▶ ❶ Purple numbers given in this chapter correspond to the location of each restaurant on the street maps. See pp312-319.

The best Restaurants

For a hearty breakfast
Chloe's Café (*see p151*); Dottie's True Blue Café (*see p137*); Kate's Kitchen (*see p152*).

For a budget lunch
Chow (*see p154*); J's Pots of Soul (*see p154*); Papalote (*see p150*); Yank Sing (*see p136*).

For a mid-afternoon coffee
Café Abir (*see p153*); Caffe Roma (*see p144*); Ritual Roasters (*see p149*).

For a blowout dinner
Fleur de Lys (*see p142*); Gary Danko (*see p145*); Michael Mina (*see p132*); Slanted Door (*see p136*);

For the late-night munchies
Bob's Donut Shop (*see p142*); Tart to Tart (*see p156*).

the week or even the hour of the day, being found lounging about the jostle of tables and chairs at all times, enviably careless of whatever the hell else it is they're meant to be doing. Buzzing about the new baby with their fellow mums, reading the news or lamenting the sad state of local politics, café denizens come in as many shapes and sizes as their cafés.

INFORMATION
This restaurant section is organised first by neighbourhood (the areas follow those found in our Sightseeing chapters) and then by cuisine. The cuisine categories are, by necessity, quite broad. 'American', for example, includes both new-wave Californian eateries and old-school grills, while 'Asian' covers such options as Japanese, Chinese, Thai, Vietnamese, Korean and Asian-fusion. The 'Cafés' designation is perhaps the most contentious: it covers places where you'd feel happy stopping in just for a pastry and a coffee, though many also serve full meals. When you're not in a sweetcakes mood, the city's taquerias (*see p150* **The Latin quarter**) are cheap and cheerful.

Downtown

Union Square & around

Many posh eateries around Union Square have reputations far above their deserts. **Farallon** (450 Post Street, between Powell & Mason Streets, 956 6969, www.farallonrestaurant.com) and **Postrio** (545 Post Street, between Taylor & Mason Streets, 776 7825, www.postrio.com) have cachet, but the food doesn't always match the hype, and it can come with a hefty price tab. Eating at lunchtime is usually better value.

Cafés, delis & diners

Although made over into a bistro, the **Café de la Presse** (*see below*) still serves as a café too.

Caffe Kuleto's

Villa Florence Hotel, 221 Powell Street, at Geary Street (397 7720/www.kuletos.com). BART & Metro to Powell/bus 2, 3, 4, 15, 30, 38, 45, 76 & Market Street routes/cable car Powell-Hyde or Powell-Mason. **Open** 7am-11pm Mon-Fri; 8am-11pm Sat, Sun. **Main courses** $5-$15. **Credit** AmEx, DC, Disc, MC, V. **Map** p315 M6 ❶
Located near the shops of Union Square, this is a nice, sophisticated spot for recharging the shopping batteries. An annex of the popular Kuleto restaurant, the café features fresh-prepared Italian pastries, as well as fresh juices and the full array of coffees. For lunch, choose from pizza by the slice, panini, antipasti and rich desserts.

French

Café Claude

7 Claude Lane, off Sutter & Bush Streets, between Kearny Street & Grant Avenue (392 3515/www. cafeclaude.com). Bus 2, 3, 4, 15, 30, 38, 45, 76. **Open** 11.30am-10.30pm Mon-Sat; 5.30-10.30pm Sun. **Main courses** *Lunch* $7-$13. *Dinner* $7-$27. **Credit** AmEx, DC, Disc, MC, V. **Map** p315 M5 ❷
Owner Stephen Decker purchased Le Barbizon café in Paris and shipped it to San Francisco one piece at a time. The result, set in an alleyway and resplendent with French style and attitude, is as close to a true French café as can be found in America. Signature dishes include salad niçoise and steak tartare. Live jazz is played at the weekend.

Café de la Presse

352 Grant Avenue, at Bush Street (398 2680/www. cafedelapresse.com). Bus 2, 3, 4, 15, 30, 38, 45, 76. **Open** 7am-10pm daily. **Main courses** $12-$20. **Credit** AmEx, DC, Disc, MC, V. **Map** p315 M5 ❸
Recently given a splendid refurbishment, this former café is now a full-service bistro, serving classic French-inspired fare along with an assortment of café-style choices so as not to completely alienate its

established café clientele. Located close to the Chinatown Gateway, the café still stocks a bevy of foreign newspapers and magazines.

Fifth Floor

Hotel Palomar, 12 4th Street, at Market Street (348 1555/www.hotelpalomar.com). BART & Metro to Powell/bus 27, 30, 45 & Market Street routes/cable car Powell-Hyde or Powell-Mason. **Open** 7-10am, 5.30-9.30pm Mon-Thur; 7-10am, 5.30-10.30pm Fri; 8-11am, 5.30-10pm Sat; 8-11am Sun. **Main courses** $30-$45. **Credit** AmEx, DC, Disc, MC, V. **Map** p315 M6 ❹
One of the city's great dining experiences: an idyllic blend of romance and chic, exemplified by the zebra-print rug beneath your feet as you stroll to your table. Chef Melissa Perello offers a daily changing menu made with ingredients she selects herself. Preparations are unfussy, leaving the ingredients as the stars. Service is flawless and unobtrusive, the wine list is amazing, and the desserts are beautiful.

Masa's

648 Bush Street, between Stockton & Powell Streets (989 7154). Bus 2, 3, 4, 27, 38, 76/cable car Powell-Hyde or Powell-Mason. **Open** 5.30-9.30pm Tue-Sat. **Main courses** *Set menu* $79/4 courses; $75-$90/ 6 courses; $120/9 courses. **Credit** AmEx, DC, Disc, MC, V. **Map** p315 M5 ❺
Masa's was the first notable restaurant to combine SF haute cuisine with a French dining aesthetic. Current chef Gregory Short has maintained the high level of care taken by his predecessors, ensuring the Masa's experience remains one worth having and paying for. His artful presentations of French-inspired fare are always mouth-watering, often playful.

International

Michael Mina

Westin-St Francis Hotel, 335 Powell Street, at Geary Street (397 9222/www.michaelmina.net). BART & Metro to Powell/bus 2, 3, 4, 15, 30, 38, 45, 76 & Market Street routes/cable car Powell-Hyde or Powell-Mason. **Open** 5.30-10pm Mon-Sat; 5.30-9.30pm Sun. **Main courses** *Set menus* $88/ 3 courses; $135/7 courses. **Credit** AmEx, DC, Disc, MC, V. **Map** p315 M5 ❻
This spare-no-expense room introduced Union Square to famed chef Mina, who micromanaged the look of the restaurant much like he does his artistic food. Meals are offered in a three-course menu, each with three preparations of a theme, or as a seven-course tasting menu. It can be as confounding as it is dazzling, and some patrons seem overawed, but mostly Mina impresses. Quality special-occasion dining. **Photo** *p133.*

Italian & pizza

Scala's

Sir Francis Drake Hotel, 432 Powell Street, between Post & Sutter Streets (395 8555/ www.scalasbistro.com). Bus 30, 45/cable car

Powell-Hyde or Powell-Mason. **Open** 8am-midnight daily. **Main courses** $12-$25. **Credit** AmEx, DC, MC, V. **Map** p315 M5 ❼
This bustling bistro is frequented by tourists staying in Union Square and locals attracted by robust, reasonably priced, Med food. Reliable choices range from the daily risotto to fresh-made pasta. The signature 'earth and surf', a melange of calamari, rock shrimp, onion, fennel and green beans, is a favourite. The wine list is well chosen from nearby regions with occasional surprises from beyond the borders.

Latin American

Colibrí Mexican Bistro
438 Geary Street, between Taylor & Mason Streets (440 2737/www.colibrimexicanbistro.com). Bus 2, 3, 4, 27, 38, 76/cable car Powell-Hyde or Powell-Mason. **Open** 11.30am-10pm Mon; 11.30am-11pm Tue-Thur; 11.30am-midnight Fri; 10am-midnight Sat; 10am-10pm Sun. **Main courses** $10-$16. **Credit** AmEx, MC, V. **Map** p314 L5 ❽
A refreshing addition to the area, serving unpretentious, delicious and atypical Mexican fare. Dishes are presented tapas-style, with unfamiliar regional flavours. The selection includes brilliant tortilla soup, tamarind-sautéed shrimp served with corn cakes, and a fire-roasted *chile relleno* that will have you raving almost before you put down your fork.

Handsome **Michael Mina**. *See p132.*

Financial District

American

Sam's Grill
374 Bush Street, between Montgomery & Kearny Streets (421 0594). Bus 15, 45, 76. **Open** 11am-9pm Mon-Fri. **Main courses** $10-$35. **Credit** AmEx, DC, Disc, MC, V. **Map** p315 M5 ❾
Sam's has been satisfying San Franciscan appetites for 130 years. The restaurant holds fast to history, with a friendly atmosphere and a charming dining room panelled in dark wood and punctuated by bright-white tablecloths. The American menu is largely driven by seafood, but it's worth opting for such local specialities as the wonderful Hangtown Fry. At lunch, don't pass on the burgers.

Fish & seafood

Aqua
252 California Street, between Battery & Front Streets (956 9662/www.aqua-sf.com). Bus 1, 10, 12, 15, 41/cable car California. **Open** 11.30am-2pm, 5.30-10.30pm Mon-Thur; 11.30am-2pm, 5.30-11pm Fri; 5.30-11pm Sat; 5.30-9.30pm Sun. **Main courses** Lunch $15-$25. *Set dinner menus* $68/3 courses; $65-$95/7 courses. **Credit** AmEx, DC, Disc, MC, V. **Map** p315 N4 ❿
This sleek, handsomely appointed space is enlivened by floral arrangements and good-looking servers. Chef Laurent Manrique took over recently and injected new life into a seafood restaurant that was once without peer. The seasonal menu includes local and imported fish, prepared with brilliant flourishes. The wine list has won awards; service is exemplary.

French

Jeanty at Jack's
615 Sacramento Street, at Montgomery Street (693 0941/www.jeantyatjacks.com). Bus 1, 10, 12, 15, 41/cable car California. **Open** 11.30am-10.30pm Mon-Fri; 5-10.30pm Sat, Sun. **Main courses** $10-$28. **Credit** AmEx, MC, V. **Map** p315 M4 ⓫
The 'Jack's' of the name is a brasserie that opened in 1864; the 'Jeanty' is chef Philippe, who's consolidated his French-won reputation over the last eight years by directing proceedings at his excellent bistro in the Napa Valley town of Yountville. The two have combined to create one of the city's better and more authentic French restaurants. Don't leave without trying the steak tartare.

Plouf
40 Belden Place, between Bush & Pine Streets (986 6491/www.ploufsf.com). Bus 15, 45, 76. **Open** 11.30am-3pm, 5.30-10pm Mon-Thur; 11am-3pm, 5.30-11pm Fri; 5.30-11pm Sat. **Main courses** $14-$25. **Credit** AmEx, MC, V. **Map** p315 M5 ⓬
Set in an alleyway beneath the towers of the Financial District, this charming, wildly chaotic restaurant is named after the French word for the sound a pebble makes when dropped into water. No dining experience here is complete without a bucket

After a fashion

San Francisco likes its trends. Indeed, few major trends of any kind – from fashion to music to corporate management – have failed to make it here, to be tried, embraced and then discarded like a used bottle of ion-infused spring water. Food is no exception. At the forefront of many culinary trends, the town has been at the tail-end of several more.

Widespread appreciation of fine food gained its footing here in the 1970s, when Alice Waters of Berkeley's **Chez Panisse** (*see p159*) became famous for her 'California cuisine'. In essence, Waters combined the use of local seasonal ingredients and traditional recipes with cross-cultural influences. The trend spread like wildfire; from fine French to snappy seafood, most chefs prepared their signature dishes with some influence from California cuisine.

Mixing fresh ingredients and traditional recipes soon progressed into the mixing of traditional recipes from different regions. 'Fusion' grew fast and furious during the go-go 1980s, fuelled by a mind-boggling assortment of East-meets-West concept restaurants. Combining Japanese and Italian cuisine may not have been the best food, but that didn't stop people from trying it. In some instances, fusion worked: witness the abundance of French-Thai and Cal-Asian restaurants still thriving. But the public grew quickly disenchanted with food so conceptual it required lengthy explanations.

Restaurants began moving back to the basics, and the con-fusion food of the early 1990s was supplanted by comfort eating at the beginning of the new millennium, as chefs began adding down-home classics – fried chicken, mashed potatoes, macaroni cheese – to their menus. Granted, they were given gourmet touches, but they still felt like home. And in the crazy days of the dot-com boom, home is where many longed to be.

As good as many of these boom-era restaurants were, most were also wildly pricey. When the bottom fell out of the economy, hitting San Francisco on the perpendicular, big-ticket dining drained away. The rooms that survived often did so only by revamping their strategy. Plate-sized steaks gave way to petite portions and small plates became the fashion. Created in the tradition of tapas, the trend wasn't limited to Spanish cuisine: small plates were globally influenced and universally embraced. French, Asian, American: all cuisine types were given the small-plate treatment.

Despite everything, diners remain loyal to food to which they can relate. Nuevo Latino, artisan ingredients and slow food have all had their moment, but San Francisco is no town for snake-oil salesmen. If a trend is good, it lasts; if not… well, the public can be unforgiving. That's probably why comfort is still on the menu, and also doubtless why California cuisine is still so popular. It continues to be a source of inspiration for chefs whose ideas now take additional inspiration from regions far and wide. Maybe the cycle has come all the way round to the beginning.

of the speciality steamed mussels, but the ever-changing array of fish is also excellent. The fish and chips is a definite winner.

International

Kokkari Estiatorio

200 Jackson Street, at Front Street (981 0983/ www.kokkari.com). Bus 1, 10, 12, 41. **Open** 11.30am-10pm Mon-Thur; 11.30am-11pm Fri; 5-11pm Sat. **Main courses** $15-$35. **Credit** AmEx, DC, Disc, MC, V. **Map** p315 N4 ⑬

Kokkari serves what it describes as 'Hellenic cuisine'. It's quite outstanding, though highly priced, and unlike what most people think of when it comes to Greek food. The *pikilia*, an appetiser plate featuring three traditional Greek dips with fresh pittas, is a good place to start. For mains, grilled lamb chops, pan-roasted halibut steaks and moussaka stand out.

The Embarcadero

American

Americano

Hotel Vitale, 8 Mission Street, at the Embarcadero (278 3777/www.hotelvitale.com/dining). BART & Metro to Montgomery/bus 2, 3, 4, 31 & Market Street routes. **Open** 6.30-10.30am, 11.30am-2.30pm, 5.30-10pm Mon-Thur; 6.30-10.30am, 11.30am-2.30pm, 5.30-11pm Fri; 7.30am-3pm, 5.30-11pm Sat; 7.30am-3pm, 5.30-10pm Sun. **Main courses** $11-$28. **Credit** AmEx, DC, Disc, MC, V. **Map** p315 O4 ⑭

This stylish restaurant in the new Hotel Vitale (*see p48*) offers seasonally fresh, Italian-inspired food, served with Californian flair. Chef Paul Arenstam has a deft touch, allowing the ingredients to work. Try grilled panini at lunch, Sonoma duck breast with prunes at dinner, and own-made gelato for dessert.

Eat, Drink, Shop

Boulevard

*1 Mission Street, at Steuart Street (543 6084/
www.boulevardrestaurant.com). BART & Metro to
Montgomery/bus 2, 3, 4, 31 & Market Street routes.*
Open 11.30am-2pm, 5.30-10pm Mon-Thur; 11.30am-
2pm, 5.30-10.30pm Fri; 5.30-10.30pm Sat; 5.30-10pm
Sun. **Main courses** *Lunch* $18-$25. *Dinner* $28-$39.
Credit AmEx, DC, Disc, MC, V. **Map** p315 O4 ⓯
Since 1993 this handsome room has been one of San
Francisco's most consistently reliable restaurants:
from service to cooking, there's seldom a misstep.
Always packed, it attracts locals and visitors with
waterfront views and hearty food. Self-taught chef
Nancy Oakes specialises in elaborate New American
dishes: pork chops, steaks and risottos are always
on offer. Wood-roasted dishes are another strength.

Fog City Diner

*1300 Battery Street, at Greenwich Street (982
2000/www.fogcitydiner.com). Metro F to Lombard
& Embarcadero/bus 10.* **Open** 11am-10pm Mon-
Thur; 11am-11pm Fri; 10.30am-11pm Sat; 10.30am-
9pm Sun. **Main courses** $8-$29. **Credit** AmEx,
MC, V. **Map** p315 N2 ⓰
From outside, this looks like a generic, if very handsome, restoration of a classic 1950s diner. Inside, the
decor is swisher, and the menu lurches from burgers and steaks to crab cakes and grilled salmon. The
menu's too long for its own good, and prices are
higher than they should be, but you can eat well.

Frisson

*244 Jackson Street, between Battery & Front Streets
(956 3004/www.frissonsf.com). Bus 1, 10, 12, 41.*
Open 6-11pm Mon-Wed, Sun; 6pm-midnight Thur-
Sat. **Main courses** $18-$26. **Credit** AmEx, DC,
Disc, MC, V. **Map** p315 N4 ⓱
Be prepared to people-watch and to be watched by
people: this is a social showcase, from its disarm-
ingly modern decor to the playful interpretations of
French-Californian cuisine. There is a tendency here,
both in the kitchen and among the cooler-than-you
clientele, to overdo things, but staples such as slow-
cooked chicken are outstanding. There's a good
selection of wines by the glass.

Globe Restaurant

*290 Pacific Avenue, at Battery Street (391 4132).
Bus 1, 10, 12, 41.* **Open** 11.30am-1am Mon-Fri;
6pm-1am Sat; 6pm-midnight Sun. **Main courses**
$12-$27. **Credit** AmEx, MC, V. **Map** p315 N3 ⓲
Still one of the best-kept secrets in the area, this
dining room has an exposed-brick look that imparts
an urban, New York feel to the place. A popular
hangout for off-duty chefs, the menu offers such
standards as wood-oven pizzas and grilled salmon,
prepared with fresh ingredients and without complications. The Globe is best known for innovative
meat dishes: try the T-bone steak for two.

Market Bar

*1 Ferry Building, at the Embarcadero (434
1100/www.marketbar.com). BART & Metro to
Montgomery/bus 1, 9, 14, 31 & Market Street*
routes. **Open** 11.30am-10pm Mon-Thur; 11.30am-
11pm Fri; 9am-10pm Sat, Sun. **Main courses** $10-
$25. **Credit** AmEx, DC, MC, V. **Map** p315 O4 ⓳
This casual brasserie features hearty California cuisine and some Italian fare. The bustling room, with
its dark wood panels, is well suited to the excellent
seafood: soul-warming bouillabaisse and *cioppino*.
Dinner begins with fresh bread, plopped directly on
the paper tablecloths; it typically finishes with a
lovely dessert, such as chocolate-croissant pudding.

Taylor's Refresher

*1 Ferry Building, at the Embarcadero (1-866 328
3663/www.taylorsrefresher.com). BART & Metro to
Montgomery/bus 1, 9, 14, 31 & Market Street
routes.* **Open** *Summer* 10.30am-9pm daily. *Other
times* 10.30am-8pm daily. **Main courses** $3-$14.
Credit AmEx, MC, V. **Map** p315 O4 ⓴
A little over 50 years after the original opened its
drive-thru window in the Napa Valley, the second
branch of Taylor's Refresher set up shop in the Ferry
Building. The decor at the diner is rather more modern than at the still-extant original, and the menu a
little posher in spots (ahi tuna burger, anyone?).
However, the basics – burgers, fries, malts and
shakes – remain absolutely peerless.

Asian

Butterfly

*Pier 33, at Bay Street (864 8999/www.butterflysf.
com). Metro F to Bay & the Embarcadero/bus 10,
15.* **Open** 11.30am-3pm, 5-10pm Mon-Fri; 11am-3pm,
5-10pm Sat, Sun. **Main courses** $9-$39. **Credit**
AmEx, Disc, MC, V. **Map** p315 M2 ㉑
Although chef-owner Robert Lam's pan-Asian
cuisine is good, it's nearly incidental to the stylish
surroundings: beautiful views of the Bay without
and the beautiful crowd within. Culinary highlights
include the duck confit spring roll appetiser and the
'ponzu'-grilled hanger steak main.

Longlife Noodle Company

*139 Steuart Street, at Mission Street (281 3818).
BART & Metro to Montgomery/bus 2, 3, 4, 31 &
Market Street routes.* **Open** 11am-3pm Mon-Fri.
Main courses $4-$8. **Credit** MC, V. **Map** p315 O4 ㉒
The quality of food at this modern noodle joint, the
first in a mini-chain that extends to the Metreon
Center, Berkeley and beyond, can be unreliable, and
dish names will have purists wincing. But when the
food is good, it's good enough, and the prices make
it a decent option if you're just after a quick bite.

Ozumo

*161 Steuart Street, at Mission Street (882 1333/
www.ozumo.com). BART & Metro to Montgomery/
bus 2, 3, 4, 31 & Market Street routes.* **Open**
11.30am-midnight Mon-Fri; 5.30pm-midnight Sat, Sun.
Main courses $12-$38. *Sushi omakase* from $100.
Credit AmEx, DC, Disc, MC, V. **Map** p315 O4 ㉓
There aren't enough 'e's in sleek to describe this
beautiful contemporary Japanese restaurant, where
some 6,000sq ft (560sq m) of design panache swaddle

Eat, Drink, Shop

an equally chic crowd. The front area holds a bar and lounge serving an exhaustive menu of sakes and rare teas. Amble past the robata grill – the meat, fish and vegetables from the robata menu are the real attractions – and you'll come to an enormous main dining room, with sushi bar and Bay Bridge views.

Slanted Door

1 Ferry Building, at Embarcadero (861 8032/www. slanteddoor.com). BART & Metro to Montgomery/ bus 1, 9, 14, 31 & Market Street routes. **Open** 11am-2.30pm, 5.30-10pm Mon-Thur, Sun; 11am-2.30pm, 5.30-10.30pm Fri, Sat. **Main courses** $8-$27. **Credit** AmEx, MC, V. **Map** p315 O4 ㉔

Chef Charles Phan has, with great success, moved his white-hot restaurant to a corner of the Ferry Building. It's stylish, with sleek lines and great views of the Bay, but the attraction remains Phan's incredible, inventive Vietnamese-inspired food. There isn't a bad choice on the menu, though the shaking beef, the spicy short ribs and the shrimp-and-crab spring rolls continue to stand out. A must.

Yank Sing

Rincon Center, 101 Spear Street, at Mission Street (957 9300/www.yanksing.com). BART & Metro to Montgomery/bus 2, 3, 4, 31 & Market Street routes. **Open** 11am-3pm Mon-Fri; 10am-4pm Sat, Sun. **Main courses** *Dim sum* $3-$8. **Credit** AmEx, DC, MC, V. **Map** p315 O4 ㉕

The purveyors of some of the finest dim sum in town. The quality of the food explains how the place manages to thrive in the corner of a massive office complex. Non-English-speaking waitresses roll out an endless array of steaming dumplings, filled with everything from pork to vegetables; an on-the-go business crowd snaps them up with speed.

Other locations: 49 Stevenson Street, Financial District (541 4949).

International

Café de Stijl

1 Union Street, at Front Street (291 0808). Metro F to Green & the Embarcadero/bus 10. **Open** 7am-5pm Mon-Fri; 8.30am-2.30pm Sat. **Main courses** $7-$10. **Credit** AmEx, Disc, MC, V. **Map** p315 N3 ㉖

Named after the 20th-century Dutch art movement, de Stijl is a lively café with sleek, architecturally mindful decor and a wide-ranging menu. Middle Eastern dishes are a speciality, as is Tuscan-style roast chicken and the bowl-sized lattes.

The Tenderloin

Asian

Asia de Cuba

Clift Hotel, 495 Geary Street, at Taylor Street (929 2300/www.clifthotel.com). Bus 2, 3, 4, 27, 38, 76/cable car Powell-Hyde or Powell-Mason. **Open** 7am-2.30pm, 5.30-10.30pm Mon-Wed, Sun; 7am-2.30pm, 5.30pm-midnight Thur-Sat. **Main courses** $23-$69. **Credit** AmEx, DC, MC, V. **Map** p314 L6 ㉗

Ever popular, especially with out-of-towners, this swishy Starck-designed room at the Clift (*see p48*) is worth popping into just to see what all the fuss is about. The menu is good for groups, with many dishes (including the excellent paella) designed to be shared. Rich, sweet sauces characterise most items on the intensely flavoured Chino-Latino menu. Also here is the Redwood Room bar (*see p161*).

Incredible Vietnamese food at **Slanted Door**.

Eat, Drink, Shop

Breakfast in America: **Dottie's True Blue Café**.

Cafés, delis & diners

Dottie's True Blue Café

522 Jones Street, at O'Farrell Street (885 2767).
Bus 2, 3, 4, 27, 38, 76. **Open** 7.30am-3pm Mon,
Wed-Sun. **Credit** Disc, MC, V. **Main courses**
$6-$12. **Map** p314 L6 ㉘

You may have to wait a little to be seated for your
breakfast: maybe huevos rancheros, perhaps pancakes, possibly a funky omelette or huge scramble
of cheese and veg. However, when it arrives, it may
well be one of the best breakfasts you've ever tasted.
A quintessential piece of West Coast Americana.

International

Cortez Restaurant & Bar

*550 Geary Street, between Taylor & Jones Streets
(292 6360/www.cortezrestaurant.com). Bus 2, 3,
4, 27, 38, 76.* **Open** 5.30-10.30pm daily. **Main
courses** $11-$18. **Credit** AmEx, DC, MC, V.
Map p314 L6 ㉙

This stylish place seems an anomaly on an unseemly
stretch of Geary Street. The room is modern and
energetic, filled with well-dressed patrons eager to
experience the assortment of small plates, which
range from the Far East to the American West. Wash
down the maze of tasties with a speciality cocktail.

Millennium

*Savoy Hotel, 580 Geary Street, at Jones Street
(345 3900/www.millenniumrestaurant.com).
Bus 2, 3, 4, 27, 38, 76.* **Open** 5.30-9pm Mon-Thur,

Sun; 5.30-10pm Fri, Sat. **Main courses**
$19-$21. **Credit** AmEx, DC, Disc, MC, V.
Map p314 L6 ㉚

Casual, elegant Millennium is still setting the pace
when it comes to vegetarian and vegan cooking in
SF, doing things with vegetables that you'd never
dream possible. The food, both the *carte* and the $62
tasting menu, changes frequently, driven by the
freshest available ingredients; it's accompanied by
one of the best all-organic wine lists in the US.

Shalimar

*532 Jones Street, at O'Farrell Street (928 0333).
Bus 2, 3, 4, 27, 38, 76.* **Open** noon-3pm, 5.30-
11.30pm daily. **Main courses** $5-$8. **No credit
cards. Map** p314 L6 ㉛

Locals have other favourites, but this is perhaps the
best of the Indian and Pakistan in this preternaturally grubby corner of the Tenderloin. The dishes
here are fairly spicy, turned out at speed and at predictably keen prices. The room's not much to look
at, but you'll only have eyes for the food.
Other locations: 1409 Polk Street, at Pine Street
(776 4642).

Civic Center

American

Indigo

*687 McAllister Street, at Gough Street (673
9353/www.indigorestaurant.com). Bus 5, 47, 49.*
Open 5-11pm Tue-Sun. **Main courses** $15-$20.
Credit AmEx, MC, V. **Map** p318 J7 ㉜

Eat, Drink, Shop

The key to Indigo's success is good food, well priced and served in an edgy, chic environment that defies modishness. The lounge-like setting features a long, open kitchen, from which emerges a broad mix of inventive New American dishes. The three-course evening special prix fixe (offered 5-7pm) is one of the best deals in town at just $28.

Zuni Café
1658 Market Street, at Franklin Street (552 2522). Metro to Van Ness/bus 6, 7, 66, 71. **Open** 11.30am-midnight Tue-Sat; 11am-11pm Sun. **Main courses** $10-$35. **Credit** AmEx, MC, V. **Map** p318 K8 ③
At Zuni, one of the most reliable eateries in town, chef Judy Rodgers's Cal-Ital food manages to be both memorable and transparently simple. The art-filled setting can be quite a scene before and after cultural events in the vicinity, but the sourdough bread and oysters on an iced platter, the roast chicken for two and the pizzettas from the wood-fired oven are attractions by themselves.

Asian

Tulan
8 6th Street, at Market Street (626 0927). BART & Metro to Powell/bus 14, 26 & Market Street routes. **Open** 11am-9pm Mon-Sat. **Main courses** $5-$9. **No credit cards. Map** p318 L7 ③
Other restaurants around town put a modern American spin on Vietnamese cuisine, serving the food in chic surroundings and upping the charges in the process. Tulan, though, keeps things authentic, scruffy and cheap: the menu sticks to Vietnamese basics, the room hasn't been decorated in decades (in a neighbourhood that could generously be described as downtrodden) and the prices are gloriously low.

Cafés, delis & diners

Saigon Sandwich Café
560 Larkin Street, between Turk & Eddy Streets (474 5698). Bus 19, 31. **Open** 7am-5.30pm Mon-Sat; 7.30am-5pm Sun. **Main courses** $2-$5. **No credit cards. Map** p314 K6 ③
Still the Civic Center's best unsung spot, this dingy, tiny room is typically jammed with foodies and federal workers who file in for huge sandwiches at rock-bottom prices. The bare-bones menu is made up almost entirely of Vietnamese banh mi sandwiches, which are prepared with such ingredients as roast pork with a chilli sauce.

French

Jardinière
300 Grove Street, at Franklin Street (861 5555/ www.jardiniere.com). BART & Metro to Civic Center/ bus 21, 47, 49 & Market Street routes. **Open** 5-10.30pm Mon-Wed, Sun; 5-11.30pm Thur-Sat. **Main courses** $25-$45. **Credit** AmEx, DC, Disc, MC, V. **Map** p318 K7 ③

This beautiful, whimsically shaped restaurant is still one of the best high-dollar special-occasion spots in the state. Chef Traci des Jardins continues to seek out the best and most environmentally friendly local ingredients. Starters can be a meal in themselves, but save room for memorable mains (or try the $75 tasting menu). The wine list has pages of sparkling wine.

SoMa & South Beach

Yerba Buena Gardens & around

American

Public
1489 Folsom Street, at 11th Street (552 3065/www. thepublicsf.com). Bus 9, 12, 27, 47. **Open** 6-9.30pm Tue-Sat. **Main courses** $17-$25. **Credit** AmEx, MC, V. **Map** p318 L8 ③
A deft mix of fine-dining sophistication and night-club energy, Public is built into a historic brick building that makes it feel as if it's been here longer than it has. In the kitchen, American-Italian comfort is the theme. Highlights might include braised duck leg with pappardelle mushrooms, and pan-roasted rib-eye with a nice balsamic glaze. The stylish bars are open long after the kitchen closes.

Town Hall Restaurant
342 Howard Street, at Fremont Street (908 3900/ www.townhallsf.com). Bus 10, 76. **Open** *Lunch* 11.30am-2.30pm, 5.30-10pm Mon-Thur; 11.30am-2.30pm, 5.30-11pm Fri; 5.30-11pm Sat; 5.30-10pm Sun. **Main courses** $10-$25. **Credit** AmEx, MC, V. **Map** p315 O5 ③
This little slice of New England, a collaboration between the legendary front-of-house man Doug Washington and Postrio chefs Mitchell and Steven Rosenthal, is a great-looking spot. The menu reads the American classics; highlights include bacon-wrapped quail with cheddar grits, cedar-planked salmon served with jambalaya and, at lunch, a beautiful pork tenderloin sandwich. **Photo** *p140.*

XYZ
W Hotel, 181 3rd Street, at Howard Street (817 7836/www.xyz-sf.com). BART & Metro to Montgomery/bus 12, 15, 30, 45, 76. **Open** 6.30-10.30am, 11.30am-2.30pm, 6-10.30pm Mon-Thur; 6.30-10.30am, 11.30am-2.30pm, 6-11pm Fri; 8am-2.30pm, 6-11pm Sat; 8am-2.30pm, 6-10.30pm Sun. **Main courses** $18-$38. **Credit** AmEx, DC, Disc, MC, V. **Map** p315 N6 ③
Adjacent to the lobby of the W (*see p52*), XYZ holds fast to its austere decor and sophisticated clientele. The most recent in a long line of talents in the kitchen, chef Paul Piscopo has injected new life to the space, with a tempting menu of modern California fare with

Eat, Drink, Shop

Get connected

Eat, Drink, Shop

San Francisco is such a tech-friendly town that it's sometimes hard not to feel naked when walking into a café without a laptop. Every café worth its salt has some sort of wireless network; what's more, many of them are free to use for anyone with their own machine (in contrast to the pay-to-surf network at Starbucks, for example). For more on the internet in San Francisco, *see p288*; for a list of local Wi-Fi hotspots, see http://metrofreefi.com/. However, even if you haven't brought a computer with you, there are still a number of spots around town where travellers without a laptop can get online, check email and maybe even send a virtual postcard to the folks back home.

The nicest of the central internet cafés is **Golden Gate Perk** near Union Square (401 Bush Street, at Kearny Street, 362 3929, www.ggperk.com; *pictured*), which supplements free wireless access with several workstations ($1.50/10mins). The range of iMacs at **Quetzal** (1234 Polk Street, at Bush Street, Polk Gulch, 673 4181, www.cofffeeandcocoa.com) go for a similar rate (16¢/min), though wireless access isn't free. The **Brainwash** café (*see p140*) has two connected computers ($3/20mins, $5/40mins, $7/hr). And down in the Haight, head to **Rockin' Java** (1821 Haight Street, at Shrader Street, 831 8842, www.rockinjava.com), where access costs $1/10mins.

French Provençal touches. The seasonally changing menu might include the likes of seared Sonoma duck breast or rabbit ravioli. The wine list is excellent.

Asian

For something with extra sizzle, dine with the 'gender illusionists' of **Asia SF** (*see p220*).

Azie

826 Folsom Street, at 4th Street (538 0918/www. restaurantlulu.com). Bus 12, 30, 45. **Open** 5.30-10.30pm Mon-Thur; 5.30-11.30pm Fri; 5-11.30pm Sat; 5-10.30pm Sun. **Main courses** $16-$26. **Credit** AmEx, DC, Disc, MC, V. **Map** p319 N7 ㊵

Possessing a beautiful dining room, with a soaring ceiling, flowing red drapery and swanky lighting fixtures, this cool restaurant and lounge has managed to withstand both a fickle public and the economic downturn to become a dependable outpost for inventive French-inspired Asian dishes. Azie's presentations are artfully geometric, with the series of small plates combining into an interesting and ultimately satisfying meal.

Cafés, delis & diners

If you're in the area and stuck for eating ideas, the café at **SFMOMA** (*see p81*) makes a good place for a quick lunch.

Town Hall Restaurant. *See p138.*

Brainwash

1122 Folsom Street, at Langton Street (861 3663/ www.brainwash.com). Bus 12, 19. **Open** 7am-11pm daily. **Main courses** $5-$10. **Credit** MC, V. **Map** p319 M8

Part laundromat, part bar/café and part performance space, this popular spot remains one of the premier singles hangouts in town. People bring along their dirty linens and a wandering eye as they peruse the array of potential mates and occasionally the menu of soups, salads and burgers. On most evenings, the atmosphere is brightened by live music (generally at a neighbourly volume), poetry readings or improv comedy (all ages, no cover).

French

Le Charm

315 5th Street, at Folsom Street (546 6128/ www.lecharm.com). Bus 12, 30, 45. **Open** 11.30am-2.30pm Mon; 11.30am-2.30pm, 5.30-9.30pm Tue-Thur; 11.30am-2.30pm, 5.30-10pm Fri; 5.30-10pm Sat; 5-8.30pm Sun. **Main courses** *Lunch* $8-$13. *Dinner* $18-$25. **Credit** AmEx, MC, V. **Map** p319 N7

One of the few places in town where you can enjoy eating your way through an authentic French bistro menu without having to make a massive cash outlay. Alongside an excellent standard *carte*, Le Charm has a three-course prix fixe menu ($28) that may include main courses such as pan-roasted calf's liver or grilled steak-frites. The pick of the desserts is generally the tarte tatin. There's only a tiny wine list, but it is well chosen.

International

Thirsty Bear Brewing Company

661 Howard Street, between 2nd & 3rd Streets (974 0905/www.thirstybear.com). BART & Metro to Montgomery/bus 12, 15, 30, 45, 76. **Open** 11.30am-10pm Mon-Thur; 11.30am-midnight Fri; noon-midnight Sat; 5-10pm Sun. **Main courses** $10-$20. *Tapas* $5-$10. **Credit** AmEx, DC, MC, V. **Map** p315 N6

Thirsty Bear is known for its microbrewed beers, sure, but also for its rotating selection of good Spanish tapas, including the famed *kokotxas* (fish cheeks), and numerous paellas. Patrons are often corporate clones out for an after-work beer and quick bite, but don't let that put you off: everybody feels at home here, and the beer is outstanding. Pool tables and dartboards offer further diversion.

Italian & pizza

LuLu

816 Folsom Street, between 4th & 5th Streets (495 5775/www.restaurantlulu.com). Bus 12, 30, 45. **Open** 11.30am-10pm Mon-Thur, Sun; 11.30am-11pm Fri, Sat. **Main courses** $7-$30. **Credit** AmEx, DC, MC, V. **Map** p319 N7

LuLu majors in delicious, rustic, Italian-influenced cuisine, including specialities from the wood-fired oven, rotisserie and grill. Pizzas, pasta and shellfish come on large platters, designed to be shared. LuLu's wine bar next door offers a more intimate alternative; executive chef Jody Denton also owns Azie (*see p139*) and the LuLu Petite deli in the Ferry Building (362 7019).

South Park & South Beach

American

Acme Chop House

24 Willie Mays Plaza, corner of King & 3rd Streets (644 0240/www.acmechophouse.com). Metro N to 2nd & King/bus 10, 15, 30, 45. **Open** 11am-2.30pm, 5.30-9pm Tue, Wed; 11am-2.30pm, 5.30-10pm Thur, Fri; 5.30-10pm Sat; 5.30-9pm Sun. **Main courses** *Lunch* $11-$20. *Dinner* $20-$50. **Credit** AmEx, DC, MC, V. **Map** p319 O7

Traci des Jardins of Jardinière (*see p138*) runs the menu at this large, comfortable restaurant at the ballpark, and her commitment to sustainability and organically raised meat sets the place apart from most steakhouses. Beef is tender and perfectly prepared, and the raw bar (oysters, mussels and fresh shrimp) makes a fine start to a meal. Needless to say, it gets crowded on game days.

Bacar

448 Brannan Street, between 3rd & 4th Streets (904 4100/www.bacarsf.com). Metro N to 4th & King/bus 15, 30, 45, 76. **Open** 5.30-11pm Mon-Thur; 11.30am-2.30pm, 5.30pm-midnight Fri;

5.30pm-midnight Sat; 5.30-10pm Sun. **Main courses** $15-$35. *Set lunch menu* $22/3 courses. **Credit** AmEx, DC, MC, V. **Map** p319 O7
Bacar is a cork-dork's Valhalla: some 100 of the 1,000 varietals are available by the glass. The 'wine wall' is the most eye-catching aspect of this remarkable three-level converted warehouse, but of late the food has also come into its own. Wood-fired pizzas are the best bet, although the mesquite-grilled meat, seared diver scallops and smoked sturgeon are also highlights on the approachable US and Med menu.

Jack Falstaff
598 2nd Street, at Brannan Street (836 9239/ www.plumpjack.com). Metro 2nd & King/bus 12, 15, 30, 45, 76. **Open** 11.30am-2pm, 5.30-10pm Mon-Thur; 11.30am-2pm, 5.30-11pm Fri; 5.30-11pm Sat; 5.30-10pm Sun. Also open for lunch on game days Sat, Sun. **Main courses** *Lunch* $12-$20. *Dinner* $20-$35. **Credit** AmEx, DC, MC, V. **Map** p315 O6
A big hit near the ballpark, this smart-looking new restaurant from the folks behind PlumpJack Wines (*see p189*) has an urban appeal that doesn't forsake comfort or hospitality. The often-changing menu features reassuring food, prepared with organic touches and a slow-food approach. Highlights include pan-roasted Liberty Farm duck and coriander-crusted tuna. Finish with an artisan cheese plate.

Paragon
701 2nd Street, at Townsend Street (537 9020/www. paragonrestaurant.com). Metro N to 2nd & King/bus 10, 15, 30, 45, 76. **Open** 11.30am-2.30pm, 5.30-10pm Mon-Fri; 5.30-11pm Sat. Also open for lunch on game days Sat, Sun. **Main courses** $12-$19. **Credit** AmEx, DC, Disc, MC, V. **Map** p319 P7
Before Giants games, fans press at the huge bar here shoulder to shoulder. The attractive dining room is similarly energy-charged. The classic American brasserie fare is rustic and reliable; steaks and seafood come with hearty sides, such as mashed potato or vegetable gratin.

Cafés, delis & diners

Butler & the Chef
155 South Park, at 3rd Street (896 2075/www. oralpleasureinc.com/cafe). Bus 10, 15. **Open** 8am-4pm daily. **Main courses** $8-$15. **Credit** AmEx, Disc, MC, V. **Map** p319 O7
This *très* French little café is always crowded with locals who queue for the fresh-made breakfast pastries and wonderful breads. Breakfast on *pain au chocolat* or sip a Pernod while chatting with Pierre, the amiable owner. The Butler & the Chef also runs a warehouse of French antiques (290 Utah Street, at 16th Street, Potrero Hill, 626 9600).

Town's End Restaurant & Bakery
2 Townsend Street, at Embarcadero (512 0749). Metro N to Brannan/bus 10, 15. **Open** 7.30am-2pm, 5.30-9pm Tue-Fri; 5.30-9pm Sat. **Main courses** $10-$18. **Credit** AmEx, DC, Disc, MC, V. **Map** p315 P6

'Bewitched with the rogue': **Jack Falstaff.**

This comfortable, unpretentious space near the ballpark offers hearty fare at good prices. Fresh-made baked goods are the highlight, but weekend breakfasts are also popular: it's one of the few spots in the area where you can get that first meal of the day.

French

La Suite
100 Brannan Street, at Embarcadero (593 5900/ www.lasuitesf.com). Metro N to Brannan/bus 10, 12, 15, 108. **Open** 5.30-11pm Mon-Thur, Sun; 5.30pm-midnight Fri, Sat. **Main courses** $19-$28. **Credit** AmEx, MC, V. **Map** p315 P6
This waterfront brasserie has great views of the bridge and the water from its bank of expansive windows, and luxurious, warm-toned decor. The menu offers a tempting assortment of seafood, steaks and grilled mains, all prepared with French aplomb. Start with a towering plate of *fruits de mer* and move on to something like rack of lamb or roasted halibut. Service can be abrupt.

International

Coco 500
500 Brannan Street, at 4th Street (543 2222/ www.coco500.com). Metro N to 4th & King/bus 15, 30, 45, 76. **Open** 11.30am-10pm Mon-Thur; 11.30am-11pm Fri; 5.30-11pm Sat. **Main courses** $9-$16. **Credit** AmEx, DC, Disc, MC, V. **Map** p319 N7
This SoMa restaurant is a reinvention of sorts for its popular proprietor, Loretta Keller, whose penchant for Parisian hospitality has given way to a small

plate style. Mediterranean-influenced dishes prepared with organic, today-fresh ingredients range from light pizzas from a wood-fired oven to beef-cheek mole, and whole fish with fennel saffron sauce.

Italian & pizza

Zuppa
564 4th Street, between Bryant & Brannan Streets (777 5900). Metro N to 4th & King/bus 15, 30, 45, 76. **Open** 5.30-11pm daily. **Main courses** $18-$32. **Credit** AmEx, MC, V. **Map** p319 N7
Despite the long banquettes that flank the dining room, and the post-work young professionals and adventurous Mission hipsters who sit in them, the rustic, fresh-made southern Italian cuisine steals the show at Zuppa. Almost everything on the menu is excellent, especially the house-cured meats offered at each table. The wine list is all-Italian all the time.

Latin American

Tres Agaves
130 Townsend Street, between 2nd and 3rd Streets, (227 0500/tresagaves.com). Metro N to 2nd & King/bus 12, 15, 30, 45, 76. **Open** 11am-1am Mon-Thur; 11am-2am Fri; 10am-2am Sat; 10am-1am Sun. **Main courses** $13-$18. **Credit** AmEx, Disc, MC, V. **Map** p319 O7
Tequila expert Julio Bermejo has teamed with impresario Eric Rubin, chef Joseph Manzare and rocker Sammy Hagar for this homage to the Mexican state of Jalisco, home to the town of Tequila. The cavernous brick-and-timber space houses ample bar space for Bermejo to serve his inventive cocktails, while the display kitchen turns out gourmet regional Mexican cuisine around the clock.

Nob Hill & Chinatown

Nob Hill & Polk Gulch

Cafés, delis & diners

Bob's Donut Shop
1621 Polk Street, at Sacramento Street (776 3141). Bus 47, 49, 76/cable car California. **Open** 24hrs daily. **No credit cards. Map** p314 K5
The space can be a bit depressing, not somewhere you want to linger over a cup of coffee and conversation, but this round-the-clock hole in the wall serves some of the best doughnuts ($1-$2.50) in town. The sugary wheels have been the late-night salvation of many a clubber, and the coffee is good and strong.

FC Nook
1500 Hyde Street, at Jackson Street (447 4100/ www.cafenookcom). Bus 1, 12, 27/cable car

Powell-Hyde. **Open** 7am-10.30pm Mon-Thur; 7am-11pm Fri; 8am-11pm Sat; 8am-10.30pm Sun. **Main courses** $4-$8. **Credit** MC, V. **Map** p314 K4
This unassuming little spot in Polk Gulch has quickly gained popularity for its easy-going atmosphere, good prices and wireless internet access. The menu is an assortment of bagels, soups and sandwiches, plus a selection of small-plate-style appetisers. For the evenings, there's a list of sakes and wines.

Fish & seafood

Swan Oyster Depot
1517 Polk Street, between California & Sacramento Streets (673 1101). Bus 47, 49, 76/cable car California. **Open** 8am-5.30pm Mon-Sat. **Main courses** $5-$16. **No credit cards. Map** p314 K5
Don't miss this Polk Gulch institution: half fish market, half counter-service hole in the wall, it's been wholly delighting locals since 1912. The best time to visit is November to June, when local Dungeness crab is in season. But at any time, the selections are straight-from-the-water fresh. Specialities include clam chowder and an obscenely large variety of oysters, best downed with a pint of local-brewed Anchor Steam beer. You can buy shellfish to take away.

French

Dining Room
Ritz-Carlton Hotel, 600 Stockton Street, at California Street (773 6198/www.ritzcarlton.com). Bus 1, 15, 30, 45/cable car California. **Open** 6-9pm Tue-Thur; 5.30-9.30pm Fri, Sat. **Main courses** *Set menus* $68/3 courses; $89/4 courses; $115/5 courses. **Credit** AmEx, DC, Disc, MC, V. **Map** p315 M4

Imperial Tea Court. *See p143.*

The Dining Room has a global reputation and a waitstaff-to-diner ratio of almost 1:1. Opulent without being over the top, it is, if anything, a little too serious. The modern French menu is inventive and artfully executed by chef Ron Siegel (the first non-Japanese to win the Iron Chef contest), as are the famous seasonal speciality menus, such as the annual white-truffle festival. Master sommelier Stephane Lacroix will guide you to an appropriate wine; the bar list of single malts is one of the largest in the US.

Fleur de Lys

777 Sutter Street, between Jones & Taylor Streets (673 7779/www.fleurdelyssf.com). Bus 2, 3, 4, 27, 38, 76. **Open** 6-9.30pm Mon-Thur; 5.30-10.30pm Fri, Sat. **Main courses** *Set menus* $70/3 courses; $78/4 courses; $88/5 courses. **Credit** AmEx, DC, MC, V. **Map** p314 L5 **59**

A fine dining experience so memorable that it's been duplicated in Las Vegas. Chef Hubert Keller's cuisine is deserving of a wider audience because of his vast repertoire: his menu is lush, even exorbitant. It all plays out like a symphony, a feast for the eyes as much as the palate, enhanced by service that is attentive without being overbearing. Perhaps the best pull-out-all-the-stops restaurant in town.

Chinatown

American

Alfred's Steakhouse

659 Merchant Street, between Kearny & Montgomery Streets (781 7058/www.alfredssteakhouse.com). Bus 1, 12, 15, 30, 45. **Open** 5.30-9pm Mon-Thur, Sun; 5.30-10pm Fri, Sat. **Main courses** $15-$40. **Credit** AmEx, DC, Disc, MC, V. **Map** p315 M4 **60**

With decades of experience as one of the city's best steakhouses, Alfred's feels like a bit of San Francisco gone by but continues to prove itself worthy of a fiercely loyal fanbase. The chief attractions are giant Chicago ribeyes, tender T-bones and a porterhouse that covers the dish, but the fish and pasta are also from the top drawer. The bar, which mixes superlative Martinis, stocks more than 100 single malts.

Asian

San Francisco's best Chinese food is actually found in the Richmond (*see p155*), but there are still worthwhile spots in Chinatown. The Chinese crowd at **Dol Ho's** (808 Pacific Avenue, at Stockton Street, 392 2828) speaks volumes about the food's authenticity, and **House of Nanking** (919 Kearny Street, at Jackson Street, 421 1429), while touristy, never disappoints with its food.

R&G Lounge

631 Kearny Street, at Clay Street (982 7877/www.rnglounge.com). Bus 1, 12, 15, 30, 45. **Open** 11am-9.30pm daily. **Main courses** $10-$28. **Credit** AmEx, DC, MC, V. **Map** p315 M4 **61**

Always busy and often chaotic, R&G Lounge has two levels for dining, neither of them much to look at. The Hong Kong-style food is authentic, emphasising seafood that mostly comes direct from in-house tanks. People come from miles around for the deep-fried salt-and-pepper crab and barbecue pork.

Yuet Lee

1300 Stockton Street, at Broadway (982 6020). Bus 12, 15, 30, 41, 45. **Open** 11am-3am Mon, Wed-Sun. **Main courses** $5-$15. **No credit cards. Map** p315 M3 **62**

Terrific seafood and the opportunity to indulge in some small-hours dining attract sundry restaurant folk to this tiny, bright-green Chinese eaterie. The roasted squab with fresh coriander and lemon, sautéed clams with black bean sauce, and 'eight precious noodle soup', made with eight kinds of meat, are all worth trying. Lighting is glaringly unflattering and the service matter-of-fact.

Cafés, delis & diners

Imperial Tea Court

1411 Powell Street, at Broadway (788 6080/www.imperialtea.com). Bus 12, 15, 30, 41, 45/cable car Powell-Mason. **Open** 11am-6.30pm Mon, Wed-Sun. **Main courses** $6-$10. **Credit** AmEx, MC, V. **Map** p314 L3 **63**

There are few better places in the city for tea. This serene, wood-panelled tea house offers a vast array of teas, served to the accompaniment of birds chirping in cages. Presented in the traditional Chinese *gaiwan* (a covered cup), teas include Fancy Dragon Well, Silver Needle and Snow Water; they're all available to take away. Don't expect serious food, though traditional nibbles are served. **Photo** *p142*. **Other locations**: 27 Ferry Market Place, Ferry Building, Embarcadero (544 9830).

North Beach to Fisherman's Wharf

North Beach

American

Moose's

1652 Stockton Street, between Union & Filbert Streets (989 7800/www.mooses.com). Bus 12, 15, 30, 39, 41, 45. **Open** 5.30-10pm Mon-Wed; 11.30am-2.30pm, 5-11pm Fri, Sat; 10am-2.30pm, 5-10pm Sun. **Main courses** $10-$33. **Credit** AmEx, DC, MC, V. **Map** p315 M3 **64**

Long-time restaurateurs Ed and Mary Etta Moose have created a uniquely San Franciscan environment here, and the storied Mooseburger keeps right on satisfying a motley assortment of local celebs, business types and big-ego politicos. A full bar, an open kitchen serving consistently good California cuisine and an extensive wine list are big draws; Sunday brunch is excellent.

Washington Square Bar & Grill

1707 Powell Street, at Union Street (982 8123). Bus 12, 15, 30, 39, 41, 45/cable car Powell-Mason. **Open** 11.30am-10pm Mon, Tue; 11.30am-11pm Wed-Fri; 10.30am-3pm, 5-11pm Sat; 10.30am-3pm, 5-10pm Sun. **Main courses** $17-$24. **Credit** AmEx, MC, V. **Map** p314 L3 ➎

Many loyalists were shocked when the Washbag changed identities a few years back, but happily the erstwhile Cobalt soon switched back. Now, it is again playing its familiar role as watering hole and reliable American-Italian restaurant. The best dishes are classics, such as double-cut pork chops. Live nightly jazz lends the place an energetic tone.

Asian

House

1230 Grant Avenue, at Columbus Avenue & Vallejo Street (986 8612/www.thehse.com). Bus 12, 15, 30, 41, 45. **Open** 11.30am-3pm, 5.30-10pm Mon-Thur; 11.30am-3pm, 5.30-11pm Fri; 5-11pm Sat; 5-10pm Sun. **Main courses** *Lunch* $8-$14. *Dinner* $15-$21. **Credit** AmEx, DC, MC, V. **Map** p315 M3 ➏

This no-frills (though often ear-shatteringly loud) Chinese fusion dining room works wonders with fresh, seasonal produce and East-meets-West preparations. The Chinese chicken salad with sesame soy illustrates the menu: light, tangy and big enough to be a meal on its own. The menu changes often, resisting trends while remaining decidedly sophisticated, and wines are at rock-bottom prices.

Cafés, delis & diners

Caffe Puccini

411 Columbus Avenue, at Vallejo Street (989 7033). Bus 12, 15, 30, 39, 41, 45. **Open** 6am-11.30pm daily. **Main courses** $5-$8. **No credit cards. Map** p315 M3 ➐

Owner Graziano Lucchese, a North Beach institution, is from the same town as the composer after whom he named this intimate North Beach café; he's been known to regale customers with tales from the Old Country. His café is warm and welcoming, serving an inexpensive assortment of vast sandwiches stuffed with salami, prosciutto and mortadella.

Caffe Roma

526 Columbus Avenue, between Green & Stockton Streets (296 7942). Bus 12, 15, 30, 39, 41, 45. **Open** 6.30am-7pm Mon-Fri; 6.30am-9pm Sat; 7am-8pm Sun. **Credit** ($10 minimum) AmEx, MC, V. **Map** p314 L3 ➑

Some say it's the strongest coffee in the city – it's certainly the most coveted. Espressos, long coffees and a range of gelati are served in a large, airy space, great for sipping, thinking and explaining your latest conspiracy theory. Hint: JFK's still alive.

Caffe Trieste

601 Vallejo Street, at Grant Avenue (982 2605/ http://caffetrieste.com). Bus 12, 15, 30, 39, 41, 45. **Open** 6.30am-11pm Mon-Thur, Sun; 6.30am-midnight Fri, Sat. **Main courses** $5-$10. **No credit cards. Map** p315 M3 ➒

Here's one of the city's great cafés, a former hangout for Kerouac and Ginsberg and, it's believed, the spot where Coppola worked on the screenplay for *The Godfather.* The dark walls are plastered with photos of opera singers and famous regulars. There are muffins, pastries and sandwiches to eat, and the lattes are legendary, as are the opera sessions held here on a Saturday afternoon.

Mama's on Washington Square

1701 Stockton Street, at Filbert Street (362 6421). Bus 12, 15, 30, 39, 41, 45. **Open** 8am-3pm Tue-Sun. **Main courses** $6-$15. **No credit cards. Map** p314 L3 ➓

The weekend queue is part of the fun at this wildly popular North Beach mainstay, with its mix of locals and tourists milling about with newspapers. Once seated, you'll be faced with such temptations as a giant made-to-order 'm'omelette' or the Monte Cristo sandwich. Service is swift and familiar.

Mario's Bohemian Cigar Store

566 Columbus Avenue, at Union Street (362 0536). Bus 12, 15, 30, 39, 41, 45. **Main courses** $4-$9. **Credit** MC, V. **Map** p314 L3 ⓫

Despite its name, you can't buy a cigar at Mario's, nor will you be allowed to smoke one. Instead sip a flavoured Italian soda and watch the neighbourhood while perusing a light menu of focaccia sandwiches and salads, own-made biscotti, beer and coffee. Mario's location means it's always packed, so lunch may be slow in coming, but there's no more essential North Beach café.

International

Helmand

430 Broadway, between Kearny & Montgomery Streets (362 0641). Bus 12, 15, 30, 41, 45. **Open** 5.30-10pm Mon-Thur, Sun; 5.30-11pm Fri, Sat. **Main courses** $10-$17. **Credit** AmEx, MC, V. **Map** p315 M3 ⓬

Cheap and widely recommended, the Helmand is still the city's only Afghan restaurant. Influenced by the flavours of India, Asia and the Middle East, the food here is deliciously aromatic, with marinades and fragrant spices giving each dish unique character. Specialities include leek ravioli and baked baby pumpkin and scallion.

Iluna Basque

701 Union Street, at Columbus Avenue (402 0011/ www.ilunabasque.com). Bus 12, 15, 30, 39, 41, 45/ cable car Powell-Mason. **Open** 5.30-11pm Mon-Thur, Sun; 5.30pm-midnight Fri, Sat. **Main courses** $8-$14. *Tapas* $4-$10. **Credit** AmEx, DC, Disc, MC, V. **Map** p314 L3 ⓭

A bowl, freshly baked by the **Boudin** family. *See p146.*

With views of Washington Square, this lively restaurant has become a fast favourite among locals, as much for its fun atmosphere as for its memorable Basque-influenced tapas. Graze your way through plates of delightful delicacies, from empanadas to Spanish tortillas and a traditional cassoulet of sausage and lamb chop. The service can be patchy, but the food is worth suffering for.

Italian & pizza

For North Beach's best Italian cafés, *see p144*.

Enrico's Sidewalk Café

504 Broadway, at Kearny Street (982 6223/ www.enricossidewalkcafe.com). Bus 12, 15, 30, 41, 45. **Open** 11.30am-11pm Mon-Thur, Sun; 11.30am-midnight Fri, Sat. **Main courses** $9-$29. **Credit** AmEx, MC, V. **Map** p315 M3 ⑦
A noisy and friendly joint, Enrico's is quintessential North Beach, one of those places where locals and tourists happily bump elbows. Pasta, pizza and such specialities as Niman Ranch seven-hour lamb stew fill out a menu that's heavy with appetisers. A long wooden bar specialises, oddly, in Mojitos, while the outdoor patio offers some prime people-watching and, most nights, live jazz.

Sodini's

510 Green Street, at Grant Avenue (291 0499). Bus 12, 15, 30, 41, 45. **Open** 5-10pm Mon-Thur; 5-11pm Fri, Sat. **Main courses** $13-$20. **Credit** MC, V. **Map** p315 M3 ⑦
Sodini's is small and darkly romantic, jamming patrons close together to feather their servers to squeeze past with platters of sloppy pasta and rib-sticking lasagne. The place's popularity suffers not at all for being a bit off the beaten track, so visitors should arrive earlier than they intend to eat and sign the list; they can then drop over to a neighbourhood bar while waiting for their table. Once inside, the Chianti is cheap and in plentiful supply.

Tommaso's Ristorante Italiano

1042 Kearny Street, at Pacific Avenue (398 9696). Bus 12, 15, 30, 41, 45. **Open** 5-10.30pm Tue-Sun. **Main courses** $11-$23. **Credit** AmEx, DC, Disc, MC, V. **Map** p315 M3 ⑦
Tommaso's is known city-wide for its simple Italian food, which has been served family-style in a tiny, boisterous room since 1935. The wood-fired pizzas and calzones deserve their reps and the house red is surprisingly good. No affectations, no frills and no reservations. Join the queue and keep your eyes peeled: you never know who might walk in.

Latin American

FC Impala

501 Broadway, at Kearny Street (982 5299/www. impalasf.com). Bus 12, 15, 30, 41, 45. **Open** 5-11pm daily. **Main courses** $12-$18. **Credit** AmEx, MC, V. **Map** p315 M3 ⑦
In the otherwise honky-tonk heart of North Beach, this buzzing, popular restaurant is surprisingly chic. It aims to raise Mexican cuisine to a higher level and, in many aspects, it succeeds. Mains focus on fish dishes, slow-roasted meats and Mexican classics; the crowd eats them up with as much enthusiasm as it does the lounge-style atmosphere, a combination of candlelight and DJ-spun music. The bar is open until 2am.

Fisherman's Wharf

American

Gary Danko

800 North Point Street, at Hyde Street (749 2060/ www.garydanko.com). Metro F to Fisherman's Wharf/bus 10, 19, 30, 47/cable car Powell-Hyde. **Open** 5.30-10pm daily. **Main courses** Set menus $59/3 courses; $71/4 courses; $81/5 courses. **Credit** AmEx, DC, Disc, MC, V. **Map** p314 K2 ⑦

Eat, Drink, Shop

Superstar chef Danko has created a fabulous – and fabulously understated – spot for fine dining near the wharf. The best way to experience his dexterity and genius is via the tasting menus, which change seasonally but might include chickpea-crusted black grouper starter, beef medallion with orzo risotto as a main, and farmhouse artisan cheeses to finish. A more casual adventure can be found at the bar.

Asian

Ana Mandara

981 Beach Street, at Polk Street (771 6800/ www.anamandara.com). Metro F to Fisherman's Wharf/bus 10, 19, 30, 47/cable car Powell-Hyde. **Open** 11.30am-2pm, 5.30-9.30pm Mon-Thur; 11.30am-2pm, 5.30-10.30pm Fri; 5.30-10.30pm Sat; 5.30-9.30pm Sun. **Main courses** *Lunch* $11-$20. *Dinner* $17-$32. **Credit** AmEx, DC, Disc, MC, V. **Map** p314 J2 ⑦

Although located in tourist-laden Ghirardelli Square, this fabulous French-Vietnamese restaurant could hold its own in the foodiest of neighbourhoods. The room is beautiful, with soaring ceilings and a staircase that sweeps you to a chic lounge. The sumptuous and beautifully presented specialities are all enriched with the aromas and flavours of Vietnam. The room turns into a nightclub on some Thursdays.

Cafés, delis & diners

Boudin Sourdough Bakery & Café

2890 Taylor Street, at Jefferson Street (776 1849/ www.boudinbakery.com). Metro F to Pier 39/bus 10, 15, 30, 39, 47/cable car Powell-Mason. **Open** *Café* 8am-10pm Mon-Thur, Sun; 8am-11pm Fri, Sat. *Bistro* 11.30am-9pm Mon-Thur, Sun; 11.30am-10.30pm Fri, Sat. **Main courses** $7-$12. **Credit** AmEx, MC, V. **Map** p314 L1 ⑥⓪

Locals brag that sourdough bread was invented in the city, but it's more impressive that the Boudin family has been making it since 1849. Their flagship store, a relaxing alternative to ear-busting crab and seafood stands along the Wharf, offers such delights as sourdough pizzas and clam chowder served in a hollowed-out sourdough bowl. **Photo** *p145.*

Other locations: throughout the Bay Area.

Fish & seafood

Alioto's

8 Fisherman's Wharf, at Taylor & Jefferson Streets (673 0183). Metro F to Pier 39/bus 10, 15, 30, 39, 47/ cable car Powell-Mason. **Open** 11am-11pm daily. **Main courses** $10-$28. **Credit** AmEx, DC, Disc, MC, V. **Map** p314 K1 ⑥①

Crack one open

Much of the legend of Fisherman's Wharf is attributable to the sweet and tasty Dungeness crab fished off the shores of San Francisco. For generations, families retained the same stalls at the Wharf; some Italian fishermen never bothered to learn English, as their entire lives were centred on the Wharf and neighbouring North Beach. Both baseball legend Joe DiMaggio and former mayor Joe Alioto were sons of local fishermen.

These days, locals are loath to tread in Fisherman's Wharf, its streets awash with tourist-trap stores and knock-off fashions. But the start of Dungeness crab season in early to mid November draws even the most reluctant San Franciscans to the docks. At times, you can simply buy the crabs directly off the boat, take 'em home and cook 'em up. But it's just as easy – and virtually as cheap (at least half what it costs in local restaurants) – to sample a freshly cracked crab right in the Wharf from one of the many vendors that line the sidewalks near the marina.

In February, the **San Francisco Crab Festival** takes over the town. Restaurants – nay, entire neighbourhoods – are given over to crab-themed menus and events. Some of the more traditional presentations take place around the Wharf and North Beach, while the more adventurous recipes can be found in the Mission district's cultural melting pot. Every Friday in February, the **Mission Crab Festival** packs restaurants with crab lovers enjoying Moroccan, Senegalese, Mexican, Italian, French, Cajun and down-home American takes on luscious lumps of crabmeat.

Outside of the festival, the best time to get crackin' is December and January, when the supply of crabs is the greatest (and cheapest) and the meat the sweetest. Dungies can be found all over the city, but outside the wharf the best place to sample them is undoubtedly the legendary **Swan Oyster Depot** (*see p142*). The family-run operation makes a prime Crab Louie, but they'll also serve it up all on its lonesome. It's no coincidence that San Francisco's other gustatory institutions accompany the dish so well. Bellying up to the vast marble counter at Swan's for a serving of crabmeat, with some drawn butter, a chunk of crusty sourdough and some equally buttery Chardonnay or a draft Anchor Steam beer, is truly an 'only in San Francisco' culinary experience.

Alioto's began as a sidewalk stand serving crab and shrimp cocktails in a paper cup to passers-by. Now, more than seven decades later, it's a hugely popular restaurant owned by a prominent local family. The room offers an amazing view of the Bay, which is enough to draw in hordes of tourists year-round, but the kitchen still manages to turn out decent (if pricey) seafood, as well as fish-centred Sicilian specialities. The wine list is outstanding.

Blue Mermaid

Argonaut Hotel, 471 Jefferson Street, at Hyde Street (771 2222/www.bluemermaidsf.com). Metro F to Fisherman's Wharf/bus 10, 19, 30, 47/cable car Powell-Hyde. **Open** 7am-9pm Mon-Thur, Sun; 7am-10pm Fri, Sat. **Main courses** $8-$24. **Credit** AmEx, DC, Disc, MC, V. **Map** p314 K2 ⊕

Designed to recall the history of the working wharf, this rustic-looking restaurant is set into the corner of the impressive Argonaut Hotel (*see p58*). The menu is great for San Francisco's fogged-in days, with hearty chowders spooned up from large cauldrons: specialities include New England clam, sweetcorn and Dungeness crab varieties. It's a great spot for families.

Russian Hill

American

Tablespoon

2209 Polk Street, between Vallejo & Green Streets (268 0140/www.tablespoonsf.com). Bus 12, 19, 27, 47, 49, 76. **Open** 6pm-midnight Mon-Sat; 5-10pm Sun. **Main courses** $17-$22. **Credit** AmEx, Disc, MC, V. **Map** p314 K4 ⊕

The concept of offering well-above-par food at neighbourhood prices might seem obvious, but it's much easier said than done. At Tablespoon, it's delivered with some panache: four-star service at casual prices. The food is inventive, maybe too inventive at times, but appeals to the home-cooking heart; roast pork tenderloin is a standout. The bar attracts a young, hip crowd.

Asian

Sushi Groove

1916 Hyde Street, between Union & Green Streets (440 1905). Bus 41, 45/cable car Powell-Hyde. **Open** 5.30-10pm Mon-Thur, Sun; 5.30-10.30pm Fri, Sat. **Main courses** $13-$16. *Sushi* $4-$10. **Credit** AmEx, MC, V. **Map** p314 K3 ⊕

If you don't mind sitting elbow to elbow in a dining room that's roughly the size of a postage stamp, join the stylish clientele at this creative and highly charged sushi restaurant. The decor is postmodern, the mood music is drum 'n' bass, and the original rolls and salads are mostly very good indeed. Fresh crab, sea urchin and eel join the familiar mackerel, tuna and salmon. The impressive sake selection is worth the trip in itself.

Cafés, delis & diners

La Boulange de Polk

2310 Polk Street, at Green Street (345 1107). Bus 12, 19, 27, 47, 49, 76. **Open** 7am-6.30pm Tue-Sun. **Main courses** $3-$9. **No credit cards.** **Map** p314 K3 ⊕

In the style of a Parisian boulangerie, this spot in Russian Hill serves beautiful pastries and tasty fresh-baked bread. The best place to watch a morning unfold is from one of the inviting pavement tables, but they can be difficult to acquire, especially at the weekend.

Other locations: Boulangerie Bay Bread, 2325 Pine Street, Pacific Heights (440 0356).

Fish & seafood

Pesce

2227 Polk Street, between Green & Vallejo Streets (928 8025). Bus 12, 19, 27, 47, 49, 76. **Open** 5-10pm Mon-Thur; 5-11pm Fri; noon-4pm, 5-11pm Sat; noon-4pm Sun. **Main courses** $15-$32. **Credit** AmEx, Disc, MC, V. **Map** p314 K4 ⊕

Modest and comfortable, Pesce is a great place to make a mess with your local speciality *cioppino*. This simple restaurant and bar proves that fabulous seafood doesn't have to be fancy or expensive, making it wildly popular with those lucky enough to live nearby. Starters include excellent mussels, cod cakes and calamari; main courses tend to be Italian.

French

La Folie

2316 Polk Street, between Union & Green Streets (776 5577/www.lafolie.com). Bus 12, 19, 27, 47, 49, 76. **Open** 5.30-10.30pm Mon-Sat. **Main courses** *Set menus* $60/3 courses; $75/4 courses; $85/5 courses. **Credit** AmEx, DC, Disc, MC, V. **Map** p314 K3 ⊕

If you want to find out why chef Roland Passot enjoys a passionate following, opt for the five-course discovery menu ($85) and sample his ever-changing selection of classic French fare, prepared with seasonally fresh ingredients. The Provençal decor and attentive staff add to the charm of this delightful French-Californian eaterie. The newer Green Room is a good option for intimate dining.

Le Petit Robert

2300 Polk Street, at Green Street (922 8100/www.le petitrobert.com). Bus 12, 19, 27, 47, 49, 76. **Open** 11.30am-10pm Mon-Fri; 10am-10pm Sat, Sun. **Main courses** $10-$20. **Credit** MC, V. **Map** p314 K3 ⊕

With an air of casual sophistication, this high-ceilinged room is easily able to accommodate both boisterous parties and romantically inclined couples. The menu features above-par French classics, including salad niçoise with steak tartare; the less adventurous are catered for with some approachable basics. The wine list has many affordable selections and good choices by the glass.

Eat, Drink, Shop

International

Zarzuela

2000 Hyde Street, at Union Street (346 0800). Bus 41, 45/cable car Powell-Hyde. **Open** 5.30-10pm Tue-Thur; 5.30-10.30pm Fri, Sat. **Main courses** $12-$16. **Credit** Disc, MC, V. **Map** p314 K3 ⑥

The tapas are always a treat at cosy Zarzuela, where the Spanish cuisine is served amid bullfight posters and maps of Spain. Old standbys such as grilled eggplant filled with goat's cheese, sautéed shrimps in garlic and olive oil, and fried potatoes with garlic and sherry vinegar never disappoint.

The Mission & the Castro

The Mission

American

Delfina

3621 18th Street, between Dolores & Guerrero Streets (552 4055). BART 16th Street/bus 26, 33. **Open** 5.30-10pm Mon-Thur, Sun; 5.30-11pm Fri, Sat. **Main courses** $11-$24. **Credit** MC, V. **Map** p318 J10 ⑨

In all the fusion-food madness, chef/owner Craig Stoll favours simplicity over whimsy, and tradition over fashion. Yet his food is never ordinary: fresh-made pasta, fish and braised meats all burst with flavour; you actually want to order the chicken. The menu changes daily, reflecting Stoll's desire to stay on his toes; it's a pity the staff don't always seem to share his ambition. The Delfina Pizzeria (437 6800) is just next door; guess what the speciality is. **Photo** *p149*.

Luna Park

694 Valencia Street, at 18th Street (553 8584/www. lunaparksf.com). BART 16th Street/bus 14, 26, 33, 49. **Open** 11.30am-2.30pm, 5.30-10.30pm Mon-Thur; 11.30am-2.30pm, 5.30-11.30pm Fri; 11.30am-3pm, 5.30-11.30pm Sat; 11.30am-3pm, 5.30-10pm Sun. **Main courses** $9-$17. **Credit** AmEx, MC, V. **Map** p318 K10 ㉛

The notion of serving no-nonsense food at decent prices in a place where people want to linger has been so successful there are now clones in New York and LA. That Luna Park is tiny (50 seats) doesn't deter locals from queuing; a vibrant lounge bar catches the spillover. Expect swift, courteous service and an accessible selection of hearty dishes, including flat-iron steak and fries, the amazing tuna poke and earthy stomach-fillers such as the 'pot on fire' stew.

Slow Club

2501 Mariposa Street, at Hampshire Street (241 9390/www.slowclub.com). Bus 9, 33. **Open** 7.30am-2.30pm, 6.30-10pm Mon-Thur; 7.30am-2.30pm,

6.30-11pm Fri; 10am-2.30pm, 6.30-11pm Sat; 10am-2.30pm Sun. **Main courses** $8-$20. **Credit** MC, V. **Map** p319 M10 ㉜

With its remote location and hip hideaway vibe, this is a true locals' spot. Slow Club's understated charm makes it one of the coolest places in town. Typical mains include pan-seared sea bass and fresh linguine bolognese. There are no reservations, but a cosy bar area makes waiting tolerable. The dinner menu changes nightly; the weekend brunch is great.

Universal Café

2814 19th Street, between Bryant & Florida Streets (821 4608). Bus 27. **Open** 5.30-10pm Tue-Thur; 5.30-10.30pm Fri; 9.30am-2.30pm, 5.30-11pm Sat; 9am-2.30pm Sun. **Main courses** $9-$24. **Credit** AmEx, DC, MC, V. **Map** p318 L11 ㉝

Universal Café has become a staple in the area, beloved for its laid-back, industrial-look dining room and fresh, interesting food. It's a popular spot for a weekend breakfast, when you can enjoy potato pancakes at an outside table; lunch features focaccia sandwiches, salads and tiny pizzas. Dinner brings higher prices, but a decent menu.

Asian

Firecracker

1007 Valencia Street, at 21st Street (642 3470). Bus 26. **Open** 5.30-10.30pm Tue-Thur; 5.30-11pm Fri, Sat; 5-10pm Sun. **Main courses** $9-$16. **Credit** DC, Disc, MC, V. **Map** p318 K11 ㉞

With flame-red walls and, often, an ear-splitting din, Firecracker lives up to its name. The place has withstood Asian-inspired food trends and carved a niche for itself with Chinese standards: spring rolls, dumplings and the seafood specialities are popular orders. Reliable when fun is the order of the evening.

Nihon

1779 Folsom Street, at 14th Street (552 4400/ www.nihon-sf.com). BART 16th Street/bus 9, 12. **Open** 6pm-midnight Mon-Sat. **Main courses** $14-$23. **Credit** AmEx, MC, V. **Map** p318 L9 ㉟

With its emphasis on scene and style, this new sushi lounge has given this out-of-the-way location a bit of life. The space features edgy design, with conversation-starters in each of three areas: a bar, a lounge and a bottle-service room. The menu has nicely presented renditions of Japanese small plates, as well as fresh sushi and sashimi. At the bar, a menu of more than 120 whiskies is a big plus.

Cafés, delis & diners

Atlas Café

3049 20th Street, at Alabama Street (648 1047/ www.atlascafe.net). Bus 27. **Open** 6.30am-10pm Mon-Fri; 8am-8pm Sat, Sun. **Main courses** $4-$9. **No credit cards. Map** p317 L11 ㊱

This comfortable, popular café is one of the Mission's great hangouts, with people lining up for fresh breakfast pastries in the morning and settling

Eat, Drink, Shop

At **Delfina**, the complications stay in the kitchen. *See p148.*

into fresh-roasted lattes for the afternoon and evening. A daily list of grilled sandwiches includes many vegetarian specialities, and there are also soups and salads. Music on Thursday evenings and Saturday afternoons is often of the bluegrass variety. On nice days, try for a sunny seat on the patio at the back (where dogs are allowed).

Ritual Roasters

1026 Valencia Street, between 21st & 22nd Streets (641 1024/www.ritualroasters.com). Bus 26. **Open** 7am-11pm Mon-Fri; 8am-11pm Sat; 8am-8pm Sun. **Credit** MC, V. **Map** p318 K11 ⓞ

In the Bay Area, where coffee is regarded with religious concern, it might seem heretical to open a coffee shop at which the beans are imported from Oregon. But Portland's Stumptown roastery is virtually a cult, and the eager denizens of the Mission have guzzled the fresh coffee and espresso with fanatic enthusiasm. The room itself is a fairly standard café; some are here to talk, but most to surf.

St Francis Fountain

2801 24th Street, at York Street (826 4200). Bus 27. **Open** 8am-9pm daily. **Main courses** $4-$8. **No credit cards. Map** p319 M12 ⓞ

An almost classical link from old Mission to new, this ancient soda fountain has undergone a new lease of life in recent years thanks to the attention lavished on it by its new owners. The menu offers a few nods to the 21st century, but it's mainly a wonderfully retro experience, from the formica tabletops to the magnificent mac and cheese and ice-cream sodas.

French

Ti Couz Creperie

3108 16th Street, between Valencia & Guerrero Streets (252 7373). BART 16th Street/bus 14, 26, 33, 49. **Open** 11am-11pm Mon-Fri; 10am-11pm Sat, Sun. **Main courses** $5-$12. **Credit** MC, V. **Map** p318 K10 ⓞ

Watch before you taste: here classic Breton buckwheat galettes (savoury) and crêpes (sweet) are cooked captivatingly before your eyes. All kinds of urbanite pop in to try more than 100 fillings, from smoked salmon to lemon and brown sugar. Next door, Ti Couz Two has seafood and a full bar.

International

Andalu

3198 16th Street, at Guerrero Street (621 2211/ www.andalusf.com). BART 16th Street/bus 14, 26, 33, 49. **Open** 5.30-10pm Mon-Tue, Sun; 5.30-11pm Wed, Thur; 5.30-11.30pm Fri, Sat. **Main courses** *Tapas* $3-$14. **Credit** AmEx, DC, MC, V. **Map** p318 J10 ⓞ

This spacious room is anchored by a long bar at the back, a great spot when you're waiting for a table. But as soon as you sit down, your focus will shift from crowd to cuisine. The 'small plates' – order tapas-style – are given an inventive twist, with such surprises as glazed turkey lettuce cups, prosciutto-stuffed chicken breast and Coca Cola-braised short ribs. Save room for fresh-made donuts.

Foreign Cinema

2534 Mission Street, between 21st & 22nd Streets (648 7600/www.foreigncinema.com). BART 24th Street/bus 14, 26, 48, 49, 67. **Open** 6-11pm Mon-Thur; 6pm-midnight Fri; 11am-5pm, 6pm-midnight Sat; 11am-5pm, 6-11pm Sun. **Main courses** $16-$30. **Credit** AmEx, MC, V. **Map** p318 K11 ⓞ

The opening of a bar, Laszlo, has helped contribute to the steady stream of customers into Foreign Cinema, but the food has also remained well above par. The place is dominated by the screen on one side of the outdoor courtyard dining room, on which classic films are projected each night; there are speakers at each table if you want to listen. But the food remains the focus, a frequently updated list of classically rooted Mediterranean favourites and a massive range of stellar oysters.

The Latin quarter

Silver Torpedo, UFL (Urban Food Log), La Bomba… Whatever the nickname, the Mission burrito is a glory to behold, a steamed tortilla packed with meat (optional), cheese, rice, beans, guacamole and spicy, peppery salsa. Originally consumed by field workers, the tortilla is essentially an edible-sack lunch: it was called a *burrito* ('little donkey') because it carried everything. On 29 September 1969, the first Mission burrito was sold at Valencia Street's still-extant **La Cumbre Taqueria** (515 Valencia Street, at 16th Street, 863 8205): the revolution had begun.

The Mission is packed with burrito joints, walk-up counters dishing up immense hunks of food for a meagre few bucks. Some of the more accessible ones, among them mega-taqueria **Pancho Villa** (3071 16th Street, at Valencia Street, 864 8840) and the respected **El Toro** (598 Valencia Street, at 17th Street, 431 3351), are both good and authentic. However, the best ones are a bit further afield. Consistent champion **Taqueria San Francisco** (2794 24th Street, at York Avenue, 641 1770) slings exquisite *carne asada* (grilled beef) into lightly grilled, warm and flaky tortillas, while **Taqueria Cancun** (2288 Mission Street, near 19th Street, 252 9560) does a particularly fine vegetarian burrito. Pair the slabs at **El Farolito** (2779 Mission Street, at 24th Street, 826 4870)

with the refreshing cantaloupe *agua fresca* – 'fresh water' flavoured with fruit juice. And at **Papalote** (3409 24th Street, at Valencia Street, 970 8815, www.papalote-sf.com), the ingredients are fresher and the decor is more colourful, but the price is still right.

While the Mission simply means Mexican food to many locals and visitors, there's more to it than that. These days, the neighbourhood is home to eateries covering most of South and Central America, as well as the so-called Nuevo Latino fusion movement, which weds traditional Latin American cuisine with American, Asian and continental food. The **Balompie Café** (3349 18th Street, at Capp Street, 648 9199) and the more upscale **Panchitas #3** (3115 22nd Street, at S Van Ness Avenue, 821 6660) serve Salvadorean favourites such as *pupusas*, thick tortillas stuffed with meat, beans, cheese or *loroco*, a fresh green herb. **San Miguel** (3520 20th Street, near Mission Street, 826 0173) offers choice Guatemalan fare, while at **El Majahual** (1142 Valencia Street, between 22nd & 23rd Streets, 821 7514), a Colombian husband and his Salvadorean wife offer flavourful, inexpensive food. At the other end of the price spectrum, the Nuevo Latino take on Peruvian cuisine served up at **Limón** (524 Valencia Street, between 16th & 17th Streets, 252 0918, limon-sf.com) has garnered awards, and deservedly so.

Eat, Drink, Shop

Italian & pizza

Pauline's Pizza
*260 Valencia Street, between Brosnan & 14th Streets
(552 2050). Bus 26.* **Open** 5-10pm Tue-Sat. **Main
courses** $10-$23. **Credit** MC, V. **Map** p318 J9 ⓶
Pauline's inventive, thin-crust pies all come with top-
quality ingredients: roasted peppers, perhaps, or
goat's cheese, edible flowers, exotic vegetables, even
several without tomato sauce. The pesto pizza (basil
and pesto are baked into the crust) is renowned.

Latin American

El Nuevo Frutilandia
*3077 24th Street, between Folsom & Treat Streets
(648 2958). Bus 12, 48, 67.* **Open** 11.30am-3pm,
5.30-9pm Tue-Thur; 11.30am-3pm, 5.30-10pm Fri;
noon-10pm Sat; noon-9pm Sun. **Main courses**
$6-$13. **Credit** MC, V. **Map** p318 L12 ⓷
Near Balmy Alley, this tiny, noisy eaterie specialises
in Cuban and Puerto Rican food. There are meat-filled
plantain and yucca fritters, vegetarian yucca with
garlic, black beans and rice, and the speciality *higa-
do a la Frutilandia*, succulent calf's liver.

The Castro

For other good Castro eateries, *see pp219-220.*

American

Chow
*215 Church Street, at Market Street (552 2469).
Metro F, J, K, L, M to Church/bus 22, 37.* **Open**
11am-11pm Mon-Thur; 11pm-midnight Fri; 10am-
midnight Sat; 10am-10pm Sun. **Main courses**
$7-$14. **Credit** Disc, MC, V. **Map** p318 J9 ⓸
Chow is a no-gimmick spot, serving hugely popular,
well-priced, straight-ahead American fare. The
menu ranges widely from roast chicken and burgers
to Asian pak choi noodles, and the kitchen succeeds
at most things it attempts. Staff are pally, and the
portions are huge.
Other locations: Park Chow, 1240 9th Avenue,
Sunset (665 9912).

Home
*2100 Market Street, at Church Street (503 0333/
www.home-sf.com). Metro F, J, K, L, M to Church/
bus 22, 37.* **Open** 5-11pm Mon-Thur, Sun; 5pm-
midnight Fri, Sat. **Main courses** $8-$18. **Credit**
AmEx, Disc, MC, V. **Map** p318 H9 ⓹
One of the Castro's can't-go-wrong spots, this sceney
place has big-city atmosphere but small-town comfort. The crowd tends to be on the make, but that
doesn't interfere with good conversation over generous portions of well-prepared classic American fare.
Roast chicken and meatloaf are right at home alongside seafood specialities and vegetable spring rolls.
Other locations: 2032 Union Street, at Buchanan
Street (931 5006).

Mecca
*2029 Market Street, at Dolores & 14th Streets
(621 7000/www.sfmecca.com). Metro to Church/
bus 22, 37.* **Open** 5-11pm Tue-Thur, Sun; 5pm-
midnight Fri, Sat. **Main courses** $19-$29.
Credit AmEx, DC, MC, V. **Map** p318 J9 ⓺
Always in harmony with the surroundings, the food
at this big, bustling and unswervingly fashionable
restaurant has been taken to the next level by chef
Stephen Barber. His world-influenced menu features
some wonderfully flavourful spare ribs, a divine
seared ahi and one of the best New York strip steaks
you'll find in San Francisco. Back at the bar, the
mood gets ever looser as the cocktails flow and the
DJ works his platters. This is the de facto headquarters of Castro cuisine.

Noe Valley

American

Firefly
*4288 24th Street, at Douglass Street (821 7652/
www.fireflyrestaurant.com). Metro J to Church &
24th/bus 24, 35, 48.* **Open** 5.30-9.30pm Mon-Thur;
5.30-10pm Fri, Sat; 5.30-9pm Sun. **Main courses**
$18-$25. **Credit** AmEx, MC, V. **Map** p317 G12 ⓻
White-topped tables aglow with soft lights and a
room buzzing with good conversation make this
neighbourhood spot well worth seeking out. The
eclectic menu might feature fried chicken (among
the best in town), rack of lamb crusted with garlic
and herbs, or rib-sticking chicken and dumplings.
There are always a number of inventive seasonal
vegetarian selections. From Sunday to Thursday,
it's also good value: three courses go for just $30.
Warm, romantic and utterly charming.

Asian

Alice's
*1599 Sanchez Street, at 29th Street (282 8999).
Metro J to Church & 29th/bus 24, 26.* **Open**
11am-9.15pm Mon-Thur; 11am-10pm Fri, Sat;
noon-9.15pm Sun. **Main courses** $8-$11. **Credit**
MC, V.
Banish any thought of Arlo Guthrie from your mind:
it's worth trekking to Alice's restaurant for the spicy
Hunan and Mandarin cooking. The clean and airy
setting enhances such dishes as asparagus salmon
in a black bean sauce or delicate orange beef; and
the spicy fried string beans will sear you in only the
best possible way.

Cafés, delis & diners

Chloe's Café
*1399 Church Street, at 26th Street (648 4116).
Metro J to Church & Clipper.* **Open** 8am-3pm
Mon-Fri; 8am-3.30pm Sat, Sun. **Main courses**
$6-$10. **No credit cards.**

Eat, Drink, Shop

Tiny Chloe's is a neighbourhood staple for Noe Valley residents, who arrive in droves for the brunch at weekends. The tables outside are popular, but inside there's an equally friendly hubbub.

Lovejoy's Tea Room

1351 Church Street, at Clipper Street (648 5895/ www.lovejoystearoom.com). Metro J to Church & Clipper/bus 48. **Open** 11am-6pm Wed, Thur, Sat, Sun; 11am-7pm Fri. **Main courses** $5-$13. **Credit** MC, V.

Select from Lovejoy's six different teas, including the Queen's Tea ($18.95) and the Wee Tea ($8.25) for children. They're all served in a room furnished with a jumble of antiques and odd knick-knacks.

Miss Millie's

4123 24th Street, between Diamond & Castro Streets (285 5598). Metro J to Church & 24th/ bus 24, 35, 48. **Open** 6-10pm Wed-Fri; 9am-2pm, 6-10pm Sat; 9am-2pm Sun. **Main courses** $8-$15. **Credit** MC, V. **Map** p317 H12 ⑩

The familiar ambience and gracious waitstaff make having breakfast here like spending a morning at your favourite aunt's house. Renowned for its lemon ricotta pancakes and hearty brunches, Millie's also offers great french toast, omelettes and classic American standards. Vegetarians will also find much to love. The best seats for brunch are at the outdoor patio tables.

The Haight & Around

Cole Valley

Asian

Eos Restaurant

901 Cole Street, at Carl Street (566 3063/www. eossf.com). Metro N to Carl & Cole/bus 6, 37, 43. **Open** 5.30-10pm Mon-Thur, Sun; 5.30-11pm Fri, Sat. **Main courses** $6-$16. **Credit** AmEx, MC, V. **Map** p317 E10 ⑩

The best of East-West fusion, served in a comfortably spare, highly designed restaurant. Classically trained chef/owner Arnold Eric Wong produces dishes such as tea-smoked Peking Duck and tamarind chilli-glazed spare ribs, backed up by one of the Bay Area's best wine lists. The same menu is served in the wine bar next door (101 Carl Street).

French

Zazie

941 Cole Street, at Parnassus Street (564 5332/ www.zaziesf.com). Metro N to Carl & Cole/bus 6, 37, 43. **Open** 8am-2.30pm, 5.30-9.30pm Mon-Thur; 8am-2.30pm, 5.30-10pm Fri; 9am-3pm, 5.30-10pm Sat; 9am-3pm, 5.30-9.30pm Sun. **Main courses** $8-$16. **Credit** AmEx, MC, V. **Map** p317 E10 ⑩

Zazie isn't quite all things to all people, but it isn't far off. It serves gentle breakfasts on a weekday morning, a small variety of lunch dishes (pasta, sandwiches), a more French menu for dinner and a much-cherished weekend brunch. Some see the place as a café, others view it as a bistro, but classification is hardly the point – it manages to pull in easygoing Cole Valley locals almost all through the day.

Lower Haight

American

RNM

598 Haight Street, at Steiner Street (551 7900/www. rnmrestaurant.com). Bus 6, 7, 22, 66, 71. **Open** 5.30-10pm Tue-Thur; 5.30-11pm Fri, Sat. **Main courses** $14-$25. **Credit** MC, V. **Map** p318 H8 ⑪

A slice of New York's SoHo translated for a laid-back Californian crowd. The high-style dining room (complete with massive chandelier) belies the food, which is almost entirely without pretension and mostly off-the-chart delicious. Don't miss ahi on roasted garlic crostini or the Maine lobster with white corn risotto. Alongside the regular *carte* is a list of 'small plates'.

Asian

Thep Phanom

400 Waller Street, at Fillmore Street (431 2526). Bus 6, 7, 22, 66, 71. **Open** 5.30-10.30pm daily. **Main courses** $9-$16. **Credit** AmEx, DC, Disc, MC, V. **Map** p317 H9 ⑫

If you're smart, you'll make an advance reservation at Thep Phanom; if you're a genius, you'll order the *tom ka gai* (coconut chicken soup) as a starter when you arrive. The 'angel wings' – fried chicken wings stuffed with glass noodles – are another universally popular choice. Often hailed as the best Thai restaurant in San Francisco.

Cafés, delis & diners

Grind Café

783 Haight Street, at Scott Street (864 0955). Bus 6, 7, 22, 66, 71. **Open** 7am-8pm Mon-Sat; 8am-8pm Sun. **Main courses** $5-$8. **No credit cards**. **Map** p317 H9 ⑬

This casual spot is populated by too-cool-for-school denizens of the Lower Haight, likely to be spending the morning leafing through Sartre or sweating off a hangover. The best eats are the vegetable-packed omelettes and stacks of pancakes. The café's open-air patio hosts smokers and dog owners.

Kate's Kitchen

471 Haight Street, between Fillmore & Webster Streets (626 3984). Bus 6, 7, 22, 66, 71. **Open** 9am-2.45pm Mon; 8am-2.45pm Tue-Fri; 8.30am-3.45pm Sat, Sun. **Main course** $5-$9. **No credit cards. Map** p317 H8 ⑭

A buzzing spot that's an excellent choice when you've a mountain of Sunday papers through which to wade. Ease into the day with the assistance of a giant bowl of granola, a huge omelette or the signature dish of hush puppies (drop pancakes made of cornmeal). Lower Haight's unofficial brunch HQ.

The Western Addition

Cafés, delis & diners

Café Abir
1300 Fulton Street, at Divisadero Street (567 7654). Bus 5, 21, 24. **Open** 6am-12.30am daily. **Main courses** $5-$8. **No credit cards. Map** p317 G7 **115**
This laid-back café is one of the most popular spots in the area, and the friendly staff and well-chosen house music mean it's as much about nightlife as morning life these days. The large café is supplemented by an organic grocery store, a bar, a coffee roastery and an international newsstand. Choose from the freshly made sandwiches and deli salads, or just get a bagel to accompany your latte and a copy of the *Times* (which comes in London, New York and Los Angeles varieties).

Japantown

Asian

Mifune
Japan Center, 1737 Post Street, between Webster & Buchanan Streets (922 0337/www.mifune.com). Bus 2, 3, 4, 22, 38. **Open** 11am-9.30pm Mon-Thur, Sun; 11am-10pm Fri, Sat. **Main courses** $10-$14. **Credit** AmEx, DC, Disc, MC, V. **Map** p314 H6 **116**
The motto here is 'It's okay to slurp your noodles', which gives you a good sense of the atmosphere and focus. Good for kids and great for vegetarians, here you'll find the lowly noodle prepared in at least 30 different ways. Orders come quickly, and the food is that magic combination: inexpensive and delicious.

Seoul Garden
22 Peace Plaza, Geary Boulevard, at Laguna Street (563 7664/www.seoulgardenbbq.com). Bus 2, 3, 4, 22, 38. **Open** 11am-11pm daily. **Main courses** $7-$25. **Credit** AmEx, MC, V. **Map** p314 H6 **117**
A good choice when all the Japanese places are too crowded (which is often), here you grill marinated beef at your table while nibbling at the myriad little dishes that typically make up Korean cuisine.

Out of this world

San Franciscans are a people of appetites, both sexual and gustatory. When one dines about town, it's often difficult to tell which of these drives they're indulging, as groans and moans of ecstasy erupt from tables. Having fetishised their food, locals consistently need to take it to another level to 'get off', and there are many opportunities to do so in this theatre of the menu-maniacal.

The standard deviance is the co-mingling of cultures known as fusion (*see p134* **After a fashion**). Most often this has meant American-Asian and French-Asian cuisine, but in San Francisco, it came to encompass some surprising combinations. Exhibit A: the marinated tofu burrito. Once a curio, it's now something of an institution, and can be found at a number of taquerias throughout the city: try Hayes Valley's **Las Estrellas** (330 Gough Street, at Hayes Street, 552 1312), **Loco Taco** in the Lower Haight (292 Divisadero Street, at Page Street, 255 8225) or the Mission's **Pancho Villa** (3071 16th Street, at Valencia Street, 864 8840).

Other examples of fusion cuisine are, if anything, even more extreme. At **Henry's Hunan** (924 Sansome Street, at Broadway Street, 956 7727), you can order 'Polish sausage, Hunan style'. That's right: kielbasa

stir-fry. In the Sunset, **Art's Cafe** (747 Irving Street, between 8th & 9th Avenues, 665 7440) has mixed Korean food with US diner fare. Try the tofu kimchee sausage omelette, which weds Korea's traditional spicy pickled cabbage with good old American meat.

The new institution of the 'bar chef' has also taken cocktail creation to the next level. What started with the muddled fresh mint of the Cuban Mojito and the ascendancy of the Appletini has yielded concoctions such as the Balsamic Moroccan Mary served at **Aziza** (5800 Geary Boulevard, at 22nd Avenue, 752 2222), a knockout Bloody Mary made with spicy organic tomato juice, fresh lime, a dash of balsamic vinegar and the secret Moroccan ingredient: harissa. Some of the other standouts on their wacked-out cocktail menu are the Meyer Lemon Basil Drop and the Tarragon-Cardamom Caipirinha.

Even the more upscale restaurants can't resist a little fun. At the **Campton Place Hotel** (*see p43*), the *amuse-bouches* are legendarily cheeky, but the menu itself has been known to throw out some WTF gems. Chilled cantaloupe soup with lobster ice-cream, anyone? Or how about olive oil ice-cream with anchovy garnish, topped with a parmesan cracker?

Ella's is full again. *See p156.*

Hayes Valley

American

J's Pots of Soul

*203 Octavia Street, at Page Street (861 3230).
Bus 21, 47, 49.* **Open** 9am-2.30pm Tue-Sun. **Main
courses** $4-$7. **No credit cards**. **Map** p318 J8
The gritty character of this area may soon go the
way of the one-dollar cup of coffee. But, hopefully,
this great little spot will withstand the influx of new
homes and businesses along the newly installed
Octavia Boulevard and Hayes Green. The hearty
soul food and southern-fried comfort fare are rib-
sticking good; specialities include sweet potato
pancakes, fried chicken and hush puppies.

Cafés, delis & diners

Citizen Cake

*399 Grove Street, at Gough Street (861 2228/www.
citizencake.com). BART & Metro to Civic Center/
bus 21, 47, 49 & Market Street routes.* **Open** 8am-
10pm Tue-Fri; 10am-10pm Sat; 10am-5pm Sun.
Main courses *Lunch* $10-$15. *Dinner* $20-$30.
Credit AmEx, MC, V. **Map** p318 J7

Quite possibly the hippest place for dessert in town,
this swanky eaterie sells gorgeous sweet things to
a crowd of well-dressed and good-looking patrons.
As good as the cakes and pies are, the excellent – if
slightly pricey – lunch and dinner menus are also
worth exploring.

French

Absinthe

*398 Hayes Street, at Gough Street (551 1590/www.
absinthe.com). BART & Metro to Civic Center/bus
21, 47, 49 & Market Street routes.* **Open** 11.30am-
midnight Tue-Fri; 11am-midnight Sat; 11am-10.30pm
Sun. **Main courses** $10-$30. **Credit** AmEx, DC,
Disc, MC, V. **Map** p318 J7
The spirit of bohemian France is reborn in San
Francisco as a boisterous brasserie. The restaurant's
grand feel is starting to come into its own, and the
French menu offers reliable favourites, including
excellent coq au vin and cassoulet. Try the seafood
platter to start. You can't get absinthe here, but
'Death in the Afternoon' (Pernod and champagne)
has a similar effect. Minus the blindness.

International

Suppenküche

*601 Hayes Street, at Laguna Street (252 9289/www.
suppenkuche.com). Bus 21, 49.* **Open** 5-10pm Mon-
Sat; 10am-2.30pm, 5-10pm Sun. **Main courses** $10-
$20. **Credit** AmEx, Disc, MC, V. **Map** p318 J8
If you're hungry for something that's going to last
you all day, Suppenküche is a good choice. Its menu,
which covers spätzle, schnitzels and dense, dark
breads, is authentically German. While the food isn't
for the faint of belly, there is a decent range of
options for vegetarians. An impressive array of
flavoursome German beers is served in tall steins;
seating is on benches.

Latin American

Espetus

*1686 Market Street, at Gough Street (552 8792/
www.espetus.com). Metro to Van Ness/bus 6, 7,
66, 71.* **Open** 11.30am-3pm, 5-10pm Mon-Thur;
11.30am-3pm, 5-11pm Fri; noon-3pm, 5-11pm Sat;
noon-9pm Sun. **Main courses** *Set lunch* $12
(3 meats), $19 (7 meats) Mon-Fri; $35 Sat; $29
Sun. *Set dinner* $29 Mon-Thur, Sun; $35 Fri,
Sat. **Credit** AmEx, MC, V. **Map** p318 K8
San Francisco's first Brazilian-style steakhouse is
also a one-of-a-kind dining experience. It's a meat-
lover's paradise, wherein attendant servers, adorned
head-to-toe in white, cruise through the restaurant
wielding skewers laden with straight-from-the-fire
pork, steak, shrimp and lamb, awaiting your
request. All the while, the evocative strummings and
patterings of Brazilian jazz unfurl in the background. An impressive, authentic take on the
increasingly popular churrascaria.

Sunset, Golden Gate Park & Richmond

Richmond

American

Q Restaurant
225 Clement Street, at 3rd Avenue (752 2298).
Bus 1, 2, 4, 38, 44. **Open** 11.30am-3pm, 5-11pm
Mon-Fri; 10am-11pm Sat; 10am-10pm Sun. **Main
courses** $8-$16. **Credit** MC, V. **Map** p312 C6 **123**
A delightful restaurant, serving some of the tastiest
comfort food in town. The name comes from its earlier ambitions as a barbecue joint, but the kitchen
now runs to grilled steaks and seafood, pasta and
some of the city's top fried chicken. A good wine list
and eclectic decor make Q one of a kind.

Asian

Khan Toke
*5937 Geary Boulevard, between 23rd & 24th
Avenues (668 6654). Bus 2, 29, 38.* **Open** 5-10.30pm
daily. **Main courses** $5-$12. **Credit** AmEx, MC, V.
One of the city's most attractive Thai restaurants,
Khan Toke is often overlooked by locals. More fools
them. Slip off your shoes, sit on the floor (or, rather,
on a low chair with a padded back support) and
enjoy fiery, colourful curries with excellent noodles,
plus a good selection of sauvignon blancs.

Mayflower
6255 Geary Boulevard, at 27th Avenue (387 8338).
Bus 2, 29, 38. **Open** 11am-2.30pm, 5-9.30pm Mon-
Fri; 10am-2.30pm Sat, Sun. **Main courses**
$8-$12. *Dim sum* $2-$6. **Credit** MC, V.
Perhaps best known for its terrific mid-morning dim
sum, the Mayflower also serves some good house-
speciality seafood, fine clay-pot dishes and great
roast chicken or duck. Alongside the broad range of
Cantonese options, you'll find Mongolian beef –
another perennial favourite. The restaurant is large,
noisy and family-oriented; arrive after 8pm if you
want to avoid the dinner hordes.

Ton Kiang
*5821 Geary Boulevard, between 22nd & 23rd
Avenues (387 8273/http://tonkiang.net). Bus 2,
29, 38.* **Open** 10.30am-10pm Mon-Thur; 10.30am-
10.30pm Fri; 9.30am-10.30pm Sat; 9am-10pm Sun.
Main courses $7-$25. **Credit** AmEx, DC, MC, V.
This large restaurant's stock-in-trade is quality
hakka cuisine, a traditional style of Chinese gypsy
cooking. Favourite dishes include the authentic salt-
baked chicken served with a ground garlic and
ginger paste. Around Chinese New Year there's a
delicious seasonal menu, and dim sum is very popular on weekend mornings.

Cafés, delis & diners

Blue Danube Coffee House
306 Clement Street, at 4th Avenue (221 9041).
Bus 1, 2, 4, 38, 44. **Open** 7am-10pm Mon-Thur,
Sun; 7am-11pm Fri, Sat. **Main courses** $5-$8.
No credit cards. Map p312 C6 **124**
One of the city's first hipster coffee houses, Danube
still enjoys a loyal following after a quarter of a century. It's a great spot for ducking into on a foggy
afternoon: grab a latte or a pint, and sit watching
passers-by from the large streetside windows.

International

Chapeau!
1408 Clement Street, at 15th Avenue (750 9787).
Bus 2, 28. **Open** 5-10pm Tue-Thur, Sun; 5-10.30pm
Fri, Sat. **Main courses** $15-$20. **Credit** AmEx, DC,
Disc, MC, V. **Map** p312 A6 **125**
This place is a proper little charmer, with cosy bistro
decor and friendly staff. The Provençal fare is just
as comforting, with excellent coq au vin, onion soup
and duck à l'orange. There's a fine brunch on
Sundays, which makes an ideal opportunity for
exploring the bubbly list. 'Hat!', appropriately
enough, is more or less French for 'Wow!'.

Golden Gate Park

Park Chow (1240 9th Avenue, 665 9912), sister-
restaurant to the estimable **Chow** (*see p151*), is
handy for Golden Gate Park, as are the **Beach
Chalet** and **Park Chalet** (*see p111*).

Sunset

American

PJ's Oyster Bed
*737 Irving Street, between 8th & 9th Avenues
(566 7775/www.pjsoysterbed.com). Metro N to
Irving & 9th/bus 6, 43, 44, 66.* **Open** 11.30am-
2.30pm, 5-10pm Mon-Thur, Sun; 11.30am-2.30pm,
5-11pm Fri, Sat. **Main courses** $10-$22. **Credit**
AmEx, DC, MC, V. **Map** p316 C10 **126**
In what used to be a fish market, you'll find a noisy,
friendly neighbourhood seafood restaurant that
makes some of San Francisco's freshest and most
authentic Cajun food. The seafood is displayed on
ice, with oysters shucked to order, and portions are
generous. The place is always packed. The jovial
chef, sporting Mardi Gras beads, eventually slips out
from the kitchen to jaw with his customers.

Asian

Ebisu
*1283 9th Avenue, between Irving Street & Lincoln
Way (566 1770/www.ebisusushi.com). Metro N to
Irving & 9th/bus 6, 43, 44, 66.* **Open** 11.30am-2pm,

Eat, Drink, Shop

5-10pm Mon-Wed; 11.30am-2pm, 5-11pm Thur,
Fri; 11.30am-11pm Sat; 11.30am-10pm Sun. **Main
courses** $10-$19. *Sushi* $3-$12. **Credit** AmEx, DC,
MC, V. **Map** p316 C10 ②

Still jealously defended by many as the best sushi
in town, Ebisu has legions of fans, which usual
translates into a wait for a table. Put your name on
the list and get a drink at the bar with a light heart,
because you're going to enjoy house specialities like
the 'pink Cadillac' (salmon sushi roll), seafood salad
and the '49er roll. Good as the sushi is, you can happily forgo it for the traditional Japanese cooked food.

Cafés, delis & diners

Java Beach Café

*1396 La Playa Boulevard, at Judah Street (665
5282). Metro N to Ocean Beach.* **Open** 5.30am-11pm
Mon-Fri; 6am-11pm Sat, Sun. **Main courses** $5-$8.
Credit MC, V.

Java Beach is funky and civilised, with the wetsuits
and grand Pacific views making it feel a bit like LA's
Hermosa Beach – minus the permatans. Surfers,
cyclists and ordinary passers-by pop in for a basic
sandwich, some soup or maybe a pastry.

Tart to Tart

*641 Irving Street, between 7th & 8th Avenues
(504 7068). Metro N to Irving & 7th/bus 6, 43,
44, 66.* **Open** 6am-2am daily. **Main courses**
$4-$6. **Credit** MC, V. **Map** p316 C10 ②

There are few late-night options in the Inner Sunset,
one of the city's best unsung neighbourhoods,
perhaps because residents are mainly families. No
matter: at Tart to Tart you can get freshly made
cookies and cakes, above-average salads and sandwiches, and more tarts than you could comfortably
sample over the course of a month.

Pacific Heights to the Golden Gate Bridge

Pacific Heights

American

Harris'

*2100 Van Ness Avenue, at Pacific Avenue (673
1888/www.harrisrestaurant.com). Bus 12, 27, 47,
49, 76.* **Open** 5.30-9.30pm Mon-Fri; 5-10pm Sat;
5-9pm Sun. **Main courses** $22-$75. **Credit**
AmEx, DC, Disc, MC, V. **Map** p314 J4 ②

Unchanged for a couple of decades (even the most
recent refurb was little more than a dusting down),
Harris' offers classy old-style dining. Sink into your
booth, start with a strong cocktail, then proceed with
a textbook Caesar salad (put together at your table),
a prime piece of carefully aged steak and a baked
potato with all the trimmings. Hefty desserts follow.

Cafés, delis & diners

Ella's

*500 Presidio Avenue, at California Street (441
5669/www.ellassanfrancisco.com). Bus 1, 3, 4, 43.*
Open 7am-5pm Mon-Fri; 8.30am-2pm Sat, Sun.
Main courses $7-$12. **Credit** AmEx, MC, V.
Map p313 F5 ⑬

This stylish corner restaurant in Presidio Heights is
famed for its weekend brunch. The wait can be long,
but it's well worth it. Favourites include the chick-
en hash with eggs and toast, or the potato scramble,
which is prepared with a frequently changing list of
fresh ingredients. The thick and perfectly crisped
French toast is tremendous. **Photo** *p154*.

French

Florio

*1915 Fillmore Street, between Bush & Pine Streets
(775 4300/www.floriosf.com). Bus 1, 2, 3, 4, 22.*
Open 5.30-10.30pm Mon-Wed; 5.30-11pm Thur-Sat;
5.30-10pm Sun. **Main courses** $14-$28. **Credit**
AmEx, MC, V. **Map** p313 H5 ⑬

A quintessential local bistro, Florio is warm and welcoming, with just the right degree of refinement.
Dark wood and white tablecloths set the tone for the
French-inspired rural cooking. The steak-frites (ask
your server) and the roast chicken and fries (to be
shared by two) are always soul-warming on a foggy
evening. Service is swift and neighbourly.

Galette

*2043 Fillmore Street, between Pine & California
Streets (928 1300). Bus 1, 2, 3, 4, 22.* **Open** 9am-
3pm Mon-Fri; 9am-5pm Sat, Sun. **Main courses**
$3-$7. **Credit** MC, V. **Map** p313 H5 ⑬

Duck in here to escape the hustle and bustle of
Fillmore Street and experience some truly authentic
Gallic cuisine. Crêpes are the star attraction, made
fresh to order and crisped to perfection. You can
even order a bowl of French cider as the ideal accompaniment. Grab one of the few outdoor seats for
prime people-watching action.

International

Chez Nous

*1911 Fillmore Street, at Pine Street (441 8044).
Bus 1, 2, 3, 4, 22.* **Open** 11.30am-3pm, 5.30-10pm
Mon-Thur, Sun; 11.30am-3pm, 5.30-11pm Fri, Sat.
Main courses *Tapas* $4-$13. **Credit** AmEx, MC,
V. **Map** p313 H6 ⑬

This neighbourhood eaterie is small enough to seem
always crowded, sometimes frustratingly so. It's a
recommendation, of sorts, for the delicious, tapas-
like plates of Mediterranean food served here, which
is typified by Moroccan spiced duck confit and a luscious salad niçoise. The bread is unbelievably fresh,
coming straight from the owner's bakery around the
corner. If a table takes too long to materialise, you
can always ask to sit at the bar.

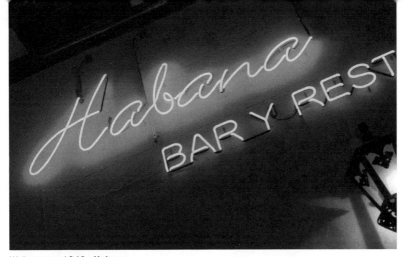

Welcome to 1940s **Habana**.

Latin American

Fresca

2114 Fillmore Street, at California Street (447 2668). Bus 1, 2, 3, 4, 22. **Open** *Lunch* 11am-3pm, 5-10pm Mon-Thur; 11am-3pm, 5-11pm Fri; 11am-11pm Sat. 11am-10pm Sun. **Main courses** $7-$20. **Credit** AmEx, DC, Disc, MC, V. **Map** p313 H5
Fresca claims to be SF's only ceviche bar, but has a broader menu than you might expect. Try tangy halibut ceviche or flambéed pisco prawns to start, followed by grilled ribeye with fries and plantains or sweet soy-roasted trout. The place can be very loud and tables are crammed together, but the quality of the Peruvian food makes up for any discomfort. **Other locations**: 3945 24th Street, Noe Valley (695 0549); 24 West Portal Avenue, Sunset (759 8087).

Habana

2080 Van Ness Avenue, at Pacific Avenue (441 2822/www.habana1948.com). Bus 12, 27, 47, 49, 76. **Open** 5.30-10pm Mon-Thur, Sun; 5.30-11pm Fri, Sat. **Main courses** $18-$20. **Credit** AmEx, DC, Disc, MC, V. **Map** p314 J4
Created to evoke Cuba in 1948, Habana's awkward space is full of banana palms and tons of wrought iron. Luckily, the surroundings are compensated for by some very nice modern interpretations of Cuban classics. Three seasonal ceviches start things off nicely, while the main-course highlight is a delicious *ropa nueva*, whimsical braised beef ragout served with cumin-marinated skirt steak with chimmichurri sauce. Don't miss the coconut flan.

Cow Hollow

American

PlumpJack Café

3127 Fillmore Street, between Greenwich & Filbert Streets (563 4755/www.plumpjack.com). Bus 22, 28,
43, 76. **Open** 11.30am-2pm, 5.30-10pm Mon-Fri; 5.30-10pm Sat, Sun. **Main courses** *Lunch* $12-$16. *Dinner* $25-$34. **Credit** AmEx, DC, MC, V. **Map** p313 G3
The success of PlumpJack Wines (*see p189*) inspired the opening of this high-profile, special-occasion eaterie. A blend of new ideas and old money (co-owner Gavin Newsom is the city's mayor), it produces outstanding California cuisine, with a penchant for interesting seafood and Mediterranean recipes, such as pan-roasted organic wild Pacific steelhead with quinoa pilaf, grilled portobello mushroom, roast baby beets and red wine sauce.

Asian

Betelnut

2030 Union Street, between Webster & Buchanan Streets (929 8855/www.betelnutrestaurant.com). Bus 22, 28, 43, 76. **Open** 11.30am-11pm Mon-Thur, Sun; 11am-midnight Fri, Sat. **Main courses** $5-$18. **Credit** DC, Disc, MC, V. **Map** p313 H4
This cool-looking spot has managed to retain its popularity by combining a relatively exotic South Pacific concept and consistent execution. Sidestep the sometimes-can't-be-bothered attitude up front, squeeze into the crowd of good-looking people at the bar and peruse a menu that's made for grazing. The best bet is to keep ordering small plates (tea-smoked duck, braised short ribs, papaya salad) until either your waistline or your credit card goes pop.

French

Baker Street Bistro

2953 Baker Street, between Lombard & Greenwich Streets (931 1475). Bus 28, 29, 41, 43, 45, 76. **Open** *Lunch* 11.30am-2.30pm Tue-Fri; 9am-2.30pm Sat, Sun. *Dinner* 5.30-9.30pm Mon; 5.30-10.30pm Tue-Sat; 5-9.30pm Sun. **Main courses** $8-$19. **Credit** AmEx, MC, V. **Map** p313 F3

Why so glum? **César** is a roaring success. *See p159.*

Wood floors, lots of sunlight and a temperate outdoor patio attract a loyal clientele, but the place's good looks are complemented by great French food and unbelievable prices: the three-course prix fixe is only $14.50. Close to the Palace of Fine Arts (*see p119*).

The Marina & the waterfront

American

Greens
Building A, Fort Mason Center, Marina Boulevard, at Buchanan Street (771 6222/www.greensrestaurant. com). Bus 10, 19, 28, 30, 47, 49. **Open** 5.30-9pm Mon; noon-2.30pm, 5.30-9pm Tue-Sat; 10.30am-2pm Sun. **Main courses** $16-$22. **Credit** AmEx, Disc, MC, V. **Map** p313 H2
Vegans and carnivores alike extol the virtues of venerable Greens, with its great views of the Golden Gate Bridge and award-winning, all-vegetarian menu. Fresh produce and an extensive wine list complement hand mesquite-grilled vegetables and wood-fired pizzas topped with wild mushrooms. If you don't fancy queuing, pick up sandwiches or soups from the takeaway counter, open from 8am (9am Sun).

Cafés, delis & diners

Grove
2250 Chestnut Street, at Avila Street (474 4843). Bus 30, 76. **Open** 7am-11pm Mon-Fri; 8am-11pm Sat, Sun. **Main courses** $7-$10. **Credit** AmEx, MC, V. **Map** p313 G3

This happening spot is a true outpost of café culture. As well as coffee, beer, wine and comfort food (lasagne, chicken pot pie), patrons can enjoy chess, checkers and backgammon. The Fillmore Street location offers the same kind of woodsy interior and big cappuccinos, but for a less trend-conscious clientele. **Other locations**: 2016 Fillmore Street, Pacific Heights (474 1419).

International

Isa
3324 Steiner Street, between Chestnut & Lombard Streets (567 9588/www.isarestaurant.com). Bus 22, 30. **Open** 5-10pm Tue-Thur; 5-10.30pm Fri, Sat. **Main courses** $5-$18. **Credit** MC, V. **Map** p313 G3
Expect such interesting fare as roast mussels with shallots and white wine, or hanger steak with tarragon mustard and roast garlic potatoes from the tapas-like menu at Isa. Cosy, with a secluded back patio, it is winningly free of Marina affectations.

Latin American

Los Hermanos
2026 Chestnut Street, at Fillmore Street (921 5790). Bus 22, 30. **Open** 10.30am-9.30pm Mon-Sat. **Main courses** $5-$8. **No credit cards. Map** p313 G3
Chaotic but friendly, with people shouting orders from three rows back, this nondescript spot thinks it's in the Mission. You'll find authentic Mexican food, including enormous, freshly made burritos.

The East Bay

A solid case can be made that the roots of San Francisco's current high culinary standing are grounded across the Bay. **Chez Panisse** (*see below*) is the headline-maker, but there are other dining options that make a jaunt over the bridge a mighty powerful temptation.

Oakland

American

Bay Wolf

3853 Piedmont Avenue, between 40th Street & MacArthur Boulevard (1-510 655 6004/www.bay wolf.com). AC Transit 51, 57, 59. **Open** 11.30am-2pm, 6-9pm Mon-Thur; 11.30am-2pm, 5.30-9.30pm Fri; 5.30-9.30pm Sat; 5.30-9pm Sun. **Main courses** $12-$25. **Credit** AmEx, MC, V.

Opened by Michael Wild in 1975, this comfortable East Bay staple is situated in a beautifully revamped Craftsman-style house. Wild is renowned for his duck specialities, which form part of a tempting blend of California and Mediterranean fare, using freshest seasonal produce. In nice weather, the best seats are on the enclosed redwood deck out front.

Italian & pizza

Oliveto

5655 College Avenue, at Shafter Avenue (1-510 547 5356/www.oliveto.com). BART Rockridge. **Open** *Café* 7am-9pm Mon; 7am-10pm Tue-Fri; 8am-10pm Sat; 8am-9pm Sun. *Restaurant* 11.30am-2pm, 5.30-9pm Mon; 11.30am-2pm, 5.30-9.30pm Tue, Wed; 11.30am-2pm, 5.30-10pm Thur, Fri; 5.30-10pm Sat, 5-9pm Sun. **Main courses** *Café* $6-$13. *Restaurant* $14-$28. **Credit** AmEx, DC, MC, V.

This warm, welcoming restaurant in Oakland's upscale Rockridge area, features soul-warming northern Italian fare that is almost entirely handmade, right down to the trademark olive oil. The speciality is house-cured, grilled and spit-roasted meat, but menus change daily to showcase the freshest available ingredients. A café menu features pizzas and baked goods from the wood-fired oven.

Berkeley

American

Chez Panisse

1517 Shattuck Avenue, between Cedar & Vine Streets (1-510 548 5525/www.chezpanisse.com). BART Downtown Berkeley. **Open** *Restaurant sittings* 6-6.30pm, 8.30-9.30pm Mon-Sat. *Café* 11.30am-3pm, 5-10.30pm Mon-Thur; 11.30am-3.30pm, 5-11.30pm Fri, Sat. **Main courses** *Restaurant set menu* $50-$75. *Café* $15-$25. **Credit** AmEx, DC, Disc, MC, V.

This is where chef/owner Alice Waters created California cuisine more than 30 years ago. Her modest, wood-framed restaurant still reigns supreme, serving impeccable prix fixe dinners downstairs in the restaurant and more casual à la carte meals in the upstairs café. Ingredients are always fresh, local, organic and of the very best quality. The excellent wine list combines French and Californian options, but you can also bring your own if you're prepared to pay the $20 corkage (two-bottle limit).

European

César

1515 Shattuck Avenue, between Cedar & Vine Streets (1-510 548 5525/www.barcesar.com). BART Downtown Berkeley. **Open** noon-11pm Mon-Thur, Sun; noon-11.30pm Fri, Sat. **Main courses** *Tapas* $4-$12. **Credit** AmEx, Disc, MC, V.

It was pretty daring to locate César right next door to Chez Panisse (*see above*), but the place has more than held its own despite the competition. It no doubt helps that the ambience here is very different (lively, thanks in part to the presence of a bar area), but the food, a collection of Spanish-influenced tapas made from high-quality ingredients, also impresses. In short, a good bet. **Photo** *p158*.

Rivoli

1539 Solano Avenue, between Neilson Street & Peralta Avenue (1-510 526 2542/www.rivoli restaurant.com). **Open** 5.30-9.30pm Mon-Thur; 5.30-10pm Fri; 5-10pm Sat; 5-9pm Sun. **Main courses** $17-$25. **Credit** AmEx, Disc, MC, V.

Rivoli is a charming, intimate and neighbourly Italian-inspired restaurant, run by talented chef Wendy Brucker. The menu offers simple versions of classic dishes, prepared with seasonal organic produce; though it changes every three weeks, the portobello mushroom fritters (Brucker's signature dish), Caesar salad and a great hot fudge sundae remain a constant presence.

Walnut Creek

American

Lark Creek Inn

1360 Locust Street, at Diablo Street (1-925 256 1234/www.larkcreek.com). **Open** 11.30am-2.30pm, 5.30-10pm Mon-Fri; 5-10pm Sat; 10am-2pm, 5-9pm Sun. **Main courses** $18-$40. **Credit** AmEx, MC, V.

Chef Bradley Ogden and restaurateur Michael Dellar have established a Walnut Creek branch of their growing Lark Creek empire to cater for the sophisticated tastes of growing numbers of SF émigrés. The charming dining room maintains a bustling neighbourhood feel, and the kitchen prepares American fare with considerable imagination. Fish, fowl and grilled meats are all served in huge portions, along with signature Lark Inn dishes, such as the famed clam chowder.

Eat, Drink, Shop

Bars

If you can't find a bar to suit in SF, you can't be drinking about it hard enough.

The state of California is responsible for over 90 per cent of the wine produced in the US. The ever-thirsty citizenry of San Francisco, however, seem happy to imbibe whatever they find in front of them. More so than any other big city in the state, this is a drinking town.

The one characteristic shared by local drinkers is their lack of fear. More likely to be found in a Bacchanalian revel than cowering beneath the sommelier's withering gaze, San Franciscans spend more on booze than the citizens of any other US city. Their devotion to the dram means local alcohol production isn't limited to wine: the region is home to a goodly number of breweries and micro-distilleries, along with many brewpubs and a few speciality bars dedicated to more exotic tipples.

WHERE TO DRINK

Generalists will delight in the number and variety of bars here, but each locale has bars that fit its personality. The hangouts around the **Financial District** suit the suits who frequent them, while those around the **Tenderloin** and the **Civic Center** tend towards the earthy (and, from time to time, seedy). **North Beach**, *the* place to drink back in the days of the Beats, is now best avoided on weekends, when the bridge-and-tunnel crowd invades. The scene is smart, sometimes even chi-chi, in **Nob Hill** and **Pacific Heights**. **Haight-Ashbury** draws a down-to-earth, occasionally crunchy crowd; denizens of the **Lower Haight** may have more ink on their skin, but they're a friendly bunch.

However, the **Mission** is still the best place to booze it up. Home to artists, musicians and much of the city's Latino population, the area is powered by a bohemian engine that also drives its nightlife. Choose from beer gardens or cocktails on roof decks, Irish pubs or Mexican *cervecerias*, chic style bars and a host of dives that are pure Americana.

BOOZE AND THE LAW

You have to be aged 21 or over to buy and consume alcohol in California (bring ID even if you look older), which can be sold only

> ► ❶ Pink numbers given in this chapter correspond to the location of each bar on the street maps. *See pp312-319*.

The best Bars

For outdoor refreshment
Take a trip to the the hip **Medjool Sky Terrace** (*see p167*), the beer garden at punkabilly **Zeitgeist** (*see p167*) or the verdant lawn at the **Park Chalet** (*see p170*).

For local brews
Grab a pint of cask-conditioned ale at **Magnolia** (*see p168*), sample Bay Area brews at **Toronado** (*see p169*), or celebrate the **21st Amendment** (*see p163*) with a beer made on site.

For uptown cocktailing
The **Redwood Room** (*see p161*), **Top of the Mark** (*see p164*), **Matrix** (*see p170*), **Bix** (*see below*) and the **Bubble Lounge** (*see p161*) come with various levels of swank.

For down and dirty drinkin'
On the opposite side of the coin, the **500 Club** (*see p167*), **Club Mallard** (*see p172*) and **Place Pigalle** (*see p170*) all offer a rather baser booze bonanza. *See also p162* **Crawling the Tenderloin**.

For the tiki experience
The **Tonga Room** (*see p164*) is a rather more upscale (and tame) hangout than earthier **Trad'r Sam** (*see p170*).

between 6am and 2am. However, many bars choose to remain closed until late afternoon, and last call is often around 1.15am-1.30am. Staff are obliged to confiscate unconsumed alcoholic drinks after 2am, and don't take kindly to being messed around.

Downtown

The Financial District

Bix
56 Gold Street, between Montgomery & Sansome Streets (433 6300/www.bixrestaurant.com). Bus 10, 12, 15, 41. **Open** 5.30-10.30pm Mon-Thur, Sun; 11.30am-11.30pm Fri, Sat. **Credit** AmEx, DC, Disc, MC, V. **Map** p315 N4 ❶

Eat, Drink, Shop

The secretive locale and supper-club menu of Bix, named for owner Doug 'Bix' Beiderbeck ('very vaguely related' to 1920s and '30s jazz cornet legend Bix Beiderbecke), evoke the opulence of the Jazz Age. The room combines the glamour of Harlem's Cotton Club with the splendour of a cruise liner's dining room so effectively that you half expect to spy Rita Hayworth sipping a Martini in a booth.

Bubble Lounge

714 Montgomery Street, between Washington & Jackson Streets (434 4204/www.bubblelounge.com). Bus 1, 10, 12, 15, 41. **Open** 5.30pm-2am Mon-Fri; 6.30pm-2am Sat. **Credit** AmEx, DC, MC, V. **Map** p315 N4

After the stock market closes, stockbrokers and short-skirted executives tickle their noses with an incredible selection of sparkling wines and champagnes at this upscale hangout. The booze is paired with fine pâté, salads and caviar for a top-drawer taste of the Wall Street of the West.

The Tenderloin

Also in the area is the **Hemlock Tavern** (*see p235*), best known as a music venue but with a fine bar out front at which there's no cover. *See also p162* **Crawling the Tenderloin**.

Edinburgh Castle

950 Geary Street, between Larkin & Polk Streets (885 4074/www.castlenews.com). Bus 2, 3, 4, 19, 38, 47. **Open** 5pm-2am daily. **Credit** MC, V. **Map** p314 K6

Upstairs sits a small cultural venue, playing host to local bands, DJ nights, literary readings and even the odd play (the stage version of *Trainspotting* had its debut here), while downstairs is a raffish, capacious boozer. The patrons are an unpretentious mix of mods, musos and the occasional expat, some munching on fish 'n' chips (delivered in rolled-up newspaper). The highlight of the drinks selection is a vast and affordable range of single malt whiskies.

Redwood Room

Clift Hotel, 495 Geary Street, at Taylor Street (775 4700/www.clifthotel.com). Bus 2, 3, 4, 27, 38, 76/cable car Powell-Hyde or Powell-Mason. **Open** 5pm-2am daily. **Credit** AmEx, DC, MC, V. **Map** p314 L6

No time was wasted in adding a bar to the Clift (*see p48*) after the repeal of Prohibition in 1933, and the magnificent result has been a fixture for high-end cocktailing ever since. Although the decor shifted from art deco to postmodern under Schrager, the bar is neither tacky nor too flamboyant, its towering walls still panelled in redwood thought to have come from a single tree. A DJ spins four nights a week for a well-dressed and moneyed crew. **Photo** *p163*.

SoMa & South Beach

Close by SBC Park is the **Hotel Utah** (*see p235*), a good music venue with a great bar.

Butter

354 11th Street, between Folsom & Harrison Streets (863 5964/www.smoothasbutter.com). Bus 9, 12, 27, 47. **Open** 6pm-2am Tue-Sat. **Credit** AmEx, DC, Disc, MC, V. **Map** p318 L9

With the pun-on-Beck motto 'two turntables and a microwave', Butter combines chill-room vibe (complete with DJ) with trailer-trash kitsch and food. After several years on the scene, Butter's still packing people in, and its magic-formula repast of a corn dog, a Twinkie and a tin of Pabst Blue Ribbon may just prove to be the Elixir of Life.

Catalyst Cocktails

312 Harriet Street, between Bryant & Brannan Streets (621 1722/www.catalystcocktails.com). Bus 12, 19, 27, 47. **Open** 4pm-2am Tue-Sat. **Credit** MC, V. **Map** p319 N8

Sipping cocktails beneath the spires of Catalyst's art deco bar is a bit like making a toast under a miniature Statue of Liberty, but there's much to celebrate here, including a daunting four-page cocktail menu:

Bix. *See p160.*

Eat, Drink, Shop

Walk Crawling the Tenderloin

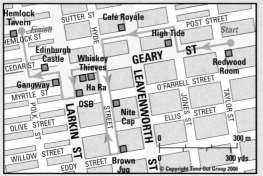

Further treats are found further west along Geary. Between Hyde and Leavenworth sits **Whiskey Thieves** (No.839, 409 2063), a brash hole in the wall notable mostly for the fact that, thanks to its owner-operated status, it allows its patrons to smoke. Whiskey Thieves only arrived on the street in 2005, and the disparity between it and ragged old near-neighbour the **Ha-Ra** (No.875, 673 3148) could hardly be greater. Bartender Carl has a reputation for truculence, which he plays up to like nobody's business for an audience that rarely reaches double figures. He's a pussycat really.

Still, if the grouching grows old, there are other options. The mix of weary workers and gassing hipsters at **OSB** (it stands for O'Farrell Street Bar; 800 Larkin Street, 567 9326) is amusingly dissimilar to the gay-heavy crowds, leavened further by the occasional tranny, that gathers at **Gangway** (841 Larkin Street, 776 6828). A block away, young guns and raving expats suck back single malts at the **Edinburgh Castle** (*see p161*), while beer's the beverage of choice at Korean bar **Hanaro** (939 Geary Street, 928 4066). In the unlikely event you're still capable of walking in a straight line at this point, you're just a block and a half from the **Hemlock Tavern** (*see p235*) and the assorted bars on and around Polk Street. But isn't it time you went home already?

Time was when the Tenderloin's unsavoury reputation kept the derelicts and the determined bohos in and everyone else out. Still packed with unpretentious, seedy booze-holes, it's now also decorated with a number of new-breed dive bars that come complete with top-shelf liquors and DJ nights. The contrast is entertaining, educational and best experienced via a long and fancy-free crawl around this most alcoholically unbalanced of areas.

Starting at the area's north-eastern edge will allow for the most extreme variation in saloon style. At the **Redwood Room** in the Clift Hotel (*see p161*), moneyed yuppies make the scene with cocktails in one hand and cellphones in the other. Few of them make the block-long walk to the **High Tide** (600 Geary Street, 771 3145), a scruffy old corner bar that grows buzzily popular with hipsters on weekends.

Even fewer of them head south from the High Tide into the edgy Tenderloin proper and insalubrious but undeniably characterful bars such as the **Nite Cap** (699 O'Farrell Street, 776 5711) and the **Brown Jug** (496 Eddy Street, 441 8404). Both look more dangerous than they actually are. Even so, this sketchy little pocket of town (south of Geary, north of Market, east of Taylor) is home to some of the city's sleaziest dives. Approach with caution, and contrast with the likes of the **Café Royale** (800 Post Street, 441 4099), a sophisticated new-breed bar-gallery on the other side of Geary where the attractions include free wireless internet access and regular live jazz.

sup a Ukrainian Quaalude or a Love and Chaos, a mix of Jim Beam and cream soda with a Twizzlers Licorice Straw. Handily located across from the city jail.

Hi Dive

Pier 28½, Embarcadero, at Bryant Street (977 0170/www.hidive.net). Metro N to Folsom & Embarcadero/bus 12. **Open** 11.30am-11.30pm Mon-Sat; 10am-11pm Sun. **Credit** MC, V. **Map** p315 P5 ●
Once a dive patronised by dock workers and sailors on shore leave, the Hi Dive has recently been renovated, but still draws a low-key crowd. A fine pit stop during a walk down the Embarcadero, it's right on the water, and gets lively – or, depending on your mood, crowded – before and after Giants games.

21st Amendment

563 2nd Street, between Bryant & Brannan Streets (369 0900/www.21st-amendment.com). Metro 2nd & King/bus 12, 15, 30, 45, 76. **Open** 11.30am-midnight Mon-Thur, Sun; 11.30am-1am Fri, Sat. **Credit** AmEx, Disc, MC, V. **Map** p315 O6 ●
Named in honour of the constitutional diktat repealing Prohibition, this brewpub gets packed with Giants fans looking to load up on good, nicely priced booze – a mix of own-label beers and guests – before getting soaked by the exorbitant beer prices inside the stadium. At other times, it's a standard brewpub, with decent food and a convivial atmosphere.

W Hotel

181 3rd Street, at Howard Street (817 7836/www.starwoodhotels.com). BART & Metro to Montgomery/bus 12, 15, 30, 45, 76. **Open** 7pm-2am Tue-Sat. **Credit** AmEx, DC, Disc, MC, V. **Map** p315 N6 ●
The two bars at this trendy hotel (*see p52*) are packed with beautiful people. The first bar is a circular affair in the lobby, while the main room, next to XYZ (*see p138*), lies behind a beaded curtain above. Some find the atmosphere a bit competitive, but the scene shifts nightly and banquettes upstairs encourage an intimate vibe. **Photo** *p164*.

Nob Hill & Chinatown

Nob Hill & Polk Gulch

C Bobby's Owl Tree

601 Post Street, at Taylor Street (776 9344/www.theowltree.com). Bus 2, 3, 4, 27, 38, 76/cable car Powell-Hyde or Powell-Mason. **Open** 5pm-1am Wed-Sat. **No credit cards.** **Map** p314 L5 ●
Stuffed owls, paper owls, china owls, cardboard owls. Paintings of owls. An owl clock. Owl-shaped drinks menus. A stained-glass owl. There are probably 400 owls in this small, cosy and eccentrically beautiful bar, which is the length and width of a school bus. Rumour has it that the theme is

Take a seat at the **Redwood Room**. *See p161*.

connected to the Bohemian Club, a secret society whose headquarters are located in the ivy-covered building across the street. But camp, acerbic owner Bobby isn't letting on. Drinks are a little pricey.

Le Colonial
20 Cosmo Place, between Jones & Taylor Streets (931 3600/www.lecolonialsf.com). Bus 2, 3, 4, 27, 38, 76. **Open** 5.30-10pm Mon-Wed, Sun; 5.30-11.30pm Thur-Sat. **Credit** AmEx, DC, MC, V. **Map** p314 L5 ⓫
Designed to approximate Vietnam circa 1920, when the country was still a French colony, this elegant hideaway has a sizeable dining room, while the stylish upstairs lounge serves tropical drinks, exotic teas and a menu highlighting Vietnamese fusion cuisine. The comfortable couches invite cocktailing and more in a lush environment of palm trees, rattan furniture and shuttered windows.

Red Room
Commodore Hotel, 825 Sutter Street, between Jones & Leavenworth Streets (346 7666/www.jdvhospitality. com). Bus 2, 3, 4, 27, 38, 76. **Open** 5pm-2am Mon-Sat; 7pm-2am Sun. **No credit cards**. **Map** p314 L5 ⓬
Enough to inspire a craving in any vampire, this slick hotel bar is entirely blood red: the walls, the tables, the semicircular bar, even one of the many speciality Martinis. It's wildly popular but tiny – an uncomfortable combination at weekends. Come during the week when it's cosier.

Tonga Room
Fairmont, 950 Mason Street, between California & Sacramento Streets (772 5278/www.fairmont.com). Bus 1/cable car California or Powell-Mason. **Open** 5pm-midnight Mon-Thur, Sun; 5pm-1am Fri, Sat. **Credit** AmEx, Disc, MC, V. **Map** p314 L4 ⓭
Despite the all-you-can-eat happy-hour dim sum, the sarong-clad waitresses and the enormous, exotic cocktails (Bora Bora Horror, anyone?), the real attraction at this long-lived tiki bar is the spectacle of house musicians performing off-key covers of cheesy pop songs while afloat on a raft on the Tonga's indoor 'lagoon'. There's even an indoor thunderstorm every 20 minutes, complete with rain.

Top of the Mark
Mark Hopkins Inter-Continental Hotel, 1 Nob Hill, at California & Mason Streets, Nob Hill (392 3434/ www.ichotelsgroup.com). Bus 1/cable car California, Powell-Hyde or Powell-Mason. **Open** 5pm-midnight Mon-Thur, Sun; 4pm-1am Fri, Sat. **Admission** $10 after 9pm Fri, Sat. **Credit** AmEx, DC, Disc, MC, V. **Map** p314 L5 ⓮

W. *See p163.*

Neatly named for its location at the summit of the Mark Hopkins Inter-Continental Hotel, Top of the Mark offers spectacular panoramic views of San Francisco. It's worth a quick visit just to check the view and sip a cocktail from the extensive '100 Martinis' menu, but arrive early in the evening to avoid the cover charge and the dress code (look smart or drink elsewhere).

Chinatown

Li Po

916 Grant Avenue, between Washington & Jackson Streets (982 0072). Bus 1, 12, 15, 30, 45. **Open** 2pm-2am daily. **No credit cards.** **Map** p315 M4 ⓫
A fun spot for a pick-me-up when you're done with the junk shops on Grant Avenue. Li Po is basically a dive, but the cave façade and giant, tattered Chinese lantern inside set it nicely apart from its neighbours. It'll take you back to Barbary Coast-era San Francisco with no risk of being shanghaied by anything except the potent cocktails.

Mr Bing's

201 Columbus Avenue, at Pacific Avenue (362 1545). Bus 12, 15, 30, 41, 45. **Open** 10am-2am daily. **No credit cards. Map** p315 M4 ⓰
This shambles of a bar doesn't look like much from the outside, and looks like even less once you're through the door. But, thanks partly to its highly conspicuous location, it's a prince among dives, frequented by a mix of idling Chinese, haggard old North Beach bums and those who are simply, plainly desperate for a drink. For dive bar devotees, this is rarely less than entertaining.

Tunnel Top

601 Bush Street, at Stockton Street (986 8900/ www.tunneltop.com). Bus 30, 45/cable car Powell-Hyde or Powell-Mason. **Open** 5pm-2am daily. **No credit cards. Map** p315 M5 ⓱
The two-storey Tunnel Top perches above the Stockton Tunnel between Chinatown and Union Square, and looks a little shabby from the outside. Inside, however, the decor is urban-decay cool; films are projected against rust-coloured walls, while a DJ soundtracks the conversation. Outside is the spot where Sam Spade surveys the scene of his partner's murder at the beginning of *The Maltese Falcon.*

North Beach to Fisherman's Wharf

North Beach

Rogue Ale's Public House

673 Union Street, between Powell Street & Columbus Avenue (362 7880/www.rogue.com). Bus 12, 15, 30, 39, 41, 45. **Open** 11am-midnight Mon-Thur, Sun; 11am-2am Fri, Sat. **Credit** AmEx, Disc, MC, V. **Map** p314 L3 ⓭

Oregon microbrewery Rogue Ale's bold land grab is evidenced by this ale house, devoted to its staggering array of brews. The standard selection of ambers and lagers is supplemented by such gems as chilli-pepper-tinged Chipotle Ale, Smoke Ale (with strong flavours of smokehouse almonds), Coffee Stout and Iron Chef Morimoto's Black Obi Soba Ale.

Rosewood

732 Broadway, at Stockton Street (951 4886). Bus 12, 15, 30, 41, 45. **Open** 5.30pm-2am Tue-Fri; 7pm-2am Sat. **Credit** MC, V. **Map** p315 M3 ⓳
This stylish bar, opened in early 2001, boasts rosewood panelling and is furnished with low black leather benches. Located on a neglected commercial strip at the edge of North Beach and Chinatown, with no sign outside, it's not been overrun, and remains one of the best places in the city to sip a cocktail while DJs spin low-key tunes.

Royale

1326 Grant Avenue, between Green & Vallejo Streets (433 4247). Bus 12, 15, 30, 41, 45. **Open** 6pm-2am daily. **Credit** MC, V. **Map** p315 M3 ⓴
Royale's carefully styled interior, bathed in the azure glow of accent lighting, is at once contemporary and soothing. Solid cocktails, handsome blue suede banquettes and a top-notch jukebox heavy on horns (ska, jazz, jam) make the madness of the weekend Broadway crowds seem a world away.

San Francisco Brewing Company

155 Columbus Avenue, at Pacific Avenue (434 3344/www.sfbrewing.com). Bus 12, 15, 30, 41, 45. **Open** 11.30am-1am Mon-Fri; 11.30am-1.30am Sat, Sun. **Credit** AmEx, MC, V. **Map** p315 M4 ㉑
Housed in a restored 1907 saloon, complete with a mahogany bar and belt-driven fans, this brewpub offers microbrews, pub grub and even free tours. Formerly the Andromeda Saloon, it was here that gangster 'Baby Face' Nelson was captured. The scene is more staid today, but it's hard to pass up the $1 brews from 4pm to 6pm and midnight to 1am.

Spec's

William Saroyan Place, at Broadway (421 4112). Bus 12, 15, 30, 41, 45. **Open** 4.30pm-2am Mon-Fri; 5pm-2am Sat, Sun. **No credit cards. Map** p315 M3 ㉒
Spec's is the quintessential old-school San Francisco bar: one part North Beach bohemian and one part Wild West saloon, with a dash of weirdness for good measure. Tucked away in a false alley (you'll see what we mean), nearly every inch is covered with dusty detritus from around the world. If you're feeling a bit peckish, a basket of saltines and a wedge of gouda can be had for a mere $2.

Tony Nik's

1524 Stockton Street, at Green Street (693 0990). Bus 12, 15, 30, 39, 41, 45. **Open** 4pm-2am daily. **Credit** MC, V. **Map** p315 M3 ㉓
This venerable lounge, essentially a long bar with a few extra seats, opened the day after Prohibition was repealed in 1933, and keeps the old-time vibe

Look down on the world at **Vesuvio**.

Eat, Drink, Shop

alive thanks to Atomic Age decor and the comfortably hip and friendly environs. They take their cocktails seriously here: there's always a surprise lurking behind the bar if the right mixologist is on duty.

Tosca Café

242 Columbus Avenue, between Broadway & Pacific Avenue (986 9651). Bus 12, 15, 30, 41, 45. **Open** 5pm-2am Tue-Sun. **No credit cards. Map** p315 M3 ②

Formica-topped tables, massive copper espresso machines, Caruso warbling from an ancient jukebox… Bars with interiors this lush deserve to double as movie sets. The house speciality, a blend of coffee, steamed milk and brandy, really packs a punch. The bada-bing Italian ambience and Hollywood-connected owner have drawn the likes of Bono and Sean Penn to the private pool room.

Vesuvio

255 Columbus Avenue, between Broadway & Pacific Avenue (362 3370/www.vesuvio.com). Bus 12, 15, 30, 41, 45. **Open** 6am-2am daily. **No credit cards. Map** p315 M4 ②

A funky old saloon with a stained-glass façade, Vesuvio preserves the flavour of an earlier era. It's next to the famous City Lights bookshop (*see p179*), just across Jack Kerouac Alley (the writer was a regular here), and its walls are covered with beat memorabilia. Sit on the narrow balcony and check out the scene downstairs and on the street.

The Mission

Argus Lounge

3187 Mission Street, at Valencia Street (824 1447/ www.arguslounge.com). Bus 12, 14, 26, 27, 49, 67. **Open** 4pm-2am Mon-Sat; 5pm-midnight Sun. **No credit cards.**

Known by some as the Peacock because of the illuminated feather out front (there's no other sign), the Argus is far enough down Mission to escape the gentrifying masses. A clean, simple hangout, it draws a happy crowd, including local indie-rock heroes. A superlative jukebox and back-room pool table add to quirky touches such as a working 1950s exercise belt. Shake it, baby.

Attic

3336 24th Street, between Mission & Bartlett Streets (643 3376). BART 24th Street/bus 14, 26, 48, 49, 67. **Open** 5pm-2am daily. **No credit cards. Map** p318 K12 ㉖

This skinny little hangout opens out the further from the front door you go, but it never really loses its intimacy. When DJs aren't spinning tunes alternately spiky and mellow, the bartender's iPod gets set to 'shuffle', which usually starts a conversation or two. Drinks are strong and keenly priced.

Beauty Bar San Francisco

2299 Mission Street, at 19th Street (285 0323/ www.beautybar.com). BART 16th Street/bus 14, 26, 33, 49. **Open** 5pm-2am Mon-Fri; 7pm-2am Sat, Sun. **Credit** MC, V. **Map** p318 K11 ㉗

This little cocktail bar, modelled after its sister bar in New York, is decorated with bric-a-brac salvaged from a Long Island hair salon. Instead of a couch, curl up on a Naugahyde salon chair, with hairdryer still attached. On Wednesday to Saturday evenings, buy a $10 cocktail and get a free manicure.

Dalva

3121 16th Street, at Albion Street (252 7740). BART 16th Street/bus 14, 26, 33, 49. **Open** 4pm-2am daily. **No credit cards. Map** p318 J10 ㉘

An unspoiled oasis of cool in the manic Mission bar scene, Dalva worships good music. The jukebox, named Orpheus, carries a wonderfully diverse array of sounds, from Cuban music to tiki kitsch. When it's not on, DJs spin drum 'n' bass, jazz, soul, funk, salsa, and other odds and sods.

Doc's Clock

2575 Mission Street, at 22nd Street (824 3627). BART 24th Street/bus 14, 26, 48, 49, 67. **Open** 6pm-2am daily. **No credit cards. Map** p318 K12 ㉙

This place was formerly a total dive but, in common with many bars around here, has had a kindly refit. The mahogany bar has been buffed up, the booze selection has expanded, and the CD changer spits out anything from Air to Sufjan Stevens for the hipster crowd. Just down the road is the similarly brushed-up Mission Bar (2695 Mission Street, 647 2300), which lacks both the shuffleboard table and the magnificent neon sign of Doc's Clock, but adds some of the area's strongest drinks.

500 Club
500 Guerrero Street, at 17th Street (861 2500). BART 16th Street/bus 26, 33. **Open** noon-midnight daily. **No credit cards. Map** p318 J10 ⓪
Vying with Doc's Clock for the title of the Mission's best marquee, the 'Five Hunge' is everybody's favourite dive. Cavernous Naugahyde booths, a punk jukebox, a pool table and cheap, stiff drinks keep the place brimming with an incredibly various crowd. Pull up a stool at the long, long bar and don't make any plans to leave.

Knockout
3223 Mission Street, at Valencia Street (550 6994/ www.theknockoutsf.com). Bus 12, 26, 27, 49, 67. **Open** 5pm-2am Tue-Sat; 4pm-midnight Sun. **No credit cards.**
Patrons won't be seeing the freakshows of yore at this old hangout, recently wrestled from the hands of the locally notorious ringmaster of punk Circus Redickuless, but Knockout takes on all challengers, hosting everything from reggae to rockabilly. Its once-grungy corners have been given the white-glove treatment just in time to host weekly bingo evenings.

Medjool Sky Terrace
2522 Mission Street, between 21st & 22nd Streets (550 9055/www.medjoolsf.com). BART 24th Street/ bus 14, 26, 48, 49, 67. **Open** 6-10pm Mon-Thur, Sun; 6-11pm Fri, Sat. **Credit** AmEx, MC, V. **Map** p318 K11 ㉛
This two-building complex, topped by Medjool's massive roof deck, contains a restaurant, a café and an excellent hostel. However, weather permitting, the deck is the primary draw. Sip cocktails, draft beer or wine, and scoff scaled-down, lighter fare from the restaurant's menu while taking in some of the Mission's best views.

Phone Booth
1398 S Van Ness Avenue, at 25th Street (648 4683). BART 24th Street/bus 12, 14, 48, 49, 67. **Open** 1pm-2am Mon-Fri, Sun; 2pm-2am Sat. **No credit cards. Map** p318 K12 ㉜
While the bars on Mission Street draw people in their late twenties and hipsters in their thirties, this corner spot attracts a crowd closer to college age. Its tiny dimensions mean it often appears more popular than it is, but most drinkers are too bombed on the cheap booze to notice. Ageing British punks and new wavers will find plenty to like on the jukebox.

Sadie's Flying Elephant
491 Potrero Avenue, at Mariposa Street (551 7988/ www.flyingelephant.com). Bus 9, 33. **Open** 4pm-2am daily. **No credit cards. Map** p319 M10 ㉝
A dive bar with a heart of gold, Sadie's offers comfy couches, a superb jukebox, free popcorn and two pool tables. Most of the walls are made up of large

The sporting life: **Doc's Clock**. *See p166.*

blackboards: patrons are encouraged to contribute their own graffiti, chalk murals, epitaphs, admonitions, hexes and/or pearls of wisdom. Philanthropic activities (monthly benefits, neighbourhood trash pick-ups) make this a worthy place to binge as well.

Treat Street Cocktails
3050 24th Street, at Treat Avenue (824 5954). Bus 12, 48, 67. **Open** 5pm-2am daily. **No credit cards. Map** p318 L12 ㉞
Fans of cult TV show *Northern Exposure* will surely appreciate the look of this hangout, where the decorations include deer heads and fishing trophies. It's something of an anomaly given the bar's location on the city's most Hispanic corner, which is probably what draws the erudite-looking thirtysomething clientele.

Zeitgeist
199 Valencia Street, at Duboce Avenue (255 7505). Bus 26. **Open** 9am-2am daily. **No credit cards. Map** p318 K9 ㉟
Sited on the border between SoMa and the Mission, Zeitgeist is one of the hippest and most mellow bars in town, popular with bikers (Hondas rather than Harleys), bike messengers and people from every walk of alternative life. On sunny evenings, it's hard to find a seat at the benches and tables in the giant beer-garden-meets-junkyard back patio. The jukebox places special emphasis on underground punk.

Eat, Drink, Shop

Smoke 'em if you got 'em

The Californian rules on smoking in public places are among the most draconian in the world. Smoking is outlawed in restaurants, cafés and bars; any bar found allowing it, or any patron found doing it, is in for a big fine. However, like any good rule, this one has its exceptions; while limited, there are still a few options left for diehard smokers.

The loophole exists because the original 1995 and 1998 laws were designed to ban smoking in the workplace. What this effectively means is that all bar-owners who employ a staff must also outlaw smoking; however, those who run their own bars can do as they please, since, goes the theory, they have no employees to protect. And so it goes that around a dozen bars across town openly allow smoking throughout their premises.

The newest smoking bar in the city is the multiple-owner-operated **Whiskey Thieves** (*see p162* **Crawling the Tenderloin**), a lively, sometimes lairy hole in the wall that's the young sister bar to the **Thieves Tavern** (3349 20th Street, at Shotwell Street, 401 8661), a quiet corner taproom in the Mission. The most central is the Financial District's **Occidental Cigar Club** (471 Pine Street, between Kearny & Montgomery Streets, 834 0485) which, despite its name, welcomes those puffing on nothing stronger than a Kool. And the most stylish is **Amber** (718 14th Street, at Church Street, 415 626 7827), a fashionable lounge just off Market Street. Other bars are scattered helpfully around town, among them **O'Keefe's** in the Richmond (598 5th Avenue, at Balboa Street, 751 1449) and the **Seastar** out by China Basin (2289 3rd Street, at 20th Street, 552 9144).

Aside from the above-mentioned joints, all of which legally offer smokers solace, a small number of hangouts still permit puffing on the QT. We can't tell you where they are, but among them are several of the Tenderloin's seamiest dives and a handful of places in the Mission. If you think you might have struck lucky, wait for the bartender's nod.

The Castro

The majority of decent bars in the Castro are gay-oriented, though a number do draw a mixed crowd. For a full list of gay and lesbian hangouts in the area, *see pp217-226*; for the **Café du Nord**, which serves double-duty as both bar and music venue, *see p234*.

Lucky 13

2140 Market Street, between Church & Sanchez Streets (487 1313). Metro F, J, K, L, M to Church/ bus 22, 37. **Open** 4pm-2am Mon-Thur; 2pm-2am Fri-Sun. **No credit cards. Map** p318 H9 ㉟
Dark, spacious and always busy, Lucky 13 has long been a favourite with those who crave the aura of a punk/biker bar without the perceived risk. There's pinball, pool and foosball, but the main entertainments are people-watching and draining pints from one of the best German beer selections in the Bay Area. There are even Black Forest liqueurs.

The Haight & around

Haight-Ashbury

Hobson's Choice

1601 Haight Street, at Clayton Street (621 5859/ www.hobsonschoice.com). Bus 6, 7, 33, 43, 66, 71. **Open** 2pm-2am Mon-Fri; noon-2am Sat, Sun. **Credit** Disc, MC, V. **Map** p317 E9 ㊲

At this 'Victorian punch bar' (their description), bartenders ladle out tall glasses of tasty rum punch; the menu boasts more than 70 kinds of rum. Fresh, grilled kebabs from the neighbouring Asqew Grill soak up the booze as it settles in the bellies of the collegiate-cum-jam-band set that fills the place.

Magnolia

1398 Haight Street, at Masonic Avenue (864 7468/ www.magnoliapub.com). Bus 6, 7, 33, 43, 66, 71. **Open** noon-midnight Mon-Thur; noon-1am Fri; 10am-1am Sat; 10am-11pm Sun. **Credit** AmEx, Disc, MC, V. **Map** p317 F9 ㊳
The decor plays up to the building's history: built in 1903, it was a focal point of hippy culture in the 1960s, before being taken over by quasi-legendary local dessert maven Magnolia Thunderpussy, in whose honour the brewpub is now named. A solid bar menu complements the own-brewed beer selection, which – unusually – includes some cask ales.

Persian Aub Zam Zam

1633 Haight Street, between Clayton & Belvedere Streets (861 2545). Bus 6, 7, 33, 43, 66, 71. **Open** 3.30pm-2am Mon-Fri; 2pm-2am Sat, Sun. **No credit cards. Map** p317 E9 ㊴
This tiny bar became a legend under notoriously cantankerous owner Bruno Mooshei, who inherited it from his father and waged a one-man campaign to keep it exactly as it must have been circa World War II. Mooshei died in 2000, but the place was bought by long-time patrons devoted to keeping its Casablanca aura intact. In a word? Characterful.

Eat, Drink, Shop

Lower Haight

Mad Dog in the Fog

530 Haight Street, between Fillmore & Steiner Streets (626 7279). Bus 6, 7, 22, 66, 71. **Open** *3pm-2am Mon-Fri; 11am-2am Sat, Sun.* **No credit cards. Map** p318 H8 ⓴

Anglophiles and expats pack the Mad Dog for its twice-weekly pub quizzes and football broadcasts. Strong selections of 20 beers on tap and another 30 in bottles back up the menu of pub grub, which includes English breakfasts (the 'Greedy Bastard' is $7) for those late-risers after a little hair of the dog.

Nickie's BBQ

460 Haight Street, between Fillmore & Webster Streets (621 6508/www.nickies.com). Bus 6, 7, 22, 66, 71. **Open** *9pm-2am Mon-Sat.* **No credit cards. Map** p318 H8 ㉑

No longer a barbecue joint, Nickie's now serves up a heapin' helping of spicy-sweet soul and deep funk. The down-home atmosphere makes it a good groove, but at weekends it can get absurdly crowded with drunken louts and the ladies who tolerate them. Still, in a neighbourhood that doesn't have a club scene, it's the perfect place to get on the floor if you feel the need after some pre-game cocktails down the block.

Noc Noc

557 Haight Street, between Fillmore & Steiner Streets (861 5811). Bus 6, 7, 22, 66, 71. **Open** *5pm-2am daily.* **Credit** *MC, V.* **Map** p318 H8 ㉒

If Dr Seuss and Trent Reznor had gone into the bar business together, this is what they'd have come up with. The decor is described as 'post-apocalyptic industrial', and the whole place has an peculiarly organic Gaudi feel. Always plunged in near darkness and with a mellow chill-room vibe, Noc Noc attracts a multi-ethnic lot.

Toronado

547 Haight Street, between Fillmore & Steiner Streets (863 2276/www.toronado.com). Bus 6, 7, 22, 66, 71. **Open** *11.30am-2am daily.* **No credit cards. Map** p317 H8 ㉓

This noisy hangout is a beer drinker's delight. A board posted on the wall shows the massive, ever-changing selection of draughts (which includes local brews and Belgian imports), while the blackboard behind the bar highlights bottled beer and non-alco options. Patrons are encouraged to bring in fresh sausages from Rosamunde Sausage Grill next door.

Hayes Valley

Hotel Biron

45 Rose Street, at Market Street (703 0403/www.hotelbiron.com). Metro to Van Ness/bus 6, 7, 66, 71. **Open** *5pm-2am daily.* **Credit** *AmEx, MC, V.* **Map** p318 K8 ㉔

Home to a wine bar and gallery, this stylish yet unpretentious hotel is named for the Rodin museum in Paris. The walls showcase the work of local

Take a tequila at **Tommy's**. *See p170.*

artists; the impressive wine list boasts 80 wines by the bottle and 35 or so by the glass, plus a selection of beers and a small but appealing menu of cheeses, caviar and olives. A great, low-key place for drinkers who like to talk.

Jade Bar

650 Gough Street, at McAllister Street (869 1900). Bus 5, 47, 49. **Open** *5pm-2am Mon-Sat; 8pm-2am Sun.* **Credit** *AmEx, MC, V.* **Map** p318 J7 ㉕

Restaurateur Greg Medow calls his lounge 'three bars in one' thanks to the distinct personality of each of its three modest floors. Signature cocktails go down easy in the shag-shod loft; the stylish main-floor bar comes with orchids in highlighted nooks; and a 20ft waterfall trickles into the basement lounge. Male patrons will appreciate being able to keep an eye on their drink even while in the gents, thanks to a one-way mirror that overlooks the bar.

Place Pigalle

520 Hayes Street, between Laguna & Octavia Streets (552 2671/www.place-pigalle.com). Bus 21, 49. **Open** 4pm-2am daily. **Credit** AmEx, MC, V. **Map** p318 J8 ⑯

While the decor says 'at-risk youth drop-in centre', the well-selected wine and beer menu says otherwise. Both conspire to keep the vibe laid-back. The crowd is eclectic: gay and straight, bohemian and yuppie, young and not-so-young. The back room (with pool table) doubles as an art gallery.

Sunset, Golden Gate Park & Richmond

Richmond

In addition to the bars listed below, the Richmond and the Sunset are characterised by Irish joints; in the Sunset, head to the historic **Little Shamrock** (907 Lincoln Way, at 9th Avenue, 661 0060). For something a bit grander, try the **Beach Chalet** for cocktails or the **Cliff House** for views (*see p115*).

Park Chalet

1000 Great Highway, at Fulton Street (386 8439/ www.parkchalet.com). Bus 5, 18, 31, 38. **Open** 9am-11pm daily. **Credit** AmEx, Disc, MC, V.

Younger sibling of the well-known Beach Chalet (*see p111*), the Park Chalet doesn't have the views of Ocean Beach (it backs on to Golden Gate Park), but it does have a beautiful expanse of lush lawn and beautifully landscaped local flora. On sunny days, lounge in one of its Adirondack chairs while enjoying a pint (or several) of the house-brewed beer.

Tommy's Mexican Restaurant

5929 Geary Boulevard, between 23rd & 24th Avenues (387 4747/www.tommysmargarita.com). Bus 2, 29, 38. **Open** noon-midnight Mon, Wed-Sun. **Credit** AmEx, MC, V.

Though there is a restaurant attached to the bar, it's all about the tequila, on which Julio Bermejo, son of founder Tommy, is a global authority. Ask Bermejo for advice on which of the 240-plus varieties to sample; then sip, don't shoot. The house Margarita, made with fresh Peruvian limes (they get through 3,000lbs a month), agave nectar and top-shelf tequila, is a doozy; order it with rocks but no salt. **Photo** *p169*.

Trad'r Sam

6150 Geary Boulevard, between 25th & 26th Avenues (221 0773). Bus 2, 29, 38. **Open** 10am-2am daily. **No credit cards.**

A local favourite since 1939, this unabashedly traditional tiki bar serves the kind of cocktails that can only be described as dangerous. Planter's Punch, Mai Tais, Singapore Slings, the ever-popular Volcano & Goldfish Bowl... there's a guaranteed hangover under every tiny umbrella.

Pacific Heights to the Golden Gate Bridge

Presidio Heights

G Bar

Laurel Inn, 444 Presidio Avenue, between Sacramento & California Streets (409 4227/www.jdvhospitality. com). Bus 1, 3, 4, 43. **Open** 7pm-midnight Tue; 6pm-2am Wed-Sat. **Credit** AmEx, MC, V. **Map** p313 F5 ⑰

If you're saddened that San Francisco doesn't look like LA, head to the Laurel Inn in Presidio Heights, and specifically its hotel bar. The place was a nondescript motel until the folks behind the Commodore (home to the Red Room, *see p164*) and the Phoenix (where you'll find the Bambuddha Lounge, *see p239*) got hold of it. The bar here now has a neo-1950s look and bachelor-pad atmosphere.

Cow Hollow

For weekend partiers in Cow Hollow and the Marina, life is unchanged since their frat and sorority house days. Located on Fillmore Street around the junction with Greenwich Street, the **City Tavern** (No.3200, 567 0918), the **Balboa Café** (No.3199, 921 3944) and **Eastside West** (No.3154, 885 4000) are collectively known as the Triangle, and get packed on weekends with yuppies performing the mating ritual.

Liverpool Lil's

2942 Lyon Street, between Lombard & Greenwich Streets (921 6664). Bus 28, 29, 41, 43, 45, 76. **Open** 11am-2am Mon-Fri; 10am-2am Sat, Sun. **Credit** MC, V. **Map** p313 F3 ⑱

The façade looks like it's made out of driftwood, and the main decorative touches are old sports photos and paintings of jazz greats. No matter: this is the Marina's least pretentious bar. The crowd ranges from old-timers having their morning Scotch to well-heeled newcomers nipping in for a pint. There's a considerable pub menu.

Matrix

3138 Fillmore Street, between Filbert & Greenwich Streets (563 4180/www.plumpjack.com). Bus 22, 28, 43, 76. **Open** 5.30pm-2am daily. **Credit** AmEx, MC, V. **Map** p313 G3 ⑲

At the original Matrix, you might have seen Hunter S Thompson in the bathroom sucking LSD off a stranger's sleeve, or the Grateful Dead playing an impromptu set. These days, though, the bar belongs to SF mayor Gavin Newsom and his Plumpjack group, and the Matrix draws label-conscious fashionistas and financiers who sip from the pricey cocktail menu at what is really a high-style pick-up joint.

Mauna Loa

3009 Fillmore Street, at Union Street (563 5137). Bus 22, 28, 43, 76. **Open** 2pm-2am Mon-Fri; noon-2am Sat, Sun. **No credit cards. Map** p313 G4 ⑳

Tales of the city Heinold's

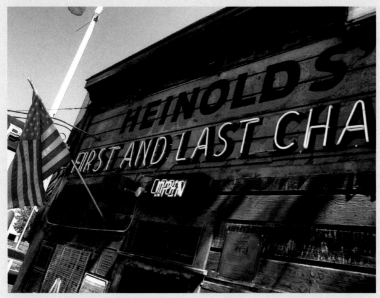

As legend has it, **Heinold's First & Last Chance** (*see p172*) was built from the salvaged timbers of a whaling ship right on the Oakland docks. It figures. A sailors' bunkhouse for three years before being bought by Johnny Heinold in 1883 for the princely sum of $100, it's a positively Melvillian structure inside and out. The one-room shack opened for business as a bar on 1 June 1883, its name inspired by the fact that it was – and, indeed, still is – the first place to find a drink on coming ashore, and the last place to get one when shipping out.

A young Jack London did his homework at these tables, and Heinold paid for the writer's college tuition until he was lured out of the classroom and back to the seas. It was here that London began writing both *The Sea Wolf* and *The Call of the Wild*, and here that he sealed the deals to purchase each of his three ships. Robert Louis Stevenson, Ambrose Bierce and President William Howard Taft are among a long list of luminaries who have taken their refreshment within these walls.

Although it only takes two rounds to fulfil the premise of Heinold's name, it pays to linger a while to get a grip on history, if not

the bar itself. It's hard not to feel that you're drinking with the ghosts of a thousand voyages. The wide, precariously sloping floorboards have been polished to a sheen by a century of foot traffic, and even though the bar is on dry land, it's difficult to shake the feeling of being at sea: the entire room dips in the middle and the bar, made in 1883 by a ship's carpenter, is canted at a sharp grade, a result of the 1906 earthquake.

As evening falls, the barman ignites the original gas lamps; the soft glow reveals that virtually every timber of the place has been shellacked by 100 years' worth of pot-bellied stove, tobacco and gas-lamp smoke. The room is littered with mementos, from a picture of the bar as it looked in 1894 to the money of servicemen shipping out to war. Tradition held that if they left a few dollars behind, they'd guarantee themselves a drink on their return. The unclaimed cash is a sobering reminder that some never made it back. Still, sitting at one of the tables with a belt of Old Overholt rye whiskey and a pint of Anchor Steam, you may well find yourself preparing to set sail yourself, if only to catch the ferry back to San Francisco.

Originally opened by a Hawaiian in the late 1950s, Mauna Loa has morphed into perhaps the only bar in the Marina that could be considered divey; the crowd, at least, is far more down to earth than you'll find at the Triangle. A pool table, foosball and Pop-A-Shot entertain patrons, but on weekends it's tough to manoeuvre your cue through the crush.

The East Bay

Oakland

Alley

3325 Grand Avenue, between Elwood & Lake Park Avenues (1-510 444 8505). BART 19th Street, then bus 12. **Open** 4pm-2am Tue-Sat. **No credit cards.**
The Alley is designed to look like a shanty-town street, complete with knickers strung between building façades and jagged fences separating the booths. At the end of the bar is a piano surrounded by bar stools, each with a mic. Anyone is free to take a seat and join the singalong that takes place every Thursday through Saturday night. Don't worry if you're not sure of the words: neither is the pianist.

Heinold's First & Last Chance

Jack London Square, at Webster Street (1-510 839 6761/www.heinoldsfirstandlastchance.com). BART Oakland City Center/12th Street, then bus 58, 72L, 301. **Open** noon-midnight Mon-Thur; noon-1am Fri, Sat; 11am-10pm Sun. **No credit cards.**
One of California's most historic bars is still going strong, more than a century after it first opened its doors. *See p171* **Tales of the city.**

Ruby Room

132 14th Street, between Madison Oak Streets (1-510 444 7224). BART Oakland City Center/12th Street, then bus 13, 59, 82. **Open** 5pm-2am daily. **Credit** AmEx, MC, V.
Neither the fantastic jukebox nor the new-wave DJs seem able to entice people on to the tiny dancefloor, but everyone hums or sings along. The crowd is young, hip, tattooed and pierced, and happy to while away the hours in Ruby Room's dim, smoky, womb-like space, all red walls and black ceiling.

Berkeley

Albatross Pub

1822 San Pablo Avenue, between Delaware & Hearst Streets (1-510 843 2473/www.albatross pub.com). BART Downtown Berkeley, then AC Transit bus 51. **Open** 6pm-2am Mon, Tue, Sun; 4.30pm-2am Wed-Sat. **No credit cards.**
The welcoming atmosphere at Berkeley's oldest pub allows its diverse crowd to take part in a range of activities. For the (relatively) active, there's a huge variety of board games, four separate dart stalls, a pool room and regular live music. For the supine? A fireplace, a large range of beers, free popcorn, reading lamps and a host of quiet corners.

Blake's on Telegraph

2367 Telegraph Avenue, between Durant Avenue & Channing Way (1-510 848 0886/www.blakes ontelegraph.com). BART Downtown Berkeley. **Open** 11.30am-2am Mon-Sat; 11.30am-1am Sun. **Credit** AmEx, Disc, DC, MC, V.
A Berkeley institution, Blake's has grown up with the university. Three floors handle overflow crowds on days when Cal teams play, but on other days, the space offers something for everyone: you may find a ska band hopping in the basement, a crowd from the local fraternity on the main floor and a mellow vibe upstairs. Each floor has its own bar.

Jupiter

2181 Shattuck Avenue, at Allston Way (1-510 843 8277/www.jupiterbeer.com). BART Downtown Berkeley. **Open** 11.30am-1am Mon-Thur; 11.30am-1.30am Fri; noon-1.30am Sat; 1pm-midnight Sun. **Credit** MC, V.
The copper bar, the interior walls clad in patterned tin siding, the pews (rescued from a local church), the two-storey outdoor beer garden… there's much to love about this pub even before you've thought about which of the 34 locally brewed draft beers to drink, and whether to supplement it with a pizza from the wood-fired oven. Beer-lovers take note: Jupiter is the dream-bar creation of one of the founders of the hallowed Triple Rock (1920 Shattuck Avenue, at Hearst Avenue, 1-510 843 2739, www.triplerock.com), which claims to be one of the first brewpubs in the US and is still worth a look.

Albany

Club Mallard

752 San Pablo Avenue, between Portland & Washington Avenues (1-510 524 8450/ www.clubmallard.com). BART El Cerrito Plaza. **Open** 2pm-2am Mon-Fri; noon-2am Sat, Sun. **Credit** MC, V.
The good-natured crowd at the half log-cabin, half tiki-style Mallard are more congenial than the salty folk that frequent the Hotsy Totsy and the Ivy Room just along the street. The two pool tables on the main floor cost only 25¢, with more tables upstairs for hire by the hour. The eclectic jukebox ranges from funk and reggae to campy lounge tunes, heightening the surreal atmosphere.

Schmidt's Tobacco Trading & Pub

1492 Solano Avenue, between Santa Fe & Curtis Avenues (1-510 525 1900). BART El Cerrito Plaza. **Open** noon-midnight Mon-Wed, Sun; noon-1am Thur-Sat. **No credit cards.**
An impressive array of tobaccos and accessories welcomes the weary to this smoker-centric outpost. Rolling machines are made available for patrons to twist up a smoke of their own while quaffing fresh-pulled pints. Pull an overstuffed chair up in front of the living room fireplace and inhale the pungent aromas from your neighbour's leaf, or play one of the house-supplied board games.

Eat, Drink, Shop

Shops & Services

Shopping bliss, whether you're a label addict or a bargain hound.

Macy's. *See p175.*

Eat, Drink, Shop

Much like its social scene, San Francisco's shopping circuit is at once radically diverse and soothingly homogenous. Impossibly edgy thrift-chic boutiques exist within shouting distance of department store behemoths, international couture and the ever-present Gap. They mostly remain cordial rivals, but things do sometimes get prickly in this most independent-minded of cities (*see p188* **Corporate punishment**).

When scouring the city for the latest It bag, It coat or It iPod accessory, don't be afraid to travel around town. Along with Union Square, posher neighbourhoods such as Nob Hill and Pacific Heights are great for high-end designer chic. However, if your tastes extend to (for example) independent designers, two-of-a-kind shoes and collectable tracksuits, head for hipper residential areas such as the Lower Haight, the deep Mission and even low-profile Laurel Heights. For a primer on commercial geography, *see p176* **Where to shop**.

Since all things old are inevitably new again one day, it never hurts to check out the used-goods stores in San Francisco: the second-hand scene is mighty here. It's not unusual to find customised clothes amid the racks of jeans and jackets cast asunder by the resolutely trendy, or out-of-print rare books amid the hot new paperbacks; there are bargains everywhere you

Don't miss Shops

Acorn Books
More than a shop, it's almost a family, and it has a stupendous range of used books. *See p178.*

Erica Tanov
Wonderful clothes, made from gorgeous fabrics. *See p184.*

Flight 001
Who knew luggage could be so sexy? *See p187.*

Sephora
When your look needs a cosmetic adjustment, but you can't bear the bullying shop assistants. *See p191.*

Swallow Tail
Furnish your home with things you've never seen before. *See p190.*

Villains
A low-pressure environment for getting your party togs got. *See p184.*

The best London bars & restaurants, just a click away.

Subscribe today and enjoy over 3,400 constantly updated reviews from *Time Out*'s acclaimed *London Eating & Drinking, Cheap Eats, Bars Pubs & Clubs* Guides and *Time Out London weekly*.

timeout.com/restaurants

Time Out's online bar & restaurant guide

look. If you'd rather stick to the new goods, the important thing to keep in mind is that no matter how fabulous the salesperson says your purchase looks, the returns policy probably doesn't care either way. Shop with confident discretion.

TAX & DUTY

Local sales tax, currently 8.5 per cent, will be added to all purchases. You can avoid paying this if you live out of state and either arrange shipment by US mail or courier or get the shop to do it for you. If you are taking goods out of the country, remember you'll be liable for duty and tax on goods worth more than a certain amount (£145 for the UK).

Department stores

Most of these stores extend their opening hours between Thanksgiving and Christmas.

Gump's

135 Post Street, between Grant Avenue & Kearny Street, Union Square & Around (984 9439/www. gumps.com). BART & Metro to Montgomery/bus 2, 3, 4, 15, 30, 38, 45, 76 & Market Street routes/cable car Powell-Hyde or Powell-Mason. **Open** 10am-6pm Mon-Sat; noon-5pm Sun. **Credit** AmEx, DC, Disc, MC, V. **Map** p315 M5.

Established in 1861, Gump's is the place where mon-eyed San Franciscans buy wedding presents, china and a variety of baubles, from black pearls to cus-tom green peridot necklaces. A thoroughly elegant shopping experience for those who believe a silver service for less than twelve is simply unthinkable.

Macy's

170 O'Farrell Street, between Powell & Stockton Streets, Union Square & Around (397 3333/www. macys.com). BART & Metro to Powell/bus 2, 3, 4, 15, 30, 38, 45, 76 & Market Street routes/cable car Powell-Hyde or Powell-Mason. **Open** 10am-9pm Mon-Sat; 11am-7pm Sun. **Credit** AmEx, DC, Disc, MC, V. **Map** p315 M6.

The definitive department store: what Macy's lacks in grace, it makes up for in discounts. Join the fray and pick up home furnishings, shoes and accessibly luxurious women's fashions care of DKNY, Theory, Calvin Klein and Michael Kors. **Photo** *p173*.

Neiman Marcus

150 Stockton Street, between Geary & O'Farrell Streets, Union Square & Around (362 3900/www. neimanmarcus.com). BART & Metro to Powell/bus 2, 3, 4, 15, 30, 38, 45, 76 & Market Street routes/cable car Powell-Hyde or Powell-Mason. **Open** 10am-7pm Mon-Wed, Fri, Sat; 10am-8pm Thur; noon-6pm Sun. **Credit** AmEx, DC. **Map** p315 M5.

Now commonly referred to as 'Needless Markup', Neiman Marcus was revered by old San Francisco society back when labels said 'Exclusively for Neiman Marcus'. Today, luxury of the mink-covered coat-hanger variety can still be yours, along with new designer and diffusion labels (Prada to Blahnik).

Nordstrom

San Francisco Centre, 865 Market Street, at 5th Street, Union Square & Around (243 8500/www. nordstrom.com). BART & Metro to Powell/bus 27, 30, 45 & Market Street routes/cable car Powell-Hyde or Powell-Mason. **Open** 9.30am-9pm Mon-Sat; 10am-7pm Sun. **Credit** AmEx, DC, Disc, MC, V. **Map** p315 M6.

Even retail snobs have to admit that bourgeois old Nordstrom has something for everyone. The expan-sive men's section includes Ben Sherman, Ted Baker and even a bar-lounge; in the vast women's depart-ment, you'll find silk camisoles, designer handbags, swish maternity wear and, most notably, a majestic shoe section; the biannual shoe sales are mob scenes.

Saks Fifth Avenue

384 Post Street, at Powell Street, Union Square & Around (986 4300/www.saksfifthavenue.com). BART & Metro to Powell/bus 2, 3, 4, 30, 45, 76 & Market Street routes/cable car Powell-Hyde or Powell-Mason. **Open** 10am-7pm Mon-Wed, Fri, Sat; 10am-6pm Sun. **Credit** AmEx, DC, Disc, MC, V. **Map** p315 M5.

The San Francisco branch of this upmarket store is airier and less claustrophobic than most of its ilk. The second floor offers designers such as Marc Jacobs, Ann Demeulemeester, Gucci and Moschino, but two floors up you'll find less pricey, but just as trendy lines, by Katayone, Miu Miu and Tocca. At the menswear store, the most cutting-edge creations are to be found on the fifth floor.

Other locations: *Menswear* 220 Post Street, Union Square & Around (986 4300).

Shopping centres

If you're after tourist tat, look no further than the inexplicably popular **Fisherman's Wharf** (Jefferson Street, between Hyde & Powell Streets, 626 7070, www.fishermans wharf.org) or nearby **Pier 39** (Beach Street & Embarcadero, 705 5500, www.pier39.com).

Embarcadero Center

Sacramento Street, between Battery & Drumm Streets, Financial District (772 0700/www.embarca derocenter.com). BART & Metro to Embarcadero/ bus 1, 2, 10, 14, 15, 31 & Market Street routes/cable car California. **Open** 10am-7pm Mon-Fri; 10am-6pm Sat; noon-5pm Sun. **Map** p315 N4.

Come here to get your retail fix in professional, calm environs. Major chains (Banana Republic, Gap, Victoria's Secret, Nine West) sit comfortably ensconced in the Embarcadero towers, which also host the bulk of the city's lawyers and financiers; expect heavy cellphone use and power lunching.

Ghirardelli Square

Beach Street, between Larkin & Polk Streets, Fisherman's Wharf (775 5500/www.ghirardelli sq.com). Metro F to Fisherman's Wharf/bus 10, 15, 30, 39, 47/cable car Powell-Hyde or Powell-Mason. **Open** *Apr-May* 10am-7pm Mon-Thur; 10am-8pm Fri, Sat; 11am-6pm Sun. *June-Aug* 10am-9pm Mon-Sat;

Where to shop

UNION SQUARE & AROUND
The heart of the city. The square itself is walled in by grand emporiums (**Saks Fifth Avenue**, **Neiman Marcus**, **Tiffany & Co**) and populist retail giants (**Macy's**, **Niketown**, **Levi's**). Many of the neighbouring streets hold similar enterprises (**Gap**, **Banana Republic**, **Apple Store**). However, by eschewing the tourist bustle of the square itself, shoppers can find designer boutiques (**Christian Dior**, **Gucci**, **agnès b**), as well as funkier franchises (**Urban Outfitters**, **Camper**, **H&M**), in the side streets and alleys close by.

THE EMBARCADERO
The staggeringly popular Ferry Building hosts a well-attended **farmers' market** (*see p189*). However, locals know to go on a more civilised weekday, to pick up cheeses, wines and other gifts from the stores permanently ensconced in the handsome structure.

CHINATOWN
A thriving, insular community, Chinatown is stuffed to the gills with commercial enterprises. On Grant Avenue, tourists collect knick-knacks, porcelain, lanterns, embroidered jackets and other chinoiserie. A block away, on Stockton Street, locals peruse the fresh fish markets, herbal apothecaries and vegetable stands. Hidden gems include the **Sam Bo Trading Co** see *p178*.

NORTH BEACH
Upper Grant Avenue has evolved from a sleepy corner of North Beach to a bona fide mecca for those with a few dollars to drop on local couture. Columbus Avenue, meanwhile, is home to the legendary **City Lights** bookstore (*see p179*), though if your tastes run to more salacious publications, there's always **Big Al's** (556 Broadway, 391 8510).

THE MISSION
The diversity of the Mission was challenged by an influx of dot-com yuppies, but it remains a bastion of bohemian chic. Mission Street is dominated by Mexicana, but the bookstores,

clothes retailers and CD shops on Valencia Street make it a real hipster haven. A recent influx of vintage shops and young designers has cropped up along 24th Street.

THE CASTRO
Popular with the young, the hip, the gay and the fit, who pour themselves into club-worthy threads at **Citizen Clothing** (*see p184*).

THE HAIGHT
Many revile Haight Street as a washed-out hippie enclave, but there are fashion finds among the peasant skirts. Used-clothing stores abound, as do progressive boutiques and the unassailable hipness of **Villains** (*see p184*). Oh, and great music stores, chief among them the amazing **Amoeba** (*see p194*).

JAPANTOWN
The **Japan Center** mall (*see p106* **Walk**) houses Japanese-language bookshops, sushi bars, noodle joints and purveyors of Japanese iron, bronze and incense that will lend a touch of authenticity to your new meditation room.

HAYES VALLEY
Modern knick-knacks, $300 sweaters and trendy-as-all-get-out homewares boutiques dominate this enclave of gentility. Stroll down Gough Street as far as Market Street for the antiques stores, then cross Market to around Brady Street for everything from imported ribbons to Eames chairs.

PACIFIC HEIGHTS & COW HOLLOW
In Cow Hollow, Union and Chestnut Streets offer dozens of retail opportunities, if you can stomach the high prices and apathetic sales girls. Running towards Pacific Heights off Union Street, Fillmore Street is a more mature district, offering classy selections of clothing, beauty products and second-hand gems.

BERKELEY
A liberal college town with all the trimmings: excellent bookstores, terrific music shops and a goodly variety of used clothing.

10am-6pm Sun. *Sept-Mar* 11am-7pm Mon-Thur; 10am-8pm Fri, Sat; 11am-6pm Sun. **Map** p314 J2.
At the home of the Ghirardelli chocolate company, gorge yourself on ice-cream drizzled with chocolate made on the premises, then wander the square, where you'll find tourist outposts Crazy Shirts, Ghiradelli Ts and, incongruously, Ann Taylor.

Metreon
4th Street, at Mission Street, SoMa (369 6000/www. metreon.com). BART or Metro to Powell/bus 14, 15, 30, 45 & Market Street routes. **Open** 10am-10pm daily. **Map** p315 N6.
For technophiles who feel most at home among the pixilated, the thriving Metreon delivers. Experience

No need to be tense: **Past Perfect** has the treasures you need. *See p178.*

gargantuan plasma screens at Sony Style, test-drive the latest video games at the PlayStation store, or get your anime on at the BanDai shop, where such curious toys as Astro Boy and Cowboy BeBop are available for viewing. But the real draw is 15 cinemas, including a monolithic Sony IMAX screen.

San Francisco Centre
865 Market Street, at 5th Street, Union Square & Around (512 6776/www.westfield.com). BART & Metro to Powell/bus 27, 30, 45 & Market Street routes/cable car Powell-Hyde or Powell-Mason. **Open** 9.30am-8pm Mon-Sat; 11am-6pm Sun. **Map** p315 M6.
Spiral escalators wind slowly up this vast vertical mall, enticing shoppers with mid-priced chain stores including J Crew, Abercrombie & Fitch, French Connection, BCBG and Club Monaco. Nordstrom (*see p175*) resides on top like a society matron; express elevators whizz you straight there past the rest of the retail riff-raff.

Antiques & collectibles

In the serpentine streets (Kansas, Henry Adams, 16th and Brannan) that surround the **Design Center** on Potrero Hill, you'll find upmarket places that cater to interior designers and decorators. Several are clustered in the **Jackson Square Historical District** (for the Jackson Square Art & Antique Dealers Association, see www.jacksonsquaresf.com

or call 398 8115), while the antique and novelty shops in **Hayes Valley** at Gough and Market Streets are a frequent haven for stylists and photographers. In the Mission, **Studio 24** (part of Galeria de la Raza, for which *see p212*) embraces everything from contemporary kitsch to Latin American folk art, while the now revitalised stretch of Polk Street on Russian Hill (between Pacific and Green Streets) is rich with shops selling furniture and collectibles.

African Outlet
524 Octavia Street, between Hayes & Grove Streets, Hayes Valley (864 3576). Bus 21, 47, 49. **Open** 10.30am-7pm daily. **Credit** AmEx, MC, V. **Map** p318 J7.
This gorgeous jumble of tribal artefacts and antiques – brilliantly coloured textiles, jewellery and beads, sculpture, fetishes, ceremonial masks – has been gathered by a Nigerian expat and his wife, who delight in explaining their pieces. You may have trouble hearing them over the blasting reggae.

Aria
1522 Grant Avenue, between Filbert & Union Streets, North Beach (433 0219). Bus 15, 30, 39, 41. **Open** 11am-6pm Mon-Sat; noon-5pm Sun. **No credit cards. Map** p315 M3.
The ultimate curiosity shop, with everything coated in just the right amount of dust. Bill Haskell's treasure trove includes a little bit of everything from

Eat, Drink, Shop

PHOTOGRAPHY

INFORMA

Sam Bo Trading Co

51 Ross Alley, between Stockton Street & Grant Avenue, Chinatown (397 2998). Bus 1, 12, 15, 30, 41, 45/cable car Powell-Hyde or Powell-Mason. **Open** 11am-5.30pm daily. **Credit** MC, V. **Map** p315 M4.
The best things in Chinatown are found down side streets, this tiny shop of Buddhist and Taoist religious items among them. Like a secret shrine, Sam Bo sells buddhas, ceremonial candles, incense and intriguing paper goods that are to be burned in honour of ancestors or to request a favour of the gods.

Tibet Shop

4100 19th Street, at Castro Street, Castro (982 0326/www.tibetshopsf.com). Metro F, K, L, M to Castro/bus 24, 33, 35, 37. **Open** 10am-6pm Mon-Sat; noon-5pm Sun. **Credit** AmEx, MC, V. **Map** p317 H11.
Incense, singing bowls, carved skulls, prayer beads, lapis lazuli, turquoise, silver, coral necklaces and clothing from Tibet come together in this shop, run by a disciple of the Dalai Lama.

Books & magazines

San Francisco has such a strong literary history (*see pp32-35* **Literary San Francisco**) that it's no wonder bookstores are in high demand. Many antiquarian booksellers are clustered at **49 Geary Street**, near Union Square, but the heaviest concentration of used bookshops is in the **Mission**: sci-fi fans should try **Abandoned Planet** (518 Valencia Street, between 16th & 17th Streets, 861 4695), while the politically minded are directed to **Modern Times** (888 Valencia Street, between 19th & 20th Streets, 282 9246, www.mtbs.com). Speciality stores around town include the **San Francisco Mystery Bookstore** (4175 24th Street, between Castro & Diamond Streets, Noe Valley, 282 7444, www.sfmysterybooks.com) and **William Stout Architectural Books** (804 Montgomery Street, between Jackson Street & Pacific Avenue, Financial District, 391 6757, www.stoutbooks.com). And don't miss Berkeley's **Telegraph Avenue**, home to numerous excellent stores.

Acorn Books

1436 Polk Street, between Pine & California Streets, Polk Gulch (563 1736/www.acornbooks.com). Bus 1, 19, 47, 49, 76/cable car California. **Open** 10.30am-8pm Mon-Sat; noon-7pm Sun. **Credit** AmEx, Disc, MC, V. **Map** p314 K5.
A large selection – and by 'large', we mean more than 100,000 volumes – of rare books in every genre, plus superlative collections of vintage sci-fi magazines, postcards and comics.

Booksmith

1644 Haight Street, between Clayton & Belvedere Streets, Haight-Ashbury (1-800 493 7323/863 8688/www.booksmith.com). Metro N to Carl &

Cody's Books. *See p179.*

everywhere: German marionettes, Victorian mirrors, World War II photos and eerie 19th-century mannequins – all illuminated by original Nelson lamps.

Dishes Delmar

558 8882/www.dishesdelmar.com. **Open** by appt.
Burt Tessler and his partner have assembled a pristine collection of mid-20th-century American dishware in their Haight Victorian: Fiesta, Harlequin and Lu-Ray all feature. Visits are by appointment, but it's often possible to stop by on the same day.

Past Perfect

2224 Union Street, between Fillmore & Steiner Streets, Cow Hollow (929 7651). Bus 22, 41, 45. **Open** 11.30am-7pm daily. **Credit** MC, V. **Map** p313 G4.
This expansive showroom contains goods sold by dozens of dealers – everything from ties to mannequins – but standards are high throughout. So are the prices, needless to say, but you get what you pay for. Great for browsers. **Photo** *p177.*

Cole/bus 6, 7, 33, 43, 66, 71. **Open** 10am-9pm
Mon-Sat; 10am-6pm Sun. **Credit** AmEx, Disc, MC,
V. **Map** p317 E9.
The Haight's best bookshop hosts many authors'
readings and events, and stocks a decent selection
of magazines, both literary and obscure.

City Lights

*261 Columbus Avenue, at Jack Kerouac Alley,
between Broadway & Pacific Avenue, North Beach
(362 8193/www.citylights.com). Bus 12, 15, 30, 41,
45.* **Open** 10am-midnight daily. **Credit** AmEx, Disc,
MC, V. **Map** p315 M3.
The legacy of Beat anti-authoritarianism lives on in
this publishing company and bookshop, co-founded
by poet Lawrence Ferlinghetti in 1953. Be sure to
head upstairs to the Poetry Annex, where books by
the Beats sit beside contemporary small-press works
and the photocopied ravings of 'shroom-addled
hippies. Readings here are real events: 2006 will see
celebrations of the 50th anniversary of the publication of Ginsberg's seminal *Howl and Other Poems*.

Cody's Books

*2454 Telegraph Avenue, at Haste Street, Berkeley
(1-510 845 7852/www.codysbooks.com). BART
Downtown Berkeley/bus 7, 40, 51.* **Open** 10am-
10pm daily. **Credit** AmEx, Disc, MC, V.
One of the staunchest and most successful independent bookstores in the US. Its tradition of
supporting writers who might not otherwise be
heard continues with regular readings by authors
ranging from unknown to legendary, while non-
reading days see bookworms huddled in the stacks
perusing the latest greats to have missed the bestseller lists. Its spiritual home remains Berkeley, but
it now has a branch in San Francisco. **Photo** *p178*.
Other locations: 730 4th Street, Berkeley (1-510 559
9500); 2 Stockton Street, Union Square & Around
(773 0444).

Get Lost Travel Books,
Maps & Gear

*1825 Market Street, at Pearl Street, Hayes Valley
(437 0529/www.getlostbooks.com). Metro to Van
Ness/bus 26.* **Open** 10am-7pm Mon-Fri; 10am-6pm
Sat; 11am-5pm Sun. **Credit** AmEx, DC, Disc, MC, V.
Map p318 J9.
This excellent enterprise on the fringes of Hayes
Valley offers a compelling assortment of travel
guides and literature, plus various other bits and
pieces to help you on your way (maps, accessories
and the like).

Green Apple Books & Music

*506 Clement Street, at 6th Avenue, Richmond (387
2272/www.greenapplebooks.com). Bus 1, 2, 4, 38,
44.* **Open** 10am-10.30pm Mon-Thur, Sun; 10am-
11.30pm Fri, Sat. **Credit** Disc, MC, V. **Map** p312 C6.
Paradise regained for used-book lovers. This long-
standing inner Richmond store has a staggering
selection of new and used titles, crammed together
in glorious disarray (don't miss the fiction and music
annex a few doors down). Packed on Sundays.

Kayo Books

*814 Post Street, between Hyde & Leavenworth
Streets, Tenderloin (749 0554/www.kayobooks.com).
Bus 2, 3, 4, 19, 38, 47.* **Open** 11am-6pm Wed-Sun.
Credit AmEx, Disc, MC, V. **Map** p314 L5.
This emporium of pulp delivers the goods for
those who like their mysteries hard-boiled,
their juveniles delinquent and their porn quaintly
smutty. Specialities include vintage paperbacks and
dime-store novels from the 1940s to the '70s, and
exploitation ephemera of all levels of debasement.

Moe's

*2476 Telegraph Avenue, between Dwight Way &
Haste Street, Berkeley (1-510 849 2087). BART
Downtown Berkeley/bus 7, 40, 51.* **Open** 10am-11pm
daily. **Credit** AmEx, Disc, MC, V.
Another Berkeley literary landmark, Moe's has
some 100,000 volumes spread over four floors, which
means you're nearly as likely to find a 17th-century
bible as a first edition of *Naked Lunch*. The fourth
floor holds antiquarian, out-of-print and art books.

Smoke Signals

*2223 Polk Street, between Vallejo & Green Streets,
Polk Gulch (292 6025). Bus 19, 41, 45, 47, 49,
76/cable car Powell-Hyde.* **Open** 8am-8pm Mon-Sat;
8am-6pm Sun. **Credit** AmEx, DC, Disc, MC, V.
Map p314 K4.
Homesick expats can smooth the process of assim-
ilation with the latest *Le Monde* or Italian *Vogue*
from this international news-stand. It also has a comprehensive selection of national and local papers,
design annuals and obscure literary journals.

Stacey's

*581 Market Street, between 1st & 2nd Streets,
Financial District (1-800 926 6511/421
4687/www.staceys.com). BART & Metro to
Montgomery/bus 2, 3, 4, 31 & Market Street routes.*
Open 8.30am-7pm Mon-Fri; 11am-6.30pm Sat.
Credit AmEx, DC, Disc, MC, V. **Map** p315 N5.
The city's oldest and largest independent bookshop
(established in 1923), Stacey's offers an impressive
selection of signed books, makes excellent staff rec-
ommendations, and co-sponsors lectures (from the
likes of Gore Vidal) with the Commonwealth Club.

Foreign-language bookshops

San Francisco is one of the most multicultural
cities in the US, good news for anyone after
foreign-language books. In the Mission, on
Valencia Street, **Dog Eared Books** (No.900,
at 20th Street, 282 1901, www.dogearedbooks.
com), **La Casa del Libro** (No.973, at 20th
Street, 285 1399) and **Modern Times** (*see
p178*) all sell Spanish-language newspapers
and *libros en Español*; in Japantown, the
magnificent **Kinokuniya** (1581 Webster
Street, between Post & Geary Streets, 567
7625, www.kinokuniya.com) is the city's
largest Japanese-language bookshop; and

Eat, Drink, Shop

Italians pick up the latest *Diabolik* at **Cavalli Italian Bookstore** in North Beach (1441 Stockton Street, at Columbus Avenue, North Beach, 421 4219). Tenderloin's **European Book Company** (925 Larkin Street, between Geary & Post Streets, 474 0626, www.european book.com) stocks publications in several different languages.

Computers & electronics

San Francisco remains at the helm of technological advancement, and prices here are keen. Be sure that your item will still work when you get home (electricity requirements vary between countries), and beware of Downtown stores advertising cheap cameras and other electronics: if a deal seems too good to be true, it probably is.

Chains dominate the commercial landscape. Locals love the low prices at **Circuit City** (1200 Van Ness Avenue, at Post Street, 441 1300, www.circuitcity.com). PC nuts will find plenty to tempt at **Franklin Covey** (350 California Street, between Sansome & Battery Streets, Financial District, 397 1776, www.frank lincovey.com), but both the store and the goods it sells are rather left in the shade by the sleek and hugely popular **Apple Store** (1 Stockton Street, at Ellis Street, Union Square & Around, 392 0202, www.apple.com).

Fashion

Children

Kids Only

1608 Haight Street, at Clayton Street, Haight-Ashbury (552 5445). Metro N to Carl & Cole/bus 6, 7, 33, 43, 66, 71. **Open** 10.30am-6.30pm Mon-Fri; 10am-6pm Sun. **Credit** AmEx, DC, Disc, MC, V. **Map** p317 E9.
Why should adults have all the fun? Here's where to get the kids tooled up with leopard-print blankets, handmade caps and tie-dye worthy of the Dead.

Laku

1069 Valencia Street, between 21st & 22nd Streets, Mission (695 1462). BART 24th Street/bus 14, 26, 48, 49, 67. **Open** 11.30am-6.30pm Tue-Sat; noon-5pm Sun. **Credit** MC, V. **Map** p318 K11.
Exquisite, intricate little slippers and coats, sewn by Laku's owner from velvet and shantung silk on a machine in the back of the shop. For baby royalty.

Murik

73 Geary Street, at Grant Avenue, Union Square & Around (395 9200/www.murikwebstore.com). BART & Metro to Powell/bus 2, 3, 4, 15, 30, 38, 45, 76 & Market routes/cable car Powell-Hyde or Powell-Mason. **Open** 10am-6pm daily. **Credit** AmEx, MC, V. **Map** p315 M5.

Sweet, affordable togs, using simple folk motifs, plain colours or geometric patterns. We like the onezees with an angel towing a heart over Golden Gate Bridge.

Designer

Unsurprisingly, San Francisco is home to branches of pretty much all the major high-end labels, with many ensconced in premises on or near Union Square. Among them are ever-elegant **Prada** (140 Geary Street, between Grant Avenue & Stockton Street, 391 8844, www.prada.com), chi-chi **Chanel** (155 Maiden Lane, between Grant Avenue & Stockton Street, 981 1550, www.chanel.com), smooth **Armani** (278 Post Street, at Stockton Street, 434 2500, www.armani.com), still-popular **Versace** (60 Post Street, at Kearny Street, 616 0604, www.versace.com) and extravagant, and not altogether tasteful, **Gucci** (200 Stockton Street, at Geary Street, 392 2908, www.gucci.com).

AB Fits

1519 Grant Avenue, between Union & Filbert Streets, North Beach (982 5726/www.abfits.com). Bus 15, 30, 39, 41. **Open** 11am-6.30pm Tue-Sat; noon-6pm Sun. **Credit** AmEx, MC, V. **Map** p315 M3.
The jean-ius of Howard Gee and Christopher Louie is to mix the familiar brands (Earl, Dope, Levi's Red, Seven) with ones that are more rarefied (hand-loomed inky jeans with silver buttons by Japan's Hollywood Ranch Market) or just plain fabulous (Blueline from Rome). You'll also find separates and accessories by designers like Fresh Hype.
Other locations: 40 Grant Avenue, Union Square & Around (391 3360).

Dema

1038 Valencia Street, between 21st & 22nd Streets, Mission (206 0500). BART 24th Street/bus 14, 26, 48, 49, 67. **Open** 11am-7pm Mon-Fri; noon-7pm Sat; noon-6pm Sun. **Credit** Disc, MC, V. **Map** p318 K11.
For those moments when your inner mod is crying out for a 1960s swing coat or denim bias-cut skirt, owner Dema Grim is on hand to guide you round a collection that's equal parts flair and insouciance.

Diana Slavin

3 Claude Lane, between Sutter & Bush Streets, Union Square & Around (677 9939/www.diana slavin.com). BART & Metro to Montgomery/bus 2, 3, 4, 15, 30, 38, 45, 76/cable car Powell-Hyde or Powell-Mason. **Open** 11am-7pm Tue-Fri; noon-5pm Sat. **Credit** AmEx, MC, V. **Map** p315 M5.
In this haberdasher's for women, Slavin designs and displays her trademark fashions: menswear-inspired clothing in rich, subtle colours and lush fabrics. Cutler & Gross glasses and Clergerie shoes complete the look.

Metier

355 Sutter Street, between Stockton Street & Grant Avenue, Union Square & Around (989 5395). BART & Metro to Powell/bus 2, 3, 4, 15, 30, 38,

A fashion Mission

Emerge from the BART subway with a newcomer's wide-eyed gaze, and the Mission looks thoroughly, overwhelmingly Mexican. Burrito joints line Mission Street, murals beam down from surrounding walls, and the sound of Spanish-language karaoke seeps out from Latino dive bars.

While the area does still provide refuge to immigrants from south of the border, the Mission grows more anglicised by the day. East and west of Mission Street, you're more likely to hear people conversing in English than Spanish; in the bars, Pabst Blue Ribbon is as widely drunk as Corona. The changes in the neighbourhood have extended to the commercial enterprises based here. Mission Street still hosts Mexican businesses, but Valencia Street is now a hipsters' paradise. Dotted around the area are all kinds of new business, but hyper-cool clothing stores dealing in vintage and/or vintage-inspired threads are in the ascendancy.

Just two blocks from the 16th and Mission BART station sits **Fabuloid** (3386 18th Street, at Mission Street, 355 0400, www.fabuloid.com), which fits into the latter category. Clothing here, all new, is sumptuously designed in a variety of fabrics, from French lace to Italian cashmere. It's a world apart from the **Community Thrift Store** (623 Valencia Street, between 17th & 18th Streets, 861 4910), but the long-standing charity retailer is usually worth a browse if you've a little time on your hands. If you don't find what you need, try the 1950s- and '60s-dominated **Retro Fit** (910 Valencia Street, at 20th Street, 550 1530), which can hook you up with a madras plaid workshirt or swingin' mod mini-dress before you can say 'The Avengers'. The window displays alone are worth a visit.

Close by, **Minnie Wilde** (3266 21st Street, between Valencia & Lexington Streets, 642 9453, www.minniewilde.com) has opened a second shop, selling her modern take

on vintage clothes: classic belts in rainbow colours, blousey tops, sleeveless dresses and – believe it or not – Jordache jeans. Just down the road is all-conquering used-clothes chain **Buffalo Exchange** (see p184).

It's a bit of a trek from here to **Mixed Use** (2917 24th Street, between Alabama & Florida Streets, 970 0560), but it's worth it for the vintage clothing and furniture. Nab one of co-owner Darshan Amrit's signature designs (Amrit, in a nice touch, also provides in-store alterations) or look through the painstakingly selected collection of vintage and one-of-a-kind wear. Just down the block is **Virginia Howells** (2839 24th Street, at Bryant Street, 647 2082; pictured), a spare, quiet place that stocks vintage goods altered with stunning detail and originality. If you've made it this far, take a load off your feet and reward yourself with a Coke float yards away at the historic **St Francis Soda Fountain & Candy Store** (2801 24th Street, at York Street; see p149), a vintage establishment of a different stripe.

Eat, Drink, Shop

45, 76/cable car Powell-Hyde or Powell-Mason. **Open** 10am-6pm Mon-Sat. **Credit** AmEx, MC, V. **Map** p315 M5.
Touted as a 'premier Downtown design boutique', Metier is indeed Serious Fashion. From slouchy sophistication care of Cathy Waterman to lingerie by Cosabella or contemporary sterling-silver creations from the renowned jewellery-makers Ten Thousand Things, the 'hot mum' set at last has a place to call home. **Photo** p182.

Susan
3685 Sacramento Street, between Locust & Spruce Streets, Presidio Heights (922 3685). Bus 1, 3, 12, 22, 24. **Open** 10.30am-6.30pm Mon-Fri; 10.30am-6pm Sat. **Credit** AmEx, MC, V. **Map** p313 E5.
This is the shop for which metrosexuals were made. Just read the labels: Yohji, Comme des Garçons, Dolce & Gabbana, Helmut Lang, Marni, Margiela and Prada. Sister shop the Grocery Store (3615 Sacramento Street, 928 3615) sells diffusion lines.

Metier makes light work of seriously cool designs. *See p180.*

Discount

The Bay Area has several sizeable outlet malls, but they're well outside town. An hour north on Highway 101, **Petaluma Village Premium Outlets** (2200 Petaluma Boulevard N, 1-707 778 9300, www.premiumoutlets.com) has 60 shops, including Liz Claiborne, Gap Outlet, Off 5th-Saks Fifth Avenue and Brooks Brothers, while **Napa Premium Outlets** (Highway 29 to 1st Street exit, 629 Factory Stores Drive, 1-707 226 9876, www.premium outlets.com), about 90 minutes from the city, has Barneys New York, Timberland, J Crew and Kenneth Cole, among others. For a complete list of stores, check the website.

Jeremy's

2 South Park, off 2nd Street, between Bryant & Brannan Streets, SoMa (882 4929/www.jeremys. com). Bus 10, 15. **Open** 11am-6pm Mon-Sat; 11am-5pm Sun. **Credit** AmEx, MC, V. **Map** p315 O6.

Jeremy's sits on a sunny corner of South Park, hawking designer wares at discount-store prices. It's a label-whore's dream come true, especially the shoes. Jimmy Choo pumps, Prada slides and Dolce & Gabbana boots can be found on the tables out front – and, if you look carefully, smaller cubbyholes in the rear. There's also excellent menswear, ties and accessories. The Berkeley location sells more casual clothing.

Other locations: 2967 College Avenue, Berkeley (1-510 849 0701).

Loehmann's

222 Sutter Street, between Grant Avenue & Kearny Street, Union Square & Around (982 3215/www. loehmanns.com). BART & Metro to Montgomery/ bus 2, 3, 4, 15, 30, 38, 45, 76/cable car Powell-Hyde or Powell-Mason. **Open** 9am-8pm Mon-Fri; 9.30am-8pm Sat; 11am-7pm Sun. **Credit** AmEx, Disc, MC, V. **Map** p315 M5.

Communal dressing rooms, eh? Don't be put off, the prices make Loehmann's worth a look. Designer clothes (DKNY, Versace, Moschino) hang from the rafters; you can get more than 50% off activewear.

General

San Franciscans love shops with a bit extra – more character, a touch of pizzazz – and it's these we list below. Tourists, though, tend to go with what they know, which is why the monoliths are so keenly represented on and around Union Square. Posh, preppy **Banana Republic** rules almost a full city block (256 Grant Avenue, at Sutter Street, 788 3087, www.bananarepublic. com); cheap and casual **Old Navy** has a vast store on Market Street (No.801, at 4th Street, 344 0375, www.oldnavy.com); and **Gap** is ubiquitous (890 Market Street, at 5th Street, 788 5909, www.gap.com). Other familiar chains include cheery **Bebe** (San Francisco Centre, 543 2323, www.bebe.com), long-standing **Guess** (90 Grant Avenue, at Geary Street, 781 1589), Brit import **French Connection** (101 Powell Street, at Ellis Street, 677 4317, www.frenchconnection.com),

Find your dream outfit in the perfect atmosphere at **Ambiance**.

girly-girl group **Betsey Johnson** (160 Geary Street, at Stockton Street, 398 2516, www.betseyjohnson.com) and snarky women's label **BCBG Max Azria** (331 Powell Street, at Union Square, 362 7360, www.bcbg.com).

Ambiance

1458 Haight Street, between Masonic Avenue & Ashbury Street, Haight-Ashbury (552 5095/www. ambiancesf.com). Metro N to Carl & Cole/bus 6, 7, 33, 43, 66, 71. **Open** 10am-7pm Mon-Sat; 11am-7pm Sun. **Credit** AmEx, MC, V. **Map** p317 F9.
If you've got an occasion, Ambiance has the perfect ensemble for it: its glowing collection of retro-style dresses and saucy skirts is even arranged by colour for your convenience. Staff are beyond friendly.
Other locations: 1864 Union Street, Cow Hollow (923 9797); 3825 24th Street, Noe Valley (647 7144).

American Rag

1305 Van Ness Avenue, between Bush & Sutter Streets, Polk Gulch (474 5214). Bus 2, 3, 4, 47, 49, 76/cable car California. **Open** 10am-9pm Mon-Sat; noon-8pm Sun. **Credit** AmEx, MC, V. **Map** p314 K5.
After an outfit that says casual without suggesting distressed? American Rag is less daunting than a used-clothing shop but a cut above institutions such as Diesel. Riffle the racks of used and new threads safe in the knowledge the poly-blend button-down you eventually choose will be a one and only.

Anthropologie

880 Market Street, between Powell & Stockton Streets, Union Square & Around (434 2210/www. anthropologie.com). BART & Metro to Powell/bus 2,
3, 4, 14, 15, 30, 45 & Market Street routes/cable car Powell-Hyde or Powell-Mason. **Open** 10am-8pm Mon-Sat; 10am-7pm Sun. **Credit** AmEx, Disc, MC, V. **Map** p315 M6.
Indulge your desire for beaded cardigans, A-line skirts and fuzzy fur-lined jackets, plus home furnishings, decadent scented candles, cute pyjamas and coquettish lingerie. The sale racks are at the back.
Other locations: 750 Hearst Avenue, Berkeley (1-510 486 0705).

Behind the Post Office

1510 Haight Street, between Ashbury & Clayton Streets, Haight-Ashbury (861 2507). Metro N to Carl & Cole/bus 6, 7, 33, 43, 66, 71. **Open** 11am-7pm daily. **Credit** AmEx, MC, V. **Map** p317 F9.
Space is at a premium here, but this tiny boutique packs in the style with vibrant T-shirts, edgy new designers and killer shoes, all at moderate prices. Even better, the expert opinions of the owners are worth their weight in carefully fitted denim.

Brown Eyed Girl

2999 Washington Street, at Broderick Street, Pacific Heights (409 0214/www.shopbrowneyedgirl. com). Bus 1, 3, 22. **Open** 11am-7pm Mon-Sat; noon-5pm Sun. **Credit** AmEx, Disc, MC, V. **Map** p313 F5.
Housed in a renovated Victorian, this pastel-hued shop for moneyed 20-year-olds has designer denim, hard-to-find indie lines (Lotta, Flicker, Jeff Gallea) and an endless array of $60 clingy tees. Be wary of the Union Street branch: it's aimed at 'tweens, and prices can be high.
Other locations: 2120 Union Street, Cow Hollow (351 2122).

Citizen Clothing

536 Castro Street, between 18th & 19th Streets, Castro (558 9429/www.bodyclothing.com). Metro F, K, L, M to Castro/bus 24, 33, 35, 37. **Open** 10am-8pm Mon-Sat; 11am-7pm Sun. **Credit** AmEx, Disc, MC, V. **Map** p317 H11.

Citizen is all about utilitarian chic, meaning Paul Frank and Adidas appear alongside Kenneth Cole and Gucci accessories. Boys seeking something a bit more sporty head round the corner to sibling establishment **Body** (4071 18th Street, 861 6111).

Diesel

101 Post Street, at Kearny Street, Union Square & Around (982 7077/www.diesel.com). BART & Metro to Montgomery/bus 2, 3, 4, 15, 30, 38, 45, 76/cable car Powell-Hyde or Powell-Mason. **Open** 10am-8pm Mon-Fri; 10am-7pm Sat; noon-6pm Sun. **Credit** AmEx, DC, Disc, MC, V. **Map** p315 M5.

Not just a zillion styles of jeans, retro sneakers and edgy separates, spread over three floors, but also the StyleLab line for those extra-experimental types who, for whatever ridiculous reason, fancy jeans made out of astronaut suits.

Dylan

1506 Vallejo Street, at Polk Street, Russian Hill (931 8721/www.dylanboutique.com). Bus 12, 19, 27, 47, 49, 76. **Open** 11am-7pm Mon-Sat; 11am-6pm Sun. **Credit** AmEx, MC, V. **Map** p314 K4.

San Francisco native (and daughter of steamy romance novelist Danielle Steel) Samantha Traina is the chief buyer for this beautiful shop. Her industry has resulted in a dizzying spread of top designers: you'll find Original Penguin hoodies, True Religion jeans and Rebecca Taylor suits.

Erica Tanov

2408 Fillmore Street, between Jackson & Washington Streets, Pacific Heights (674 1228). Bus 3, 12, 22, 24. **Open** 11am-6pm Mon-Sat; 11am-5pm Sun. **Credit** AmEx, MC, V. **Map** p313 H5.

Antique fabrics are the highlight here – and they're multitasking. Get bed linens, delicate lingerie, imported sweaters and adorable children's clothes. **Other locations**: 1827 4th Street, Berkeley (1-510 849 3331).

Girl Stuff

2255 Polk Street, between Green & Vallejo Streets, Polk Gulch (409 2426). Bus 19, 47, 49, 76. **Open** 10am-7pm Tue-Fri; 10am-6pm Sat; 10am-5pm Sun. **Credit** MC, V. **Map** p314 K4.

The name is appropriate: this little boutique is nothing but girlie. You'll find hair accessories, adorable shoes (from Hollywould to Dr Scholl's) and charming, if pricey, baby clothes for the toddler fashion mafia.

Ooma

1422 Grant Avenue, between Green & Union Streets, North Beach (627 6963). Bus 15, 30, 39, 41, 45. **Open** 11am-7pm Tue-Sat; noon-5pm Sun. **Credit** AmEx, Disc, MC, V. **Map** p315 M3.

The name stands for 'Objects Of My Affection'; ebullient proprietor Kate's fine eye for the latest local designer threads makes it all but impossible to leave empty-handed. 'Flirty' pretty much describes the whimsical, almost promiscuous fashions on offer.

Rabat

4001 24th Street, at Noe Street, Noe Valley (282 7861). Bus 24, 35, 48. **Open** 10am-6.30pm Mon-Fri; 10am-6pm Sat; 11am-5.30pm Sun. **Credit** AmEx, Disc, MC, V. **Map** p317 H12.

Sparkly chic is what Rabat's about. A huge variety of shoes, accessories and women's clothing provides reams of material for you to work with, and staff are happy to suggest ways to coordinate it all. **Other locations**: 2080 Chestnut Street, Marina (929 8688).

Rin

2111 Union Street, at Webster Street, Cow Hollow (922 8040). Bus 22, 41, 45. **Open** 11am-7pm Mon-Sat; noon-6pm Sun. **Credit** AmEx, MC, V. **Map** p313 H4.

The rails at this subterranean boutique feature adorable Tocca dresses, Fever jeans and Ruth cocktail dresses. The owners have hit on the brilliant wheeze of throwing regular wine-and-shopping parties: they've been a huge hit, not least because everyone looks fabulous after a glass or two.

Urban Outfitters

80 Powell Street, at Ellis Street, Union Square & Around (989 1515/www.urbanoutfitters.com). BART & Metro to Powell/bus 2, 3, 4, 15, 30, 38, 45, 76 & Market Street routes/cable car Powell-Hyde or Powell-Mason. **Open** 9.30am-9.30pm Mon-Sat; 10.30am-9pm Sun. **Credit** AmEx, Disc, MC, V. **Map** p315 M6.

Sturdy Ben Sherman trousers, adorable Free People cardigans, old-school T-shirts, funky jewellery and tons of jeans, new and recycled, at seriously affordable prices. Perfect for those just out of college, or those who wish they were. **Other locations**: 2590 Bancroft Way, Berkeley (1-510 486 1300).

Villains

1672 Haight Street, between Clayton & Cole Streets, Haight-Ashbury (626 5939). Metro N to Carl & Cole/bus 6, 7, 33, 43, 66, 71. **Open** 11am-7pm daily. **Credit** AmEx, DC, Disc, MC, V. **Map** p317 E9.

You'll find cropped trousers, experimental fabrics and tiny T-shirts that scream 'I party!' Next door is a great selection of covetable shoes, from limited-release Adidas to spiked heels straight out of a Joan Jett vid. Clothes and accessories for men and women.

Vintage & second-hand

For more vintage and second-hand options in the Mission, see p181 **A fashion Mission**.

Buffalo Exchange

1555 Haight Street, at Clayton Street, Haight-Ashbury (431 7733/www.buffaloexchange.com). Metro N to Carl & Cole/bus 6, 7, 33, 71. **Open** 11am-8pm daily. **Credit** MC, V. **Map** p317 F9.

The gear at **Dark Garden** either fits or it doesn't. *See p187.*

Buffalo Exchange didn't achieve its lofty station as a national trade-in chain by its gentle touch: locals are used to looks of near-contempt when attempting to get rid of those stone-washed Gap reverse-cut jeans. Still, the range is vast.
Other locations: 1210 Valencia Street, Mission (647 8332); 2585 Telegraph Avenue, Berkeley (1-510 644 9202).

CostumeParty!
1058 Hyde Street, at California Street, Nob Hill (885 3377). Bus 1, 27/cable car California.
Open 11am-7pm Mon-Sat; noon-6pm Sun.
Credit DC, MC, V. **Map** p314 K5.
As is the case at most vintage haunts on Fillmore, the pickings here are much richer than at shops in less upmarket districts such as the Haight and the Mission. CostumeParty! has a theatrical bent, with a focus on costumes and formal attire.

Crossroads Trading Company
2231 Market Street, between Noe & Sanchez Streets, Castro (552 8740/www.crossroadstrading. com). Metro F, J, K, L, M to Church/bus 22, 37.
Open 11am-7pm Mon-Thur; 11am-8pm Fri, Sat; noon-7pm Sun. **Credit** MC, V. **Map** p318 H10.
People who still haven't got over that 1980s retro thing should pop into the Market and Haight Street branches of this favourite local chain; the Fillmore branch of Crossroads Trading is best for jeans, dresses and vintage pieces.
Other locations: throughout the city.

GoodByes
3483 Sacramento Street, between Laurel & Walnut Streets, Presidio Heights (674 0151). Bus 1, 4. **Open** 10am-6pm Mon-Wed, Fri, Sat; 10am-8pm Thur; 11am-5pm Sun. **Credit** Disc, MC, V. **Map** p313 E5.
Another beneficiary of distance from the Haight/ Mission scene. Cast-off from some of the town's most upscale closets might include a barely worn Miu Miu sweater or a little Chanel suit.
Other locations: *Menswear* 3464 Sacramento Street, Presidio Heights (346 6388).

Schauplatz
791 Valencia Street, between 18th & 19th Streets, Mission (864 5665). BART 16th Street/bus 14, 26, 33, 49. **Open** 1-7pm Mon, Wed-Sun. **Credit** DC, MC, V. **Map** p318 K11.
The second-hand gear on offer here is more artfully collated than elsewhere in the Mission. In German, *schauplatz* means 'happening place'; the name makes sense when you spy Italian Riviera sunglasses, intricately beaded Moroccan mules or a Swedish policeman's leather jacket.

Ver Unica
437B Hayes Street, between Gough & Octavia Streets, Hayes Valley (431 0688/www.ver-unica.com). Bus 21, 47, 49. **Open** 11am-7pm Mon-Sat; noon-6pm Sun. **Credit** DC, MC, V. **Map** p318 J8.
Ver Unica is where people with a proper pay cheque go to buy second-hand: it stocks unique retro finds, not cast-offs crammed together on dusty shelves.

Wasteland

1660 Haight Street, between Clayton & Cole Streets, Haight-Ashbury (863 3150). Metro N to Carl & Cole/bus 6, 7, 33, 43, 66, 71. **Open** 11am-8pm Mon-Sat; noon-7pm Sun. **Credit** AmEx, MC, V. **Map** p317 E9.

Possibly the most popular used clothier in town, Wasteland sells second-hand clothing with history, including a rich supply of vintage costume jewellery, fancy gowns and worn-in leather jackets.

Fashion accessories & services

Handbags

If the following don't provide the chic clutch or giant hobo bag you're after, try **Gimme Shoes** (*see p188*) or the department stores (*see p175*).

Coach

190 Post Street, at Grant Avenue, Union Square & Around (392 1772/www.coach.com). BART & Metro to Powell/bus 2, 3, 4, 15, 30, 38, 45, 76 & Market Street routes/cable car Powell-Hyde or Powell-Mason. **Open** 10am-8pm Mon-Sat; 11am-6pm Sun. **Credit** AmEx, DC, Disc, MC, V. **Map** p315 M5.

The logo fabric in the window of this pristine designer outlet gives no sense of the high-quality leather or suede totes, satchels and accessories within. The returns policy is incredible: staff will hand you a new bag if but a single stitch comes out. **Other locations**: 1 Embarcadero Center, Financial District (362 2518); San Francisco Centre, 865 Market Street, Union Square & Around (543 7152).

Kate Spade

227 Grant Avenue, between Post & Sutter Streets, Union Square & Around (216 0880/www.katespade. com). BART & Metro to Powell/bus 2, 3, 4, 15, 30, 38, 45, 76/cable car Powell-Hyde or Powell-Mason. **Open** 10am-6pm Mon-Sat; noon-5pm Sun. **Credit** AmEx, Disc, MC, V. **Map** p315 M5.

Once a neatly stitched label on a simple black nylon handbag, Kate Spade is now a full-blown lifestyle, selling luggage, shoes, fragrances, jewellery and even drinking chocolate (at $25). The bags, of course, remain exemplary.

Marc Jacobs

125 Maiden Lane, between Stockton Street & Grant Avenue, Union Square & Around (362 6500). BART & Metro to Powell/bus 2, 3, 4, 15, 30, 38, 45, 76 & Market Street routes/cable car Powell-Hyde or Powell-Mason. **Open** 10am-6pm Mon-Wed, Fri, Sat; 10am-7pm Thur; noon-5pm Sun. **Credit** AmEx, Disc, MC, V. **Map** p315 M5.

Terminally cool Marc Jacobs is now artistic director for Louis Vuitton, but he keeps his own lines fresh and just affordable enough for the under-30s. The bags sit on glowing shelves, drawing you in with their utilitarian glamour.

Jewellery

Metier (*see p180*) also has a divine selection of contemporary and vintage jewellery.

Macchiarini Designs

1453 Grant Avenue, between Green & Union Streets, North Beach (982 2229/www.macreativedesign.com). Bus 12, 15, 30, 41, 45. **Open** 10am-6pm Tue-Sun. **Credit** AmEx, MC, V. **Map** p315 M3.

Three generations of the Macchiarini family have been crafting African-inspired jewelry for 70 years. They also do custom wedding rings, sculpture and calligraphy. So old school that they even have a set of North Beach steps named after them.

De Vera

29 Maiden Lane, between Grant Avenue & Kearny Street, Union Square & Around (788 0828/www. deveraobjects.com). BART & Metro to Powell/bus 2, 3, 4, 15, 30, 38, 45, 76 & Market Street routes/cable car Powell-Hyde or Powell-Mason. **Open** 10am-6pm Tue-Sat. **Credit** AmEx, MC, V. **Map** p315 M5.

Federico de Vera's covetable jewellery – Egyptian glass, yellow tourmaline, carnelian, rose-cut diamond – ranges from intricate beadwork to clean-lined intaglios. Don't miss the stunning collection of objets, ancient and modern, at the sister shop on Sutter. **Other locations**: 580 Sutter Street, Union Square & Around (989 0988).

Gallery of Jewels

2115 Fillmore Street, between California & Sacramento Streets, Pacific Heights (771 5099). Bus 1, 2, 3, 4, 12, 24. **Open** 10.30am-6.30pm Mon-Sat; 11am-6pm Sun. **Credit** AmEx, Disc, MC, V. **Map** p313 H5.

Peruse local creations of silver and semi-precious stones, as well as funky beads and antique bracelets. Designs run from fresh and modern to mumsy.

Launderettes

Don't miss **BrainWash** (*see p140*), SoMa's still-popular café/bar/launderette.

Star Wash

392 Dolores Street, at 17th Street, Mission (431 2443). Metro J to Church & 18th/bus 22, 33. **Open** 7am-9pm daily. **No credit cards. Map** p318 J10.

If you don't mind having your knickers scrutinised by Bogey and Bacall (in poster form only, more's the pity), this is the place for your washing chores. Movies are screened while you sort your socks.

Leather goods & luggage

Edwards Luggage

3 Embarcadero Center, between Davis & Drumm Streets, Financial District (981 7047/www.edwards luggage.com). BART & Metro to Embarcadero/bus 1, 2, 10, 14, 15, 31, 66, 71/cable car California. **Open** 10am-7pm Mon-Fri; 10am-6pm Sat; noon-5pm Sun. **Credit** AmEx, Disc, MC, V. **Map** p315 N4.

Since 1946 Edwards has been kitting people out with everything they need to hit the road, from trim carry-ons to duffle bags and voltage convertors.
Other locations: throughout the Bay Area.

Flight 001

525 Hayes Street, between Laguna & Octavia Streets, Hayes Valley (487 1001). Bus 21, 47, 49. **Open** 11am-7pm Mon-Sat; 11am-6pm Sun. **Credit** AmEx, Disc, DC, MC, V. **Map** p318 J8.
If it's important that you travel in style, Flight 001 is the place to go. Streamlined like a jet airliner, the store sells beautiful modern designs, from Japanese metal suitcases to gorgeous accessories.

Johnson Leathers

1833 Polk Street, between Jackson & Washington Streets, Polk Gulch (775 7392/www.johnsonleather. com). Bus 12, 19, 27, 47, 49, 76/cable car Powell-Hyde. **Open** 10.30am-6.30pm Mon-Sat; noon-5pm Sun. **Credit** AmEx, DC, Disc, MC, V. **Map** p314 K4.
Both a factory and a shop, Johnson makes and sells jackets and motorbike racing suits, as well as vests, trousers and chaps, all at very reasonable prices. Alterations can be made while you wait.

Lava 9

542 Hayes Street, between Laguna & Octavia Streets, Hayes Valley (552 6468). Bus 21, 47, 49. **Open** noon-7pm Mon-Sat; noon-6pm Sun. **Credit** AmEx, MC, V. **Map** p318 J8.

Sure, you could buy off the rack, but the real treat here is spoiling yourself. Get owner Heidi Werner to spread some skins, measure you up and make you the customised jacket you always deserved.

Lingerie

Belle Cose

2036 Polk Street, between Broadway & Pacific Avenue, Polk Gulch (474 3494). Bus 12, 27, 49, 76. **Open** 11am-6.30pm Mon-Fri; 11am-6pm Sat; noon-5pm Sun. **Credit** AmEx, MC, V. **Map** p314 K4.
'Vintage lingerie' sounds pretty scary, but here it's all about the 1920s boudoir theming. While there is the odd vintage slip, nightie or corset for sale, the shop majors in new designer lingerie from Calvin Klein, Princess Tam Tam and Only Hearts.

Dark Garden

321 Linden Street, between Octavia & Gough Streets, Hayes Valley (431 7684/www.darkgarden.net). Bus 21, 47, 49. **Open** noon-6pm Mon-Wed, Fri, Sat; noon-7pm Thur. **Credit** AmEx, Disc, MC, V. **Map** p318 J8.
Autumn Carey-Adamme's métier is bespoke corsets. Select style, fabric and colour and, by the magic of 12 individual measurements, she'll make a garment to which you'll gladly submit. The off-the-rack models are seductive, and the bridal corsets remain hugely popular. **Photo** *p185.*

Racks of stacks and stacks of flats at the various branches of **Shoe Biz**. *See p188.*

Workshop

2254 Union Street, between Fillmore & Steiner Streets, Cow Hollow (561 9551). Bus 22, 41, 45. **Open** 10am-6pm Mon-Sat. **Credit** AmEx, MC, V. **Map** p313 G4.
Pass through the main shop here to Lingerie Cottage out back. There brilliant concoctions by Laura Urbinati and Capucine Puerari lie in quiet sophistication beside a year-round selection of swimsuits.

Shoes

For non-specialists with great selections, try **Behind the Post Office** (*see p183*), **Rabat** (*see p184*), **Nordstrom** (*see p175*) or the cut-price range at **Jeremy's** (*see p182*).

Bulo

437 Hayes Street, at Gough Street, Hayes Valley (864 3244/www.buloshoes.com). Bus 21, 47, 49. **Open** 11am-7pm Mon-Sat; noon-6pm Sun. **Credit** AmEx, DC, Disc, MC, V. **Map** p318 J8.
Two shops in Hayes Valley (this one for women, the other for men), plus a store on Fillmore, sell a handsome array of shoes by European designers. On big sale days (a couple of times a year), expect to stand in line for those Vic Matie pony hair knee-high boots. **Other locations**: 418 Hayes Street, Hayes Valley (255 4939); 3044 Fillmore Street, Cow Hollow (614 9959).

Gimme Shoes

50 Grant Avenue, between O'Farrell & Geary Streets, Union Square & Around (434 9242). BART & Metro to Montgomery/bus 27, 30, 31, 45 & Market Street routes. **Open** 11am-7pm Mon-Sat; noon-6pm Sun. **Credit** AmEx, Disc, MC, V. **Map** p315 M5.
A fashion-forward, gender-neutral shoe salon handily close to Union Square. Richer fare includes Paul Smith, Costume National and Miu Miu, while an impressive cache of trainers and casual shoes ranging from Adidas to Prada tempts locals from their flip-flops. **Other locations**: 416 Hayes Street, Hayes Valley (864 0691); 2358 Fillmore Street, Pacific Heights (441 3040).

Shoe Biz

1446 Haight Street, between Ashbury Street & Masonic Avenue, Haight-Ashbury (864 0990/ www.shoebizsf.com). Metro N to Carl & Cole/bus 6, 7, 33, 43, 66, 71. **Open** 11am-7pm Mon-Sat; noon-6pm Sun. **Credit** AmEx, DC, Disc, MC, V. **Map** p317 F9.
Whether you need a spike heel or a hot-pink pointy-toed flat, Shoe Biz adds a bit of punky glamour to current trends. Aside from this store, there are two more branches on Haight Street, plus stores in the Mission and the Noe Valley. Of these

Eat, Drink, Shop

Corporate punishment

You will, if you look carefully, sometimes find San Franciscans slumming for a frappuccino at Starbucks, or dipping into Blockbuster to pick up the odd video. But God help the chain-store developer who takes this as a sign that anyone's putting out a corporate welcome mat. In San Francisco, the deeply held feeling that convenience is one thing and building a Walmart in the neighbourhood is quite another ranks right up there with liberalism and a love of iPods as core belief systems.

Over the years, legions of Nimbys have created more than just waves for corporate invaders. Back in the early 1990s, for example, a mysterious arson fire gutted a construction site in the Haight on which a much-contested Walgreens drugstore was being built. Less extreme – but no less strenuous – objections were raised when Urban Outfitters tried to open a shop in the same area. Both chains moved on to friendlier climes; later, Gap, Blockbuster, Rite-Aid and Starbucks all followed suit when their attempts to infiltrate established residential districts met with more than a little hostility. As we go to press, battles are raging over plans for a massive mall along the

Embarcadero waterfront, a proposed big-box Home Depot store in the Bayshore district and a Starbucks in historic Japantown.

In recent years, several of San Francisco's most idiosyncratic neighbourhoods – North Beach, Cole Valley, Hayes Valley – have passed laws banning formulaic chain stores. Civic leaders adopted a citywide ordinance requiring franchises to prove compatibility with their destination locale to a planning commission before being granted a permit.

But it seems time and corporate ties wait for no man. While Walmart may remain persona non grata, khakis now wave from the window of a Gap store at the corner of Haight and Ashbury, and the lure of decorative candles entices upscale apartment dwellers into an enormous Pottery Barn in the staunchly independent Castro. Even in the Inner Sunset, a bastion of independent mom-and-pop stores, a successful run against Blockbuster, Rite-Aid and Boston Market eventually gave way to Burger King in 2000. But residents continue to voice their displeasure: a sign that reads 'Boycott Stinky Burger King!' hangs in perpetuity above the restaurant, even as they duck in to order a Double Whopper.

shops, trainer addicts should hurry to Shoe Biz II down the road (1553 Haight Street) for racks of rare Pumas, Adidas and New Balance. **Photo** *p187.*
Other locations: throughout the city.

Shoe repair

Anthony's Shoe Service
30 Geary Street, between Grant Avenue & Kearny Street, Union Square & Around (781 1338). BART & Metro to Montgomery/bus 2, 3, 4, 15, 30, 38, 45, 76 & Market Street routes/cable car Powell-Hyde or Powell-Mason. **Open** 8am-5.30pm Mon-Fri; 9am-5pm Sat. **Credit** AmEx, DC, Disc, MC, V. **Map** p315 M5.
Whether you're down at heel or on your uppers, let Anthony's minister to you. They'll undertake any kind of shoe repair, but the work doesn't come cheap.

Food & drink

La Boulange de Polk (*see p147*) and sister establishment **Boulangerie Bay Bread** sell great cakes and bread.

Bi-Rite Market
3639 18th Street, between Guerrero & Dolores Streets, Mission (241 9773). Metro J to Church & 18th/bus 33. **Open** 9am-9pm Mon-Fri; 9am-8pm Sat, Sun. **Credit** AmEx, MC, V. **Map** p318 J10.
Bi-Rite has been sustaining the hungry for 60 years, but only became a gourmet deli in 1997. For picnics there are Middle Eastern dips, house-smoked salmon, salads, cakes, an olive bar and more than 100 cheeses; own-made sausages and pasta sauces bring smiles to self-caterers.

Ferry Plaza Farmers' Market
Ferry Building, Embarcadero, at Market Street. BART & Metro to Montgomery/bus 1, 9, 14, 31 & Market Street routes. **Open** 10am-2pm Tue, Sun; 4-8pm Thur; 8am-2pm Sat. **Credit** MC, V. **Map** p315 O4.
Since the restored Ferry Building reopened in 2002, the Ferry Plaza farmers' market has been a sightseeing attraction in its own right. White tents spill out into the open air from both north and south arcades, with locals and tourists grazing from stalls of aged goat's cheese, freshly baked bread slathered in flavoured olive oil, organic persimmons, pasta and gourmet sausages. There's lots of bustle, especially on a Saturday; crowd-phobics should visit on a non-market day to check out the excellent food shops inside the Ferry Building.

Molinari Delicatessen
373 Columbus Avenue, at Vallejo Street, North Beach (421 2337). Bus 12, 15, 30, 41, 45. **Open** 8am-6pm Mon-Fri; 8am-5.30pm Sat. **Credit** MC, V. **Map** p315 M3.
Own-made gnocchi, meatballs and sandwiches (try the Joe's Special: mozzarella, just-sliced prosciutto and pesto). So good that it's worth tolerating the huge crowds and chaotic deli-style ordering system.

Trader Joe's
3 Masonic Avenue, at Geary Boulevard, Western Addition (346 9964/www.traderjoes.com). Bus 2, 4, 38, 43. **Open** 9am-9pm daily. **Credit** Disc, MC, V. **Map** p313 F6.
With over 2,000 unique grocery items on its label, Trader Joe's is tough to beat for variety, quality and price. Expect organic, veggie and kosher products, cut-rate wines (yes, the $1.99 Charles Shaw Cabernet, aka Two-Buck Chuck, is still available) and affable salespeople.
Other locations: 555 9th Street, SoMa (863 1292); 401 Bay Street, Fisherman's Wharf (351 1013).

Alcoholic drinks

Committed oenophiles will want to rush directly into **Wine Country** (*see pp264-270*).

Arlequin Wine Merchant
384 Hayes Street, between Franklin & Gough Streets, Hayes Valley (863 1104/www.arlequinwine.com). Bus 16, 21, 47, 49. **Open** 11am-8pm Mon-Sat; noon-6pm Sun. **Credit** AmEx, MC, V. **Map** p318 J8.
The owners of this sister establishment to Absinthe (*see p154*) are thoroughly unpretentious, yet savvy enough to satisfy any armchair quaffer. Taste (and then, most likely, buy) elusive domestic bottles and coveted imports, ranging from under $10 to over $200.

K&L Wine Merchants
638 4th Street, between Brannan & Townsend Streets, SoMa (896 1734/www.klwines.com). Metro 2nd & King/bus 12, 15, 30, 45, 76. **Open** 9am-7pm Mon-Fri; 9am-6pm Sat; 11am-6pm Sun. **Credit** AmEx, DC, MC, V. **Map** p319 O7.
The SF branch of K&L is a modest warehouse, filled with carefully selected wines and spirits. Most of the staff claim specialisations in particular regions and/or varietals, and their encyclopaedic knowledge always seems to induce a buying spree.

PlumpJack Wines
4011 24th Street, at Noe Street, Noe Valley (282 3841/www.plumpjack.com). Bus 24, 35, 48. **Open** 11am-9pm Mon-Sat; noon-6pm Sun. **Credit** AmEx, DC, Disc, MC, V. **Map** p317 H12.
Though PlumpJack only opened here in 2001, there's been a wine shop on the site since Prohibition ended. You'll find a great selection of world wines for under $10, as well as grower-produced champagne, premium sake, vintage port, Madeira and microbrews. The Fillmore Street branch is the original.
Other locations: 3201 Fillmore Street, Cow Hollow (346 9870).

True Sake
560 Hayes Street, between Laguna & Octavia Streets, Hayes Valley (355 9555/www.truesake.com). Bus 21, 47, 49. **Open** noon-7pm Mon-Sat, Sun; 11am-6pm Sun. **Credit** AmEx, DC, MC, V. **Map** p318 J8.

A beautiful and elegant place, this is the first US shop devoted entirely to sake. Owner Beau Timken is every bit as helpful and knowledgeable about the rice-fermented beverage as you might hope, even suggesting food pairings for your purchase.

Tea & coffee

The **Imperial Tea Court** (*see p143*) sells, serves and delivers a wonderful range of teas.

Graffeo Coffee Roasting Company

735 Columbus Avenue, at Filbert Street, North Beach (1-800 222 6250/986 2429). Bus 15, 30, 39, 41, 45/cable car Powell-Mason. **Open** 9am-6pm Mon-Fri; 9am-5pm Sat. **Credit** MC, V. **Map** p314 L3.
If you're awake, you'll smell it. This San Francisco institution stocks fresh coffee from around the world, roasting its beans right on the premises.

Red Blossom Tea Co

831 Grant Avenue, between Washington & Clay Streets, Chinatown (395 0868/www.redblossomtea. com). Bus 1, 9, 15/cable car California. **Open** 9.30am-6pm daily. **Credit** AmEx, MC, V. **Map** p315 M4.
Renamed and expanded in 2005, Red Blossom's been in the tea business for two decades – and it shows. Not only is there a selection of more than 100 teas (black and green? Pshaw! Get into oolong and white), but you can get advice on the art of proper brewing.

Gifts

Even those yet to be convinced that shopping is an art will find museum gift stores a lovely confluence of two fields of human endeavour. The **California Palace of the Legion of Honor** gift shop (*see p115*) has rare photography books, prints and offbeat jewellery from local designers, while the **Exploratorium** store (*see p204*) has a bundle of things to spark young imaginations. The warm, welcoming shop on the first floor of the **Asian Art Museum** (*see p78*) has re-creations of artefacts among its unique and pricey mementos, and the wares at the **SFMOMA MuseumStore** (*see p81*) are sometimes more of a draw than the museum.

Alabaster

597 Hayes Street, at Laguna Street, Hayes Valley (558 0482/www.alabastersf.com). Bus 21. **Open** 11am-6pm Mon-Wed; 11am-7pm Thur-Sat; noon-5pm Sun. **Credit** AmEx, Disc, MC, V. **Map** p318 J8.
This shop not only looks beautiful, but sells beautiful things: alabaster, of course, in the form of urns and lamps, but also little boxes, buddhas, vintage globes and even framed exotic butterflies and beetles.

Dandelion

55 Potrero Avenue, between Division & Alameda Streets, Mission (436 9500/www.tampopo.com). Bus 9. **Open** 10am-6pm Tue-Sat. **Credit** AmEx, MC, V. **Map** p319 M9.

You might not enjoy getting to this charming shop (you have to go via the seedy Mission/Potrero underpass), but it's worth it for the reasonably priced and often quite exquisite gifts, ranging from lacquerware to snail wind chimes and bronze penguins.

Nest

2300 Fillmore Street, at Clay Street, Pacific Heights (292 6199). Bus 1, 3, 12, 22, 24. **Open** 10.30am-6.30pm Mon-Sat; 11am-6pm Sun. **Credit** AmEx, MC, V. **Map** p313 H5.
A nest in the magpie sense, this shop is a beguiling compilation of tin jack-in-the-boxes, gauzy Chinese lanterns, woodcuts and adorable kids' clothes. **Other locations**: 2340 Polk Street, Polk Gulch (292 6198).

Paxton Gate

824 Valencia Street, between 19th & 20th Streets, Mission (824 1872/www.paxton-gate.com). BART 16th Street/bus 14, 26, 33, 49. **Open** noon-7pm Mon-Fri; 11am-7pm Sat, Sun. **Credit** AmEx, MC, V. **Map** p318 K11.
That kneeling cushion may be more practical, but the gardener in your life will find something from this deeply bizarre shop rather more fun. Alongside ghoulish pieces of taxidermy – mice in anthropomorphic poses, say – sits an array of traditional, handcrafted Japanese garden knives.

Swallow Tail

2217 Polk Street, between Vallejo & Green Streets, Polk Gulch (567 1555/www.swallowtailhome.com). Bus 19, 41, 45, 47, 49, 76/cable car Powell-Hyde. **Open** noon-6pm daily. **Credit** AmEx, MC, V. **Map** p314 K4.
Slightly creepy but always engaging, Swallowtail takes you through art into the realm of theatre design, with a vast range of collectibles that runs from distressed urns to a 1920s coffin caddy.

Health & beauty

Complementary & alternative medicine

Scarlet Sage Herb Co

1173 Valencia Street, between 22nd & 23rd Streets, Mission (821 0997/www.scarletsageherb.com). BART 24th Street/bus 14, 26, 48, 49, 67. **Open** 11am-6.30pm daily. **Credit** AmEx, Disc, MC, V. **Map** p318 K12.
The owners of this apothecary focus on organic Native American and more familiar European herbs, essential oils, tinctures and plant essences, with a section dedicated to homoeopathy. There's also a good selection of books on alternative healing.

Vinh Khang Herbs & Ginsengs

512 Clement Street, between 6th & 7th Avenues, Richmond (752 8336). Bus 1, 2, 4, 38, 44. **Open** 10am-7pm Mon, Wed-Sun. **No credit cards**. **Map** p312 C6.

Eat, Drink, Shop

Feel the strength of SF Chinese traditions at Vinh Khang, where herbal specialists can create a customised concoction for your ailment while you wait.

Cosmetics & skincare

Kiehl's
2360 Fillmore Street, between Washington & Clay Streets, Pacific Heights (359 9260). Bus 1, 3, 12, 22, 24. **Open** 11am-7pm Mon-Sat; 10am-6pm Sun. **Credit** AmEx, MC, V. **Map** p313 H5.
The first Kiehl's botanical apothecary opened in New York's East Village in 1851; 150 years later, the second opened in Pacific Heights. The products are gentle and justifiably beloved, with a new anti-acne line attracting the 'tween set.

Sephora
33 Powell Street, at Market Street, Union Square & Around (362 9360/www.sephora.com). BART & Metro to Powell/bus 27, 30, 31, 45 & Market Street routes/cable car Powell-Hyde or Powell-Mason. **Open** 10am-9pm Mon-Sat; 11am-7pm Sun. **Credit** AmEx, Disc, MC, V. **Map** p315 M6.
Sephora's USP is its interactive floor plan: you can touch, smell and try on most of the premier perfumes and make-up brands without suffering the hard sell. **Other locations**: 2083 Union Street, Cow Hollow (614 2704).

Shu Uemura
1971 Fillmore Street, at Pine Street, Pacific Heights (395 0953/www.shuuemura-usa.com). Bus 1, 2, 3, 4, 22. **Open** 11am-8pm Mon-Sat; 11am-6pm Sun. **Credit** AmEx, MC, V. **Map** p313 H5.
Dramatic, rich and nothing but decadent, the cosmetics at Shu Uemura will set you back a few, but it's well worth it. Some say their eyelash curler is the best in the world. They're right.

Hair salons

Backstage Salon
2134 Polk Street, between Broadway & Vallejo Street, Polk Gulch (775 1440). Bus 12, 27, 49, 76. **Open** 11am-7pm Tue-Sat. **Credit** MC, V. **Map** p314 K4.
This full-service hair salon/gallery showcases local art while providing intense colour treatments, innovative haircuts, manicures, pedicures and waxing from a rotating fleet of international stylists with unpronounceable names.

De Kroon Salon & Spa
303 Sutter Street, at Grant Avenue, Union Square & Around (398 6464). BART & Metro to Montgomery/bus 2, 3, 4, 15, 30, 45, 76. **Open** 11am-7pm Wed-Sat. **Credit** AmEx, MC, V. **Map** p315 M5.
Perched two storeys up in an airy space, De Kroon is where you get pampered any which way but cheap. Hair, nails, massage and facials ensure those self-esteem boosts so necessary when fatigue, former lovers or problem skin descend.

Kabuki Springs & Spa. See p192.

Hair Play
1599 Dolores Street, at 29th Street, Noe Valley (550 1656). Metro J to Church & 30th/bus 24, 26. **Open** noon-6pm Mon, Sun; 10am-6pm Tue,Wed, Sat; noon-8pm Thur, Fri. **Credit** MC, V.
HP's earthy interior calms, while seasoned stylists whip your hair into shape without the diva-ish attitude. Lauded as the best salon in SF, and popular with those who suffer the blessing of curly hair.

Pharmacies

For alternative remedies, try **Scarlet Sage Herb Co** or **Vinh Khang Herbs & Ginsengs** (for both, *see p190*).

Walgreens Drugstore
3201 Divisadero Street, at Lombard Street, Marina (931 6417/www.walgreens.com). Bus 28, 30, 43, 76. **Open** 24hrs daily. **Credit** AmEx, Disc, MC, V. **Map** p313 F3.

Prescriptions and general drugstore purchases are available at this pharmacy around the clock. **Other 24hr locations**: 498 Castro Street, Castro (861 6276); 25 Point Lobos Avenue, Richmond (387 0706).

Spas, saunas & bathhouses

International Orange

2044 Fillmore Street, between Pine & California Streets, Pacific Heights (563 5000/www.international orange.com). Bus 1, 3, 22. **Open** 11am-9pm Mon-Fri; 9am-7pm Sat, Sun. **Credit** AmEx, MC, V. **Map** p313 H5.

Be sure you get an appointment: the secret is out about the refined treatments and professional facials here. Try the Red Flower Japan massage, a soothing mix of botanicals that awakens your senses (or, at least, leaves you smelling decent for 48 hours).

Kabuki Springs & Spa

Japan Center, 1750 Geary Boulevard, at Fillmore Street, Western Addition (922 6000/www.kabuki springs.com). Bus 22, 38. **Open** *Men only* 10am-10pm Mon, Thur, Sat. *Women only* 10am-10pm Wed, Fri, Sun. *Mixed* 10am-10pm Tue. **Admission** *Day pass* $16-$20. *Evening pass* $20. **Credit** AmEx, Disc, MC, V. **Map** p314 H6.

This traditional Japanese bathhouse has communal tubs, a steam room, saunas, a cold plunge pool and a restful tatami room. Shiatsu, Swedish and deep-tissue massages, body scrubs and other soothing services are available by appointment. **Photo** *p191*.

Osento

955 Valencia Street, at 21st Street, Mission (282 6333/www.osento.com). BART 24th Street/bus 14, 26, 48, 49, 67. **Open** noon-midnight daily (last admission 11pm). **Admission** $12-$20. **Credit** MC, V. **Map** p318 K11.

Often thought of as catering to the lesbian community, Osento is simply a women-only bathhouse. Walk into the peaceful surroundings, leave your clothes in a locker and relax in the whirlpool. After a cold plunge, choose between wet and dry saunas, or head for the outdoor deck. Massages by appointment.

Tattoos & body piercing

Black Heart Tattoos

177 Valencia Street, at Duboce Avenue, Mission (431 2100). Bus 26. **Open** noon-8pm Mon, Wed-Sun. **Credit** AmEx, MC, V. **Map** p318 K9.

Some question the wisdom of opening a tattoo shop next to raucous Zeitgeist (*see p167*), while others applaud it. Either way, Black Heart's pros take their art seriously – it might be best to look elsewhere if you're only after a dinky dolphin for your ankle.

Body Manipulations

3234 16th Street, between Guerrero & Dolores Streets, Mission (621 0408/www.bodym.com). BART & Metro 16th Street/bus 22, 26, 53.

Open noon-7pm Mon-Wed, Sun; noon-8pm Thur-Sat. **Credit** AmEx, Disc, MC, V. **Map** p318 J10.

Screw tattoos: Body Manipulations is about body-piercing, cutting and branding – its the oldest such establishment in the US. If you do insist on being inked, they've skilled tattooists too.

Lyle Tuttle Tattooing

841 Columbus Avenue, at Lombard Street, North Beach (775 4991). Bus 15, 30/cable car Powell-Mason. **Open** noon-9pm daily. **No credit cards.** **Map** p314 L3.

The highly respected Tuttle has long since retired, but Tanja Nicklish is usually available here for those who want to add some serious plumage to their skin.

Homewares

If the following doesn't satisfy your homeware needs, some of the places listed under 'Gifts' (*see p190*) probably will. SF also boasts some fabulous design-minded furniture shops (*see p193* **Take a seat**).

Other Shop II

327 Divisadero Street, between Oak & Page Streets, Lower Haight (621 5424). Bus 6, 7, 22, 66, 71. **Open** noon-6pm daily. **Credit** MC, V. **Map** p317 G8.

Come here for retro-mod home furnishings that revitalise the Space Age – or at least remind you why it was short-lived. Primary colours, burnished chrome and a plethora of cocktail accessories.

Music

CDs, tapes & records

Though the quality and variety of music shops here means that you needn't trouble yourself with the chainstores, they do have outlets in the city. There's a sizeable **Virgin Megastore** Downtown (2 Stockton Street, at Market Street, 397 4525, www.virginmega.com) and a rather smaller **Tower Records** in North Beach (2525 Jones Street, at Columbus Avenue, 885 0500, www.towerrecords.com).

We've listed the best generalists and genre specialists below, but those with a serious vocation for 180-gram will be more at home in the Lower Haight. On Haight Street at Steiner, serious deck-heads have **Tweekin Records** (No.593, 626 6995, www.tweekin.com) and **Future Primitive Sound** (No.597, 551 2328, www.futureprimitivesound.com), while **Groove Merchant** (No.687, at Pierce Street, 252 5766) boasts bins of hard-to-find jazz, funk, soul and other dusty 12-inch delights, and a namecheck on Beastie Boys' 'Professor Booty'. There are soul and funk 45s at chaotic **Rooky Ricardo's** (No.448, at Fillmore Street, 864 7526, www.rooky ricardosrecords.com), but **Jack's Record**

Take a seat

There's an Old World snobbishness about modern design – a belief that if it isn't Danish, German or Italian, it's likely to fall apart or become passé within months. Consequently, San Francisco is not celebrated for its modern design sense: it's more a city haunted by the past than one bustling into the future. Yet any local will tell you that the city is a breeding ground for solid modern design, whether of the graphic, industrial, web or furniture varieties. As part of this trend, San Francisco plays host to a smattering of modern furniture stores that will please the design novice and the cultural sophisticate alike, offering equal stage time to local designers and the European greats.

When hunting for modern furniture in San Francisco, start in Hayes Valley, which *USA Today* recently dubbed 'the NoLita of San Francisco'. And when in Hayes Valley, start at **Friend** (401 Hayes Street, at Gough Street, 552 1717, www.friend-sf.com; *pictured*), where the owners exercise a philosophy of 'warm modern'. Relaxed and comfortable, but with a definite edge, the store hawks real finds, including furniture and lifestyle accessories by the likes of Yves Behar, Kartell and Alessi, plus local talents including Pablo Lighting, Offi, Heath Ceramics and Publique Living. **Propeller** (555 Hayes Street, between Laguna & Octavia Streets, 701 7767, www.propeller-sf.com) takes a similarly inclusive approach, selling a vibrant mix of high-end and moderately priced pieces from independent, emerging designers. Especially notable is the artwork on the walls, most of which is for sale.

The SoMa district has been at the forefront of all things modern for several years now, and while the area has quietened down since the dot-com balloon burst, the stores remain. The best is still **LIMN** (290 Townsend Street, at 4th Street, 543 5466, www.limn.com), where the stock runs from all the Italian heavyweights to smaller Japanese and

American designers. It could be a museum of contemporary design, except that everything's for sale. You can also pick up rare finds at **Embellish** (177 Brannan Street, at 1st Street, 882 7147, www.embellish-sf.com) or the more reasonably priced **Room & Board** (685 7th Street, at Townsend Street, 252 9280, www.roomandboard.com), though you'll have to keep your eyes peeled: part of a nationwide mini-chain, it has a staggering inventory that includes many middling department-store pieces, though it also runs to some good deals on wares by the likes of Herman Miller and Knoll. Across town, the Fillmore area is increasingly progressive. At **Lounge** (1942 Fillmore Street, at Pine Street, 359 9111, www.loungeinc.com) you can pick up modern modular carpet tiles, slick love seats and even an Umbra backgammon set. Close by, **Design Within Reach** (1913 Fillmore Street, at Wilmot Street, 567 1236, www.dwr.com) offers a range of mod furniture, lighting and accessories by designers to the masses.

Eat, Drink, Shop

Cellar (254 Scott Street, between Haight & Page Streets, 431 3047) has the edge for hard-to-find jazz, R&B, pop and country. Experimental electronica is the speciality at **Open Mind Music** (342 Divisadero Street, at Oak Street, 621 2244, www.openmindmusic.com), while **BPM Music Factory** (654 Fillmore Street, at Hayes Street, 487 8680) is often filled with local DJs plugging the few remaining gaps in their 12-inch libraries.

Amoeba Music

1855 Haight Street, between Shrader & Stanyan Streets, Haight-Ashbury (831 1200/www.amoeba music.com). Metro N to Carl & Cole/bus 6, 7, 33, 43, 66, 71. **Open** 10.30am-10pm Mon-Sat; 11am-9pm Sun. **Credit** AmEx, Disc, MC, V. **Map** p317 E9.

Amoeba Music remains a mighty presence. It's partly a matter of scale – 25,000sq ft of former bowling alley, to be exact – but mainly a matter of breadth: you'll find every imaginable type of music,

The sign of a first-class music store: **Aquarius Records**.

both new and used, the vast majority priced very fairly. The Berkeley branch used to be the stronger of the two, but the SF store now pips it. There are free gigs, too, with some surprisingly big names. **Other locations**: 2455 Telegraph Avenue, Berkeley (1-510 549 1125).

Aquarius Records
1055 Valencia Street, between 21st & 22nd Streets, Mission (647 2272/www.aquariusrecords.org). BART 24th Street/bus 14, 26, 48, 49, 67. **Open** 10am-9pm Mon-Wed; 10am-10pm Thur-Sun. **Credit** AmEx, Disc, MC, V. **Map** p318 K12.
This splendid little neighbourhood record store could be classed as a boutique, were the staff not so wonderfully lacking in pretension. Tiny handwritten notes attached to numerous CD covers reveal the enthusiasms of the staff; the stock, both new and used, reveals their tastes to be terrifically catholic.

Grooves Vinyl Attractions
1797 Market Street, between Pearl & McCoppin Streets, Hayes Valley (436 9933). Metro to Van Ness/bus 26. **Open** 11am-7pm daily. **Credit** AmEx, Disc, MC, V. **Map** p318 J9.
Vinyl heaven, at least if your tastes don't run far beyond the 1970s. The store is packed with oddities and curios, including tons of old soundtracks, comedy records and sets by forgotten '70s crooners.

Medium Rare Records
2310 Market Street, at 16th Street, Castro (255 7273/www.modsystem.com/mediumrare). Metro F, K, L, M to Castro/bus 24, 33, 35, 37. **Open** 11am-8pm Mon-Thur, Sun; 11am-10pm Fri, Sat. **Credit** AmEx, MC, V. **Map** p317 H10.

Arnold Conrad's lovingly assembled – and somewhat chaotically displayed – collection of vinyl is crammed into a tiny space, and meanders widely across the decades and genres, from 1950s exotica via '70s soul to '80s soundtracks. A wonderful little window into the past.

Rasputin Music
69 Powell Street, between Eddy & Ellis Streets, Union Square & Around (1-800 350 8700/ www.rasputinmusic.com). BART & Metro to Powell/bus 2, 14 & Market Street routes. **Open** 11am-8pm Mon-Thur; 11am-9pm Fri, Sat; noon-7pm Sun. **Credit** AmEx, Disc, MC, V. **Map** p315 M6.
Ads in the windows and the local alternative weeklies are keen to point out that Rasputin pays the best prices for used CDs. It's something of a surprise, then, that Amoeba still has a better range of used stock. Add in a convoluted layout (rickety elevators, jumbled shelves) and staff that can sometimes give the impression that they'd rather be somewhere else, and you have a rather irritating franchise.
Other locations: 2401 Telegraph Avenue, Berkeley (1-800 350 8700).

Ritmo Latino
2401 Mission Street, at 20th Street, Mission (824 8556). BART 16th Street/bus 14, 26, 33, 49. **Open** 10am-9.30pm daily. **Credit** Disc, MC, V. **Map** p318 K11.
If you look outside, you'll find handprints of stars like Celia Cruz and Ricky Martin. Within, friendly staff can guide you to their recorded works, or to mariachi music, *conjuntos* or whatever you fancy.

Eat, Drink, Shop

Instruments & sheet music

Clarion Music

816 Sacramento Street, at Grant Avenue, Chinatown (391 1317/www.clarionmusic.com). Bus 1, 12, 15, 30, 41, 45/cable car California. **Open** 11am-6pm Mon-Fri; 9am-5pm Sat. **Credit** AmEx, Disc, MC, V. **Map** p315 M4.

It stocks didgeridoos and African drums, sure, but Clarion takes them as a starting point before heading into truly exotic waters: affordable H'mong jaw harps, say, or an impressively costly deluxe pipa.

Haight-Ashbury Music Center

1540 Haight Street, at Ashbury Street, Haight-Ashbury (863 7327/www.haight-ashbury-music.com). Metro N to Carl & Cole/bus 6, 7, 33, 43, 66, 71. **Open** 11am-7pm Mon-Fri; 10am-6pm Sat; noon-6pm Sun. **Credit** AmEx, DC, Disc, MC, V. **Map** p317 F9.

A stop-off for local musos and visiting musicians, this shop sells new and second-hand instruments, microphones, mixers, amps and sheet music.

Opticians

Bjorn Eyeware

1954 Union Street, between Laguna & Buchanan Streets, Cow Hollow (447 4224/www.bjorneyewear. com). Bus 41, 45. **Open** 11am-7pm Mon-Sat; 11am-5pm Sun. **Credit** AmEx, MC, V. **Map** p313 H3.

In a random poll, four out of five architects said they preferred Bjorn. Working with top frame designers from Italy and France, staff produce coolly chic prescription and other designs.

City Optix

2154 Chestnut Street, between Pierce & Steiner Streets, Marina (921 1188/www.cityoptix.com). Bus 22, 28, 30, 43, 76. **Open** 10am-6pm Mon-Wed, Fri, Sat; 10am-8pm Thur; noon-5pm Sun. **Credit** AmEx, MC, V. **Map** p313 G3.

Matsuda, Oliver Peoples and LA Eyeworks frames are all sold here, and helpful staff will stop you sitting on the pair you just took off and choose you some perfect new specs after one long stare. **Other locations**: 1685 Haight Street, Haight-Ashbury (626 1188).

Pets

George

2411 California Street, at Fillmore Street, Pacific Heights (441 0564/www.georgesf.com). Bus 1, 3, 22. **Open** 11am-6pm daily. **Credit** AmEx, MC, V. **Map** p313 H5.

These Texan fox-terrier owners turned animal outfitters sell eye-catching accessories for pets to wear, eat, play with and sleep on. Buy the dog a muscle shirt, or get that demanding cat some organic catnip. People clothes and accessories include an 11-dog charm bracelet and 'Dog' patch ski hats. **Other locations**: 44 4th Street, Berkeley (1-510 644 1033).

Photography

Adolph Gasser

181 2nd Street, between Natoma & Howard Streets, SoMa (495 3852/www.gassers.com). BART & Metro to Montgomery/bus 2, 3, 4, 12, 15, 31, 76 & Market Street routes. **Open** 9am-6pm Mon-Fri; 10am-5pm Sat. **Credit** AmEx, Disc, MC, V. **Map** p315 N6.

This justly famous photographic shop has the largest inventory of photo and video equipment in NorCal. There's also a good selection of scanners and digital cameras.

Discount Camera

33 Kearny Street, between Post & Market Streets, Union Square & Around (392 1103/www.discount camera.com). BART & Metro to Montgomery/bus 2, 3, 4, 14, 15, 30, 31, 45 & Market Street routes/cable car Powell-Hyde or Powell-Mason. **Open** 8.30am-6.30pm Mon-Sat; 9.30am-6pm Sun. **Credit** AmEx, Disc, MC, V. **Map** p315 M5.

Discount Camera is recommended by concierges anxious to steer their guests away from Downtown's unscrupulous tourist traps. New and second-hand models are sold, and there's an on-site photo lab.

Sex shops

Eurotique Stormy Leather

1158 Howard Street, between 7th & 8th Streets, SoMa (626 1672/www.stormyleather.com). Bus 12, 14, 19, 26. **Open** noon-7pm daily. **Credit** AmEx, Disc, MC, V. **Map** p318 L7.

Friendly female staff will help you select your leather lingerie or adult toys. There are spanking skirts and a topless Equus suit (complete with horse's bridle), but those with more vanilla tastes can settle for a French maid outfit or a latex bustier. **Other locations**: 582C Castro Street, Castro (671 1295).

Good Vibrations

603 Valencia Street, at 17th Street, Mission (522 5460/www.goodvibes.com). BART 16th Street/bus 14, 26, 33, 49. **Open** 11am-7pm Mon-Wed, Sun; 11am-8pm Thur-Sat. **Credit** AmEx, Disc, MC, V. **Map** p318 K10.

Buy a quality vibrator without suffering a seedy sex shop ambience. Staff pride themselves on providing a clean, safe environment for buying sex toys of every kind. Stock includes the popular Hitachi Magic Wand, I Rub My Duckie and the infamous Rabbit. **Other locations**: 1620 Polk Street, Polk Gulch (345 0400); 2504 San Pablo Avenue, Berkeley (1-510 841 8987).

Smoking

Ashbury Tobacco Center

1524 Haight Street, at Ashbury Street, Haight-Ashbury (552 5556). Metro N to Carl & Cole/bus 6, 7, 33, 43, 66, 71. **Open** 10am-9.30pm daily. **Credit** AmEx, DC, Disc, MC, V. **Map** p317 F9.

Eat, Drink, Shop

Ashbury Tobacco Center. *See p195.*

The full array of psychedelic sundries are available here, at one of Haight's better head shops. In addition to the hookahs and honeybear bongs, there's a vast offering of tobacco products.

Grant's Tobacconists

562 Market Street, between Sansome & Montgomery Streets, Financial District (981 1000). BART & Metro to Montgomery/bus 1, 2, 3, 4, 15, 76 & Market Street routes. **Open** 9am-5.30pm Mon-Fri; 10am-5.30pm Sat. **Credit** AmEx, Disc, MC, V. **Map** p315 N5.

For those who view smoking as a lifestyle, Grant's offers pipes, cigars, humidors, tobacco and sundry posh accessories. The walk-in humidor is said to be stocked with 100,000 cigars.

Sport

For ski, snowboard, surf and in-line skate rentals, *see pp250-251*.

Lombardi Sports

1600 Jackson Street, at Polk Street, Polk Gulch (771 0600/www.lombardisports.com). Bus 12, 19, 27, 47, 49, 76. **Open** 10am-7pm Mon-Wed; 10am-8pm Thur, Fri; 10am-6pm Sat; 11am-6pm Sun. **Credit** AmEx, Disc, MC, V. **Map** p314 K4.

Though it does sell proper wilderness gear, affable Lombardi Sports also caters to those who weren't suckled by wolves. There's equipment and accessories for cycling, running, climbing and hiking, as well as snow-, water- and team sports, plus some fashion. Staff are knowledgeable, but a little spacey.

See Jane Run Sports

3910 24th Street, at Sanchez Street, Noe Valley (401 8338/www.seejanerunsports.com). Metro J to Church & 24th/bus 48. **Open** 11am-7pm Mon-Fri; 10am-6pm Sat; 10am-5pm Sun. **Credit** AmEx, Disc, MC, V. **Map** p317 H12.

A shop for women who run, cycle, swim, hike or do yoga, with staff who are more than happy to spend time matching you to the right shoes.

Sports Basement

1415 DeHaro Street, at 16th Street, Potrero Hill (437 0100/www.sportsbasement.com). Bus 10, 15. **Open** 9am-8pm Mon-Fri; 8am-7pm Sat, Sun. **Credit** AmEx, MC, V. **Map** p319 N10.

Size is everything at Sports Basement: this branch is in a huge warehouse, but the newer Presidio premises are even larger. The stock is end-of-line goods from top-tier brands (North Face, Teva, Pearl Izumi), offered at reductions of 30% to 60%. The shop can be tricky to find, so call ahead for directions. **Other locations**: 610 Mason Street, Presidio (437 0100).

Toys

Ambassador Toys

2 Embarcadero Center, Financial District (345 8697/www.ambassadortoys.com). BART & Metro to Embarcadero/bus 1, 2, 10, 14, 15, 31, 66, 71/cable car California. **Open** 10am-7pm Mon-Fri; 10am-6pm Sat; noon-7pm Sun. **Credit** AmEx, Disc, MC, V. **Map** p315 N4.

Does the thought of Toys 'R Us drive you to the brink of insanity? This straightforward store, which specialises in toys from outside the US, has a charming selection of dolls, books, games and animals. **Other locations**: 186 W Portal Avenue, Sunset (759 8697).

Chinatown Kite Shop

717 Grant Avenue, at Sacramento Street, Chinatown (989 5182). Bus 1, 12, 15, 30, 41, 45/cable car California. **Open** 10am-9pm daily. **Credit** AmEx, Disc, MC, V. **Map** p315 M4.

It only stands to reason that hilly, windy SF should have an excellent kite shop. Stocked with hundreds of different kites in every imaginable shape and colour, the shop is perfectly situated for you to get kitted out before heading on to Marina Green.

Sanrio

San Francisco Centre, 865 Market Street, at 5th Street, Union Square & Around (495 3056/ www.sanrio.com). BART & Metro to Powell/ bus 27, 30, 45 & Market Street routes/cable car Powell-Hyde or Powell-Mason. **Open** 10am-8pm Mon-Sat; 11am-6pm Sun. **Credit** AmEx, Disc, MC, V. **Map** p315 M6.

Sanrio made the most of spreading the *kawaii* craze worldwide from Japan in the late 1990s. This is where you'll find Hello Kitty and cute animal characters ad nauseam, plus candy, pencil boxes, irresistible toys and charmingly dated cartoon stuff.

Arts & Entertainment

Features

San Francisco Giants. *See p244.*

Festivals & Events

With a dizzying array of festivities on offer, staying in simply isn't an option.

Float on: the **San Francisco LGBT Pride Celebration Parade**. *See p199.*

You would expect a city this colourful to have a calendar stacked with fascinating and often rather fruity events. And you'll find those expectations fulfilled, no matter the time of year. Spring and summer are punctuated by weekly neighbourhood fairs and parades, the only drawback being the accompanying street closures and driving detours. When cooler and wetter autumn and winter roll around, most events move indoors, but the activity barely lets up. There's always something going on here, whether it's a family fun run through the city or a transvestite beauty contest.

The dates listed below are as accurate as possible, but check before you make plans: festivals do occasionally shift dates. For up-to-date information, consult the San Francisco Visitor Information Center (*see p293*) or local papers, including the free alternative press.

▶ For **public holidays**, see *p294*.
▶ For **film festivals**, see *p208*.
▶ For **art festivals**, see *p216*.
▶ For **gay & lesbian festivals**, see *p219*.
▶ For **music festivals**, see *pp230-232*.
▶ For **theatre festivals**, see *p252*.

Spring

St Patrick's Day Parade
From 2nd & Market Streets to Civic Center.
Date Sun before 17 Mar. **Map** p314, p315 & p318.
The city has long had a sizeable Irish-American population, but everyone gets smiling Irish eyes in time for this big wingding. The parade heads from 2nd and Market to the Civic Center, before dispersing into a host of pubs.

Sisters of Perpetual Indulgence Easter Celebrations
Mission Dolores Park, Dolores & 18th Streets, Mission (www.thesisters.org). BART 16th Street/Metro J to Church/bus 22. **Date** Easter wknd. **Map** p318 J11. *See p201* Only in San Francisco....

St Stupid's Day Parade
Usually Justin Herman Plaza, Embarcadero (www. saintstupid.com). BART & Metro to Embarcadero/ bus 1, 2, 10, 14, 15, 31 & Market Street routes/ cable car California. **Date** 1 Apr. **Map** p315 O4. *See p201* Only in San Francisco....

Cherry Blossom Festival
Japan Center, Geary Boulevard, between Fillmore & Laguna Streets, Japantown (922 6776/www.sf-osaka. org). Bus 2, 3, 4, 22, 38. **Date** Apr. **Map** p314 H6.

A joyous whirlwind engulfs the usually sleepy Japantown for two weekends in April. The Cherry Blossom Festival is a splendid celebration of Japanese cuisine, traditional arts and crafts, dance and martial arts.

Cinco de Mayo

Civic Center Plaza, between McAllister, Grove, Franklin & Hyde Streets, Civic Center (256 3005). BART & Metro to Civic Center/bus 21, 47, 49 & Market Street routes. **Date** wknd before 5 May. **Map** p318 K7.

San Francisco's Latino residents and their friends celebrate General Ignacio Zaragoza's defeat of the French army at Puebla in 1862 with this raucous weekend of parades, fireworks and music. Think St Patrick's Day with tequila.

AIDS Candlelight Memorial March & Vigil

Castro & Market Streets, Castro (331 1500/ www.aidscandlelightvigil.org). Metro F, K, L, M to Castro/bus 24, 33, 35, 37. **Date** 3rd Sun in May. **Map** p317 H10.

This annual candlelit vigil begins at 8pm with a solemn procession from the Castro along Market Street, ending on the steps of the Main Library. There, crowds gather for speeches, an awards ceremony, celebrations and remembrances.

Bay to Breakers Foot Race

From Howard & Spear Streets, SoMa, to Ocean Beach, Golden Gate Park (359 2800/www.bayto breakers.com). **Date** 3rd Sun in May.

In an effort to raise spirits during the arduous and lengthy rebuilding process that followed the 1906 earthquake and fire, Randolph Hearst's *San Francisco Examiner* started this grandaddy of all San Francisco events in 1912. At the height of its popularity, the race attracted more than 110,000 participants. These days, weekend warriors dressed as salmon, jog-walkers pushing kegs of beer in shopping carts, and footloose nude zanies run, walk or stumble from the foot of Howard Street (bay), a distance of about 7.5 miles to Ocean Beach (breakers).

Carnaval

Harrison Street, between 16th & 22nd Streets, Mission (920 0125/www.carnavalsf.com). BART to 16th or 24th Streets/bus 12, 14, 22, 27, 33, 48, 49, 53. **Admission** $5. **Date** Memorial Day wknd. **Map** p318 L10/L11.

Organisers call it 'California's largest annual multi-cultural festival'. Locals call it the best place to eyeball a dazzling parade of skimpily costumed samba dancers gyrating foxily to fizzing Latin music.

Summer

Haight Street Fair

Haight Street, between Masonic Avenue & Stanyan Street, Haight-Ashbury (666 9952/www.haightstreet fair.org). Metro N to Cole/bus 6, 7, 33, 43, 66, 71. **Date** early June. **Map** p317 E9/F9.

The best Festivals

For going up in smoke
Haight Street Fair. *See below.*

For whipping up a frenzy
Folsom Street Fair. *See p200.*

For waking the dead
Día de los Muertos. *See p202.*

It's the Summer of Love all over again, with more than 200 booths of greasy food, hippie craftwork and enough roach-clips, skins, bongs and hash pipes to fill out a Cheech and Chong script. Live music comes courtesy of local acts.

Union Street Festival

Union Street, between Gough & Steiner Streets, Cow Hollow (1-800 310 6563/www.unionstreetfestival.com). Bus 22, 41, 45. **Date** early June. **Map** p 313 H4.

This weekend-long street fair draws a six-figure crowd each June, with its artists' stands, food stalls, bands and assorted other entertainments. The event will have been going strong for 30 years in 2006.

North Beach Festival

Grant Avenue, Green Street, Stockton Street & Washington Square, North Beach (989 2220/ www.sfnorthbeach.org). Bus 15, 30, 39, 41, 45/ cable car Powell-Mason. **Date** June. **Map** p315 M3.

Whip out the beret and bang out a rhythm on the bongos, daddio – it's San Francisco's oldest street party, held in the birthplace of the beatniks. The North Beach Festival is heavy on art and crafts, but there's also live music, wine and, inevitably, plenty of top-notch Italian food.

Summer Solstice

Around the city. **Date** 21 June.

San Francisco's pagans, and the men and women who love them, meet on the year's longest day to drum, dance and celebrate. At sunset, pound along with a drum circle in Justin Herman Plaza at the Embarcadero or join the Baker Beach bonfires.

San Francisco LGBT Pride Celebration Parade

Market Street, between Embarcadero & 8th Street, Downtown (864 3733/www.sfpride.org). **Date** last Sun in June. **Map** p314, p315 & p318.

A San Francisco rite of passage – but a bit of a mouthful to say – the Lesbian, Gay, Bisexual and Transgender Pride Parade is every bit as campy as you'd expect. Local politicians cruising for the rainbow vote share the route with drag queens, leather daddies and dykes on bikes. It's the wildest, friendliest parade you'll ever witness. Arrive at least an hour early for a kerbside seat, then join the masses for a celebration at Civic Center. **Photo** *p198.*

Arts & Entertainment

Fourth of July Waterfront Festival

Between Aquatic Park & Pier 39, Fisherman's Wharf (San Francisco Visitor Information Center 777 7120). Metro F to Fisherman's Wharf/bus 10, 15, 30, 39, 47/cable car Powell-Hyde or Powell-Mason. **Date** 4 July. **Map** p314 K2.

You'll find plenty of live entertainment and food stalls here on the waterfront during the day, but be sure to stay for the spectacular fireworks display that gets under way around 9pm.

Books by the Bay

Yerba Buena Gardens, Mission Street, between 3rd & 4th Streets, SoMa (561 7686/www.booksby thebay.com). BART & Metro to Montgomery/bus 9, 12, 15, 30, 45, 76. **Date** July. **Map** p315 N6.

This weekend of open-air events is a great reflection of San Francisco's proud reputation as a literary city. You can browse booksellers' booths, stand in line for for author signings or even take part in book-panel discussions. There's also plenty on offer to keep the children entertained.

San Francisco Marathon

Around the city (284 9653/www.runsfm.com). **Date** usually 1st Sun in Aug.

The younger and more athletic cousin of Bay to Breakers Foot Race (*see p199*) has grown larger every year since its inception in 1999. The course starts at the Embarcadero and then heads round the entire city, through the Mission, the Haight, Fisherman's Wharf and the Marina.

A La Carte, A La Park

Sharon Meadow, Kezar & John F Kennedy Drives, Golden Gate Park (458 1988/advance tickets 478 2277/www.eventswestca.com). Bus 5, 7, 21, 33, 66, 71. **Tickets** $12 ($10 in advance); $10 ($8 in advance) seniors; free under-12s. **Tastings** $1-$5. **Date** late Aug/early Sept. **Map** p316 D9.

Local foodies love this chance to sample culinary creations from the Bay Area's best restaurants without having to dress up or leave a tip. More than 40 eateries are represented, along with dozens of wineries and local microbreweries.

Autumn

Ghirardelli Square Chocolate Festival

Ghirardelli Square, between North Point, Beach, Larkin & Polk Streets, Fisherman's Wharf (775 5500/ www.ghirardellisq.com). Metro F to Fisherman's Wharf/bus 10, 15, 30, 39, 47/cable car Powell-Hyde or Powell-Mason. **Date** early May. **Map** p314 J2.

Keep reminding yourself that doctors say a little chocolate is good for you, as you sample chocolate-covered strawberries, decadent brownies and chocolate cheesecake. Proceeds go to a local charity.

How Berkeley Can You Be?

Around Downtown Berkeley (www.howberkeleycanyou be.com). BART Downtown Berkeley. **Date** late Sept. *See p201* **Only in San Francisco....**

Folsom Street Fair

Folsom Street, between 7th & 12th Streets, SoMa (861 3247/www.folsomstreetfair.org). Bus 9, 12, 14, 19, 27, 47. **Date** last Sun in Sept. **Map** p318 L8.

The Queen Mother of all leather street fairs, the Folsom Street Fair is a veritable gawkfest for visitors. Don your studded jockstrap and be prepared for masks, whips, chains and – that old favourite – public fellatio. Needless to say, this might not be suitable for the whole family.

ArtSpan Open Studios

Various venues (861 9838/www.artspan.org). **Date** Oct.

Get up close to San Francisco's creative visionaries throughout the month of October. More than 900 artists' studios open up to the public, with a different neighbourhood getting to show off its work every weekend. You'll find a free map detailing participating venues and the *Directory of San Francisco Artists* in city bookshops.

Castro Street Fair

Market & Castro Streets, from 16th to 19th Streets, Castro (841 1824/www.castrostreetfair.org). Metro F, K, L, M to Castro/bus 24, 33, 35, 37. **Date** early Oct. **Map** p317 H10.

A taste of the softer side of gay life in San Francisco, this one-day fair – started in 1974 by gay city official Harvey Milk (*see pp18-19*) – features food, crafts and community activists' stalls, along with plenty of rainbow merchandise.

Fleet Week

Fisherman's Wharf & Piers 30-32, Embarcadero (705 5500/www.fleetweek.com/sf). Metro F to various stations/bus 10, 15, 30, 39, 47/cable car Powell-Hyde or Powell-Mason. **Date** Oct. **Map** p314 & p315.

Since the early 1980s, the US Navy's acrobatic Blue Angels have rattled nerves and torn up the skies over San Francisco on Columbus Day weekend. The fleet sails into San Francisco Bay on Saturday morning; a spectacular air show and free battleship tours follow. A noisy couple of days.

Exotic Erotic Ball

Cow Palace, 2600 Geneva Avenue, at Santos Street, Daly City (1-888 396 8426/www.exoticeroticball. com). Bus 9, 9AX. **Tickets** $50-$150. **Credit** MC, V. **Date** late Oct.

It's obnoxious. It's exploitative. It's the bridge-and-tunnel crowd's annual excuse to pull on the latex and fishnets and party with other desperate housewives at the world's largest indoor masquerade ball.

Halloween San Francisco

Market Street, from 15th to Castro Streets; Castro Street, from Market to 19th Streets, Castro. Metro F, K, L, M to Castro/bus 24, 33, 35, 37. **Date** 31 Oct. **Map** p317 H10.

City Hall's doomed attempts to divert joyful Halloween revellers from the traditional fray in the Castro to the staid Civic Center have proved as unpopular as last year's pumpkin pie. So pop on

Only in San Francisco...

San Francisco hosts nearly a dozen fairs and festivals each month, celebrating everything from ethnic pride to civic pride, food to film. Many of these events are fairly self-explanatory, but others – well, they're pretty much unique to the Bay Area...

Founded on the belief that idiocy must be humanity's oldest creed, the First Church of the Last Laugh honours its patron saint each April Fool's Day with the **St Stupid's Day Parade** (*see p198*). Gathering in Justin Herman Plaza, the costumed procession winds its way through the Financial District stopping at each 'station of the stupid' (some of the area's noted financial institutions) to pay tribute to the gods of commerce. The parade culminates with the Blessing of the Banker's Heart and the Pacific Sock Exchange, which inevitably descends into an unhygienic hailstorm of hosiery.

Easter is the biggest holiday on the calendar for the **Sisters of Perpetual Indulgence** (*see p198*). It was at this time of year in 1979 that this order of 'gay male nuns' (their words), outfitted in habits from a community theater production of *The Sound of Music*, began their mission of 'spreading joy, absolving guilt and serving the community' through street theatre, charity events and political activism. Each Easter, they head to Dolores Park to bestow sainthood on worthy persons and preside over Easter Bonnet and Hunky Jesus contests.

San Francisco isn't the only local city that loves to flaunt its freak flag. Each September, Berkeley celebrates itself with the **How**

Berkeley Can You Be? festival (*pictured; see p200*), the only place you'll see politicians and protesters, hippies and punks, Klingons and Stormtroopers peaceably displaying their civic pride together. Like an unholy marriage of Mardi Gras and Burning Man, the event celebrates the East Bay's bastion of liberal lunacy with a procession of costumed (and naked) participants and 'art cars' – vehicles adorned with anything from organic fruit to cannabis – parading from the corner of California Street and University Avenue to the festival grounds at Civic Center Park.

If you thought the act of juggling a trio of chainsaws was the exclusive province of carnival sideshow nuts, then November's **Berkeley Unicycling & Juggling Festival** (*see p202*) may make you think again. In addition to unicycling and juggling, exhibitions include staff twirling, bullwhipping, plate spinning, devil stick flipping, yo-yoing... in all, pretty much anything that requires a keen sense of balance and superhuman dexterity. Tutorials and workshops allow you to get in on the fun.

Walking further down the wild side, venture to the annual **Miss Trannyshack Pageant** in November (*see p202*), at which an array of gender-bending beauties face off in a showdown for the coveted Miss Trannyshack tiara. The judges, who grade contestants in categories including Swimwear and Talent, include local luminaries and minor celebrities: past judges have included Gina Schock and Jane Wiedlin from the Go-Gos. Leave your inhibitions at the door.

Arts & Entertainment

your fright wig, head for the Castro, duck through the SFPD cordon and discover a land where dressed-up drag queens and half-naked pagans cavort. Leave the booze behind, though.

Día de los Muertos
24th & Bryant Streets, Mission (826 8009). Bus 27, 33, 48. **Date** 2 Nov. **Map** p319 M12.
Marchers gather at 24th and Bryant Streets to celebrate the Mexican Day of the Dead. After a traditional blessing, the music starts and the procession begins: Aztec dancers, children in papier-mâché skeleton masks and women clutching bouquets of dead flowers. Things wind up in Garfield Square, where people leave candles at a huge community altar. Dress code: dark but showy. If you really want to blend in, paint your face a ghoulish white and bring a noise-maker.

Berkeley Unicycling & Juggling Festival
King Middle School, 1781 Rose Street, at Grant Street, Berkeley (www.berkeley.edu/~juggle/festival). BART North Berkeley. **Date** early Nov.
See p201 **Only in San Francisco....**

Miss Trannyshack Pageant
Regency Center, 1300 Van Ness Avenue, at Hemlock Street, Tenderloin (www.trannyshack.com). Bus 2, 3, 4, 47, 49, 76/cable car California. **Admission** $20-$30. **Date** Nov. **Map** p314 K5.
See p201 **Only in San Francisco....**

Holiday Lighting Festivities
Union Square, between Geary, Powell, Post & Stockton Streets, Downtown; Ghirardelli Square, 900 North Point Street, at Polk Street, Fisherman's Wharf (705 5500). **Date** late Nov. **Map** p315 M5; p314 K2.
Ring in the holiday season at Union Square, where a 67ft (20m) living white-fir tree, decorated with 2,000 lights, 400 ornaments and 500 bows, is lit up each year. A 22ft wooden menorah is also lit as part of the Jewish Hanukkah celebrations.

Run to the Far Side
Golden Gate Park (759 2690/www.calacademy. org). **Entrance fee** $20-$30. **Date** wknd after Thanksgiving. **Map** p316.
As the name suggests, participants in this annual foot race, a fundraiser for the California Academy of Sciences, dress up as their favourite Gary Larson character. Fully togged up, they then walk or run either a three- or six-mile course around beautiful Golden Gate Park.

Winter

New Year's Eve
Around the city. **Date** 31 Dec.
For many years, San Franciscans have been gathering at Union Square or Ocean Beach to ring in the New Year. The city fathers have been discouraging such impromptu revelry in recent times, however,

so be sure to check local newspapers or call the Visitor Center before heading out in your glad rags. Other traditional festivities taking place around town include a cavalcade of bands performing in tents along the Embarcadero.

San Francisco International Art Exposition
Fort Mason Center, Marina Boulevard, at Laguna Street, Marina (391 2000/www.sfiae. com). Bus 10, 22, 28, 30, 47, 49. **Tickets** $12; $10 concessions; free under-10s. **Credit** AmEx, MC, V. **Date** mid Jan. **Map** p314 H2.
A chance to see work from some 100 art galleries, representing more than 2,000 artists from 12 countries. It's a fairly highbrow event, which means that prices are considerably steeper than those at the ArtSpan Open Studios (*see p200*).

Martin Luther King Jr Birthday Celebration
Yerba Buena Gardens, Mission Street, between 3rd & 4th Streets, SoMa (771 630/http://glide.org). BART & Metro to Montgomery/bus 9, 12, 15, 30, 45, 76. **Date** Mon after 15 Jan. **Map** p315 N6.
The parade celebrating Martin Luther King's birthday follows a slightly different route every year, but it always ends with a rally in Yerba Buena Gardens, where stirring speeches and reminiscences provide a poignant conclusion to the day.

Tet Festival
Around Civic Center & the Tenderloin (885 2743). **Date** Jan-Feb.
San Francisco has a large population of Vietnamese-Americans who, along with Cambodian, Latino and African-American families, transform the city centre into a multicultural carnival.

San Francisco Tribal, Folk & Textile Arts Show
Fort Mason Center, Marina Boulevard, at Laguna Street, Marina (1-310 455 2886). Bus 10, 22, 28, 30, 47, 49. **Admission** $12; free under-16s. **No credit cards**. **Date** early Feb. **Map** p314 H2.
Part-show, part-sale: upwards of 100 folk and ethnic-art dealers sell all manner of pottery, baskets, textiles and jewellery.

Chinese New Year
Market Street, at 2nd Street, and around Chinatown (982 3071/www.chineseparade.com). **Date** Feb. **Map** p311 H3.
The start of the Chinese New Year in February offers the city's best parade that doesn't involve public nudity. With colourful beauty pageants, drumming, martial arts competitions, mountains of food on every street corner, endless firework displays and a huge procession of dancing dragons, acrobats and stilt-walkers, the party turns the city jubilant and upside down. It's also the occasion of the enormously popular Annual Treasure Hunt (www.sf treasurehunts.com), which gets nearly 1,600 people scurrying round Chinatown.

Children

San Francisco appeals to the young at heart; so much the better
if you're a child yourself.

Kids in America: **Union Square**.

From visiting the belching sea lions to whale-
watching, from running wild in Golden Gate
Park to exploring the museums and driving
down crazy Lombard Street, the City by the
Bay offers plenty of family-friendly fun. Details
of most special events and festivals can be found
in the Sunday pink section of the *San Francisco
Chronicle* (www.sfgate.com) or in *SF Weekly*
(www.sfweekly.com). If they're not enough, hire
a car or hop on the BART and find a whole new
range of activities and attractions over in the
East Bay (*see pp124-128*).

The best Kids' stuff

For hoisting the mainsail
Jeremiah O'Brien Liberty Ship. *See p205.*

For lights, camera and action
Zeum. *See p205.*

For wannabe Whitmans
826 Valencia. *See p206.*

If you're set on an adults-only evening,
let the **ABC Bay Area Childcare Agency**
(24-hour call service 309 5662) watch the kids.
A caregiver from the agency, which has been
in business for nearly 60 years, will come to
your hotel or other accommodation for $11
to $12 an hour. Adventurous young 'uns
will enjoy the monthly **Kids' Night Out**,
a safe overnight party for 5- to 13-year-olds,
supervised by the Presidio Community YMCA
(447 9615, www.ymcasf.org/Presidio).

San Francisco attractions & museums

In addition to the places reviewed below,
San Francisco's gorgeous **Main Library**
(100 Larkin Street, between Grove & Hyde
Streets; *see p78*) has a Children's Center, which
includes a storytelling room, a creative area for
crafts and performances, and even a teenagers'
drop-in section. If you're stuck for something
to do, it's worth contacting one of the 30 **local
libraries** to see what events are being put on
that week; full contact details can be found at
www.sfpl.org. Other San Francisco museums

Kitchens for kids

In this relaxed city, you'll find that kids are welcome in most restaurants. However, when they prove strangely reluctant to try that yucky tartare or boring-boring fruits de mer, it's worth having a few fallbacks up your sleeve.

One great choice is the **Mel's Drive-In** chain. There are four of these 1950s-style eateries in San Francisco, serving great burgers and fries with wish-you-were-a-kid-again shakes. The most central branch is right near Yerba Buena Gardens (801 Mission Street, at 4th Street, 227 4477); details of the others can be found at www.melsdrive-in.com. Another great source of family fare in Yerba Buena, especially if you're visiting the California Academy of Sciences, is **Bucca di Beppo** (855 Howard Street, between 4th & 5th Streets, 543 7673). Portions are huge; it's best to come with a big group.

Those investigating the west of the city will find the **Park Chalet** (1000 Great Highway, at Fulton Street; see p111) dead handy from both Ocean Beach and Golden Gate Park. On the ground floor of the building's back side, there's an outdoor area in which the kids can roam while the adults actually get a chance to enjoy their meal. There are also a couple of SF classics on the Great Highway: the recently restored **Cliff House** (1090 Point Lobos Avenue; see p115) and **Louis' Diner** (902 Point Lobos Avenue, 387 6330). Another relaxed, slightly upscale option, **Park Chow** (1240 9th Avenue, between Lincoln Way & Irving Street, 665 9912) is just outside the park and, if none of these fits the bill, there's always **Giorgio's Pizzeria** (151 Clement Street, 668 1266), just north of the panhandle, for cheesy-topped pies and family-friendly decibel levels.

At Fisherman's Wharf, a freshly cooked and cracked Dungeness crab from one of the many sidewalk stands will be fresh and, during crab season (November to May; see p146 **Crack one open**), will also cost roughly half what it might in local restaurants: it's probably worth reducing the financial risk just in case the ingrates turn out to hate the stuff. Kids with sophisticated palates might appreciate the US-Italian served at **Il Fornaio** (1265 Battery Street, in Levi's Plaza, 986 0100); they'll certainly love having a water fountain to splash around in. Children also get a kick out of the samples and free snacks at the **Ferry Plaza Farmers' Market** (Ferry Building, Embarcadero, at Market Street; see p189). While your progeny marvel at the organic oddities (Buddha lemons, Hog Island oysters), you'll simply be agog at the prices.

---

of equal interest to kids and grown-ups include the Cable Car Museum (see p84) and the San Francisco Maritime Museum (see p94).

Aquarium of the Bay

Pier 39, Embarcadero at Beach Street, Fisherman's Wharf (1-888 732 3483/www.aquariumofthebay. com). Metro F to Pier 39/bus 10, 15, 30, 39, 47/ cable car Powell-Mason. **Open** *May-Sept* 9am-8pm daily. *Oct-Apr* 10am-6pm Mon-Thur; 10am-7pm Fri-Sun. **Admission** $13.95; $7.50 3-11s; £33.95 family. **Credit** MC, V. **Map** p314 L1.

For a diver's-eye view of the Bay, visit these clear plastic acrylic underwater tunnels. Moving walkways take you through 300ft of water, past more than 23,000 aquatic creatures. Upstairs, there are several touch-tide pools with urchins and bat rays.

If you've time, combine your trip with an island hop or bay cruise. Blue and Gold Fleet (705 5555, www.blueandgoldfleet.com) offers hour-long rides and three- to four-hour-long trips to Angel Island and Alcatraz; for details, see pp93-94.

California Academy of Sciences

875 Howard Street, between 4th & 5th Streets, SoMa (321 8000/www.calacademy.org). BART or Metro to Powell/bus 14, 15, 30, 45 & Market Street routes. **Open** 10am-5pm daily. **Admission** $7; $4.50 12-17s, students, seniors; $2 4-11s; free under-4s. **Map** p315 M6.

The Academy, along with its impressive Steinhart Aquarium, is downtown until 2008, when it relocates to a new building at its former Golden Gate Park site. More than 5,000 live creatures are on show here: watch penguins gulp fish, or touch hermit crabs and starfish in the Discovery Tide Pool.

Exploratorium

3601 Lyon Street, at Marina Boulevard, Marina (563 7337/www.exploratorium.edu). Bus 28, 30, 76. **Open** 10am-5pm Tue-Sun. **Admission** $13; $10 13-17s, discounts; $8 4-12s; free under-4s. Free 1st Wed of mth. **Credit** AmEx, MC, V. **Map** p313 E2.

Housed in the landmark Palace of Fine Arts, the Exploratorium offers over 600 interactive exhibits about science, art and human perception. Pay a visit to the Tactile Dome, a geodesic hemisphere of total blackness in which you try to identify various objects; book in advance (561 0362, $16). Another highlight is the Wave Organ, located nearby on the water's edge (see p118). Sea waves rush in underneath, pushing air up through the organ's tubes to create a symphony of eerie tones and sighs.

Jeremiah O'Brien Liberty Ship
Pier 45, Embarcadero, at Taylor Street, Fisherman's
Wharf (544 0100/www.ssjeremiahobrien.com).
Metro F to Fisherman's Wharf/bus 10, 15, 30, 39,
47/cable car Powell-Mason. **Open** 10am-4pm daily.
Admission $9; $5 discounts; $4 6-14s; free under-6s;
$20 family. **No credit cards. Map** p314 K1.
There's plenty for history buffs big and small to
explore on this boat, a veteran of D-Day and the
only original ship to sail under its own steam to the
50th anniversary of the Allied invasion at
Norrmandy. From the faithfully restored engine
room to the officers' bunk rooms, it's a fascinating
bit of World War II arcana. It occasionally leaves
dock for cruises, so be sure to call ahead. At Pier 43,
between Hyde & Jefferson Streets, you'll also find a
flotilla of turn-of-the-20th-century ships, including
the three-mast, square-rigged *Balclutha*. The San
Francisco Maritime Museum (*see p94*) is nearby.

Randall Museum
199 Museum Street, off Roosevelt Way, Buena
Vista (554 9600/www.randallmuseum.org). Bus
24, 37. **Open** 10am-5pm Tue-Sat. **Admission** free.
This small museum offers panoramic views of the
city and hands-on fun for pre-teens. Visit the animal
corral or drop in for Saturday arts-and-crafts classes.

San Francisco Zoo
Sloat Boulevard, at 47th Avenue, Sunset (753
7080/www.sfzoo.org). Metro L to SF Zoo/bus 18,
23. **Open** *Main zoo* 10am-5pm daily. *Children's*
zoo Memorial Day-Labor Day 10.30am-4.30pm
daily. Labor Day-Memorial Day 11am-4pm daily.
Admission $11; $8 12-17s; $5 3-11s; free under-3s.
Free 1st Wed of mth. **Credit** AmEx, MC, V.
The zoo is currently undergoing a facelift: there's a
new three-acre African savanna, the expansive
Lemur Forest and over 1,000 other species of
mammals and birds. Combine your visit with a
walk along Ocean Beach afterwards and maybe
lunch at the Cliff House or Louis' Diner (*see p204*
Kitchens for kids). You can look out for whales
nearby in January and February.

Zeum
221 4th Street, at Howard Street, SoMa (777 2800/
www.zeum.org). Bus 12, 30, 45. **Open** 11am-5pm
Wed-Sun. **Admission** $7; $6 discounts; $5 4-18s.
Credit AmEx, MC, V. **Map** p315 N6.
Budding auteurs can direct their own videos at this
lively art and technology centre. There are also
workshops for creating sculptures and experimenting with computer-aided animation design. Nearby
you'll find a bowling alley, a children's park, an ice
rink, a garden and a carousel.

Parks & beaches

There are many child-friendly attractions near
Fisherman's Wharf (*see pp92-95*). The best
are the historic ships at Hyde Street Pier and, at
Pier 45, the relocated Musée Mécanique (*see*

p94), the submarine USS *Pampanito* (*see p95*)
and the *Jeremiah O'Brien* (*see above*). There's a
pack of rather boisterous sea lions in permanent
residence on the docks at Pier 39, where you'll
also find a carousel, a games arcade and street
performers. The wharf is also the departure
point for trips to **Alcatraz Island** (*see p93*)
and **Angel Island** (*see p94*). Organised outings
from here include the excellent **Fire Engine
Tour** (*see p65*).
  Golden Gate Park attracts flocks of adults
on weekends, but it's also very child-friendly.
Kids will want to head straight for **Stow Lake**,
where they can hike out to Strawberry Hill
or rent bicycles, paddle- and rowboats. Visit
Spreckels Lake to marvel at the model
boats (at Kennedy Drive & 35th Avenue), then
wander down to the buffalo paddock to see the
small herd of bison that have been residents in
the park since 1892. The younger set will enjoy
the main children's playground (at MLK &
Bowling Green Drives) and the nearby carousel.
For more on Golden Gate Park, *see p109*. For
a walk on the wilder side, head over to **Ocean
Beach** (*see p122* **On the beach**). If it's cold,
warm up with a hot chocolate in the Cliff House.

Other Bay Area attractions & museums

In addition to the places featured below, several
other East Bay attractions are great for kids.
The **Chabot Space & Science Museum**
(10000 Skyline Boulevard, Joaquin Miller Park;
see p125) in Oakland is possibly the next best
thing to space travel; Berkeley's **Lawrence
Hall of Science** (Centennial Drive, near
Grizzly Park Boulevard; *see p128*) is also
terrific. The **Oakland Zoo** (9777 Golf Links
Road, off I-580; *see p125*) is well worth a visit.
And if you're heading south, don't miss the
world-class **Monterey Bay Aquarium**
(886 Cannery Row, Monterey; *see p280*).

Bay Area Discovery Museum
East Fort Baker, 557 McReynolds Road, Sausalito
(339 3900/www.baykidsmuseum.org). Blue &
Gold Fleet ferry from Pier 41, or Golden Gate
ferry from Ferry Building. **Open** 9am-4pm Tue-Fri;
10am-5pm Sat, Sun. **Admission** $8.50 adults;
$7.50 children; free under-1s. Free 2nd Sat of mth
after 1pm. **No credit cards.**
This hands-on museum, located just below the north
ramp of the Golden Gate Bridge and boasting spectacular skyline views, offers kids a load of hands-
on activities. There's Lookout Cove, an expansive
outdoor area with a sea cave, climbable shipwreck
and miniature Golden Gate Bridge for kids aged
ten and younger. Tot Spot gives toddlers their own
indoor/outdoor nirvana, with a plastic trout-packed
waterway, climbing structures and animal costumes.

Arts & Entertainment

Children's Fairyland

699 Bellevue Avenue, at Lake Merritt, Oakland (1-510 452 2259/www.fairyland.org). BART 19th Street/Oakland. **Open** times vary. **Admission** $6, incl unlimited rides. **Credit** MC, V.

Legend has it that Walt Disney was so taken with this whimsical theme park when he saw it in 1950 that he decided to build his own. Kids can follow Alice down the rabbit hole, ride a tiny Ferris wheel and catch daily puppet shows. There's also a pirate ship and toddler-sized houses to climb through.

Marine Mammal Center

1065 Fort Cronkhite, Sausalito (289 7325/www. tmmc.org). Blue & Gold Fleet ferry from Pier 41, or Golden Gate ferry from Ferry Building. **Open** 10am-4pm daily. **Admission** free.

See seals and sea otters at this non-profit centre, which rescues sick or stranded animals, nurtures them back to health and returns them to the Pacific. Spring is pupping season, and when you'll see most animals. There's a gift shop (289 7373) at Pier 39.

Parks & beaches

Toddlers will love the steam trains, farm animals and carousel ride at **Tilden Park** in Berkeley (1-510 562 7275, www.ebparks.org). Kids of all ages enjoy picnics at **Lake Anza**, where the water is warm enough for a summer swim. The lake is open year-round for fishing.

Shops & entertainment

Color Me Mine

2030 Union Street, between Webster & Buchanan Streets, Cow Hollow (474 7076). Bus 22, 41, 45. **Open** 11am-6pm Mon, Sun; 11am-9pm Tue-Sat. **Credit** MC, V. **Map** p313 H4.

This DIY pottery store isn't aimed just at kids, but the children love it. Buy a clay pot, plate, mug or one of various figurines, pick up a brush and get decorating with some of the dazzling glazes on offer. The staff then fire the item for you to collect later.

826 Valencia

826 Valencia Street, between 19th & 20th Streets, Mission (642 5905/www.826valencia.org). BART 24th Street/bus 14, 26, 48, 49, 67. **Open** Drop-in tutoring 2.30-5.30pm Mon-Thur, Sun. *Pirate store* noon-6pm daily. **Admission** free. **Map** p318 K11.

Local literary lion Dave Eggers opened this non-profit kids' writing centre in 2002, a must for those travelling with young, aspiring scribes. In addition to offering workshops and free drop-in tutoring for children aged 8-18, 826 is the Bay Area's only independent pirate supply store.

Pier 39

Beach Street & the Embarcadero, Fisherman's Wharf (705 5500/www.pier39.com). Metro F to Pier 39/bus 10, 15, 30, 39, 47/cable car Powell-Mason. **Open** *Jan-Feb* 10.30am-7pm Mon-Thur,

Flying high at **Pier 39**.

Sun; 10am-9pm Fri, Sat. *Mar-mid May, mid Sept-Oct* 10am-8pm Mon-Thur, Sun; 10am-9pm Fri, Sat. *Mid May-mid Sept* 10am-9pm Mon-Thur, Sun; 10am-10pm Fri, Sat. *Nov, Dec* 10.30am-8pm Mon-Thur, Sun; 10.30am-9pm Fri, Sat. **Map** p314 L1.

A bustling tourist trap, all T-shirt shops and people flogging Celtic art and music boxes, plus the newly opened WipeOut restaurant and a working carousel. If you can handle the schlock, there are beautiful views and playful (or bickering) sea lions.

Metreon

4th Street, at Mission Street, SoMa (369 6000/www. metreon.com). BART or Metro to Powell/bus 14, 15, 30, 45 & Market Street routes. **Open** 10am-10pm daily. **Map** p315 N6.

Like it or not, preteens and teens (particularly boys) will track down this mixed bag of shopping and entertainment. There's the Games Workshop (where they can paint your toy purchases for free), a high-tech arcade (complete with virtual bowling), an anime shop and a 15-screen Loews movie complex with an IMAX theatre. Parents can take infants to screenings at 11am on Mondays.

Circus skills

The **Circus Center** (755 Frederick Street, at Arguello Boulevard, 759 8123, www.circus center.org) offers child and adult courses in acrobatics, clowning and the trapeze. Most classes last several weeks, so call for details. **Acrosports** (639 Frederick Street, at Willard Street, 665 2276, www.acrosports.org) provides gymnastics, tumbling and circus classes for children as young as two.

Arts & Entertainment

Film

From art-house indie to big-bucks blockbuster, San Francisco is one of the most movie-mad cities on earth.

With the charisma of a leading man and the allure of a Hollywood starlet, celluloid-friendly San Francisco has long been a magnet for directors and location scouts. Always groomed and ready for its close-up, the City by the Bay has starred in a plethora of films, from vintage classics like *The Maltese Falcon* and *Vertigo* to modern movies such as *Interview With the Vampire* and *The Hulk*.

Of course, San Francisco's longstanding love affair with the movies goes far beyond its reputation as one of the world's finest shooting locations. Its citizen's passionate enthusiasm for cinema and its fertile creative environment have combined to foster everything from the digital-effects revolution at Industrial Light & Magic (ILM) and Pixar Studios to the birth of the Asian-American and gay and lesbian film movements in the Bay Area. San Francisco is also home to a frightening number of directors, documentarists and auteurs.

But the real draw for visiting film junkies, at least outside of one of the city's many cinematic special events (*see p208* **Festivals**), is San Francisco's wealth of neighbourhood theatres. Built between 1910 and 1930 to serve the new residential districts that had sprouted up along the city's streetcar lines, the single-screen cinemas flourished through World War II, showing films after their initial run at the larger Market Street movie houses. While dozens have been lost over the years to land developers and fierce competition from the multiscreens, several have survived thanks to the efforts of groups such as the San Francisco Neighborhood Theater Foundation. The jewel among these picture palaces is the **Castro Theatre** (*see p209*), a glamorous blend of Spanish, Italian and Oriental decor with a glazed-tile foyer and a vertical neon sign that harks back to a time when a night at the movies was an enchanted evening.

The screening of movies isn't limited to conventional cinemas, however. If you spill soup all over yourself at movie restaurant **Foreign Cinema** (*see p149*), you can get your pants cleaned while you watch at the **Star Wash** (*see p186*) laundromat. There's even a chance to catch a flick while you're working up a sweat on the treadmill: at the **Gorilla Sports Club** (2330 Polk Street, between Green & Union Streets, Russian Hill, 292 5444, www.gorilla sports.com), housed in what was once an art deco movie house, feature films play on a big screen in the main exercise area.

INFORMATION & TICKETS

You can usually buy tickets direct from cinema box offices immediately before a screening. Many cinemas also run bargain-price matinées: contact the venue direct to confirm details. For local listings, check any of the main print media outlets: the *Chronicle*, the *Examiner*, *SF Weekly* and the *Bay Guardian* all carry film listings. Showtimes, locations and tickets are also available by phone from **Moviefone** (777 3456, www.movietickets.com), but there's a $1 surcharge per ticket.

Mainstream cinemas

Time was the San Franciscans had more than a dozen grand movie palaces to choose from; only a precious few remain, however, among them the **UA Metro 1** (2055 Union Street, at Webster Street, 931 1685, www.regalcinemas.com) in Cow Hollow and the **Castro Theatre** (*see p209*). As elsewhere, the steady decline of San Francisco's movie palaces was hastened along by the rise of the massive modern multiplexes: with its gleaming escalators and long hallways, the **AMC Kabuki 8** (1881 Post Street, at Fillmore Street, 931 9800, www.amctheatres.com) in Japantown, the 14-screen **AMC 1000 Van Ness** (1000 Van Ness Avenue, at O'Farrell Street, 931 9800, www.amctheatres.com) on the edge of the Tenderloin, and SoMa's 15-screen

The best Film

For a gilt trip
Castro Theatre. See p209.

For gourmet popcorn
Red Vic. See p209.

For subcontinental showtunes
Naz8. See p210.

Festivals Film

The Bay Area's love affair with film is amply demonstrated by the volume and variety of its film festivals. Works by local movie-makers mingle with international productions, and the quality varies from high to horrific. We've listed the major festivals, but there are other smaller seasons throughout the year.

Noir City

www.noircity.com. **Venues** Palace of Fine Arts; Balboa Theatre. **Date** Jan.
Two weeks of classic *film noir* – some famous, some obscure – with talks and other special events to add further spice.

Spike & Mike's Festival of Animation

1-858 459 8707/www.spikeandmike.com. **Venues** Victoria Theatre, Mission. **Date** late Feb-Apr.
Mainstream animators such as Nick Park have shown early works at Spike & Mike's cultish festival, but it's the 'Sick and Twisted' segment that really raises the bar.

San Francisco International Asian American Film Festival

863 0814/www.naatanet.org/festival. **Venues** various theatres. **Date** mid Mar.
One of the longest running Asian American filmmaking showcases in the US provides a meeting ground for ethnic communities of all types, from around the globe.

San Francisco International Film Festival

561 5000/www.sfiff.org. **Venues** various theatres. **Date** mid Apr-early May.
Produced by the San Francisco Film Society, this is North America's longest-running film festival (it turns 50 in 2007), and one of its best. More than 200 films are screened; the 80,000 tickets sell like hot starlets.

San Francisco International LGBT Film Festival

703 8650/www.frameline.org. **Venues** various theatres. **Date** late June.
A crucial part of the month-long Gay Pride festivities: both a potent political statement and an unbridled celebration, with features, shorts, docs and experimental works.

San Francisco Silent Film Festival

777 4908/www.silentfilm.org. **Venue** Castro Theatre, Castro. **Date** early July.
Screenings at this three-day event have musical accompaniment by a pianist, a Wurlitzer organist, or anything from Indian duos to avant-garde chamber groups.

Jewish Film Festival

621 0556/www.sfjff.org. **Venues** various theatres. **Date** late July-early Aug.
The world's largest Jewish film fest, the SFJFF spends two weeks presenting contemporary (and some archival) films on Jewish culture.

Festival ¡Cine Latino!

553 8135/www.cineaccion.com. **Venues** University of San Francisco, Western Addition. **Date** mid Sept.
The best recent works from Central and South America, from obscure pieces to major works.

MadCat Women's International Film Festival

436 9523/www.madcatfilmfestival.org. **Venues** various theatres. **Date** mid Sept & early Oct.
This radical, alternative women's film festival happens over three weeks, squeezing in pioneering films that range from earnest feminist polemics to raunchy sexploitation.

Arab Film Festival

564 1100/www.aff.org. **Venues** various theatres. **Date** late Sept-early Oct.
This inclusive mix of features, documentaries and shorts, which celebrates its tenth birthday in 2006, offers a lively and involving survey of Arab cinema of every stripe and style.

Mill Valley Film Festival

383 5256/www.finc.org. **Venues** Cine Arts Sequoia, Mill Valley; Rafael Film Center, San Rafael. **Date** early Oct.
One of the state's best-known and most influential film events offers dozens of new movies over ten days. There's also a six-day Videofest, star guests and kids' events.

Film Arts Festival of Independent Cinema

552 8760/www.filmarts.org. **Venues** various theatres. **Date** early Nov.
The essential festival for a real snapshot of NorCal independents. Programming for the six-day fest is drawn from Bay Area filmmakers, featuring documentary, experimental and traditional narrative pieces in formats that range from Super-8 shorts to high-end DV.

Arts & Entertainment

Sony Metreon (4th Street, at Mission Street, 369 6201, www.metreon.com) in SoMa have all the warm ambience, classy design and individuality of an airport lobby. Still, the screens are state-of-the-art, the seats are high-backed and very comfortable, and the sound systems are beyond reproach. Kabuki 8 also serves as the main venue for the **International Film Festival** (*see p208* **Festivals**).

Other movie houses within easy reach of the town centre and worth a visit include the Marina's funky **Presidio** (2340 Chestnut Street, between Scott & Divisadero Streets, 776 2388) and the **Embarcadero Cinema** (Building 1, Embarcadero Center, Battery Street, between Sacramento and Clay Streets, 352 0835), one of five quality movie houses that make up the **Landmark Theaters** chain (for details of the others, contact 267 4893 or visit www.landmark theater.com). The Embarcadero Cinema even serves popcorn with real butter.

Tickets at all of the cinemas mentioned above cost around $10; AmEx, MasterCard and Visa credit cards are accepted.

Repertory cinemas

San Francisco's repertory theatres often owe their charm to a winning combination of independent ownership and unique buildings, as exemplified by the **Castro Theatre**, the **Roxie** and the **Red Vic**. A repertory-film scene also thrives in the East Bay (*see p210*), and the **San Francisco Cinematheque** (*see p210*) is renowned for putting on avant-garde screenings at a variety of other venues.

Castro Theatre

429 Castro Street, at Market Street, Castro (621 6120/www.thecastrotheatre.com). Metro F, K, L, M to Castro/bus 24, 33, 35, 37. **Tickets** $8.50; $5.50 discounts. **No credit cards**. **Map** p317 H10.
One of San Francisco's finest and best-loved repertory cinemas, this movie palace was built by Timothy L Pflueger in 1922. It became a registered landmark 55 years later, affording it the proper protection. These days it's a dream space of classical murals and rare old film posters, with ceilings that shimmer with gold and films introduced to the strains of a Mighty Wurlitzer organ.

Red Vic

1727 Haight Street, at Cole Street, Haight-Ashbury (668 3994/www.redvicmoviehouse.com). Bus 6, 7, 33, 43, 66, 71. **Tickets** $8; $4 seniors & children. **No credit cards**. **Map** p317 E9.
Old sofas, popcorn in wooden bowls with butter and brewer's yeast, and a choice of films ranging from revivals to the best current movies. You're in your best friend's living room, right? Wrong. Tickets for matinées are $6; a 'punch card' effectively buys four pairs of tickets costs $25.

Roxie & Little Roxie

3117 16th Street, at Albion Street, Mission (863 1087/www.roxie.com). BART 16th Street/bus 14, 26, 33, 49. **Tickets** $8; $4 seniors & children. **No credit cards**. **Map** p318 J10.
World premières of cutting-edge documentaries, classic *films noirs* and '60s horror flicks only begins to describe the impressive range of films staged at the Roxie. Next door's Little Roxie has a great projection set-up, a terrific sound system and a programme of stuff too weird even for its wacky parent to show. Tickets cost $5 for the first show on Wednesday, Saturday or Sunday; discount cards for $22 grant admission to five screenings.

Experimental cinemas

With the opening of the **Little Roxie** (*see above*) and the construction of a new **Jewish Community Center**, times are improving for off-mainstream cinema. Longer-established venues to look out for include the 278-seat cinema in **SFMOMA** (*see p81*) and the 96-seat media screening room in the **Yerba Buena Center for the Arts** (*see p255*), where the programmes of contemporary and experimental work are often themed with the exhibitions showing at the time. However, it's the **SF Cinematheque** which remains the major driving force for innovative film in the city.

Rep gems at the **Red Vic**.

Artists' Television Access

992 Valencia Street, at 21st Street, Mission (824 3890/www.atasite.org). BART 24th Street/bus 14, 26, 48, 49, 67. **Tickets** $5-$10. **No credit cards.** **Map** p318 K11.

Experimental and unusual programming, including open screenings, usually Thursday to Sunday.

Jewish Community Center

3200 California Street, at Presidio Avenue, Presidio Heights (292 1233/www.jccsf.org). Bus 1, 3, 4, 43. **Tickets** $8-$10. **Credit** AmEx, MC, V. **Map** p313 F5.

This 450-seat theatre hosts cutting-edge international Jewish-themed films and videos, as well as the Jewish Film Festival (*see p208* **Festivals**).

San Francisco Cinematheque

Various venues (522 1990/www.sfcinematheque.org). **Tickets** $7-$10. **Credit** varies by venue.

Run by the people putting on stuff you can't see anywhere else, be it documentary, feature film, animation or whatever. The Cinematheque offers programmes twice weekly from late September until July at venues including the Yerba Buena Center (*see p255*) and the San Francisco Art Institute (*see p96*).

East Bay cinemas

The East Bay has an embarrassment of cinematic riches. As well as Berkeley's **Fine Arts Cinema** and **Pacific Film Archive**,

Oakland's venerable **Paramount Theatre**.

there's the **Parkway** in Oakland; **Naz8**, the first East Asian megaplex in the US; and a wealth of film festivals. Keep an eye on the historic, art deco **Paramount Theatre** (2025 Broadway, at 20th Street, Oakland, 1-510 465 6400, www.paramounttheatre.com), which hopes to revive its movie programming in 2006.

Naz8

Gateway Plaza Shopping Center, 39160 Paseo Padre Parkway, at Walnut Avenue, Fremont (1-510 797 2000/www.naz8.com). BART Fremont. **Tickets** $8; $5 discounts. **Credit** AmEx, MC, V.

This 3,000-seat Bollywood bonanza is just a short freeway or BART ride from SF. It mainly features first-run movies from India and Pakistan, but also shows films from Afghanistan, China, Korea, the Philippines and Taiwan. You can even gorge yourself on samosas or a pistachio kulfi.

Pacific Film Archive

2575 Bancroft Way, between Telegraph Avenue & Bowditch Street, Berkeley (1-510 642 1124/www.bampfa.berkeley.edu). BART Downtown Berkeley, then AC Transit bus 7, 51. **Tickets** $8; $4-$5 discounts. **Credit** AmEx, MC, V.

Just off the university campus, the PFA has a collection of more than 7,000 titles, including Soviet, US avant-garde and Japanese cinema. Some 650 of them are screened annually to a clued-up audience.

Parkway Theater

1834 Park Boulevard, at E 18th Street, Oakland (1-510 814 2400/www.picturepubpizza.com). BART Lake Merritt, then AC Transit bus 14. **Tickets** $5-$6; $3 matinées. **No credit cards.**

Two separate screens (one has comfy chairs, the other regulation seats), a dinner menu (with proper meals, wine and beer), a friendly atmosphere… what's not to like? Along with mainstream movies, the Parkway hosts the Thrillville (www.thrillville. net) cult-movie cabaret, plus a variety of day and evening events for different ages. Sundays are family night, and the 6.30pm screening on Monday is pinned as Baby Brigade: mothers and their young 'uns (under one year old) are welcome.

Foreign-language films

As if to demonstrate its Europhile tendencies, the city offers screenings of European films in their original languages: try the **Alliance Française** (1345 Bush Street, between Polk & Larkin Streets, 775 7755, www.afsf.com) in Polk Gulch, the **Goethe Institut** (530 Bush Street, between Grant Avenue & Stockton Street, 263 8760, www.goethe.de/ins/us) near Union Square, and the **Istituto Italiano di Cultura** (425 Washington Street, between Sansome & Battery Streets, 788 7142, www.sfiic.org) in the Financial District. You'll also want to check out the South American offerings at **Festival ¡Cine Latino!** (*see p208* **Festivals**).

Faster than a speeding Bullitt

With its breathtaking views, dramatic fog-shrouded hills and iconic architecture, San Francisco has routinely ended up stealing the spotlight from movie stars, whether in gritty cop flicks such as *Dirty Harry* or the rather sillier likes of *Mrs Doubtfire*. Still, the most famous San Francisco film remains hard-boiled crime flick **Bullitt**. Shot in 1968 at the height of the counterculture movement, this unforgettable popcorn-muncher has it all: a taut storyline, a sexy love interest and arguably the greatest car chase ever filmed.

The white-knuckle, 12-minute chase jumps back and forth across town with little regard for geography. However, fans of the film can easily rediscover the spots through which Steve McQueen (and, for the trickier scenes, stunt drivers Bud Ekins and Carey Lofton) burned rubber in his dark green Ford Mustang GT 390 fastback. The chase took two weeks to shoot, but modern-day drivers can make it to all the key locations in an afternoon, albeit at slightly more conservative speeds than did Frank Bullitt. Attrition and construction have blurred or eliminated some of the locations, but many of the hot spots remain unaltered.

The chase gets under way in earnest in the southern part of the city; first around the junction of Potrero and Cesar Chavez Streets in the Mission, and then with a hard right on to York Street. The cars then emerge at 20th and Kansas Streets, alternately climbing up and flying down mountainous Potrero Hill,

before cutting to North Beach where, at breakneck speed, the autos barrel through intersections – initially heading east on Filbert Street near Taylor Street, then past Bimbo's 365 Club (*see p232*) on Columbus Avenue – before reappearing back on Potrero Hill.

The cars resurface on Russian Hill, where the real fun begins. The menacing machines race down rollercoaster-steep Taylor Street and take impossibly sharp left-hand turns on to Filbert Street before bouncing down the brick-paved stretch of Larkin Street that turns into Francisco Street. The chase continues on Laguna Street before hitting Marina Boulevard, with its glorious sights of the Golden Gate Bridge and San Francisco Bay.

It's then back across town to Visitation Valley (Mansell and University Streets) and a fly through leafy McLaren Park. The gleaming racers then head south of the city for neighbouring Brisbane, where the chase bottoms out when the unlucky gangsters perish in a fiery crash (Guadalupe Canyon Parkway at North Hill Drive).

After you're done, swing by Bullitt's Nob Hill pad (1153 Taylor Street) and see where he hung his holster, tugged on his turtleneck and slung lines like 'It's not for you, baby' at coquettish co-star Jacqueline Bissett. Then swagger across the street to the grocery store at Taylor and Clay Streets and pick up a bundle of green onions and a fistful of frozen TV dinners, just like McQueen did.

Galleries

Diversity and provocation are deep-rooted in the SF art scene.

Art by Shaun Leonardo, on show at the **Luggage Store**. *See p213.*

San Francisco's galleries provide both browsers and collectors with a heady mix of art co-ops, social activism and those airy spaces so typical of California. Most commercial galleries are within a few blocks of **Union Square**, but you'll also find much of the emerging and experimental talent in **SoMa** or the **Mission**. A fine way to sample the range of local artists' work is during the **ArtSpan Open Studios** weekends in October; many galleries also schedule openings for **First Thursdays** (for both, *see p214* **Opening source**).

You can find works of art all over the city, often without entering a gallery. San Francisco's well-established public art programme, largely funded by the San Francisco Arts Commission (www.sfgov.org/sfac), began in 1969 and is one of the best in the country. Check out **Rigo**'s faux street signs, for example – such as *Truth*, set provocatively in Civic Center Plaza directly opposite City Hall – or **Brian Goggin**'s massive *Defenestration* (on the corner of 6th and Howard Streets), with furniture and home appliances dangling from an empty building. Inside the international airport terminal is a maze of works by leading artists.

In addition to the galleries in this chapter, the city's three major art schools are worth a visit. The **San Francisco Art Institute** (800 Chestnut Street, North Beach; *see p96*),

the **Academy of Art University** (79 New Montgomery Street, at Mission Street, SoMa, 274 2200, www.academyart.edu) and the **California College of the Arts** (1111 8th Street, at Hooper Street, SoMa, 1-800 447 1278, www.cca.edu) all host semi-regular shows; CCA also stages weekly student and faculty shows at its Potrero Hill and Oakland campuses, and its **Wattis Institute** (551 9210) has independently curated exhibitions of contemporary artists such as Steve McQueen and Paul McCarthy.

INFORMATION

Pick up a copy of either the bi-monthly *San Francisco Bay Area Gallery Guide* or the monthly *Art Now Gallery Guide – West Coast*, available in galleries all over town. Both are handy for addresses and details of individual shows or special events. *San Francisco Arts Monthly* (www.sfarts.org) has a more complete calendar of monthly exhibitions, as well as music, dance and theatre listings. Copies can be found in bookshops, hotels and museums. Admission is free to all galleries listed below.

Non-profit galleries

There's also a fabulous gallery at **Intersection for the Arts** (446 Valencia Street, between 15th & 16th Streets; *see p253*).

Arts & Entertainment

Galleries

Galería de la Raza/Studio 24
2857 24th Street, at Bryant Street, Mission (826 8009/www.galeriadelaraza.org). BART to 24th Street/bus 9, 27, 33, 48. **Open** noon-6pm Wed-Sat. **Credit** MC, V. **Map** p319 M12.
Since 1970, this tiny storefront gallery has celebrated contemporary Mexican-American culture with bi-monthly exhibitions and the ongoing (Re)Generation project. The diversity of talent on display is superb.

Lab
2948 16th Street, at Capp Street, Mission (864 8855/www.thelab.org). BART to 16th Street/bus 12, 14, 33, 49, 53. **Open** 1-6pm Wed-Sat. **Credit** MC, V. **Map** p318 K10.
Located on a seedy corner, Lab favours political and subversive photography, paintings and multimedia works. Its auctions, held several times a year, can be counted on for edgy pieces at decent prices.

Luggage Store
1007 Market Street, at 6th Street, Tenderloin (255 5971/www.luggagestoregallery.org). BART & Metro to Powell/bus 14, 16, 19, 26 & Market Street routes. **Open** noon-5pm Wed-Sat. **Credit** MC, V. **Map** p314 L6.
As well as showing modern and minimalist works by local artists, Luggage develops public murals. It stages open-mic readings (8pm Tue) at the Cultural Center (509 Ellis Street), which also offers art classes and photography workshops. **Photo** *p212*.

New Langton Arts
1246 Folsom Street, between 8th & 9th Streets, SoMa (626 5416/www.newlangtonarts.org). Bus 9, 12, 27, 47. **Open** noon-6pm Tue-Sat. **Credit** MC, V. **Map** p318 L8.
At the forefront of the visual and media arts scene, this diminutive gallery is in a first-floor loft behind an unprepossessing black façade. Best known for installations and performance pieces, it also runs lively art and photography lectures.

San Francisco Art Commission Gallery
Veterans' Memorial Building, 401 Van Ness Avenue, at McAllister Street, Civic Center (554 6080/www.sfacgallery.org). BART & Metro to Civic Center/bus 21, 47, 49 & Market Street routes. **Open** by appt Tue; noon-5pm Wed-Sat. **No credit cards**. **Map** p318 K7.
This tidy space draws from local and national artists, exhibiting all kinds of media in many contexts. It also maintains Grove Street Windows (155 Grove Street, between Van Ness & Polk Streets), where you can watch projections, soundworks and other site-specific installations in the shopfront.

66Balmy
591 Guerrero Street, at 18th Street, Mission (522 0502/www.66balmy.com). BART to 16th Street/bus 26, 33. **Open** 3-8pm Thur, Fri; noon-5pm Sat, Sun. **No credit cards**. **Map** p318 J10.
One of several Mission haunts establishing itself on the gallery circuit, 66Balmy concentrates on young local talent in its regular exhibitions.

SoMarts Gallery
934 Brannan Street, between 8th & 9th Streets, SoMa (552 2131/www.somarts.org). Bus 19, 42. **Open** 2-7pm Tue-Fri. **No credit cards**. **Map** p319 M9.
Tucked under the freeway, this is one of the city's greatest and longest-lived alternative art spaces. SoMarts hosts its own group and solo shows, but is also home to a variety of other enterprises: the Kearny Street Workshop (503 0520), the USA's oldest Asian-American arts organisation; the Mural Resource Center; and the ever-popular Open Studios (*see p214* **Opening source**).

Southern Exposure
401 Alabama Street, at 17th Street, Mission (863 2141/www.soex.org). Bus 12, 22, 27, 33, 53. **Open** 11am-5pm Tue-Sat. **Credit** MC, V. **Map** p318 L10.
Large and inclusive, SoEx is the best non-profit gallery in the city; many a young artist has been discovered after showing here. The group shows and parties are legendary, and the juried art shows draw nationally respected curators.

Commercial galleries

San Francisco has its very own 'art mall' at 49 Geary Street, gathering **Catharine Clark**, **Jack Fischer**, **Stephen Wirtz**, **Fraenkel**, **Robert Koch** and **Shapiro**. In the same high-rise, **871 Fine Art** (543 5812) is a gallery-bookstore recognised as the best place in town for out-of-print art books and catalogues. Also worth a look is the fabulous **111 Minna** (111 Minna Street, at 2nd Street, SoMa; *see p240*), and a couple of edgy spaces in the Mission: the **Needles & Pens** 'zine emporium and gallery (482 14th Street, between Guerrero & Valencia Streets, 255 1534, www.needles-pens.com) and **Adobe Book Shop**'s tiny but influential back room (3166 16th Street, at Guerrero Street, 864 3936, www.adobebooks.org).

Artist-Xchange
3169 16th Street, between Guerrero & Albion Streets, Mission (864 1490/www.artist-xchange.com). BART to 16th Street/bus 14, 26, 33, 49. **Open** noon-9pm Mon-Fri; 10am-9pm Sat; 10am-8pm Sun. **Credit** MC, V. **Map** p318 J10.

The best Galleries

For agitprop
Lab. *See left.*

For home-grown talent
Hackett-Freedman Gallery. *See p215.*

For foreign imports
Jack Hanley Gallery. *See p215.*

Opening source

The scent of fresh-painted walls, spilled pinot and crushed crackers tells you it's opening night at San Francisco's many galleries.

One of your best bets is **First Thursdays**, which happens – unsurprisingly – on the first Thursday of every month. Many city galleries throw their opening bashes on these nights; even those that don't tend to stay open later than usual. Crowds converge on Downtown galleries such as **Catharine Clark** (see below) and **Stephen Wirtz** (see p216), located in the same high-rise on Geary Street, and nearby **Hackett-Freedman** (see p215), before taking detours into SoMa to **Braunstein/Quay** (see below), **SFMOMA** (see p81) and **Yerba Buena Center for the Arts** (see p82).

In recent times, both SFMOMA and YBC have thrown opening parties outside of the First Thursday circuit, which are generally packed nose to jowl. The former's SECA awards for local artists featured bands playing in the cavernous space, while YBC's Beautiful Losers exhibit drew avant-noise groups, street artists and skateboarders, attracted by a temporary indoor ramp.

Some of the liveliest openings occur at the city's art bars, where exhibition space meets nightclub. In SoMa, there's **OnSix** (60 6th Street, between Market & Mission Streets, www.onsixgallery.com) and **111 Minna Street** (111 Minna Street, at 2nd Street; see p240); in the Tenderloin, try **Rx Gallery** (132 Eddy Street, at Mason Street; see p239); while the Western Addition has the estimable **Madrone Lounge** (500 Divisadero Street, at Fell Street, 241 0202, www.madronelounge.com). Check online for details of the regular shows.

A friendly community gallery in the heart of the Mission. Up and coming artists come here to chat, take classes, and display and sell their work.

Bomani Gallery
296 8677. **Open** by appt only.
Owned by actor Danny Glover's wife, the Bomani was one of many galleries forced out of Downtown by rent rises, and is now in a Haight Victorian. Visiting takes an effort (call to make an appointment and you'll be given the address), but it's the only SF gallery representing African-American masters and emerging artists from the Third World.

Braunstein/Quay
430 Clementina Street, between 5th & 6th Streets, SoMa (278 9850/www.bquayartgallery.com). Bus 12, 14, 26, 27. **Open** 11am-5.30pm Tue-Sat. **No credit cards. Map** p319 M7.
Braunstein/Quay is one of the city's oldest galleries for contemporary art. Founded in the early 1960s, it launched several influential artists, among them the late ceramics master Peter Voulkos, who dropped the paintbrushes in favour of clay, fibre and glass.

Canvas Gallery & Café
1200 9th Avenue, at Lincoln Way, Sunset (504 0060/www.thecanvasgallery.com). Bus 44, 71. **Open** 8am-midnight Mon-Thur, Sun; 8am-2am Fri, Sat. **Credit** AmEx, DC, MC, V. **Map** p316 C10.
A lively hangout on the edge of Golden Gate Park that benefits from the Inner Sunset's student population. Canvas is industrial in feel, yet comfortable. It attracts its fair share of laptop loiterers but remains a popular venue for young, emerging artists; the road to success is paved with coffee and pastries, not just affordable art.

Catharine Clark Gallery
49 Geary Street, between Kearny Street & Grant Avenue, Union Square (399 1439/www.cclarkgallery. com). BART & Metro to Powell/bus 2, 3, 4, 15, 30, 38, 45, 76 & Market Street routes/cable car Powell-Hyde or Powell-Mason. **Open** 10.30am-5.30pm Tue-Fri; 11am-5.30pm Sat. **Credit** AmEx, MC, V. **Map** p315 M5.
Clark has a keen eye for modern art with legs: many works by her sculptors, painters and mixed-media artists walk straight into regional museums. The three-room gallery shows art ranging from kinetic sculptures to figurative paintings.

City Art
828 Valencia Street, at 19th Street, Mission (970 9900/www.cityartgallery.org). BART to 16th Street/ bus 14, 26, 33, 49. **Open** noon-9pm Wed-Sun. **Credit** AmEx, MC, V. **Map** p318 K11.
A no-frills, quirky collective that's commercial in intent but has the panache of a non-profit organisation. The gallery is full of art by co-op members, who also staff the place during the month-long exhibitions. Prices are affordable, and there are gems among the mixed bag of works on show.

Crown Point Press
20 Hawthorne Street, between Howard & Folsom Streets, SoMa (974 6273/www.crownpoint.com). BART & Metro to Montgomery/bus 12, 15, 30, 45, 76. **Open** 10am-6pm Tue-Sat. **Credit** MC, V. **Map** p315 N6.
The world's leading publisher of etchings. Richard Tuttle, Laura Owens and other established artists work in studios on the premises; their prints are shown in a large, airy, inviting space. The gallery is upstairs in a landmark brick building; there's a fine restaurant, Hawthorne Lane, on the ground floor.

Galleries

Dolby Chadwick

Suite 205, 210 Post Street, between Stockton Street & Grant Avenue, Union Square (956 3560/www. dolbychadwickgallery.com). BART & Metro to Powell/ bus 2, 3, 4, 15, 30, 38, 45, 76 & Market Street routes/cable car Powell-Hyde or Powell-Mason. **Open** 10am-6pm Tue-Fri; 11am-5pm Sat. **Credit** AmEx, MC, V. **Map** p315 M5.

Don't be intimidated by the creaky ride up in the old lift: the gallery couldn't be friendlier. Tall windows frame a view as compelling as the clean-lined still lifes on the walls. There are paintings, drawings and monotypes by emerging and mid-career artists, many priced at under $1,000.

Gallery Paule Anglim

14 Geary Street, at Market Street, Union Square (433 2710/www.gallerypauleanglim.com). BART & Metro to Powell/bus 2, 3, 4, 15, 30, 38, 45, 76 & Market Street routes/cable car Powell-Hyde or Powell-Mason. **Open** 10am-5.30pm Tue-Fri; 10am-5pm Sat. **No credit cards**. **Map** p315 M5.

The unimpressive exterior gives no indication of the light-filled, airy interior of Paule Anglim, which simultaneously accommodates a major and a minor show. Expect everything from Bay Area innovators such as David Ireland and Barry McGee to international superstars like Louise Bourgeois and Philip Guston.

Hackett-Freedman Gallery

Suite 400, 250 Sutter Street, between Kearny Street & Grant Avenue, Union Square (362 7152/www. realart.com). BART & Metro to Montgomery/bus 2, 3, 4, 15, 30, 38, 45, 76/cable car Powell-Hyde or Powell-Mason. **Open** 10.30am-5.30pm Tue-Fri; 11am-5pm Sat. **No credit cards**. **Map** p315 M5.

Another of the city's 'art towers', 250 Sutter is full of galleries. Hackett-Freedman has a comprehensive stable of artists from the major West Coast schools: Bay Area figurative and realist, California colourist, and expressionist works are all represented. A one-stop visual-art tour of California.

Jack Fischer Gallery

49 Geary Street, between Kearny Street & Grant Avenue, Union Square (956 1178/www.jackfischer gallery.com). BART & Metro to Powell/bus 2, 3, 4, 15, 30, 38, 45, 76 & Market Street routes/cable car Powell-Hyde or Powell-Mason. **Open** 10.30am-5.30pm Tue-Sat. **No credit cards**. **Map** p315 M5.

Fischer has built a solid reputation on work by self-taught artists. In the often self-congratulatory art world, it's refreshing to see artists with little or no formal technique but immense talent. The work here is often categorised as 'outsider art'.

Jack Hanley Gallery

389 & 395 Valencia Street, at 15th Street, Mission (522 1623/www.jackhanley.com). BART to 16th Street/bus 14, 26, 33, 49. **Open** 11am-6pm Tue-Sat. **No credit cards**. **Map** p318 K9.

The Jack Hanley Gallery is considered the pre-eminent exhibition space in San Francisco for young international artists, including many from European countries. An unassuming space, it has hosted many rising stars, among them Simon Evans, Chris Johanson and Keegan McHargue.

John Berggruen

228 Grant Avenue, between Post & Sutter Streets, Union Square (781 4629/www.berggruen.com). BART & Metro to Montgomery/bus 2, 3, 4, 15, 30, 38, 45, 76 & Market Street routes/cable car Powell-Hyde or Powell-Mason. **Open** 9.30am-5.30pm Mon-Fri; 10.30am-5pm Sat. **No credit cards**. **Map** p315 M5.

The premier destination for blue-chip art. Founded in the mid 1970s, Berggruen, with its smooth white walls and sleek blond floors, has played host to some of the biggest names in contemporary art, including Ellsworth Kelly, Alexander Calder, David Hockney, Damien Hirst, Edward Ruscha and Frank Stella.

Linc Real Art

1632C Market Street, between Franklin & Gough Streets, Hayes Valley (503 1981/www.lincart.com). Metro to Van Ness/bus 6, 7, 66, 71. **Open** noon-6pm Tue-Sat. **Credit** AmEx, MC, V. **Map** p318 K8.

Intimate and warm, this gallery quickly made a name for itself by showcasing playful works by young and emerging artists. It hosts events and art classes, and is one of the few places in the city where you'll find inexpensive rare art books.

Modernism

685 Market Street, between 3rd & New Montgomery Streets, Financial District (541 0461/www.artnet.com/ modernism.html). BART & Metro to Montgomery/ bus 2, 3, 4, 31 & Market Street routes. **Open** 10am-5.30pm Tue-Sat. **Credit** AmEx, MC, V. **Map** p315 N5.

Paintings by Ada Sadler at **Dolby Chadwick**.

Arts & Entertainment

Festivals Art

In July, the work of emerging artists can be enjoyed on the **Introductions & Summer Art Walk**. This presented by the San Francisco Art Dealers Association (278 9818, www.sf ada.com), a non-profit group made up of 40 Bay Area galleries. September's **Mission Art Walk** (www.missionartwalk.org), which takes in street murals and galleries, is a edgier and somewhat livelier version of the same.

Every autumn, the parking lot outside the wonderful **SoMarts Gallery** (*see p213*) is the site of the annual **Big Deal** charity art fair, a unique opportunity to snap up work by top SF and international artists for a paltry sum. It's put together by **Visual Aid** (777 8242, www.visualaid.org), a non-profit organisation that has supported Bay Area artists with life-threatening illnesses since 1989.

The **ArtSpan Open Studios** (934 Brannan Street, at 8th Street, 861 9838, www.art span.org), held city-wide throughout October, is a very worthwhile event if you're interested in seeking out young artists. And if you're willing to travel, then head to the **Headlands Center for the Arts** (944 Fort Barry, Sausalito, 331 2787, www.headlands.org) in spring and autumn for its twice-annual arts events. Both the bucolic setting and the high-quality work make the drive across the Golden Gate Bridge well worth it.

Modernism grapples with the age-old conundrum of how to show fine art that attracts high prices while maintaining a hospitable atmosphere. And loses. If you're not rich and conservatively dressed, you won't feel comfortable. A shame: the art is amazing.

Shooting Gallery

839 Larkin Street, at Geary Street, Tenderloin (931 8035/www.shootinggallerysf.com). Bus 2, 3, 4, 19, 38, 47. **Open** noon-7pm Tue-Fri; noon-5pm Sat; also by appt. **Credit** AmEx, MC, V. **Map** p314 K6.

An antidote to intimidating galleries, Justin Giarla's Shooting Gallery shows the artists he really likes – Robert Williams, Ed Roth, Von Dutch, David Perry, Robert Crumb, Spain Rodriguez, Isabel Samaras – in a welcoming and unpretentious setting. Provocative, funny and clever urban art is also the theme in White Walls, Giarla's larger second gallery next door.

Steel Gallery

3524 Sacramento Street, between Laurel & Locust Streets, Presidio Heights (885 1655/www.steelgallery inc.com). Bus 1, 3, 4. **Open** 10am-6pm Tue-Sat. **Credit** MC, V. **Map** p313 E5.

An avid collector for years, romantic novelist Danielle Steel opened her own gallery in 2003 and concentrates on showing her favourite artists, such as Wendy Robushi and Sofia Harrison. The mission statement (collecting 'bright, exciting, well thought out pieces' that bring 'happiness, and are fun to live with') may set your teeth on edge, but the shows are impressive.

Stephen Wirtz Gallery

49 Geary Street, between Kearny Street & Grant Avenue, Union Square (433 6879/www.wirtzgallery. com). BART & Metro to Powell/bus 2, 3, 4, 15, 30, 38, 45, 76 & Market Street routes/cable car Powell-Hyde or Powell-Mason. **Open** 9.30am-5.30pm Tue-Fri; 10.30am-5.30pm Sat. **No credit cards. Map** p315 M5.

All is silent save for the click, click, click of expensive heels on polished wooden floors. The contemporary, conceptual paintings and sculpture on display invariably prompt discussion – the gallery often launches young artists to major shows – and there's a feeling of sophistication and restraint in the work, not just in the atmosphere.

Photography galleries

San Francisco Camerawork (863 1001, www.sfcamerawork.org) exhibitions are shown at New Langton Arts (*see p213*).

Fraenkel Gallery

49 Geary Street, between Kearny Street & Grant Avenue, Union Square (981 2661/www.fraenkel gallery.com). BART & Metro to Powell/bus 2, 3, 4, 15, 30, 38, 45, 76 & Market Street routes/cable car Powell-Hyde or Powell-Mason. **Open** 10.30am-5.30pm Tue-Fri; 11am-5pm Sat. **Credit** MC, V (books only). **Map** p315 M5.

Well known for showing major 20th-century photographers, the Fraenkel uses photography as a nexus of interchange between media, showing sculpture or film alongside the works on paper.

Robert Koch Gallery

49 Geary Street, between Kearny Street & Grant Avenue, Union Square (421 0122/www.kochgallery. com). BART & Metro to Powell/bus 2, 3, 4, 15, 30, 38, 45, 76 & Market Street routes/cable car Powell-Hyde or Powell-Mason. **Open** 10.30am-5.30pm Tue-Sat. **Credit** MC, V. **Map** p315 M5.

This reliable, established gallery favours works with an environmental edge. You'll find experimental pieces alongside a selection of 19th-century artists.

Shapiro Gallery

49 Geary Street, between Kearny Street & Grant Avenue, Union Square (398 6655). BART & Metro to Montgomery/bus 38, 80 & Market Street routes. **Open** by appt only. **Credit** MC, V. **Map** p315 M5.

This refined gallery deals primarily in vintage and contemporary black-and-whites.

Gay & Lesbian

We're here. We're queer.

Trannyshack. *See p225.*

In February 2004, more than 4,000 lesbian and gay couples, dressed in glorious gowns and swanky tuxedos, made a mad dash for the City Hall altar. New mayor Gavin Newsom had proclaimed that the state statute prohibiting gay marriage violated California's constitution. It was to be a fleeting victory (*see p224* **I do... I don't... I do... I don't**), but the announcement set off a jubilant three-month celebration – a 'Winter of Love'. Del Martin and Phyllis Lyon, legendary lesbian activists who've been together for 51 years, were the first to wed.

As Armistead Maupin, the city's chronicler of gay life par excellence, wrote, San Francisco 'was probably always destined to lead the century's last great fight for human rights'. From the excoriating energy of Ginsberg's *Howl* to the revolutionary Daughters of Bilitis, from bar culture to the heady days of gay liberation, the city has been a sort of lightning rod for the upheavals associated with queer liberation. The place where, in 1977, Harvey Milk won a historic seat on the Board of Supervisors, a seat that proliferated into five in the 'Lavender Sweep' of the mid 1990s. Civil rights struggles are a kind of nimbus here, establishing precedent-setting laws for domestic partners and equal benefits. 'Gaybies' are so common as to barely merit comment.

NEIGHBOURHOODS

Polk Street, the Tenderloin, Haight-Ashbury and SoMa were the neighbourhoods of choice for gays and lesbians in the 1970s, but the **Castro** – with its street fair, flourishing restaurants and bars, and talismanic **Castro Theatre** (*see p209*) – soon took over. Maupin once referred to the district as the 'gay ghetto', but the Castro remains a vibrant home to trendy, exorbitantly expensive homes (and young families), its storied streets brimming with pride flags, bars, eateries and shops.

Middle-class lesbians with kids and dogs have settled in quiet, cheery residential neighbourhoods such as **Bernal Heights** and **Glen Park**. Affluent queers thrive in villagey and ultra-gentrified **Noe Valley**, filled with chic shops and some superb restaurants. The **Mission**, the city's thriving Latino birthplace, is home to less well-heeled queer inhabitants.

Arts & Entertainment

Gay men still gravitate towards **SoMa**, which was inhabited mostly by artists and leathermen until the invasion of dot-commers in the late 1990s. It is still home to almost all of the gay clubs and many good gay bars, sex clubs and dance joints frequented by the brawny and well-toned. **Duboce Triangle** (between Market, Waller and Castro Streets), **Hayes Valley**, the **Haight** and **Potrero Hill** all also draw queer folk.

RESOURCES & INFORMATION

Queer San Francisco past and present can be explored at the Reading Room in the **Center** (1800 Market Street, at Octavia Street, 865 5520, www.sfcenter.org), and at the **James C Hormel Gay & Lesbian Center** at the Main Library (*see p78*), the world's first queer research centre to have been established in a public institution. **Cruisin' the Castro** (*see p65*) is a mazy walking tour, hosted by 'Leader of the Pack' Kathy Amendola, that covers the history of SF's famous gay neighbourhood. Another walking tour comes courtesy of Humboldt State University professor and gay activist Eric Rofes (gmhs3@aol.com), who runs walking tours of the Folsom Street area that focus on what's seen as the golden era in the gay leather scene. SoMa is home to the **International Museum of Gay and Lesbian History** (Suite 300, 657 Mission Street, between 3rd & 4th Streets, 777 5455, www.glbthistory.org, $2-$4, closed Mon & Sun), which has riveting exhibits of history, culture and the arts as well as extensive archives. Back in the Castro, head to **A Different Light** (489 Castro Street, at 18th Street, 431 0891, www.adlbooks.com), the best gay bookstore in town.

The best resources for up-to-date information on everything from new shows, films and clubs to religious services and the leather calendar are the free newspapers, notably the *San Francisco Bay Times* and the *BAR* (*Bay Area Reporter*). You'll find them in cafés, bookstores and street-corner boxes. The Center organises meetings and events, as well as gathering information. The **Women's Building** (*see p100*), decorated with a great mural, is a hub of resources and services. Queer-about-town Larry-bob Roberts regularly updates his voluminous website listings: click 'event listings' at www.holytitclamps.com. The non gay-specific *Bay Guardian*, *SF Weekly* and *San Francisco Chronicle* are also worth a look.

Where to stay

For places to stay across the city, *see pp42-63*; noteworthy gay-owned, gay-friendly or simply delightful places in the Castro and beyond are listed below.

The Castro

Beck's Motor Lodge

2222 Market Street, at 15th Street, CA 94114 (621 8212/fax 421 0435). Metro F, J, K, L, M to Church/bus 22, 37. **Rates** $89-$112 double. **Credit** AmEx, Disc, MC, V. **Map** p318 H10.
Relatively cheap rates, a sun deck, private baths and, above all, a prime Castro location help Beck's retain its popularity. Inside you'll find the tacky carpets, glasses sealed in plastic and garish soft furnishings typical of a quintessential American motel. It has a reputation for being a very cruisey place to stay.

Inn on Castro

321 Castro Street, at Market Street, CA 94114 (861 0321/http://innoncastro.com). Metro F, K, L, M to Castro/bus 24, 33, 35, 37. **Rates** $80-$160 double; $185 suite. **Credit** AmEx, Disc, MC, V. **Map** p318 H10.
A beautifully restored Edwardian, with eight rooms and four apartments decorated with contemporary furnishings, original modern art and elaborate flower arrangements. The sumptuous breakfast includes delicious own-made muffins and fresh fruit.

Parker Guest House

520 Church Street, at 18th Street, CA 94114 (1-888 520 7275/621 3222/fax 621 4139/www. parkerguesthouse.com). Metro J to Mission Dolores Park/bus 22, 33. **Rates** $129-$189 double; $209 suite. **Credit** AmEx, Disc, MC, V. **Map** p318 J10.
An exquisitely renovated 21-room mini-mansion, dating to 1909. Rooms come with terrycloth robes, down comforters and new all-tile baths. There are gorgeous gardens, a steam spa room and a communal lounge with fireplace and a baby grand. On warm days, guests can take breakfast on to the deck.

24 Henry Guesthouse & Village House

24 Henry Street, between Sanchez & Noe Streets, CA 94114 (1-800 900 5686/864 5686/fax 864 0406/www.24henry.com). Metro F, J, K, L, M to Church/bus 22, 37. **Rates** $65-$129 double. **Credit** AmEx, MC, V. **Map** p318 H9.

The best Gay places

For pillow talk
Parker Guest House. *See right.*

For table talk
La Méditerranée. *See p220.*

For body talk
Badlands. *See p222.*

Festivals Gay

June's month-long **Gay Pride** (*see p199*), the largest gay carnival in the world, is the highlight of the year. It ends in high style with the boisterous Saturday night women-only **Dyke March** (241 8882, www.dyke march.org/sfo), complete with onlookers of any gender cheering from the sidelines, and Sunday's **Pride Parade**. The crowds stream up Market Street to Civic Center Plaza to watch the leather-and-lace Dykes on Bikes leading the parade with their full-throttled Harley power and roar.

The centrepiece of Pride is Frameline's **San Francisco International Lesbian & Gay Film Festival** (*see p208* **Festivals**), a two-week festival of shorts, documentaries and features. Still racy, September's leather-besotted **Folsom Street Fair** (*see p200*) is

the second largest gay event in SF; the **Dore Up Your Alley Fair** (861 3247, www.folsomstreetfair.com/alley), a cruisey and risqué S&M festival in August, also attracts thousands. The Castro's other major street celebration is **Halloween** (*see p200*). If you're thinking of going, wear a costume, or risk the scorn of patrolling homecoming queens.

On a more sombre note, there's the **AIDS Candlelight Vigil** (*see p199*) in May, with a walk along Market Street to the Main Library; the **AIDS Walk San Francisco** (www.aidswalk.net/sanfran) in July; and **World AIDS Day** on December 1 (www.artistsagainst aids.com), which sees events throughout the city. You can also view portions of the **AIDS Memorial Quilt** (www.aidsquilt.org), now celebrating its 20th anniversary.

All are welcome to this B&B, a handsome Victorian in the heart of the Castro. Of five furnished rooms, one has an en suite bathroom; the others share a double shower room with separate toilet. The Village House (4080 18th Street), another Victorian, has five beautiful rooms, with shared and private bath.

Willows Inn

710 14th Street, between Sanchez & Church Streets, CA 94114 (431 4770/fax 431 5295/www.willows sf.com). Metro F, J, K, L, M to Church/bus 22, 37. **Rates** $95-$135 double; $145 suite. **Credit** AmEx, DC, Disc, MC, V. **Map** p318 H9.
This converted Edwardian has 12 comfy rooms with bentwood willow and antique furnishings. Baths are shared, but all rooms have vanity sinks. Soft kimono bathrobes are provided, and complimentary breakfast and cocktails are served daily. No smoking.

Other neighbourhoods

Hayes Valley Inn

417 Gough Street, at Hayes Street, Hayes Valley, CA 94102 (431 9131/www.hayesvalleyinn.com). Bus 21, 47, 49. **Rates** $73-$105 double. **Credit** AmEx, DC, MC, V. **Map** p318 J8.
A lovely, European-style, 28-room pension in the centre of lively and chic Hayes Valley. There's a bar, pets are welcome, and rooms have their own sink. A kitchen and parlour room are available to guests, but baths are shared.

Restaurants & cafés

GLBT diners are welcome throughout the city, but these are a few of our favourite eateries, some with a determinedly queer milieu.

The Castro

Bagdad Café

2295 Market Street, at Noe Street (621 4434). Metro F, K, L, M to Castro/bus 24, 33, 35, 37. **Open** 24hrs daily. **Main courses** $7-$15. **No credit cards**. **Map** p318 H10.
A bustling diner with a bird's-eye view of the busy Market–Noe intersection, this is a decent option for a sandwich, vegetarian lasagne or post-bar breakfast.

Blue

2337 Market Street, at 16th Street (863 2583). Metro F, K, L, M to Castro/bus 24, 33, 35, 37. **Open** 11.30am-11pm Mon-Thur; 11.30am-11.30pm Fri; 10am-11pm Sat; 10am-10pm Sun. **Main courses** $6-$18. **Credit** AmEx, MC, V. **Map** p318 H10.
Down-home cooking in a tiny, hip diner. Slide into a smooth black booth, gaze on the beauties passing by and nosh on gourmet macaroni cheese, own-made meat loaf or pork chops.

Castro Country Club

4058 18th Street, at Hartford Street (552 6102/ www.castrocountryclub.org). Metro F, K, L, M to Castro/bus 24, 33, 35, 37. **Open** 11am-11pm Mon-Thur; 11am-1am Fri; 10am-1am Sat; 10am-11pm Sun. **No credit cards**. **Map** p318 H11.
A great alternative to boozy nights, this club is home to clean and sober queers. There's a sitting room, a coffee bar and café, a room for board games, a video theatre and a backyard patio. The front steps are Castro central's gossip parlour and cruise lookout.

Catch

2362 Market Street, at Castro Street (431 5000/www.catchsf.com). Metro F, K, L, M to Castro/bus 24, 33, 35, 37. **Open** 11.30am-3pm, 5.30-9.30pm Mon, Tue;

Arts & Entertainment

11.30am-3pm, 5.30-10pm Wed, Thur; 11.30am-3pm, 5.30-11pm Fri; 11am-3.30pm, 5.30-11pm Sat; 11am-3.30pm, 5.30-9.30pm Sun. **Main courses** $9-$23. **Credit** AmEx, DC, MC, V. **Map** p318 H10.
This seafood restaurant has an enclosed, heated outside deck and live piano music. Dishes are well turned out, but not exceptional. No one seems to mind, though: the bar fills up with local yuppies on a date (or looking for one) and gym rats. You'll need to book at weekends.

Firewood Café

4248 18th Street, between Collingwood & Diamond Streets (252 0999/http://firewoodcafe.com). Metro F, K, L, M to Castro/bus 24, 33, 35, 37. **Open** 11am-11pm daily. **Main courses** $7-$14. **Credit** MC, V. **Map** p317 G11.
There's sometimes a queue outside the door for evening meals here, but the loyal customers are willing to wait. Menu standouts are the roast chicken, so tender it melts in the mouth; pasta dishes; and European-style thin-crust pizza. Eat in or phone to take out. A little slice of queer heaven.

La Mediterranée

288 Noe Street, between Market & 16th Streets (431 7210/www.cafelamed.com). Metro F, K, L, M to Castro/bus 24, 33, 35, 37. **Open** 11am-10pm Mon-Fri; 11am-11pm Sat, Sun. **Main courses** $7-$10. **Credit** AmEx, MC, V. **Map** p318 H10.
A well-established success, due in no small part to brilliant use of fresh ingredients. Everything's keenly priced, with terrific houmous and baba ganoush, plus an excellent filo-dough combination plate with Armenian potato salad. The warm interior makes the place feel like a genuine Mediterranean escape. **Other locations**: 2210 Fillmore Street, Pacific Heights (921 2956); 2936 College Avenue, Berkeley (540 7773).

Samovar

498 Sanchez Street, at 18th Street (626 4700/www.samovartea.com). Metro F, K, L, M to Castro/bus 24, 33, 35, 37. **Open** 10am-10pm daily. **Main courses** $5-$10. **Credit** MC, V. **Map** p318 H10.
The Castro's only tearoom, this tranquil spot quickly became a hit with locals searching out a quiet Zen-like refuge. There are over 100 teas, plus healthy, Asian-inspired small plates. Come for high tea during the week (from 3 to 6pm) or weekend brunch (from 10am to 3pm).

2223 Restaurant & Bar

2223 Market Street, between Noe & Sanchez Streets (431 0692/http://2223restaurant.com). Metro F, K, L, M to Castro/bus 24, 33, 35, 37. **Open** 6-10pm Mon-Thur; 6-11pm Fri, Sat; 10am-2pm, 6-10pm Sun. **Main courses** $15-$20. **Credit** AmEx, DC, MC, V. **Map** p318 H10.
Expect vibrant dishes that awaken all the senses at this sleek restaurant. There are Med, Mexican and Caribbean influences on the menu, and excellent pizza, pasta and fish. It's one of the more popular places for the queer crowd, so the din may intrude on romantic *tête-à-têtes*. Sunday brunch is a winner.

Other neighbourhoods

Asia SF

201 9th Street, at Howard Street, SoMa (255 2742/www.asiasf.com). Bus 12, 14, 19, 26. **Open** *Restaurant* 6-10pm Mon-Wed; 5-10pm Thur-Sun. *Club* 7pm-3am Fri, Sat. **Main courses** $10-$20. **Credit** AmEx, DC, Disc, MC, V. **Map** p318 L8.
Those lovely ladies who serve you? They're not. Not women, that is, nor drag queens. The sexy creatures who bring the food and dance seductively atop the long red bar are 'gender illusionists'. The food is inventive Cal-Asian, with small plates and shareable portions. A restaurant, lounge and club all in one, Asia SF's crowd is a compellimg mix of local party-goers and wide-eyed businessmen. Reservations a must.

Emma's Coffee House

1901 Hayes Street, at Ashbury Street, Haight (221 3378). Bus 21, 43. **Open** 6am-8pm daily. **No credit cards. Map** p317 F8.
Two iMacs are available for customer use (first 15mins free with purchase; $2 for every 15mins after that). Food and drinks-wise, prepare yourself for the real deal: robustly strong Italian-style coffee, made exactly the right way. Saunter upstairs to the lounge for a perfectly quiet place to read.

Liberty Café

410 Cortland Avenue, between Bennington & Wool Streets, Bernal Heights (695 8777). Bus 24. **Open** 11am-3pm Tue-Thur; 11am-3pm, 5.30-9.30pm Fri; 10am-2pm, 5.30-9.30pm Sat; 10am-2pm, 5.30-9pm Sun. **Main courses** $6-$15. **Credit** AmEx, Disc, MC, V.
A neighbourhood gem that serves exquisite home-style American food. The chicken pot pie is a sensual delight, and the desserts are among the best in the city, from the voluptuous banana cream pie to a luscious strawberry shortcake with whipped cream.

Mabel's Just for You Café

732 22nd Street, at 3rd Street, Potrero Hill (647 3033/www.justforyoucafe.com). Bus 15, 22, 48. **Open** 7.30am-3pm Mon-Fri; 8am-3pm Sat, Sun. **Main courses** $5-$11. **No credit cards. Map** p319 P11.
The popularity of the original version of this dyke-run café prompted the owners to move to bigger quarters in Dogpatch, close to the Bay. The house speciality is a Cajun-style breakfast, with superb grits and fluffy pancakes. Before 8.30am, you can get a full eggs-and-toast breakfast for about $3.

PastaGina

741 Diamond Street, at 24th Street, Noe Valley (282 0738). Bus 35, 48. **Open** 10am-9pm Mon-Fri; 10am-8.30pm Sat, Sun. **Main courses** $5-$10. **Credit** AmEx, DC, MC, V. **Map** p317 G12.
An exceptional gourmet take-out joint selling yummy fresh pasta and classy salads (Tuscan bean, calamari and so on), as well as Sonoma chicken, Thai vegetarian rolls, organic red beets with basil, sauces, dips, cheeses from various countries, and European and Californian wines.

Arts & Entertainment

Tutu hot to handle

If, during the holiday season, you should find yourself weighed down with the world's troubles, afflicted with an inexorable dullness of spirit, and feeling yourself, as Melville once said, 'growing grim about the mouth', don't take to the sea. Instead, grab your tutu if you have one, and perhaps a wand, and head for the San Francisco Lesbian/Gay Freedom Band's annual **Dance-Along Nutcracker**, a dazzlingly wacky jamboree that's just celebrated its 20th anniversary.

The Dance-Along is participatory *Nutcracker* with a fanciful twist. And what a gambol it is. While there are professional performers dancing on stage to, say, 'The Waltz of the Flowers', the second half of the ballet is a different story. Whenever the sign reading 'All Dance' flashes up above the stage, everybody – frisky kids, arrow-straight lawyers, cross-dressing grannies – makes a rush from their seats to the aisles to prance about on

point as a sylph, execute a splashy pirouette or do a little of the shake-out-the-leg step kick. Some even sway with rumba hips, do a little ballroom, or even samba.

The dancing is optional, of course, and it's terrific fun just watching. However, it's a riot if you do as the locals do. And they do more or less anything, clad in old wedding gowns, chiffon tutus and heaven knows what else. The band members start swathed in tuxes and cummerbunds, but transform themselves after intermission into the silliest of attire. Only in SF would you be able to indulge your fantasy for such delicious ludicrousness.

The whole shebang is staged by the exuberant San Francisco Lesbian/Gay Freedom Band, the first openly gay musical organisation in the world. It also performs at Pride, and has a free Community Concert Series. For details about the band and its performances, check out www.sflgfb.org.

Tartine

600 Guerrero Street, at 18th Street, Mission (487 2600/www.tartinebakery.com). BART 16th Street/ bus 26. **Open** 8am-7pm Mon; 7.30am-7pm Tue, Wed; 7.30am-8pm Thur, Fri; 8am-8pm Sat; 9am-8pm Sun. **Main courses** $3-$8. **Credit** AmEx, Disc, MC, V. **Map** p318 J10.

The selection of fresh-baked morning buns, lemon cream tarts, ham and cheese croissants, croque monsieur, pastries, cakes, tea cakes, cookies, bars and loaves will leave you gasping for air. Unmissable.

Bars

The Castro

The Café (*see p225*) is also good for a drink.

Badlands

4121 18th Street, at Castro Street (626 9320). Metro F, K, L, M to Castro/bus 24, 33, 35, 37. **Open** 2pm-2am daily. **No credit cards. Map** p318 H11.

Even those wistful for the old beloved Badlands come to this newly sparkling hotspot. Beautifully renovated, the legendarily cruisey bar now attracts a younger crowd, thanks to its excellent dancefloor.

Bar on Castro

456 Castro Street, between 18th & Market Streets (626 7220). Metro F, K, L, M to Castro/bus 24, 33, 35, 37. **Open** 5pm-2am Mon-Fri; noon-2am Sat, Sun. **No credit cards. Map** p318 H10.

Dizzyingly crammed with a multitude of pretty boys, frugging to thumping dance music, elbow to elbow. After-work crowds congregate for the weekday happy hour (4-8pm Mon-Thur).

Coffee and cocktails at the **Orbit Room**.

Daddy's

440 Castro Street, at 18th Street (621 8732/www. daddysbar.com). Metro F, K, L, M to Castro/bus 24, 33, 35, 37. **Open** noon-2am daily. **No credit cards. Map** p318 H11.

The Castro's reigning bar for leathermen and bears. The denizens partake of daily drink specials and swoon over Sunday football games. It really packs the punters in for the Folsom Street Fair (*see p200*).

Harvey's

500 Castro Street, at 18th Street (431 4278/www. harveyssf.com). Metro F, K, L, M to Castro/bus 24, 33, 35, 37. **Open** 11am-2am Mon-Fri; 9am-2am Sat, Sun. **Credit** AmEx, MC, V. **Map** p318 H11.

Site of an infamous brawl with cops during the 1979 White Night riot (*see p40*), this bar-restaurant – named after Harvey Milk – is now pervaded by a spirit of bonhomie. Memorabilia and photos line the walls; Monday is a popular trivia quiz night.

Midnight Sun

4067 18th Street, at Hartford Street (861 4186/ www.midnightsun.sf). Metro F, K, L, M to Castro/ bus 24, 33, 35, 37. **Open** 2pm-2am Mon-Fri; 1pm-2am Sat, Sun. **No credit cards. Map** p318 H11.

The big draw at Midnight Sun – aka Midnight Scum, Midnight Slum and Midnight Shun – is videos: classic and contemporary music cross-cut with comedy clips, *The Sopranos* or *Sex and the City*. Two-for-one cocktails are on offer during the week (2-7pm), and weekends are a boy fest.

The Mix

4086 18th Street, at Hartford Street (431 8616). Metro F, K, L, M to Castro/bus 24, 33, 35, 37. **Open** noon-2am Mon-Fri; 8am-2am Sat, Sun. **No credit cards. Map** p318 H11.

This rough-and-ready sports bar is a haven for queer jocks and those who adore them. Fervent fans pack the place to root for the '49ers, and sunny weekends see the back-patio grill cooking up burgers and hot dogs. The windows face 18th, perfect for ogling.

Moby Dick's

4049 18th Street, at Hartford Street (no phone). Metro F, K, L, M to Castro/bus 24, 33, 35, 37. **Open** 2pm-2am Mon-Fri; noon-2am Sat, Sun. **No credit cards. Map** p318 H11.

A true neighbourhood bar, Moby Dick's is exactly as it has been since the 1980s. It's popular with pool players (though there's only one table) and pinball addicts (four machines at the back), though big windows and a prime Castro location afford ample street cruising too. Drink specials and Margaritas are served all week, and there's Sex on the Beach on Sundays.

Orbit Room

1900 Market Street, at Laguna Street (252 9525). Metro to Van Ness/bus 6, 7, 66, 71. **Open** 2pm-2am daily. **No credit cards. Map** p318 J9.

This high-ceilinged art deco retreat with pedestal tables is a coffee house by day and cocktail bar by night. The crowd is quite young, a mix of straights

Arts & Entertainment

and queers, with some uptown lesbians thrown into the mix. Good music, café food and the city's best cocktail mixologist make it a relaxing place to flutter away a gentle evening. **Photo** *p222*.

Pilsner Inn

25 Church Street, at Market Street (621 7058). Metro F, J, K, L, M to Church/bus 22, 37. **Open** 10am-2am daily. **No credit cards. Map** p318 J9.

It all happens here, especially on the back patio (where the heaters cope with frigid San Francisco evenings). A local favourite among youngish beauty boys, who play pool, pinball and computer games, or listen to the retro-ish jukebox and actually chat. There's a wide choice of draft beer and customers can wait at the front for opening tables at Chow (*see p151*).

Twin Peaks

401 Castro Street, at Market Street (864 9470/ www.twinpeakstavern.com). Metro F, K, L, M to Castro/bus 24, 33, 35, 37. **Open** noon-2am Mon-Wed; 8am-2am Thur-Sun. **No credit cards. Map** p318 H10.

The snug Twin Peaks was one of the first gay bars in the US to brave the public gaze with street-level windows. Nowadays, habitués are mostly older, enjoying a quiet chat, good music and even a game of cards. The antique bar serves everything but bottled beer.

Whiskey Lounge

4063 18th Street, at Hartford Street (255 2733/ www.redgrill.com). Metro F, K, L, M to Castro/bus 24, 33, 35, 37. **Open** 5pm-midnight Mon-Sat; 10am-midnight Sun. **Credit** AmEx, MC, V. **Map** p318 H11.

Set above the Red Grill (tasty Asian-influenced comfort food) in a renovated Victorian, the Whiskey Lounge is a throwback to more elegant times. Soft lighting, plush leather seats and a classy ambience.

The Mission

Not strictly a gay bar, **El Rio** (3158 Mission Street, at Cesar Chavez Street; *see p235*) draws queers to its riotous music nights. Mango, the monthly lesbian Saturday party, has a huge following, and Sunday Salsa is very queer.

Esta Noche

3079 16th Street, at Mission Street (861 5757). BART 16th Street/bus 14, 22, 26, 33, 49, 53. **Open** 1pm-2am daily. **No credit cards. Map** p318 K10.

In business for decades, this gay-Latino-drag-sports bar attracts a gregarious, diverse clientele. There's a pool table for the daytime and animated drag shows and rousing lip-synching at night. Music mixes US and Latino pop, cumbia and merengue, and the place doubles as a welcome mat for Latino queens new to town. The street outside can be menacing.

Lexington Club

3464 19th Street, at Lexington Street (863 2052). BART 16th Street/bus 14, 26, 33, 49. **Open** 5pm-2am Mon-Thur; 3pm-2am Fri, Sat. **No credit cards. Map** p318 K11.

The city's only lesbian-owned, lesbian-operated bar, 'Where every night is ladies' night'. Primarily for the younger set, the Lexington has a pool table (free on Mondays) and full bar; crimson walls and church-pew seating give the place a ready-for-anything atmosphere. There's no dancing, but theme nights include Sister Spit's rowdy performances.

SoMa

Eagle Tavern

398 12th Street, at Harrison Street (626 0880/ www.sfeagle.com). Bus 9, 12, 27, 42. **Open** noon-2am daily. **No credit cards. Map** p318 L9.

A venerable gay bar offering all-male leather action, random mud-wrestling, goings-on in the beer garden and a chance to cosy up to local gay – and straight – indie rockers and punkheads such as Pansy Division, Erase Errata and Enorchestra. Check the website for a schedule of events.

Hole in the Wall

289 8th Street, between Howard & Folsom Streets (431 4695/www.holeinthewallsaloon.com). Bus 12, 19, 27, 47. **Open** noon-2am daily. **No credit cards. Map** p318 L8.

This 'Nasty Little Biker Bar', a SoMa institution, is a magnet for the biker crowd, locals and tourists. There's a beautifully re-felted pool table, video games, pinball and rock 'n' roll oldies on repeat.

Lone Star Saloon

1354 Harrison Street, between 9th & 10th Streets (863 9999). Bus 12, 19, 27, 47. **Open** noon-2am Mon-Fri; 9am-2am Sat, Sun. **No credit cards. Map** p318 L8.

Once unabashed 'bear country', the Lone Star has of late become more of a fashion show for beauty bears. But it's still a jolly place with pinball machines, a pool table and a rear patio for smoking, and authentic bear types can still be hunted here.

Powerhouse

1347 Folsom Street, between 9th & 10th Streets (552 8689/www.powerhouse-sf.com). Bus 12, 19, 27, 47. **Open** 4pm-2am daily. **No credit cards. Map** p318 L8.

White-hot and cruisey, Powerhouse is one of the city's most popular gay bars. Entertainment includes buzz-cut nights, underwear or bare-chest parties, wrestling, leather nights and S&M lessons. Call or check online for details.

Other neighbourhoods

Aunt Charlie's Lounge

133 Turk Street, at Taylor Street, Tenderloin (441 2922/www.auntcharlieslounge.com). BART & Metro to Powell/bus 27, 30, 45 & Market Street routes/cable car Powell-Hyde or Powell-Mason. **Open** noon-midnight Mon-Thur; noon-2am Fri; 10am-2am Sat; 10am-midnight Sun. **No credit cards. Map** p314 L6.

I do... I don't... I do... I don't

A famous *New Yorker* cartoon depicts a couple reading a newspaper article about gay marriage. The punchline: 'Haven't these people suffered enough?' Yet despite any ambivalence about the institution of marriage in general, gay matrimony is now at the centre of America's moral debate about social justice and anti-discrimination legislation.

Gay marriage attracted widespread notice around the country in 2004 when Gavin Newsom swept into office in San Francisco and directed officials to issue marriage licences to same-sex couples. Over 4,000 marriages took place during the 'Winter of Love', but all were later nullified by the California Supreme Court, which ruled that the mayor had exceeded his authority.

The issue, though, refused to die. California assemblyman Mark Leno, a gay Democrat, wrote the Marriage Equality Bill, supporting equal rights for the institution of marriage. In an historic vote in September of the same year, California become the first US state legislative body to legalise same-sex marriage, with the State Assembly narrowly approving a bill that defines marriage as gender-neutral and between 'two persons'.

Less than a month after California's bold recognition of gay unions, however, Republican governor Arnold Schwarzenegger quickly lowered the boom – as Kate Kendell, executive director of the National Center for Lesbian Rights, sneered, 'Who's the girly man now?' – and vetoed the same-sex marriage bill, thus depriving gays and lesbians of more than 1,000 federal 'inalienable' rights and responsibilities. Schwarzenegger argued that the issue should be decided not by legislative action but in the courts, or through another vote by the people. The Terminator claimed the bill to be in conflict with Proposition 22, an infamous ballot initiative passed in California in 2000 that defined marriage as between a man and a woman (though its legality is now being challenged in the courts).

In late 2005, conservative groups began collecting signatures that back a variety of proposed constitutional amendments to the California Constitution: banning gay marriage, for one thing, but also stripping domestic partner rights from same-sex couples placed on the 2006 ballot. Gay-rights groups are gearing up for what could turn out to be the most important civil rights battle of the era.

Sports nights, stiff drinks, old-fashioned drag shows and lip-synching on weekends and a long-standing Tenderloin location make this a popular spot with the loyal attendees. The drag shows are a sweet entertainment, featuring all kinds of endearing personas.

Chaise Lounge

309 Cortland Avenue, at Bocana Street, Bernal Heights (401 0952). Bus 24. **Open** 5pm-2am daily. **No credit cards.**
Recently opened and beautifully renovated, this girl bar attracts a heterogeneous clientele. The nightly entertainment varies from live blues and jazz singers to DJs spinning every kind of music. Happy hour is 5-8pm, Monday to Friday.

Lion Pub

2062 Divisadero Street, at Sacramento Street, Pacific Heights (567 6565). Bus 1, 24. **Open** 4pm-2am daily. **No credit cards. Map** p313 G5.
The only gay bar in chi-chi Pacific Heights and the oldest in the city to have remained in continuous operation. Easy to miss on the first floor of a renovated Victorian, it's the place for queers with an eye for moneyed honeys and Martha Stewart-type decor.

Marlena's

488 Hayes Street, at Octavia Street, Hayes Valley (864 6672). Bus 21, 49. **Open** noon-2am Mon-Fri; 10am-2am Sat, Sun. **No credit cards. Map** p318 J8.
An eclectic crowd (including drag queens on the weekends) shows up for the superb Martinis at this treasured former speakeasy. A fold-down Murphy stage lends an eccentric, cosy ambience. There are drag shows every second and fourth Saturday.

Martuni's

4 Valencia Street, at Market Street, Hayes Valley (241 0205). Muni to Van Ness/bus 6, 7, 66, 71. **Open** 2pm-2am daily. **Credit** MC, V. **Map** p318 J8.
Martuni's is a warm, inviting piano bar with an open mic. The Martinis are enormous, the music mostly show tunes, and the clientele extremely various. The only gay bar to have thrived in the vicinity.

Wild Side West

424 Cortland Avenue, at Wool Street, Bernal Heights (647 3099). Bus 24. **Open** 1pm-2am daily. **No credit cards.**
Probably the city's longest-lived lesbian bar, Wild Side West really sees itself as just a neighbourhood bar. The walls are a shifting art installation, the patio is perfect for live music or poetry, and the clientele is happily mixed. The ace jukebox plays Joplin, Patsy Cline and – naturally – 'Walk on the Wild Side'.

Nightclubs

The dance scene changes with bewildering rapidity, so call ahead, check websites or get club-scene mags *Odyssey* and *Gloss* to make sure a particular night is happening. Most clubs are 21 and over, so bring valid photo ID. For more nightclubs, *see pp238-242*.

The Castro

The Café

2367 Market Street, at Castro Street (861 3846). Metro F, K, L, M to Castro/bus 24, 33, 35, 37. **Open** 3pm-2am daily. **Admission** varies. **No credit cards. Map** p318 H10.
There's dancing every night at the Café, the Castro's largest and most popular club. Once the area's only women's bar, it now mainly attracts boys from outlying areas, but lasses show up during the day, on weeknights and (especially) Sunday afternoons. The music blends house, hip hop and salsa. There are two bars, a dancefloor and a patio, plus pinball, pool and computer games. Expect to queue at busy times.

SoMa

Mezzanine (444 Jessie Street, at 6th Street; *see p240*) is a also big hit with the boys.

The Endup

401 6th Street, at Harrison Street (357 0827/www. theendup.com). Bus 12, 27, 47. **Open** 10pm-4.30am Thur; 10pm-6am Fri; 6am-1pm, 10pm-4am Sat; 6am-4am Sun. **Admission** $6-$12. **No credit cards. Map** p319 M7.
A fixture since 1973, the Endup boasts Fag Fridays, plus a Saturday-morning club from 6am until 1pm, and the legendary T-Dance from 6am on Sundays, with drag queens and straight ravers revelling together. Roller Girl (third Sat of the month) grants the ladies drink specials and free entry before 11pm.

The Stud

399 9th Street, at Harrison Street (252 7883/www. studsf.com). Bus 12, 19, 27, 47. **Open** hours vary. **Admission** free-$15. **No credit cards. Map** p318 L8.
Now (whisper it) nearly 40 years old, the Stud still has dancing all week (except temporarily, due to repairs, Mondays). The crowd is mainly gay and male, but the club prides itself on being 'omnisexual'. Wondrous Heklina hosts the best drag in town on Tuesdays at Trannyshack; it's top-40 pop on Thursdays; there's indie pop/electro/goth on Fridays; and Saturdays are deep house. **Photo** *p217*.

Other neighbourhoods

In the Mission, girls can explore ladies-only events, including the New Indie Rock Girrrl Night, at **26 Mix** (3024 Mission Street, at 26th Street, 826 7378, www.26mix.com).

Space 550

550 Barneveld Avenue, at Apparel Way, Bernal Heights (550 8286/www.space550.com). Bus 24. **Open** 10pm-4am daily. **Admission** varies. **No credit cards.**
Three ample dancefloors, live performances and seductive go-go dancers attract crowds of hip partygoers and sexy Latino queers to this warehouse club. Cream, every second Sat, is for lusty lesbians.

Arts & Entertainment

Entertainment & culture

The Castro

The **Castro Theatre** (429 Castro Street, at Market Street; *see p209*) comes alive for gay and camp screenings: you haven't lived until you've seen *Valley of the Dolls* or *All About Eve* here. It also stages a regular *Sound of Music* singalong and, on Christmas Eve, the SF Gay Men's Chorus singing 'Home for the Holidays'.

Comedy Showcase

The Center, 1800 Market Street, at Octavia Street (541 5610/www.qcomedy.com). Metro to Van Ness/ bus 6, 7, 47, 49, 66, 71. **Shows** 2nd Mon of mth. **Admission** $8-$15. **Map** p318 J8.

What's so funny about queers? QComedy at the Center will tell you at its monthly shows. The ebullient Nick Leonard hosts and performs regularly; top-flight comics Heather Gold, Charlie Ballard and Aundre the Wonderwoman also ppear often.

The Mission

Brava! For Women in the Arts

Theatre Center, 2781 24th Street, between York & Hampshire Streets (641 7657/www.brava.org). BART 24th Street/bus 9, 27, 33, 48. **Tickets** free-$50. **Credit** MC, V. **Map** p319 M12.

Housed in a old vaudeville theatre, Brava is one of few theatres that specialise in work by women of colour and lesbian playwrights. Check the website for shows.

In Bed with Fairy Butch

12 Galaxies, 2565 Mission Street, at 22nd Street (339 8000/www.fairybutch.com). BART 24th Street/bus 14, 26, 48, 49, 67. **Tickets** $15-$20. **Open** times vary. **No credit cards**. **Map** p318 K12.

On first and third Saturdays, charming Fairy Butch hosts an erotic cabaret for dykes, trannies and their friends. The evening ends with a drag show by FB's alter ego, Shirley U Gest. After the show, the DJ spins disco, 1980s tunes and hip hop.

Theatre Rhinoceros

2926 16th Street, between Mission Street & South Van Ness Avenue (861 5079/www.therhino. org). BART 16th Street/bus 14, 22, 33, 49, 53. **Tickets** $15-$30. **Credit** MC, V. **Map** p318 K10.

Describing itself as the world's oldest continually producing, professional queer theatre, Rhino creates theatre that is genuinely inviting rather than self-segregating. Its productions comprise comedy, reinterpreted classics (Shaw's *The Philanderer* in 2005), original drama and the occasional musical.

Other neighbourhoods

The **Magic Theatre** (Fort Mason, Marina Boulevard; *see p253*) hosts a lesbian playwright festival every January and showcases queer plays through the year. Groundbreaking gay theatre is staged at the **New Conservatory Theatre** (25 Van Ness Avenue, between Fell & Oak Streets, Hayes Valley; *see p254*).

Empire Plush Room

York Hotel, 940 Sutter Street, between Leavenworth & Hyde Streets, Nob Hill (392 4400/www.plush room.com). Bus 2, 3, 4, 27, 38, 76. **Open** hours vary. **Admission** $20-$60. **Credit** AmEx, MC, V. **Map** p314 K5.

Romantic and soul-stirring cabaret, in a chic and jazzy setting. Shows are primarily held Wednesdays to Sundays and often feature big names: recent performers have included Lorna Luft and Mary Wilson.

Sports, health & fitness

All San Francisco's workout spaces (*see p248*) are queer-friendly, but those listed below are especially gay-oriented. All offer daily (around $12-$20) and weekly ($40-$50) memberships; call for details.

Gold's Gym Castro

2301 Market Street, at Noe Street, Castro (626 4488/ www.goldsgym.com). Metro F, K, L, M to Castro/ bus 24, 33, 35, 37. **Open** 5am-midnight Mon-Thur; 5am-11pm Fri; 7am-8pm Sat, Sun. **Credit** AmEx, Disc, MC, V. **Map** p318 H10.

Cruisey, with a steamy steam room. Friendly staff and a fierce sound system make this well-equipped gym popular with both gay boys and lesbians.

Magnet

4122 18th Street, at Collingwood Street, Castro (581 1600/www.magnetsf.org). Metro F, K, L, M to Castro/bus 24, 33, 35, 37. **Open** noon-6pm Tue, Sat; 3-9pm Wed-Fri. **Map** p317 G11.

In response to rising HIV and STD rates among the city's queer men, community health groups have rallied to create Magnet. This welcoming space looks more like an upscale café than a health clinic. There are hangout areas, internet access, and free, anonymous HIV and STD testing and counselling.

Muscle System

2275 Market Street, between Sanchez & Noe Streets, Castro (863 4700/www.musclesystem.com). Metro F, K, L, M to Castro/bus 24, 33, 35, 37. **Open** 5am-midnight Mon-Fri; 7am-10pm Sat; 8am-8pm Sun. **Credit** MC, V. **Map** p318 H10.

*The Castro sweat palace: all gay, and men only.

World Gym

290 De Haro Street, at 16th Street, Potrero Hill (703 9650/www.worldgym.com). Bus 10, 19. **Open** 5am-midnight Mon-Fri; 6am-10pm Sat; 7am-10pm Sun. **Credit** AmEx, MC, V.

The gym of gyms, World is where serious work is done. There are classes in almost everything, including yoga, boxing, Thai boxing, kickboxing, ju-jitsu and spin. The clientele takes in the whole of heterogeneous San Francisco. Fabulous.

Music

From Delius to Deerhoof and most points in between.

If you're going to San Francisco, be fully prepared to hang with some of the most passionate, hip and adventurous artists and audiences in the country. Like its grande dame Victorians and rocked-out bike messengers, San Francisco endures, managing to maintain its reputation as a hard-partying port in the storm of millennial change. Artists, writers and musicians have been coming here for decades, from the first Gold Rush to the most recent dot-com money-grab. Both rock and classical scenes in the city reflect this: the city's cultural circuit is one of the most forward-thinking in the US.

The inflated expectations of the recent venture capitalist-funded years may have burst, but the Bay Area still yields one of the highest levels of rock concert attendance in the country. Only New York and LA, both industry cities, attract more bands than SF, while few towns draw as many famous classical musicians and international touring performers.

INFORMATION & TICKETS

The best overall sources of information are the *San Francisco Bay Guardian* (www.sfbg.com) and *SF Weekly* (www.sfweekly.com), both of which carry extensive listings. In addition, check www.sfgate.com, the *San Francisco Chronicle*'s website, and www.sfstation.com.

Classical & opera

The exploratory impulse that courses through much of the city's cultural landscape extends to its classical scene. San Francisco's major orchestra and opera company are both renowned for their challenging projects, and a number of the city's smaller ensembles have built their reputations on contemporary music. However, there's plenty of familiar repertoire on show at venues large and small. Area ensembles also make a concerted effort to reach new audiences, which means virtuosic performances are presented at fair prices in venues ranging from the modern (Louise M Davies Symphony Hall) to the historic (St Patrick's Church).

Ticketing can be complicated. Several of the larger ensembles sell tickets via subscription packages, and the most popular shows do sell out. However, individual tickets are available for most concerts; even on nights listed as sell-outs, there are usually a few seats available on

the evening. A handful of the smaller venues don't sell tickets ahead of time, but try to book in advance (by phone or online) if possible.

Major companies & venues

San Francisco Opera

War Memorial Opera House, 301 Van Ness Avenue, at Grove Street, Civic Center (864 3330/ www.sfopera.com). BART & Metro to Civic Center/ bus 21, 47, 49 & Market Street routes. **Box office** 10am-6pm Mon-Sat. **Tickets** $25-$235. **Credit** AmEx, MC, V. **Map** p318 K7.

Inaugurated in 1923, the SF Opera achieved great renown at the start of the 21st century for its bold programming under Pamela Rosenberg, its general director. After joining in 2001, Rosenberg brought the company into rude artistic health (if not necessarily great financial shape), overseeing triumphs such as the 2005 première of John Adams' *Doctor Atomic*. However, Rosenberg declined to renew her contract, and will hand over to David Gockley in 2006; it should be interesting to see where he leads the company. The fall season runs early September to November, the summer season from May to July.

The SF Opera is based in the War Memorial Opera House, a grand Beaux Arts building designed by City Hall architect Arthur Brown Jr and built in 1932

The best Live music

Café du Nord
The feel of a Prohibition-era speakeasy and a taste for daring sounds. *See p234.*

Louise M Davies Symphony Hall
The San Francisco Symphony perform at this striking glass edifice. *See p228.*

Rickshaw Stop
Hip local bands, oddball events and hot, hard-edged DJ nights. *See p236.*

Yerba Buena Center for the Arts Theater
Some of the most exciting contemporary music and dance in the US. *See p228.*

Yoshi's at Jack London Square
The Bay Area's best jazz can be found over the bridge in Oakland. *See p231.*

Arts & Entertainment

as a memorial to the soldiers who fought in World War I. The 3,176-seat auditorium is modelled on European opera houses, with a vaulted ceiling, a huge art deco metal chandelier and a marble foyer. An $84.5m revamp in 1997 not only restored the elegant building (restorers found clouds painted on the ceiling when they scraped away the grime), but installed up-to-date electronics and stage gear. The San Francisco Ballet (*see p256*) also performs here.

San Francisco Performances

Various venues (398 6449/www.performances.org). **Box office** 9.30am-5pm Mon-Fri. **Tickets** $20-$50. **Credit** MC, V.

Directed with imagination and enthusiasm by Ruth Felt, this independent promoter puts on a pro-gramme of over 200 concerts each year in a wide variety of styles: the 2005-06 season included concerts by baritone Thomas Hampson and the Philip Glass Ensemble. Most concerts are held at the Herbst Theatre (*see p253*) or the Yerba Buena Center for the Arts Theater (*see below*), but there are also events at the likes of St John's Presbyterian Church in Berkeley (*see below*) and the Hotel Rex (*see p45*).

San Francisco Symphony

Louise M Davies Symphony Hall, 201 Van Ness Avenue, at Hayes Street, Civic Center (864 6000/www.sfsymphony.org). BART & Metro to Civic Center/bus 21, 47, 49 & Market Street routes. **Tickets** $20-$107. **Credit** MC, V. **Map** p318 K7.

Formed to boost public morale shortly after the 1906 earthquake and fire, the San Francisco Symphony performed its first concert in 1911. Today, under the dynamic direction of Michael Tilson Thomas, the orchestra is internationally recognised for its innovative work, winning several Grammy awards in the process. Its current series of Mahler concerts has won the ensemble particular acclaim.

The Symphony is based at the Louise M Davies Symphony Hall, commonly known simply as the Davies. Opened in 1980 and renovated in 1992, the striking, multi-tiered, curved-glass edifice boasts flawless acoustics and clear sight-lines. There isn't a bad seat in the house, even the 40 in the centre terrace section behind the orchestra that sell for just $20 and go on sale two hours before most performances (call for details). In addition to SF Symphony concerts, look out for events in the Great Performers series, which imports world-renowned soloists, conductors and ensembles for one-night stands. **Photo** *p229*.

Yerba Buena Center for the Arts Theater

701 Mission Street, at 3rd Street, SoMa (978 2787/www.ybca.org). BART & Metro to Montgomery/bus 9, 12, 15, 30, 45, 76. **Box office** noon-5pm Tue-Sun. **Tickets** $20-$100. **Credit** AmEx, MC, V. **Map** p319 N6.

This 757-seat auditorium plays host to some of the most exciting contemporary music and dance companies in the country, among them the Kronos Quartet and the San Francisco Contemporary Music

Players (for both, *see below*). Designed by modernist architect James Stewart Polshek, the exterior of the cube-shaped theatre is covered in aluminium panels that catch the ever-changing local light.

Church venues

A number of churches host recitals and chamber concerts, often featuring young local musicians and frequently for free. Among them are the **Old First Presbyterian Church** (1751 Sacramento Street, between Polk Street & Van Ness Avenue, 776 5552, www.oldfirst.org) on the edge of Pacific Heights; the **First Unitarian Universalist Church** (1187 Franklin Street, at Geary Street, 776 4580, www.uusf.org) near the Civic Center, famous for its Bartok birthday concert on the third Sunday in March; and Nob Hill's **Grace Cathedral** (*see p84*).

St Patrick's Church (*see p81*) hosts concerts at 12.30pm every Wednesday and every other Tuesday (www.noontimeconcerts.org).

The intimate **St John's Presbyterian Church** in Berkeley (2727 College Avenue, between 1st & Garber Streets) hosts numerous events throughout the year, with the popular **Chamber Music Sundaes** series (584 5946, www.chambermusicsundaes.org) among the highlights. Held over seven or eight Sunday afternoons from November to June, it features members of the SF Symphony playing varied programmes; tickets are around $20 each.

Other ensembles & venues

Aside from the players listed above, a number of groups call the city home. Among them are the **Philharmonia Baroque Orchestra** (252 1288, www.philharmonia.org), which performs baroque and classical repertoire on original instruments. The orchestra's season consists of six programmes a year (September to April), which they 'tour' to the Herbst Theatre (*see p253*) and Berkeley's First Congregational Church (*see p229*), plus locations in Palo Alto and Contra Costa. The 17-member **New Century Chamber Orchestra** (357 1111, www.ncco.org) has a similar set-up, playing roughly six times a year at the Florence Gould Theater in the California Palace of the Legion of Honor as well as at St John's Presbyterian Church in Berkeley (*see above*) and beyond.

Two local ensembles are in demand across the world. The **Kronos Quartet** (731 3533, www.kronosquartet.org) focuses on new works, many of them composed for the group. The 34-year-old **San Francisco Contemporary Music Players** (978 2787, www.sfcmp.org) is also in the vanguard of modern music, commissioning new works from both young

Arts & Entertainment

Michael Tilson Thomas conducts the San Francisco Symphony. *See p228.*

and established composers. The music performed by the all-male, Grammy-winning a cappella group **Chanticleer** (252 8589, www.chanticleer.org) is less challenging, but performed with no less skill. All three ensembles tour for much of the year but play in the Bay Area regularly: Kronos and the SFCMP at the Yerba Buena Center, and Chanticleer, whose Christmas programme is particularly terrific, at a wide variety of local venues.

Two groups give the SF Opera some small measure of competition. Donald Pippin's **Pocket Opera** (972 8930, www.pocketopera.org) presents operas in English; performances are generally held at the Florence Gould Theater in the California Palace of the Legion of Honor (*see p115*). The **Lamplighters Musical Theatre** (227 4797, www.lamplighters.org) has been presenting lighter works, including more Gilbert and Sullivan than strictly necessary, for half a century. The company performs at the Yerba Buena Center and the Herbst Theatre. Finally, look out for the **San Francisco Conservatory of Music** (564 8086, www.sfcm.edu), which will be showcasing its young talent at a new Civic Center facility from late 2006.

Berkeley & Oakland

Just over the Bay Bridge, the **Berkeley Symphony Orchestra** (1-510 841 2800, www.berkeleysymphony.org) plays half a dozen concerts a year at Zellerbach Hall on the UC Berkeley campus; Kent Nagano is their long-time director. Zellerbach Hall also offers concerts by everyone from John Adams to Cecilia Bartoli as part of **Cal Performances** (1-510 642 9988, www.calperfs.berkeley.edu).

Nearby, **Berkeley Opera** (1-510 841 1903, www.berkeleyopera.org) stages three productions a year at the Julia Morgan Theater (2640 College Avenue). Other East Bay venues include the **First Congregational Church** in Berkeley (2345 Channing Way, 1-510 848 3696, www.fccb.org); Oakland's **Mills College** (5000 MacArthur Boulevard, 1-510 430 2296, www.mills.edu), where the Center for Contemporary Music has a global reputation; and the **Paramount Theatre** (2025 Broadway, Oakland), home to the **Oakland East Bay Symphony** (1-510 444 0801, www.oebs.org) and the **Oakland Symphony Chorus** (1-510 207 4093, www.oakland-sym-chorus.org).

Jazz & blues

West Coast jazz found a foothold here with the advent of beat culture. Although the scene isn't as strong as it might be, the Bay Area does continue to turn out musicians: the Berkeley High Jazz Ensemble, a high-school programme, has spawned the likes of Joshua Redman and David Murray. Things look set to improve further in 2007, when **Yoshi's** (*see p231*) hopes to establish a presence on Fillmore Street.

In addition, the **Fillmore Auditorium** (*see p232*), the **Hemlock Tavern** (*see p235*), the **Great American Music Hall** (*see p232*) and the **Intersection for the Arts** (*see p253*) stage sporadic jazz shows. *See also p230* **Festivals**.

TICKETS

Booking ahead isn't always necessary at SF's jazz and blues venues. However, on weekends and for big names, an advance reservation is always a good idea; **Yoshi's** is frequently busy even during the week.

Biscuits & Blues

*401 Mason Street, at Geary Street, Union Square
(292 2583/www.biscuitsandblues.com). Bus 2, 3, 4,
27, 38, 76/cable car Powell-Hyde or Powell-Mason.*
Open 7pm-1am daily. **Shows** 8.30pm or 9pm daily;
also 10.30pm some nights. **Admission** $7.50-$20.
Credit AmEx, Disc, MC, V. **Map** p318 L5.
This subterranean nightclub/restaurant is a pretty
basic affair. Partly due to its location, it attracts a
portion of middle-aged tourists and suburbanites,
and can get fairly stuffy when crowded. However,
it's still the best place in town to catch mainstream
blues, played for genuinely excited crowds. The
American food is served with a Southern accent.

Boom Boom Room

*1601 Fillmore Street, at Geary Boulevard, Fillmore
(673 8000/www.boomboomblues.com). Bus 2, 3, 4, 22,
38.* **Open** 8pm-2am Tue-Sun. **Shows** 9pm Tue-Sun.
Admission $5-$20. **Credit** MC, V. **Map** p314 H6.
Formerly Jack's Bar, an SF fixture for more than 50
years, the Boom Boom Room has been remade as a
classy version of a blues joint: John Lee Hooker gave
the club his name and, until his death in 2001, held
court up front. These days, the venue attracts solid
blues, roots, funk, R&B and groove-oriented acts,
with an occasional surprise rock-star dropping in.

Elbo Room

*647 Valencia Street, between 17th & 18th Streets,
Mission (552 7788/www.elbo.com). BART 16th
Street/bus 14, 26, 33, 49.* **Open** 5pm-2am daily.
Shows 9pm or 10pm daily. **Admission** $5-$10.
No credit cards. Map p318 K10.
Although the Elbo has been commandeered by yuppies, it continues to be a place to hear good music on
a lively stretch of Valencia Street. You're likely to
hear jazz (usually with a beat-driven edge), pure
funk, soul or Latin jazz in the open-raftered space
upstairs, but hip hop, hard rock, metal and random
whacked-out experimentalism also appear. On
Sundays, it's the legendary Dub Mission DJ night.

Festivals Jazz

The free **Fillmore Street Jazz Festival**
(1-800 731 0003, www.fillmorejazzfestival.
com) in early July consists of two days
of local acts; the end of the month sees
the week-long **North Beach Jazz Festival**
(www.nbjazzfest.com), which stages local
musicians in a variety of locations. From
June to October, **SF Jazz Summerfest**
(www.sfjazz.org) runs around 25 free early-
evening and lunchtime shows in outdoor
locations inside and outside the city. Then,
from mid October to early November, come
the big guns at the **San Francisco Jazz
Festival** (788 7353, www.sfjazz.org), an
terrific series of shows throughout town.

Peter Lang at **Biscuits & Blues**.

Jazz at Pearl's

*256 Columbus Avenue, between Broadway & Pacific
Avenue, North Beach (291 8255/www.jazzatpearls.
com). Bus 12, 15, 30, 41, 45.* **Open** from 7.30pm
Mon-Thur, Sun; from 8pm Fri, Sat. **Shows** 8.30pm,
10.30pm Mon-Thur, Sun; 9pm, 11pm Fri, Sat.
Admission $10-$25. **Credit** VIP ticket holders
only. **Map** p315 M3.
This intimate venue (just 25 tables) is the last jazz
house left standing in North Beach, once the home
for a hoppin' mid-century scene. However, it's a
great little place. Singer Kim Nalley and husband
Steve Sheraton bought the club from former owner
Pearl Wong in 2003 and now book acts such as Pete
Escovedo, Voz do Brasil and Mark Murphy.

Rasselas Jazz

*1534 Fillmore Street, at Geary Boulevard,
Fillmore (346 8696/www.rasselasjazzclub.com).
Bus 2, 3, 4, 22, 38.* **Open** 6pm-midnight Mon-
Thur, Sun; 6pm-2am Fri, Sat. **Shows** 8pm Mon-
Thur; 6pm, 9.30pm Fri; 9.30pm Sat; 6pm Sun.
Admission $7 Fri, Sat. **Credit** AmEx, MC, V.
Map p314 H6.

Like the Fillmore Historic Jazz District it's designed to anchor, Rasselas suffers from unadventurous programming, yet still manages to draw lively crowds on weekends. The decor – high ceilings, bachelor-pad furniture and a crackling fireplace behind the band – is suggestive of a 1960s playboy den, and combos usually get the weekend crowds of African-American revellers and white yuppies on their feet.

Saloon
1232 Grant Avenue, at Columbus Avenue, North Beach (989 7666). Bus 12, 15, 30, 41, 45. **Open** noon-2am daily. **Shows** 9.30pm daily. **Admission** $5. **No credit cards. Map** p315 M3.
A beer hall that scandalised the neighbourhood when it was established in 1861 (it's now the oldest continuously operating bar in town), the Saloon has survived earthquakes and shifting musical tastes, and remains a no-nonsense, rough-edged joint with a busy, bluesy calendar. Psychedelic-era rockers gracing the stage might include former members of Jefferson Airplane and Country Joe & the Fish.

Yoshi's at Jack London Square
510 Embarcadero West, at Jack London Square, Oakland (1-510 238 9200/www.yoshis.com). Bus 72. **Open** *2pm, 8pm shows* from 2hrs before showtime. *10pm shows* 30mins before showtime. **Shows** 8pm, 10pm Mon-Sat; 2pm, 8pm Sun. **Admission** $15-$25. **Credit** AmEx, Disc, MC, V.
This handsome, refined enterprise is the best jazz joint in the Bay Area, possibly along the entire West Coast. Its separate dining room does good business on the strength of its Japanese food, but the main attraction is the music, a cultured line-up of big names (working the weekend slots) and newcomers (earlier in the week). Book in advance.

Rock, pop & hip hop

Although San Francisco started to recover relatively quickly after the tech-world bust, the music scene faced a longer hangover. Clubs and rehearsal spaces bit the dust, and musicians headed to Oakland and beyond. Although the moneyed masses that once snapped up tickets to emerging artists' shows as though they were stock options have fled, the scene has held on without them. New halls such as the **Independent** sprang up; dance clubs such as the **Mezzanine** (*see p240*) built proper stages; and new spots such as the **Rickshaw Stop** and **12 Galaxies** have begun to draw flash trendoids, cool schoolers and even a few serious listeners to once-quiet neighbourhoods.

The scene's continued success can be chalked up to a cross-genre cadre of youthful musicians and promoters who continue to form bands and put on stage shows all over: at clubs and other music events, sure, but also at galleries and warehouses. SF boasts one of the most exciting underground scenes in the US, the likes of the

Lovemakers breaking out on to major labels or, as with hip hopper E-40 and electronica terrorist Kid 606, making it on their own imprints. As Slim Moon, the owner of influential Seattle label Kill Rock Stars, recently testified, 'The Bay Area has the most fruitful scene going, and it produces many of the most interesting, fun and challenging bands in America.' The rosters on that label, and sister imprint 5 Rue Christine, bear witness to his enthusiasm: Deerhoof, Nedelle, Xiu Xiu, Gold Chains and Gravy Train!!!! all hail from the Bay Area.

The variety on that list of alternative acts is indicative of the eclecticism on offer throughout the city. Public perception of the SF sound is still stuck in the 1960s, when the likes of Jefferson Airplane drew young pilgrims; more recently, the Dead Kennedys, Metallica and the Black Rebel Motorcycle Club have added to the city's reputation for noisy guitar rock. However, the Bay Area also has a potent hip hop scene, while Oakland is a hotbed of electronic experimentation informed by indie-rock aesthetics, thanks to acts such as humorous Matmos side project Soft Pink Truth.

For events, *see below* and *p232* **Festivals**.

TICKETS
For larger concerts – pretty much anything at the 'Major venues' below – it's worth buying tickets in advance. Where possible, buy from the venue's own box office to avoid the booking fees levied by **Ticketmaster** (421 8497, www.ticketmaster.com). Advance purchase isn't always necessary for the venues listed under 'Bars & clubs' on *pp234-237*, but it's never a bad idea if you want to be on the safe side. Always call ahead or look at venue websites before making a special trip.

Festivals Roots

The **San Francisco Blues Festival** (979 5588, www.sfblues.com, $25/day), held over a weekend in late September at the Great Meadow by Fort Mason, is the oldest event of its type in the US. The line-ups at **Hardly Strictly Bluegrass** (www.strictly bluegrass.com, free entry), staged on the first weekend in October at Speedway Meadow in Golden Gate Park, are stunning: among the 50-plus acts who played in 2005 were Doc Watson, Dolly Parton, Ralph Stanley and Gillian Welch. The **San Francisco Bluegrass & Old-Time Festival**, held around town for a week in February (www.sfbluegrass.org), is also worth a look.

Major venues

The venues detailed below all host concerts on a regular basis. In addition, though, a handful of larger arenas stage the occasional show, among them **SBC Park** (*see p244*), the **Nob Hill Masonic Center** and the cavernous **Bill Graham Civic Auditorium** (99 Grove Street, at Polk Street, 974 4060, www.billgraham civic.com) in San Francisco; the **Oakland Arena** (*see p244*); and the **Greek Theatre** in Berkeley (1-510 642 9988,www.calperfs. berkeley.edu). A little further out, the **Shoreline Amphitheatre** in Mountain View (1-650 967 3000, www.shorelineamp.com), the **Chronicle Pavilion** in Concord (1-925 363 5701, www.chroniclepavilion.com) and the **HP Pavilion** in San José (1-408 287 9200, www.hppsj.com) also stage big-name shows from time to time, especially during the summer months. Check venue websites or contact Ticketmaster (*see p231*) for tickets.

Bimbo's 365 Club

1025 Columbus Avenue, at Chestnut Street, North Beach (474 0365/www.bimbos365club.com). Bus 30/cable car Powell-Mason. **Box office** 10am-4pm Mon-Fri. **Tickets** $15-$50. **Credit** (advance bookings only) MC, V. **Map** p314 L2.
Bimbo's began life as a Market Street speakeasy in 1931, moving to North Beach two decades later. The venue is still owned by the descendants of Agostino

Festivals Rock

On Sundays from June to August, the **Stern Grove Festival** (www.sterngrove.org) stages everything from rock to opera (but, happily, no rock opera) in an idyllic amphitheatre set in a grove of eucalyptus trees; admission is free. Probably the biggest rock festival of the year in SF is **Noise Pop** (www.noisepop.com), a week-long, city-wide series of indie shows in February. Tickets are available for individual gigs, but there's also a festival pass available (around $130). June's similarly spreadeagled **Mission Creek Music & Arts Festival** (www.mcmf.org) also concentrates on alternative rock, albeit with a more experimental edge and a more local focus. And, speaking of experimental, lovers of the avant-garde ought to investigate August's **San Francisco Electronic Music Festival** (www.sfemf.org), which invites composers such as George Lewis and Zeena Parkins to consort with luminaries from the SF electronica scene.

'Bimbo' Giuntoli, one of its original owners, and has been nicely preserved, with a mermaid theme running throughout. Rita Hayworth once worked the boards as a dancer, but these days you're more likely to see Prefuse 73 spinning vinyl, or touring acts such as the Go! Team working up the crowd.

Fillmore Auditorium

1805 Geary Boulevard, at Fillmore Street, Fillmore (24hr hotline 346 6000/www.thefillmore.com). Bus 2, 3, 4, 22, 38. **Box office** 10am-4pm Sun; also 7.30-10pm show nights. **Tickets** $20-$50. **Credit** AmEx, MC, V. **Map** p314 H6.
The 1,200-capacity Fillmore was built in 1912, but is better known as the venue in which Bill Graham launched his rock-promotion empire. The rosters who play the gorgeous room tend to be on the verge of making it massive. *See p233* **Tales of the city**.

Grand

1300 Van Ness Avenue, at Sutter Street, Tenderloin (673 5716). Bus 2, 3, 4, 19, 38, 47, 49, 76. **Box office** Ticketmaster only. **Tickets** $20-$50. **Credit** AmEx, MC, V. **Map** p314 K5.
Formerly a Masonic temple, a dance studio, a Polish arts foundation and a movie theatre, this gorgeous Beaux Arts-style ballroom, with a horseshoe-shaped balcony, hardwood floors and fin-de-siècle teardrop chandeliers, now stages everything from opera to rock, jazz gigs to dance events. The landmark 1909 building incorporates the quasi-legendary Avalon Ballroom, which once hosted shows by Janis Joplin and Country Joe & the Fish.

Great American Music Hall

859 O'Farrell Street, between Polk & Larkin Streets, Tenderloin (885 0750/www.musichallsf. com). Bus 2, 3, 4, 19, 38, 47. **Box office** 10.30am-6pm Mon-Fri. **Tickets** $10-$25. **Credit** MC, V. **Map** p314 K6.
Originally a bordello, then a highfalutin nightclub operated by notorious fan dancer Sally Rand, the grande dame of the city's smaller venues is as beautiful today as at any point in its 100-year history. The lavish room, done out with huge mirrors, rococo woodwork and gold-leaf trim, is these days run by the owners of Slim's (*see p233*), who present a cutting-edge roster of well regarded local and touring musicians (many of the indie-rock ilk). Try to snag one of the coveted seats on the upper balcony.

Independent

628 Divisadero Street, at Hayes Street, Western Addition (771 1421/www.theindependentsf.com). Bus 21, 24. **Box office** 11am-6pm Mon-Fri. **Tickets** $10-$25. **Credit** MC, V. **Map** p317 G8.
New owners have given this venerable black box the makeover it deserved, with work that included the installation of a stellar sound and light system. In accordance with the varied sounds in the club's storied past, the calendar is filled with a mix of touring rock, pop, jazz, Americana, jam and otherwise undefinable offerings such as Sunn0))), Maktub, the Boredoms and Israel Vibration.

SF Weekly Warfield

982 Market Street, at Mason Street, Tenderloin (775 7722/www.bgp.com). BART & Metro to Powell/ bus 27, 31 & Market Street routes. **Box office** 10am-4pm Sun; also 7.30-10pm show nights. **Tickets** $20-$50. **Credit** AmEx, MC, V. **Map** p315 M6.

Another grand old theatre, this one dating back to 1922, that's been converted into a rock and pop venue in later life. A step up from the Fillmore in terms of capacity, the ornate, 2,100-seat room hosts major national and international acts, many making their last stop on the circuit before vaulting to arena-sized venues. It's very well designed: even the back balcony seats have good views of the stage.

Slim's

333 11th Street, between Folsom & Harrison Streets, SoMa (255 0333/www.slims-sf.com). Bus 9, 12, 27, 47. **Tickets** $8-$35. **Credit** MC, V. **Map** p318 L9.

It might be one of San Francisco's more important music venues, but the 550-capacity Slim's isn't one of its most comfortable: most patrons have to stand, sight lines are compromised by the floor-to-ceiling

Tales of the city The Fillmore

It was constructed as the Majestic Ballroom in 1911. However, it wasn't until more than half a century later, with the serendipitous convergence of the San Francisco counter-culture and a canny German-born orphan, that the **Fillmore Auditorium** (*see p232*), as it was then known, made its global reputation. While the name Wolfgang Grajonca may not ring any bells, Bill Graham – the name he assumed when he moved to the US as a teenager in the 1940s – is synonymous not only with the local rock revolution of the 1960s, but with the whole business of concert promotion.

Graham moved to San Francisco in the early 1960s and began promoting theatre events. However, a series of coincidences led him towards the rock world at a time when the local scene was beginning to bubble. He soon took over the then-ailing Fillmore and dedicated himself to the venue, combining new technology (light shows, psychedelic projections) with his adventurously compiled bills. The venue's reputation grew apace.

Although he had a grand vision for the Fillmore, the orphan Graham always wanted it to feel like home. He looked after everything, leaving bowls of apples in the hallway and once feeding breakfast to 1,200 people. Musically, he loved odd juxtapositions, pairing his headliners with unusual supports: Cream once played on a bill with jazzer Gary Burton, and Miles Davis opened for the Grateful Dead. He also brought classic blues and jazz acts to the very navel of the psychedelic era, among them Muddy Waters, Chuck Berry (whose opening act was the then-obscure Steve Miller Blues Band) and even Count Basie.

The local acts he promoted are a who's who of the 1960s counterculture. Jefferson Airplane, Janis Joplin and the Grateful Dead (whose first gig at the Fillmore actually occurred before Graham took over the venue)

flourished under his wing, but international groups such as Cream also credited him as a key influence. Around this time, a broke young Mexican urchin would sneak into shows without paying. Graham repeatedly booted him out until he heard the kid play guitar, whereupon he hired Carlos Santana for his first ever show in 1968.

Graham's empire soon expanded. In March 1968, he opened the Fillmore East in New York; several months later, he shifted the Fillmore to a larger venue at Market and Van Ness Streets and renamed it the Fillmore West (it's now a Nissan car dealership). But the encroachment of record companies into promotion soon made Graham shutter his clubs and concentrate on promoting concert tours and other projects.

Graham always felt deeply affectionate towards the old Fillmore, and began presenting shows there again in 1988. His second tilt didn't last long: the 1989 earthquake damaged the venue, and in 1991, before it could be restored, Graham died in a helicopter crash. However, his now-massive Bill Graham Presents company was inspired to restore the Fillmore, refashioning the spectacular ballroom with state-of-the-art sound and lighting, and reopening it as a full-time venue in 1994.

These days, the Fillmore is operated by global giant Clear Channel, a company not noted for its sympathies towards either artistic history or countercultural diversity. It does, however, keep the room in beautiful shape. A bowl of free apples still stands in the hallway, while the handsome upstairs lounge features a gallery of posters from Fillmore gigs dating back decades. The posters, commissioned by Graham from some of the finest graphic designers of the era and given out free after each show, are now collectors' items. Much like the venue itself.

Arts & Entertainment

Café du Nord, here hosting fiery local
singer-songwriter Terese Taylor.

pillars and, on busy nights, it gets pretty steamy.
The schedule is mostly made up of rock bands, who
play alongside a smattering of hip hop acts, reggae
groups and rootsy singer/songwriters.

Bars & clubs

Several other bars and nightclubs around the
city host worthwhile music nights. Among
them are the **Eagle**, a gay bar that hosts punk
and hardcore shows, and **Kimo's**, a landmark
gay bar that now stages shows of varying
quality by local and touring rock acts in its
upstairs room. For gay nightlife, *see pp217-226*.

   Note that for all venues listed here, opening
hours and showtimes can vary: 'usually 9pm'
means the occasional show may begin at
8.30pm or even 8pm. Always call or check
online (most venues keep their websites
bang up to date) before setting out.

Ashkenaz Music & Dance
Community Center

*1317 San Pablo Street, at Gilman Street, Berkeley.
(1-510 525 5054/www.ashkenaz.com). BART
Downtown Berkeley, then bus 9.* **Open/shows**
times vary. **Admission** $4-$20. **No credit cards**.
Jam band groupies and folk fans will find plenty to
love at this East Bay institution, which has been
putting the groove in groovy since 1973. It's just
steps away from the 924 Gilman Street Project (*see*

p236), but music store aisles away in terms of genre.
Known for its folk dance nights, Grateful Dead trib-
utes and zydeco bands, the centre also serves up
Western swing, African, Balkan and klezmer sounds.

Bottom of the Hill

*1233 17th Street, at Missouri Street, Potrero Hill
(621 4455/www.bottomofthehill.com). Bus 22, 53.*
Open 8.30pm-2am Mon, Tue, Sat, Sun; 4pm-2am
Wed-Fri. **Shows** usually 9pm daily. **Admission**
$5-$20. **Credit** MC, V. **Map** p319 N10.
This little club, wedged among warehouses at the
bottom of Potrero Hill, has long been a favourite
with the indie-rock crowd. It features local and
touring acts most nights, as well as occasional name
acts (Mars Volta, the Beastie Boys) hankering to
play an intimate show. Underground bands that
play here one year may become cult sensations or
even major stars the next. The decor is classic dive,
with quirky touches.

Café du Nord/
Swedish American Hall

*2170 Market Street, between Church & Sanchez
Streets, Castro (861 5016/www.cafedunord.com).
Metro F, J, K, L, M to Church/bus 22, 37.*
Open 1hr before show-2am. **Shows** times vary,
daily. **Admission** $7-$20. **Credit** AmEx, MC, V.
Map p318 H9.
Several SF nightspots carry the feel of a Prohibition-
era speakeasy, but none captures the spirit quite as
well as the Café du Nord. Mind you, it does have a

decent Margaritas and a friendly crowd of straights and queers. Other nights you might encounter experimental rock, DJs or, in summer, outdoor films.

Freight & Salvage Coffee House
1111 Addison Street, at San Pablo Avenue, Berkeley. (1-510 548 1761/www.thefreight.org). BART Downtown Berkeley. **Box office** noon-7pm daily. **Open** from 7.30pm, days vary. **Shows** usually 8pm, days vary. **Admission** $16-$25. **No credit cards**.
The venerable, booze-free Freight is a much-loved outpost of traditional music in all its incarnations, from folk to gospel. The monthly calendar might include sets from Ralph Stanley, Ricky Skaggs, Odetta, Dar Williams and Dan Bern, plus Hawaiian slack-key players, Iraqi oud pluckers, Hungarian violinists or austere Appalachian mandolinists.

Hemlock Tavern
1131 Polk Street, at Post Street, Tenderloin (923 0923/www.hemlocktavern.com). Bus 2, 3, 4, 19, 38, 47. **Open** 4pm-2am daily. **Shows** 9.30pm daily. **Admission** $5-$10. **No credit cards**. **Map** p314 K6.
Out front, the Hemlock looks like a capacious, matey watering hole, a lively mix of young tastemakers, art snobs and yuppies playing pool, yapping at the central bar or puffing in the open-air smoking 'room'. Out back, however, a newly expanded but still intimate room plays host to some of the more edgy and intelligent musical programming in the city. The roster is built around hipster-friendly artists such as Wolf Eyes, Deerhoof and… next year, who knows?

Hotel Utah
500 4th Street, at Bryant Street, SoMa (546 6300/ www.thehotelutahsaloon.com). Bus 15, 30, 45, 47, 76. **Open** 11.30am-2am Mon-Sat; 6pm-2am Sun. **Shows** usually 9pm daily. **Admission** free-$10. **Credit** MC, V. **Map** p319 N7.
The down-and-dirty days of the Barbary Coast are ingrained in the timbers of this 1908 watering hole, which has previously welcomed the likes of Marilyn Monroe, Bing Crosby and a variety of gangsters and beatniks. Now gaining a fresh lease of life, the Utah is both a characterful bar and a fair music room, hosting indie rock, singer-songwriters and the occasional curiosity. **Photo** *p237*.

Make-Out Room
3225 22nd Street, between Mission & Valencia Streets, Mission (647 2888/www.makeoutroom. com). BART 24th Street/bus 14, 26, 48, 49, 67. **Open** 6pm-2am daily. **Shows** usually 9pm daily. **Admission** $5-$10. **No credit cards**. **Map** p318 K12.
One of the best places in town to see smallish bands, the Make-Out Room attracts a laid-back, alternative and youthful crowd on its regular live music nights. The decor lives up to the name: there's a bearskin rug on one wall and a stag's head on another, with a rainbow of bras strung from the antlers. The atmosphere, in common with many Mission bars, is that of a cheery dive.

head start: it actually was one. The subterranean front room, which hosts cultured alternative acts, has red velvet walls and a 40ft mahogany bar that bustles with scenesters. Owner Guy Carson also books the likes of Cat Power and Joanna Newsom to play the quaint, larger Swedish American Hall upstairs.

Cherry Bar
917 Folsom Street, at 5th Street, SoMa (974 1585/ www.thecherrybar.com). Bus 9, 12, 27, 30, 45, 76. **Open** 8pm-2am Tue-Sun. **Shows** times vary. **Admission** $5-$10. **Credit** *Bar only* MC, V. **Map** p319 M7.
Once the venerable Covered Wagon Saloon, the Cherry still proudly maintains its dive-joint roots. However, it's a little smarter these days, and runs a wider spectrum of entertainments, everything from Britrock nights to Miss Kitty's Scratching Post, a lively party servicing queer women and trannies.

El Rio
3158 Mission Street, at Cesar Chavez Street, Mission (282 3325/www.elriosf.com). Bus 12, 26, 27, 49, 67. **Open** *Mar-Nov* 5pm-2am Mon-Thur; 3pm-2am Fri-Sun. *Dec-Feb* 5pm-2am Mon-Thur, Sat, Sun; 3pm-2am Fri. **Shows** times vary. **Admission** free-$10. **No credit cards**.
Head to the El Rio on a Sunday afternoon from March to November and make your way to the garden, where you'll find SF's most diverse and lively salsa party: a local tradition for 25 years and counting. There's an outdoor barbecue, dancing lessons,

924 Gilman Street Project

924 Gilman Street, between 7th & 8th Streets, Berkeley (1-510 525 9926). BART Downtown Berkeley, then bus 9. **Open/shows** from 8pm Fri, Sat, sometimes Sun. **Admission** $5-$7. **No credit cards**.

This all-ages, alcohol-free institution, run by a collective, is internationally renowned among punks. Green Day started out playing here, but these days, since the club has a policy against booking major-label bands, you're more likely to catch the likes of Dr Know, MDC and This Bike Is a Pipe Bomb, along with committed locals such as Octis and Vholtz. Punk rock fanzine *Maximumrocknroll* runs the occasional record swap.

Pound SF

Pier 96, 100 Cargo Way, near 3rd Street, Hunter's Point (826 5009/www.poundsf.com). Bus 15. **Open** times vary. **Shows** times vary. **Admission** $5-$30. **No credit cards**.

Hidden in the furthest reaches of one of the city's sketchiest neighbourhoods (take a cab), on a pier with a view of giant cranes and the bay, Pound is your basic black box, but the management has invested in decent lights and sound. It books mainly hard rock, punk and metal bands, but with the occasional hip hop and indie act.

Red Devil Lounge

1695 Polk Street, at Clay Street, Polk Gulch (921 1695/www.reddevillounge.com). Bus 1, 19, 27, 47, 49, 76. **Open** usually 8pm-2am daily. **Shows** usually 9pm daily. **Admission** $5-$10. **No credit cards**. Map p314 K4.

This corner venue, done out with Gothic touches, has recently ramped up its music offerings, which sit alongside club nights in a fairly busy calendar. The line-ups aren't often cutting edge, but the venue does stage crowd-pulling acts such as the English Beat, Fastball and Digital Underground.

Rickshaw Stop

155 Fell Street, at Franklin Street, Hayes Valley (861 2011/www.rickshawstop.com). BART & Metro to Van Ness/bus 21, 47, 49 & Market Street routes. **Open** 7pm-2am Wed-Sat. **Shows** times vary. **Admission** $5-$10. **No credit cards**. Map p318 K8.

Doing its best to fill a sparse strip near Civic Center, the Rickshaw taps a cool collegiate/rec-room vibe with its crash-pad decor of fat mod plastic loungers, foosball table and odalisque-via-Target lighting. Come for the laid-back hipster ambience and low-priced snack menu, but stay for hep local bands, oddball events (mixtape trading night) and hot, hard-edged DJ nights of electro, mash-ups and glam.

Starry Plough

3101 Shattuck Avenue, at Prince Street, Berkeley (1-510 841 2082/www.starryploughpub.com). BART Downtown Berkeley. **Open** 11am-2am Mon-Sat; 4pm-2am Sun. **Shows** usually 9.30pm Thur-Sat. **Admission** free-$12. **Credit** AmEx, MC, V.

Talented local indie-rock and folk acts, such as 20 Minute Loop and Sean Smith, and nationally famous cult singer-songwriters, among them Penelope Houston and Vic Chesnutt, consort at this comfy, friendly pub that fronts on to a leafy, residential strip of Shattuck Avenue. There are also regular poetry slams and Irish sessions.

New weird SF

It's little wonder the city that spawned the Summer of Love, Ken Kesey's acid tests and Jefferson Airplane's 'White Rabbit' should provide a home to many of the major players in what *The Wire* dubbed 'New Weird America'. The psychedelic folk and rock that emanated from the city four decades ago will always have its fans, but recently younger musicians have picked up that ball and run with it, creating a music by turns heavy and gentle, yet with roots firmly planted in the 1960s.

On-again-off-again city resident (and long-time SF Art Institute student) **Devendra Banhart**, who's made quite a splash with his original take on blues and folk, might be considered the crown prince of the movement. That said, Banhart's former backing band **Vetiver** has garnered plenty of attention with its gorgeous chamber folk, while former touring companion **Joanna Newsom**, a distant relation of Mayor Gavin

Newsom, has made indie boys, girls and critics swoon with her dark lyrics, girlish granny wail and delicate harp playing.

Newsom, a Mills College dropout, is actually from northern California, as are **Comets on Fire**. The group, who hail from behind the so-called Redwood Curtain in Eureka, continues to stun with its powerful mix of ear-bleeding jams, avant-rock and aural experimentation. Other groups on the rich, jammy side of heavy psych are **Om** and Comets' Santa Cruz juniors **Residual Echoes**; both stand in stark contrast to the stirring solo guitar folk of **Six Organs of Admittance**, aka Comets' Ben Chasny, which has drawn comparisons to the likes of John Fahey. Other artists in a similar vein include back-to-the-land psych-slowcore mavens **Bright Black**, the Buffalo Springfield high-on-field-recordings folk-rock of **Skygreen Leopards**, and Harry Nilsson-meets-the-Velvets psych-popster **Kelley Stoltz**.

Upcoming local Americana act the Bittersweets play the **Hotel Utah**. *See p235.*

Stork Club

2330 Telegraph Avenue, between 23rd & 24th Streets, Oakland (1-510 444 6174/www.storkclub oakland.com). BART 19th Street/Oakland. **Open** 4pm-2am Tue-Sat; 6pm-2am Sun. **Shows** usually 9pm Tue-Sun. **Admission** $5. **No credit cards**.
Located on a slightly sketchy stretch of Telegraph Avenue, this quirky, two-room bar is the place in the East Bay to hear those edgy touring artists – lots of punk, hardcore and indie acts – who might also play at the Hemlock Tavern while they're in the area.

StudioZ.tv

314 11th Street, at Folsom Street, SoMa (252 7666/ www.studioZ.tv). Bus 9, 12, 27, 47. **Open/shows** times vary. **Admission** free-$15. **No credit cards**. **Map** p318 L8.
Happily, StudioZ.tv is a better venue than its name suggests. The space hosts everything from the regular Club Dread reggae night and south Asian fusion jams to political fund-raisers and hip hop poetry slams. Done out with exposed red-brick walls, high ceilings and hardwood floors, the huge main room, several mezzanines and full bars provide the ideal blank slate for the city's ambitious party organisers.

Thee Parkside

1600 17th Street, at Wisconsin Street, Potrero Hill (503 0393/www.theeparkside.com). Bus 10, 22, 53. **Open** noon-2am daily. **Shows** times vary. **Admission** free-$15. **No credit cards**. **Map** p319 N10.
This roadhouse started out as a lunch spot for dot-com cube farmers. When the pink slips began to flutter, Thee Parkside has found new life as a rowdy joint specialising in roots, punk, country and garage rock. Things get sweaty in the main room, where the so-called stage abuts the door. In the tiki patio out back, beer drinkers heat up with a bit of ping-pong.

12 Galaxies

2565 Mission Street, at 21st Street, Mission (970 9777/www.12galaxies.com). BART 24th Street/ bus 14, 26, 48, 49, 67. **Open** show nights only. **Shows** 9pm, nights vary. **Admission** $5-$25. **No credit cards**. **Map** p318 K11.
The sight lines are all swell at this relatively new club: check out the live music from the art deco-style bar, hunker down in a shadowy seat by the stage, or look down from the second-floor mezzanine. The likes of Alejandro Escovedo have bunked down for residencies, though the lineup tends to be heavy on local talents such as Kelley Stoltz and the Mass.

Nightclubs

Some dance, some only drink and pose, but most go home happy.

Light up the dancefloor at **Suite One8one**. *See p240.*

Few cities have ever seen a greater or quicker transference of wealth than San Francisco in the 1990s. Young adults flocked here from all over the country, many making millions almost overnight, and left their mark in just about every one of the city's industries.

Much like the housing market, clubland got a little out of control. Dance clubs opened left and right, age-old dive bars started levying cover charges, and cafés and pubs were overtaken by dot-coms hosting IPO parties. These kids had money to spend, and needed places to spend it. If you had two turntables and a crate of vinyl, you could steadily make a few hundred bucks a night, pumping half of it back into your friend's upstart house store in the Lower Haight.

The trend was short-lived. A few years ahead, many of the once-thriving venues have closed, either because of impossible-to-keep-up rents, noise violations or, more probably, the drastic exodus of young money when the tech party went kerplunk. Though a few new venues have opened along and across from venerable Slim's and DNA Lounge, SoMa's 11th Street corridor is a shadow of its former self.

Still, San Franciscans will never let their party scene die. When the circuit was plagued by police crackdowns, activists set up groups such as the **Popular Noise Foundation** (www.popularnoise.org), the **San Francisco Late Night Coalition** (www.sflnc.com) and **Save Local Music** to boost the scene. In a move unusual for US civic politics, the city council responded by creating a seven-member Entertainment Commission to regulate and promote nightlife, simultaneously taking the power to issue entertainment-related permits from the San Francisco Police Department.

Dancing isn't always central to a night out. The city's so-called 'cabaret laws' play havoc with promoters looking to license their venues for dancing. Up-and-up club owners try to secure Place of Entertainment licenses, which allow dancing. That said, authorities tend to turn a blind eye to those without licenses until more serious illegal activities draw their attention. If you're looking to shake it, **Milk**, **Ruby Skye** and **Mezzanine** are all good bets. At most other spots, however, patrons are often more likely to pose against the wall with drink in hand than get down and dirty to the DJ's offerings. More typically in the style of New York than LA or Miami, the SF club scene aims for style first, shameless good times second.

INFORMATION

Both print and online versions of *SF Weekly* and the *San Francisco Bay Guardian* have extensive clubs listings. However, it's also worth visiting Amoeba Music, Tweekin Records, Aquarius Records or BPM Music Factory (for all, *see pp192-194*) to pick up flyers and free CD-sized magazines advertising goings-on.

It's also worth checking online for details of under-the-radar events. The discussion boards at **Craigslist** (www.craigslist.org) and **SF Raves** (www.sfraves.org) are both useful, while the **Squid List** (www.laughingsquid.org) is the first place techno hippies look for multimedia extravaganzas. Other sites, among them **Nitevibe** (www.nitevibe.com) and **Illstatic** (www.illstatic.com), offer well-culled, succinctly written party listings. However, the daddy of them all is **Flavorpill** (http://sf.flavorpill.net), its weekly dispatch outlining the best of San Francisco's cultural happenings.

Admission prices depend on the night, but usually vary from nothing to $25. Many clubs stay open well past last orders, but by law they can't serve alcohol between 2am and 6am. Some clubs are strictly 21 and over; if you're under 21, check the club's policy before you go.

LATE-NIGHT TRANSPORT

The Muni Owl Service operates on the Muni Metro L and N lines and on the 5, 14, 22, 24, 38, 90, 91 and 108 bus lines from 1am until 5am. All other lines stop at 12.30am. BART runs roughly until midnight. For taxi companies, *see p283*.

Downtown

Union Square & around

Harry Denton's Starlight Room

Sir Francis Drake Hotel, 450 Powell Street, between Post & Sutter Streets (395 8595/www.harrydenton. com). BART & Metro to Powell/bus 2, 3, 4, 30, 45, 76 & Market Street routes/cable car Powell-Hyde or Powell-Mason. **Open** 6pm-2am daily. **Admission** $10 after 8pm Wed-Fri; $15 after 8.30pm Sat. **Credit** AmEx, MC, V. **Map** p315 M5.

Both of Harry Denton's venues are a love 'em or leave 'em affair. Set aside the stunning 21st-floor view over Union Square, the multiple mirrors and the floral carpets, and you're left with a room of dressed-up social and financial climbers dancing to 'Mustang Sally'. Meanwhile, Harry Denton's Rouge (1500 Broadway, at Polk Street, 346 7683) offers the delights of Vegas-style showgirls jiggling on the bar and mingling with the starry-eyed punters.

Ruby Skye

420 Mason Street, between Geary & Post Streets (693 0777/www.rubyskye.com). BART & Metro to Powell/bus 2, 3, 4, 38, 76 & Market Street routes/ cable car Powell-Hyde or Powell-Mason. **Open** 9pm-3am Thur-Sat. **Admission** $10-$30. **Credit** AmEx, Disc, MC, V. **Map** p314 L5.

Converted from an elegant 1890s theatre, Ruby Skye has retained a good many of its ornate Victorian touches, while gaining thoroughly modern sound and light systems in the translation. But with its huge dancefloor and parade of surgically enhanced women, the whole scene feels like it's been imported from LA. Not surprisingly, it's a second home for rave-circuit big names like Sasha and Digweed.

The Tenderloin

Bambuddha Lounge

Phoenix Hotel, 601 Eddy Street, at Larkin Street (885 5088/www.bambuddhalounge.com). Bus 19, 31. **Open** 6-11pm Tue-Thur; 6pm-2am Fri, Sat. **Admission** free-$20. **Credit** AmEx, MC, V. **Map** p314 K6.

This nouveau south-east Asian hangout is sleek and minimal. Gentle lighting complements the numerous conversation-promoting nooks and bamboo daybeds alongside the cabaña-style pool, while the glittering bar and roaring fireplace area are inviting spots in which a see-and-be-seen crowd sits back and enjoys DJs spinning acid jazz, funky disco and other downtempo sounds. **Photo** *p241*.

Rx Gallery

132 Eddy Street, between Mason & Taylor Streets (756 8825/www.rxgallery.com). BART & Metro to Powell/bus 27, 31 & Market Street routes/cable car Powell-Mason. **Open** 3-7pm Wed; 5pm-2am Thur-Sat. **Admission** free-$10. **No credit cards. Map** p314 L6.

The best Nightlife

Arrow

Divey drinking at its best. *See p240.*

Bambuddha Lounge

Vintage swank for visiting rock stars. *See above.*

Mighty

Fresh sounds on a flawless system. *See p241.*

Milk DJ Bar & Lounge

SF hip hop's ground zero. *See p242.*

Rx Gallery

A perfect blend of art and techno. *See above.*

Arts & Entertainment

On weekdays, this subtly lit gallery/soju-and-wine bar showcases innovative and occasionally interactive works by multimedia artists. Weekends, however, are taken over by SF's best DJs; nights such as Kontrol bring in underground electronic acts from all over the world, and make the 'no dancing' signs occasionally posted on the wall laughable.

Suite One8one

181 Eddy Street, at Taylor Street, Tenderloin (345 9900/www.suiteone8one.com). BART & Metro to Powell/bus 27, 31, 38 & Market Street routes. **Open** 9pm-4am Thur-Sat. **Admission** $20. **Credit** AmEx, MC, V. **Map** p314 L6.
The ultra-swank Suite One8one has quickly become one of SF's hottest spots, but it's not for everyone. Some cologne-soaked folks are suckers for a $20 cover, and that's potentially the appeal. Past the rather surly doormen, three floors boast a series of plush rooms and VIP areas. However, the pedestrian music, not to mention the rather snooty crowd, can leave one feeling a bit empty. **Photo** *p238*.

SoMa & South Beach

For gay and lesbian bars and nightclubs in SoMa, among them the **Stud**, *see pp217-226.*

Arrow

10 6th Street, at Market Street (255 7920). BART & Metro to Powell/bus 14, 26, 31 & Market Street routes. **Open** 9pm-2am daily. **Admission** $2-$7. **Credit** AmEx, MC, V. **Map** p318 L7.
The street outside is as grungy as they come, but the vibe inside this funky dive, complete with a tiny but pristine dance area, is as cool as art school. Hipsters groove to indie rock and new-wave DJs, and up-and-coming electronic-dance bands. The venue is also a favourite among the local muso and music-writer crowd, looking for the next cool thing and cheap beer in cans. There's not much signage: look out for the neon arrow marking the entrance.

DNA Lounge

375 11th Street, between Folson & Harrison Streets (626 1409/www.dnalounge.com). Bus 9, 12, 27, 47. **Open** 9pm-2am Tue-Thur; 9pm-4am Fri, Sat. **Admission** $5-$20. **No credit cards. Map** p318 L9.
Goth kids flock to SoMa for all manner of musical fetishes and countercultural indulgences. But none of their nights is complete without a stop in at DNA. This long-time fixture has undergone massive remodelling over the years and now hosts DJ nights and concerts by the likes of Laibach. However, the wonderful stage set-up, viewable from both the dancefloor and the recessed mezzanine, has turned even hip hop acts on to this gem of a nightspot.

Mezzanine

444 Jessie Street, at 6th Street (820 9669/www. mezzaninesf.com). BART & Metro to Powell/bus 14, 26 & Market Street routes. **Open** 10pm-2am Fri; 10pm-7am Sat; other nights vary. **Admission** free-$30. **No credit cards. Map** p319 M7.

This 900-capacity club and art gallery has two long bars bordering the ample dancefloor and lofty space upstairs. Local DJs and even some live acts hold court on the weekends, while touring techno acts such as Richie Hawtin and Miss Kittin make it their sole stop in SF. Could it be that massive sound system, often thought of as the city's best?

111 Minna

111 Minna Street, between 2nd & New Montgomery Streets (974 1719/www.111minnagallery.com). BART & Metro to Montgomery/bus 12, 14, 15, 30, 45, 76 & Market Street routes. **Open** 5-10pm Wed, Thur; 5pm-2am Fri, Sat. **Admission** $3-$15. **Credit** AmEx, MC, V. **Map** p315 N5.
This concrete box, located down an alley just south of Market Street, is an art gallery by day but a truly happening dance club by night. It draws an unusual hybrid clientele – serious rave yuppies – but is popular with all kinds of dance-music enthusiasts thanks to a music policy that travels from garage to Afrobeat, stopping at all stations in between.

Paradise Lounge

1501 Folsom Street, at 11th Street (864 3086/ www.paradiseloungesf.com). Bus 9, 12, 27, 47. **Open** 9.30pm-4am Fri, Sat. **Admission** varies. **Credit** MC, V. **Map** p318 L8.
Once the premier showcase for local bands, the Paradise had a major makeover a couple of years back, jettisoning its three stages and being transformed into a two-storey dance club. It's proved a successful conversion, as guests routinely wait in queues to dance the night away to everything from Latin jazz to deep house to rock and techno.

Six

60 6th Street, at Jessie Street (863 1221/www. clubsix1.com). BART & Metro to Powell/bus 14, 26 & Market Street routes. **Open** 9pm-2am Tue-Sat. **Admission** $2-$12. **No credit cards. Map** p318 L7.
Behind the doors of this venue, located on one of the city's grubbiest blocks (go in a group or avoid looking rich or touristy), you'll find a high-ceilinged chill-out room/bar with a low-ceilinged dancefloor below. DJs have been known to spin house, dub, dancehall and whatever else may be filling floors at the moment. The upstairs space features paintings and photography by local and international artists.

Sno-Drift

1830 3rd Street, at 16th Street (431 4766/www. sno-drift.com). Bus 15. **Open** 10pm-4am Mon, Wed-Sun. **Admission** $5-$20. **Credit** AmEx, MC, V. **Map** p319 P9.
Located on a barren commercial strip near SBC Park, the Sno-Drift is easy to spot: foreign movies are beamed on to the windows. Inside, the cocktail lounge has the feel of a swingin' '60s ski lodge, with a circular fireplace, a deer statue and a long, curved bar behind which sit cocktail glasses chilling atop mountains of crushed ice. Come early or during the week if you don't like crowds.

Sublounge

628 20th Street, between 3rd & Illinois Streets (552 3603/www.sublounge.com). Bus 15, 22. **Open** 6pm-2am Wed-Sat. **Admission** $5-$10. **Map** p319 P11.
Sublounge is inauspiciously located between a taqueria and some warehouses. Club kids from all over the city, however, strap in to the deep-cool decor and take off in relaxed but playful mood: genuine aeroplane seats are scattered beneath the space-ace bachelor-pad light fixtures, while deep house, hip hop, indie pop and funky beats provide the in-flight entertainment.

Ten 15 Folsom

1015 Folsom Street, at 6th Street (431 7444/www. 1015.com). Bus 12, 27, 42. **Open** 9.30pm-7am Thur, Fri; 10pm-7am Sat; 10pm-5.30am Sun. **Admission** free-$20. **No credit cards**. **Map** p319 M7.
San Francisco's meat-and-potatoes dance club, Ten 15 is always a safe bet, whether you want to go dancing before, during or after hours. The three rooms each have their own vibe – move through space and time without changing venues. You'll find the same suburban crowd of pick-up artists and bimbos as in any big club, but they don't overwhelm the place.

330 Ritch

330 Ritch Street, between Brannan & Townsend Streets (541 9574). Metro N to 2nd & King/bus 15, 27, 30, 45, 47, 76. **Open** 5pm-2am Wed-Fri; 10pm-2am Sat, Sun. **Admission** free-$10. **Credit** AmEx, MC, V. **Map** p319 O7.
The young crowd seems right at home in this spacious yet intimate spot, tucked away down an alley. The sounds include hip hop and classic soul, but Thursdays belong to long-running Popscene, a Britpop night (spot the scooters out front) that often features touring bands on the tiny stage – if you've got a British accent, you'll make friends easily.

The Mission & the Castro

The Mission

Amnesia

853 Valencia Street, between 19th & 20th Streets (970 0012). Bus 14, 26, 49. **Open** 6pm-2am daily. **Admission** free-$10. **No credit cards**. **Map** p318 K11.
Amnesia is still resisting the party-hearty armies that take over most of this stretch of the Mission at weekends. Instead, it draws a diverse, friendly, multi-ethnic crowd, and the DJ spins suitably eclectic sounds. With a nice selection of Belgian brews and friendly staff to boot, the patrons at the bar are as likely to be neighbourhood regulars as they are curious tourists checking out the action.

Mighty

119 Utah Street, at 15th Street (626 7001/www. mighty119.com). Bus 9, 22, 53. **Open** 10pm-4am Fri, Sat; 8pm-4am Sun. **Admission** free-$15. **No credit cards**. **Map** p319 M9.

Bambuddha Lounge. *See p239.*

The slick interior and flawless sound system led *URB* magazine to name Mighty as the 'Best New Club in America', but the place has also received plenty of accolades from the locals. Indeed, it's such a well-tuned space that Austin DJ D:Fuse recorded his *People_3* live set there. Rave it up at the main stage or take it easy in the chill-out room at the back.

Pink

2925 16th Street, between S Van Ness Avenue & Capp Street (431 8889/www.pinksf.com). BART 16th Street/bus 14, 22, 26, 53. **Open** 9pm-2am Mon-Sat. **Admission** free-$10. **Credit** MC, V. **Map** p318 K10.
A favourite spot for fans of DJ culture, Pink is a narrow bar with a small dancefloor, uncomfortably crowded during the weekend. Although the drinks

prices might seem to cater to the upper echelon, music is still the club's focus; the venue frequently hosts international DJs with very little fanfare.

The Castro

For gay and lesbian bars and nightclubs in the Castro, *see pp217-226*.

Hey DJ!

The music nurtured here during the 1960s has been well documented. However, in more recent years, the city has sprouted an amazing crop of talented mixmasters. Heck, they even teach the stuff at school here: see www.norcaldjmpa.com. The earnings for home-grown decksmen and -women aren't as sizeable as they were in the heady 1990s, but kids are still taking to the Technics with more enthusiasm than they do Stratocasters. Some spin to tight crowds at Dalva (*see p166*) and Delirium (3139 16th Street, between Valencia & Guerrero Streets, Mission, 552 5525); others prefer the comforts of their bedroom, from which they've been known to blast bass to the neighbours down the street. Either way, the scene thrives.

House music started in Chicago, but its deep, trancey strains were perfected and popularised on the West Coast. **Mark Farina** and **Miguel Migs**, the local kings of the genre, both run nights throughout the city; check www.om-records.com and www.naked-music.com, their respective labels' websites, for their whereabouts. Hip hop is also a staple of the Bay Area's nocturnal landscape: **Dan the Automator** is known to pop up at Milk (*see p242*) alongside Triple Threat scratchers **Apollo**, **Vinroc** and **Shortkut**, whose roving parties can be tracked through True Skool's webpage (www.true-skool.org).

SF's musical history is steeped in experimentalism, and the town is still a hotspot for abstract electronica and minimal techno. Broker/Dealer DJs **Ryan Fitzgerald** and **Ryan Bishop** can often be found holding court at the monthly Pop event at Rx Gallery (*see p239*), while friends **Kid 606** and **Gold Chains** make the rounds at rock clubs and far-flung locations (see www.tigerbeat6.com for their events). If you're up for a mix, Popscene's **Aaron Axelsen** and **Omar Perez** know their way around every style imaginable.

Haight-Ashbury

Milk DJ Bar & Lounge

1840 Haight Street, between Shrader & Stanyan Streets (387 6455/www.milksf.com). Bus 6, 7, 33, 43, 66, 71. **Open** 7pm-2am daily. **Admission** free-$10. **No credit cards. Map** p317 E9.

For years, the Haight-Ashbury district was ground zero for the city's rock scene, but these days, hip hop is creeping in and proving itself as a Haight Street mainstay, due in no small part to Milk's hip hop- and R&B-friendly bookers. Hip, modern decor and a decent-sized dancefloor characterise the space; and big-name guests such as DJ Shadow have been known to drop in at events put on by True Skool and Future Primitive Sound.

Lower Haight

Underground SF

424 Haight Street, between Fillmore & Webster Streets (864 7384/www.undergroundsf.com). Bus 6, 7, 22, 66, 71. **Open** 9pm-2am Tue-Sat. **Admission** free-$10. **Credit** MC, V. **Map** p318 H8.

Just down the street from Nickie's BBQ (*see p169*), on a somewhat sketchy stretch of Lower Haight, the club formerly known as the Top is little more than a converted dive with a smallish dancefloor. But set the Underground's looks aside and pay attention instead with your ears: it has a deservedly good reputation as a centre of turntable culture, and is the go-to place for the many discerning queers who love disco-funk but hate ABBA.

The Western Addition

Madrone Lounge

500 Divisadero Street, at Fell Street (241 0202/www.madronelounge.com). Bus 21, 24. **Open** 6pm-midnight Mon, Sun; 6pm-2am Tue-Sat. **Admission** free-$5. **Credit** MC, V. **Map** p317 G8.

This cosy room on the edge of the Lower Haight draws its share of students from the nearby USF and UCSF campuses, primarily for its regular happy hours but also for its laid-back vibe. It's tiny, so when local bands notify USF's college radio station, KUSF 90.3 FM, of their concerts here, they have little trouble filling the joint.

Hayes Valley

The best bet for lively nightlife in the area is unquestionably the **Rickshaw Stop** (*see p236*). Located on the edge of Hayes Valley, it supplements programme of live music with hot club gatherings. Nights such as Fallout, Club ID and Blow-Up draw a heavy hipster contingent, the venue always throws a great party. Arrive early for the authentic rickshaw-cart seating.

Arts & Entertainment

Sports & Fitness

Whether you're a player or a spectator, you've come to the right place.

The **San Francisco Giants** take on the NY Mets at America's loveliest ballpark. *See p244.*

No doubt about it: San Franciscans are a cultured bunch. But they still find time to step away from the galleries, recork the chardonnay and put down the opera glasses long enough to tug on a well-worn baseball cap, grab a 'We're No.1' foam finger and hit the sports bars. Since back in the early 1900s, when prize-fighting was king and the city sandlots began spawning out professional baseball players, including a whole family of DiMaggios, San Francisco has been a hotbed for sports. Football's **49ers** (*see p244*) and baseball's **Giants** (*see p244*), who play only a home run (aka 'splash hit') away from the Bay, inspire fierce loyalty.

However, they don't have it all their own way. The triumphs of their scrappy Oakland counterparts (football's **Raiders**, for which *see p244*, and baseball's **Athletics**, for which *see p244*) have given rise to a splendid cross-bridge rivalry in recent years. San Jose, an hour away on a good traffic day, has a professional hockey team (the **Sharks**; *see p246*) to add to Oakland's **Golden State Warriors** (*see p244*), a pro basketball team on the rise at last after a bleak decade of mediocrity.

The wealth of tempting landscape means that there's plenty of opportunity for outdoor activities. Runners have the annual **Bay to Breakers** (*see p199*) foot race every May, and the superb paths at the **Marina** and round **Lake Merced** all year round. Biking is popular both in the city, particularly in **Golden Gate Park**, and beyond it, especially in the **Marin Headlands** (*see pp259-260*), while devotees of aerobics or cross-training will find a health club on nearly every corner. Skiers and

The best Sports

For getting on your bike
San Francisco Bicycle Coalition. See p247.

For baseball by the bay
San Francisco Giants. See p244.

For contemplating your navel
Yoga Tree. See p251.

snowboarders even have the option of taking off to the mountains (*see pp271-274*). If it's all too much, there are plenty of yoga classes to help you restore your inner balance (*see p251*).

Spectator sports

For information on local events, head to the *Chronicle*'s website at www.sfgate.com/sports, or check the 'Sporting Green' section of the *San Francisco Chronicle*, which has a calendar of local sporting events and media broadcasts. If you can stomach the phone-ins, KNBR (680 or 1050 AM, www.knbr.com) is good for news.

If it's convenient, buy tickets in person from the team's stadium in order to avoid booking fees and surcharges. If that's not possible, call the team direct or buy tickets from its website. And if they're sold out, try **Tickets.com** (1-415 478 2277, www.tickets.com) or **Ticketmaster** (421 8497, www.ticketmaster.com), who both work with the major teams. Other brokers include **Premier Tickets** (1-800 376 6876, www.premiertickets.com), **Entertainment Ticketfinder** (1-800 523 1515, www.ticketfinder.com) and **Mr Ticket** (1-800 424 7328, www.mrtix.com). Be warned: scams abound, especially with scalpers, so be on your guard.

Auto racing

Infineon Raceway

Intersection of Highways 37 & 121, Sonoma (1-800 870 7223/www.infineonraceway.com). **Open** *Box office* 8am-5pm Mon-Fri & race days. **Tickets** $10-$85. **Credit** Disc, MC, V.
Home to everything from NASCAR to monster-truck rallies, Infineon is a fun slice of Americana located just an hour away from the city.

Baseball

The two Bay Area teams could not be more different. While the National League's **San Francisco Giants** have a roster stacked with veterans, a middle-class following and a lovely Downtown stadium, the American League's **Oakland Athletics** (*see p245* **Walking back to happiness**) favour youngsters, draw a more working-class fanbase and play in a concrete shell in the middle of nowhere. Fans should head directly for the Giants' SBC Park (the name seems likely to change in 2006, after SBC bought AT&T and announced it would be adopting its name), where the old-fashioned design and bay views combine to create one of the most beautiful sports stadia in the country. However, though Oakland's McAfee Coliseum is no competition for its SF rival, and the controversial Giants slugger Barry Bonds

is a bigger star than anyone across the bay, the A's have been the better team in recent years. The season runs from April to September, with play-offs in October.

Oakland Athletics *McAfee Coliseum, 7000 Coliseum Way, Nimitz Freeway, at Hegenberger Road, Oakland (1-510 568 5600/www.oakland athletics.com). BART Coliseum/Oakland Airport.* **Open** *Box office* 9am-6pm Mon-Fri; 10am-4pm Sat; 2hrs before game. **Tickets** $10-$40. **Credit** AmEx, Disc, MC, V.
San Francisco Giants *SBC Park, 24 Willie Mays Plaza, at 3rd & King Streets, South Beach (972 2000/www.sfgiants.com). Metro N to 2nd & King/bus 10, 15, 30, 45.* **Open** *Box office* 8.30am-5.30pm Mon-Fri; 2hrs before game Sat, Sun. **Tickets** $12-$72. **Credit** Disc, MC, V. **Map** p319 P7.

Basketball

San Francisco might not have a pro basketball team, but Oakland does: the perennially poor **Golden State Warriors**, who play in the Oakland Arena behind the Coliseum. The NBA season runs from November until the middle of April, whereupon the Warriors go home and spend some time with their families while their rivals go to the play-offs. Rather more dramatic is the exciting college season, which runs from December through the 'March Madness' of the NCAA tournament. **Stanford** (1-800 782 6367, www.gostanford.com) and the **University of California at Berkeley** (1-800 462 3277, www.calbears.com) are both members of the Pac-10 and can usually be relied on to produce competitive teams.

In the summer, the **Kezar Pavilion** (Waller and Stanyan Streets, Haight) hosts a free Pro-Am league that showcases top local college talent and the occasional NBA star. If you think you've got game, check out the pick-up contests across the city: the best hoops are at **James Lick Middle School** (Clipper & Castro Streets, Noe Valley).

Golden State Warriors *Oakland Arena, 7000 Coliseum Way, Oakland (1-510 986 2200/www.nba.com/warriors). BART Coliseum/Oakland Airport.* **Open** *Box office* 10am-6pm Mon-Fri; 10am-4pm Sat. **Tickets** $10-$1,000. **Credit** AmEx, MC, V.

Football

The Bay separates the NFL's **San Francisco 49ers** from the **Oakland Raiders**, and their supporters remain fanatically opposed. The 49ers' record of selling out every home game for nearly 25 years (single-game seats are available if you're quick) was brought under threat in recent years: the team followed a 2-14 season in 2004 with an equally futile performance in 2005 in front of a restless fanbase.

Walking back to happiness

Throughout its four decades, the Oakland A's baseball club has fielded a number of controversial superstars, among them Reggie Jackson, Rickey Henderson and Jose Canseco. These days, however, the best-known – and most polarising – member of the organisation isn't a player at all, but A's general manager **Billy Beane** (*pictured*). In a sport that loves its traditions and is terminally suspicious of new ideas, Beane's innovative approach to running a baseball team has ruffled more than a few feathers. Even more galling to the traditionalists is that Beane's methods actually seem to work.

As delineated in detail in Michael Lewis's fascinating 2003 book *Moneyball: The Art of Winning an Unfair Game*, Beane typically relies more on statistical spreadsheets than scouting reports to evaluate players, believing that oft-ignored stats like a batter's on-base average or a pitcher's WHIP ratio (walks and hits per innings pitched) offer more insight into a player's ability than sexier categories like batting or earned-run average. Though

the A's budgetary restrictions prevent Beane from stocking the line-up with high-priced sluggers, he's kept the team competitive by fielding an ever-changing roster of hot young prospects and bargain-priced cast-offs. Despite competing against heavily bankrolled organizations like the Anaheim Angels and the Texas Rangers, the A's have managed to be competitive in the AL West in recent years, and won it in 2000, 2002 and 2003.

Still, not everyone agrees that Beane's system is a sure-fire recipe for success. The A's have yet to make it to the World Series on Beane's watch; and while Beane disciple Theo Epstein guided the Boston Red Sox to a world championship in 2004, he did so with a considerably larger budget at his disposal. Much to the chagrin of Beane-haters everywhere, other teams are increasingly incorporating Beane's ideas into their own dealings, using his own methods to beat Oakland. No matter: Beane will almost certainly go down in baseball history as one of this era's most influential figures.

Despite being a marginally more successful team in recent years (though it's all relative when you're this bad), the Raiders rarely sell out their home games in advance, and tickets can usually be obtained even minutes prior to kick-off. If you happen to find yourself in the 'Black Hole', home to Oakland's most rabid and creatively outfitted fans (think Darth Vader on a bad day), you'll be terrified. Possibly amused,

but most likely terrified. The 'Big Game' between Stanford and Cal in November is the annual highlight of the college football season.

Oakland Raiders *McAfee Coliseum, 7000 Coliseum Way, Nimitz Freeway, at Hegenberger Road, Oakland (1-510 864 5000/www.raiders.com). BART Coliseum/Oakland Airport.* **Open** *Box office* 10am-6pm Mon-Fri; 10am-4pm Sat; 2hrs before game Sun. **Tickets** $47-$91. **Credit** AmEx, Disc, MC, V.

Cyclists ride down by the **Marina**...

Arts & Entertainment

San Francisco 49ers *Monster Park, Giants Drive, at Gilman Avenue, Bayview (656 4900/ www.sf49ers.com). Ballpark Express 9X from Sutter & Sansome Streets, 28X from Funston & California Streets, or 47X on Van Ness Avenue.* **Tickets** $64. **Credit** V.

Hockey

Ice hockey came to the Bay Area more than a decade ago, courtesy of the National Hockey League's **San Jose Sharks**. Although the novelty has now worn off – an NHL lockout suspended play for a year – the team still attracts a decent core of fans to the 'Shark Tank'. The season runs from October to April, followed by two months of play-offs.

San Jose Sharks *HP Pavilion, 525 West Santa Clara Street, at Autumn Street, San Jose (1-408 287 9200/www.sj-sharks.com). CalTrain to San Jose Diridon Station.* **Open** *Box office 9.30am-5.30pm Mon-Fri; from 3hrs before game Sat, Sun.* **Tickets** $17-$115. **Credit** AmEx, MC, V.

Horse racing

Bay Meadows Racecourse *2600 S Delaware Street, at Palm Avenue, San Mateo (1-650 574 7223/www.baymeadows.com). CalTrain to Bay Meadows.* **Open** *Race days Apr-June, Aug-Nov. Box office 9.30am-7pm Wed-Sat.* **Tickets** $3-$15. **Credit** AmEx, Disc, MC, V.
Golden Gate Fields *1100 Eastshore Highway, Albany (1-510 559 7300/www.goldengatefields .com). BART North Berkeley, then AC Transit shuttle bus.* **Open** *Race days Nov-Apr Wed-Sun. Box office 9.30am-7pm Mon-Fri; 9am-5pm Sat.* **Tickets** $3-$15. **Credit** MC, V.

Active sports & fitness

Every Thursday, the *Chronicle* publishes a supplement called 'Outdoors', full of listings and information on open-air activities. For

special events, it's also worth trying the Visitor Information Center (*see p293*). **CitySports** (www.citysportsmag.com), a regional magazine available in gyms and sports shops, carries information on participatory sports. Note: if you're hiring expensive equipment, photo ID or a credit card is usually required for the deposit.

Bowling

Presidio Bowling Center *Building 93, at Montgomery Street & Moraga Avenue, Presidio (561 2695). Bus 29.* **Open** *9am-midnight Mon-Thur, Sun; 9am-2am Fri, Sat.* **Rates** $3.75-$5/game. *Shoe rental* $3. **Credit** MC, V. **Map** p312 D3.
Yerba Buena Bowling Center *750 Folsom Street, between 3rd & 4th Streets, SoMa (777 3727/www. skatebowl.com). BART & Metro to Montgomery/bus 12, 15, 30, 45, 76.* **Open** *10am-10pm Mon-Thur, Sun; 10am-midnight Fri, Sat.* **Rates** $3.50-$5/game. *Shoe rental* $3. **Credit** MC, V. **Map** p315 N6.

Cycling

If you're looking to get around San Francisco quickly, hop on a bike. Hemmed in by the peninsula, the city doesn't sprawl like most major conurbations, and while it's certainly hilly (going up can be exhausting, coming down can be heart-in-mouth terrifying), the steepest inclines are easily avoided. Biking in the city is a singularly memorable experience, taking in majestic sea views, the aroma of eucalyptus trees and the glorious Golden Gate Park.

Bike stores dot the centre of town, and bike lanes are widespread. Bicycles can be taken free of charge on BART, except for peak hours (7-9am and 4-6pm weekdays); the ferries will also take you and your bike across the rough Bay waters. All major outdoor public events in San Francisco are required by law to offer free and secure bike parking – there's even a free valet bike park for every Giants home game.

... and over **Golden Gate Bridge**.

The only downers are typical of most major urban areas: theft, which is common, and traffic, which can be nasty. Always secure your bike with a U-lock when parking it, and don't leave it outside overnight (many hotels will be able to store it if you ask nicely). Back on the roads, SUVs, Hummers and other such monstrosities are notorious for disregarding anything smaller than they are; take care.

Many tourists head to Fisherman's Wharf and rent bikes for day-rides across the Golden Gate Bridge, but there's even more entrancing biking elsewhere in the Bay Area. The endless trails in the **Marin Headlands** (*see pp259-260*) offer unmatched sights and pulmonary exertions: the mountain bike was born on the paths of **Bolinas Ridge** in Marin County and **Railroad Grade** along Mount Tamalpais. For more information, call the Golden Gate National Recreation Area Visitor Center (331 1540) or the Pantoll Ranger Station (388 2070).

For more on cycling in the city, contact the terrific **San Francisco Bicycle Coalition** (www.sfbike.org). Among other resources, the Coalition publishes an immeasurably useful map of the city with all gradients marked on it, so you can avoid the worst of the hills. You can download a PDF at the Coalition's website, or purchase a printed copy online or from any bike store around town ($4). Ray Hosler's *Bay Area Bike Rides* (Chronicle, $14.95) is another very worthwhile read.

Bike Hut

Pier 40, Embarcadero at 1st Street, SoMa (543 4335/www.thebikehut.com). Metro N to Brannan/ bus 10, 15. **Open** 10am-6pm daily. **Rates** $5/hr or $20/day. **Map** p319 P7.
This excellent little enterprise, staffed by volunteers (who train kids from deprived backgrounds in bike mechanics while on the job), rents and repairs bicycles from a location just south of the Bay Bridge.

Blazing Saddles

2715 Hyde Street, at North Point Street, Fisherman's Wharf (202 8888/www.blazingsaddles.com). Metro F to Fisherman's Wharf/bus 10, 19, 30, 47/cable car Powell-Hyde. **Open** from 8am daily. **Rates** $7/hr or $28-$48/day. **Credit** MC, V. **Map** p314 K2.
Bikes rented to tourists with a yen for cycling the eight miles from Fisherman's Wharf over the Golden Gate Bridge to Sausalito. Guided tours are also offered. **Other locations**: throughout the city.

Golden Gate Park Skate & Bike

3038 Fulton Street, between 6th & 7th Avenues, Richmond (668 1117). Bus 5, 21, 31, 33. **Open** 10am-6pm Mon-Fri; 10am-7pm Sat, Sun. **Rates** *Bikes* $5/hr or $25/day. *Skates* $5/hr or $20/day. **Credit** MC, V. **Map** p316 C8.
Bikes, rollerskates and in-line skates are all available for rent (helmet and knee and elbow pads included), and you can take skateboarding lessons.

Mike's Bikes

1233 Howard Street, between 8th & 9th Streets, SoMa (241 2453/www.mikesbikes.com). Bus 9, 12, 27, 47. **Open** 11am-7pm Mon-Fri; 10am-6pm Sat, Sun. **Credit** MC, V. **Map** p318 L8.
Mike's doesn't offer rentals, but is an excellent one-stop shop for bikes, clothing and other accessories.

Solano Avenue Cyclery

1554 Solano Avenue, Albany (1-510 524 1094/ www.solanoavenuecyclery.com). BART El Cerrito Plaza, then AC Transit bus 43. **Open** 11am-7pm Mon-Fri; 10am-6pm Sat; noon-5pm Sun. **Rates** $35/day. **Credit** Disc, MC, V.
Near Berkeley, this is a great place to launch into the East Bay trails. Ask about the Nimitz Bike Path.

Golf

Golden Gate Park Course

John F Kennedy Drive, at 47th Avenue, Golden Gate Park (information 751 8987/reservations 750 4653). Bus 5, 18, 31, 38. **Open** dawn-dusk daily. **Rates** *Non-residents* $14-$18. **No credit cards.**

The Golden Gate Park Course is a handsome little nine-hole par-three municipal number, reasonably priced and located above Ocean Beach.

Harding Park Golf Course

Harding Road & Skyline Boulevard, Lake Merced (information 664 4690/reservations 750 4653/www. harding-park.com). Bus 18, 88. **Open** dawn-dusk daily. **Rates** *Non-residents* $80-$138. **Credit** MC, V.
Arguably one of the best municipal courses in the country, Harding Park has recently benefitted from a fabulous renovation, and hosted the prestigious WGC AmEx tournament in 2005. Tee times are available up to 30 days ahead with a $10 surcharge. Also here is the nine-hole, par-32 Fleming Course (non-residents $22-$27).

Lincoln Park Golf Course

300 34th Avenue, at Clement Street, Lincoln Park (information 221 9911/reservations 750 4653). Bus 18. **Open** dawn-dusk daily. **Rates** *Non-residents* $31-$36. **No credit cards.**
The wonderful view of the Golden Gate Bridge from the 17th hole has made Lincoln Park one of the most photographed courses in the US.

Mission Bay Golf Center

1200 6th Street, at Channel Street, China Basin (431 7888). Bus 15. **Open** 11.30am-10pm Mon; 7am-10pm Tue-Sun. **Map** p319 O9.
For your pleasure, a 300yd (274m), two-tiered driving range, putting greens, a restaurant and a discount golf shop. And you'll love the 360° panoramic view of Downtown, the freeway, East Bay and the south San Francisco hills.

Presidio Golf Course

300 Finley Road, at Arguello Gate, Presidio (561 4653/www.presidiogolf.com). Bus 28. **Open** dawn-dusk daily. **Rates** $50-$108. **Credit** AmEx, MC, V. **Map** p312 C5.
Former presidents Roosevelt and Eisenhower both played this 18-holer– the second oldest course west of the Mississippi – when it was owned by the Army. Built in 1885, it finally opened to the public in 1995 following a makeover by Arnold Palmer and co.

Gyms

San Franciscans love their corner gyms every bit as much as their corner cafés and bars. Each neighbourhood seems to have at least one; some have many. Here are a few of the best.

Embarcadero YMCA

169 Steuart Street, at Mission Street, Financial District (957 9622/www.ymcasf.org). BART & Metro to Montgomery/bus 2, 3, 4, 31 & Market Street routes. **Open** 5.30am-9.45pm Mon-Fri; 8am-7.45pm Sat; 9am-5.45pm Sun. **Rates** $15/day. **Credit** MC, V. **Map** p315 O4.
San Francisco has plenty of YMCAs, but this is the only one which can boast a waterfront view. A day pass will give you access to aerobics classes, free

weights, Cybex and Nautilus machines, racquetball and basketball courts, and the 25m (82ft) swimming pool. For the pass, you'll need photo ID.

Koret Health & Recreation Center

University of San Francisco, 2130 Fulton Street, at Stanyan Street, Richmond (422 6821/www.usfca. edu/koret). Bus 5, 31. **Open** 6am-10pm (pool closes at 9pm) Mon-Fri; 8am-8pm (pool closes at 6pm) Sat, Sun. **Rates** $15/day. **Credit** MC, V. **Map** p317 E8.
Koret has an Olympic-sized pool, a gym and six racquetball courts, though for the latter you'll need to bring your own equipment.

24 Hour Fitness Center

1200 Van Ness Avenue, at Post Street, Cathedral Hill (776 2200/www.24hourfitness.com). Bus 2, 3, 4, 19, 38, 47, 49, 76. **Open** 24hrs daily. **Rates** $15/day. **Credit** MC, V. **Map** p314 K6.
This chain has several branches around the city, all offering a variety of facilities and classes. For other locations, check online or call 1-800 249 6756.

Hiking

Walking San Francisco's splendid hills is a delight, with both the Presidio and Golden Gate Park offering decent walking opportunities. Less than a half-hour outside the city lie trails with stunning views and fragrant paths. Just across the Golden Gate Bridge, the short and easily hiked **Morning Sun Trail** rises from a parking lot at Spencer Avenue (exit off US 101 north). The trail offers lovely views east towards the city over the Bay and Angel Island, and west to the thundering Pacific. Alternatively, take Golden Gate Transit bus 10 to Mill Valley for the day-long **Dipsea Trail** to Stinson Beach. The **Bootjack Trail** to the summit of Mount Tamalpais is popular too. Call the Pantoll Ranger Station (388 2070) for trail information. The **Bay Area Sierra Club** (1-510 848 0800, www.sanfrancisco bay.sierraclub.org) in Berkeley has a wealth of useful knowledge.

Horse-riding

If you want equestrian action, horses and tours are offered at the **Sea Horse & Friendly Acres Ranch** (1-650 726 9903, www.seahorseranch.com) near Half Moon Bay and the **Chanslor Stables** (1-707 875 3333, www.chanslor.com) next to Bodega Bay.

In-line skating

Sunday skating in **Golden Gate Park** is hard to beat: the beach at one end, sunny meadows along the way and no motor vehicles anywhere to be seen. For wide smiles – without the wide polyester collars – join the mix of in-line

Embarcadero: keep on running...

skating, disco twirling and breakdancing near 6th Avenue on JFK Drive. Skates are available for rent at **Golden Gate Park Skate & Bike** (*see p246*), or for purchase from **Skates on Haight**. On Fridays, join the **Midnight Rollers** night-time skate, which leaves Ferry Plaza opposite the Ferry Building at 9.15pm sharp; for information, see www.cora.org.

Skates on Haight

1818 Haight Street, at Stanyan Street, Haight-Ashbury (752 8375/www.skatesonhaight.com). Metro N to Cole & Carl/bus 7, 33, 66, 71. **Open** 9am-6pm Mon-Fri; 11am-6pm Sat, Sun. **Credit** AmEx, MC, V. **Map** p317 E9.
Skates on Haight was at least partly responsible for launching the worldwide skateboarding craze during the 1970s. Stock these days includes in-line skates, roller skates and snowboards.
Other location: 1219 Polk Street, at Sutter Street, Tenderloin (447 1800).

Rock climbing

Devoted climbers travel to **Lake Tahoe** and **Mount Shasta**, but **Yosemite** is the state's climbing mecca, with lessons available year-round. *See pp271-274*. While you're still in the city, warm up at Mission Cliffs...

Mission Cliffs

2295 Harrison Street, at 19th Street, Mission (550 0515/www.mission-cliffs.com). Bus 12, 27. **Open** 6.30am-9pm Mon-Fri; 9 am-7pm Sat, Sun. **Rates** $10-$18/day. **Credit** AmEx, Disc, MC, V. **Map** p318 L11.
This 14,000sq ft (4,300sq m) of urban wilderness and polished jungle gym runs beginner's lessons from noon until 7.30pm on weekdays.

Running

Crissy Field is highly popular with runners, and it's easy to see why. Each step of the route from Fort Mason past Marina Green along the Golden Gate Promenade is a postcard, leading all the way to historic Fort Point beneath the

bridge. The **Embarcadero** offers another lovely path beneath the city's other beautiful bridge, and **Golden Gate Park** offers a third option, with the track at Kezar Stadium on the eastern edge providing a good spot for sprints.

For something more sociable, the **San Francisco Dolphin South End Runners**, founded in 1966, has group runs at 9.30am every Sunday, in which non-members can take part for $5. Call 978 0837 or check out www.dserunners.com for more details. Annual foot races include the **Bay to Breakers** (*see p199*) run in May and the **San Francisco Marathon** (*see p200*) in July.

Sailing, kayaking & rowing

There are numerous boating, sailing and kayaking outfits in the Bay Area and along the Pacific coastline; all offer equipment, lessons and trips. Rowing opportunities range from single sculls to whale-boat racing; for details call **Open Water Rowing** (332 1091, www.owrc.com) in Sausalito or **South End Rowing Club** (776 7372, www.south-end.org) in San Francisco. For the romantic dabbler, pedalos and rowing boats are available for rent at **Stow Lake** in Golden Gate Park.

Cal Adventures

UC Aquatic Center, 100 University Avenue, at Shorebird Park, Berkeley Marina (1-510 642 4000/ www.oski.org). BART Downtown Berkeley, then AC Transit bus 9. **Open** noon-sunset Wed-Fri; 7.30am-sunset Sat, Sun. **Rates** *Kayaks* $12/hr. *Sailboats* $15/hr. **Credit** Disc, MC, V.
Cal Adventures rents out 15ft Coronados on the South Sailing Basin. Those without proper certification must be accompanied by an instructor, at a cost of an additional $60.

California Canoe & Kayak

409 Water Street, at Franklin Street, Jack London Square, Oakland (1-510 893 7833/www.calkayak. com). BART Oakland City Center/12th Street. **Rates** *Kayaks* $15/hr. *Canoes* $25/hr. **Credit** MC, V.
One of the Bay Area's best locations for hiring and buying kayaks and seagoing gear. Lessons and day trips navigate the nearby Oakland Estuary.

Sea Trek

Schoonmaker Point Marina, at Libertyship Way, Sausalito (332 4465/www.seatrekkayak.com). Blue & Gold Fleet ferry from Pier 41, or Golden Gate ferry from Ferry Building. **Open** 9am-4pm Mon-Fri; 8.30am-4pm Sat, Sun. **Rate** *Kayak rental* $15-$25/hr. *Tours* $65-$135. **Credit** AmEx, Disc, MC, V.
Sea Trek hosts summer camps for kids, books expeditions to Alaska and Baja, and supports waterway conservation. Beginner's classes in kayaking, guided tours and moonlight paddles are available; rental covers everything from pro gear to wave-rider kayaks suitable for novices.

Arts & Entertainment

Shark attack!

If you're expecting Bay Area beaches to live up to your *Baywatch* fantasies, you're in for a shock. The waves may be big but they're also cold, the sands are often rocky, and offshore waters are home to a sizeable contingent of sharks. And not just any old sharks. We're talking Great Whites here. But don't bin the swimsuit yet. The locals feel happy living with their finned neighbours; in fact, some surfers are alarmingly blasé about them. Once you know a few facts, you might feel the same.

First, a shark's natural prey is seals. They don't want to eat humans. Second, the Great Whites tend to hang out in particular places (Marin County's south-facing coast, the mouth of Tomales Bay, off Stinson Beach, Año Nuevo, Salmon Creek) and at certain times (August is when they spawn in Tomales Bay; October and November is when they migrate past the Farallon Islands). Third, they don't want no trouble. So don't swim solo, take off anything glittery and stay away from fins – you should be fine. When a shark is sighted, lifeguards clear everyone out of the water.

So you can relax? Well, no. Rip tides are a real danger. (Warning signs offer the frank statement: 'People have died swimming here.') Formed by breaking waves pulling strongly away from the shore, rip tides are commonplace at most Bay Area beaches. You should stay away from any water that looks especially foamy, as this is a sign that two currents are battling each other. If you do get caught in a rip, don't waste strength swimming against it towards the shore. Just tread water until someone rescues you, or swim parallel to the beach until you're out of the rip, whereupon you can swim safely ashore. The locals' golden rule? Never turn your back on the ocean.

Spinnaker Sailing

Pier 40, South Beach Harbor, Embarcadero, at Townsend Street, South Beach (543 7333/www. spinnaker-sailing.com). Metro N to Brannan/bus 10, 15. **Open** 8.30am-5.30pm daily. **Rates** *Boat rental* $140-$735/day. **Credit** AmEx, MC, V. **Map** p319 P7.
Professional instruction, boats from 22ft (7m) to 80ft (24m), and a great location near the ballpark.

Skateboarding

The police have done a pretty thorough job of eliminating skate rats from once-favourite sites such as Justin Herman Plaza and Pier 7 on the Embarcadero, though you'll be able to sniff out a Safeway parking lot or two and any number of downtown concrete ramps. If you're posing or want to learn, invest in helmet, gloves, knee and elbow pads at DLX listed below. Dusting up on the slang won't hurt either.

DLX

1831 Market Street, at Guerrero Street, Lower Haight (626 5588/www.dlxsf.com). Metro F, J, K, L, M to Church/bus 6, 7, 26, 66. **Open** 11am-7pm Mon-Sat; 11am-6pm Sun. **Credit** AmEx, MC, V. **Map** p318 J9.
DLX (née Deluxe) is the mother of all skateboarding shops in SF, and has a comprehensive range of clothes, boards, accessories and stickers.

Skiing & snowboarding

The slopes could be hit and run in a day trip, but most people prefer to spend at least a weekend in the Sierras. For leading resorts around **Lake Tahoe**; *see pp259-260*. During the season (November to April), most ski shops have calendars of events package deals. Check www.goski.com for listings of all the major California resorts.

FTC Ski & Sports

1360 Bush Street, between Larkin & Polk Streets, Nob Hill (673 8363). Bus 2, 3, 4. **Open** 10am-7pm Mon-Fri; 10am-5pm Sat, Sun. **Credit** AmEx, MC, V. **Map** p314 K5.
A great selection of skis, snowboards and all the accoutrements, as well as deals on used equipment.

SFO Snowboarding

618 Shrader Street, at Haight Street, Haight-Ashbury (386 1666/www.sfosnow.com). Bus 6, 7, 33, 43, 66, 71. **Open** 11am-7pm Mon-Sat; 11am-6pm Sun. **Map** p317 E9.
Boards, boots, bindings and more for rent, plus an array of cold-weather clothes for sale.

Sullivan's Ski World

5323 Geary Boulevard, at 17th Street, Richmond (751 7070). Bus 38. **Open** 10am-6.30pm Mon-Fri; 10am-6pm Sat; 10am-5pm Sun. **Credit** AmEx, Disc, MC, V. **Map** p316 A7.
For more than 50 years, Sullivan's has been selling everything you need for a ski trip to Tahoe. There is a four-day minimum on rentals.

Surfing

Here are the facts: the waves around San Francisco are dangerous – not a good place to learn (*see p250* **Shark attack!**). An hour north

Arts & Entertainment

of San Francisco on Highway 1, **Stinson Beach** has gentler waves and fewer surfers, while the experts head to **Mavericks** in Santa Cruz. But whether you're a pro headed to Ocean Beach and beyond or a newbie boogie-boarding the black-sand beaches of Marin County, Wise Surfboards is the first choice for gear.

Wise Surfboards

800 Great Highway, at Cabrillo Street, Ocean Beach (750 9473/www.wisesurfboards.com). Bus 5, 18, 31, 38. **Open** 9am-6pm daily. **Credit** AmEx, MC, V. Located right on Ocean Beach, this shop sells boards, wetsuits and various accessories, and hosts a 24-hour surf information phoneline (273 1618), updated several times daily.

Swimming

The ocean is usually too chilly and turbulent for a proper swim, but there are plenty of pools in town, including those at the **Embarcadero YMCA** and the **Koret Center** (for both, *see p248*). The most central pools can be found at **Hamilton Recreation Center** (Geary Boulevard & Steiner Street, 292 2001) and the **North Beach Pool** (Lombard and Mason Streets, 274 0200). For your nearest municipal pool, check the White Pages under 'City Government Offices: Recreation and Parks'.

Tennis

Indoor tennis is almost exclusively a members-only affair, but there are plenty of outdoor courts. **Golden Gate Park** has several (near the Stanyan Street entrance, 753 7001), and there are busy courts at **Mission Dolores Park** (*see p100*). Both locations are free and open from sunrise to sunset. You can find a full list of tennis facilities in the 'Neighbourhood Parks' section of SBC Yellow Pages.

Whale watching

Whale watching happens during the migration season (Nov-Dec and late Mar/early Apr), and occurs primarily just north and south of San Francisco. On occasion, it can be as easy as taking a pair of binoculars to the shore and having a look. Mendocino and Monterey are popular viewing spots, but we recommend the tip of **Point Reyes** (*see p263*), an hour's drive north of the city. You might see glorious humpback and blue whales, as well as sea lions.

Oceanic Society Expeditions

Fort Mason Center, Laguna & Beach Streets, Marina (474 3385/www.oceanic-society.org). Bus 10, 19, 28, 30, 47, 49. **Open** 9am-5pm Mon-Fri. **Rates** *Voyages* $75-$78. **Credit** AmEx, MC, V. **Map** p314 H2.

A cut above most tourist trips – the staff are experts in natural history and marine life. On weekends (from June to November), a full-day trip heads 26 miles west to the Farallon Islands, home of the largest seabird rookery in the continental US. Along the way, whales can often be seen.

Windsurfing

San Francisco is a popular windsurfing centre; the 30-plus launch sites include **Candlestick** and **Coyote Points**, as well as **Crissy Field**, the site of several international competitions.

City Front Boardsports

2936 Lyon Street, at Greenwich Street, Cow Hollow (929 7873/www.boardsports.com). Bus 41, 45. **Open** noon-7pm Mon-Fri; 10am-6pm Sat, Sun. **Credit** Disc, MC, V. **Map** p313 F4. With locations in Berkeley and Marin County, City Front is the place to go if you're a seasoned windsurfer with your own wetsuit and harness. Complete sailing rigs cost around $50 to rent. **Other locations**: 1601 University Avenue, Berkeley (1-510 843 9283); 113 3rd Street, nr East Francisco Boulevard, San Rafael (288 9283).

Yoga

For many San Franciscans, yoga is as vital as coffee at work and drinks afterwards. The city's myriad yoga schools offer a variety of styles, for students of all levels; the Yoga Society (285 5537) is good for general info.

Bikram's Yoga College of India

2nd Floor, 910 Columbus Avenue, at Lombard Street, North Beach (3465400/www.bikramyoga.com). Bus 15, 30, 39/cable car Powell-Mason. **Open** *Classes* 9am, 4.30pm, 6.30pm Mon-Fri; 9am, 4.30pm Sat, Sun. **Rates** $10/class. **Credit** MC, V. **Map** p314 L2. Yogic exercises based on the 'hot yoga' techniques of Bikram Choudhury, who introduced his style to the US in 1971. Bring a towel, though: the classes take place in a sweltering room.

Mindful Body

2876 California Street, at Broderick Street, Pacific Heights (931 2639/www.themindfulbody.com). Bus 1, 24. **Open** 7am-9pm Mon-Fri; 8am-7pm Sat, Sun. **Rates** $13/class. **Credit** MC, V. **Map** p313 G5. The popular Ashtanga class builds endurance, strength and flexibility.

Yoga Tree

1234 Valencia Street, at 23rd Street, Mission (647 9707/www.yogatreesf.com). BART 24th Street/bus 14, 26, 48, 49, 67. **Open** call for class schedule. **Rates** $14/class. **Credit** AmEx, MC, V. **Map** p318 K12. Popular with beginners and good for drop-ins, Yoga Tree has four locations around town and offers daily classes as well as workshops, massage and retreats. **Other locations**: throughout the city.

Arts & Entertainment

Theatre & Dance

From blockbuster to avant-garde, San Francisco makes a song and dance of it.

The *Black Rider*, at the **American Conservatory Theatre**. See p253.

Nothing beats the frisson of live performance, and San Francisco and the Bay Area can keep you on the edge of your seat every night of the week. In contrast to silver-screen-obsessed LA, this is a city of performing arts addicts. Despite the crises brought on by the dot-bomb, small theatres and performing arts spaces have been steadily reclaiming ground abandoned by the retreating forces of the virtual economy.

Given the awesome gravitational pull of New York and LA, it's remarkable how much first-rate talent stays and prospers here. Handsome old houses have helped make SF a desirable launching pad for Broadway-bound plays and musicals. However, regional and fringe theatres also develop new works by both emerging and established playwrights: it was a small, little-known SF company that first produced Tony Kushner's *Angels in America*. The city is also home to a vibrant modern dance scene, taking in everything from the **San Francisco Ballet** (*see p256*) to several ethnic dance ensembles.

INFORMATION & TICKETS

The *Chronicle*'s Sunday 'Datebook' section is accessible online at www.sfgate.com and has extensive listings. *San Francisco Weekly* and the *San Francisco Bay Guardian*, two weekly free sheets, also run reviews and listings. For online listings, check www.bayinsider.com, www.sfarts.org and www.laughingsquid.org.

Prices vary wildly: tickets for some leftfield shows are just $5, but you could pay 30 times that for a blockbuster. To avoid booking fees, call the theatre's own box office, or book online at its website. If you're willing to take a chance, the **TIX Bay Area** booth in Union Square (433 7827, http://tix.theatrebayarea.org) sells half-price tickets for many shows on the day of the performance. It opens at 11am from Tuesday to Friday, and at 10am on weekends. Some venues sell through **Ticketmaster** (512 7770, www.ticketmaster. com); other agencies, some of which charge big fees, include **Mr Ticket** (775 3031, www.mrticket.com), **Tickets.com** (776 1999, www.tickets.com), and **City Box Office** (392 4400, www.cityboxoffice.com). Some theatres run 'pay-what-you-can' schemes on Thursdays (or, at the Magic Theatre, Tuesdays).

Mainstream theatres

A handful of theatres host major touring shows. **Best of Broadway** (www.bestofbroadway-sf.com) offers imports from the Great White Way in three beautiful old rooms: the grand **Orpheum** (1192 Market Street, at Hyde Street) and the 2,300-seat art deco **Golden Gate Theatre** (1 Taylor Street, at Golden Gate Avenue), which both specialise in musicals, and the elegant, intimate **Curran Theatre**

(445 Geary Street, between Mason & Taylor Streets), runs non-musical Broadway and pre-Broadway fare. For information on all three, call 551 2000; for tickets, which typically run from $20 to around $95, call Ticketmaster.

The **Herbst Theatre** (401 Van Ness Avenue, at Grove Street, 392 4400), a cosy 900-seater, hosts local and out-of-town guests, many as part of the **San Francisco Performances** series (*see p228*). Finally, both the 80-year-old **Marines' Memorial Theatre** (609 Sutter Street, at Mason Street, 771 6900) and the **Post Street Theatre** (450 Post Street, between Powell and Mason Streets, 771 6900) present off-Broadway, regional and local productions.

Regional theatres

American Conservatory Theater

Geary Theater, 415 Geary Street, between Mason & Taylor Streets, Tenderloin (information 834 3200/ box office 749 2228/www.act-sfbay.org). Bus 2, 3, 4, 27, 38/cable car Powell-Hyde or Powell-Mason. **Tickets** $12-$80. **Credit** AmEx, MC, V. **Map** p314 L6.
Since opening in 1967, the ACT has been staging modern classics and new works by the likes of David Mamet, earning it a solid reputation, though it's also known for its fine conservatory: alumni include Annette Bening and Denzel Washington. In addition to ACT shows, the exquisite Geary Theater usually also hosts one or two touring productions per season (recently, *Urinetown* and *The Black Rider*) and stages *A Christmas Carol* every year. **Photo** p252.

Magic Theatre

Building D, Fort Mason, Marina Boulevard at Buchanan Street, Marina (441 8822/www.magic theatre.org). Bus 10, 22, 28, 30, 47, 49. **Tickets** $20-$50. **Credit** AmEx, Disc, MC, V. **Map** p314 H2.
Drawing its name from a line in Herman Hesse's *Steppenwolf*, the Magic Theatre has impressed locals over its 40-year history with stagings of ground-breaking works by the likes of Sam Shepard. Since 1977, the theatre has resided within stunning ocular reach of the Golden Gate Bridge, where its two 150-seat houses offer an intriguing mix of new works by both emerging playwrights and leading lights.

<table>
<tr><td>**The
best**</td><td>**Theatre**</td></tr>
</table>

For a blockbuster
Best of Broadway. See p252.

For frolics on the fringe
EXITheater. See right.

For dance, ancient and modern
San Francisco Ballet. See p256.

Fringe theatres & companies

For gay theatre and cabaret, *see p226*.

Asian American Theater Company

New Langton Arts Theater, 1246 Folsom Street, between 8th & 9th Streets, SoMa (information 543 5738/tickets 1-800 838 3006/www.asianamerican theater.org). Bus 12, 27, 42. **Tickets** $10-$25. **Credit** AmEx, MC, V. **Map** p318 L8.
Started by ACT in 1973, AATC fosters work that speaks to the experience of Americans of Asian and Pacific Island descent. Phillip Kan Gotanda and David Henry Hwang are among the theatrical talents nurtured in its first 30 years; both have recently returned to collaborate with the next generation. The emphasis is on new work, and quality can vary wildly.

Beach Blanket Babylon

Club Fugazi, 678 Green Street, between Columbus Avenue & Powell Street, North Beach (421 4222/ www.beachblanketbabylon.com). Bus 12, 15, 30, 41, 45. **Tickets** $25-$75. **Credit** MC, V. **Map** p314 L3.
The longest-running musical revue in theatrical history, *Beach Blanket Babylon* sells its formulaic blend of songs, puns and outrageous headgear with such irresistible conviction that it's become an institution. Featuring an array of tabloid-friendly 'guest stars' from popular culture and the news, this queer eye on the straight world celebrated its 30th year in 2004. Evening performances are for over-21s only.

Crowded Fire

Various venues (675 5995/www.crowdedfire.org). **Tickets** $15-$25. **Credit** MC, V.
Founded in 1997, Crowded Fire is a small but ambitious company that mixes premières with often hard-hitting interpretations of politically charged modern plays by the likes of Caryl Churchill. Socially relevant but with a strong aesthetic bent, the company takes its name from Abbie Hoffman's definition of free speech as the right to yell 'Theatre!' in a crowded fire.

EXITheater

156 Eddy Street, between Mason & Taylor Streets, Tenderloin (931 1094/www.sffringe.org). BART & Metro to Powell/bus 27, 30, 45 & Market Street routes. **Tickets** $10-$20. **No credit cards**. **Map** p314 L6.
This three-stage set-up offers eclectic, provocative shows, from new one-acts to work by well-known authors; Dan Carbone's absurdist *There Be Monsters!* was a recent highlight. The main location has the added attraction of Lily, the sweet and sleepy pooch who guards the door; there's a fourth stage nearby at 277 Taylor Street.

Intersection for the Arts

446 Valencia Street, between 15th & 16th Streets, Mission (information 626 2787/box office 626 3311/ www.theintersection.org). BART 16th Street/bus 14, 26, 33. **Tickets** $9-$15. **Credit** MC, V. **Map** p318 K10.
The oldest alternative space in the city, Intersection is a powerhouse, combining the talents of resident theatre group Campo Santo with visiting playwrights

Arts & Entertainment

such as Denis Johnson and John Steppling. The small theatre isn't hugely comfortable – there are only folding chairs – but performances are intense. There's a great art gallery upstairs.

Last Planet

351 Turk Street, at Hyde Street, Tenderloin (440 3505/www.lastplanettheatre.com). BART & Metro to Civic Center/bus 21, 47, 49 & Market Street routes. **Tickets** $10-$18. **Credit** MC, V. **Map** p314 L6.

Last Planet occupies a high-ceilinged corner of an old, decorative 1928 YMCA building. The 100-seat house has been comfortably renovated, with good sight lines and an exceptionally large stage. Edgy modern pieces by established playwrights, including many an overlooked gem from the dreamier fringes of contemporary drama, are filtered through the company's audacious and rather arch sensibility.

Lorraine Hansberry Theatre

620 Sutter Street, between Mason & Taylor Streets, Nob Hill (474 8800/www.lorrainehansberrytheatre.com). Bus 2, 3, 4, 27, 38, 76/cable car Powell-Hyde or Powell-Mason. **Tickets** $16-$32. **Credit** AmEx, Disc, MC, V. **Map** p314 L5.

The best-known African-American theatre group in the Bay Area produces four or five plays each year, either by black playwrights or dealing with issues affecting the black community. They usually include a must-see musical Christmas offering, such as Langston Hughes's *Black Nativity*.

Marsh

1062 Valencia Street, at 22nd Street, Mission (information 826 5750/tickets 1-800 838 3006/www.themarsh.org). BART 24th Street/bus 14, 26, 49. **Tickets** $8-$22. **Credit** MC, V. **Map** p318 K12.

The Marsh works hard to present new works, priding itself on allowing performers to take risks. Acts here often move on to larger venues in the Bay Area or countrywide (Josh Kornbluth's monologues were launched here), but proceed with caution if you're after a sure thing. The sister venue in Berkeley (2120 Allston Way, at Shattuck Avenue) offers similar fare.

New Conservatory Theatre

25 Van Ness Avenue, between Fell & Oak Streets, Hayes Valley (861 8972/www.nctcsf.org). BART & Metro to Civic Center/bus 21, 47, 49 & Market Street routes. **Tickets** $10-$35. **Credit** AmEx, Disc, MC, V. **Map** p318 K8.

The resident company at this well-designed theatre complex is best known for its annual Pride Season, featuring works about the gay community, and a series of musicals. Recent highlights include the world première of Terrence McNally's *Crucifixion*.

Off-Market Theatres

965 Mission Street, between 5th and 6th Streets, SoMa (896 6477/www.offmarkettheater.com). BART & Metro to Powell/bus 14, 27, 30, 45 & Market Street routes/cable car Powell-Hyde or Powell-Mason. **Tickets** $10-$20. **Credit** varies. **Map** p319 M7.

Arts & Entertainment

Pyromania

Mark Pauline's salt-and-pepper hair and horn-rimmed glasses make him look like a caricature of the Ideal Man of the 1950s. However, appearances can be deceptive: behind this mild-mannered exterior lies the deranged creator of **Survival Research Laboratories** (www.srl.org), purveyors of 'The Most Dangerous Show on Earth' since 1978.

SRL's motto is a nod to PT Barnum's 'Greatest Show on Earth' line, but the key word is 'dangerous'. So dangerous, in fact, that Pauline's right hand had to be surgically reconstructed, when most of his fingers were blown off by one of his creations in 1982. (One of his big toes was transplanted to his hand as a makeshift thumb.) His workshop is a Frankenstein's laboratory of mayhem littered with the detritus of military cast-offs and dismembered industrial hardware.

Performances truly are a spectacle. Paying crowds of thousands routinely leave SRL shows dumbstruck, terrified and sometimes the victims of collateral damage. Regulars bring their own protective gear, including earplugs, safety goggles and even hospital

masks, to counter the assault. But that's precisely the point: to inject an element of terror and danger into onlookers' lives. The shows are not only not intended to be 'safe', they're intended to be a kind of loosely controlled chaos. Gargantuan killer robots and jet-powered death machines (covered with animal hides, bones and sometimes flesh) might clash in warehouses, at piers and parking lots; five pulse-jet engines are arrayed in a circle to create a howling vortex into which fuel is fed, producing a tornado of flames named the Hurricane of Fire.

Performances are designed to walk the fine line of legality. Much adolescent contemporary art attempts to corral sexually explicit material to do its work for it; SRL is a threat not just to propriety, but to law and order itself. Provocative in every sense of the word, this is not simply outsider art, but outlaw art of the highest order. Perhaps unsurprisingly, almost every city in which they have performed has banned them. Seattle, Phoenix, Austin and even their hometown San Francisco refuse to allow them back. For now.

Yerba Buena Center for the Arts.

This SoMa theatre/gallery complex recently opened in space made available to low-budget arts groups in the wake of the dot-com bust. Various smaller companies and troupes appear, but the main stage and the 50-seat studio are now respectively run by the Custom Made Theatre Company (262 0477, www.custommade.org) and the improvisational Lila Theatre (820 1467, www.lilatheatre.org).

Project Artaud Theater

450 Florida Street, between 17th & Mariposa Streets, Mission (626 4370/www.artaud.org). Bus 22, 27, 33. **Tickets** $5-$25. **Credit** MC, V. **Map** p318 L10.
The non-profit Project Artaud offers a variety of new works, often boundary-pushing and hybrid in character, and including everything from one-person plays to modern dance. Two other member theatres share parts of the block-long structure: the Traveling Jewish Theatre (www.atjt.com), with its recently arrived co-resident group foolsFURY (www.foolsfury.org); and Theater of Yugen/Noh Space (www.theatreofyugen.org), specialists in eastern-influenced theatre, Butoh and performance art.

SF Playhouse

536 Sutter Street, between Powell & Mason Streets, Nob Hill (677 9596/www.sfplayhouse.org). Bus 2, 3, 4, 27, 38, 76/cable car Powell-Hyde or Powell-Mason. **Tickets** $18-$36. **Credit** AmEx, MC, V. **Map** p315 M5.
A newcomer to the theatre district, SF Playhouse benefits from its savvy management by a team of seasoned theatre artists. A mid-sized repertory house with high-end sophistication, it's already attracting prime local acting and production talent. The 2005-2006 season opened with a well-received staging of Arthur Miller's *The Crucible*, but you're unlikely to go too far wrong with anything on the menu.

Word for Word

Various venues (437 6775/www.zspace.org). **Tickets** $15-$32. **Credit** MC, V.
Well suited to a famously literary city, this professional theatre company 'brings literature to its feet' by staging short stories by acclaimed authors such as Michael Chabon and Tobias Wolff. The thrilling inventiveness and talent brought to bear on such pop-up book productions has earned the company acclaim from both literature lovers and lazy readers.

Yerba Buena Center for the Arts

701 Mission Street, at 3rd Street, SoMa (978 2787/www.ybca.org). BART & Metro to Montgomery/bus 9, 12, 15, 30, 45, 76. **Tickets** $5-$100. **Credit** AmEx, MC, V. **Map** p315 N6.
This angled, blue-tiled box, one of the city's most striking performance spaces, boasts a wide variety of events, ranging from the Afro Solo Festival to holiday-season must-see *The Velveteen Rabbit*. *See also p82 and p228.*

East Bay theatres & companies

See also p254 **Marsh**.

Aurora Theatre Company

2081 Addison Street, at Shattuck Avenue, Berkeley (1-510 843 4822/www.auroratheatre.org). BART Downtown Berkeley. **Tickets** $28-$45. **Credit** AmEx, MC, V.
Based in a custom-designed 150-seat theatre over in Berkeley, Aurora produces a top-notch five-play season, running the gamut from Shakespeare to Neil LaBute via new translations of Henrik Ibsen. Meticulously crafted small theatre.

Berkeley Repertory Theater

2025 Addison Street, between Shattuck Avenue & Milvia Street, Berkeley (information 1-510 647 2900/tickets 1-510 647 2949/www.berkeleyrep.org). BART Downtown Berkeley. **Tickets** $39-$55. **Credit** AmEx, Disc, MC, V.
The acclaimed Berkeley Rep works here within a 400-seat thrust-stage auditorium and a newer 600-seat proscenium space. Seasons usually comprise a classic drama and several new works, as well as better-known plays by contemporary writers. New neighbour Rita Moreno recently wowed in an excellent revival of Terrence McNally's *Master Class*.

California Shakespeare Theater

Bruns Amphitheatre, 100 Gateway Boulevard, off Cal State 24, Orinda (1-510 548 9666/www.calshakes.org). BART Orinda, then free shuttle bus. **Tickets** $30-$55. **Credit** AmEx, MC, V.
Cal Shakes regularly draws on the best Bay Area and national talent in its inventive presentations of Shakespeare and other classic writers, such as the recent staging of David Edgar's much-admired take on Dickens's *Nicholas Nickleby*. The superb 545-seat Bruns Amphitheatre, opened in 1991 amid sensual

Arts & Entertainment

Festivals Theatre

From June until September, the **San Francisco Mime Troupe** (285 1717, www.sfmt.org) perform political musicals about the evils of genetic engineering and dot-com gentrification in parks around the city. Check online for details. September sees two other events: the two-week **San Francisco Fringe Festival** (931 1033, www.sffringe.org), which features getting on for 300 performances by local, national and international theatre groups, and the **San Francisco Shakespeare Festival** in the Presidio (558 0888, www.sfshakes.org, three weeks of the Bard out in the open air.

rolling hills and the picnic-ready grounds of an adjacent eucalyptus grove, is beautiful, but be sure to pack a coat: with nightfall often comes the foggy ocean air.

Shotgun Players

Ashby Stage, 1901 Ashby Avenue, at Martin Luther King Jr Way, Berkeley (1-510 841 6500/www. shotgunplayers.org). BART Ashby. **Tickets** $15-$30. **Credit** MC, V.

Newly ensconced in its own spiffy space, Shotgun began as an 'underground' theatre (under a Berkeley pizza parlour, to be exact) but is now one of the more popular mid-size companies in the Bay Area. Under Patrick Dooley's bold leadership, it engages in a wide variety of material, from re-imagined Greek tragedies to Dylan Thomas's verse play *Under Milk Wood* and even premières, such as the award-winning *Dog Act* by Liz Duffy Adams.

Dance

In addition to the companies listed below, there is a strong tradition of ethnic dance in SF. The **Lily Cai Chinese Dance Company** (474 4829, www.ccpsf.org) has been blending ancient forms with modern dance since 1988; **Chitresh Das Dance Company** (333 9000, www. kathak.org) performs narrative-driven Kathak dance, one of the six main Indian classical dance forms; and Carolena Nericcio's **Fat Chance Belly Dance** (431 4322, www.fcbd.com) has been performing an 'American Tribal' style of traditional Middle Eastern dancing since 1987.

Alonzo King's Lines

Yerba Buena Center for the Arts; see p255 (information 863 3040/tickets 978 2787/www. linesballet.org). **Tickets** $20-$50.

This excellent contemporary ballet company has been performing primarily new works and tours extensively, both in the US and internationally. It performs two seasons annually at Yerba Buena.

Cal Performances

Zellerbach Hall, UC Berkeley campus, Berkeley (1-510 642 9988/www.calperfs.berkeley.edu). BART Downtown Berkeley. **Tickets** $10-$250. **Credit** AmEx, Disc, MC, V.

An adjunct of UC Berkeley, Cal Performances offers a smattering of everything: dance, music and drama. In the former category, it regularly presents companies from around the country and the globe, such as Alvin Ailey, Twyla Tharp and Mark Morris.

Joe Goode Performance Group

Yerba Buena Center for the Arts; see p255 (information 561 6565/tickets 978 2787/www. joegoode.org). **Tickets** $20-$38.

The JGPG has pushed modern dance to new heights, pursuing with gusto its founder's mission to explore contemporary issues, from gender to AIDS. The company also holds workshops for community groups, including at-risk youth and battered women. It performs at the Yerba Buena Center every June.

ODC

3153 17th Street, between Shotwell Street and Van Ness Avenue, Mission (863 9834/www.odcdance.org). BART 16th Street/bus 14, 22, 33, 49, 53. **Tickets** $10-$40. **Credit** AmEx, MC, V. **Map** p318 K10.

Founded in 1971, in Ohio's Oberlin College, the Oberlin Dance Collective clambered on a yellow bus and headed for San Francisco in 1976. Since then, the group has focused on creating innovative works of modern dance, but has also used its business savvy to open its own school, gallery and theatre, which stages a variety of works all year round; ODC itself also performs twice a year at the Yerba Buena Center for the Arts.

San Francisco Ballet

War Memorial Opera House, 301 Van Ness Avenue, between Grove & McAllister Streets, Civic Center (information 861 5600/tickets 865 2000/www.sf ballet.org). BART & Metro to Civic Center/bus 21, 47, 49 & Market Street routes. **Tickets** $12-$135. **Credit** AmEx, MC, V. **Map** p318 K7.

Founded in 1933, this is the longest-running professional US ballet company. In 1939 it presented the first full-length US production of *Coppélia*, followed in 1940 by the country's first complete *Swan Lake* and first full-length *Nutcracker* (1944). The company is based in the War Memorial Opera House (*see p227*); its annual season (February to May) is typically an even blend of traditional pieces and new works.

Smuin Ballets

Yerba Buena Center for the Arts; see p255 (information 495 2234/tickets 978 2787/www. smuinballet.org). **Tickets** $35-$50.

How many ballets can claim a film appearance, let alone in *Return of the Jedi*? Founded in 1994 by Michael Smuin, former director of the SF Ballet (*see above*), this innovative group wowed the crowds with *Dancin' with Gershwin* in 2001 and *To the Beatles Revisited* in 2002. Performances take place in winter and late spring at the Yerba Buena Center.

Trips Out of Town

Features

Muir Woods. *See p261.*

Getting Started

Get out of town!

Ask any resident of San Francisco why they live where they live, and high on their list of reasons will be the world that surrounds their city. San Francisco isn't just a world-class city: it's also ringed on three sides by varied and inviting landscape. North of San Francisco lie cute villages, rugged countryside, gourmet restaurants and an array of world-famous wineries; to the south sit more delightful small towns, some breathtaking coastline and great opportunities for sports as varied as surfing and golf. Everything is within easy, day-tripping reach; the only problem the locals have is making the time to see it all.

Close to San Francisco are the sleepy fishing villages, wildlife refuges and amazing redwoods of **Marin County** (*see pp259-263*), or **Wine Country** (*see pp264-270*), with its vineyards and spas. Further afield lie the celebrated golf courses of the **Monterey Peninsula** (*see pp278-280*), the exhilarating ski slopes and watersports of **Lake Tahoe** (*see p271*) and the soaring peaks of **Yosemite** (*see p273*).

For more information, or to plan your trip in advance, contact the tourist information centres listed in this chapter; they're generally very well organised, have good websites and will send out a visitor pack on request. All phone numbers are listed as if dialled from San Francisco. For a map of the Bay Area and surrounding coast, *see p306*.

TRANSPORT
While a car is a hindrance when staying in San Francisco, it's virtually a necessity when travelling outside it. BART (*see p283*) connects San Francisco with the East Bay, while Golden Gate Transit has a regular schedule of bus services to and from many Marin County destinations; you can also use Greyhound buses, Amtrak (via Oakland station), a charter tour or even take the ferries. But if your budget permits, rent a car; it's simply the easiest way to explore the area. For rental firms, *see p285*.

Trips Out of Town

The best Trips

For drinking and driving
Head into **Wine Country**. See pp264-270.

For hiking and biking
Take a trip over the Golden Gate Bridge to the wilds of **Marin County**. See pp259-261.

For skiing and sightseeing
Drive first to **Lake Tahoe** and then south to **Yosemite**. See pp271-274.

For more on the state of California, pick up the 416-page **Time Out California** (UK: Ebury, £13.99; US: PGW, $19.95), available from www.timeout.com and from all good bookstores.

Heading North

Just over the Golden Gate Bridge, wilderness awaits.

The stunning, rugged **Marin Headlands**, just north of San Francisco.

The Golden Gate Bridge sometimes seems the only link between bustling San Francisco and languid **Marin County**. The city's wealthy northern neighbour, Marin extends from **Sausalito**, a quarter-hour by car from San Francisco, to **Bodega Bay** and inland to **Novato**; the protected parkland that sprawls across the county leaves it virtually immune to overpopulation. Of the county's towns, those on the east side (**Tiburon**, Sausalito, **Mill Valley**) tend to be well heeled and staid, while those on the western coast (**Stinson Beach**, **Point Reyes Station** and, notoriously, **Bolinas**) are more bohemian.

Sausalito to Larkspur

The first exit north of the Golden Gate Bridge, **Vista Point**, offers amazing views. Pull off at the following exit, Alexander Avenue, for the **Bay Area Discovery Museum** (see p205), an interactive museum geared towards youngsters that's snuggled in Fort Baker, at the northern foot of the bridge. Just north, the **Marin Headlands** offer nearly endless opportunities for outdoor activity, as well as breathtaking views of the city and the wide-open Pacific Ocean. Here, too, is the **Marine Mammal Center** (289 7325, www.tmmc.org), a sanctuary for injured seals and sea lions.

Sausalito, the southernmost Marin County town, is not as quaint as its reputation suggests, but it is picturesque, with a maze of tiny streets stretching from the shoreline all the way up to US 101. Originally a fishing village, the town is now home to prosperous artists, yacht owners and well-off businessfolk. The ferry from San Francisco's Pier 41 or Ferry Building, which provides great views of the Golden Gate Bridge and Alcatraz from the top deck, docks Downtown, all manicured gardens and pretty bungalows. Along North Bridgeway, opposite Spring Street, is the turn-off for the **San Francisco Bay Model Visitor Center** (see p260). Across Richardson Bay is tiny downtown **Tiburon**. Again, there are no real sights, just the temptation to enjoy a lingering meal at one of the harbour-view restaurants on Main Street. However, it's also notable as the departure point for the ferry to **Angel Island**.

Sausalito. *See p259.*

Marin County lacks a real centre: though sizeable, Marin City, Corte Madera and Fairfax aren't very interesting unless you're shopping for a BMW or a hot tub. It is, however, worth taking the North San Pedro Road exit off US 101 towards **San Rafael**. On the north side of the city is Frank Lloyd Wright's grand **Marin Civic Center** (Avenue of the Flags, 499 6400, www.marincenter.org), fondly nicknamed 'Big Pink', while a post-war replica of **Mission San Rafael Arcangel** sits on 5th Avenue. Smaller than the 1817 original, the mission has a cemetery that contains the mortal remains of once-rebellious, then-contrite Chief Marin.

From there, head to **Mill Valley**, at the bottom of Mount Tamalpais, where yuppies enjoy charming boutiques and restaurants, as well as a prestigious film festival (*see p208* **Festivals**). You'll also find picnic-friendly **Tennessee Beach** (331 1540), accessible from Highway 101. Take the Mill Valley/Shoreline Highway exit towards Stinson Beach, then turn left on Tennessee Valley Road, which ends in the parking area a mile from the beach. The **Miwok Livery Stables** (701 Tennessee Valley Road, 383 8048, www.miwokstables. com) are also around here. Quaint **Larkspur** is still little frequented by tourists, though it's still visited by them more often than is the nearby **San Quentin Prison**.

San Francisco Bay Model Visitor Center

2100 Bridgeway, at Olive Street, Sausalito (332 3870/www.spn.usace.army.mil/bmvc). **Open** *Labor Day-Memorial Day* 9am-4pm Tue-Sat. *Memorial Day-Labor Day* 9am-4pm Tue-Fri; 10am-5pm Sat. **Admission** free.

This two-acre 1:5-scale hydraulic model of San Francisco Bay and delta was built in 1957 as a means of demonstrating how navigation, recreation and ecology interact. As such, it prevented the construction of various dams that would have disastrously altered the bay's tidal range. There are walkways over the model, from which you can watch a complete lunar day in under 15 minutes.

Where to eat, drink & stay

Bridgeway, Sausalito's main drag, proffers excellent seafood at **Horizons** (No.558, 331 3232, www.horizonssausalito.com, $15-$28). In **Tiburon**, try Main Street: most come to eat, drink Margaritas and take in the views from **Guaymas** (No.5, 435 6300, www. guaymas.com, mains $15-$25), or for the excellent weekend brunch at **Sam's Anchor Café** (No.27, 435 4527, mains $15-$25), which invites you to accompany some hard liquor on to the waterfront deck.

Larkspur's highly regarded **Lark Creek Inn** (234 Magnolia Avenue, 924 7766, www. larkcreek.com, closed lunch Sat, mains $19-$31) is a lovely Victorian house with giant sloping skylights, in a grove of redwoods. Its organic salads and vegetables come from the farmers' market. **Left Bank** (507 Magnolia Avenue, 927 3331, www.leftbank.com, mains $14-$30) is a quasi-Parisian bistro. The first-rate **Marin Brewing Company** (1809 Larkspur Landing Circle, 461 4677, www.marinbrewing.com) is a good spot for a brew and some bar food. In Mill Valley, visit ski-lodge-style **Buckeye Roadhouse** (15 Shoreline Highway, 331 2600, www.buckeyeroadhouse.com, mains $12-$30), which offers upscale all-American food.

If you're in this part of the world, you're likely day-tripping. However, one great alternative to lodging in San Francisco is to stay at the **Inn Above Tide** in Sausalito (30 El Portal, 1-800 893 8433, 332 9535, www. innabovetide.com, $265-$865), where all the pleasingly handsome bayside rooms offer wonderful views of San Francisco.

Getting there

By car

Take US 101 across the Golden Gate Bridge. For Sausalito (8 miles from San Francisco), take the Alexander Avenue or Spencer Avenue exit. For Mill Valley (10 miles) and Larkspur, take the East

Blithedale exit; you can also reach Larkspur by the Paradise Drive or Lucky Drive exits. For Tiburon, turn off here but follow the signs to Highway 131.

By bus

Golden Gate Transit runs bus services from San Francisco to Sausalito (route 10), Tiburon and Mill Valley (routes 10, 70 or 80 to Marin City, then route 15) and for Larkspur (routes 70 or 80 to Corte Madera, then routes 18 or 22), but taking the ferry and connecting to a bus there is usually far quicker. See schedules at www.goldengate.org.

By ferry

Golden Gate Transit ferries run daily from the Ferry Building on the Embarcadero to Sausalito and Larkspur; the Blue & Gold Fleet sails to Tiburon from the Ferry Building, and to Sausalito and Angel Island from Pier 41, Fisherman's Wharf.

Tourist information

Mill Valley *Mill Valley Chamber of Commerce, 85 Throckmorton Avenue (388 9700/www.millvalley. org).* **Open** *9am-noon Tue-Fri, or by appt.*
Sausalito *Sausalito Chamber of Commerce & Visitor Center, Bay 2, Suite 250, 10 Liberty Ship Way (331 7262/www.sausalito.org).* **Open** *Chamber of Commerce 9am-5pm Mon-Fri. Historical Exhibit & Visitor Centre (331 1093).* **Open** *11.30am-4pm Tue-Sun.*

Angel Island

The largest island in the San Francisco Bay is a delightful, wild place with a fascinating history. Camp Reynolds, in the east of the island, was established in 1863 by Union troops to protect the bay against a Confederate attack; later, from 1910 to 1940, the west of the island became the site of a US government immigration station set to screen immigrants under the terms of the 1882 Chinese Exclusion Act. Known as 'the Ellis Island of the West', Angel Island was notorious. Boatloads of Chinese immigrants were detained for months so officials could interrogate them; many were eventually sent home, never having touched the mainland. During World War II, Angel Island was an equally unwelcome home to German and Japanese POWs. The military remained in control through the '50s and '60s, when the island served as a Nike missile base (still closed to the public), but in 1963 the land was finally ceded to the government as a state park.

Ayala Cove, where the ferry docks, has a visitors' centre (435 1915) and also marks the beginning of the five-mile Perimeter Trail, which will take you past the immigration station, wooden Civil War barracks and other military remnants hidden among the trees. At 797 feet (243 metres), the peak of **Mount Livermore** affords a panoramic view of the bay from the island's centre. There's a wonderful diversity of bird and animal species on the island, from deer to seals, pelicans to hummingbirds. You'll also find **Quarry Beach**, a sheltered sunbathing strip popular with kayakers. Those who don't want to walk can take the tram tour and anyone who wants to stay overnight can pitch up at the campsite. For details of camping, guided tours, and bike or kayak rental, see www.angelisland.org; if you do want to camp, book well in advance.

Getting there

By ferry

The Angel Island ferry (435 2131, $7.50-$10 return) runs from Tiburon, daily in summer and weekends only in winter. Schedule information can be found at www.angelislandferry.com.

Mount Tamalpais & Muir Woods

Mount Tamalpais State Park covers 6,200 acres (ten square miles) on the western and southern slopes of the peak. Visible from as far away as Sonoma, the mountain itself soars to nearly 2,600 feet (almost 800 metres), but its rise is so steep it seems far taller. Beautiful at any time of day, it's magnificent at sunset. The roads that snake over Mount Tam, while challenging, are great for hiking and for bicycling; indeed, the mountain bike was invented here. The **Mount Tamalpais Interpretive Association** (258 2410, www.mttam.net) offers organised group hikes. If you're feeling adventurous, call the **San Francisco Hanggliding Center** (1-510 528 2300, www.sfhanggliding.com).

Nearby **Muir Woods National Monument** (388 7059, www.visitmuirwoods.com, $3) contains majestic groves of towering coastal redwoods, many over 500 years old. You'll find several miles of trails here, of which one, the mile-long Main Trail Loop, is accessible to the disabled. Redwood Creek is lined with madrone and big-leaf maple trees, wildflowers (even in winter), ferns and wild berry bushes. Deer, chipmunks and a variety of birds live peacefully among the redwoods, while the creek is a migratory route for steelhead trout and silver salmon. To avoid crowds, visit on weekday mornings and late afternoons.

Where to eat, drink & stay

The restaurant at the English-styled **Pelican Inn** (10 Pacific Way, 1-415 383 6000, closed dinner Mon, mains $15-$25) is not great, but it's

Trips Out of Town

the best eating option near the beach. It's also a fine hotel (from $201): quaint rooms have canopied beds, balconies and private bathrooms. Rugged travellers should try the 100-year-old **West Point Inn** (646 0702, www.westpointinn.com, $35), a collection of five rustic cabins that's a two-mile hike up Mount Tam from **Pantoll Ranger Station** (388 2070). Guests bring their own sleeping bags and cook grub in a communal kitchen. There's no electricity, but nothing beats the views.

Getting there

By car

Take US 101 across the Golden Gate Bridge, then turn on to Highway 1. Muir Woods is 15 miles from San Francisco.

By bus

Launched in 2005, a free shuttle bus, No.66, runs from Marin City to Muir Woods on weekends and holidays from Memorial Day to Labor Day. Otherwise, Golden Gate Transit bus 63 goes from Marin City to Stinson Beach and local trailheads from mid Mar to mid Dec, and to Audubon Canyon Ranch from Mar to July.

Tourist information

Mount Tamalpais *Mount Tamalpais State Park (388 2070/www.parks.ca.gov)*. **Open** 7am-sunset daily.
Muir Woods *Muir Woods Visitor Center (388 2595/www.visitmuirwoods.com)*. **Open** 8am-sunset daily. **Admission** $3.

Stinson Beach & Bolinas Beach

The drive from Mill Valley to Stinson Beach along **Panoramic Highway** is long and filled with dangerous hairpin bends, with deer apt to make appearances frighteningly close to the road. Nonetheless, the route is gorgeous, with redwoods casting shadows on to the road and ferns dotting the ground along the way, and takes you to affluent and pleasantly new age **Stinson Beach**. Stinson was only connected to Sausalito by a dirt road in 1870; prior to that, sole access was by boat, and there's still a delicious sense of isolation. Stinson is home to **Shakespeare at Stinson** (868 1115, www.shakespeareatstinson.org), a theatre company that puts on shows in a 155-seat outdoor theatre from May to October.

A good reason to visit is the **beach**, prettier and much warmer than San Francisco's Ocean Beach. Lifeguards are on duty May through October, and there's a 50-acre park with more than 100 picnic tables. All-nude **Red Rock Beach** (www.redrockbeach.com) is a bare half mile south of downtown. Just north of Stinson

Beach is the pristine **Bolinas Lagoon Preserve** (4900 Highway 1, 868 9244, www.egret.org). The Alice Kent Trail leads to an observation point, from which you can see egrets and great blue herons.

Between the lagoon and the Pacific is **Bolinas**, a beachside hamlet far enough off the beaten track for locals to find it worthwhile binning road signs to dissuade outsiders. But if you can, navigate your way into town and to the beach, which has small enough waves to be a great spot for novice surfers: try **Bolinas Surf Lessons** (2 Mile Surf Shop, 22 Brighton Avenue, 868 0264, www.surfbolinas.com). The water is also excellent for kayaking and fishing; camping, campfires and dogs are allowed on the beach. The town is a haven for writers and artists, as the **Bolinas Museum** (48 Wharf Road, 868 0330, www.bolinasmuseum.org, closed Mon-Thur) makes clear. At the banding station of nearby **Point Reyes Bird Observatory** (900 Mesa Road, 868 1221, www.prbo.org), the public can watch biologists catch and release birds, using special 'mist' nets, every day except Mondays from May to late November, and on Wednesday, Saturday and Sunday mornings during winter.

Where to eat, drink & stay

The thing to eat in Stinson is, of course, seafood: try the **Stinson Beach Grill** (3465 Highway 1, 868 2002, mains $10-$25) for posh dining or the lunches at **Sand Dollar Restaurant** (3458 Shoreline Highway, 1-415 868 0434, mains $9-$32). Bolinas has only a few choice spots: on Wharf Road, try the **Coast Café** (No.46, 868 2224, www.bolinashotel.com, closed Mon, mains $8-$20) or the **Blue Heron Inn** (No.11, 868 1102, www.blueheronbolinas.com, reservations only, closed Tue & Wed, mains $15-$23). For a pint, the **Saloon at Smiley's** (*see below*) has been in the business for more than 150 years, and claims to be the second oldest bar in California.

Accommodation-wise, Stinson's cute and simple **Sandpiper** (1 Marine Way, 1-877 557 4737, 868 1632, www.sfbay.net/sandpiper, $95-$195) has rooms and cabins within walking distance of the waves, while the funky **Stinson Beach Motel** (3416 Highway 1, 868 1712, www.stinsonbeachmotel.com, $85-$200) is in the town centre. If you'd like the comforts of home by the beach in Bolinas, rent one: phone ahead for the address of the **Beach House** (927 2644, www.bolinasbeach.net), where up to four people can be accommodated for $190-$200 a night. Otherwise, try **Smiley's Schooner Saloon & Hotel** (41 Wharf Road, 868 1311, $76-$87).

Getting there

By car
Take US 101 across the Golden Gate Bridge and then, at Marin City, pick up Highway 1. This will lead you to Stinson Beach and (follow the signs) to Bolinas.

By bus
Golden Gate Transit's 63 service runs from Marin City to Stinson Beach. The West Marin Stagecoach (www.marin-stagecoach.org) operates four buses a day from Marin City to Stinson Beach and Bolinas.

Point Reyes National Seashore

If you head north from Stinson Beach on Highway 1, you'll come to the **Bear Valley Visitor Center** (*see below*) near Olema. The centre acts as the entry point for the most famous parcel of land in these parts: the vast wilderness of **Point Reyes National Seashore**. This protected peninsula is an extraordinary wildlife refuge, with sea mammals, waterfalls and miles of unspoilt beaches. From the visitor centre, you can either head west towards the coast for **Drake's Beach**, or go north via Inverness to the tip of the peninsula: **Point Reyes Lighthouse** (669 1534, closed Tue, Wed) is a perfect lookout for whale-watching. Several trails also start here, including the popular Chimney Rock. Nearby **Inverness** is picturesque, with many homes still owned by the families that built them, while tiny **Point Reyes Station** bustles along its three-block Downtown; both were visited in 2005 by Prince Charles and Camilla on their US tour. Make a note to check in at the **Cowgirl Creamery** (80 4th Street, 663 9335, www.cowgirlcreamery.com), where you can try a bounty of fine local cheeses.

Natural historians and those with more energy than is good for them should press on along Highway 1 to **Tomales Bay**. There, **Blue Waters Kayaking** (12938 Sir Francis Drake Boulevard, at the Golden Hinde Inn, 669 2600, www.bwkayak.com) offers half- or full-day paddle trips, and (by appointment) romantic full-moon tours.

Where to eat, drink & stay

In Point Reyes Station, the **Station House Café** (Main Street, 663 1515, www.station housecafe.com, closed Wed, mains $7-$20) is a mellow place that serves California cuisine, while the **Pine Cone Diner** (60 4th Street, 663 1536, www.pineconediner.com, mains $3-$7) is a sweet, much-treasured retro spot for breakfast or lunch.

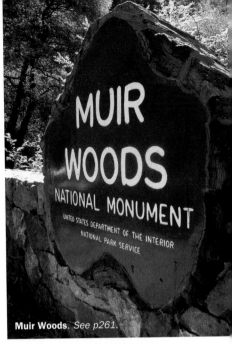

Muir Woods. *See p261.*

Built as a hunting and fishing lodge, **Manka's Inverness Lodge** (30 Callender Way, Inverness, 669 1034, www.mankas.com, $215-$565) serves as both a terrific restaurant (dinner only, closed Jan-mid Feb) and a lodging place, with eight rooms, a suite, two cabins and a dramatic 1911 boathouse over the water. Breakfast is served to lodge guests only.

Since 1876, Olema has been home to the charming **Olema Inn** (10000 Sir Francis Drake Boulevard, 663 9559, www.theolemainn.com, $145-$185). In Point Reyes, try art-heavy **Abalone Inn** (12355 Sir Francis Drake Boulevard, 663 9149, 1-877 416 0458, www. abaloneinn.com, $110-$150) or **Knob Hill** (40 Knob Hill Road, 663 1784, doubles $70-$160).

Getting there

By car
Take US 101 across the Golden Gate Bridge, then Highway 1. Point Reyes is 32 miles from SF.

By bus
There is no direct public transport to Point Reyes.

Tourist information

Point Reyes National Seashore *Bear Valley Visitor Center (464 5100/www.nps.gov/pore).* **Open** 9am-5pm Mon-Fri; 8am-5pm Sat, Sun. *Lighthouse Visitor Center Point (669 1534/www.nps. gov/pore).* **Open** 10am-4.30pm Mon, Thur-Sun, weather permitting.

Wine Country

Where beautiful country makes beautiful wines.

It takes only an hour to drive from San Francisco to Napa and Sonoma Counties, but it really is another world out here. Rolling hills planted with lush rows of tangled vines attest to the region's major industry, but it's the nature of the place that really shocks the system after frantic Frisco. This is not high country, but it's certainly *haute* California.

Since pioneering Hungarian farmer Agoston Haraszthy de Mokcsa planted his 500-acre Buena Vista wine estate in the middle of the 19th century, Wine Country has changed hugely. From modest beginnings, the wine industry has become masterful at marketing itself. It's not just wine they sell so successfully – what Wine Country does better than any of the state's other wine-producing regions is sell a lifestyle: idyllic, cultured, romantic and deluxe.

It's a lifestyle to which five million visitors a year aspire. Summer here is ridiculously busy, so the best times to visit are spring, when the hills are verdant and the vineyards carpeted with mustard flowers, and autumn, when the burnished light and auburn vine leaves lend the place a calming ambience.

NAPA AND SONOMA

The region is separated into the Napa and Sonoma Valleys, located on either side of a low-lying mountain range. Of the two, **Napa** is the largest, the most famous and the most popular. **Sonoma** is far smaller and slower, retaining much of its bucolic charm, but Napa no longer lays sole claim to tarted-up cow towns: Sonoma has its share of chic hotels and shops. And no town in either valley is more than a stone's throw from countryside dotted with vines and cows. Most higher-priced wineries are in Napa, but alongside industry behemoths are smaller wineries, many family-owned. Even in Napa you'll find 'crossroads wineries', off the main route, that don't charge for tastings, a practice now standard at the majority of tasting rooms.

Wining here is as important as dining. Many wineries have picnic areas, but it's courteous to buy a bottle to enjoy with your feast at the gratis table. Plenty of restaurants allow BYOB: check the corkage fee when booking, and do purchase something from the wine list if you're planning to consume more than one bottle.

Most wineries are open daily. They generally charge a nominal amount for tastings of several wines and, in some cases, a tour. For a guide to the labels and grapes, *see below* **Grape expectations**. The classic Wine Country route winds through both valleys. Drive up Highway 29 to Calistoga, hitting the towns of Napa, Yountville, Oakville, Rutherford and St Helena on the way. From Calistoga, head west for 12

Grape expectations

Not all Californian wines are widely available outside the state, so here's a guide to which label does what. Huge volume of fruit and flavour is the hallmark of today's Californian wines; common varieties include crisp chardonnays, big cabernet sauvignons, soft merlots, sauvignon blancs, pinot noirs, rieslings and the versatile zinfandel.

Napa labels

Bouchon (pinot, chardonnay); **Carneros Creek** (pinot noir); **Chimney Rock** (chardonnay, cabernet); **Clos Pégase** (cabernet, chardonnay, merlot, petite syrah, port); **Cuvaison** (cabernet, chardonnay); **Joseph Phelps** (chardonnay); **Opus One** (cabernet); **Pine Ridge** (chardonnay, cabernet, merlot); **Robert Sinskey** (pinot noir); **Silver Oak** (cabernet); **Stag's Leap** (cabernet, chardonnay, sauvignon blanc).

Sonoma labels

Cline (zinfandel); **Dry Creek** (chardonnay); **Field Stone** (cabernet, petite syrah); **Foppiano** (petite syrah, zinfandel); **Geyser Peak** (chardonnay); **Gundlach Bundschu** (merlot, pinot noir, chardonnay, cabernet, zinfandel); **Lambert Bridge** (fumé blanc, pinot noir, zinfandel); **Matanzas Creek** (chardonnay); **Pezzi King** (pinot noir, zinfandel, cabernet); **Roche** (chardonnay, pinot noir); **Shug** (pinot noir).

Clos Pegase: giving the finger to their rivals in Napa Valley. *See p267.*

miles to Fulton, taking Petrified Forest Road to Highway 101, and then take Route 12 south through the Sonoma Valley.

Napa Valley

The 30-mile-long Napa Valley, on the east side of the Mayacamas Mountains, was originally settled by the Wappo Indian tribe several centuries ago. The Gold Rush of the 1850s saw its population grow, with Europeans as well as Californians; Prussian immigrant Charles Krug introduced grapes here in 1861.

The valley, bisected by the Napa River, runs from the San Pablo Bay's fertile Carneros region north to Calistoga. There are now 250 commercial vineyards here, along with smaller 'custom crush' wineries. Many are situated on the often-busy **Highway 29** (aka the St Helena Highway), which runs up the centre of the valley; along the way, towns and villages offer dining and shopping opportunities. Boutique wineries are found mostly on the **Silverado Trail**, a more scenic and less cramped artery to the east, or on the lanes that criss-cross the valley. Alternatively, take the **Wine Train** (1-707 253 2111, www.winetrain.com), which runs between Napa and St Helena or Rutherford. Rides on the lovingly restored pre-1950s Pullman coaches start at $47.50.

Towns & attractions

Once a blue-collar town, Napa has grown increasingly tourist-oriented over the last few years. Most of the changes have centred on historic Downtown, where the national attention paid to the opening of **COPIA** (*see below*) helped stimulate plenty of investment. It's a livelier place than ever.

North of here, things get more genteel. **Yountville** is white-collar territory, with posh restaurants and immaculate hotels and upscale shops. The tidy towns of **Rutherford** and **Oakville** are both dominated by the wineries that surround them, but **St Helena**, further north, has real charm, and can be enjoyed in a more modest way than its shiny veneer suggests. It's Wine Country's most popular town, and home to the **Robert Louis Stevenson Silverado Museum** (*see p265*).

Calistoga is one of Wine Country's more interesting place, because it barely relies on the wine industry: it's the geothermal springs that draw visitors. The town is awash with spas offering treatments, from dips in mineral pools to baths in volcanic ash. Among them are the charming, 50-year-old **Dr Wilkinson's Hot Springs Resort** (1507 Lincoln Avenue, 1-707 942 4102, www.drwilkinson.com, rooms $109-$199, treatments $55-$137) and the **Golden Haven** (1713 Lake Street, 1-707 942 6793, www.goldenhaven.com, rooms $79-$199, treatments $45-$155); for more, check with the Chamber of Commerce. The town's other draw is the little **Old Faithful Geyser** (www.oldfaithfulgeyser.com), one of only three geysers on earth that blast out water and steam at regular intervals – around every 40 minutes – to heights from 60 to 100 feet (around 20 to 30 metres).

COPIA: The American Center for Wine, Food & the Arts

500 1st Street, Napa (1-800 512 6742/1-707 259 1600/www.copia.org). **Open** 10am-5pm Mon, Wed-Sun. **Admission** $12.50; $7.50-$10 discounts; free under-12s. **Credit** AmEx, Disc, MC, V.

A vast $50m facility, COPIA puts a new spin on the museum concept in its celebrations of eating, drinking and living well. Art and interactive

Trips Out of Town

exhibits line the walls; cooking demonstrations crop up on the calendar, as do concerts and other performances in the outdoor amphitheatre. There are, of course, daily wine tastings, a well-stocked gift shop and a couple of good eating options, including Julia's Kitchen (1-707 265 5700). **Photo** *p268.*

Robert Louis Stevenson Silverado Museum

1490 Library Lane, St Helena (1-707 963 3757).
Open noon-4pm Tue-Sun. **Admission** free.
No credit cards.
Robert Louis Stevenson, who honeymooned on Mount St Helena, came over all poetic about Napa's natural splendours – and its wines – in books such as *The Silverado Squatters.* The collection here includes manuscripts, his wedding ring and marriage licence, and the last words he ever wrote.

Wineries

Traffic permitting, you're rarely more than a ten-minute drive from a winery in the Napa Valley. Though Napa itself doesn't have any, it does have a number of fine tasting rooms, led by the **Vintner's Collective** (1245 Main Street, 1-707 255 7150, www.vintnerscollect ive.com). The notable wineries south-west of the town, along or off the Carneros Highway towards Sonoma, include **Domaine Carneros** (1240 Duhig Road, 1-707 257 0101, www. domaine.com), where the pinot you'll be sipping is sparkling: the winery is a satellite of Taittinger. The views are spectacular, as they are from the terrace at off-the-beaten-track **Artesa Vineyards & Winery** (1345 Henry Road, 1-707 224 1668, www.artesawinery.com).

The leading winery near Yountville is **Domaine Chandon** (1 California Drive, 1-707 944 2280, www.chandon.com), which offers an excellent tour ($5) introducing visitors to its interpretation of méthode champenoise. Good local wineries sit close by on the Silverado Trail: at **Pine Ridge** (No.5901, 1-707 575 9777, www.pineridgewinery.com), you can enjoy barrel-to-bottle tastings and a caves tour (by appointment). Oakville is home to the popular **Robert Mondavi Winery** (7801 St Helena Highway, 1-707 226 1335, www.robertmondavi winery.com, reservations recommended), a good bet for first-timers, and the unstuffy **PlumpJack** (620 Oakville Crossroad, 1-707 945 1220, www.plumpjack.com).

Another cluster of wineries draws oenophiles to Rutherford. **Mumm** (8445 Silverado Trail, 1-707 967 7700, www.mummcuveenapa.com) has a collection of Ansel Adams photographs, while Francis Ford Coppola's **Niebaum-Coppola Winery** (1991 St Helena Highway, 1-707 968 1161, www.niebaum-coppola.com) has memorabilia from the great man's movies. **St Supéry** (8440 St Helena Highway, 1-707 963 4507, www.stsupery.com) encourages novices with tastings suitable for first-timers.

The list of wineries in St Helena is led by historic **Beringer** (2000 Main Street, 1-707 963 7115, www.beringer.com), where events

Trips Out of Town

run from a $5 half-hour tour to a glorious two-hour Saturday picnic ($65). **Charles Krug** (2800 Main Street, 1-800 682 5784, www.charleskrug.com), founded in 1861, enhances its wines with summer chocolate tastings; **Burgess Cellars** (1108 Deer Park Road, 1-707 963 4766, www.burgesscellars.com, tastings by appointment only) is a beautiful mountainside winery. Two relative curios are **Prager** (1281 Lewelling Lane, 1-707 963 7678, www.pragerport.com), where the speciality is port, and the **Silverado Brewing Company** (3020A St Helena Highway, 1-707 967 9876, www.silveradobrewingcompany.com), for those more interested in the grain than the grape. Up the road in Calistoga, try **Clos Pegase** (1060 Dunaweal Lane, 1-707 942 4981, www.clospegase.com); for the wines, sure, but also for the architecture (by Michael Graves) and the sculpture garden.

Where to eat & drink

As well as a chic hotel (the **Napa River Inn**; *see p268*), a new jazz club (**DG's**, 1-707 253 8474), a pastry shop and a day spa, the restored Napa Mill in Napa houses several fine eateries. 'Global comfort food' is no oxymoron at **Celadon** (500 Main Street, 1-707 254 9690, mains $17-$26), with the likes of flash-fried calamari and braised Moroccan lamb, while Greg Cole's **Angèle** (540 Main Street, 1-707 252 8115, mains $20-$32) is a favourite spot

for terrace drinks and French country cooking. The river patio of the **Napa General Store** (540 Main Street, 1-707 259 0762, mains $7-$15) is good for salads, sandwiches and thin pizzas.

Yountville is renowned around the world as the home of the **French Laundry** (6640 Washington Street, 1-707 944 2380, set menu $175), regularly identified as the greatest restaurant on earth. Prices are immense, and you'll have to book two months in advance, but you'll get a world-class meal. Thomas Keller, lord of the Laundry, also runs urbane **Bouchon** (6534 Washington Street, 1-707 944 8037, mains $20-$25), where the French menu is priced more moderately. Philippe Jeanty's the other big name, with the casual **Bistro Jeanty** (6510 Washington Street, 1-707 944 0103, mains $20-$34) his signature spot. In Rutherford, the **Rutherford Grill** (1180 Rutherford Road, 1-707 963 1792, mains $10-$29) wins out with reasonable prices and American fare.

St Helena options are plentiful: for breakfast, try the **Model Bakery** (1357 Main Street, 1-707 963 8192, mains $4-$7); for lunch, there's **Ana's Cantina** (1205 Main Street, 1-707 963 4921, mains $8-$11) or the 1949-vintage **Taylor's Refresher** (933 Main Street, 1-707 963 3486, mains $4-$12), offering terrific 1950s-style burgers and shakes. For dinner, **Martini House** (1245 Spring Street, 1-707 963 2233, mains $25-$32) celebrates Napa's bounty with top-quality cooking and, at the downstairs Wine Cellar bar, a huge list of wines.

Scenes from Wine Country.

Trips Out of Town

Beyond the grapevine: **COPIA** (*left*; *see p265*), and wine retailers in **Sonoma** (*see p269*).

Calistoga's restaurants are mainly concentrated on Lincoln Avenue: sturdy American classics dominate at **Brannan's** (No.1374, 1-707 942 2233, mains $19-$31) and the great **Flatiron Grill** (No.1440, 1-707 942 1220, mains $12-$22).

Where to stay

Lodgings around Napa run the gamut from quaint Queen Anne-style B&Bs to full resorts. The sleek, luxurious **Carneros Inn** (4048 Carneros Highway, 1-707 299 4900, www.the carnerosinn.com, $400-$1,200), just south-west of Napa, fits into the latter category: its 86 ultra-modern cottages have fireplaces, flat-panel televisions and outdoor showers. In the Napa Mill, you'll find the deluxe, 66-room **Napa River Inn** (500 Main Street, 1-877 251 8500, 1-707 251 8500, www.napariverinn.com, $180-$500). The **Oak Knoll Inn** (2200 E Oak Knoll Avenue, 1-707 255 2200, www.oakknollinn.com, $285-$550) is one of the valley's most luxurious B&Bs; while, if you've had enough of all things quaint, the **John Muir Inn** (1998 Trower Avenue, 1-800 522 8999, 1-707 257 7220, www.johnmuir napa.com, $105-$225) is an above-par motel.

There are fewer budget options in Yountville; the high-class **Vintage Inn** (6541 Washington Street, 1-800 351 1133, 1-707 944 1112, www. vintageinn.com, rates $310-$550) is one of several deluxe hotels. In Rutherford, spend your hard-earned cash at the **Auberge du Soleil** (180 Rutherford Hill Road, 1-800 348 5406, 1-707 963 1211, www.aubergedusoleil. com, rates $550-$3,500), one for special occasions. Along St Helena's Main Street, try the Victorian-era **St Helena Hotel** (No.1309, 1-707 963 4388, www.hotelsthelena.com, $95-$325); the luxurious **Inn at Southbridge** (No.1020, 1-800 520 6800, 1-707 967 9400, www.innatsouthbridge.com, $255-$615); or the delightful **El Bonita Motel** (No.195, 1-800 541 3284, 1-707 963 3216, www.elbonita.com, $89-$289), a mix of art deco and a French colonial look that's something of a bargain by St Helena standards. Located outside town, the **Meadowood Napa Valley** complex (900 Meadowood Lane, 1-800 458 8080, 1-707 963 3646, www.meadowood.com, $450-$625) contains a hotel, separate cottages, restaurants as well as a swanky fitness centre and spa. California's oldest spa, the **White Sulphur Springs Inn** (3100 White Sulphur Springs Road, 1-800 963 8873, 1-707 963 8588,

www.whitesulphursprings.com, $95-$210)
provides hotel-style rooms and creekside
cottages. For Calistoga lodgings, *see p265*.

Wherever you want to stay, book well in
advance, especially in summer. If you do get
stuck, try **Napa Valley Reservations** (1-800
251 6272, www.napavalleyreservations.com).

Tourist information

Calistoga *Calistoga Chamber of Commerce, Suite
9, 1458 Lincoln Avenue (1-707 942 6333/www.
calistogachamber.com)*. **Open** 10am-5pm Mon-Fri;
10am-4pm Sat; 11am-3pm Sun.
Napa *Napa Valley Conference & Visitor Center,
1310 Napa Town Center (1-707 226 7459/
www.napavalley.com)*. **Open** 9am-5pm daily.
St Helena *St Helena Chamber of Commerce, 1010
Main Street (1-800 799 6456/www.sthelena.com)*.
Open 10am-5pm Mon-Fri; 11am-3pm Sat.
Yountville *Yountville Chamber of Commerce, 6516
Yount Street (1-707 944 0904/www.yountville.com)*.
Open 10am-3pm daily.

Sonoma Valley

The Sonoma Valley, which runs about 23 miles
north from San Pablo Bay, is home to about
200 wineries. However, the main attraction
of a Sonoma tour is the valley itself, with its
working farms and rustic barns. The county's
topography is diverse, from beaches to redwood
forests and rolling hills. It's also agriculturally
rich, and the areas around towns such as Glen
Ellen and Sebastopol brim with farms.

Towns & attractions

Although its central plaza is now ringed by
restaurants, bookshops, a cinema (the delightful
70-year-old **Sebastiani Theatre**) and food
shops, the town of **Sonoma** retains the feel
of old California. The town was founded in 1823
as the **Mission San Francisco Solano** (363
3rd Street West, 1-707 938 9560), today part
of the loose affiliation of humbly atmospheric
sites known as **Sonoma State Historic
Park**. The town hall and Bear Flag Monument
mark the site where the Californian Bear Flag
first flew: for the 25 days of the riotous Bear
Flag Revolt in 1846, this was the capital of the
independent Republic of California. Close by
to the north, the small town of **Glen Ellen**
was once the home of Jack London, adventurer,
farmer, autodidact and author; **Jack London
Historic State Park** contains the charred
remains of Wolf House, the author's huge home.

Its population is twice that of the city of
Napa, but **Santa Rosa** manages to retain a
low-key appeal. Historic Railroad Square is the
city's busy downtown area, but the real visitor
attraction is the park on the corner of Santa
Rosa and Sonoma Avenues: **Luther Burbank
Home & Gardens** (*see below*). Also here is the
Charles M Schulz Museum (2301 Hardies
Lane, 1-707 579 4452, www.schulzmuseum.org),
commemorating the man who created Snoopy,
Charlie Brown and the whole *Peanuts* gang.

Further north is **Healdsburg**, a high-priced,
highfalutin boutique town where Bay Area
boomers come to drop some serious cash. Find
a spot around the fountain in the main plaza
and watch the opposite ends of the spectrum
in motion: middle-aged white guys in suits and
luxury SUVs rubbing up against Mexican day
labourers waiting for their next job. Gourmet
food stores, artisan bakeries and sleek eateries
bring in the herds, but the **Healdsburg
Museum** (221 Matheson Street, 1-707 431
3325), with Pomo Indian baskets and other
cultural artefacts, is pretty authentic.

Luther Burbank Home & Gardens

*Santa Rosa Avenue, at Sonoma Avenue (1-707 524
5445/www.lutherburbank.org)*. **Open** *Apr-Oct* 10am-
3.30pm Tue-Sun. **Admission** $4; $3 discounts; free
under-12s. **No credit cards.**
America's most renowned horticulturist, Burbank
developed more than 800 new varieties of plant during his life. His former house and grounds are now
a national historic landmark. Docent tours (booking
isn't necessary) and themed gardens explain and
demonstrate this botanical pioneer's work.

Wineries

Sonoma County's quaint, family-owned
wineries are more secluded than many of their
Napa neighbours, giving visitors the sensation
of having escaped from the real world. The
Sonoma County Wineries Association
(1-800 939 7666, 1-707 586 3795, www.sonoma
wine.com), located near US 101 in Rohnert Park,
organises winery tours and daily tastings.

Sonoma's history is intertwined with that
of the Californian wine industry, which began
at what is now the **Historic Buena Vista
Winery** (18000 Old Winery Road, 1-800 926
1266, www.buenavistawinery.com). Of the
nearly 40 wineries in the valley, several are
near the city's main plaza. **Bartholomew Park
Winery** (1000 Vineyard Lane, 1-707 935 9511,
www.bartholomewparkwinery.com) is great for
picnics; **Sebastiani Vineyards** (389 4th Street
East, 1-707 938 5532, www.sebastiani.com) may
not be the most charming winery, but it gives
another perspective on the ubiquitous family.

The Carneros area includes southern Sonoma
as well as Napa; wineries take advantage of
the cooler climate to produce excellent pinot
noir grapes and sparkling wines. The **Viansa
Winery** (25200 Arnold Road, 1-707 935 4700,

www.viansa.com), a Tuscan-style winery on a knoll, sells Italian food and has a two-bedroom cottage available to rent.

The pick of the viticulture in and around Glen Ellen includes the **Arrowood Vineyards & Winery** (14347 Sonoma Highway, 1-707 935 2600, www.arrowoodvineyards.com) and the **Benziger Family Winery** (1883 London Ranch Road, 1-707 935 3000, www.benziger. com), which makes its wines using bio-dynamic farming methods devised in the 1920s by Rudolf Steiner. Nearby **Kenwood** is synonymous with the **Kenwood Vineyards** (9592 Sonoma Highway, 1-707 833 5891, www. kenwoodvineyards.com), known for wine made from grapes grown on Jack London's former ranch (novelist Haruki Murakami drinks a bottle from here on his birthday each year). The original barn, now the tasting room and shop, dates from before Prohibition.

The area around Santa Rosa boasts several fine vineyards. **Kendall-Jackson Wine Center & Garden** (5007 Fulton Road, 1-707 571 8100, www.kj.com) is just outside the city in Fulton and has a state-of-the-art tasting room and education centre. Just north of Healdsburg, in the Alexander Valley area up towards Geyserville, are the **Murphy-Goode Estate** (4001 Highway 128, 1-707 431 7644, www.murphygoodewinery.com) and **Geyser Peak** (22281 Chianti Road, 1-707 857 9400, www.geyserpeakwinery.com).

Where to eat & drink

In Sonoma, Carlo Cavallo does a bang-on job at **Sonoma-Meritáge** (165 W Napa Street, 1-707 938 9430, closed Tue, mains $10-$25), his diverse menu focusing on southern French and northern Italian cuisine. For a spicy change, try **Maya** (110 E Napa Street, 1-707 935 3500, mains $11-$24), a casual spot serving great Mexican fare. Picnickers get supplies from **Artisan Bakers** (750 W Napa Street, 1-707 939 1765) or the **Vella Cheese Company** (315 2nd Street East, 1-707 938 3232).

In Kenwood, the 17-year-old **Kenwood Restaurant & Bar** (9900 Sonoma Highway, 1-707 833 6326, mains $12-$24) turns out commendable California fare. In Santa Rosa, try hip and inexpensive **Tex Wasabi's** (515 4th Street, 1-707 544 8399, mains $10-$20), a jumble of barbecue style and Japanese sushi, or two steadfastly popular options on Center Street in Healdsburg: **Ravenous** (No.420, 1-707 431 1302, closed Mon, Tue & lunch Wed-Sun, mains $14-$23) and **Zin** (No.344, 1-707 473 0946, mains $14-$25), with the latter's applewood-smoked pork chop a real favourite. The fabulous **Hotel Healdsburg** (*see below*)

is home to award-winning chef Charlie Palmer's **Dry Creek Kitchen** (No.317, 1-707 431 0330, mains $28-$35), where the changing menus are based on fresh seasonal ingredients.

Where to stay

In Sonoma, try the **Sonoma Hotel** (10 West Spain Street, 1-800 468 6016, 1-707 996 2996, www.sonomahotel.com, $95-$245) and the comfy **El Dorado Inn** (400 1st Street West, 1-707 996 3030, www.hoteleldorado.com, $145-$165). To spoil yourself, the **Ledson Hotel** (480 1st Street East, 1-707 996 9779, www.ledsonhotel.com, $350-$395) has six ultra-deluxe rooms at prices to match. In Kenwood is the historic **Kenwood Inn & Spa** (10400 Sonoma Highway, 1-800 353 6966, 1-707 833 1293, www.kenwoodinn.com, $350-$700), a luxurious resort that has recently enjoyed a major renovation. Glen Ellen is home to the **Jack London Lodge** (13740 Arnold Drive, 1-707 938 8510, www.jacklondonlodge.com, $70-$170), a straight-ahead motel.

Santa Rosa's nicest option is the 44-room **Vintners Inn** (4350 Barnes Road, 1-707 575 7350, www.vintnersinn.com, $210-$395), a prime place to stay for some proper Wine Country relaxation. The **Gables** (4257 Petaluma Hill Road, 1-800 422 5376, 1-707 585 7777, www.thegablesinn.com, $175-$250) is a lovely old Victorian Gothic inn, on several secluded acres. In Healdsburg, a number of decent motels off the freeway will serve as a good base if you don't want to blow your entire budget on accommodation, but for high-flyers, the **Hotel Healdsburg** (25 Matheson Street, 1-800 889 7188, 1-707 431 2800, www.hotel healdsburg.com, $260-$790) is pure luxury.

Tourist information

Healdsburg *Healdsburg Chamber of Commerce & Visitors Bureau, 217 Healdsburg Avenue (1-707 433 6935/www.healdsburg.org).* **Open** 9am-5pm Mon-Fri; 9am-3pm Sat; 10am-2pm Sun.
Santa Rosa *Santa Rosa CVB, 9 4th Street (1-707 577 8674/www.visitsantarosa.com).* **Open** 9am-5pm Mon-Thur, Sat; 9am-6pm Fri; 10am-5pm Sun.
Sonoma *Sonoma Valley Visitors Bureau, 453 1st Street East (1-707 996 1090/www.sonomavalley. com).* **Open** 9am-5pm daily.

Getting there

By car
Wine Country is an hour by car from SF (44 miles) over the Golden Gate along US 101. Turn east at Ignacio to Highway 37 and take Highway 121 north. From here, Highway 12 takes you along Sonoma Valley, while Highway 29 leads along Napa Valley.

Heading East

Out to the mountains of the Sierra Nevada.

Lake Tahoe

Reaching a maximum depth of 1,636 feet (500 metres), 22-mile-long **Lake Tahoe** is the tenth deepest lake in the world and the second deepest in the US. It is blessed with remarkable water clarity, a result of the pure High Sierra streams and snow melt that drain into it. Much of the lake's 72 miles of shoreline – two-thirds of which lie inside California's boundary line, with one-third in Nevada – have been divvied up into exclusive parcels of private property, but there's still plenty here to enjoy.

From March to early November, it's easy to drive the 72-mile perimeter of the lake, much of it served by public transport. The **Tahoe Rim Trail** (call 1-775 298 0012 for information) provides extensive trails to explore on foot, horse or by bike. On the California side you'll find such attractions as the **Sugar Pine Point State Park** (1-530 525 7982), near Meeks Bay, and further south the **Emerald Bay State Park** (1-530 541 3030), which overlooks the bay of the same name. There are plenty of beaches around the lake, among them **Sand Harbour**, **Zephyr Cove** and **Camp Richardson**, though only during August and September is the water, fed by snow melt, warm enough for swimming. And for a bird's-eye view of the area, take a trip with **Lake Tahoe Hot Air Balloons** (1-530 544 1221, www.laketahoe balloons.com) from South Lake Tahoe, or in the sightseeing cable cars operated by **Heavenly Valley** (1-775 586 7000, www.skiheavenly.com).

The north end of Lake Tahoe is roughly a three-and-a-half hour drive from San Francisco via Sacramento on I-80. The other route, via US 50, leads to the south shore. The two shores are geographically close, but culturally far apart. At **Tahoe City**, the main settlement on the north shore, the lodgings and restaurants are casual and mellow. However, down in **South Lake Tahoe**, on the California-Nevada border, things are very different, thanks to the presence of some looming, all-hours hotel-casinos. Drive from one to the other along the lake's west side, and you'll pass three state parks: **Sugar Pine Point**, **DL Bliss** and **Emerald Bay**. Hikers, bikers and cross-country skiers come here to enjoy miles of trails, and campers toast marshmallows under starry skies. For more information on all, see www.parks.ca.gov.

On the beach in **Lake Tahoe**.

Truckee, an Old West railroad town about 12 miles north of the lake, is worth a visit for its wooden sidewalks, historic station and wooden-framed shopfronts. While you're there, head over to **Donner Memorial State Park**, a few miles west of Truckee off Highway 80. It's named after a doomed group of pioneers, who suffered misfortune after misfortune as they attempted to cross the pass here in the viciously cold winter of 1842; starvation drove some of them to cannibalism. It's an affecting place.

Skiing

The ski season varies each year, but usually starts in December and lasts until late April. Two of the most popular ski areas are **Squaw Valley** (1-530 583 6985, www.squaw.com), site of the 1960 Winter Olympics, and **Alpine Meadows** (1-800 441 4423, 1-530 583 4232, www.skialpine.com). Alpine is more family-oriented and has better snowboarding, while Squaw is glitzier, with more exciting runs. Other options include **Boreal** (1-530 426 3666, www.borealski.com), whose lower prices attract snowboarders; **Northstar** (1-530 562 1010, www.skinorthstar.com) at Tahoe, which has excellent beginners' slopes; and **Sugar Bowl** (1-530 426 9000, www.sugarbowl.com), where there's a creaky old gondola that takes you to the base lodge. Lift passes tend to be expensive, but most resorts offer half-day passes for the afternoon and, sometimes, mid-week specials.

If you're not confident about your ability, invest in a lesson, which generally include the cost of a lift pass for the day. If you're driving and are not tied to a particular schedule, avoid going on Friday afternoons: San Franciscans tend to leave work early to get a head start to the slopes. Likewise, Sunday evenings can be a nightmare if you're trying to get back into the city. You can even get some skiing in as a day trip: it means leaving town at 6am, but you'll be among the first to experience the day's fresh powder snow when the lifts open at 9.30am.

Where to eat & drink

Gourmet dining is rare in Tahoe, but you'll find loads of unpretentious, friendly restaurants. The bigger restaurant chains are in the casinos, along with Vegas-style 'all-you-can-eat' buffets. In north Tahoe, try the historic **River Ranch Lodge** near Alpine Meadows (1-530 583 4264, www.riverranchlodge.com, closed lunch Mon-Fri, mains $17-$32). Diners can choose between sitting indoors or taking a spot on the patio by the Truckee River's white water. The **Bridge Tender Tavern** (65 W Lake Boulevard, 1-530 583 3342, mains $7-$10) has delectable burgers and a great river view.

On the south shore, the intimate **Café Fiore** (1169 Ski Run Boulevard, 1-530 541 2908, closed lunch, mains $15-$30) is the spot for special occasions, with fabulous Italian cuisine (book ahead). Those on a more modest budget should try the non-trad Mexican food at the **Cantina** (765 Emerald Bay Road, 1-530 544 1233, mains $9-$15) and wash it down with one of their celebrated Margaritas.

In Truckee, try **Moody's Bistro**, beneath the Truckee Hotel (10007 Bridge Street, 1-530 587 8688, mains $18-$28) which has a louche, (live) jazz-driven atmosphere and an impeccably sourced, Californian menu.

Where to stay

On the north shore, Tahoe City overflows with condo complexes offering vacation lodging. For something more interesting, try **Mayfield House** (236 Grove Street, 1-530 583 1001, www.mayfieldhouse.com, $125-$260), a quality B&B in a remodelled mansion. The 19 river-view rooms at the **River Ranch Lodge** (1-530 583

4264, www.riverranchlodge.com, $70-$180) are hard to come by but worth it; the same goes for the **Sunnyside Lodge** outside Tahoe City (1850 W Lake Boulevard, 1-530 583 7200, www.sunnysideresort.com, $100-$300).

On the west shore, **Tahoma Meadows B&B** (6821 W Lake Boulevard, 1-530 525 1553, www.tahomameadows.com, $95-$245) gets plenty of repeat business for its 14 cabins. For lakefront lodging, stay at the **Shore House B&B** (7170 N Lake Boulevard, Tahoe Vista, 1-530 546 7270, www.tahoeinn.com, $190-$290), legendary for its gourmet breakfasts.

South Lake Tahoe's big spot is **Caesar's Tahoe Resort Casino** (1-775 588 3515, www.caesars.com, $69-$200). Many south shore lodgings offer free shuttle buses to the casinos: try the **Inn by the Lake** (1-800 877 1466, 1-530 542 0330, www.innbythelake.com, $98-$228) or **Driftwood Lodge** (1-530 541 7400, $40-$160) for good value rooms and easy transport. At the higher end, book a stay at one of five rooms or three cabins at the **Black Bear Inn** (1-877 232 7466, 1-530 544 4451, www.tahoeblackbear.com, $200-$255), a luxurious B&B built in the 1990s with an old-style Tahoe look. South of Tahoe, **Kirkwood Ski & Summer Resort** (off Highway 88, 1-800 967 7500, www.kirkwood. com, $125-$269) is a family-oriented ski resort with both hotel- and condo-style lodging.

Truckee has some decent mid-range B&B options, notably the eight-room **Richardson House** (10154 High Street, 1-530 587 5388, www.richardsonhouse.com, $100-$175), high above Truckee's historic district, and **River Street Inn** (10009 E River Street, 1-530 550 9290, www.riverstreetinntruckee.com, $100-$160), a historic B&B that's been renovated to a comfortable and chintz-free standard.

Getting there

By car

A car is your best means of transport for exploring Lake Tahoe, especially if you're skiing. It takes 3.5hrs from San Francisco, traffic and weather permitting. To reach the north shore, follow I-80 east over the Bay Bridge all the way to Truckee, then take Highway 89 to Tahoe City. To reach the south shore, take I-80 to Sacramento, then turn off on to US 50.

By bus

Greyhound buses (1-800-229-9424, www.greyhound. com) stop in Truckee and Reno and take about 6hrs. Fares are about $69 return; buses to Truckee run 3-4 times a day; Reno buses are more frequent.

By train

Amtrak (1-800 872 7245, www.amtrak.com) leaves once a day from Emeryville at 8.40am. It arrives in Truckee at just after 3pm and Reno at 4pm (it costs from $32 one way).

By air

Reno-Tahoe International Airport, 58 miles north-east of the lake, is served by several airlines. United (1-800 241 6522, www.united.com) has frequent daily flights from $150 return. The South Tahoe Express (1-800 446 6128) offers a regular daily shuttle bus and limo service to South Lake Tahoe from the airport for around $38 return.

Tourist information

Donner Memorial State Park Visitors' Centre
12593 Donner Pass Road, Truckee (1-530 582 7892/www.parks.ca.gov). **Open** *June-Aug* 10am-4pm daily. *Sept-May* 9am-4pm daily.
North Lake Tahoe Chamber of Commerce
380 North Lake Boulevard, Tahoe City (1-530 581 6900). **Open** 9am-5pm Mon-Fri; 9am-4pm Sat, Sun.
South Lake Tahoe Chamber of Commerce
3066 Lake Tahoe Boulevard, South Lake Tahoe (1-530 541 5255/www.tahoeinfo.com). **Open** 9am-5pm Mon-Sat.

Yosemite

The most enchanting, intoxicating, stunning, breathtaking… many adjectives can be applied to **Yosemite National Park**, all superlatives. The park covers some 1,200 square miles of forest, alpine meadows, sheer granite cliffs, lush waterfalls and undisturbed wildlife. Park elevations range from 2,000 feet (600 metres) to over 13,000 feet (4,000 metres). Highway 120 runs east–west the entire length of the park, climbing to 9,945 feet (3,031 metres) at **Tioga Pass**, the highest automobile pass in California.

Visit in the less crowded off-season, if possible, from October to May. In spring, the wild flowers are in bloom, and in winter, snowcapped peaks are majestic (though parts of the park are inaccessible). If you must visit in high season, try to avoid the perpetually packed Yosemite Valley. You don't need reservations to visit (although you should certainly book lodgings in advance): you can drive in at any time. The $20 entrance fee per vehicle is good for seven days. However, be aware that the park is massive, with more than 250 miles of roads criss-crossing its 1,200 square miles. To see even a respectable chunk, you'll need a few days.

Most people head straight for seven-mile-long **Yosemite Valley**, where most of the park services and places to stay are located. It's both touristy and more of a proper town than first-timers expect; indeed, it's estimated that more than half of Yosemite's visitors see only Yosemite Valley, even though the Valley makes up less than one per cent of the park. Yosemite is all about views: as you drive into the valley, **El Capitan** is the first dramatic sight, a sheer rock wall 3,000 feet (914 metres) high. Look out for tiny, ant-like figures slowly crawling up its grey granite face: it's one of the most popular climbing spots in the US.

For non-valley sites, head for **Crane Flat** and **Tuolumne Meadows** (via Highway 120), **Glacier Point** (near Badger Pass) and the **Hetch Hetchy Reservoir** (north of Big Oak Flat). You'll get a bird's-eye view from Glacier Point and a spectacular view of the Sierras from

Yosemite.

Trips Out of Town

Tunnel View. Though the roads are engineered as scenic drives, the best way to experience the park is on foot, which allows you to escape into your own solitary experience.

There are hiking trails throughout the park. **Mist Trail** is the most popular: it's three miles to Vernal Falls and back, or a seven-mile round trip to Nevada Falls. Standing beneath the pounding water of Yosemite Falls is heart-stopping, with an ambitious hike to the top of **Yosemite Point** (a round trip of just under seven miles). The hike to **Glacier Point** is just as challenging, but you can cheat by driving there instead. Then there's the hike to **Half Dome** (16-mile round trip), which is strictly for the hardcore, as you have to cling to cables anchored into a sheer rockface for the last half mile). Allow ten to 12 hours. Minimum.

Back-country backpacking is the best way to avoid the crowds and get the most out of the park. However, the park has a visitor quota, so make sure you plan ahead. The **Yosemite Mountaineering School** (1-209 372 8344, www.yosemitemountaineering.com) offers excellent classes for beginners (from $120 per day), as well as five-day climbs. Alternatively, you can rent rafts to float down the valley's winding **Merced River** (available from Curry Village in Yosemite Valley, near the put-in point; 1-209 372 8319) or hire horses from summer stables at Yosemite Valley (1-209 372 8348), Tuolumne Meadows (1-209 372 8427) and Wawona (1-209 375 6502).

Between November to March you can take advantage of the terrific **winter sports**. Practise figures-of-eight with a head-on view of Half Dome at Curry Village's outdoor ice rink (1-209 372 8341). Rent downhill or cross-country skis, or a snowboard, and carve a few S-turns down the slopes at family-oriented **Badger Pass Ski Area** (www.badgerpass.com, closed early spring-late autumn, lift tickets $15-$38).

Some safety advice. First, stay away from cliff edges and watch for storm clouds: injuries and fatalities are regularly caused by people taking nosedives over the falls or getting hit by lightning while climbing. Second, take a decent map, compass and sensible shoes. Third, heed the warnings about bears and lock food and cosmetics in bear-safe boxes. And fill up your car before arriving; there's no petrol in the park.

Where to eat & drink

Three main areas of the Valley can satisfy your stomach's cravings: Yosemite Lodge, Yosemite Village and Curry Village.

Mountain Room is the best of the handful of restaurants at Yosemite Lodge, serving grills and other hearty main courses. Try to get a table near the windows for a spectacular view of Yosemite Falls. The neighbouring **Food Court** is a good option if you are in a hurry. In Yosemite Village, **Degnan's Deli** is busy at lunchtime, with made-to-order sandwiches, salads and soups. **Degnan's Café** serves ice-cream and coffee, while upstairs is the **Loft**, a pizza joint that only opens in summer. And Curry Village also has a variety of options, from cheap-and-easy category burritos and pizza to the grand, jacket-and-tie required **Ahwahnee Hotel**, whose Sunday brunches are legendary. Reservations are a must; phone 1-209 372 1489.

Where to stay

The seven lodgings available inside the park run the gamut from slum-like to extravagant. Try to avoid **Housekeeping Camp** ($67), a collection of duplex units that are a strange hybrid of cabin and campsite. A more civilised choice is the 260-room **Yosemite Lodge** ($97-$162), which has all the charm (and facilities) of a chain motel but is unbeatable for its central location. Those with money to blow should consider the **Ahwahnee Hotel** ($379), a National Historic Landmark built in 1927 of huge timbers and river rock.

Reservations for lodgings are all made at **Yosemite Reservations** (1-559 252 4848, www.yosemitepark.com). For rooms from May to September, make reservations six months to a year in advance. At other times, it's not hard to book a room in the Valley, especially midweek. Rates drop outside peak season.

Getting there

By car

Highway 41 leads from the south, Highway 140 from the west (the best entrance), and Highway 120 from the north-west. Highway 120 (the Tioga Road) is the only road across the park, but closes in winter (approx Nov to May) due to snow. Allow 4hrs from SF.

By bus

Gray Line (558 9400, www.graylinesanfrancisco.com) run one-day tours from $115, while Green Tortoise (1-800 867 8647, www.greentortoise.com) runs 2- and 3-day camping tours (from $154).

By train

Each morning, Amtrak trains 712 and 714 from Oakland to Merced (1-800 872 7245, www.amtrak.com, $25-$35 one way, 3hrs) connect with a Via Adventures bus to Yosemite.

Tourist information

General information is available from the National Park Service on 1-209 372 0200 and at www.nps.gov/yose. www.yosemitepark.com is also useful.

Heading South

Rugged coastline, fine food and one of Californian's great man-made attractions.

Monterey Bay Aquarium. *See p279.*

Half Moon Bay & the coast

Half Moon Bay is a small, easygoing seaside town with a rural feel to it. Quaint Main Street is good for a wander, with bookshops, florists and antiques shops, but the town is most famous for its pumpkins at Hallowe'en and Christmas trees. If you're on Highway 84, drop in on the **San Gregorio General Store** (1-650 726 0565, www.sangregoriostore.com), eight miles south of Half Moon Bay. Serving the local community since 1889, it's a hybrid bar, music hall and gathering place.

Continuing south from Half Moon Bay, you'll find probably the best of the region's beaches: **San Gregorio State Beach**, a strip of white sand distinguished by sedimentary cliffs. At Half Moon Bay and Highway 1, the **Sea Horse & Friendly Acres Ranch** (*see p248*) offers beach horseback rides for a range of levels. Another 15 miles down the coast are the historic buildings and rolling farmlands of **Pescadero**, with locals still tending their artichoke fields and strawberry patches. Then there's **Mavericks**: right in the middle of Half Moon Bay and about half a mile offshore, it's one of the gnarliest big-wave surf spots in the world.

Where to eat, drink & stay

In Half Moon Bay, cosy **Pasta Moon** (315 Main Street, 1-650 726 5126, www.pastamoon.com, mains $17-$29) serves elegant own-made pasta dishes. Old-school **Main Street Grill** (435 Main Street, 1-650 726 5300, closed dinner, mains $5-$12) and the bistro fare at **Rogue Chefs** (No.730, 1-650 712 2000, www.rogue chefs.com, closed dinner Mon, Tue, Sun, mains $17-$28) are both excellent. **Half Moon Bay Brewing Company** (390 Capistrano Avenue, Princeton-by-the-Sea, 1-650 728 2739, www.hmb brewingco.com, mains $9-$14) boasts views of the harbour, plus excellent burgers.

There's no shortage of places to stay in and around Half Moon Bay. The grandest is the **Ritz-Carlton** (1 Miramontes Point Road, 1-800 241 3333, 1-650 712 7000, www.ritzcarlton.com, $295-$875), on a bluff overlooking the rugged coastline. About 25 miles south of here, the **Costanoa Coastal Lodge & Camp** (2001 Rossi Road, 1-877 262 7848, 1-650 879 1100, www.costanoa.com) is more rustic resort than campground: there are individual wooden cabins ($95-$185) and a 40-room lodge ($165-$350), but you can also pitch a tent ($40-$55).

Trips Out of Town

Getting there

By car

Half Moon Bay is 30 miles south of San Francisco on Highway 1, about a 45min drive.

By train & bus

Take a BART train to Daly City (15min journey), pick up SamTrans bus 110 to Linda Mar and transfer to bus 294 for Half Moon Bay.

Tourist information

Tourist information

Half Moon Bay *Half Moon Bay Coastside Chamber of Commerce, 1st floor, 520 Kelly Avenue, Half Moon Bay (1-650 726 8380/www.hmbchamber.com).* **Open** 9am-5pm Mon-Fri.

Silicon Valley

Silicon Valley runs south-east from the base of San Francisco Bay. Routinely dismissed as mere sprawl, it actually offers fine strolling in the pretty downtowns of upscale **Los Altos**, **Los Gatos** and **Saratoga**. More substantial pleasures are found in **Palo Alto**, the site of Stanford University. Here the 20 bronzes that comprise the on-campus **Rodin Sculpture**

Santa Cruz. *See p277.*

Garden, associated with the Cantor Arts Center (328 Lomita Drive, 1-650 723 4177, tours 11.30am Sat, 3pm Sun), make a neat diversion.

Despite all the concrete, **San Jose** is the most appealing Silicon Valley town for visitors. Attractions include the interactive **Children's Discovery Museum** (180 Woz Way, 1-408 298 5437, www.cdm.org, closed Mon, $7) and nearby **Monopoly in the Park** (Guadalupe River Park, West Fernando Street, 1-408 995 6487, www.monopolyinthepark.com). The latter, a 930-square-foot (86-square-metre) board game, is the closest ordinary people get to buying property in Silicon Valley; you'll have to reserve a game in advance. The **San Jose Museum of Art** (110 S Market Street, 1-408 271 6840, http://sjmusart.org, closed Mon) has a collection of nearly 1,400 pieces, most from the latter 20th century. There's good shopping, too, with S Bascom Avenue boasting **Streetlight Records** (No.980, 1-888 330 7776) and, for pop-culture collectibles, **Time Tunnel Toys** (No.532, 1-408 298 1709, closed Mon & Sun).

Rosicrucian Egyptian Museum & Planetarium

1342 Naglee Avenue, at Park Avenue, San Jose (1-408 947 3636/www.egyptianmuseum.org). **Open** 10am-5pm Mon-Fri; 11am-6pm Sat, Sun. *Planetarium shows* 2pm Mon-Fri; 2pm, 3.30pm Sat, Sun. **Admission** $9, $5-$7 discounts. **Credit** AmEx, MC, V.
Located in Rosicrucian Park, this museum has the biggest Egyptian collection on the West Coast. There are six real mummies, a collection of more than 4,000 ancient artefacts and full-scale replica tombs. The planetarium reopened in March 2004: its free 35-minute show explores 'The Mithraic Mysteries', connecting the Roman cult to modern astronomy.

Winchester Mystery House

525 South Winchester Boulevard, San Jose (1-408 247 2101/www.winchestermysteryhouse.com). **Open** from 9am daily; tour times vary by season. **Admission** free. *Tours* $16.95-$24.95; $13.95-$21.95 discounts. **Credit** Disc, MC, V.
Haunted by the ghosts of those killed by the namesake rifle, widow-heiress Sarah Winchester spent 38 years continuously building this 160-room mansion to placate the malevolent spirits. Flashlight tours on Friday the 13th and Hallowe'en are extra creepy, but at any time the oddity of the place (a staircase heads into a bare ceiling, a window is set in the floor) is impressive. Still, the small museum celebrating the gun might be seen, given the widow's fears, to be a little insensitive.

Where to eat, drink & stay

Given all the expense accounts, it's no surprise to find quality restaurants here. Palo Alto offers new American cuisine at **Zibibbo** (430 Kipling Street, 1-650 328 6722, mains $14-$30) and a **Spago** (265 Lytton Avenue, 1-650 833

1000, www.wolfgangpuck.com, closed Sun & lunch Sat, mains $10-$40); in San Jose, try highly regarded chop house **AP Stumps** (163 W Santa Clara Street, 1-408 292 9928, www.apstumps.com, mains $15-$40).

If want to stay, downtown San Jose has a **Ramada Inn** (455 S 2nd Street, 1-408 298 3500, www.ramada.com, $105-$147) and the classy **Hotel De Anza** (233 W Santa Clara Street, 1-408 286 1000, www.hoteldeanza.com, $129-$249), with its Hedley Club Lounge you can sit by the fire and take in piano jazz.

Getting there

By car

San Jose is about 50 miles south of San Francisco on Highway 101.

By train

CalTrain travels every 30mins from San Francisco to San Jose, making several stops along the way, including Palo Alto. CalTrain also runs the Baby Bullet commuter train from SF to San Jose.

Tourist information

San Jose *San Jose CVB, 408 Almaden Boulevard (1-408 295 9600/1-800 726 5673/www.sanjose.org). Open 9am-5pm Mon-Fri.*

Santa Cruz

Established as a mission at the end of the 18th century, **Santa Cruz** is now a beach town well known for being easygoing and politically progressive. The **University of California at Santa Cruz** takes the lead; its students can often be found down at robustly independent **Bookshop Santa Cruz** (1520 Pacific Avenue, 1-831 423 0900, www.bookshopsantacruz.com). Owner and ex-Santa Cruz mayor) Neil Coonerty has been waging a war on local mediocrity with 'Keep Santa Cruz Weird' merchandise.

All that remains of Misión la Exaltación de la Santa Cruz is the Neary-Rodriguez Adobe in **Santa Cruz Mission State Historic Park**; commonly known as **Mission Adobe** (1-831 425 5849, closed Mon-Wed in winter, $1-$2), it once housed the mission's Native American population. Down the street is **Mission Plaza** (1-831 426 5686, closed Mon), a complete 1930s replica. The **Santa Cruz Museum of Natural History** (1305 East Cliff Drive, 1-831 420 6115, www.santacruzmuseums.org, closed Mon, $1.50-$2.50) contains info about the Ohlone people who once populated the area. The culturally inclined can visit the **Santa Cruz Museum of Art & History** (*see below*), while pop-culture fans will be unable to resist the **Mystery Spot** (465 Mystery Spot Road, 1-831 423 8897, $5), a few miles north

of the city in the woods off Highway 17. It's a 150-foot (46-metre) patch of earth that has been confounding the laws of physics and gravity since its discovery in 1939. Kitsch nonsense.

Bang on the beach, the **Santa Cruz Beach Boardwalk** (400 Beach Street, 1-831 423 5590, closed Mon-Fri Sept-May, unlimited rides $26.95) is an amusement park that hails back to the city's 19th-century heyday and contains, among other things, a vintage carousel and a classic wooden rollercoaster. The Boardwalk's **Cocoanut Grove Ballroom** (1-831 423 2053) is another remnant, with live music for weekends and holidays bringing it back to life. Continuing the beach theme, the lighthouse contains the engaging **Surfing Museum** (West Cliff Drive, 1-831 420 6289, www.santacruzsurfingmuseum.org, closed Tue & Wed, hours vary in winter), while right outside the lighthouse is **Steamer Lane**, one of the best surfing spots in the state.

Fans of towering redwoods should head north into the Santa Cruz Mountains to **Big Basin Redwoods State Park** (21600 Big Basin Way, Boulder Creek, 1-831 338 8860, www.bigbasin.org) or the **Henry Cowell Redwoods State Park** (101 North Big Trees Park Road, Felton, 1-831 335 4598), which has a tree you can drive through. Also to the north, a mile past Western Drive on Highway 1, you'll find the 4,500 acres of former dairy farm **Wilder Ranch State Park** (1-831 423 9703). Centred on a quaint compound of historic Victorian houses and gardens, the park also has 34 miles of trails.

Some 50 wineries are scattered across the area, most open to the public but free of the crowds that put some off Wine Country (*see pp264-270*). The best of the Santa Cruz-based wineries are **Bonny Doon** (10 Pine Flat Road, 1-831 425 3625, www.bonnydoonvineyard.com) and award-winning **Storrs** (303 Potrero Street, 1-831 458 5030, www.storrswine.com).

Santa Cruz Museum of Art & History

McPherson Center, 705 Front Street, at Cooper Street (1-831 429 1964/www.santacruzmah.org). Open 11am-5pm Tue-Sun. Admission $5; $3 students, seniors; $2 12-17s; free under-12s. Free 1st Fri of mth. Credit MC, V.

This fair art museum features rotating exhibitions, as well as a permanent display of early Santa Cruz artefacts, and a historical library. The museum also offers tours of the Evergreen Cemetery, one of the region's first Protestant burial grounds.

Where to eat, drink & stay

High above Santa Cruz Yacht Harbor, the **Crow's Nest** (2218 East Cliff Drive, 1-831 476 4560, mains $14-$24) offers magnificent views

Trips Out of Town

and great seafood. Downtown has a whole world of options, among them the hip **Mobo Sushi** (105 S River Street, 1-831 425 1700, www.mobosushirestaurant.com, sushi $3-$6) and premier Mexican **El Palomar** (1336 Pacific Avenue, 1-831 425 7575, mains $8-$20). On the Eastside, there's fabulous wood-fired pizza to be had at **Engfer Pizza Works** (537 Seabright Avenue, 1-831 429 1856, closed Mon, pizzas $8-$15), as well as a ping pong table and an exotic array of old-time sodas. And you're spoilt for cheap choices. One of the best is the **Saturn Café** (145 Laurel Street, 1-831 429 8505, mains $6-$8), the kind of vegetarian spot even meat-eaters are impressed with, and serves an outlandishly huge chocolate dessert.

Santa Cruz has many dreary motels, but there are some charming spots. The **Babbling Brook Inn** (1025 Laurel Street, 1-831 427 2437, www.babblingbrookinn.com, $142-$317) is surrounded by an acre of leafy gardens with tall redwood trees and, naturally, a garrulous watercourse. Overlooking the sea, the **Pleasure Point Inn** (2-3665 East Cliff Drive, 1-831 469 6161, www.pleasurepointinn.com, $225-$295) is modern, upscale and well appointed. The Gothic Victorian **Compassion Flower Inn** (216 Laurel Street, 1-831 466 0420, www.compassion flowerinn.com, $115-$175) is a handsome old B&B also notable for being one of the first medical-marijuana-friendly hotels in the US.

Getting there

By car
Santa Cruz is 74 miles south of San Francisco on I-280 (take Highway 17 to I-85 to get to I-280).

By train & bus
Amtrak shuttle buses link San Jose and Santa Cruz. Greyhound buses leave San Francisco for Santa Cruz about four times a day.

Tourist information

Santa Cruz *Santa Cruz County CVB, 1211 Ocean Street, nr Washburn Avenue (1-831 425 1234/1-800 833 3494/www.scccvc.org).* **Open** 9am-5pm Mon-Fri; 10am-4pm Sat, Sun.

The Monterey Peninsula

Settled by Spanish explorer Sebastián Viscaíno in 1602, **Monterey** wasn't colonised until 168 years later with the arrival of Junípero Serra, who established the second of his 23 missions here. For the Spanish, the town was a crucial settlement, and remained important when the Mexicans seceded from Spain in 1822 and assumed stewardship over California; it was

at **Custom House** (*see below*) 24 years later that the American flag was raised in California for the first time with any degree of permanency.

Monterey's unlikely journey from capital of Alta California to sardine capital of the world took several generations, during which the town, and neighbouring **Pacific Grove**, briefly became popular resorts. The fishing industry drove the economy for the first part of the 20th century; when the fish and the money both ran out, the fishermen left the place to the tourists, and Monterey is now one of the most popular towns for visitors on the west coast.

Monterey

All downtown Monterey's low-key attractions are scattered around its fringes, meaning that **Calle Principal** and **Alvarado Street**, the two main drags, are populated chiefly with restaurants and shops. Stroll south, and you'll find the **Monterey Museum of Art** (559 Pacific Street, 1-831 372 5477, www.monterey art.org, closed Mon & Tue, $5) which has an august permanent collection containing pieces by Ansel Adams. Continuing north along Alvarado Street, meanwhile, leads you towards the water and the pleasures of the spreadeagled **Monterey State Historic Park** (1-831 649 7118, www.parks.ca.gov).

Once you've found the pedestrianised plaza, head for the visitor centre inside the **Stanton Center** to pick up a map of the area's assorted historic buildings; among them are the **Custom House**, an adobe building dating back over 175 years, and the **Larkin House**, a curious but unquestionably attractive structure built by a Yankee merchant in the late 1840s. You can see as many or as few of these buildings as you choose as part of the two-mile **Path of History** self-guided walk, for which leaflets are dispensed at the Stanton Center. The Center can also provide information for the guided tours of Old Monterey itself.

Adjoining **Fisherman's Wharf** is smaller than the version in San Francisco, but is just like it in one regard: it fails to live up to its name. The fishermen who once drove the town's economy long ago drew in their nets for the final time, leaving their former base to the tourists. Fisherman's Wharf is now merely a collection of shops and restaurants, working a tired spell on a steady stream of easily impressed visitors.

Thought Fisherman's Wharf was touristy? You're going to be in for a shock when you get to **Cannery Row**. This stretch of waterside road was once home to robust fishing industry immortalised by John Steinbeck in a 1945 novel. Steinbeck would be appalled to see it now, its old buildings converted into bars, gift shops

The honking seals of **Monterey**. See p278.

and hokey attractions that trade off his name in a variety of inventively crass ways. However, there is one redeeming feature: the celebrated **Monterey Bay Aquarium**.

Monterey Bay Aquarium

886 Cannery Row (1-831 648 4800/www.mbayaq. org). **Open** *Memorial Day-Labor Day* 9.30am-6pm daily. *Labor Day-Memorial Day* 10am-6pm daily. **Admission** $21.95; $10.95-$19.95 discounts; free under-3s. **Credit** AmEx, MC, V.
Striking the perfect balance between education and entertainment, the Monterey Bay Aquarium pulls off the enviable trick of appealing to adults as much as kids. Two decades after its opening, it's never looked better: a new entrance hall has alleviated some of the chaos that ensues on busy mornings, and though the Skywalk is less grand than its name suggests, the gangway linking the two halves of the aquarium – the original buildings and the Outer Bay Wing – has made navigation easier.
The centrepiece of the museum is still the vast Kelp Forest exhibit, crammed with marine life both prosaic and exotic. However, it's fast being usurped in the popularity stakes by the exhibits in the Outer Bay Wing. On the ground floor is Sharks: Myth & Mystery, which supplements the crowd-pleasing fish (including some funky hammerheads and a very neat stingray exhibit; we won't spoil the surprise) with displays on a more cultural tack. Above it, on the second floor, is the Outer Bay, a breathtaking collection of fish in a tank that holds a cool million gallons of water. Get here to see feeding time. Among the other inhabitants of the building are the perennially cute sea otters. However, it's all change in the original wing, with a number of the exhibits revamped. By the way, if any of the tanks look a bit murky, there's a good reason: the water in many exhibits comes in

direct from the Pacific. The water is filtered during the day to increase visibility but unfiltered out of hours; either way, cloudiness varies. **Photo** *p275.*

Pacific Grove & Carmel

Just down the road from Monterey lies the sweet little town of **Pacific Grove**, a more moneyed settlement than its neighbour and a far less touristy one to boot. Its downtown (around the junction of Lighthouse Avenue and Forest Street) is largely unencumbered by gift shops and galleries; its restaurants are no more expensive than they need to be. Pick up a walking tour leaflet from the Chamber of Commerce (*see p280*) for details on the histories of the town's century-old private residences.

The **Pacific Grove Museum of Natural History** (165 Forest Avenue, 1-831 648 5716, www.pgmuseum.org, closed Mon & Sun) is home to an interesting exhibition on the Monarch butterflies that spend winters here (ask at the visitor centre for details of where to see them). The town wears its nickname, Butterfly Town USA, with pride. However, Pacific Grove's main attraction is its craggy coastline. Catch it on a grey day, and the coast hugging Ocean View Boulevard is awesome, waves beating furiously against the rocks. On bluer days, it's more serene; several parks and viewpoints offer the chance to picnic while watching sea lions laze the day away.

Just south of Pacific Grove is the **17-Mile Drive**, a privately owned road, established in 1881, that takes drivers alongside some breathtaking coastal scenery. So breathtaking,

Trips Out of Town

in fact, that the road's owners charge drivers around $10 just to see it. Also here is **Pebble Beach Golf Links** (1-800 654 9300, www.pebblebeach.com); regarded by many as one of the world's finest courses, it's also, at $400 a round, one of the most expensive.

The southern point of the 17-Mile Drive is the infuriating town of **Carmel-by-the-Sea**. If this formerly charming but now merely cutesy idyll proves anything, it's that money doesn't buy taste. The shops in the centre hawk chintzy souvenirs and frumpy clothes; the restaurants serve generally mediocre food at inflated prices; and the galleries for which the town is famed deal only in art of the most preternaturally ghastly kind. However, while a walk around Carmel's centre is a maddening experience, the village's undeniable aesthetic charm excised by the pomposity of its residents, the town does have two splendid beaches: **Carmel Beach**, at the western end of Ocean Avenue, and, down the coast, the less crowded and more pleasant **Carmel River State Beach** (1-831 649 2836), which also includes a bird sanctuary. A word of warning: both beaches might look idyllic, but tides can be lethal. Swimming is a bad idea.

Where to eat & drink

Your best bet in downtown Monterey is chic **Montrio** (414 Calle Principal, 1-831 648 8880, www.montrio.com, closed lunch, mains $9-$32), where the Californian cuisine lives up to the stylish room in which it's served. It's an egalitarian place, too, popular with the Gold Card crew but also with local couples and tourists. **Stokes** (500 Hartnell Street, 1-831 373 1110, closed lunch Mon-Fri, mains $10-$25) has retained its favoured status with locals for two reasons: one, it's off the beaten path for tourists, despite being housed in a gorgeously converted 170-year-old adobe house, and two, the Mediterranean cuisine is wonderfully flavourful.

There's a high hit-rate of quality to quantity in Pacific Grove. You'll find daisy-fresh fish creations at smart-casual **Passionfish** (701 Lighthouse Avenue, 1-831 655 3311, www.passionfish.net, closed lunch, mains $12-$25) and some fair Mediterranean-influenced food at **Fandango** (223 17th Street, 1-831 372 3456, www.fandangorestaurant.com, mains $15-$30). In Carmel, the best of a mixed bunch is the **Flying Fish** (Carmel Plaza, 1-831 625 1962, closed lunch, mains $15-$30).

Where to stay

There are a number of individualistic lodgings closer to downtown Monterey. The largest is the **Monterey Plaza** (400 Cannery Row, 1-800 368 2468, 1-831 646 1700, www.woodsidehotels.com/monterey, $179-$470), a plush oceanside hotel-spa that strikes a decent balance between comfortable luxury and corporate efficiency. The most appealing is the **Old Monterey Inn** (500 Martin Street, 1-800 350 2344, www.oldmontereyinn.com, $200-$400), an immaculate B&B set on a quiet street. Also worth a look is the elegant **Spindrift Inn** (475 Cannery Row, 1-800 841 1879, 1-831 646 8900, www.spindriftinn.com, $179-$409), which bears nary a trace of its former incarnation as a whorehouse. But the best bargain is the century-old **Monterey Hotel** (406 Alvarado Street, 1-800 966 6490, 1-831 375 3184, www.montereyhotel.com, $89-$249), good value given its central location.

Over in Pacific Grove, try the **Martine Inn** (255 Ocean View Boulevard, 1-831 373 3388, 1-800 852 5588, www.martineinn.com, $145-$365). Owned by Don Martine, who spends his spare time restoring classic cars (he's happy to show them off), the hotel has over 20 rooms with unique antique fixtures. Also here is the **Jabberwock Inn** (598 Laine Street, 1-888 428 7253, 1-831 372 4777, www.jabberwockinn.com, $155-$275), a fab B&B in a century-old mansion that's gently themed around the works of Lewis Carroll. Great breakfasts, too. The best bet in Carmel is the **Mission Ranch** (26270 Dolores Street, 1-800 538 8221, 1-831 624 6436, www.missionranchcarmel.com, $110-$290), where the tastefully decorated rustic rooms look out over handsome countryside. The property is co-owned by Clint Eastwood.

Getting there

By car

Monterey is 110 miles from San Francisco if you take US 101 to CA-17 to Highway 1, and a bit further if you take Highway 1 all the way. Plan on a 2-3hr drive. It's 5 miles to Monterey from Carmel, and 6 miles to Pacific Grove.

Tourist information

Carmel *Carmel Chamber of Commerce, San Carlos Street, between 5th & 6th Streets (1-800 550 4333/ 1-831 624 2522/www.carmelcalifornia.org).* **Open** 9am-5pm Mon-Fri.

Monterey *Monterey Visitor Center, Lake El Estero, at Franklin & Camino El Estero (1-888 221 1010/ 1-831 649 1770/www.montereyinfo.org).* **Open** *Apr-Oct* 9am-6pm Mon-Sat; 9am-5pm Sun. *Nov-Mar* 9am-5pm Mon-Sat; 10am-4pm Sun. There's also a smaller visitor centre in the Stanton House.

Pacific Grove *Pacific Grove Chamber of Commerce, cnr of Central & Forest Avenues (1-800 656 6650/1-831 373 3304/www.pacificgrove.org).* **Open** 9am-5pm Mon-Fri.

Directory

Cable cars. *See p284.*

Directory

Getting Around

San Francisco International Airport (SFO)

1-650 821 8211/www.flysfo.com.
SFO lies 14 miles south of the city, near US 101. The International terminal, which opened in 2000, is a grand, gleaming spot, but the airport as a whole is nice, with above-par shops and some enlightened museum displays (see www.sfoarts.org).

If you're staying downtown, take the **train** from the BART station in the International terminal (accessible from all terminals via SFO's free Airtrain). The journey to town costs $4.95 and takes 30mins; trains leave SFO from 4am to 10.15pm. BART is a far better bet than the three SamTrans **bus** routes – the KX, the 292 and the 24-hour 397 – that serve SFO (fares vary from $1.50 to $4); the buses can take ages to make the journey from the airport to the city.

Shuttle vans, which hold 8-12 people and offer door-to-door service, are a more direct option. Shuttles operate on a walk-up basis at the airport, though you must book for your return journey. Firms running shuttle vans include **Bay Shuttle** (564 3400), **SuperShuttle** (558 8500) and **American Airporter Shuttle** (202 0733, 1-800 282 7758); the airport's website has a full list. The fare into San Francisco will be $10-$17; ask about discounted rates for two or more travellers in the same party. Vans leave regularly from the upper level of the terminal: follow the red 'passenger vans' signs outside the baggage-claim area.

Taxis run to and from SFO, though they're pricey: expect to pay around $40 plus tip, though you might be able to haggle a flat rate.

For a **limousine**, use the toll-free white courtesy phones located in the terminal to summon a car (walk-up service isn't permitted). The fare will likely be at least $50 plus tip.

Mineta San Jose International Airport (SJC)

1-408 501 7600/www.sjc.org.
Efficient SJC is the airport of choice for many Silicon Valley travellers. However, those without cars but with San Francisco lodgings face a lengthy and/or pricey journey to the city.

Without a car, the best way to get to San Francisco from SJC is by **train**. Ride the Airport Flyer bus (20mins) from the airport to Santa Clara station, then take the Caltrain service to San Francisco station (4th & King Streets, $6.50, 90mins). Door-to-door **shuttle vans**, available on a walk-up basis, are quicker, but cost up to $80. A **taxi** will set you back $120 plus tip.

Oakland International Airport (OAK)

1-510 563 3300/ www.flyoakland.com.
The ride into San Francisco from Oakland Airport is simple by **train**. The AirBART bus shuttle links the airport to the Coliseum/Oakland Airport BART station; the ride costs $2 and takes 20-30mins. From the station, take the next Daly City or Millbrae train to San Francisco ($3.15; about 25mins to Downtown). Note: this is generally not a safe option for lone passengers at night. Instead, take one of the myriad **shuttle vans**, available on a walk-up basis, or a very expensive taxi/limo ride.

Airlines

Air Canada *1-888 247 2262/ www.aircanada.com.*
America West *1-800 235 9292/ www.americawest.com.*
American Airlines *1-800 433 7300/www.aa.com.*
British Airways *1-800 247 9297/ www.britishairways.com.*
Continental *domestic 1-800 523 3273/international 1-800 231 0856/ www.continental.com.*
Delta *domestic 1-800 221 1212/ international 1-800 241 4141/ www.delta.com.*
Northwest *domestic 1-800 225 2525/international 1-800 447 4747/ www.nwa.com.*
Southwest *1-800 435 9792/ www.southwest.com.*
United Airlines *domestic 1-800 864 8331/international 1-800 538 2929/www.united.com.*
US Airways *domestic 1-800 428 4322/international 1-800 622 1015/ www.usairways.com.*
Virgin Atlantic *1-800 862 8621/ www.virginatlantic.com.*

San Francisco's mass-transit network is comprehensive and efficient. Buses, streetcars and cable cars are run by the San Francisco Municipal Railway, aka **Muni** (673 6864, www.sfmuni.com), while the Bay Area Rapid Transit rail network, aka **BART** (989 2278, www.bart.gov) connects San Francisco to Oakland, Berkeley and beyond. Maps and timetables are available online, and free leaflets available at stations offer details on popular routes and services. However, Muni's system-wide *Street & Transit Map*, costing $3 and available from bookshops, drugstores and the SFCVB (*see p293*), is a sound investment. Further details on Bay Area transit, including route guidance, can be found at **www.511.org** or **www.transitinfo.org**, or by calling **511** from a local phone.

For information about single fares on the modes of transport in San Francisco, *see pp283-284*. However, if you plan to travel often in the Bay Area, the new **TransLink** card may help: the reuseable ticket is valid on all major transit networks, including Muni, BART and Caltrain. Tag the TransLink card when you start your journey (and, on BART, when you exit). The cost of the ride will be deducted, and any remaining value can be used on your next trip. When the card runs low, add funds at machines around the transit network. It's hoped TransLink will be widely available during 2006 and 2007; for more, see www.translink.org.

Until then, there are other options. The **Passport**, valid for unlimited travel on all Muni vehicles (but not BART trains), is aimed at tourists. Passports are valid for one day ($11), three days ($18) and seven days ($24), and are sold at the CVB (*see p293*), the cable car ticket booths downtown at Powell and Market and in Fisherman's Wharf at Beach and Hyde, Montgomery metro station, the TIX booth in Union Square, the Muni offices (949 Presidio Avenue) and SFO.

At $15, the **weekly Muni pass** is cheaper than the equivalent Passport, but comes with two caveats: one, the pass only runs Monday to Sunday (seven-day Passports begin on any day of the week), and two, there's a $1 surcharge for each cable car ride. The **monthly Muni pass** ($45), valid from the first of the month until three days into the following month, is also valid on the eight BART stations within the city of San Francisco, but not beyond (so you'll have to pay extra to get to Oakland, Berkeley and SFO). Weekly and monthly passes are available at the locations listed above, with the exception

of TIX and the Muni offices. Holders of a **CityPass** (*see p64*) also get free travel on Muni vehicles.

BART

Bay Area Rapid Transit is a $5-billion network of five high-speed rail lines serving San Francisco, Daly City, Colma and the East Bay. It's modern and efficient, run by computers at Oakland's Lake Merritt station, with announcements, trains, ticket dispensers, exit and entry gates all automated. BART is of minor use for getting around San Francisco – it only has eight stops in the city, four on Market Street, two on Mission and two further south – but it's the best way to get to Berkeley and Oakland.

Fares vary by destination, from $1.25 to $7.45. Machines at each station dispense reusable tickets encoded with the amount of money you entered (cash and credit cards are both valid). Your fare will be deducted from this total when you end your journey, and any remaining value will be valid for future trips. You can add value to the card at all ticket machines.

Stations are marked with blue and white signs at street level. Trains run from 4am on weekdays, 6am on Saturday and 8am on Sunday, and shut down around midnight.

Buses

Muni's orange and white buses are the top mode of public transport in SF. Relatively cheap, they can get you to within a block or two of almost anywhere in town. Bus stops are marked by a large white rectangle on a street with a red kerb; a yellow marking on a telephone or lamp post; a bus shelter; and/or a brown and orange sign listing buses that serve that route.

A single journey on a Muni bus is $1.50; seniors, 4-17s and the disabled pay 50¢, while under-4s travel free. Exact change is required. Free transfers, which let passengers connect with a second Muni bus or streetcar route at no extra charge, are valid for 90 minutes after the original fare was paid. (The transfer tokens serve as your ticket/receipt; always ask for one when you board.)

Major bus routes

San Francisco's bus network is comprehensive but complicated, especially to newcomers to the city. The Muni maps are very useful, but for quick reference, here are some key routes.

5, 6, 7, 9, 21, 71 These six routes run down Market Street from the Financial District to Civic Center; for ease of use, we've used the shorthand '**Market Street routes**' for them in our Downtown listings. Route **5** continues through the Western Addition to the northern edge of Golden Gate Park; routes **6, 7** and **71** head into the Haight, with the **6** then running into the Sunset and the **71** taking the southern edge of Golden Gate Park; route **9** runs south down Potrero Avenue in the Mission and all the way to the edge of the city; and route **21** cuts through the Hayes Valley to the north-east corner of Golden Gate Park.

14 Runs the length of Mission Street; good for riding between the Mission and Downtown.

38 Apart from a stretch in central San Francisco, where the one-way system means it's forced east down O'Farrell Street, this route runs the length of Geary Street/Boulevard.

45 After stopping at SBC Park, SFMOMA, Union Square, Chinatown and North Beach, this useful route then heads west along Union Street through Cow Hollow to the Presidio.

49 Links Fort Mason, Polk Gulch, the Tenderloin, Civic Center and the Mission along Van Ness Avenue, before heading further south.

Directory

Buses run 5am-1am during the week, 6am-1am on Saturdays and 8am-1am on Sundays. From midnight to 5am, a skeleton crew runs the Owl, nine lines on which buses run every half-hour.

Cable cars

There are 44 cable cars in San Francisco, 27 in use at peak hours, moving at top speeds of 9.5mph on three lines: California (California Street, from the Financial District to Van Ness Avenue), Powell-Mason and Powell-Hyde (both from Market Street to Fisherman's Wharf).

Lines operate from 6.30am to midnight daily. If you don't have a Muni pass or CityPass, buy a $5 one-way ticket from the conductor (under-5s go free). Transfers are not valid. The stops are marked by pole-mounted brown signs with a cable car symbol; routes are marked on Muni bus maps. *See also p68* **The cable guys**.

Ferries

Ferries are used mainly by suits during peak hours, but they double as an inexpensive tourist excursion across the Bay to Sausalito, Tiburon or Larkspur (*see pp259-263*). There are also ferries from San Francisco to Alcatraz and Angel Island in San Francisco Bay (*see pp93-94*).

Blue & Gold Fleet (information 773 1188, tickets 705 5555, www.blueandgold fleet.com) runs boats to Sausalito, Alcatraz and Angel Island from Pier 41 at Fisherman's Wharf. Commuter services to Alameda, Oakland (both $5.50 one way), Tiburon and Vallejo (both $7.50) leave from the Ferry Building on the Embarcadero. The competing **Golden Gate Transit Ferry Service** (455 2000, www.goldengate.org),

meanwhile, runs services from the Ferry Building to Sausalito and Larkspur (both $6.45 one way).

Streetcars

The Muni Metro streetcar – or tram – is used rarely by tourists, though it's a very useful service. Five lines (J, K, L, M and N) run under Market Street in Downtown and above ground elsewhere, while the F line runs beautiful vintage streetcars on Market Street and along the Embarcadero as far as Fisherman's Wharf. Fares are the same as on Muni's buses, and transfers are valid.

Along Market, Muni makes the same stops as BART; past the Civic Center, routes branch out towards the Mission, the Castro, Sunset and beyond. Lines run 5am-midnight.

Taxis

Taxi travel in San Francisco is relatively cheap, since the city is relatively small. The base fare is $2.85, with an additional charge of 45¢ per one-fifth of a mile ($2.25 a mile); there's a $2 surcharge for all rides starting at SFO.

The problem is that there simply aren't enough cabs in San Francisco, especially during morning and evening rush hours and sometimes late at night. If you're downtown, your best bet is to head for one of the bigger hotels; alternatively, if you're shopping or at dinner, to ask the shop or restaurant to call a cab for you. If you're in an outlying area, phone early to request one and ask how long you'll need to wait.

City Wide Dispatch *920 0700.*
DeSoto *970 1300.*
Luxor *282 4141/www.luxorcab.com.*
Metro *920 0715.*
National *648 4444.*
Veteran's *552 1300.*
Yellow *626 2345/ www.yellowcabsf.com.*

Outside San Francisco

The **CalTrain** commuter line (1-800 660 4287, www. caltrain.com) connects San Francisco with San Jose and ultimately Gilroy. Fares are calculated by the number of zones through which the train travels; fares range from $2 to $9.50; discounts, ten-ride tickets, and daily and monthly passes are all available.

Several companies run bus services around the rest of the Bay Area. **AC Transit** (817 1717, www.actransit.org) runs buses trans-bay and to Alameda and Contra Costa Counties; buses A to Z go across the Bay Bridge to Berkeley and Oakland. **Golden Gate Transit** (455 2000, www.goldengate.org) serves Marin and Sonoma Counties from Sausalito to Santa Rosa. And **SamTrans** (1-800 660 4287, www.sam trans.org) looks after San Mateo County, with a service to downtown San Francisco.

Driving

Three words: *don't do it.* It's not so much that the traffic in San Francisco is bad – it's no worse (and, it should be added, not much better) than any average US city. However, the hills are hellish (remember, you're not Steve McQueen and this isn't *Bullitt*), the streetcars are a bitch and the parking is horrendous. There's very little street parking, and private garages charge up to $15/hr.

However, if you must drive, be aware of a few things. The speed limit is 25mph; seatbelts are compulsory. Cable cars always have the right of way. When parking on hills, set the handbrake and 'kerb' the front wheels (towards the kerb if facing downhill, away if facing uphill). Always park in the direction of the traffic, and never block driveways. Don't park at kerbs coloured white (passenger drop-off zones), blue (drivers with disabilities only), yellow (loading and unloading commercial vehicles only) or red (bus stops or fire hydrants). Green kerbs allow only ten-minute parking. And if you venture across the water, make sure you have enough cash to pay the toll ($5 for the Golden Gate Bridge and $3 for the Bay Bridge), levied on the return trip.

For information on the latest highway conditions, call the 24-hour **CalTrans Highway Information Service** on 511, or check online at www.dot.ca.gov.

Breakdown services

Members of the **American Automobile Association** (**AAA**; 1-800 222 4357, www.aaa.com), and members of affiliated clubs such as the British AA, receive free towing and roadside service.

Fuel stations

There aren't a huge number of stations in the city limits. However, if you're running low, there's an **Arco** at Mission and 14th Streets, a **Union 76** on Harrison Street just before the Bay Bridge on-ramp, and a **Shell** at Fell and Steiner Streets.

Parking

There are garages around town, but you'll pay for the privilege of parking in them. Inquire about discounted (or 'validated') rates, but before you park, always ask your hotel: few have their own lots, but many have an arrangement with a nearby garage.

If you're parking during the day, look out for the few large city lots where you can plug a parking meter by the hour (keep your quarters handy). Otherwise, there are garages at the following locations; with

the exception of the Mission garage, closed midnight to 6am, all are open 24 hours.

Financial District *Between Battery, Drumm, Clay & Sacramento Streets.* **Map** p315 N4.
Union Square *333 Post Street (enter on Geary Street), between Stockton & Powell Streets.* **Map** p3315 M5.
SoMa *833 Mission Street, between 4th & 5th Streets.* **Map** p315 M6.
North Beach *766 Vallejo Street, between Stockton & Powell Streets.* Map p314 L3.
Chinatown *651 California Street, at Kearny Street.* **Map** p315 M4.
Mission *3255 21st Street, between Bartlett & Valencia Streets.* **Map** p318 K11.
Western Addition *1610 Geary Boulevard, between Webster & Laguna Streets.* **Map** p314 H4.
Marina *2055 Lombard Street, between Webster & Fillmore Streets.* **Map** p313 H3.

Vehicle hire

Most car-hire agencies are at or near the airport, though some have satellite locations Downtown. Call around for the best rate, and book well ahead if you're planning to visit at a holiday weekend. Every firm requires a credit card and matching driver's licence; few will rent to under-25s. Prices won't include tax, liability insurance or collision damage waiver (CDW); US residents may be covered on their home policy, but foreign residents will need to buy insurance.

Alamo *US: 1-800 462 5266/263 8411/www.goalamo.com. UK: 0870 400 4562/www.alamo.co.uk.*
Avis *US: 1-800 230 4898/261 5595/www.avis.com. UK: 0870 606 0100/www.avis.co.uk.*
Budget *US: 1-800 527 0700/736 1212/www.budget.com. UK: 0870 153 9170/www.budget.co.uk.*
Dollar *US: 1-866 434 2226/1-800 800 3665/www.dollar.com. UK: 0800 085 4578/www.dollar.co.uk.*
Enterprise *US: 1-800 261 7331/365 6662/www.enterprise.com. UK: 0870 350 3000/www.enterprise.com/uk.*
Hertz *US: 1-800 654 3131/220 9700/www.hertz.com. UK: 0870 844 8844/www.hertz.co.uk.*
National *US: 1-800 227 7368/261 5391. UK: 0116 217 3884. Both: www.nationalcar.com.*
Thrifty *US: 1-800 847 4389/896 7600/www.thrifty.com. UK: 01494 751600/www.thrifty.co.uk.*

Cycling

San Francisco is a real cycling city. A grid of major cycle routes across the town is marked by oval-shaped bike-and-bridge markers. North–south routes use odd numbers; east–west routes even; full-colour signs indicate primary cross-town routes; neighbourhood routes appear in green and white. The Yellow Pages has a map of the routes, but you can also call the Bicycle Information Line on 585 2453 for details. Daunted by the hills? Pick up the *San Francisco Bike Map & Walking Guide*, which indicates the gradients of the city's streets; for details, *see p246*. There are also two scenic cycle routes: one from Golden Gate Park south to Lake Merced, the other heading north from the southern end of Golden Gate Bridge into Marin County.

You can take bicycles on BART free of charge (except at rush hour). Bike racks on the front of certain Muni buses take up to two bikes. On CalTrain, cyclists can bring their bikes on cars that display yellow bike symbols. You can also stow bikes in lockers at CalTrain stations. For more on cycling in San Francisco, including other tips for riding in town and a list of shops offering bike rentals, *see pp246-247*.

Walking

Exploring on foot is the most enjoyable and insightful way to see San Francisco. In a city with more than its share of road rage, pedestrians walk unimpeded, often arriving sooner than their petrol-consuming counterparts. For walking tours of the city, covering everything from the shops of Chinatown to old Victorian houses, *see p65*.

Resources A-Z

Addresses

Addresses follow the standard US format. The room and/or suite number usually appears after the street address, followed on the next line by the city name and the zip code.

Age restrictions

Buying alcohol 21
Drinking alcohol 21
Driving 16
Sex (heterosexual couples) 18
Sex (homosexual couples) 18
Smoking 18

Attitude & etiquette

If you're here on banking business, a suit may be in order, but otherwise, dressing down is fine. Few restaurants in town operate a dress code, though some bars forbid jeans, sneakers and/or tank tops.

Business

San Francisco is a world-class vacation and business city. Around 1.5 million people a year come for conventions; plenty of others arrive here on day-to-day business. Many banking companies are based here (Wells Fargo, Charles Schwab); other big industries include bio-medical technology, telecommunications, law, shipping and some of the giants in new technology.

Conventions

Big conventions are held at the **Moscone Convention Center** (747 Howard Street, between 3rd & 4th Streets, SoMa, 974 4000, www.moscone.com), situated on two SoMa blocks. The busiest times for conventions are usually mid January (when the city hosts the MacWorld Expo), May and September.

Courier services

DHL *1-800 225 5345/www.dhl.com.* Credit AmEx, Disc, MC, V.
Federal Express *1-800 463 3339/ www.federalexpress.com.* Credit AmEx, DC, Disc, MC, V.
UPS *1-800 742 5877/www.ups.com.* Credit AmEx, MC, V.

Office services

Copy Central *705 Market Street, at 3rd Street, Financial District (882 7377/www.copycentral.com). BART & Metro to Montgomery/ bus 2, 3, 4, 31 & Market Street routes.* Open 7.30am-10pm Mon-Thur; 7.30am-7pm Fri; 10am-6pm Sat; noon-6pm Sun. Credit AmEx, DC, Disc, MC, V. Map p315 M5.
Kinko's *369 Pine Street, at Montgomery Street, Financial District (834 1053/www.kinkos.com). Bus 1, 10, 12, 15, 41/cable car California.* Open 7am-11pm Mon-Fri; 10am-6pm Sat, Sun. Credit AmEx, DC, Disc, MC, V. Map p315 N5.
Mail Boxes Etc *268 Bush Street, between Montgomery & Sansome Streets, Financial District (765 1515/ www.mbe.com). Bus 1, 10, 12, 15, 41/ cable car California.* Open 8.30am-5.30pm Mon-Fri. Credit AmEx, DC, Disc, MC, V. Map p315 N5.
Office Depot *33 3rd Street, at Market Street, Financial District (777 1728/www.officedepot.com). BART & Metro to Montgomery/bus 2, 3, 4, 31 & Market Street routes.* Open 8am-7pm Mon-Fri; 10am-5pm Sat. Credit AmEx, Disc, MC, V. Map p315 M5.

Useful organisations

The **San Francisco Main Library** (*see p78*) has access to vast amounts of business-related information. You don't need a library card for in-house print research or to read back-dated newspapers. The research desk staff are terrific; phone 557 4400 for assistance.

Law Library
401 Van Ness Avenue, at McAllister Street, Civic Center (554 6821/ www.ci.sf.ca.us/sfll). BART & Metro to Civic Center/bus 21, 47, 49 & Market Street routes. Open 8.30am-5pm Mon-Fri. Map p318 K7.
Open to the public for research, but only San Francisco-based lawyers can borrow books and materials.

Mechanics' Institute Library
57 Post Street, between Montgomery & Kearny Streets, Financial District (393 0101/www.milibrary.org). BART & Metro to Montgomery/ bus 2, 3, 4, 31 & Market Street routes. Open 9am-9pm Mon-Thur; 9am-6pm Fri; 10am-5pm Sat; 1-5pm Sun. Admission *Non-members* $10/day; $35/wk. Membership $95/yr. Map p315 N5.
Many of the same data sources as the Main Library but in only a fraction of the space. Its true source of fame, however, lies in its chess room (421 2258, www.chessclub.org), the best place in town for a quiet game.

Travel advice

For current information on travel to a specific country—including the latest news on health issues, safety and security, local laws and customs – contact your home country's government department of foreign affairs. Most have websites with useful advice for would-be travellers.

Australia
www.smartraveller.gov.au

Canada
www.voyage.gc.ca

New Zealand
www.mft.govt.nz/travel

Republic of Ireland
http://foreignaffairs.gov.ie

UK
www.fco.gov.uk/travel

USA
www.state.gov/travel

Consulates

For a complete list, consult the Yellow Pages.

Australian Consulate-General
Suite 200, 625 Market Street, at New Montgomery Street, CA 94105 (536 1970/www.austemb.org). BART & Metro to Montgomery/ bus 2, 3, 4, 31 & Market Street routes. **Map** p315 N5.
British Consulate-General *Suite 850, 1 Sansome Street, at Market Street, CA 94104 (617 1300/www. britainusa.com/sf). BART & Metro to Montgomery/bus 2, 3, 4, 31 & Market Street routes.* **Map** p315 N5.
Consulate-General of Canada *Suite 1288, 580 California Street, at Kearny Street, CA 94104 (834 3180/www.dfait-maeci.gc.ca). Bus 1, 10, 12, 15, 41/cable car California.* **Map** p314 N4.
Consulate-General of Ireland *33rd Floor, 100 Pine Street, at Front Street, CA 94111 (392 4214/www. irelandemb.org). BART & Metro to Embarcadero/bus 2, 3, 4, 31 & Market Street routes.* **Map** p315 N4.
New Zealand Consulate *Suite 700, 1 Maritime Plaza, Front Street, at Clay Street, CA 94111 (399 1255/ www.mfat.govt.nz). BART & Metro to Embarcadero/bus 1, 2, 10, 14, 15, 31 & Market Street routes/cable car California.* **Map** p314 N4.

Consumer

Attorney General: Public Inquiry Unit
1-800 952 5225/http://ag.ca.gov/ consumers.
Call to complain about consumer law enforcement or any other agency.

Better Business Bureau
1-510 238 1000/www.goldengate bbb.org.
The BBB provides information on the reliability of a company and a list of companies with good business records. It's also the place to call to file a complaint about a company.

Customs

International travellers go through US Customs directly after Immigration. Give the official the filled-in white form you were given on the plane.

Foreign visitors can import the following goods duty free: 200 cigarettes or 50 cigars (not Cuban; over-18s) or 2kg of smoking tobacco; one litre of wine or spirits (over-21s); and

up to $100 in gifts ($800 for returning Americans). You must declare and maybe forfeit plants or foodstuffs. Check **US Customs** online for details (www.cbp.gov/xp/cgov/travel). **UK Customs & Excise** allows returning travellers to bring in £145 worth of goods.

Disabled

Despite its topography, San Francisco is disabled-friendly; California is the national leader in providing facilities for the disabled. All public buildings are required by law to be wheelchair-accessible; most city buses can 'kneel' to make access easier; the majority of city street corners have ramped kerbs; and most restaurants and hotels can accommodate wheelchairs. Privileges include free parking in designated (blue) areas and in most metered spaces; display a blue and white 'parking placard' for both. Still, what a building is supposed to have and what it actually has can be different; wheelchair-bound travellers should call the **Independent Living Resource Center** (543 6222, www.ilrcsf.org).

Braille Institute
1-800 272 4553.
Volunteers can connect anyone who has sight difficulties with services for the blind throughout the US.

California Relay Service
TTD to voice 1-800 735 2929/ voice to TTD 1-800 735 2922. **Open** 24hrs daily.
Relays calls between TTD and voice callers.

Crisis Line for the Handicapped
1-800 426 4263. **Open** 24hrs daily.
Phoneline/referral service with advice on many issues.

Electricity

US electricity voltage is 110-120V 60-cycle AC. Except for dual-voltage, flat-pin plug shavers, foreign appliances will usually need an adaptor.

Emergencies

Ambulance, fire or police *911.*
Coast Guard *399 3547.*
Poison Control Center *1-800 876 4766.*

Gay & lesbian

Community United Against Violence
333 4357/www.cuav.org.
A group assisting GLBT victims of domestic violence or hate crimes.

New Leaf
626 7000/www.newleafservices.org. **Open** 9am-8pm Mon-Fri.
A GLBT counselling service that deals with a variety of issues.

Parents, Families & Friends of Lesbians & Gays (P-FLAG)
921 8850/www.pflagsf.org. **Open** 24hr answerphone.
A helpline offering support for families and friends of gay and lesbian teens and adults.

Health & medical

For complementary medicine, *see p190*; for opticians, *see p191*; for pharmacies, *see p195*.

Accident & emergency

Foreign visitors should ensure they have full travel insurance: health treatment can be pricey. Call the emergency number on your insurance before seeking treatment; they'll direct you to a hospital that deals with your insurance company. There are 24hr emergency rooms at the locations listed below.

California Pacific Medical Center *Castro Street, at Duboce Avenue, Lower Haight (600 6000). Metro N to Duboce & Church/bus 24, 37.* **Map** p318 H9.
St Francis Memorial Hospital *900 Hyde Street, between Bush & Pine Streets, Nob Hill (353 6300). Bus 2, 3, 4, 27, 38, 76.* **Map** p314 K5.
San Francisco General Hospital *1001 Potrero Avenue, between 22nd & 23rd Streets, Potrero Hill (206 8111). Bus 9, 33, 48.* **Map** p319 M12.
UCSF Medical Center *505 Parnassus Avenue, between 3rd & Hillway Avenues, Sunset (476 1000). Metro N to UCSF/bus 6, 43.* **Map** p316 D10.

Directory

Clinics

Haight-Ashbury Free Clinics, Inc

558 Clayton Street, at Haight Street, Haight-Ashbury (487 5632/www. hafci.org). Bus 6, 7, 33, 43, 66, 71. **Open** *Appointments* call for details. *Drop-in clinic* from 4.45pm Mon; from 8.45am, 4.45pm Tue; from 8.45am Wed. **Map** p317 E9.
Health care, including a variety of speciality clinics, is provided to the uninsured on a sliding-scale basis; most patients pay little or nothing. Spanish and Hindi are also spoken.

Lyon-Martin Women's Health Services

1748 Market Street, between Octavia & Gough Streets, Upper Market (565 7667/www.lyon-martin.org). Metro to Van Ness/bus 6, 7, 66, 71. **Open** *Appointments* call for details. **Credit** MC, V. **Map** p318 J8.
Named after two founders of the modern lesbian movement in the US, this clinic offers affordable health care for women and transgender patients.

St Anthony Free Medical Clinic

121 Golden Gate Avenue, at Jones Street, Tenderloin (241 2600/www. stanthonysf.org). BART & Metro to Powell/bus 14, 26 & Market Street routes. **Open** *Drop-in clinic* 8am-noon, 1-4.30pm Mon-Fri. **Map** p314 L6.
Free medical services for those with or without insurance. Arrive early.

Contraception & abortion

Planned Parenthood Clinics

815 Eddy Street, between Van Ness Avenue & Franklin Street, Tenderloin (1-800 967 7526/www. plannedparenthood.org). BART & Metro to Civic Center/bus 31, 42, 47, 49. **Open** 9am-3pm Mon-Fri. **Credit** MC, V. **Map** p314 K6.
In addition to contraception, Planned Parenthood's multilingual staff provides low-cost general health-care services, HIV testing and gynaecological exams; with the exception of the morning-after pill, all are by appointment only.

Dentists

1-800 Dentist

1-800 336 8478/www.1800dentist. com. **Open** 24hrs daily.
Dental referrals.

University of the Pacific School of Dentistry

2155 Webster Street, at Sacramento Street, Pacific Heights (929 6400). Bus 1, 2, 3, 4, 22. **Open** 8.30am-5pm Mon-Fri. **Map** p313 H5.
Supervised dentists-in-training provide a low-cost service.

HIV & AIDS

AIDS-HIV Nightline

434 2437. **Open** 5pm-5am daily.
Hotline offering emotional support.

California AIDS Foundation

1-800 367 2437. **Open** 9am-5pm Mon, Wed-Fri; 9am-9pm Tue.
Information and advice.

Helplines

Alcoholics Anonymous *674 1821/www.alcoholics-anonymous.org.* **Open** 24hrs daily.
Drug Crisis Information *362 3400/hearing-impaired 781 2224.* **Open** 24hrs daily.
Narcotics Anonymous *621 8600/www.na.org.* **Open** 24hrs daily.
SF General Hospital Psychiatric Helpline *206 8125.* **Open** 24hrs daily.
SF Rape Treatment Center *206 3222.* **Open** 8am-5pm Mon-Fri.
Suicide Prevention *781 0500/ www.sfsuicide.org.* **Open** 24hrs daily.
Talk Line Family Support *441 5437/www.sfcapc.org.* **Open** 24hrs daily.
Victims of Crime Resource Center *1-800 842 8467.* **Open** 8am-6pm Mon-Fri.
Women Against Rape Crisis Hotline *647 7273.* **Open** 24hrs daily.

ID

Even if you look 30, you'll need photo ID (preferably a driver's licence with a photo) to get into the city's bars, or to buy alcohol in a restaurant or shop.

Immigration

Immigration regulations apply to all visitors to the US. During the flight, you will be issued with an immigration form to present to an official on the ground. You'll have your fingerprints and photograph taken as you pass through. If you have a foreign passport, expect close questioning. For more on passports, *see p289* **Passport update**; for visas, *see p294*.

Insurance

Non-nationals should arrange comprehensive baggage, trip-cancellation and medical insurance before they leave. US citizens should consider doing the same. Read the small print: consequences of security scares, including cancelled flights, may not be covered.

Internet

Getting online here is very easy these days. Most hotels (*see pp42-62*) offer some form of in-room high-speed access – via cable or wireless networks – for travellers with laptops; a number of hotels also provide at least one public computer. In addition, a number of cafés and even a few bars across the city offer 'free' wireless access (you pay for your drink, but not the connection), and the city has even set up a handful of wireless 'hotspots', where anyone can connect to an open network; the most famous is in Union Square. If you don't have a laptop, head to the Main Library (*see p78*), which has several terminals available for free, or to one of the city's internet cafés (*see p139* **Get connected**). For more on getting online in the city, see www.bawug.org or http:// metrofreefi.com.

Left luggage

Leaving luggage has got trickier since 9/11. However, larger hotels may allow you to leave bags, while at SFO, you can store everything from bags to bicycles at the Airport Travel Agency (1-650 877 0422, 7am-11pm daily), on the Departures level of the International Terminal.

Legal help

Lawyer Referral Service
989 1616/www.sfbar.org.
pen 8.30am-5.30pm Mon-Fri.
Callers are referred to attorneys and
mediators for all legal problems.

Libraries

For San Francisco Main
Library, see p78; for business
libraries, see p286.

Lost property

Property Control
850 Bryant Street, between 6th
& 7th Streets, SoMa (553 1377).
Bus 12, 19, 27, 47. Open 8.30am-
4.30pm Mon-Fri. Map p319 M8.
Make a police report – then hope.

Airports
For items lost en route, contact the
specific airline. If you leave a bag at
the airport, it may get destroyed, but
it's worth calling the numbers below.

**San Francisco International
Airport** 1-650 821 7014.
Open 8am-8pm Mon-Fri.
**Mineta San Jose International
Airport** 1-408 277 5419.
Open 7am-6pm Mon-Fri.
Oakland International Airport
1-510 563 3982. Open 8.30am-5pm
daily.

Public transport
The **Muni** lost-and-found office is on
923 6168. For **BART**, phone 1-510
464 7090; for **AC Transit**, try 1-510
891 4706; call 257 4476 for **Golden
Gate Transit**; and for **SamTrans**,
dial 1-800 660 4287.

Taxis
Phone the relevant firm (see p284).

Media

The San Francisco media
exists not only to report what's
going on, but to confirm the
inhabitants' collective belief
that they're living in the most
trend-setting quadrant of the
globe. The city supports only
one major newspaper, the
San Francisco Chronicle, as
well as a faltering tabloid,
the Examiner. Livelier are the
alternative weekly tabloids, the
San Francisco Bay Guardian
and SF Weekly. The best
media, though, are based out
of town. The San Jose Mercury
News remains the best read,
and Oakland's KTVU (channel
2) gets the best news ratings.

Newspapers

Local papers are listed below.
For broader coverage, try the
regional edition of the New
York Times ($1) or the national
edition of the Los Angeles
Times ($1). USA Today (75¢)
makes good fishwrap; it's
distributed free in many hotels.

San Francisco Chronicle
www.sfgate.com/chronicle.
Complaining about the Chron (50¢)
has become a San Francisco cliché.
The region's largest circulation paper,
it's the only real choice for local news
since the Hearst Corporation bought
it for $660 million in 2000 and closed
down the Examiner, its only rival
(it's since re-emerged as a tabloid, but
it's hardly a rival). The sports writing
is generally engaging, and both the
'Datebook' culture section and the
presence of a few good columnists
make it a decent Sunday read, but
the Chron still lacks the punch and
vigour of a big-city newspaper.

San Francisco Examiner
www.examiner.com.
This free tabloid is sometimes good
for a laugh or a sensational story.

San Jose Mercury News
www.mercurynews.com.
If you're thirsting for news outside
San Francisco, this paper (25¢) offers
the Bay Area's best overall news
reporting, business and sport; its
business coverage of Silicon Valley
and internet commerce is first-rate.

Alternative weeklies

San Francisco Bay Guardian
www.sfbg.com.
One of a pair of free weekly arts
tabloids that battle for supremacy in
San Francisco, this thick, lively rag

Passport update

People of all ages who enter the US on the Visa Waiver
Progam (VWP; see p294) are now required to carry their own
machine-readable passport, or MRP. MRPs are recognisable
by the double row of characters along the foot of the data
page. All burgundy EU and EU-lookalike passports issued
in the UK since 1991 (and still valid) should be machine
readable. Some of those issued outside the country may
not be, however; in this case, holders should apply for a
replacement even if the passport has not expired. Check at
your local passport-issuing post office if in any doubt at all.

The US requirement for passports to contain a 'biometric'
chip applies only to those issued from 26 October 2006.
By then, all new and replacement UK passports should be
compliant, following a gradual phase-in. The biometric chip
contains a facial scan and biographical data.

Though it is being considered for 2008 (when ID cards
may be introduced), there is no current requirement for UK
passports to contain fingerprint or iris data. The application
process remains as it was, except for new guidelines that
ensure the photograph you submit can be used to generate
the facial scan in the chip.

Further information for UK citizens is available at www.
passport.gov.uk or 0870 521 0410. Nationals of other
countries should check well in advance of their trip whether
their passport meets the requirements for the time of their
trip, at http://travel.state.gov/visa and with the issuing
authorities of their home country.

mixes a progressive stance – it eagerly annoys the conservative local establishment by exposing cronyism, graft, fraud and double standards – with arts coverage. Available free from newspaper boxes and in bars, restaurants, cafés and coffeeshops.

SF Weekly

www.sfweekly.com.
Lighter on politics and issue-oriented pieces than the *BG*, the *Weekly* betters it with its arts coverage, more comprehensive than that of its rival. In common with many alternative weeklies, some of the pieces could stand to lose 1,000 words here or there, but the writing is generally strong. Highlights include a personal ads section so steamy it would make an exhibitionist blush. Available in the same places that carry the *BG*.

San Francisco Bay Times

www.sfbaytimes.com.
A free fortnightly tabloid directed at the gay and lesbian community. It features listings, commentary, classified advertisements and personals. Find it in coffeeshops and bookstores in the Castro.

BAR (Bay Area Reporter)

www.ebar.com.
Similar to the *Bay Times*, the free weekly *BAR* features listings and news that affects the gay community. Copies can be found in most of the same places as the *Bay Times*.

Street Sheet

Written by the homeless and sold by them for $1. No need to look for it: it will come looking for you.

Magazines

San Francisco Magazine (www.sanfran.com) is a lively glossy monthly covering everything from local politics to the dining scene. Literary periodical *Zyzzyva* (www.zyzzyva.org), produced three times a year, offers short stories, poetry, creative non-fiction and original art. Francis Ford Coppola's quarterly *Zoetrope: All-Story Magazine* publishes short fiction and one-act plays. The quarterly *Juxtapoz* preaches to the alt-arts crowd. *The Believer* is a literary and culture monthly associated with *McSweeney's* and Dave Eggers.

Television

The Bay Area has affiliates of all three major networks: ABC (local station is KGO, found on channel 7), NBC (KNTV, channel 11) and CBS (KPIX, channel 5). KRON (channel 4) is devoted to Bay Area news and syndicated sitcoms; KTVU (channel 2) is part of the Fox TV network. PBS, the Public Broadcasting Service, has stations in San Francisco (KQED, on channel 9), in San Jose (KTEH, channel 54) and in San Mateo (KCSM, channel 60).

Radio

San Francisco's constantly changing radio profile reflects a number of ongoing difficulties: attracting enough listeners in a competitive market, and outsmarting weather and geography, which combine to undermine reliable radio signals. But Bay Area radio is still spectacular.

The weaker, non-commercial stations lie to the left of the FM dial; the powerhouses with the loudest ads cluster on the right. AM is mostly reserved for talk, news and sports broadcasts, with a few foreign-language, oldie and Christian stations peppering the mix.

News & talk

For news, **KGO-AM** (810 AM; www.kgoam810.com), NPR-affiliated **KQED** (88.5 FM; www.kqed.org) and **KALW** (91.7 FM; www.kalw.org) remain your best bets. **KCBS** (740 AM; www.kcbs.com) runs solid news and priceless traffic reports (every 10mins). Berkeley-based **KPFA** (94.1 FM; www.kpfa.org) offers a jumble of talk programming during the day. A welcome recent addition is left-wing Air America, on **KQKE** (960 AM; www.quakeradio.com). For sports, try **KNBR** (680 AM; www.knbr.com)

Classical & jazz

KDFC (102.1 FM; www.kdfc.com) is the best classical station in the city, but its programming is conservative. There's less choice for jazz fans: the most popular 'jazz' station in the city is **KKSF** (103.7 FM; www.kksf.com), which deals only in elevator-friendly smooth jazz.

Dance, hip hop & soul

KMEL (106.1 FM; www.106kmel.com) is the Bay Area's foremost station for hip hop. **KYLD** (94.9 FM; www.wild949.com) is a party station. For something different, tune in to non-profit **KPOO** (89.5 FM, www.kpoo.com), where innovative hip hop and hardcore rap alternate with cool blues shows on weekend nights.

Rock & pop

KLLC (97.3 FM; www.radioalice.com) dominates the airwaves with its mix of mid-1990s comfort-rock and endless plays of the latest Maroon 5 **KITS** (105.3 FM; www.live105.com), offers a more alternative mix; **KFOG** (104.5 FM; www.kfog.com) plays the classic-rock card. Those in search of more eclectic listening tune in to college and independent stations such as **KFJC** (89.7 FM; www.kfjc.org), UC Berkeley's **KALX** (90.7 FM; http://kalx.berkeley.edu) and **KUSF** (90.3 FM; http://kusf.org), where you'll find all manner of diverse and distinctive sounds.

Money

The US dollar ($) is divided into 100 cents (¢). Coin denominations run from the copper penny (1¢) to the silver nickel (5¢), dime (10¢), quarter (25¢) and less-common half-dollar (50¢). There are also two $1 coins: the silver Susan B Anthony and the gold Sacagawea. Notes or 'bills' are the same green colour and size; they come in denominations of $1, $5, $10, $20, $50 and $100. The $20 and $50 have recently been redesigned with features that make them hard to forge, including, for the first time, some subtle colours other than green and black. Old-style bills remain legal currency.

ATMs

There are ATMs throughout the city: in banks, stores and even bars. ATMs accept Visa, MasterCard and American Express, as well as other cards, but almost all charge a usage fee. If you don't remember your PIN, most banks will dispense cash to cardholders. Wells Fargo offers cash advances at all of its branches.

Directory

Banks & bureaux de change

Most banks are open from 9am to 6pm Monday to Friday and from 9am to 3pm on Saturday. Photo ID is required to cash travellers' cheques. Many banks don't exchange foreign currency, so arrive with some US dollars. If you arrive after 6pm, change money at the airport. If you want to cash travellers' cheques at a shop, note that some require a minimum purchase. You can also obtain cash with a credit card from certain banks, but be prepared to pay interest rates that vary daily.

American Express Travel Services

455 Market Street, at 1st Street, Financial District (536 2600/www. americanexpress.com/travel). BART & Metro to Montgomery/ bus 2, 3, 4, 31 & Market Street routes. **Open** 9am-5.30pm Mon-Fri; 10am-2pm Sat. **Map** p315 N5.
AmEx will change travellers' cheques and money, and also offers (for AmEx cardholders only) poste restante.

Western Union

1-800 325 6000/www.westernunion. com. **Open** 24hrs daily.
The old standby for bailing travellers out of trouble. Get advice on how to get money wired to you and where to pick it up. You can also wire money to anyone outside the state over the phone, using your MasterCard or Visa. Expect to pay a huge commission when sending money.

Credit cards

Bring at least one major credit card: they are accepted – often required – at nearly all hotels, restaurants and shops. The cards most accepted in the US are American Express, Diners Club, Discover, MasterCard and Visa.

Lost or stolen cards

American Express Cards 1-800 992 3404. Travellers' cheques 1-800 221 7282.
Diners Club 1-800 234 6377.
Discover 1-800 347 2683.
MasterCard 1-800 622 7747.
Visa Cards 1-800 847 2911. Travellers' cheques 1-800 227 6811.

Police stations

Central Station 766 Vallejo Street, between Stockton & Powell Streets, North Beach (315 2400). Bus 12, 15, 41, 45/cable car Powell-Mason. **Map** p315 M3.
Southern Station 850 Bryant Street, between 6th & 7th Streets, SoMa (553 1373). Bus 12, 19, 27, 47. **Map** p319 M8.

Postal services

Post offices mostly open from 9am to 5.30pm Monday to Friday, 9am to 2pm Saturday. All close on Sundays. Phone 1-800 275 8777 for information on your nearest branch. Stamps can be bought at any post office and also at some hotel receptions, vending machines and ATMs. Stamps for postcards within the US cost 23¢; for Europe, the charge is 70¢. For couriers and shippers, see p286.

Poste Restante (General Delivery)

Main Post Office, 101 Hyde Street, at Golden Gate Avenue, Civic Center (1-800 275 8777). BART & Metro to Civic Center/bus 21, 47, 49 & Market Street routes. **Open** 10am-2pm Mon-Sat. **Map** p318 L7.
If you need to receive mail in SF and you're not sure where you'll be staying, have the envelope addressed with your name, c/o General Delivery, San Francisco, CA 94102, USA. Mail is only kept for ten days from receipt, and you must present some photo ID to retrieve it.

Religion

SF is teeming with temples, whether Baptist or Buddhist, Nazarene or Satanic. For more, see the Yellow Pages.

Calvary Presbyterian
2515 Fillmore Street, at Jackson Street, Pacific Heights (346 3832/ www.calvarypresbyterian.org). Bus 3, 12, 24. **Map** p309 E3.
Cathedral of St Mary of the Assumption 1111 Gough Street, at Geary Boulevard, Western Addition (567 2020/www.stmarycathedral sf.org). Bus 2, 3, 4, 38. **Map** p314 J6.
Glide Memorial
330 Ellis Street, at Taylor Street, Tenderloin (771 6300/www.glide. org). Bus 1, 15, 30, 45/cable car California. **Map** p314 L6.

Grace Cathedral
1100 California Street, at Taylor Street, Nob Hill (749 6300/www. gracecathedral.org). Bus 1, 27/ cable car California. **Map** p314 L5.
Old St Mary's Cathedral 660 California Street, at Grant Avenue, Chinatown (288 3800/www.oldsaint marys.org). Bus 1, 15, 30, 45/cable car California. **Map** p315 M5.
St Boniface Catholic Church 133 Golden Gate Avenue, at Leavenworth Street, Tenderloin (863 7515/www.sfarchdiocese.org). BART & Metro to Civic Center/bus 27, 30, 45 & Market Street routes. **Map** p318 L7.
St Paul's Lutheran Church 930 Gough Street, between Turk & Eddy Streets, Western Addition (673 8088). Bus 31, 47, 49. **Map** p314 J6.
Temple Emanu-el
2 Lake Street, at Arguello Boulevard, Presidio Heights (751 2535/www. emanuelsf.org). Bus 1, 4, 33, 44. **Map** p312 D6.
Zen Center
300 Page Street, at Laguna Street, Lower Haight (863 3136/www.sfzc. org). Bus 6, 7, 66, 71. **Map** p318 J8.

Safety & security

Crime is a reality in all big cities, but San Franciscans generally feel secure in their town. There is really just one basic rule of thumb you need to follow: use your common sense. If a neighbourhood doesn't feel safe to you, it probably isn't. Only a few areas warrant caution during daylight hours and are of particular concern at night. These include the Tenderloin (north and east of Civic Center); SoMa (near the Mission/6th Street corner); Mission Street between 13th and 18th Streets; and the Hunter's Point neighbourhood near 3Com Park. Golden Gate Park should be avoided at night. Many tourist areas, most notably around Union Square, are sprinkled with homeless people who beg for change but are basically pretty harmless.

If you're unlucky enough to be mugged, your best bet is to give your attackers whatever they want, then call the police from the nearest pay phone by dialling 911. (Don't forget to get the reference number on

Directory

the claim report for insurance purposes and to get travellers' cheque refunds.) If you are the victim of a sexual assault and wish to make a report, call the police, who will escort you to the hospital for treatment. For helplines that serve victims of rape or other crimes, *see p288.*

Smoking

Smokers may rank as the only group of people who are not especially welcome in San Francisco. The city is party to some of the stiffest anti-smoking laws in the US: smoking is banned in all public places, including banks, sporting arenas, theatres, offices, the lobbies of buildings, shops, restaurants, bars, and any and every form of public transport. There are many small hotels and B&Bs that don't allow you to light up anywhere inside (and, boy, do they get cross if you do). On the other hand, a select few bars cheerfully ignore the law.

Study

California's higher education system is a hierarchy that starts with publicly funded community colleges and city colleges at the lower end of the scale, followed by California State Universities, which cater primarily to undergraduates and do not grant doctorates, and then, at the top of the pile, the University of California system, which includes formal, research-oriented universities with rigorous entry demands (increasingly so, given recent funding cuts). There are also many private – and pricey – universities, among them Stanford and the University of San Francisco.

In general, universities in the United States are much more flexible about part-time studying than their European counterparts. Stipulations for non-English-speaking students might include passing the TOEFL (Test of English as a Foreign Language); most students also have to give proof of financial support.

Visas & ID cards

To study in the Bay Area (or, for that matter, anywhere in the United States), exchange students should apply for a J-1 visa, while full-time students enrolled in a degree programme must apply for an F-1 visa. Both are valid for the duration of the course and for a limited period thereafter.

Foreign students need an International Student Identity Card (ISIC) as proof of student status. This can be bought from your local travel agent or student travel office. In San Francisco, an ISIC can be bought at either of the two STA Travel offices (530 Bush Street, between Grant Avenue and Stockton Street, 421 3473; 36 Geary Street, between Kearny Street and Grant Avenue, 391 8407). You'll need proof you're a student, ID and a passport-size photo.

Tax

Sales tax of 8.5 per cent is added on to the label price in shops within city limits, and 8.25 per cent in surrounding cities. Hotels charge a 14 per cent room tax and the same percentage on hotel parking.

Telephones

Dialling & codes

The phone system is reliable and, for local calls, cheap. Long-distance, particularly overseas, calls are best paid for with a rechargeable, pre-paid phonecard ($6-$35) available from vending machines and many shops. You can use your MasterCard with AT&T (1-800 225 5288) or Sprint (1-800 877 4646).

Direct dial calls

If you are dialling outside your area code, dial 1 + area code + phone number; on pay phones an operator or recording will tell you how much money to add. All phone numbers in this guide are given as if dialled from San Francisco; hence, Berkeley numbers have the 1-510 prefix, while Marin County numbers have no prefix.

Collect calls

For collect or when using a phone card, dial 0 + area code + phone number and listen for the operator/ recorded instructions. If you're completely befuddled, dial 0 and plead your case with the operator.

Area codes

San Francisco & Marin County 415
Oakland & Berkeley 510
The peninsula cities 650
San Jose 408
Napa, Sonoma & Mendocino Counties 707

International calls

Dial 011 followed by the country code. If you need operator assistance with international calls, dial 00.

Australia 61
Germany 49
Japan 81
New Zealand 64
UK 44

Public phones

Public pay phones only accept nickels, dimes and quarters, but check for a dialling tone before you start feeding in your change. Local calls usually cost 35¢, though some companies operate pay phones that charge exorbitant prices, The rate also rises steeply as the distance between callers increases (an operator or recorded message will tell you how much to add).

Operator services

Operator assistance 0
Emergency (police, ambulance and fire) 911
Local and **long-distance directory enquiries** 411
Toll-free numbers generally start with 1-800, 1-888 or 1-877, while pricey pay-per-call lines (usually phone-sex numbers) start with 1-900; don't confuse them.

Telephone directories

Directories in San Francisco are divided into Yellow Pages (classified) and White Pages (business and residential), and are available at many public phones, in hotels and at libraries around the city. They contain a wealth of travel information, including area codes, event calendars, park facilities, post office addresses and city zip codes. If you can't find a directory in the phone booth you're using, dial 411 (for directory assistance) and ask for your listing by name (and, if you have it, the address).

Mobile phones

San Francisco, like most of the continental US, operates on the 1900 GSM frequency. Travellers from Europe with tri-band phones will be able to connect to one or more of the networks here with no problems, assuming their service provider at home has an arrangement with a local network; always check before travelling. European travellers with dual-band phones, however, will need to rent a handset upon arrival.

Check the price of calls before you go. Rates may be hefty and, unlike in the UK, you'll probably be charged for receiving as well as making calls. It might be cheaper to rent or buy a mobile phone while you're in town – try the agency below, or check the Yellow Pages. Alternatively, you can simply get a pre-paid SIM card when you arrive.

AllCell Rentals

1-877 724 2355/www.allcellrentals. com. **Open** 24hrs daily. **Credit** AmEx, DC, Disc, MC, V.
Rentals of mobile, GSM and satellite phones and pagers. You pay for daily, weekly or monthly rental ($4.95-$69.95), plus the airtime ($1.45 per minute). There also may be a delivery fee, depending on the product you rent.

Time & dates

San Francisco is on **Pacific Standard Time**, which is three hours behind Eastern Standard Time (New York) and eight hours behind Greenwich Mean Time (UK). Daylight Savings Time, which is almost concurrent with British Summer Time, runs from the first Sunday in April, when the clocks are rolled ahead one hour, to the last Sunday in October. Going from the west to east coast, Pacific Time is one hour behind Mountain Time and two hours behind Central Time, three hours behind Eastern Time.

British readers should note that in the US, **dates** are written in the order month, day, year: 2.5.98 is February 5, not May 2.

Tipping

Unlike in Europe, tipping is a way of life in the US: many locals in service industries rely on gratuities as part of their income, so you should tip accordingly. In general, tip bellhops and baggage handlers $1-$2 a bag; tip cab drivers, waiters and waitresses, hairdressers and food delivery people 15-20 per cent of the total tab; tip valets $2-$3; and tip counter staff 25¢ to 10 per cent of the order, depending on its size. In restaurants, you should tip at least 15 per cent of the total bill and usually nearer 20 per cent; most restaurants will add this to the bill automatically for a table of six or more. In bars, bank on tipping around a buck a drink, especially if you want to hang around for a while. If you look after the bartender, they'll look after you; tipping pocket change may leave you dry for a while.

If you get good service, leave a good tip; if you get bad service, leave little and tip the management with words.

Toilets/restrooms

Restrooms can be found in prime tourist areas such as Fisherman's Wharf and Golden Gate Park, as well as in shopping malls. If you're caught short, don't hesitate to enter a restaurant or a bar and ask to use its facilities.

In keeping with its cosmopolitan standing, San Francisco has installed 20 of the French-designed, self-cleaning JC Decaux lavatories throughout the high-traffic areas of the city. Keep an eye out for these forest-green commodes (they're usually plastered with high-profile advertising). Admission is 25¢ for 20min; after that, you may be fined for indecent exposure, because the door pings open automatically. Be aware that some people use the toilets for purposes other than those for which they were designed.

Tourist information

One of the attractions of San Francisco is that there are many wonderful places to visit beyond the city itself. For full listings of the best of these options, including details on tourist offices, *see pp258-280.*

San Francisco Visitor Information Center

Lower level of Hallidie Plaza, corner of Market & Powell Streets (391 2000/http://onlysf.sfvisitor.org). *BART & Metro to Powell/bus 27, 30, 45 & Market Street routes/cable car Powell-Hyde or Powell-Mason.* **Open** 9am-5pm Mon-Fri; 9am-3pm Sat, Sun. **Map** p315 M6.
Located in Downtown, this is the visitor centre for the efficient and helpful San Francisco Convention & Visitor Bureau. You won't find any parking, but you will find tons of free maps, brochures, coupons and advice. The number above gives access to a 24hr recorded message listing daily events and activities; you can also use it to request free information about hotels, restaurants and shopping.

Directory

Climate

	Average high	Average low	Average rain
Jan	56°F (13°C)	46°F (8°C)	4.5in (11.4cm)
Feb	60°F (15°C)	48°F (9°C)	2.8in (7.1cm)
Mar	61°F (16°C)	49°F (9°C)	2.6in (6.6cm)
Apr	63°F (17°C)	50°F (10°C)	1.5in (3.8cm)
May	64°F (17°C)	51°F (10°C)	0.4in (1cm)
June	66°F (19°C)	53°F (11°C)	0.2in (0.5cm)
July	66°F (19°C)	54°F (12°C)	0.1in (0.25cm)
Aug	66°F (19°C)	54°F (12°C)	0.1in (0.25cm)
Sept	70°F (21°C)	56°F (13°C)	0.2in (0.5cm)
Oct	69°F (20°C)	55°F (13°C)	1.1in (2.8cm)
Nov	64°F (18°C)	51°F (10°C)	2.5in (6.4cm)
Dec	57°F (14°C)	47°F (8°C)	3.5in (8.9cm)

Berkeley Convention & Visitors Bureau

2015 Center Street, between Shattuck & Milvia Streets, Berkeley, CA 94704 (1-800 847 4823/1-510 549 7040/www.visitberkeley.com). BART Downtown Berkeley. **Open** 9am-5pm Mon-Fri.
A block from the Downtown Berkeley BART station. Staff can post a visitors' guide on request.

Oakland Convention & Visitors Bureau

463 11th Street, between Broadway & Washington Streets, Oakland, CA 94609 (1-510 839 9000/www. oaklandcvb.com). BART 12th Street/ City Center. **Open** 8.30am-5pm Mon-Fri.
Located in opposite the City Hall in downtown Oakland. Phone them if you would like to be sent a visitors' guide to Oakland.

Visas

Under the current **Visa Waiver Scheme**, citizens of 27 countries, including the UK, Ireland, Australia and New Zealand, do not need a visa for stays of less than 90 days (for business or pleasure). Visitors are required to have a machine-readable passport that's valid for the full 90-day period and a return or open standby ticket. Mexicans and Canadians don't usually need visas but must have legal proof of their citizenship. All other travellers must have

visas. However, given current security fears, it's advisable to double-check requirements before you set out. For more, *see p286* **Travel advice**, *p288* **Immigration** and *p289* **Passport update**; *see also below* **Work**.

Visa application forms and complete information can be obtained from the nearest US embassy or consulate. It's wise to send in your application at least three weeks before you plan to travel. If you require a visa more urgently you should apply via the travel agent who is booking your ticket.

For further information on visa requirements, see http:// travel.state.gov. UK citizens can call the Visa Information Line: 09042 450100 (£1.20/ min) or look online at www.usembassy.org.uk.

When to go

Climate

San Francisco may be in California, but its climate, like its politics, is all its own. When planning a trip, don't anticipate the normal seasons, climatically, at least. Spring and autumn are relatively predictable, with warm days and cool nights. During the summer, however, days are

often chilly, but the nights are usually mild. In midwinter, what seems like months of rain will break for a week of sun. In general, temperatures rarely stray above 80°F (27°C) or below 45°F (7°C).

San Francisco is small, but the weather varies wildly between neighbourhoods. The city's western terrain is flat, and so fog often covers Golden Gate Park and the Sunset and Richmond areas. However, the fog is often too heavy to climb further east, so the areas east of Twin Peaks – the Mission, the Castro, Noe Valley – are often sunny just as Golden Gate Park is shrouded in fog. Add in the wind that whips in to Fisherman's Wharf, and you may experience four seasons in one day.

Public holidays

New Year's Day (1 Jan); **Martin Luther King Jr Day** (3rd Mon in Jan); **President's Day** (3rd Mon in Feb); **Memorial Day** (last Mon in May); **Independence Day** (4 July); **Labor Day** (1st Mon in Sept); **Columbus Day** (2nd Mon in Oct); **Veterans' Day** (11 Nov); **Thanksgiving Day** (4th Thur in Nov); **Christmas Day** (25 Dec).

Work

For foreigners to work legally in the US, a US company must sponsor your application for an **H-1 visa**, which enables you to work in the country for up to five years. For the H-1 visa to be approved, your prospective employer must convince the Immigration Department that there is no American citizen qualified to do the job as well as you. Students have a much easier time. UK students can contact the **British Universities North America Club** (BUNAC) for help in arranging a temporary job and the requisite visa (16 Bowling Green Lane, London, EC1R 0QH; 020 7251 3472, www. bunac.org/uk).

Further Reference

Fiction & poetry

Isabel Allende
Daughters of Fortune
A delightfully written piece centred on the Gold Rush and one young woman's search for love in a tumultous city.
James Dalessandro *1906 A Novel*
A fictionalised, though grippingly researched, account of San Francisco's catastrophic year of earthquake and fire.
Dave Eggers *A Heartbreaking Work of Staggering Genius*
A beautiful memoir of bringing up a younger brother, wrapped in fun postmodern flim-flam.
Jim Fadiman
The Other Side of Haight
This enjoyable book details the early psychedelic experiments in the Haight-Ashbury neighbourhood.
Allen Ginsberg
Howl and Other Poems
Grab your chance to read the rant that caused all the fuss way back in the 1950s.
Glen David Gold
Carter Beats the Devil
A sleight-of-hand comedy thriller set in 1920s San Francisco.
Dashiell Hammett
The Maltese Falcon
One of the greatest detective writers and one of the world's best detective novels, set in a dark and dangerous San Francisco.
Jack Kerouac *On the Road; The Subterraneans; Desolation Angels; The Dharma Bums*
Famous for a reason: bittersweet tales of drugs and sex in San Francisco and around the world, from the best Beat of them all.
Jack London *Tales of the Fish Patrol; John Barleycorn*
Early works from London, set in the writer's native city. For his musings on the Sonoma Valley, pick up *Valley of the Moon*.
Armistead Maupin
Tales of the City (6 volumes)
This witty soap opera, later a very successful TV series, follows the lives and loves of a group of San Francisco friends.
Frank Norris *McTeague*
Working-class life and loss set in unromanticised Barbary Coast days. A cult classic of the 1890s.
James Patterson *1st to Die*
A detective, diagnosed with a terminal illness, struggles to catch a serial killer in San Francisco.
Domenic Stansberry
The Last Days of Il Duce
A fearsome, authentic piece of *noir* fiction, set in North Beach.

John Steinbeck
The Grapes of Wrath
Grim tales of California in the Great Depression by the master of American fiction.
Amy Tan *The Joy Luck Club*
A moving story of the lives and loves of two generations of Chinese-American women living in San Francisco.
Alfredo Vea *Gods Go Begging*
A San Francisco murder trial has ties to the Vietnam War.
William T Vollmann
Whores for Gloria
The boozy story of a middle-aged alcoholic whose fall into decrepitude occurs in the seamy underbelly of the Tenderloin.
Tom Wolfe *The Electric Kool-Aid Acid Test; The Pump House Gang*
Alternative lifestyles in trippy, hippy, 1960s California.

Non-fiction

Walton Bean
California: An Interpretive History
An anecdotal account of California's shady past.
Po Bronson
The Nudist on the Late Shift
An unblinking treatise on the Silicon Valley scene.
Herb Caen *Baghdad by the Bay*
Local gossip and lightly poetic insight from the much-missed *Chronicle* columnist.
Carolyn Cassady
Off the Road: My Years with Cassady, Kerouac and Ginsberg
Not enlightened feminism, but an interesting alternative examination of the Beats.
Joan Didion
Slouching Towards Bethlehem; The White Album
Brilliant essays examining California in the past couple of decades by one of America's most respected authors.
Timothy W Drescher
San Francisco Bay Area Murals
A well-resourced book with plenty of maps and 140 photos.
Lawrence Ferlinghetti & Nancy J Peters *Literary San Francisco*
The city's literary pedigree examined by the founder of City Lights books.
Robert Greenfield *Dark Star: An Oral Biography of Jerry Garcia*
The life and (high) times of the Grateful Dead's late frontman.
Emmett Grogan
Ringolevio: A Life Played for Keeps
Part-memoir, part-social history, part-fable, *Ringolevio* traces the story of Grogan, one of the founders of the Diggers, from New York to 1960s Haight-Ashbury. Fantastic.

Michael Lewis *Moneyball: The Art of Winning an Unfair Game*
Oakland A's GM Billy Beane may go down as one of the most influential baseball executives of the last half-century. This vital book profiles Beane and his team.
Beth Lisick
Everybody into the Pool
A tremendously enjoyable and occasionally laugh-out-loud funny collection of essays about Lisick's journey from child to adult in the Bay Area.
Malcolm Margolin
The Ohlone Way
How the Bay Area's original inhabitants lived, researched from oral histories.
John Miller (ed) *San Francisco Stories: Great Writers on the City*
Contributions by Herb Caen, Anne Lamott, Amy Tan, Ishmael Reed and many others.
Ray Mungo
San Francisco Confidential
A gossipy look behind the city's closed doors.
John Plunkett & Barbara Traub (eds) *Burning Man*
Photo-heavy manual to the the annual insanity that is the Burning Man Festival.
Marc Reisner *Cadillac Desert: A Dangerous State*
The role of water in California's history and future; a projection of apocalypse founded on shifting tectonics and hairtrigger irrigation.
Nathaniel Rich *San Francisco Noir*
San Francisco's cinematic history gets re-examined in this beautifully written piece, which falls somewhere between guidebook, cultural criticism and academic tract.
Richard Schwartz *Berkeley 1900*
An in-depth account of the early origins of complex and controversial Berkeley.
Joel Selvin *San Francisco: The Magical History*
Tour of the sights and sounds of the city's pop music history by the *Chronicle*'s music critic.
Randy Shilts
And the Band Played On
Shilts' crucial work is still the most important account of the AIDS epidemic in San Francisco.
John Snyder *San Francisco Secrets: Fascinating Facts About the City by the Bay*
This amusing collection of city trivia comes complete with facts and figures galore.
Gertrude Stein
The Making of Americans
This autobiographical work includes an account of Stein's early childhood in Oakland.

**Tom Stienstra & Ann Marie
Brown** *California Hiking*
What it says: an outstanding guide
to over 1,000 hikes all over the state.
Stienstra is the outdoors columnist
for the *San Francisco Chronicle*.
Other books in the excellent
Fogohorn Outdoors series on
California cover camping, hiking,
biking and fishing.
Robert Louis Stevenson
*An Inland Voyage; The Silverado
Squatters*
Autobiographical narratives
describing the journey from Europe
to western America.
Bonnie Wach
San Francisco As You Like It
City tours to suit pretty much all
personalities and moods, from Ivy
League shoppers to cheapskate
fitness-freak vegetarians.

Film

Birdman of Alctraz (1961)
Hopelessly overlong and laughably
inaccurate, but, thanks largely to
Burt Lancaster's likeable title turn,
a decent film regardless.
Bullitt (1968)
This Steve McQueen film boasts
the all-time greatest San Francisco
car chase.
Chan Is Missing (1982)
Two cab drivers search for a man
who stole their life savings in this
movie, which gives an authentic,
insider's look at Chinatown.
The Conversation (1974)
Gene Hackman's loner surveillance
expert gets a little deeper than he
planned in Coppola's classic. The
opening scene, shot in Union Square,
is a cinematic *tour de force*.
Crumb (1994)
An award-winning film about the
comic book master and misanthrope
Robert Crumb.
Dark Passage (1947)
This classic thriller starts in Marin
County, where Bogart escapes from
San Quentin Prison, and ends up in
Lauren Bacall's SF apartment.
Dirty Harry (1971)
Do you feel lucky?
The Graduate (1967)
Hoffman at his best, with shots of
Berkeley as well as a a cool wrong-
direction shot on the Bay Bridge.
Harold and Maude (1971)
Bay Area scenery abounds in this
bittersweet cult classic about an
unbalanced boy who falls in love
with an elderly woman.
Jimi Plays Berkeley (1970)
Stirring footage of the town during
its radical days, plus Hendrix at his
very best.
The Maltese Falcon (1941)
Hammett's classic made into a
glorious 1940s thriller, full of great
street scenes.

Mrs Doubtfire (1993)
Relentlessly hammy Robin Williams
plays a divorcee posing as a nanny to
be near his kids.
Pacific Heights (1990)
Pity the poor landlord: Michael
Keaton preys on doting yuppie
parents-to-be.
San Francisco (1936)
Ignore the first 90 minutes of
moralising and sit back to enjoy the
Great Quake.
So I Married An Axe Murderer
(1993)
This San Francisco-set romantic
comedy features Mike Meyers giving
an immensely funny send-up of
1950s beat culture.
The Sweetest Thing (2002)
Gross-out movie meets chick flick,
with Cameron Diaz.
The Times of Harvey Milk
(1984)
This Oscar-winning documentary
focuses on the first 'out' gay
politician in the United States.
Vertigo (1958)
A veteran cop becomes obsessed
with a mysterious blonde. A die-cast
San Francisco classic.
**The Voyage Home:
Star Trek IV** (1986)
The gang come to SF to to save
some whales in this flick, the best
of the series.
The Wedding Planner (2000)
This update of the classic screwball
comedy is a bit clunky, but J-Lo is
immaculately cast.
**The Wild Parrots of Telegraph
Hill** (2000)
A delightful documentary about
Mark Bittner and the North Beach
birds who love him dearly.

Music

**Big Brother and the Holding
Company** *Cheap Thrills* (1968)
Classic Janis Joplin, housed in a
classic Robert Crumb sleeve. Tracks
include 'Ball and Chain' and 'Piece
of My Heart'.
Black Rebel Motorcycle Club
Take Them On, On Your Own (2003)
They smoke, they wear leather
jackets. Rebels, huh?
Chris Isaak *Heart Shaped World*
(1989)
What a 'Wicked Game' to be so good-
looking, with a voice like that.
Creedence Clearwater Revival
Willie and the Poor Boys (1969)
Classic southern rock with a San
Francisco touch.
The Dead Kennedys *Fresh Fruit
for Rotting Vegetables* (1980)
Excellent, angry SF punk.
Deerhoof *The Runners Four* (2005)
A surprisingly straightforwward set
from the local critics' darlings. For
something a little more out-there, try
1999's *Holdy Paws*.

Digital Underground
Sex Packets (1990)
Terrific, if slightly dated, hip hop.
Erase Errata
At Crystal Palace (2003)
Angular, uplifting rock from the
queens of the underground.
Gold Chains
Young Miss America (2003)
Bay Area hip hop, 21st-century style.
The Grateful Dead
Dick's Picks Vol.4 (1996)
Jerry Garcia and the boys in their
1970 prime at the Fillmore East.
Jefferson Airplane
Surrealistic Pillow (1967)
Folk, blues and psychedelia. Grace
Slick helps define the SF sound.
Joshua Redman *Wish* (1993)
Quality jazz from the Bay Area tenor
saxophonist.
Kid 606 *The Action Packed
Mentallist Brings You the Fucking
Jams* (2003)
This demented set of cut-ups and
samples is as close as this sonic
terrorist has ever come to accessible.
Primus *Pork Soda* (1993)
Wryly intelligent punk-funk in the
Zappa tradition.
Sly and the Family Stone
Stand! (1969)
Funk-rock masters. If you haven't
heard this, you haven't really heard
the 1960s.

Websites

www.craigslist.org
How San Franciscans hook up.
Hilarious and enlightening.
http://onlysf.sfvisitor.org
The CVB's site is packed with
information on the town.
www.mistersf.com
A delicious collection of local
oddballs, notorious history and
contemporary culture.
www.oaklandhistory.com
Pretty much what the title suggests,
and pretty interesting to boot.
www.sanfranciscomemories.com
Wonderful photographs of the city in
days gone by.
www.sfbg.com
The online edition of the *San
Francisco Bay Guardian*.
www.sfgate.com
The *San Francisco Chronicle* online.
www.sfheritage.org
This site focuses on the city's
architectural heritage.
www.sfstation.com
Upcoming events, clubs, parties, film
and restaurant reviews and more.
www.sfweekly.com
Listings, reviews and features.
www.streetcar.org
The past and present of SF's classic
streetcars, now on the F line.
www.transitinfo.org
Very useful for all forms of Bay Area
public transport.

Directory

Index

Advertisers' Index

Please refer to the relevant pages for contact details

Place of interest and/or entertainment	▢
Hospital or college	▢
Railway station	▢
Parks	▢
River	▢
Interstate Highway	🛡
US Highway	(101)
State or Provincial Highway	①
Main road	▬
Airport	✈
Church	✚
Area name	CASTRO
Hotels	❶
Restaurants	❶
Bars	❶

Maps

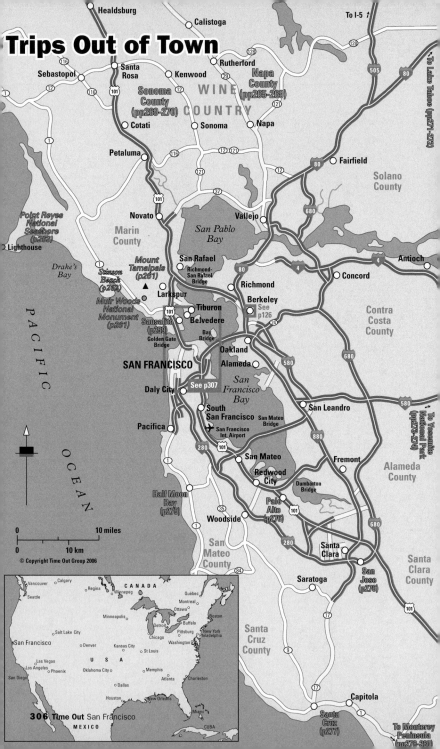

Trips Out of Town

Healdsburg
Calistoga
To I-5
Santa Rosa
Rutherford
Sebastopol
Kenwood
Napa County (pp265-269)
WINE COUNTRY
Sonoma County (pp269-270)
Cotati
Sonoma
Napa
Petaluma
Fairfield
Solano County
Novato
Vallejo
Point Reyes National Seashore (p263)
Marin County
San Pablo Bay
Antioch
Lighthouse
Drake's Bay
San Rafael
Richmond-San Rafael Bridge
Richmond
Concord
Mount Tamalpais (p261)
Larkspur
Berkeley
See p126
Contra Costa County
Muir Woods National Monument (p261)
Tiburon
Belvedere
Sausalito (p259)
Golden Gate Bridge
Bay Bridge
Oakland
Alameda
SAN FRANCISCO
San Francisco Bay
PACIFIC OCEAN
Daly City
See p307
San Leandro
South San Francisco
San Mateo Bridge
Pacifica
San Francisco Int. Airport
Fremont
Alameda County
San Mateo
Redwood City
Dumbarton Bridge
To Yosemite National Park (pp273-274)
To Lake Tahoe (pp271-272)
Half Moon Bay (p275)
Woodside
Palo Alto (p276)
Santa Clara
Santa Clara County
San Mateo County
Saratoga
San Jose (p276)
Santa Cruz County
Capitola
Santa Cruz (p277)
To Monterey Peninsula (pp278-280)

0   10 miles
0   10 km
© Copyright Time Out Group 2006

CANADA
Vancouver Calgary Regina Winnipeg Québec
Seattle Ottawa Montreal
Minneapolis Boston
Salt Lake City Detroit Buffalo New York
San Francisco Denver Chicago Pittsburg Philadelphia
Kansas City St Louis Washington DC
Las Vegas U S A Memphis
Los Angeles Phoenix Oklahoma City Atlanta Charleston
San Diego Dallas
Houston New Orleans
Miami
MEXICO CUBA

City Overview

San Francisco by Area

San Francisco Bay

Crissy Field

Palace of Fine Arts & Exploratorium

Marina Green

Fort Mason

MARINA BOULEVARD

MARINA

Moscone Playground

BAY STREET

101

RICHARDSON AVENUE

LOMBARD STREET

Cow Hollow Playground

COW HOLLOW

PRESIDIO

VALLEJO STREET

Presidio Golf Course

West Pacific Avenue

PACIFIC HEIGHTS

Alta Plaza Park

California Pacific Medical Center

Mountain Lake Park

PRESIDIO HEIGHTS

CALIFORNIA STREET

PINE STREET

BUSH STREET

UCSF Medical Center

Japan Center

CALIFORNIA STREET

GEARY EXPRESSWAY

Kaiser Medical Center

CLEMENT STREET

ARGUELLO BOULEVARD

GEARY BOULEVARD

WESTERN ADDITION

GEARY BOULEVARD

RICHMOND

University of San Francisco

TURK STREET

GOLDEN GATE AVENUE

BALBOA STREET

FULTON STREET

Alamo Square

Painted Ladies

PARK PRESIDIO BOULEVARD

FULTON STREET

University of San Francisco

MASONIC AVENUE

FELL STREET

OAK STREET

LOWER HAIGHT

St Mary's Medical Center

FELL STREET

Panhandle

DIVISADERO STREET

Golden Gate Park

Sharon Meadow

OAK STREET

HAIGHT-ASHBURY

Buena Vista Park

Duboce Park

DUBOCE AVENUE

STANYAN STREET

ASHBURY STREET

BUENA VISTA TERRACE EAST

UCSF Davies

Muni Metro Church

LINCOLN WAY

Corona Heights Park

CASTRO STREET

MARKET STREET

SUNSET

PARNASSUS AVENUE

COLE VALLEY

17th STREET

Muni Metro Castro

CASTRO

University of California San Francisco

DIAMOND STREET

Street Index

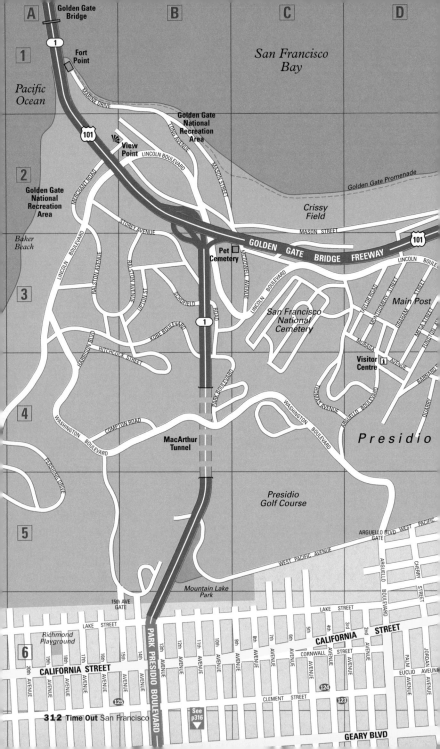

E · **F** · **G** · **H**

❶ Hotels pp42-62
❶ Restaurants & Cafés pp131-159
❶ Bars pp160-172

0   500 m
0   500 yds
© Copyright Time Out Group 2006

1

Wave Organ

Golden Gate Yacht Club

Fort Mason Center

139

A B C D

Marina Small Craft Harbor

Parking

MARINA GREEN DRIVE

Marina Green

Great Meadow

YACHT ROAD

MASON STREET

DOYLE DRIVE

MARINA BOULEVARD

MARINA BLVD

2

MARINA GATE

JEFFERSON STREET

CASA WAY

RICO WAY

BEACH STREET

FILLMORE STREET

NORTH POINT STREET

BAY STREET

FRANCISCO ST

OCTAVIA STREET

MARINA

Exploratorium

Palace of Fine Arts

BEACH STREET

BOULEVARD

CERVANTES

MALLORCA

AVILA STREET

PIERCE STREET

ALHAMBRA STREET

TOLEDO WAY

Moscone Playground

CHESTNUT STREET

MAGNOLIA STREET

RICHARDSON

GORGAS AVENUE

NORTH POINT STREET

CAPRA WAY

SCOTT STREET

BAY STREET

142

3

EDIE ROAD

Letterman Digital Arts Center

GORGAS GATE

AVENUE

FRANCISCO STREET

CHESTNUT STREET

DIVISADERO STREET

BRODERICK STREET

140

141

LOMBARD STREET

MOULTON STREET

57

N BLVD

LETTERMAN DRIVE

LOMBARD GATE

48 138

101

59

COW HOLLOW

PIXLEY

136

49

WEBSTER STREET

137

LAGUNA STREET

CHARLTON COURT

LOMBARD STREET

Cow Hollow Playground

GREENWICH STREET

SCOTT STREET

PIERCE STREET

STEINER STREET

FILLMORE STREET

50

BUCHANAN STREET

SCARTHUR

SIMONDS LOOP

FILBERT STREET

58

SHAFTER RD

PRESIDIO BOULEVARD

UNION STREET

4

PISTOL

WEST BROADWAY

GREEN STREET

VALLEJO STREET

BROADWAY

PACIFIC HEIGHTS

See p314

Julius Kahn Playground

PRESIDIO GATE

PACIFIC AVENUE

54

PACIFIC AVENUE

JACKSON STREET

Alta Plaza Park

California Pacific Medical Center

5

PRESIDIO HEIGHTS

SPRUCE STREET

LOCUST STREET

LAUREL STREET

WALNUT STREET

PRESIDIO AVENUE

LYON STREET

BAKER STREET

WASHINGTON STREET

CLAY STREET

SACRAMENTO STREET

CALIFORNIA STREET

SCOTT STREET

PIERCE STREET

STEINER STREET

FILLMORE STREET

WEBSTER STREET

BUCHANAN STREET

134

132

ST PACIFIC AVENUE

47

56

130

131

133

HEATHER AVE

IRIS AVENUE

MANZANITA AV

COLLINS ST

PINE STREET

BUSH STREET

JAPANTOWN

Peace Plaza

116

Laurel Hill Playground

SPRUCE STREET

LAUREL STREET

MASONIC AVE

SUTTER STREET

UCSF Medical Center

Hamilton Recreation Center

Japan Center

117

AVENUE

POST STREET

Kaiser Medical Center

GEARY EXPRESSWAY

Fillmore Jazz District

6

GEARY BOULEVARD

See p317

ANZA ST

TERRA VISTA AVE

ST JOSEPH'S

O'FARRELL STREET

ELLIS STREET

Kimbell Playground

EDDY STREET

Time Out San Francisco **313**

M   N   O   P

1

❶ Hotels pp42-62
❶ Restaurants & Cafés pp131-159
❶ Bars pp160-172

0   500 m
0   500 yds
© Copyright Time Out Group 2006

Cruise Ship Terminal

THE EMBARCADERO

San Francisco Bay

2

TELEGRAPH HILL

Coit Tower

GRANT
AVENUE
COLUMBUS
BROADWAY
KEARNY STREET
MONTGOMERY STREET
BATTERY STREET
SANSOME STREET
THE EMBARCADERO
FRONT STREET
DAVIS STREET

3

Macchiarini Steps

JACK KEROUAC ALLEY

CHINATOWN

Jackson Square

Chinese Culture Center

Portsmouth Square

ROSS ALLEY
WAVERLY PL

MERCHANT ST

Transamerica Pyramid

GOLD ST

FINANCIAL DISTRICT

Golden Gateway Center

Embarcadero Center

Ferries to North Bay

Justin Herman Plaza

Ferry Building

4

Old St Mary's Cathedral

Wells Fargo History Museum

Bank of California

Merchant's Exchange

COMMERCIAL ST

Cable Car

Rincon Center

STEUART STREET

Contemporary Jewish Museum (until 2007)

San Francisco-Oakland Bay Bridge

Bank of America

Chinatown Gateway

CLAUDE LANE

Pacific Coast Stock Exchange

FRONT STREET
DAVIS STREET
MAIN STREET
SPEAR STREET

Muni Metro BART Embarcadero

Muni Metro Folsom

80

5

SF Museum of Craft & Design

Crocker Galleria

MARKET STREET

Transbay Terminal & Greyhound Bus Depot

BEALE STREET
FREMONT STREET
1st STREET

Muni Metro BART Montgomery

Union Square

MAIDEN LANE

Museum of the African Diaspora

NEW MONTGOMERY ST
MISSION STREET
MINNA STREET
NATOMA STREET
HOWARD STREET
TEHAMA STREET
CLEMENTINE ST

26
28
7

6

Cartoon Art Museum

Center for the Arts

SFMOMA

2nd STREET

HARRISON STREET

SOUTH BEACH

Cable Car

SF Centre

Moscone Center North

Yerba Buena Gardens

Metreon

3rd STREET
4th STREET

HAWTHORNE STREET

FOLSOM STREET

SOMA

THE EMBARCADERO

Muni Metro BART Powell

Old Mint

California Academy of Sciences (until 2008)

Zeum

Moscone Center South

5th STREET
MISSION STREET

JAMES LICK SKYWAY

BRYANT STREET
BRANNAN STREET

South Park

Muni Metro Brannan

See p319

80

A 125

B

C 124 CLEMENT STREET 123

D

Richmond
Tennis Courts

MENT STREET

GEARY BOULEVARD 7

Argonne
Playground

ANZA STREET

BALBOA STREET 8

21st AVENUE
20th AVENUE
19th AVENUE
18th AVENUE
17th STREET
CABRILLO AVENUE
16th AVENUE
15th AVENUE

FULTON STREET

PARK PRESIDIO BOULEVARD

GEARY BOULEVARD

ANZA STREET

© Copyright Time Out Group 2006

500 m
500 yds

❶ Hotels pp42-62
❶ Restaurants & Cafés pp131-159
❶ Bars pp160-172

GEARY BOULEVARD

ARGUELLO BOULEVARD

Columbarium

Rossi
Playground

ROSSI AVENUE
WILLARD STREET NORTH

ANZA STREET

BALBOA STREET

RICHMOND

13th AVENUE
12th AVENUE
11th AVENUE
9th AVENUE
8th AVENUE
7th AVENUE
6th AVENUE
5th AVENUE
CABRILLO AVENUE
4th AVENUE
3rd AVENUE
2nd AVENUE

McAllister ST

FULTON STREET

CONSERVATORY DRIVE

Conservatory
of Flowers

JOHN F KENNEDY DRIVE

JOHN F KENNEDY DRIVE

de Young
Museum

TEA GARDEN DRIVE

California Academy
of Sciences
(reopens 2008)

CONCOURSE DRIVE

MIDDLE DRIVE EAST

BOWLING GREEN DR

AIDS
Memorial Grove

Sharon
Meadow

Boat House

Japanese
Tea Garden

STOW LAKE DRIVE E

Stow
Lake

Strawberry
Hill

CROSS OVER DRIVE

Golden Gate Park

MARTIN LUTHER KING JR DRIVE

Children's
Playground

Strybing Arboretum &
Botanical Gardens

ARGUELLO DRIVE

Kez
Pavi

County Fair
Building

MARTIN LUTHER KING JR DRIVE

MARTIN LUTHER KING JR DRIVE

KEZAR DRIVE

LINCOLN WAY 9

LINCOLN WAY 10

22nd AVENUE
21st AVENUE
20th AVENUE
19th AVENUE
18th AVENUE
17th AVENUE
16th AVENUE
15th AVENUE
14th AVENUE
13th AVENUE
12th AVENUE
11th AVENUE
10th AVENUE
9th AVENUE
8th AVENUE
7th AVENUE
6th AVENUE
5th AVENUE
4th AVENUE
3rd AVENUE
2nd AVENUE

LINCOLN WAY

HUGO STREET
IRVING STREET

127
126 128

IRVING STREET

JUDAH STREET

JUDAH STREET

PARNASSUS AVENUE

UCSF
Medical Center

KIRKHAM STREET

KIRKHAM STREET

LAWTON STREET 11

LAWTON STREET

SUNSET

LAWTON STREET

Mount Sutros

Shriners
Children's
Hospital

MORAGA STREET

13th AVENUE

MORAGA STREET

CRESTMONT DRIVE

21st AVENUE
19th AVENUE
18th AVENUE
16th AVENUE
15th AVENUE
14th AVENUE
11th AVENUE
9th AVENUE

ORTEGA STREET

NORIEGA STREET

OAK PARK DRIVE

WARREN DRIVE

NORIEGA STREET 12

7th AVENUE

ORTEGA ST

ORTEGA STREET

PACHECO STREET

7th AVENUE

Laguna Honda
Reservoir

CLARENDON AVENUE

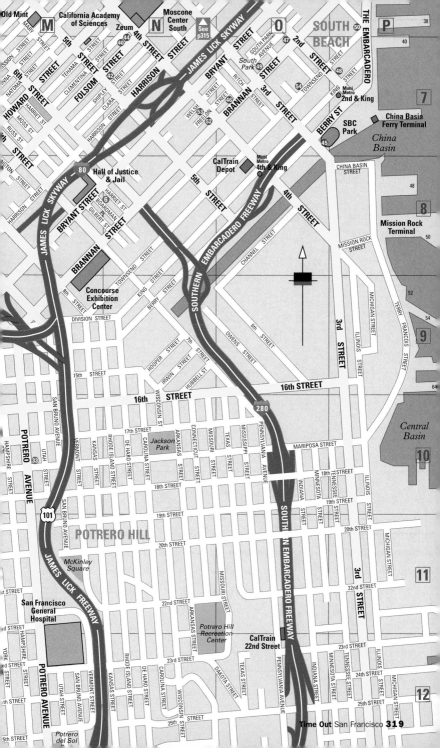

Downtown San Francisco
Public Transport

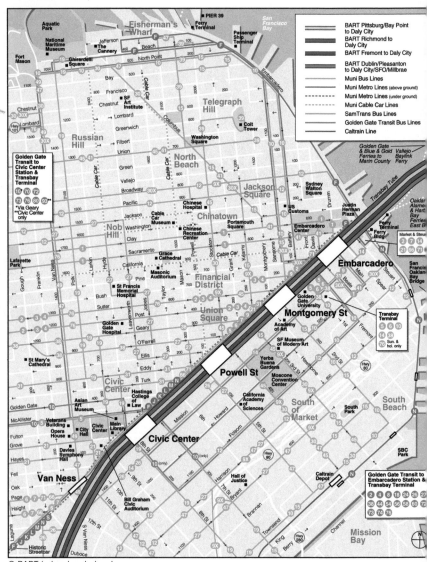

© BART/reineckandreineck.com